WORLD ENEMY NO. 1

Also by Jochen Hellbeck

Stalingrad:
The City That Defeated the Third Reich

Revolution on My Mind:
Writing a Diary Under Stalin

WORLD ENEMY NO. 1

NAZI GERMANY, SOVIET RUSSIA, AND THE FATE OF THE JEWS

Jochen Hellbeck

PENGUIN PRESS | NEW YORK | 2025

PENGUIN PRESS
An imprint of Penguin Random House LLC
1745 Broadway, New York, NY 10019
penguinrandomhouse.com

Image credits appear on page 517.

Designed by Amanda Dewey

Names: Hellbeck, Jochen author
Title: World enemy no. 1 : Nazi Germany, Soviet Russia,
and the fate of the Jews / Jochen Hellbeck.
Other titles: World enemy number one
Identifiers: LCCN 2025027727 (print) | LCCN 2025027728 (ebook) |
ISBN 9780593657386 hardcover | ISBN 9780593657393 ebook
Subjects: LCSH: Jews—Persecutions—Soviet Union | Propaganda,
Anti-communist | Holocaust, Jewish (1939–1945)—Soviet Union |
Soviet Union—History—German occupation, 1941-1944 |
World War, 1939-1945—Atrocities—Soviet Union
Classification: LCC DS134.85 .H45 2025 (print) | LCC DS134.85 (ebook)
LC record available at https://lccn.loc.gov/2025027727
LC ebook record available at https://lccn.loc.gov/2025027728

Printed in the United States of America
1st Printing

The authorized representative in the EU for product safety and compliance is Penguin Random House Ireland, Morrison Chambers, 32 Nassau Street, Dublin D02 YH68, Ireland, https://eu-contact.penguin.ie.

To my parents

CONTENTS

Note on Historical Place Names *xxiii*

Introduction *1*

Chapter 1. A FRONT AGAINST BOLSHEVISM *21*

Chapter 2. SWASTIKA AND SOVIET STAR *61*

Chapter 3. CROSSING THE RUBICON *104*

Chapter 4. A VIOLENCE SHAKING EUROPE *144*

Chapter 5. JEWS AND BOLSHEVIKS, STEP FORWARD! *177*

Chapter 6. MOSCOW STRIKES BACK *211*

Chapter 7. ENSLAVEMENT *253*

Chapter 8. LIBERATION *292*

Chapter 9. "HERE SHE IS, ACCURSED GERMANY!" *329*

Chapter 10. ERASURE *381*

Acknowledgments *427*

Notes *431*

Image Credits *517*

Index *519*

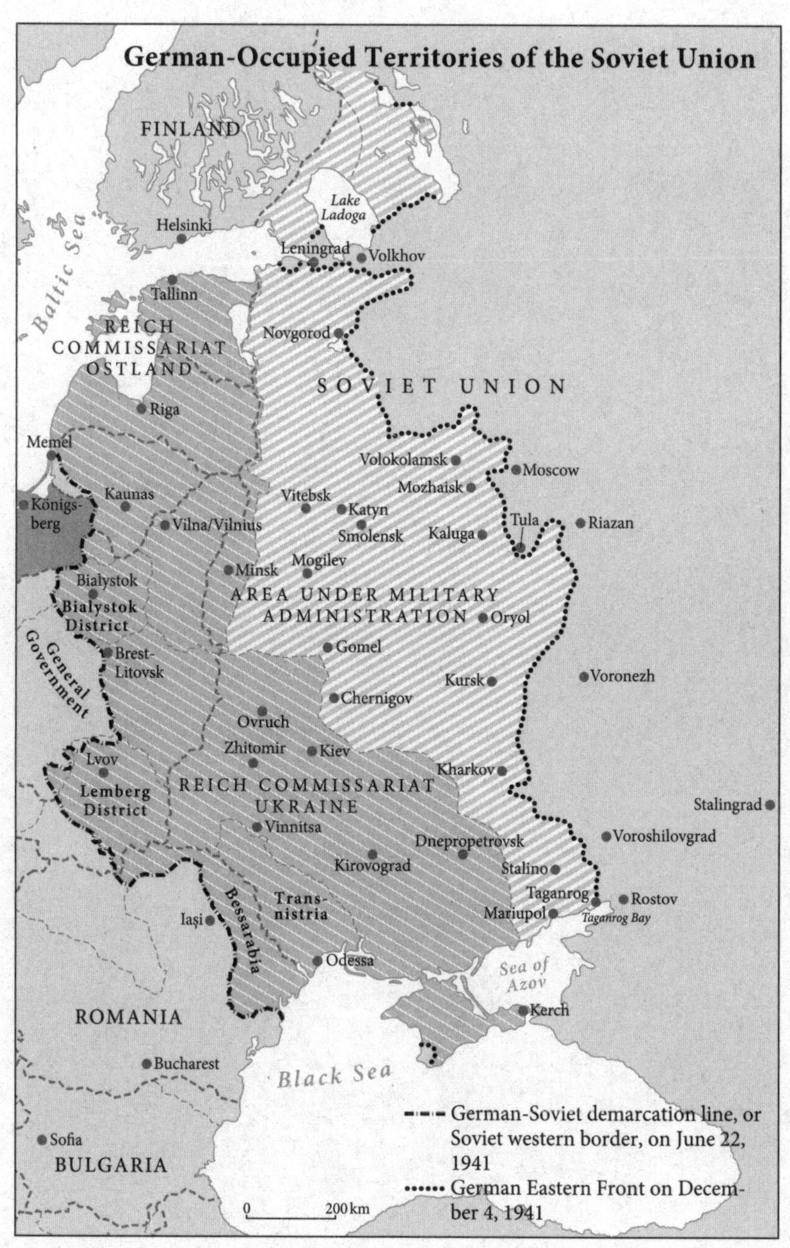
German-Occupied Territories of the Soviet Union
FINLAND
Lake Ladoga
Helsinki
Baltic Sea
Leningrad
Volkhov
Tallinn
REICH COMMISSARIAT OSTLAND
Novgorod
SOVIET UNION
Riga
Memel
Volokolamsk
Moscow
Mozhaisk
Kaunas
Königsberg
Vitebsk
Katyn
Vilna/Vilnius
Smolensk
Kaluga
Tula
Riazan
Minsk
Mogilev
Bialystok
Bialystok District
AREA UNDER MILITARY ADMINISTRATION
Oryol
General Government
Brest-Litovsk
Gomel
Voronezh
Kursk
Chernigov
Ovruch
Zhitomir
Kiev
Lvov
Lemberg District
Kharkov
REICH COMMISSARIAT UKRAINE
Stalingrad
Vinnitsa
Voroshilovgrad
Dnepropetrovsk
Kirovograd
Stalino
Taganrog
Rostov
Mariupol
Taganrog Bay
Trans-nistria
Bessarabia
Iași
Odessa
Sea of Azov
Kerch
ROMANIA
Bucharest
Black Sea
Sofia
BULGARIA
German-Soviet demarcation line, or Soviet western border, on June 22, 1941
German Eastern Front on December 4, 1941
0
200 km

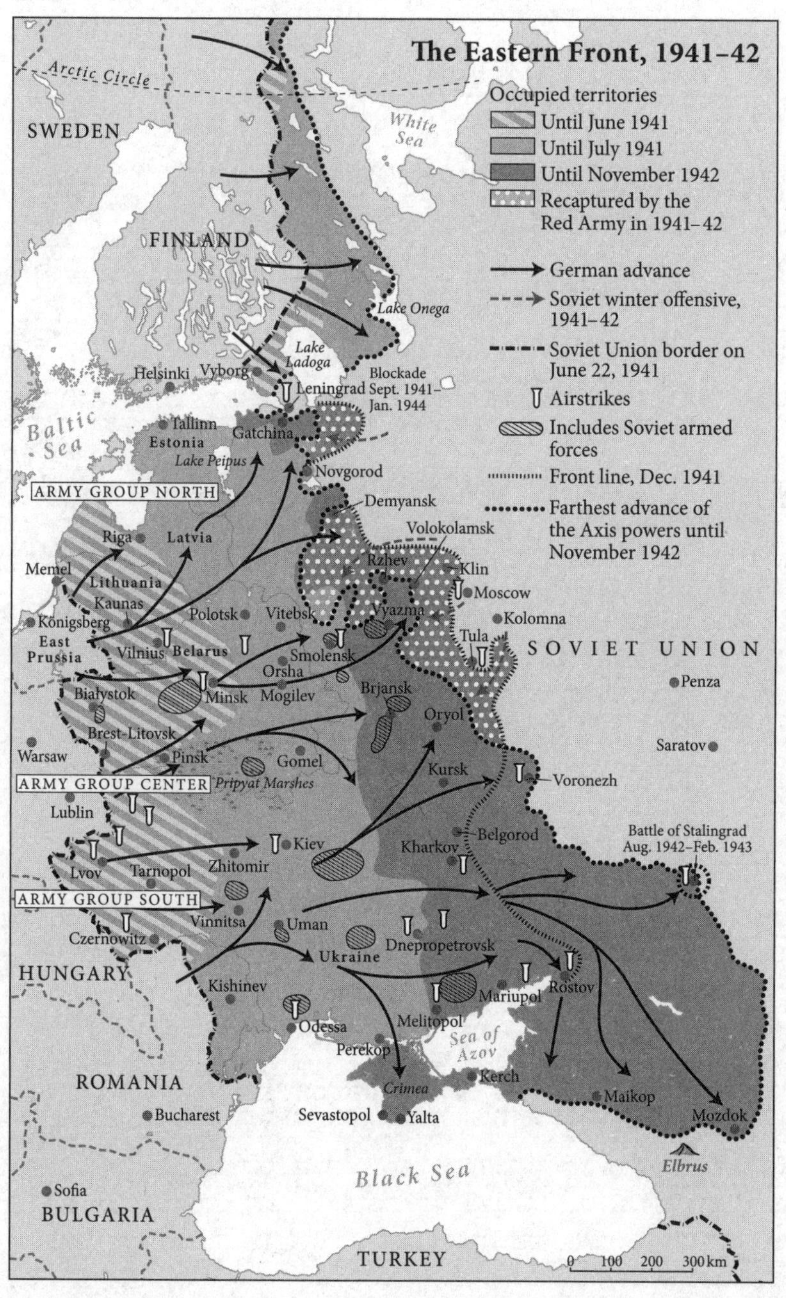

The Eastern Front, 1941–42
Occupied territories
Until June 1941
Until July 1941
Until November 1942
Recaptured by the Red Army in 1941–42
German advance
Soviet winter offensive, 1941–42
Soviet Union border on June 22, 1941
Airstrikes
Includes Soviet armed forces
Front line, Dec. 1941
Farthest advance of the Axis powers until November 1942
Arctic Circle
SWEDEN
White Sea
FINLAND
Lake Onega
Lake Ladoga
Helsinki
Vyborg
Leningrad
Blockade Sept. 1941–Jan. 1944
Baltic Sea
Tallinn
Estonia
Gatchina
Lake Peipus
Novgorod
ARMY GROUP NORTH
Demyansk
Volokolamsk
Riga
Latvia
Memel
Lithuania
Kaunas
Rzhev
Klin
Moscow
Königsberg
East Prussia
Polotsk
Vitebsk
Vyazma
Kolomna
Vilnius
Belarus
Smolensk
Tula
SOVIET UNION
Orsha
Białystok
Minsk
Mogilev
Brjansk
Penza
Oryol
Brest-Litovsk
Warsaw
Pinsk
Gomel
Saratov
ARMY GROUP CENTER
Pripyat Marshes
Kursk
Voronezh
Lublin
Belgorod
Kiev
Kharkov
Battle of Stalingrad Aug. 1942–Feb. 1943
Lvov
Tarnopol
Zhitomir
ARMY GROUP SOUTH
Vinnitsa
Uman
Czernowitz
Dnepropetrovsk
HUNGARY
Ukraine
Rostov
Kishinev
Mariupol
Odessa
Melitopol
Sea of Azov
Perekop
ROMANIA
Crimea
Kerch
Maikop
Bucharest
Sevastopol
Yalta
Mozdok
Elbrus
Black Sea
Sofia
BULGARIA
TURKEY
0 100 200 300 km

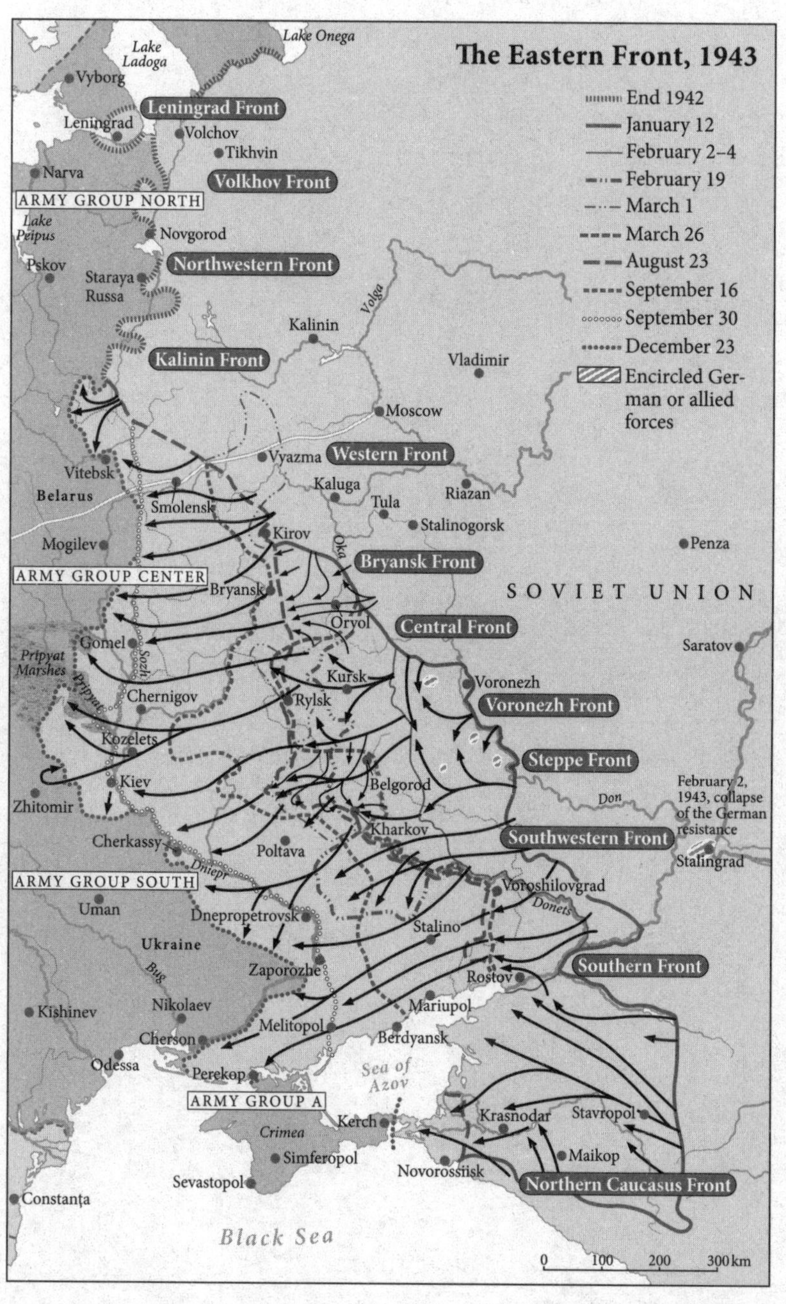
The Eastern Front, 1943
End 1942
January 12
February 2–4
February 19
March 1
March 26
August 23
September 16
September 30
December 23
Encircled German or allied forces
Lake Onega
Lake Ladoga
Vyborg
Leningrad Front
Leningrad
Volchov
Tikhvin
Narva
Volkhov Front
ARMY GROUP NORTH
Lake Peipus
Novgorod
Pskov
Staraya Russa
Northwestern Front
Volga
Kalinin
Kalinin Front
Vladimir
Moscow
Vyazma
Western Front
Vitebsk
Belarus
Smolensk
Kaluga
Tula
Riazan
Stalinogorsk
Kirov
Mogilev
Oka
Bryansk Front
Penza
ARMY GROUP CENTER
Bryansk
SOVIET UNION
Oryol
Central Front
Saratov
Gomel
Pripyat Marshes
Sozh
Pripyat
Kursk
Voronezh
Chernigov
Rylsk
Voronezh Front
Kozelets
Steppe Front
Kiev
Belgorod
Zhitomir
Don
February 2, 1943, collapse of the German resistance
Kharkov
Southwestern Front
Cherkassy
Poltava
Stalingrad
Dniepr
ARMY GROUP SOUTH
Voroshilovgrad
Uman
Donets
Dnepropetrovsk
Stalino
Ukraine
Bug
Zaporozhe
Southern Front
Rostov
Kishinev
Nikolaev
Mariupol
Melitopol
Cherson
Berdyansk
Odessa
Perekop
Sea of Azov
ARMY GROUP A
Kerch
Krasnodar
Stavropol
Crimea
Maikop
Simferopol
Novorossiisk
Northern Caucasus Front
Sevastopol
Constanța
Black Sea
0 100 200 300 km

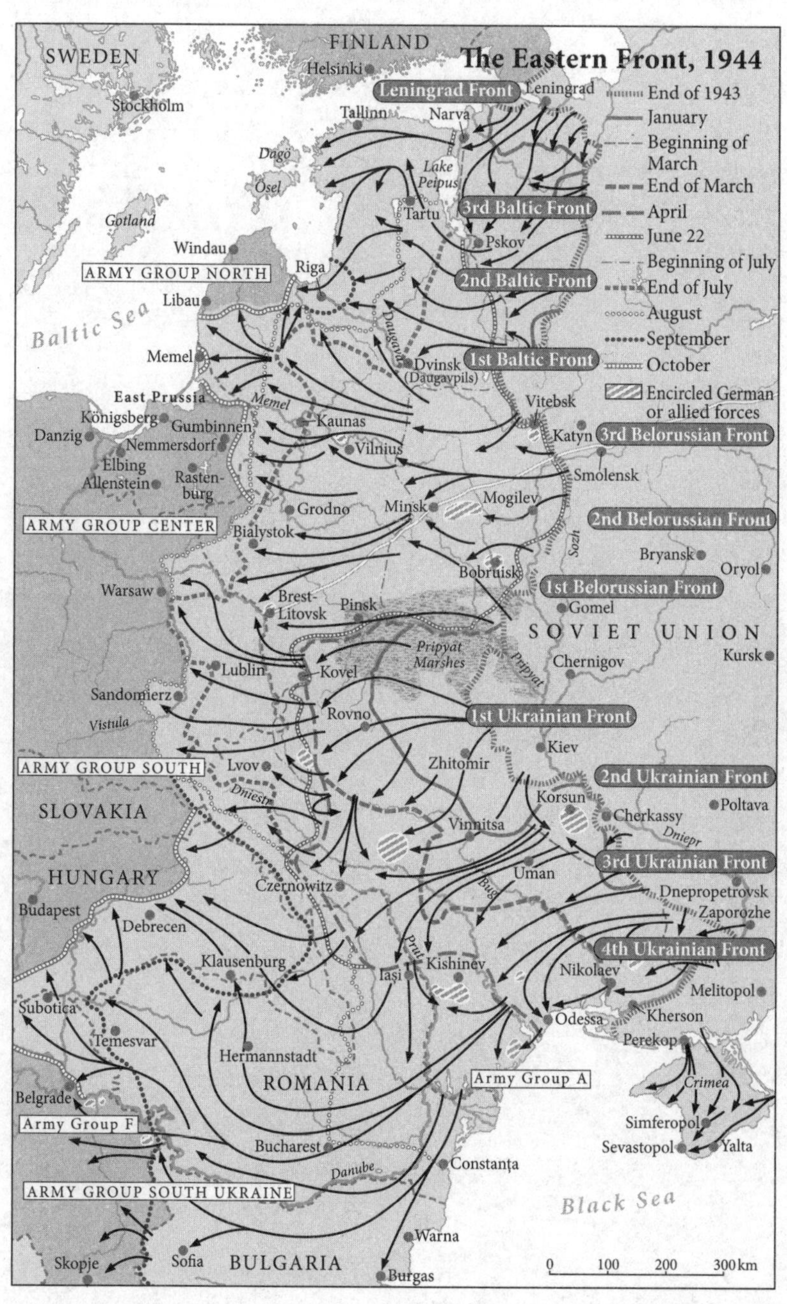

The Eastern Front, 1944
End of 1943
January
Beginning of March
End of March
April
June 22
Beginning of July
End of July
August
September
October
Encircled German or allied forces
SWEDEN
FINLAND
Helsinki
Stockholm
Leningrad Front
Leningrad
Tallinn
Narva
Dagö
Ösel
Lake Peipus
Tartu
3rd Baltic Front
Pskov
Gotland
Windau
ARMY GROUP NORTH
Riga
2nd Baltic Front
Libau
Baltic Sea
Daugava
Memel
Dvinsk (Daugavpils)
1st Baltic Front
East Prussia
Königsberg
Gumbinnen
Danzig
Nemmersdorf
Elbing
Allenstein
Rastenburg
Kaunas
Vilnius
Vitebsk
Katyn
3rd Belorussian Front
Smolensk
Mogilev
Minsk
Grodno
ARMY GROUP CENTER
Bialystok
2nd Belorussian Front
Sozh
Bryansk
Oryol
Bobruisk
Warsaw
1st Belorussian Front
Brest-Litovsk
Pinsk
Gomel
SOVIET UNION
Pripyat Marshes
Pripyat
Kursk
Lublin
Kovel
Chernigov
Sandomierz
Vistula
Rovno
1st Ukrainian Front
Kiev
Zhitomir
ARMY GROUP SOUTH
Lvov
2nd Ukrainian Front
SLOVAKIA
Dniestr
Korsun
Cherkassy
Poltava
Vinnitsa
Dniepr
3rd Ukrainian Front
HUNGARY
Uman
Bug
Czernowitz
Dnepropetrovsk
Zaporozhe
Budapest
Debrecen
4th Ukrainian Front
Klausenburg
Prut
Iași
Kishinev
Nikolaev
Melitopol
Subotica
Odessa
Kherson
Temesvar
Perekop
Hermannstadt
Crimea
ROMANIA
Army Group A
Belgrade
Army Group F
Simferopol
Sevastopol
Yalta
Bucharest
Constanța
Danube
ARMY GROUP SOUTH UKRAINE
Black Sea
Warna
Skopje
Sofia
BULGARIA
Burgas
0 100 200 300 km

The Eastern Front, 1945
SWEDEN
(neutral)
DENMARK
Baltic Sea
Memel
Tilsit
Königsberg
Insterburg
Gotenhafen
Danzig
Elbing
Rastenburg
Allenstein
Stralsund
Rostock
Wismar
Schwerin
Swinemünde
Kolberg
Neustrelitz
Stettin
Stargard
Havelberg
Berlin
Potsdam
Magdeburg
Seelow
Landsberg
Bromberg
Thorn
Schwerin an der Warthe
Frankfurt/Oder
Posen
Vistula
Oder
Warthe
Cottbus
Torgau
Leipzig
Elbe
Glogau
Kalisch
(Lodz)
Litzmannstadt
Warsaw
Bialystok
District
Dresden
Görlitz
Breslau
Radom
Lublin
Aussig
Karlsbad
Prague
Pilsen
Tschenstochau
General Government
Gleiwitz
Kattowitz
Troppau
Cracow
Tarnow
Przemysl
Protectorate of
Bohemia
and Moravia
Brno
SLOVAKIA
Linz
Salzburg
Obersalzberg
Vienna
Bratislava
Ostmark
Graz
Budapest
HUNGARY
Tisza
Danube
Maribor
Lower
Styria
Carinthia
and Carniola
Triest
Zagreb
Rijeka
(Fiume)
Save
Drau
CROATIA
Adriatic
0 50 100 150 km
Territories held by the Soviet Union until December 16, 1944
Territorial gains until January 17, 1945
Front on March 22, 1945
Front on April 19, 1945
Territories held by German troops on May 6, 1945
Border of the Greater German Reich

Concentration Camps and Other Nazi Murder Sites
NORWAY
Stockholm
Göteborg
SWEDEN
DENMARK
North Sea
Copenhagen
Baltic Sea
Libau
Memel
Kiel
Rostock
Danzig
Elbing
Fuhlsbüttel
Hamburg
Bremerhaven
NETHERLANDS
Bremen
Fallingbostel
Bergen-Belsen
Ravensbrück
Stettin
Graudenz
Sachsenhausen
Bromberg
Amsterdam
Celle
Hannover
Berlin
Posen
Magdeburg
Potsdam
Kulmhof
Litzmannstadt
(Lodz)
Cottbus
Kassel
Cologne
Buchenwald
Leipzig
Dresden
Breslau
Ohrdruf
Weimar
Gross-Rosen
Tschenstochau
GERMAN REICH
Chemnitz
Theresienstadt
Gleiwitz
Frankfurt
Prague
Luxembourg
Homburg (Saar)
Flossenbürg
Pilsen
Protectorate
Bohemia and
Moravia
Auschwitz-
Birkenau
Saarbrücken
Mannheim
Zweibrücken
Karlsruhe
Nuremberg
Brno
Strasbourg
Stuttgart
Regensburg
SLOVAKIA
Ulm
Moosburg
Mauthausen
FRANCE
Freiburg
Dachau
Linz
Vienna
Bratislava
Munich
Salzburg
Basel
Zurich
Budapest
Innsbruck
Bern
Graz
SWITZERLAND
Klagenfurt
HUNGARY
(allied with Germany)
Meran
Zagreb

Concentration Camps and POW Camps
Large Ghettos*
Other Killing Places
*In the occupied territories of the Soviet Union, the establishment of a ghetto was tantamount to the almost immediate extermination of its Jewish inhabitants.
Tallinn
Klooga
ESTONIA
Viljandi
Tartu
Novgorod
Pskov
Kalinin
Moscow
LATVIA
Riga
Rumbula
Kaiserwald
Velikiye Luki
Dvinsk Fortress
Dvinsk (Daugavpils)
Vyazma
LITHUANIA
REICH COMMISSARIAT OSTLAND
Vitebsk
Tula
Smolensk
Kaunas
Vilna
Ponary
Orsha
Roslavl
Mogilev
Bryansk
Oryol
Minsk
Maly Trostinets
Lida
Bobruisk
AREAS UNDER MILITARY ADMINISTRATION
Bialystok District
Bialystok
Baranovichi
Slonim
Gomel
SOVIET UNION
(partly occupied by the German Reich)
Pinsk
Brest-Litovsk
Sobibor
Drobytsky Yar
Kharkov
Lublin
Trawniki
Majdanek
Kovel
Syrets
Babi Yar
Kiev
Lutsk
Rovno
Zhitomir
Berdichev
Poltava
Belzec
Rawa-Ruska
Janowska
Lvov
Kremenchug
Przemysl
Tarnopol
Vinnitsa
REICH COMMISSARIAT UKRAINE
Dnepropetrovsk
Drobomil
Sambor
Rohatyn
Kamenets-Podolsky
Czernowitz
Bogdanovka
Sea of Azov
Kishinev
Odessa
Kerch
ROMANIA
(allied with Germany)
Black Sea
0
200 km
Sevastopol

Note on Historical Place Names

The spelling of place names in this book follows the spelling used in the historical sources on which it is based and thus also expresses the power dynamics of the time. Between 1940 and 1991, Lithuania, Latvia, Estonia, Belorussia (today's Republic of Belarus), and Ukraine belonged to the Soviet Union. For this period, the Russian form of all Soviet place names is used—i.e., *Babi Yar* (not *Babyn Yar*), *Kharkov* (not *Kharkiv*), *Kiev* (not *Kyiv*), *Mogilev* (not *Mahilyow*), *Rovno* (not *Rivne*), *Vitebsk* (not *Vitsebsk*), and so forth, except if the sources adopt a different spelling. The city now known as *Lviv* in Ukraine is referred to as *Lemberg* in the context of German rule. I use the Polish name, *Lwów*, in a few instances where the discussion centers on the city's predominantly Polish character between 1920 and 1944; otherwise, the spelling is *Lvov*.

The narrative parts of the book use an intuitive spelling of Slavic names, whereas the annotation transliterates these same names according to scholarly conventions: *Ilya Ehrenburg* in the text; *Il'ia Erenburg* in the notes—though only for the most part … Ehrenburg also frequently appeared in German or French sources where he is spelled as *Ilja Ehrenburg* (German) or *Ilya Ehrenbourg* (French).

Readers may wonder why the book refers to Soviet communists as *Bolsheviks* in some instances and as *Bolshevists* in others. The National Socialists and most Germans frequently referred to the Soviet rulers as *Bolshevists*, a term that conjured for them an enormous threat. Only rarely do German sources from the Nazi era use the term *Bolsheviks*. The variation in spelling in this book reflects this uneven practice.

INTRODUCTION

A few days into the German occupation of Kiev in September 1941, explosions rocked the city, blowing up office buildings and apartment blocks where German soldiers were quartered. Before their withdrawal from Kiev, Soviet forces had placed mines throughout the downtown area. Triggered by sabotage teams stationed outside the city in communication with undercover Soviet agents within it, the explosions killed some two hundred German soldiers and an unknown number of residents. The Germans on the ground immediately decided who was responsible for this terror attack: the Jews.

House searches began. On September 22, two Gestapo agents in plain clothes charged into the apartment of thirty-nine-year-old resident Olga Mukhortova-Pekker. One of them punched Olga's elderly neighbor, who stood in the doorway, while the second man threw himself at Olga, yelling, "Gangsters! Your power has ended! Tell us where your Jew-Communist husband is!" Within a week, the Germans had rounded up Kiev's Jews. Thousands of men, women, and children were led into a ravine on the city's outskirts, forced to lie down, and shot. Those who were brought later were forced to lie face down on the bodies of the dead and were shot in turn. With the help of Ukrainian auxiliaries, over the course of two days German task forces killed 33,771 Jews. In their reports of the mass killings in Kiev's Babi Yar ravine and other places, German security officials described their actions as a political operation to destroy the pillars of the Soviet order: "It can be stated positively today that the Jews, without exception, served Soviet Bolshevism."[1]

Bolshevism was one of Hitler's primary obsessions and the catalyst that provoked Nazi Germany to mount a war of extermination unprecedented in world history. The term Lenin had given to the Soviet Communist Party, "Bolshevism" was how the Nazis and other right-wing crusaders characterized the Soviet system, a system both repulsive and menacing, conjuring "Asiatic" cunning, criminality, and mass murder. Émigrés from Russia had circulated lurid accounts of leather-clad commissars dispatching thousands of helpless victims by shooting them in the neck. In the words of one such émigré, who would rise in the Nazi Party to become Germany's wartime minister for the Occupied Eastern Territories, Bolshevism was a "plague" that threatened the West's very survival. A collision with it had only two possible outcomes: "annihilation, or victory."[2]

The Führer consistently portrayed Communists as his deadliest enemies. Throughout the Weimar years, he exploited Germans' fear of a civil war, which was, above all, the fear of a Communist uprising. After coming to power, the Nazis locked up more than one hundred thousand German Communists in concentration camps created for that purpose. "Europe against Bolshevism" became their most popular rallying cry. By the late 1930s, Hitler felt ready to move against the Soviet Union, both to face down the global menace he believed Bolshevism had become and, conveniently, to seize territories in the East that were vital for Germany to realize its imperial racial destiny. On August 11, 1939, only days before Nazi Germany would sign a nonaggression pact with the Soviet Union, Hitler openly remarked: "Everything I undertake is directed against Russia. If the West is too stupid and blind to grasp this, then I shall be compelled to come to an agreement with the Russians, beat the West, and after its defeat, turn against the Soviet Union with all my forces."[3]

Hitler's other great obsession was with the Jews. He had been a fierce anti-Semite from early on in his life, but it was only with his embrace of anti-Bolshevik thought in the aftermath of World War I that his hatred of Jews became an ideology.[4] To Hitler, Bolshevism evoked not only Soviet Communism, but the nefarious goals of Jews, who had created Marxism and seized the Kremlin in a bid to invade Germany and all of Europe. The widespread conviction among the German Right that Jewish or Jewish-led Communists had masterminded their country's downfall in 1918 gave Hitler's ideas about the Jewish enemy substance and intensity.

So completely did the Soviet system embody the twin hatreds of Jews and Bolsheviks that the Nazis and other far-right movements used a neologism to refer to it: "Judeo-Bolshevism." In the Nazi imagination, the USSR was the most powerful Jewish organization in the world; they called it "World Enemy No. 1." The Soviet threat was all-encompassing: As Hitler noted with concern in 1936, the rulers in Moscow propagated the "most extreme" variant of the modern Enlightenment faith, which had first provoked the French Revolution and was now sending the world hurtling toward a global showdown.[5] Coded by the Nazis as Jewish, the Communist creed of universalism and interracial solidarity stood in the way of Hitler's plans to fulfill the German people's historical destiny as the world's master race. Germany had to either destroy the Soviet Union or suffer its own demise. As they readied their country for war, Nazi leaders never tired of denouncing Communism as a world-devouring Jewish plot. Large "anti-Bolshevik" exhibitions toured German cities during the 1930s, to expose the USSR's Semitic face and deadly designs Hundreds of thousands of German boys and men saw these ghastly ex hibits prior to joining their nation's fight on the Eastern Front. In Ma 1939, the notoriously anti-Semitic paper, *Der Stürmer*, prepared its reac ers for Germany's upcoming "punitive campaign" against Bolshevisr The war would "provide the same fate for [the Jews in Russia] that eve murderer and criminal must expect. Death sentence and execution. T Jews in Russia must be killed. They must be exterminated root a branch. Then the world will see that the end of the Jews is also the enc Bolshevism."[6]

On June 22, 1941, more than three million German soldiers, the l est army in the nation's history, invaded the USSR. "Operation barossa," Hitler announced to his generals, would play out as a giga final battle between German National Socialism and Soviet Communism. Before the campaign began, Hitler ordered the troops on the ground to disavow the international norms of warfare that German sol-liers had previously adhered to when fighting elsewhere in Europe. Spe- fically, they were to detain and mark for execution the political mmissars in the Red Army, who were believed to be the army's Jewish sterminds. German soldiers were also told to use deadly force against lians as needed. When they came face-to-face with millions of "Bol- iks," who were supposedly more beast than human, German soldiers to resort to the very cruelty and ruthlessness they had ascribed to nemy.

e invading German troops largely accepted their leaders' view of riet Union as a Judeo-Bolshevik terror regime. As they entered So- nes, the first question soldiers shouted at frightened residents *de, Kommunist?*" "We just know," an artillerist from Göttingen me to his parents, "that this war is a war between good and evil, reason and lunacy, for Bolshevism is out-of-control madness." r asked his parents not to think that he had turned into a Nazi ist. He hadn't realized, he wrote, that "the picture that has d of Russia would pale against the horrific reality."[7]

to die en masse were the Jews of the Soviet Union, Bolshe- ial backers in the eyes of the invaders. From the first days of SS commando units rounded up and executed Jewish men. n forces behind the front lines came under fire, they re- uted this hostility to Jews, who constituted a large part of of the Soviet Union's western regions. In reprisal for acts SS annihilated entire Jewish communities. Even small geted as future resistance fighters and "finished off," in he SS death squads. The Jews of the Soviet Union were tively, because they were believed to be *Soviet* Jews. As shed his generals prior to the campaign, if they failed rbarossa in his stark political terms, "then while we before us today, in thirty years we will be faced once nist foe."[8]

As they became consumed by their battle against Bolshevism, German leaders began to cast all European Jews as Bolsheviks. When Communists across Europe staged demonstrations and uprisings after Hitler's attack on the Soviet Union, Nazi officials responded by blaming "Bolsheviks" and rounding up Jews. Throughout Nazi-occupied lands, Jews were soon redefined—they were no longer racial aliens who could simply be expelled from Germanic soil, but racial-political enemies who needed to be destroyed. In this fashion, the annihilation of Jews in the Soviet Union seamlessly extended into the oppression, and then annihilation, of Jews elsewhere. On September 1, 1941, less than three months after Operation Barbarossa began, all Jews living in the German Reich were ordered to wear a yellow star on their sleeves when in public—a mandate supposedly necessitated by Jewish atrocities on the Eastern Front. Before long, the Nazi fixation on the Soviet Union as a Judeo-Bolshevik terror regime extended to their treatment of Jews everywhere.

The Nazi war on Bolshevism additionally took aim at millions of non-Jewish Soviet citizens. Wehrmacht officials typically referred to their Soviet prisoners of war as "Bolsheviks" and mistreated them so horrifically that by early 1942 more than 2 million out of a total of 3.3 million captives had died. One million Leningraders, among them 400,000 children, starved to death during the blockade of the city, a sieg that Hitler purposefully planned as an act of historical revenge, to extin guish the city in which Bolshevism had first come to power. The million Soviet civilians brought to Germany as slave workers starting i 1942 received far worse treatment than workers from other nation Alone among the foreign laborers, these Soviet workers, predominant young women, were under the jurisdiction of the Gestapo. In total, t Axis invasion and occupation took the lives of between 26 million a 27 million Soviet citizens, 15 million of them civilians. Among th were 2.6 million Jews.[10] The Nazis intended this colossal death coun be only the beginning. Blueprints for the postwar colonization of East foresaw the extinction, mostly through starvation, of tens of lions of Soviet citizens, especially urban residents, who were believ be most infected by Bolshevism.

Germany's invasion in summer 1941 nearly knocked out the Soviet state. At the time of the attack, the Red Army was undergoing an ganizational overhaul following Stalin's bloody purge of his military, d its new command structures were not yet fully in place. The Soviet tator expected Hitler to strike at some point, but the actual attack him by surprise. Operation Barbarossa dealt a devastating blow to oviet military, killing or capturing nearly six million Red Army sol- in just the first six months.

other respects, however, the USSR was prepared. For the past ten Soviet factories had been churning out tanks, cannons, and air- at rates far exceeding the estimates gathered by German intelli- Millions of young Soviet men and women underwent paramilitary during the 1930s to condition themselves for an inevitable war, Soviet state anthem called the "final battle." After Hitler took scow shone as one of the world capitals of anti-fascism, as in- from across the world teamed up with Soviet writers to coordi- tural fight against Nazism.

he Soviet reporters who joined this fight and brought it to eaders, none would prove more incisive or influential than rg. Born into a Jewish family in Kiev, the left-leaning writer t spent many years in France and Germany. Fluent in rman, he witnessed Nazism's violent expansion from up aris correspondent for the Soviet newspaper *Izvestiya*, rted from the trenches of the Spanish Civil War. In 1940, German troops invaded, barely making it to the Soviet scow, he predicted Germany's attack against the Soviet y of the invasion, the writer fired his opening volley, an a thousand editorials he would produce over the

elty of German violence in the Soviet Union stunned believed he knew all there was to know about Ger- ware that his accounts would otherwise be dis- , he packed his editorials with firm evidence of terrible German deeds. Citing German military orders and the diaries and letters of German servicemen that had been retrieved from the battlefield or found in the pockets of captured soldiers, Ehrenburg depicted German soldiers, as well as the people with whom they corresponded, as willing participants in Nazism's horrendous crimes. The German murder of Soviet Jews prompted the intensely secular writer to embrace his own Jewish roots, but Ehrenburg's editorials rarely detailed the ordeals of Jews alone. Committed universalist that he was, Ehrenburg depicted the war as a struggle between Germany, a nation that had forsaken its conscience, and a multiethnic Soviet order that was defending humanist values. Killing this enemy, Ehrenburg instructed his readers, was a moral duty.

Far from every Soviet citizen was eager to defend the USSR on those terms, though. Millions of Soviet men and women entered the war with memories of the extraordinary violence they'd suffered at the hands of their own regime. They had survived a bloody civil war, a brutal collectivization campaign, and an ensuing famine. Several million people had been caught up in waves of arrests during the 1920s and '30s. By the time of the German attack, police informants were recording widespread defeatist sentiment within Soviet society. As Wehrmacht units approached their home cities, many residents did not heed official exhortations to pack up and leave. At least some hoped that Hitler's soldiers would bring liberation; Germans, after all, had a reputation for being "cultured" and benign.

The reality of Nazi occupation shattered any such hopes and prompted people on the ground to reassess their relationship to the Soviet state. The prewar Soviet regime rivaled Nazi Germany in its ruthless persecution of perceived enemies, but unlike Germany it did not glorify its repressive acts. Stalin's police agents carried out arrests under cloak of darkness, raiding apartments of presumed "counterrevolutionaries" at night. By contrast, the Germans staged their reckonings with Judeo-Bolshevism in broad daylight, for everyone to see. Nazi commanders summoned townspeople and villagers to watch executions of suspected "bandits," and they left the bodies of the deceased hanging for weeks.

These shocking deeds, compounded by plunder, destruction, and untold humiliations inflicted on locals who were reduced to servants, slaves, or prostitutes, prompted even erstwhile critics of the Communist regime to reexamine their commitments. The Nazis' attempt to pulverize the Bolshevik system thus had the unintended effect of revitalizing the Soviet war effort. A newly discovered Soviet identity thrived in the occupied territories. The changing fortunes on the battlefields of the Eastern Front accelerated its formation.

As the Soviets fought hard and passionately, Britons and Americans avidly followed their efforts in the press. Western reporters praised "the Russians" for leading a global crusade in support of humanity against the fascist might. Soviet snipers, soldiers, and workers, predominantly women, toured Great Britain and the United States, describing how to prevail against German fascism. During the epic standoff between the Wehrmacht and the Red Army at Stalingrad, British and American newspapers continually featured heroic stories from the beleaguered city. While the U.S.-sponsored Lend-Lease program supplied the Soviet Union with vast quantities of tanks, trucks, and food, infusions of another kind traveled from East to West: stirring tales of the Soviet men and women who had stopped the hitherto undefeated German military machine. In military, human, and cultural terms, the Soviet war effort formed the center of the global resistance against Nazism. By the time the Western Allies launched the cross-Channel invasion in June 1944, the Red Army had been fighting and dying for three long years.

On their path of reconquest, Red Army soldiers crossed through Soviet towns, villages, and pastures that the enemy had ravaged during its retreat. They talked with survivors and saw gallows in marketplaces, often with corpses of suspected partisans still dangling from nooses. And they were led to ravines and anti-tank trenches on the outskirts of towns, where locals had begun to uncover mass graves filled with the bodies of mostly Jewish residents. Red Army commanders brought their soldiers to these murder sites to listen to political officers and local survivors, who offered harrowing accounts of German deeds. These vengeance meetings, as they were called, concluded with vows by the outraged soldiers to fight on and avenge the dead. In July 1944, Soviet soldiers reached Majdanek—the first death camp to be liberated by Allied troops. Six months later, the Red Army liberated Auschwitz. Thousands of troops participated in vengeance meetings held in these camps. Majdanek and Auschwitz became household names in the Soviet press.

As the Red Army pushed into Germany, Ilya Ehrenburg summoned the memory of horrendous German crimes. "Advancing toward Berlin," he wrote in *Red Star*, "are not only our divisions and armies, but also legions of petrified mothers, inconsolable widows, and children whose hair has turned gray. . . . Advancing toward Berlin are the boots, shoes, and baby slippers of those who have been gassed, among them the tiny shoes of a two-year-old. . . . Buried alive by the Germans, the children have crawled out of the pits and anti-tank trenches; they are already at the border, eager to get to Berlin. . . . These children are not going to go away. They are our conscience."[12] Although Ehrenburg cast their objective as meting out justice, many of his readers were more interested in expressing violent hatred than bringing accountability. Countless rapes and acts of destruction punctuated the Red Army's march toward Berlin, vengeful crimes in contravention of military decrees and official efforts to present the Soviet way of war as morally righteous.

By this time, virtually all Germans had come to understand the Soviet Union as their defining enemy, in tune with what Nazi propaganda had proclaimed all along. Their existential fight against the "Mongolian hordes" and the "Jewish Commissars" who supposedly instigated them had molded Germans as Aryans, valiant defenders of European culture and Bolshevism's future victims.[13] A wave of suicides roiled Germany's eastern provinces in the winter and early spring of 1945. Most of these came before the arrival of Red Army troops—they were acts of dread-filled anticipation. Aversion toward "Russians" was universal, gripping even those far from the Eastern Front. From a Hamburg suburb, a German diarist observed how liberated Soviet POWs were roaming the streets during the final weeks of the war, asking for food and resorting to force when their requests were refused. The diarist recorded the hysterical mood among the local population: "The Russians are looting!" "The

Russians are all murderers and criminals!" Local men would gather with bats and sticks, ready to defend their villages.[14]

By 1945, "the Russian" displaced the Jew or Jewish Bolshevik as the embodiment of monstrous, Asiatic evil. With nearly all of Europe's Jews killed, and the Red Army crossing into Germany, this conceptual reframing made political sense. Touting the fatherland as crucial to Europe's defense against Bolshevism, Nazi newspapers in early 1945 called on the Western Allies to switch sides and come to Germany's aid. Ehrenburg observed these maneuvers with alarm. In April 1945, with the Red Army about to seize Berlin, Ehrenburg warned that "one can win the war and lose the peace. Everyone knows this adage. The Germans, too, and as they are now losing this war, they are trying to win the peace." Ehrenburg reported on German efforts to ingratiate themselves with the American occupiers and agitate against a supposed Russian menace. He also condemned the Western press's double standard regarding Nazi violence, as British newspapers decried the barbaric killings of a few of their POWs in German captivity but made no mention of the millions of Soviet POWs who had been killed.[15] Ehrenburg's premonition proved true: The Soviet Union defeated Germany militarily, but the Germans emerged as the winners on the ideological battlefield. Their slogan "Europe against Bolshevism" would live on past the demise of the Nazi state, occluding Germany's singular crimes in the East for many years to come.

For a moment after the war, Western public opinion registered the Soviet Union's outsize losses. The lion's share of the evidence that supported the indictment of top Nazi leaders at the Nuremberg International Military Tribunal came from the Soviet Union. The last of the four Allied powers to make its case, the Soviet indictment charge culminated in the screening of film footage documenting Nazi atrocities in Russia, Ukraine, Belorussia, the Baltic republics, and Poland. The film had a devastating impact on spectators in the courtroom. "Nothing," a reporter for *The New York Times* wrote, had "brought the horror of the German occupation home to the court room as did today's picture."[16]

But the world soon became desensitized to Soviet suffering. Two weeks after the Soviet film aired at Nuremberg, Winston Churchill warned dramatically about an "iron curtain" that had descended over Eastern Europe, casting Stalin as an aggressor in the mold of Hitler. Furious, Stalin reacted by likening Churchill himself to Hitler. The sundering of the wartime alliance put an end to the joint Allied prosecution of former Nazis. Soviet leaders departed Nuremberg convinced that international legal institutions did not serve their interests and should be shunned. Western leaders in turn began to denounce their erstwhile ally as a "totalitarian" foe. In the process, the West lost sight of millions of Soviet victims of Nazi aggression.

One of the most often (mis)quoted texts about Nazi violence illustrates the workings of this dynamic. The text is theologian Martin Niemöller's confession of his moral failure during the 1930s:

> First they came for the Communists, but I was not a Communist—so I said nothing. Then they came for the Social Democrats, but I was not a Social Democrat—so I did nothing. Then they came for the trade unionists, but I was not a trade unionist. And then they came for the Jews, but I was not a Jew—so I did little. Then when they came for me, there was no one left who could stand up for me.

Originally a staunch nationalist, Niemöller had backed Hitler in 1933 before publicly denouncing the Nazi regime and being thrown in jail in 1937. After his release in 1945, Niemöller toured western Germany as a prominent preacher, imploring his countrymen to acknowledge their guilt for the Nazi crimes. Each lecture contained a variation of his confession. The churchman spoke extemporaneously, and he listed the victims in different order at different times. But every single recorded speech has the Communists at the beginning, and for good reason. Niemöller remembered well that the Nazis in power had first gone after the Communists. However, when invoking the theologian, multiple American politicians, as well as an encyclopedia of the Holocaust, moved the Jews from last to first place: "First they came for the Jews." As a parting message to visitors, the United States Holocaust Memorial Museum

United States Holocaust Memorial Museum, Washington, D.C.

in Washington, D.C., features Niemöller's self-accusation in the last room of its permanent exhibition. The museum cites the theologian in a way he never spoke, changing the word "Communists" to "socialists." In this version, the Communists are not relegated to a lower rank—they are erased from the record.[17]

My intention is to push against such amnesia and willful repression and to restore the USSR to its proper place in the history of the Second World War and the fight against Nazism. The Soviet Union was both the laboratory for the German politics of mass murder and the decisive power that defeated the Third Reich. For millions of Germans, the specter of Soviet Communism sparked murderous fantasies that they began to enact in 1941, inaugurating a wave of killing and terror unprecedented in modern history. Soviet observers seized on German atrocities to cast their own war effort as "humanity" resisting "fascist barbarism." The power of this moral narrative was instrumental in achieving Allied victory over Nazi Germany. To fully understand the Second World War, we need to set its axis firmly in the East.

World Enemy No. 1 calls for a revision of not only the geography of Nazi violence, but also its chronology. In searching for explanations of

Nazism's annihilatory thrust, many historians invoke the prehistory of anti-Semitism in Germany to tell the story of Hitler's ascent and the rise of the Nazi Party in cumulative fashion. These profoundly German-centric accounts feature the Nazi assumption of power (1933), the Nuremberg Race Laws (1935), Kristallnacht (1938), Germany's attack on Poland (1939), the creation of the Auschwitz–Birkenau death camp (1941), and the Wannsee Conference (1942) as decisive markers. Listed like station stops on a train schedule, the events suggest a point of origin, a direction, and a final destination.[18]

Such "step-by-step" readings of how Nazism grew ever more destructive obscure the centrality of Soviet Jews in the German imagination. While the Nazis depicted Jews as part of a global conspiracy and railed against "Jewish banks in New York, the Jewish-plutocratic establishment in London, and the Jews of the Kremlin in Moscow," they considered the Jews who hailed from the Soviet Union to be the greatest threat to Germany. Operation Barbarossa differed from all previous campaigns because it targeted an ostensibly Jewish state, governed by a "Jewish" Marxist-Leninist faith.[19] As supposed operatives of a huge and heavily armed Communist state, Soviet Jews were believed to wield political clout in ways other Jews and "racial aliens" did not. Germany's attack on the Soviet Union thus marked the pivotal moment when German security forces instituted a system of mass murder to kill all Soviet Jews. The German-occupied Soviet lands in turn became ground zero of the destruction of Europe's Jews.[20]

If so much of what happened on the Eastern Front and behind its front lines remains unknown and hidden, this is only partly a problem of sources. To be sure, documents authenticating the scale, let alone the texture, of German crimes in the Soviet Union are incomplete.[21] The search for precision is further hampered by restricted access to sensitive documentation in Russian archives, keeping off-limits a host of documents believed to be essential for understanding the German-Soviet war. But the primary reason the Eastern Front has not yet been revealed as the decisive arena of the war has to do with politics—specifically the anti-Communist prejudice that pervades Western scholarship.

Western anti-Communism is the reason why the Soviet Union is regularly described as an aggressor, rather than a target, let alone victim, in the history of the Second World War. Some of the most influential narratives of the war foreground the temporary pact between Hitler and Stalin and the German-Soviet rout of Poland as the most fateful marker in the history of the twentieth century. The decades-old enmity between German Nazism and Soviet Communism gets short shrift, as does the Soviet Union's crucial yearslong contribution to the anti-Hitler alliance.[22] Many studies implicate all Soviet citizens in the cynical designs of their callous dictator. This calculus writes off the moral endeavor of a people whose sacrifices in fighting Nazism exceeded that of any other nation.[23] There seems to be no room for Soviet victims in our conscience. The shocking number of Soviet citizens—twenty-six million—who lost their lives between 1941 and 1945 is widely known. But the faces and the voices of these victims of Nazism are conspicuously absent. By contrast, historians have meticulously studied the excesses of violence committed by Soviet soldiers against German civilians.[24] The fantasy of an "Asiatic flood" sweeping Europe continues to be a mainstay of the West's conception of Russia and the Soviet Union, and serves to buttress the West's understanding of itself as a bastion of order and rectitude.

The rise, starting in the 1960s, of Holocaust scholarship and its understanding of Nazism as a singular evil did little to correct this truncated memory. On the contrary, the study and commemoration of the Holocaust in Western countries have in recent decades increasingly become tied to the invocation of liberal democratic values. But liberal values are typically understood as antithetical to Communism. For that reason, the commemoration of the Holocaust in the West today tends to erase the central place of Communists, alongside Jews, as Nazism's chief victims.

Most Holocaust scholars, trained as Western or Central Europeanists with research languages that include German, French, Yiddish, and Polish, but rarely Russian, believe that the Nazis spewed hatred against all

Jews from early on, irrespective of their imagined or real political affiliation. This view misses the fact that the deadliest forms of Nazi violence targeted a presumed *political* enemy. More fundamentally, the notion that the Nazis persecuted Jews exclusively as Jews obscures the distinction Germans made between all Jews as "racial aliens"—who were to be expelled from Germanic soil as "polluters" of the German race—and those Jews whose purported Communist ideology made them additionally a formidable threat to national security.

The fateful linkage Germans created between Soviet Jews and Communists also remains understudied partly because scholars actively work to rupture it, intent on disproving Nazism's notion of Soviet Communism as a Jewish conspiracy. For instance, a team of Holocaust scholars who recently published a critical edition of German security police reports issuing from Nazi-occupied Soviet territories included a detailed commentary to render the reports legible to modern-day readers. The persistent references in the SS reports to Soviet Jews as "Bolsheviks," "criminals," or "partisans," the editors write, deserve no credence, as these ascriptions had no "objective" basis: The security police used such political language merely in order to conceal their murderous hatred toward all Jews.[25] While well intentioned, such attempts to expose Germany's wartime conception as patently fantastical and therefore unworthy of serious investigation paper over the fact that these ideas were vital motivators of the Nazi project. An intricate racial-political calculus drove German killings on the Eastern Front, as the language employed by Nazi officials and German soldiers makes abundantly clear.

To properly understand the war, the German crusade against Judeo-Bolshevism must be seen as the conflict's driving force. A visceral loathing of Marxist ideology and its Communist offspring in particular directed Nazism's most extreme violence, from the street fights incited by brown-shirted storm troopers in Berlin's working-class neighborhoods, to the mass arrests of German Communists in 1933, to Germany's eventual attack on the world's first Communist state. Nazi leaders invariably cast this fight as targeting a Jewish enemy who had invented

Communism and planned to use its power to destroy the world. Historically, this lethal anti-Communism has not received its due.*

The concerns of this book are personal for me. Born in 1966, I am West German by background and a historian of Russia by training. My father fought in the war. Drafted at age seventeen, he was sent to the Eastern Front when the Red Army was already inside Germany. A grenade splinter that tore into his leg on April 20, 1945, probably saved my father's life. He was allowed to retreat, and somehow made his way to Berlin, and from there farther south to the Elbe River. A man on a horse cart offered him a ride to Hamburg; my father got on and, by a few days, managed to escape the ring that the Red Army formed around Berlin as part of their final attack. Many years later, he joined the German Foreign Service with the intention of specializing in Russia. But with his rudimentary knowledge of Russian, he could not compete with some of his peers who spoke the language fluently, and so he chose Mandarin and became a Chinese specialist instead. All the while my father retained a strong sense of curiosity for the Soviet Union. In 1984, about to enroll as a student at Berlin's Free University, I followed my father's advice to study Russian. He predicted interesting times ahead for the Soviet order. Shortly after I began my studies, Mikhail Gorbachev came to power, and

---

* Among the few scholars who *have* foregrounded anti-Bolshevism as a driver of Nazi policies, Arno Mayer and Ernst Nolte deserve particular mention. Mayer's 1988 monograph showcases Nazism's abiding hatred of Communism, culminating in the 1941 attack on the Soviet Union. Strangely, however, Mayer parses Soviet Communists and Jews and does not engage with the German specter of the "Judeo-Bolshevik" enemy in the East. In his reading, it was in response to their failure to crush the Communist state that the Germans began to vent their "seething and exploding rage" on the Soviet Jews. This disconnect makes no sense, discursively or in the sequence of events. The mass murder of Soviet Jews did not begin in late 1941, as Mayer would have it, but as soon as German soldiers set foot on Soviet soil. When his book appeared, Mayer was attacked by historians of the Holocaust for treating the murder of the Jews as an epiphenomenon of Barbarossa, rather than the Nazis' principal aim. Amid the clamor, the book's singular merit was lost from view.

Before Mayer, Ernst Nolte was the first scholar to reveal how profoundly Nazism defined itself in opposition to Bolshevism. This insight is upended by the credence Nolte gives to Nazi propaganda, specifically Hitler's claim that his movement fought in dire defense against a primal Communist aggression. Nolte refers to anti-Communism as Nazi ideology's "rational core," and he clearly sympathizes with the side that claimed to defend Europe against a supposed Asiatic menace. Like Mayer (but independently of him), Nolte disconnects Nazi anti-Bolshevism from Nazi anti-Semitism, treating an entwined hatred as separate strands.[26]

six years later the Soviet Union dissolved. My father's collection of Russian and Soviet writers is now in my library.

My maternal grandfather was thirty-nine when World War II began. A manager of a bobbin factory in southern Germany and a member of the Nazi Party since 1937, he was never called up for military service. During the war, over a thousand mostly Soviet laborers were forced to work at the factory, which had been retrofitted to produce weapons. After French forces took the town and freed the camps, the former laborers asked to execute the SS guard who had cruelly ruled over their lives. The French gave them rifles to shoot the man. Some people then asked to shoot the director—my grandfather. But others stepped up, saying he was a good man, and so he was spared. Even so, when conversations on my mother's side of the family would turn to "the Russians," the tone was often harsh, differing from my father's more positive views. I grew up under the influence of both.

When I was fourteen, we moved from Paris to East Berlin, where my father began to work for the Permanent Representation of West Germany to East Germany, a long-winded designation for an office that West Germany refused to call an embassy, as it did not recognize East Germany as an independent state. We lived in a leafy diplomatic district in the northwest of the East German capital, and our backyard almost touched the wall of a massive Soviet war memorial. It was the largest Soviet cemetery outside of Russia and had been set up in the late 1940s on the grounds of a former forced labor camp. On my walks, I could observe parading soldiers in their dress uniforms and hear the solemn music coming from inside the memorial. But it was only many years later, well after I had taken up Russian, visited the Soviet Union, and become a historian of the Soviet Union, that I learned about the history and context of this memorial and the thousands of Soviet men and women who lie buried beneath it.

This project has been long in the making. After completing an earlier study exploring the diaries of ordinary people who lived through Stalin's industrialization and terror campaigns, I became interested in comparing life under Soviet Stalinism and German Nazism. I began with an exploration of the Battle of Stalingrad, interviewing Soviet and German veterans, and drawing on previously unknown Soviet accounts to fill out a history that has almost invariably been told through German eyes. The present book extends this research to the broader subject of the two countries at war. For both the German and the Soviet sides, I have studied numerous sources, many of them found in previously unknown documentary collections. These include political and military directives, journalistic reports, personal writings, photographs, wartime interview transcripts, as well as hundreds of letters from Red Army soldiers, many of them Jewish, who corresponded intensely with Ilya Ehrenburg throughout the war.[27]

One trove of documents proved of special interest—a vast collection of interviews conducted by a group of scholars who worked under the aegis of the Moscow historian Isaak Izrailevich Mints. Early on, Mints recognized the epochal nature of the Soviet war against the German invaders. By late 1941, he had formed a "Commission on the History of the Great Patriotic War," with the aim of creating a comprehensive record of the Soviet war effort. Practicing a form of oral history that was ahead of its time and is still impressive even by today's standards, tandem teams of scholars and stenographers traveled to the military front lines and wrote down soldiers' accounts of how the war had entered their lives.[28]

As soon as the Red Army repelled the German attack on Moscow in December 1941, Mints expanded the work of his commission to include interviews on the impact and legacy of the Nazi occupation. The project began with historians trekking to destroyed villages and towns near Moscow, where they spoke with survivors. After the turning of the military tide in early 1943, members of the commission fanned out to trail the Red Army on its path of liberation or reconquest of occupied Soviet soil. They visited smoldering towns and villages in southern and western Russia, in Ukraine, and in Belorussia, where they recorded hundreds more interviews, sometimes within weeks of the Germans' departure.[29] Six weeks after the Red Army had entered Kiev, two members of the Mints commission arrived in the Soviet Ukrainian capital and sat down to speak with Olga Mukhortova-Pekker and her husband, Solomon Pekker, both of whom had survived against all odds.

Continuing to follow the Red Army, the Moscow historians traveled on, in search of more testimonies. They made it as far as northern Germany, where in June 1945 they interviewed forced laborers who had escaped captivity only weeks before. The hundreds of interviews that the commission created vary greatly in tone and length, but common to all is an urge on the part of the interviewees to share memories of the ordeal they had just endured. Even as Soviet witnesses of Nazi atrocities often struggled for words to characterize the humiliations and tortures meted out by the occupiers, they identified themselves as historical agents rather than helpless victims. Many not only described what they had seen or suffered through but stressed their personal contribution to the fight against fascism. As these voices finally enter the public record, they will challenge received histories of Nazi aggression and annihilation, imparting them with a Soviet accent.[30]

In July 1942, after German troops conquered the port city of Sevastopol following a prolonged siege and an all-out air and land assault, a German colonel who had taken part in the storming of the Sevastopol fort praised the courage of the Soviet defenders in Berlin press conferences and on the radio. Joseph Goebbels was beside himself when he learned about this. The German propaganda minister perfectly understood the stakes. As he noted in his diary, the colonel in question had acknowledged that Bolshevism was a "catalyst of moral action" (Goebbels's words). Goebbels had always insisted that this moral force never be avowed, for doing so would unduly humanize the Soviet enemy. In response to the colonel's address, Goebbels instructed the workers in his ministry to stress the radical difference between the "heroism" of the highly developed German race and Soviet "toughness," which sprang from "primitive Slavic animality, organized into resistance by wild [Jewish] terror." The minister went on to explain: "There are living beings that are extremely resilient because they are so inferior. A street dog is more resilient than a highly bred German shepherd. But that doesn't make the street dog more valuable. A rat is also more resilient than a pet."[31] Goebbels's fear that more German commanders would go on the air and praise the Soviet war effort turned out to be unfounded. After the rout of the Sixth Army at Stalingrad, the German nation lived in growing expectation of defeat, and millions assimilated the fears that Goebbels's ministry stoked of the "Asiatic hordes" that were setting out to obliterate Germany.

Even after Nazi Germany's demise, and still to this day, Western observers have struggled to recognize Soviet institutions and values as reservoirs of moral action. Many histories of the war insist on painting Communism as no more than an oppressive official ideology, leaving little or no place for Soviet people who identified with the Stalinist state, the homeland, or socialist values, and effectively writing off a cardinal part of the Soviet war experience.[32] The most recent studies of what in Soviet times was referred to as the Great Patriotic War recast this war in national terms, distinguishing between what it meant for Russians, as opposed to Ukrainians, Belorussians, Tatars, or Bashkirs. Ethnicity unquestionably mattered in the Soviet war effort: Most soldiers and civilians identified with a specific nationality, and they were familiar with the cultural and historical distinctions that Soviet officials drew between Slavic and Central Asian nationalities, as well as between Russians and Ukrainians.[33] But to view the war primarily through national lenses, which some scholars do as they separate ethnically Ukrainian or Belorussian soldiers from Russian ones and impute that non-Russian soldiers fought for principally different political aims than their Russian counterparts, is to risk misrepresenting the actual history of the Soviet-German war.[34] Germany launched Operation Barbarossa in an attempt to destroy Soviet civilization, which Hitler identified as a Jewish enterprise and the most radical political experiment of the modern Enlightenment. If the USSR succeeded in halting and repelling Germany's attack, it did so on the strength of soldiers and civilians from a host of different ethnicities mobilized in a common fight against the German fascist invaders. Many, perhaps most, of the people who joined this war would have reflexively described themselves as Soviet people if asked who they were. These people, and their efforts, deserve our attention. They have been dismissed for far too long.

Chapter 1

A FRONT AGAINST BOLSHEVISM

Five months after Hitler's party rose to power, Theodore Abel, a thirty-six-year-old sociologist teaching at Columbia University, arrived in Germany. Together with his wife and three children, he disembarked from a transatlantic steamer in Bremen, intending to pass through Berlin to visit his parents in Poznan, as the family did every summer. But for Abel, the trip across Germany proved more absorbing than the destination. "Nazi propaganda everywhere—radio, buses cruising with speeches and music, big placards on corners, flags and uniforms everywhere," he noted in his diary on June 30, 1933, while in Berlin. Abel spoke fluent German and struck up conversations with people on the street, and in cafés and restaurants. A few confided to him with horror how the Nazis were abusing Jews and persecuting their political opposition. Most others spoke about the new regime very differently. Ardently patriotic, they credited the government with unifying and strengthening their crisis-ridden country. Hitler had restored their hope for a better future. Abel chronicled what he saw as a historic moment: Germans' enthusiastic rejection of "liberalism, democracy, tolerance, and international cooperation," and their regression to a primitive state of "national egotism and intolerance." By the time Abel returned to the United States in early September, he knew he had to write about Nazism.[1]

Abel devised an ingenious way to gather the sources necessary for his study: He planned a writing contest. Anyone, regardless of sex or age, who had identified with the Nazi movement prior to January 1933 would be invited to participate. Cash prizes, which would go as high as 125 marks—about half a month's salary at the time—would be awarded to essays that provided "the most detailed and trustworthy accounts" of individuals' personal lives, particularly during the years following the Great War, which saw the founding and rise of the National Socialist German Workers' Party (NSDAP). When Abel returned to Germany the following summer, he presented his project to officials in the Reich Propaganda Ministry as a large-scale sociological study, conducted by Columbia University to inform the American public about the history of National Socialism. Impressed, the officials sent bulletins to all local headquarters of the Nazi Party with instructions to announce the contest in the party press.[2]

By fall 1934, 683 Nazis had submitted essays, offering Abel a unique view from within the movement.[3] The group was composed mostly of men, along with several dozen women, and included respondents from a wide variety of different regions and occupations. The contestants displayed a wide array of styles and levels of sophistication as well, with some limiting themselves to a few paragraphs and others presenting their autobiography over many pages. But all authors merged their life stories with the Nazi movement. The moment they first saw Hitler, or joined his party, suffused them with renewed purpose to fight for the restoration of a great nation that had been diminished by foreign powers and internal strife.

Germany, according to most accounts, had been brought down by sinister enemy forces that had concealed their conspiratorial designs by posing as disinterested parties. Many authors began by blaming "the Jews" for bringing Germany to its knees: Jews had pushed Germany into the Great War in order to hijack its wartime economy, then orchestrated its defeat in 1918 in search of further profits.[4] But Jews did not act out in in the open, some of the writers stressed. Globally dispersed and operating behind the scenes, they were the puppet masters who controlled millions of unwitting Germans. Their most effective weapon was the

Marxist rhetoric of class struggle, which pitted Germans against Germans, sapping their national strength.[5] Multiple writers—including one Grete Kircher, who had been born to wealthy parents and was converted to Nazism by her driving instructor—claimed that "international Marxism and the Jewish problem" had combined to destroy Germany.[6] Of these two, the Marxist political parties posed the greatest threat, given their popular support and power to command uprisings and revolutions: "Our struggle was directed mainly against Marxism, which is supported by the Jews, since it was willing to defend its power to the utmost with brutal violence."[7]

More pointedly, several writers identified their principal enemy as "extreme Marxism" or "Bolshevism"—the Communist faith that was preached in Moscow and had captivated countless German Communists. Nazi autobiographers who served in the paramilitary storm troopers (*Sturmabteilung*, or SA) described their bloody street fights against a "red subhumanity" that was determined to devastate Germany.[8] One of them cast their effort to defend the fatherland against the "murderous red mob" as a matter of existential survival for its sixty million inhabitants. In the view of some, there was no sacrifice too extreme in the struggle against Bolshevism, which represented the antithesis of everything Germany stood for. "I shuddered at the thought of Germany in the grip of Bolshevism," one respondent wrote. "The slogan 'Workers of the world unite!' made no sense to me. But National Socialism, with its promise of a community of blood, barring all class struggle, attracted me profoundly."[9] Hans Schönherr, a schoolteacher from Wiesbaden, prefaced his eight-page autobiography with a succinct summary. He wanted to explain to "the great American people (1) that the horror stories about my fatherland . . . are nothing but nasty lies, and (2) that Germany and Europe can be saved from Bolshevism only by National Socialism."[10]

Much has been written about what turned Germans into Nazis. Among the contributing factors that historians have identified are militant nationalism, national humiliation, economic upheaval, Hitler's charisma, and anti-Semitism. Understood as distinct forces, these concepts reflect scholars' need for analytical clarity, but they often contribute to a misunderstanding of how ordinary Germans viewed themselves and their political project. One scholar who studied the Nazi autobiographies written at Abel's behest dismissed their descriptions of "Germany's mortal enemy" as "rantings" that "made little sense then and now."[11] The anti-Bolshevism invoked by Hitler and his followers was certainly conceptually diffuse, often conflating Marxists, Communists, and Jews. But this very imprecision proved advantageous for the Nazis, as it gave them license to strike out hard and wide. Their task, as one street fighter put it, was to "wipe the wanton grin off the Bolshevist's murderous face" and "save Germany from the bloody terror of unrestrained hordes."[12] Though fantastical and misguided, the Nazi conception of an entwined Jewish-Bolshevik enemy was an important catalyst for violent political action, and there is every reason to take it seriously.[13]

Anti-Bolshevism had energized and shaped the Nazi Party ever since its founding in 1919. From then until January 1933, a fourteen-year stretch that came to be called the "period of struggle" (*Kampfzeit*), the Nazis consistently attacked the German Communist Party (KPD), which they saw as their most organized and potent political foe. In countless clashes with the KPD, Nazi street fighters discovered their movement's sense of purpose: It was the Nazi fist that would shatter Marxism's "poisonous" and "false" creed.[14] Upon coming to power in 1933, the Nazis began a brutal reckoning with the KPD, arresting thousands of members, as well as outspoken members of the moderate Social Democratic Party (SPD), whom they also counted as Marxist "traitors." Outside Communist circles, few observers in Germany and other Western countries condemned the mistreatment of the Communist prisoners, who in 1933 constituted the vast majority of those confined in concentration camps.[15] At the same time, the Nazis' attacks on Communists provided cover for their assault on Germany's democracy, allowing them to cast it not as a power grab but rather a last-ditch defense against Bolshevism.

RED FEAR

Within months of the Bolshevik revolution in October 1917, the name of Vladimir Lenin's party had become an international political buzzword.[16] Bolshevism shook and divided the globe. Odes poured in to revolutionary Petrograd in late 1917, fervently welcoming the "party of the Bolsheviks as the sole party that is leading us, at long last, to full power for the people." Their authors were soldiers and workers, men and women, who described themselves as "worn out by bloody slaughter, starvation, and the cold of winter," while clamoring for the "total emancipation of all laborers" and "universal education for both sexes."[17] In other accounts, Bolshevism was a source of corruption and wanton destruction. Conservative media such as London's *Morning Post* denounced Lenin's new government as a regime of "cranks" and "crooks," partaking in an "orgy of passion and unreason," while *The New York Times* referred to the Bolsheviks as "human scum."[18] Betraying how much the Communist takeover of 1917 triggered memories of Jacobin *terreur*, American newspapers published fantastical reports of an electric guillotine in Petrograd that could decapitate five hundred prisoners per hour.[19] In Moscow, the writer Ivan Bunin shuddered at the spectacle of lower-class citizens making themselves heard. "Again some kind of demonstration," he wrote in February 1919, describing "banners, posters, music—hundreds of throats shouting: 'Stand up, rise up working people.'" He continued: "The voices are visceral, primitive. The women have Chuvash, Mordvinian faces, the men all look like criminals, some could have come straight from Sakhalin."[20] There was no single lens through which to view the Soviet Revolution. For many, it signified a people's will in action; for others, a brutal coup and the unleashing of a frenzied mob.

As Russia erupted into civil war, pitting revolutionary Reds against counterrevolutionary Whites, Western media reports invariably attributed the terrible violence engulfing the country to the Bolsheviks' alleged murderous designs, while largely ignoring acts of White terror. Many of these reports were penned by refugees whose property or land had been confiscated during the upheaval. Their experience resonated with politicians and businessmen in the West who feared Communist takeovers in their own countries. In Great Britain, Secretary of War Winston Churchill was filled with foreboding as war-weary troops formed soldier committees and strikes and mutinies cropped up in early 1919. Churchill was so concerned that, even after the Great War had come to a close, he pushed hard for the British military to continue its intervention in Russia to fight on behalf of the Whites. On his initiative, the British government published a report that assembled many of the already circulating accounts of the "horrors of Bolshevism."[21]

In the United States, the Senate held hearings to investigate a recent wave of strikes as a Bolshevik attempt to incite the overthrow of the federal government. Dozens of witnesses spoke, among them Russian refugees, American missionaries, and the U.S. ambassador to Russia, who claimed that the Bolsheviks killed everyone "who wears a white collar or who is educated and who is not a Bolshevik." Others alleged that the Red Army used "Chinese" executioners, and that the Soviet government sought to "nationalize" women and turn them into the communal property of men.[22] The committee concluded that Bolshevism had formed a conspiracy to control all left-wing political, industrial, and social organizations in the United States and to threaten America's system of government and free-enterprise economy.[23]

The constant refrain of counterrevolutionary reports on Bolshevism spoke of innocent Russians enduring horrific violence at the hands of frenzied alien groups: German agents, Chinese hooligans, and especially Jews. The Bolshevik party counted many members of Jewish background, most prominently Leon Trotsky, the founder of the Red Army, and Grigory Zinoviev, who headed the Communist International (Comintern), which was formed in early 1919 to promote revolution abroad. Anti-Semites in Russia and throughout the world referred to Trotsky and Zinoviev not by their revolutionary pseudonyms but by their birth names, Bronstein and Apfelbaum, in order to "unmask" the Bolshevik regime as a Jewish conspiracy.[24] The allegation was untrue: While Jews joined the nascent Communist state in large numbers, what attracted them was not a supposed Jewish agenda but the experience of past stigmatization and violence under the tsars and the hopes for universal freedom and equality.[25] Yet for many of their opponents, the fact that the Bolsheviks consistently called out acts of anti-Semitic violence only reinforced the idea that they were Jews protecting fellow Jews.[26] Less than a year into Soviet rule, a Dutch diplomat, cabling from Petrograd, urged the immediate suppression of the Communist regime. If left unchecked, in his view, Bolshevism was bound to spread over the globe, "as it is organized and carried out by Jews who have no nationality, and whose one object is to destroy for their own ends the existing order of things."[27]

Hatred of Jews was the cornerstone of White propaganda during the civil war. For lack of positive aims of their own that could match the Red promises of bread, land, and liberation featured on Soviet proclamations and leaflets, counterrevolutionary propagandists settled on indicting Soviet leaders as Jewish mass murderers.[28] A poster commissioned by White propagandists depicted a monstrous Trotsky straddling the Kremlin wall, observing with grim satisfaction the mountain of skulls rising below him, as a group of Chinese Red Army soldiers standing to the side execute yet another captive Russian peasant. Posted on the Kremlin wall is an order allegedly given by Trotsky: It commands Soviet commissars to commit "the most unjust" deeds, to increase the suffering of children and women, to make "villagers wail and cry." In the illustration, the murderous Trotsky, drenched in his victims' blood, is marked as both a Jew and a Communist: He wears the Soviet five-pointed star around his neck, but the star is yellow and interlaced like the Star of David.

The most incendiary piece of propaganda in the civil war, and one that would quickly fan out across Europe and the United States, was not a poster or a witness report. It was a booklet that claimed to lay bare a comprehensive Jewish plot for world domination. The *Protocols of the Elders of Zion*, as the text was titled, was originally fabricated by the tsarist secret police in the late nineteenth century for the purpose of delegitimizing political opposition to the tsar's regime. Presented as a speech by an unnamed leader held at an assembly of Jewish notables (the "Elders of Zion"), the book claims to detail a supposed conspiracy to subvert the

"Peace and Freedom in the Soviet Republic," Odessa, undated.

morals of the non-Jewish world and assume control over the world's banks and the press, in preparation for a final bloody coup.[29] When it was first published, the *Protocols* was quickly exposed as a hoax and soon largely forgotten. The Bolshevik revolution and the subsequent civil war made the text appear newly relevant. Shortly after the murder of the former tsar and his family in July 1918, a copy of the *Protocols* was found in the bedroom of the murdered empress. The discovery seemed to impart prophetic power to the booklet, which then circulated in multiple editions, including one in 1919 that adapted the title to *Documented Facts Proving the Origin of Bolshevism and What Bolshevism Is Striving for in Reality.*[30]

Propaganda of this sort licensed the killing of Jews as Communists. Especially in the borderlands of the former Russian and Austro-Hungarian empires, areas that counted large Jewish populations and became engulfed in nationalist strife as Lithuanians, Latvians, Poles, and Ukrainians took up arms to fight for their emerging states. The warring parties cast the Jews as Bolshevik agents and blamed them for their national misfortunes. After the Poles drove Ukrainian forces out of Lwów, Polish soldiers staged a pogrom, killing over a hundred Jewish residents. Cossacks fighting for a Ukrainian national republic carried out a pogrom in Proskurov, murdering two thousand Jews. The worst actions were committed by soldiers of General Anton Denikin's Volunteer

Army—the Whites—who were encouraged to persecute every Jew as a Bolshevik. Between 1918 and 1920, more than one hundred thousand Jews were murdered in a series of at least two thousand pogroms.[31]

"THE HOMELAND IS IN DANGER!"

In spring 1917, German military leaders had helped foment revolution in Russia by arranging for Lenin to return from Swiss exile to Russia in a sealed train. Their gambit paid off in the short term: After seizing power, the Bolsheviks sued for peace in the ongoing Great War. Along with ending the war on one of the two fronts, the Treaty of Brest-Litovsk granted Germany dominion over Ukraine, thereby realizing the nation's long-held imperial fantasies in the East. But, as some German observers noted with alarm, the treaty was unable to prevent "Russian conditions" from spreading to their own country.[32] Russia was a "source of revolutionary pestilence for the Prusso-German monarchy," a conservative newspaper warned in July.[33] As the flu pandemic swept Europe in the spring and summer of 1918, the public-health crisis further inflamed the political crisis. Germans began to refer to the flu as the "Russian plague," while Poles coined an even more pointed name: the "Bolshevik disease."[34] Eduard Stadtler, who acquired notoriety as the founder of the Anti-Bolshevik League, referred to Bolshevism as an "epidemic" and a "spiritual flu" threatening Germany's very survival.[35] On November 3, 1918, an Austrian newspaper described the revolutionary mood in Vienna as a flu-induced delirium: "Burning fever has befallen many residents, raging through their bodies, impairing their senses. . . . Like a 'red flag' the feverish blaze is flickering, finding its expression in a cry mouthed by hundreds of thousands: Revolution!"[36]

Germany lost the war on the battlefields in France, succumbing to the overwhelming number of fresh troops pouring in from the United States and the British Empire in the summer and fall of 1918.[37] Recognizing imminent defeat, on October 28 the German Admiralty ordered the fleet into battle with the British Royal Navy in a final showdown, solely for the purpose of safeguarding a notion of German honor. The sailors mutinied and demanded peace at any price, as well as the Kaiser's immediate abdication, demands that echoed those of the Russian protesters in Petrograd in early 1917. On the morning of November 9, newspapers announced the Kaiser's intention to step down. Word spread that left-wing socialists led by Karl Liebknecht, who had just been released from prison, were preparing a coup. Philipp Scheidemann, a leader of the moderate Left, rushed to the balcony of the Reichstag to proclaim the birth of the German Republic. Two hours later, Liebknecht stood in front of the Imperial Palace and declared Germany a Free Socialist Republic. On his way to the palace, Liebknecht led a procession of antiwar socialists to the Russian embassy—a gesture that many viewed as an indication of Liebknecht's "Bolshevist ambitions."[38]

In the hour of defeat and revolution, Germany was not as divided as these competing proclamations might suggest. Most politically active Germans, including those on the moderate Left, agreed that protecting their nation from "Bolshevist chaos" should be a top priority.[39] One day after Social Democrat Friedrich Ebert was made chancellor of Germany, the army's deputy chief of the General Staff called to offer the army's full support to the new government so long as both sides agreed to join forces in "combating Bolshevism." Ebert took up the offer.[40] The new republic was founded on an anti-Bolshevist pact, which the Western powers fully endorsed. As part of their fall offensive, the Allies could easily have pushed into Germany to force an unconditional surrender. But their hatred toward Germany was overpowered by their dread of Soviet Communism. If Germany were to collapse, they feared, its fall might prompt an outbreak of the "Bolshevist plague" that could spread into France.[41] "Kill the Bolshie, Kiss the Hun," Winston Churchill instructed, summarizing the British government's new priority.[42] The armistice that went into effect on November 11 took pains to protect Germany from Bolshevism, requiring German forces in the Baltic states and Ukraine to stay where they were as a deterrent against the Red Army.[43]

It was on the soil of the former tsarist empire that Germany opened its first military front against Bolshevism. Taking advantage of Germany's defeat, the Red Army, with the support of Latvian Bolsheviks, had marched into the recently independent republics of Estonia and Latvia. In desperation, the Latvian government appealed to German soldiers for support, promising them land grants as a reward.[44] Thousands reported for service in what became known as *Grenzschutz Ost* (Border Protection Service East). They called themselves the *Freikorps* (free corps), drawing on the nomenclature for the irregular units that had fought for Prussia since the eighteenth century, while in fact serving under the Supreme Army Command. The Iron Division, consisting of sixteen thousand men under the command of Major General Rüdiger von der Goltz, seized Riga in April 1919. In every Baltic city that fell into their hands, Freikorps soldiers sought to eliminate any Communists they found, whether real or imagined. Von der Goltz and his men referred to the Bolsheviks as "bandits" and "beasts" endowed with satanic powers. Young female insurgents in particular drew the counterrevolutionaries' ire—women combatants, when captured, were cruelly abused and murdered. As justification for their extreme violence, Freikorps leaders declared that they were defending "the culture of the entire world."[45]

Unlike the Russian Whites, these German forces fighting the Bolsheviks did not emphasize their enemy's alleged Jewishness. The menace they saw had a mostly Asiatic face. For instance, a German propaganda brochure published in February 1919, entitled "The True Face of Bolshevism," contained photographs of murdered civilians and priests, and alleged that thousands of Tatars and Chinese were serving among the Bolshevik troops.[46] A poster soliciting funds to support Germany's fight in the East portrayed the Bolshevik enemy as a skull with slanted eye sockets and a Genghis Khan–style mustache, underneath a Mongolian fur hat.[47] Other posters from the same period depicted the Bolshevik as a torch-wielding or bomb-throwing anarchist, marked as Russian by his tunic dress and belt.[48] German Social Democrats generally referred to Bolshevism as "Socialism asiaticus," casting it as the antithesis of German culture and European order.[49]

The Germans lost their foothold in the East in summer 1919. Angered by von der Goltz's brutal despotism, Latvians and Lithuanians joined

"The Homeland Is in Danger!" (1919)

ranks to drive their guests west.[50] Back at home, the men of the Freikorps continued to cling to their imperial fantasies and their anti-Bolshevik commitments.[51] In a book published in 1920, von der Goltz described his past "mission" to avert the "downfall of the West" by fighting the "Bolshevist Weltanschauung of Asiatic bondage."[52] His book was followed by a slew of memoirs in which Freikorps veterans mourned the lost opportunity to gain colonial lands in the East, while dwelling on their heroic efforts to fight the Bolshevik menace, often embodied in the figures of bestial "riflewomen"—"cruel furies only Bolshevism could concoct."[53] In 1921, Heinrich Himmler, a student of agronomy at the Technical University of Munich, heard von der Goltz speak. In his diary, Himmler noted: "I am more certain than ever that when there is another campaign in the East, I will join it. The East is what is most important to us. . . . We must fight and settle in the East."[54]

A second front against Bolshevism opened simultaneously inside Germany. It was formed by officers who had returned from the front lines of the Great War with the belief that soldiers' low morale and revolutionary agitation were the result of an organized conspiracy to bring down the empire. As early as October 17, 1918, in response to a motion to grant the German parliament greater political rights, Captain Gotthard Heinrici spoke of the downfall of "our entire old fatherland." "A clique of Jews and socialists now governs us, people who put the Internationale above everything else."[55] The fact that no Allied soldier set foot on German soil ahead of the armistice further nourished the belief that Germany had suffered defeat not on the battlefield, but through a "stab in the back" carried out by Jews, Marxists, and Bolshevists who had infiltrated the home front. Determined to rid Germany of the "red menace," some of the returning officers formed Freikorps units that targeted those they blamed for Germany's surrender, generally radical fringe groups that proudly called themselves Bolshevik and sought to stage a revolution in Germany. Liebknecht and Rosa Luxemburg, for example, had transformed the radical Left into a Communist party and led strikes and mass demonstrations. Government and Freikorps troops suppressed the uprising, shooting hundreds of demonstrators and hunting down their leaders. Liebknecht and Luxemburg were murdered in cold blood, but the non-Communist press claimed they had been lynched by a furious crowd. Government troops stepped up their repressions in the months that followed. Their brutal quelling of public disorder took several thousand lives.[56] The sustained violence in the capital forced the Constituent German National Assembly to meet in the town of Weimar, which would lend the shaky republic its name.

In Munich, Kurt Eisner, who campaigned as a pacifist and democrat, was attacked for publicizing documents that highlighted Germany's responsibility for the outbreak of the Great War. Eisner's detractors focused especially on his Jewish background, calling him a traitor. Particular vitriol came from the Thule Society, a nationalist and racist clandestine organization founded to counter alleged Jewish influence in Germany and establish a purely "Aryan" Reich. On February 21, 1919, just as Eisner approached the Bavarian parliament to offer his resignation after suffering a humiliating electoral loss, he was murdered by a young lieutenant, Anton Graf von Arco auf Valley. The lieutenant justified his deed, saying, "Eisner's a Bolshevist, he's a Jew, he's not a German, he doesn't seem German, he undermines every patriotic thought and feeling, he's a traitor."[57] But there was another, more personal reason, as well: Once a member of the Thule Society, Graf van Arco had been excluded after it was learned that his mother was Jewish. By committing this act, Arco sought to prove that he was a true German engaged in the struggle against Bolshevists and Jews.[58] Enemies of Germany's revolution celebrated the news of Eisner's murder. Students at the University of Munich broke out in cheers upon learning that Eisner was dead. The eminent Professor Wilhelm Röntgen was even forced to cancel his lecture.[59]

Sentiment among Munich's workers shifted further left following Eisner's demise. In March, Hungarian Communist Bela Kun had declared Hungary a Soviet Republic. Not long afterward, Communist activists in Munich proclaimed a Soviet Republic there as well. Several of their leaders were Russian and Jewish, and they had soon summoned a "Red Army" of worker activists that they called upon to fight the "White" government troops.[60] The haphazardly formed Red forces didn't stand a chance against the thirty thousand soldiers who advanced on Munich in April 1919. With government troops closing in, the revolutionaries ordered the execution of ten political prisoners, seven of them activists from the Thule Society who had infiltrated their ranks. These hostages were put up against a wall and shot.[61] Soon, though, the government troops and Freikorps men restored order in Munich with a wildly disproportionate degree of force. After quelling the uprising using flamethrowers, heavy artillery, and even airplanes, they murdered more than a thousand suspected insurgents. Any member of Munich's working class was fair game.[62]

HITLER: BECOMING AN ANTI-BOLSHEVIST

Corporal Adolf Hitler was in a north German hospital recovering from a mustard gas attack on the Western Front when he learned of the proclamation of the German Republic. As Hitler described it in his political tract *Mein Kampf*, news of the fatherland being seized by "wretched criminals" made him break down in tears, before filling him with the resolve to enter politics.[63] Available historical documentation suggests that Hitler experienced his awakening somewhat differently. Contrary to his claim in *Mein Kampf*, Hitler did not initially oppose the revolution, but joined it in Munich, where his regiment was based. He supported Eisner's government and appears in a photograph of Eisner's funeral procession, walking behind the coffin. He also served on the soldiers' council of his regiment and was reelected after the proclamation of the Munich Soviet Republic.[64] Hitler, it seems, was no anti-Bolshevik in these early days. Only after the fall of the Communist government did he join the counterrevolution, enrolling as an agitator in the army's propaganda department. Some historians believe this turnaround was driven by the survival instinct of a consummate politician; others make light of Hitler's Soviet phase, determined to portray him as an unyielding counterrevolutionary.[65] The autobiographical essays by Nazi party members that Theodore Abel collected in the 1930s make Hitler's switch appear less idiosyncratic. Many of those who would later become Nazis also felt energized by the revolution and joined leftist organizations before settling on the far right.

In summer 1919, Hitler cultivated his voice, honing an unrelenting message of anti-Semitism that had been wholly absent from his earlier life.[66] Hitler's first documented rant against Jews was dated August 1919, a month after the signing of the Versailles Treaty, which officially ended the Great War by ordering Germany to pay enormous reparations, limiting its army to one hundred thousand men, and forcing it to accept the blame for starting the war. Many Germans responded to this humiliation by blaming "the Jews."[67] Only then, and in ways that could not be seen in November 1918, did the full measure of Germany's defeat become apparent. For Hitler, the "dictate" of Versailles bore the handwriting of global financiers ruling from London, Paris, and Wall Street, all of them Jews who were conspiring to keep Germany in "servitude to interest rates" in perpetuity. They were assisted by Jewish ideologues on the Left who, allegedly, had brought down Germany from the inside. For Hitler and many others, Jews were responsible for virtually all of Germany's woes. The chairman of the Central Association of German Citizens of Jewish Faith threw his hands up in despair as he tried to list all the different charges made against Jews:

> We are supposed to have begun the war, we are supposed to have prolonged the war, we are supposed to have set conditions for the armistice, we are supposed to have made a revolution, we are to blame for the dictated peace. We are at once democrats, mainstream socialists, breakaway socialist independents, and Bolshevists.[68]

In September 1919, Hitler attended a meeting of the German Workers' Party, an ethno-nationalist (*völkisch*) splinter group that had formed a few months earlier at the initiative of the Thule Society. He spoke with the party's founder, Anton Drexler, and was given a copy of his booklet, *My Political Awakening*. Drexler's attempt to fuse nationalism and socialism in order to free the working class from the false teachings of "Jewish Marxism" and harness them for the nationalist cause appealed to Hitler, especially as it spoke to his own experience. He joined the party. Appointed chief propagandist, Hitler increased the party's membership and had it renamed the National Socialist German Workers' Party (*Nationalsozialistische Deutsche Arbeiterpartei)*. As he established himself as the NSDAP's leader, Hitler also adopted the swastika symbol from the Thule Society and purchased its newspaper, the *Völkischer Beobachter* (*Ethno-National Observer*). A meeting of the party in May 1920 attracted the attention of the Munich police:

> The speaker was Mr. Adolf Hitler, who behaved more like a comedian. Every third sentence of his couplet-like lecture contained the refrain: The Hebrews are to blame! There is hardly a dirty trick or coarse misrepresentation that the speaker did not attribute to the Jews! . . . When the speaker raised the question of how one is supposed to fend off the Jews, calls from the assembly provided the answer: Hang them! Beat them to death![69]

"Why are we anti-Semites?" Hitler asked at a party meeting in Rosenheim in August. "We are fighting the Jew mainly because of his race and his actions as a subversive factor in the life of our people."[70]

From early on, Hitler's generic anti-Semitism carried an anti-Bolshevik tinge.[71] But over time, hatred of Communism would become an increasingly central element of his vitriol. He was by no means alone in this—after the defeat of the local Soviet government, popular opinion in Munich turned staunchly anti-Bolshevik in summer 1919. The city's newspapers carried exposés detailing the "horrific" shooting of the ten hostages, complete with false claims that "Russians" had carried out the murders and that the genitals of the nine male hostages had been cut off and thrown into the garbage. "Only Bolsheviks" were believed to be capable of such ghastly crimes.[72] Accounts from the Russian civil war amplified these fears, as they suggested what horrors lay in store for Germany if Bolshevism swept westward. The Thule Society courted refugees from Russia, inviting them to hold lectures on Bolshevik terror. In this way, Hitler came into contact with a group of Baltic Germans and White Russians who had settled in Munich.[73] One of them was Alfred Rosenberg, a schoolteacher from Reval (Tallinn) who had fled the Baltics alongside retreating German troops.

Rosenberg exploited his authority as a supposed eyewitness to Bolshevism to launch a prodigious writerly career. Claiming to have traveled widely throughout Russia in 1917 and 1918, he asserted that wherever he had seen Russian Communists gathering, "90 out of 100 of them were Jews."[74] Rosenberg's first bestselling book was entitled *Plague in Russia! Bolshevism, Its Heads, Henchmen, and Victims.* It described the techniques adopted by agents of the Cheka, the Soviet secret police, who were said to employ the most sadistic torture methods imaginable, including the skinning of victims after boiling them in water. The goal of these agents, whom Rosenberg referred to as "Jewish and Chinese," was to kill off Russia's national elite.[75] In an article for the *Völkischer Beobachter* in 1921, Rosenberg presented Jewish terror in Russia as the largest crime in world history: "Over 30 million people have died through murder, starvation, and cholera." But Rosenberg's warning extended beyond Russia: Next on the Bolsheviks' agenda, he said, was a pogrom against the German people.[76]

Under Rosenberg's influence in particular, Hitler embraced anti-Bolshevism as his own mission.[77] Rosenberg's mantra that Russia was a victim of Jewish Bolshevik terror became a central tenet for the future German chancellor. In July 1922, Hitler repeated Rosenberg's claim that Soviet Communists had murdered more than thirty million people—"partly on the scaffold, partly through machine guns and similar means, partly in veritable slaughtering houses, and the rest through starvation."[78] Perhaps Rosenberg's most influential contribution to the budding Nazi movement was introducing Hitler to the *Protocols of the Elders of Zion*. This booklet had first arrived in Germany in 1918, courtesy of an anti-Semitic Russian officer who had fought for the Whites, but it was an edition published by Rosenberg in 1923 that introduced the forgery to large numbers of Germans for the first time.[79] In his introduction, Rosenberg described the revelatory power of the *Protocols*: "Many otherwise inexplicable present-day phenomena suddenly no longer seem coincidences, but consequences of a previously secret, but now exposed cooperation among the leaders of classes, parties, and peoples who only appeared to be bitterly fighting with one another."[80] Rosenberg's sense of illumination and sudden insight bears a striking resemblance to Hitler's discussion of the *Protocols* in his early speeches and writings. *Mein Kampf* abounds with metaphors of veils dropping and scales falling from the narrator's eyes to reveal the concerted actions of Jews, even as they appear to compete with one another as capitalists, Social Democrats, and Communists.[81]

Starting in the early 1920s, Hitler came to conceive of Soviet Communism as a formidable threat. "Judeo-Bolshevism's flood of dirt" required a "battering ram of German character" in opposition, he proclaimed to the party faithful in February 1922, mixing metaphors.[82] Addressing the Nazi Party paramilitary men, the SA storm troopers, in Munich later that year, Hitler predicted that Russian Bolshevism's next and "decisive battle" would prove existential for Germany.[83] "This is a life-or-death fight," he intoned in February 1923. "Either Jewish-international Marxism will survive, or Germany will. The Nazi Party was founded to ensure German victory."[84] As before, Hitler conceived of Jews as a global force operating under different guises, but he now presented Soviet Marxism, or "Bolshevism," as their most fearsome weapon.

In July 1923, Hitler saw the Soviet star as "the emblem of a race that is preparing to assume power from Vladivostok to Western Europe. The sickle is a sign of cruelty, the hammer is a sign of freemasonry. The reign of the Soviet star will be a paradise for Jews, but a slave colony for all others. The Communists' goal is not Germany's salvation but its destruction."[85]

For many of Hitler's listeners, there was compelling evidence to support his rants. Germany was in economic collapse, French forces had occupied the Ruhr Valley to enforce reparation payments, and a sustained wave of strikes had unseated two consecutive governments. Conservative observers likened Germany in summer 1923 to Russia on the verge of the Bolshevik uprising, and open calls for a "German October" from Communists in Berlin and Moscow gave their warnings credence.[86] Socialist newspapers added fuel to the fire with calls for someone to "put the most treasonous upper classes out of their misery by sticking a knife in their necks."[87] Fearing an uprising from the Left, the Social Democratic Reich chancellor unseated the governments of two federal states that ruled with Communist support. The widespread fear of revolution benefited the Nazi Party. The example set by Benito Mussolini, another erstwhile socialist turned right-wing nationalist, emboldened Hitler further; Mussolini had brought his Fascist movement to power in Italy in 1922 largely on the strength of a propaganda campaign against the perceived Communist threat. Molding himself in the image of the "Duce," Hitler insisted on being called "Führer" and prepared to step forward as Germany's savior.

Hitler chose a highly symbolic day for his coup: November 9, 1923, the fifth anniversary of the German revolution, or as he preferred to call it, the "day of the greatest crime of German history." The purpose of his movement, he said, was to decisively reject "the revolt of the lumpen and the Jews" by inaugurating Germany's "national rebirth."[88] On the morning of November 9, Hitler led several thousand Nazis through Munich, pronouncing himself Germany's dictator. The Munich march, an imitation of Mussolini's march on Rome, was poorly planned and ended ignominiously, with the temporary prohibition of the Nazi Party and the arrest of its leaders on charges of treason. But at the trial that ensued, the atmosphere in the courtroom was so strongly anti-Communist that the accused were feted as national heroes and received astonishingly light sentences.

When the Nazi Party was founded anew in 1925, November 9 became its most important holiday. While sorrowful remembrances of the fallen soldiers of the Great War had predominated in the earliest commemorations of the Nazi movement, the tone after 1925 turned decisively vengeful. November 9 was invoked as "judgment day." "The death of Marxism will be the birth of the Germany to come," a pro-Nazi general proclaimed on November 9, 1931.[89] The November holiday retained its retaliatory thrust into the years of Nazi rule. It was on the night of November 9, 1938, that the Nazis staged a violent anti-Jewish pogrom, Kristallnacht, calling it an act of retribution for the assassination of a German diplomat by a desperate Jewish refugee. When Hitler declared war on Poland on September 1, 1939, he justified the invasion as a way to wipe out the shameful memory of November 1918.[90] And in May 1941, a military directive invoked the suffering of the German nation following the collapse in 1918, so as to legitimize any and all acts of cruelty German soldiers might inflict on Soviet ("Bolshevist") civilians. "No German has forgotten this."[91]

"MARXISM MUST DIE!"

While in prison, Hitler dictated a comprehensive history of his movement and its programmatic goals to a fellow Nazi inmate.[92] At its core, *Mein Kampf* laid out the dangers confronting Germany and provided a road map to ensuring the nation's survival. Human history, in Hitler's reading, was in large measure natural history: a harsh struggle between races, the outcome of which would be either survival or annihilation. On account of their inborn qualities, Germans, or Aryans, were destined to become a "highest race" that would rule as a "master race."[93] But at the present, the workings of these natural laws were stymied by the "Jewish doctrine of Marxism," which ignored race as a marker of difference and thus rejected the "aristocratic principle of Nature, replacing the eternal privilege of power and strength by the mass of numbers and their dead weight." As such, democracy and internationalism threatened to spell the end of not only Germany but also the very principles of cultural distinction. Claiming to be nature's avenger, Hitler called on Germans to shake off Jewish rule and reassert their racial dominance.

Mein Kampf echoed the *Protocols* by positing a global Jewish conspiracy, but unlike in the earlier text, Hitler cast the conspiracy as directed specifically against the German people. As leaders of world capitalism and world Communism, Jews had spawned two ideologies that only appeared to be opposites but in reality were two sides of the same coin. Both aimed to divide Germans and keep them on their knees.[94] Of the two, the Bolshevik ideology was far more menacing. The Soviet Union was the only state where "the Jew" had openly seized power and revealed his true face as the "blood-spilling tyrant," who in his "fanatical wildness" had sent thirty million people to their deaths. And the Jews in the Kremlin were not content with subduing only the Russian people: "In Bolshevism we have to perceive the attempt of Jewry to seize control over the world."[95]

While exceedingly dire, Hitler's message also exuded confidence. Jews, he held, were only a force of destruction, unable to hold on to power. Once they had killed the Russians, the host upon whom the parasitical Jewish "vampires" were feeding, they would face their own destruction. This presented a chance for Germans, who required more living space (*Lebensraum*), to fulfill their racial destiny and secure their country's status as a great power by colonizing Russia.[96] In the present moment, however, the Soviet system remained a formidable threat, especially as it controlled a shadow army of German Communists. There could be no peace and quiet in Germany, Hitler declared behind closed doors in 1926, until "the last Marxist is converted or exterminated."[97]

The fight against Bolshevism was a fight for the restoration of the German nation. In Hitler's racial imagination, a people formed a single living and breathing organism. In this sense, the German body had been grievously wounded during the Great War, only to be weakened further by Marxism's divisive class rhetoric.[98] The task for the Nazi movement was to heal the nation by making leftists recognize that they were "part of a single people."[99] German workers who voted Communist were "deluded" but curable, on account of their healthy racial stock. They needed only to be alerted to the fact that their anthem, "The Internationale," was in reality "Moscow's song of tyranny, played on Jewish finger cymbals."[100] This coming "day of recognition" would bring about a reckoning with the racially alien, Marxist-Jewish intellectuals who conspired to turn German Communists against the Nazi cause.

Marxism, which Hitler always imagined as a Jewish doctrine, was antithetical to his understanding of Germany, and as such, it had to die. But Marxism also provided the model for Hitler's own faith. It was the sole ideology besides Nazism that Hitler recognized as a "worldview" and drew inspiration from for his own movement. In a veiled admission of his past infatuation with Leftism, Hitler, in *Mein Kampf*, describes a mass demonstration of "Marxists" he witnessed in Berlin shortly after

"The Day of Recognition—the Dawn of the Third Reich."
The lower caption reads: "Brothers of one people."
Der Angriff, *August 6, 1928.*[101]

the war: "A sea of red flags, red scarves and red flowers gave to this demonstration. . . . an aspect that was gigantic from the purely external point of view. I myself could feel and understand how easily the man in the street succumbs to the suggestive magic of a spectacle so grandiose in effect."[102] As he sought to recruit workers to his own party, Hitler copied his opponents' colors as well as their reliance on banners and chants.[103] He did so, however, with an important twist. In their mission to transform human consciousness, Communists favored written and verbal appeals—the works of Marx and Lenin in particular.[104] Even Communist street agitation worked through theater troupes, as exemplified in Berlin's popular "Red Megaphone" collective, which spoke in monologues and choruses to explain politics and history to their audiences.[105] Hitler, on the contrary, sought to appeal to his audience's emotions rather than their intellect. Hence, he embraced visual propaganda, ranging from posters to film. Such propaganda, he explained, had better prospects as it required viewers "to use their brains even less; . . . . many will more readily accept a *pictorial presentation* than *read* an *article* of any *length*."[106]

As soon as Hitler was released from prison on probation after a six-month term, he led his party on a visual conquest of Germany, enacting the script laid out in *Mein Kampf.* The Nazis, as he wrote, were to work not through conspiratorial cells of hardened revolutionaries—a reference to Lenin's party—but through armies of hundreds of thousands of "*fanatical fighters*" whose task was to impress Germans with an overwhelming show of force. "*We must teach the Marxists that the future master of the streets is National Socialism, just as it will some day be the master of the state.*"[107] This task fell to the SA. Countless German villages in the late 1920s experienced the same Sunday spectacle: Trucks with uniformed men would pull up to perform roll calls and hold parades, organize sports events, and present concerts for hours on end before concluding with a torchlight procession. Local Communists would unfailingly be taunted and terrorized. What these "propaganda marches" advertised above all were the virile and aggressive bodies of the SA fighters. They were "national socialism incarnate."[108]

Nazi Party rally in Weimar, July 1926. Hitler (upper left) in a pale trench coat is standing in a car as he reviews an SA procession. The banner proclaims: "Death to Marxism."

But it was the cities, and chiefly Berlin, that turned into the Nazis' principal battleground against Marxism. One-tenth of all German Communists lived in Berlin, and in 1932, nearly a third of all Berliners voted Communist.[109] "Berlin is red and Jewish at once," wrote one member of Berlin's newly founded Nazi chapter in 1926. "Every political event, every election documents it anew. And it must be red, because it is Jewish. The two easily complement one another: Since time immemorial Marxism and the stock exchange have been loyal brothers in arms."[110]

For the Nazi Party to conquer "Red Babylon," it had to win over its working class. In October 1926, Hitler appointed Joseph Goebbels, his most talented propagandist, to lead the Berlin party organization. Goebbels meticulously planned the "storming" of Berlin. He began in Wedding, the city's celebrated Communist district. In February 1927, Goebbels rented the Pharus Halls, a community center that Communists in Wedding referred to as their "second living room." More than a thousand people, most of them Nazis, crowded in the space to hear Goebbels speak. When the attending Communists called for the right to debate the speaker, a Nazi official retorted, "We are the ones who set the agenda." His words were a signal for SA men to start a brawl, swinging chairs and beer mugs.[111] By evening's end, a Nazi report noted, the Communists counted eighty-three "more or less heavily injured" followers, compared to three heavily wounded Nazis and a dozen others who had sustained light wounds. "The Marxist terror was bloodily suppressed," the report concluded. "Toward 11:30 p.m., an SA procession, more than five hundred men strong, set out through the streets, which were cordoned off by the police. . . . The battle was fought. A victory for National Socialism at Wedding achieved."[112]

The Nazis carried out acts of brazen aggression, which they cast as a legitimate defense against an ostensible Red Terror. A set of instructions provided to the SA in 1926 specified that their primary purpose was to attack the party's enemies. The same message appeared in the newspaper that Goebbels launched in 1927, which he called *The Attack* (*Der Angriff*). While claiming to be victims of Communist aggression, the Nazis for their own part praised the virtue of systematic and preemptive violence.[113] They resorted to violence systematically and in preemptive fashion. When the Nazi Party organized marches, it disguised some of its toughest fighters as ordinary civilians who would follow the march on the sidewalk. As soon as onlookers objected to the sight of the brownshirts, these men, often from the SS (or *Sturmstaffel*, at the time Hitler's bodyguard within the SA), would immediately assault the protesters.[114] The aggression was above all physical, rather than verbal, in contrast to that of the Communists. The purpose of the SA, the *Völkischer Beobachter* wrote, was to drown out the lyrics of "The Internationale" with the cadence of their own anthem: "The sounds of cracking wood and splintering glass, and the screams of the battle meetings. And it will remain that way until we hold power in the state. For that reason, fight to the last man, fight with the fanaticism that our opponents fear in us. Fight, fight, fight!"[115]

In this scenario of perpetual aggression, Jews as Jews barely figured. The most hated opponents were the Communists, who were understood to be controlled by Jews.[116] For the parliamentary elections in May 1928, the Nazis campaigned with a poster that showed an athletic SA trooper, his belt buckle in the form of a swastika, hammering away at the Soviet red star. Etched into the star is a yellow Star of David. "Marxism dies so that socialism may live," the poster intoned. Propaganda of this kind helped the Nazis earn their first seats in the Reichstag. One of the twelve Nazi deputies was the Great War veteran and fighter pilot ace Hermann Göring, who subsequently became Hitler's devoted lieutenant. Göring took his wife, Carin, to the ceremonial opening of the parliament. What struck Carin most was the appearance of the fifty-four Communist delegates in the plenary hall. "It was quite eerie," she wrote to her mother the following day, "to see the Red Guard gang. They throw their weight about colossally. They were all wearing uniforms adorned with the Star of David—that is, the Soviet star, which is the same thing—red armbands, etc. Young, most of them, and just raring for a fight. And some of them downright criminal types. How many in all these parties except Hitler's are Jews!"[117] That Marxism as a Jewish ideology threatened Germany's survival was not just an effective political slogan; for adherents of the Nazi movement, it was an article of faith.

"Marxism dies so that socialism may live." Nazi campaign poster, 1928.

RESCUING GERMANY

Throughout much of the 1920s, the Communists barely took notice of the Nazis, who scored a mere 2.6 percent of the popular vote in the 1928 elections. For the KPD, the main enemy remained the ruling SPD, which they reviled as "social fascists" for their role in abetting the persecution of Communists. The steady growth of the SA changed this picture. Some thirty thousand paramilitary men in uniform arrived at the party rally in Nuremberg in August 1929. In addition to parading through the city's stadium and streets, SA militants went on a rampage, demolishing a trade union building, raiding the city's Communist pubs, and attacking passengers in streetcars. As accounts of Nazi terror seeped into the Communist press, Communists came to reimagine "White fascism"—referring to the White movement in Russia's civil war—as wearing a brown shirt. The summer of 1929 marked the beginning of street battles between the Nazis and the KPD, which would escalate through the coming years. "Beat the fascists wherever you see them!" the Communist daily *Die Rote Fahne* (*Red Flag*) exhorted readers.[118]

While Hitler's storm troopers made headlines, Nazi violence on its own was not enough to propel the party into the national limelight. An unforeseen crisis came to its aid: Wall Street crashed on October 29, 1929, and in its wake, Germany's economy, built largely on U.S. short-term loans, went into free fall, wiping out all the gains made during the previous years of recovery. As wages dropped and unemployment soared, Nazi propagandists painted a clear picture of who was to blame—world Jewry—and how the crisis could be solved: through a program of national unity and regeneration. Hitler's position as an outsider—to date, his party had not participated in any of Weimar's short-lived coalition governments—made his program even more alluring. When new parliamentary elections were called for September 1930, the Nazis campaigned more strenuously than any other party, holding thirty-four thousand meetings throughout Germany during the final four weeks of the campaign. Large crowds came to hear Hitler. Among them was Gustav Hilger, a civil servant who saw Hitler in Berlin's Sports Palace on September 12, two days before the elections. "Everybody cheered the Führer when he said plain and simple that he would not yield in his fight against the numerous political parties until his idea had carried the day. I will never forget his prophecy: 'The final struggle will play out only between National Socialism and

Bolshevism.'"[119] Hans Schönherr, the teacher from Wiesbaden and participant in Abel's writing competition, attended a party rally in a tavern in nearby Mainz: "The access roads were heavily secured by police forces, for a wild pack of Social Democrats and Communists had gathered outside. For them, the Nazis were fair game who should be beaten to death wherever they were found." Schönherr was so captivated by the Nazi speakers that he applied for admission into the party before leaving the tavern.[120]

September 14, 1930, brought a political earthquake. The Nazi Party suddenly became the second-largest delegation in parliament, behind the SPD; the KPD took fourth place. When the new Reichstag convened on October 13, 1930, the 107 Nazi delegates—up from 12—marched into the chamber wearing brown shirts, swastika armbands, and tan riding breeches, in violation of an existing ban on uniforms. The same day, SA men rampaged through the streets of Berlin, smashing windows of a department store and many other shops they believed to be owned by Jews. "Down with the Jews!" they shouted.[121] But despite these and other outbursts, the German public was calmed by an oath Hitler swore in court, promising to seek power through legal and nonviolent means only. The brutality of the storm troopers notwithstanding, Hitler's assurances made him appear as a lesser evil compared to the Communists, who never gave up the call for violent revolution.

Emboldened, the Nazis vied for even greater power, positioning themselves as the staunchest opponents of the radical Left. "Us or Bolshevism"[122] was the central directive given to all Nazi propagandists in 1931. To demonstrate the party's fighting form, Hitler ordered 100,000 SA men to convene in Braunschweig in October 1931 for a two-day rally.[123] By calling up this number of men, Hitler signaled that he already fielded an army the size of the entire German military, per the restrictions imposed by the Versailles Treaty. While the actual number fell short, the 60,000 SA men who arrived in Braunschweig on trains and trucks transformed the city of 150,000 into an army camp. The violence they brought to Braunschweig was a repeat of Nuremberg 1929, but on a much greater scale. Worked up by a torch parade and military songs, SA men undertook a "punitive expedition" in Braunschweig's working-class quarters, demolishing stores and homes and provoking fights with residents. Braunschweig's "Bloody Sunday" resulted in at least two deaths and scores of injuries. Liberal papers decried the helplessness of police facing the storm troopers, while the Social Democratic newspaper *Vorwärts* carried the headline CIVIL WAR IN BRAUNSCHWEIG. The British *Daily Mail*, by contrast, credited Hitler with creating a bulwark against Bolshevism.[124] And *The New York Times* presented a largely uncritical interview with Hitler, enabling him to expound on the "more than six million communists and from six to seven million other varieties of international socialists" who represented "the advance guard in our own country of a formidable foreign power."[125]

Fears of Communism destroying the fabric of the nation in preparation for a violent seizure of power were rampant in Germany at the time Hitler spoke with *The New York Times*. They crystallized in a buzzword that started to gain enormous traction in the late 1920s: "cultural Bolshevism" (*Kulturbolschewismus*). An alarmed reviewer first used the term to denounce one of Erwin Piscator's overtly revolutionary plays at the Berlin Volksbühne. Soon, a coalition of critics, ranging from moderates to those on the extreme political Right, began to see cultural Bolshevism everywhere, from expressionist art to reform-era pedagogy.[126] Some observers maintained that the "degenerate" condition of modernist culture helped establish Bolshevism, whereas others blamed Soviet leaders in Moscow for the breakdown of "authentic" German culture.[127] Either way, as the Nazis were the most consistently anti-Communist political party, the public obsession with Bolshevism's spread played into their hands. "Anti-Cultural Bolshevism" (*Antikulturbolschewismus*), a perceptive critic noted at the time, was in negative terms what one would call Fascism in positive terms.[128]

With unemployment skyrocketing and millions of despairing Germans losing their faith in government, the Nazis further stepped up their attacks on the Left. Their strategy was to incite even more street violence, while casting themselves as the defenders of law and order against "Bolshevik chaos." Increasingly, German public opinion and German authorities came to share the Nazi view of things. When Nazi troopers raided the heavily Communist city of Altona on July 17, 1932, the brawls they provoked prompted the police to resort to firepower. Two SA men were shot. Not understanding that the shots had come from their own men, and believing they had been fired on by Communist snipers, the police shot at nearby roofs and apartment windows, killing another sixteen people. (Only in 1992 did an examination of police and court records reveal that the bullets that killed the SA men had come from the guns of policemen.[129]) Altona's "Bloody Sunday" proved a consequential event for Prussia (to which Altona belonged as an independent city, before it became part of Hamburg in 1937). German Chancellor Franz von Papen invoked the shootings to suspend Prussia's constitution and its social democratic and liberal government.[130]

Eleven days later, on July 31, the Nazis gained 37.4 percent of the popular vote in the Reichstag elections, becoming Germany's largest party. In September, von Papen's government foundered after a vote of no confidence supported by 90 percent of the newly elected Reichstag. President Paul von Hindenburg was forced to call yet another round of parliamentary elections for November. The Nazis stayed their anti-Bolshevik course, reviving images of fear that dated back to the earliest days of the German counterrevolution. Their election posters portrayed a Red Army soldier as a uniformed skeleton, bloodred, lurking in the shadows and ready to maul his unsuspecting victims. Hitler alone could save Germans from Bolshevism, the poster exclaimed.[131] In the end, the Nazis lost several percentage points in that election, a result probably of voter exhaustion and internal party squabbles, while the KPD and SPD recovered their earlier losses.

The Nazis again responded by doubling down on anti-Bolshevism. In the lead-up to the next election, scheduled for January 15, 1933, they committed resources disproportionately to the contest in the dwarf state of Lippe-Detmold. A sound victory there, they calculated, would show all Germans that the brown revolution was unstoppable. A poster produced for the campaign illustrated the stakes. It portrayed Germany's war against Bolshevism as a confrontation between two racial antipodes: the photograph of an upright Nordic type in front of a swastika, and the tilted por-

"This or That?" Illustrierter Beobachter, *January 14, 1933.*

trait of a man with stereotypical Jewish features superimposed on the Soviet star.[132] "This or That?" the poster asked of voters. Would Germany regain its virility and health, or would it suffer degradation and corruption under Bolshevik rule? By magnifying the Nordic man and contrasting his straight and clear features with his smaller, swarthy, and mocking opponent, the poster underscored the choice between darkness and light, dissolution and order. By this time, the anti-Communist character of Nazi propaganda was so familiar to Germans that the caption flagged Bolshevism without spelling out the word:

> The new year—a crossroad to the future!
> This way: we rise; that way: we plunge
> Into chaos of hordes from the east!
> This way: a new life; that way: the drive
> To wreak havoc and murder.
>
> There is only one choice—this or that!
> You hold your fate in your own hands,
> If you balk, nation, a fire will soon sweep
> Germany from end to end.

The efforts paid off—not only in Lippe, where the party won 39.5 percent of the vote, but throughout the country.[133] Chancellor Kurt Schleicher subsequently handed in his resignation on January 28. Von

Papen recommended Hitler for the post, in hopes of instrumentalizing the Nazis for his own authoritarian designs. At this stage, however, Papen and others on the conservative Right were already captives of Nazi propaganda. Despite their disdain for Hitler's plebeian movement, they fully embraced its polarizing imagery, which no party on the Right projected more forcefully than the Nazis. Virtually all the non-Nazis who backed Hitler in January 1933 desired an end to the "party system" of democratic politics, the oppression of "Jewish Marxism," and the destruction of "Bolshevism." Hitler rose to power thanks to the years he had spent building a broad anti-Bolshevik front. On the morning of January 30, he entered the president's office, wearing a dark double-breasted suit. In the course of an unceremoniously short meeting, Hindenburg entrusted him to form a new government.

RETRIBUTION

On February 1, Hitler addressed the German people on the radio, striking a dark and dystopian tone. In the wake of the Great War, the nation had lost its spiritual unity to a "tangle of political-egoistic opinions, economic interests, and ideological contradictions." But this "picture of heartbreaking internal strife," which Hitler blamed on "Marxism," was only a prelude to the even worse fate that awaited: an onslaught of Communist "madness" that would "ultimately poison and undermine the people, who had already been shaken and uprooted to their core." He had been appointed to forestall Germany's imminent annihilation by taking up the fight once more, as on the front lines of the Great War. Germany's survival hinged on a "decisive act": terminating the Communist threat.[134]

With Hitler's government lacking a majority in parliament, President Hindenburg once again disbanded the Reichstag. The new elections were set for March 5. When Hitler launched his party's campaign in the Berlin Sports Palace on February 10, he stood in front of a huge banner proclaiming "Marxism must die so that the nation will rise again."[135] As the governing party, the Nazis held a considerable edge over their opponents. On February 4, they had persuaded Hindenburg to pass a decree that allowed the banning of Communist meetings and demonstrations in the German states that were under Nazi control, forcing activists to hold meetings in secret.[136] Nazi militants beat, tortured, and killed Communists with impunity, especially after the SA was elevated to an auxiliary police force in Prussia on February 22, on the pretext of an alleged increase in "left-radical" violence. On February 23, the Berlin police, supported by the SA, raided KPD headquarters. The press release, prepared by Interior Minister Hermann Göring, announced the discovery of stockpiles of weapons, secret passageways, and leaflets summoning the population to armed revolt.[137]

Shortly before 9:00 p.m. on February 27, the Reichstag building caught fire. Policemen who rushed to the scene arrested a young Dutch Communist, Marinus van der Lubbe, who readily confessed to setting the fire in order to spark political resistance.[138] While the burning took the Nazis by surprise, it also confirmed their worst fears of an imminent Communist uprising.[139] When Hitler arrived at 10:00 p.m., his face shone purple with agitation and the heat from the fire. He brushed off the view of the police that the arson was the work of a lone "madman." "There will be no mercy now," Hitler shouted. "Anyone who stands in our way will be cut down. . . . Every Communist official will be shot where he is found. The Communist deputies must be hanged this very night. Everybody in league with the Communists must be arrested. There will no longer be any leniency for Social Democrats either."[140]

During the night of February 27–28, the police arrested four thousand Communists and suspected members of other opposition parties, working from lists that had been prepared the previous year.[141] At a cabinet meeting the next morning, Nazi ministers circulated a draft decree to be signed by Hindenburg, ordering the "prevention of Communist acts of violence endangering the state." Employing language drawn from earlier emergency decrees dating back to the government's first anti-Communist repressions in 1919, this one suspended civil liberties as well

"The Reichstag in Flames! Set on Fire by the Communists!" Nazi campaign poster for the March 1933 Reichstag elections.

as the autonomy of Germany's federal states, all of which were enshrined in the Weimar constitution. Political opponents of the state could be held in extrajudicial and indefinite "protective custody."

Nazi propaganda went into overdrive. "A 24-year-old foreign communist has set fire to the Reichstag on the instructions of the Russian and German party offices of this world plague," the *Völkischer Beobachter* printed in large letters on March 1. That evening, Göring addressed the nation by radio, providing more details on the arson attack and its wider aims. The "Communist beast," Göring claimed, planned further assaults on Berlin on the night of the election, March 5. The Nazis used the fire to smear the entire Left: "Stomp Communism! Shatter Social Democracy!" an election poster shouted, reviving memories of Munich in 1919 to evoke the suffering that Communism allied with social democracy would bring: "Good citizens made hostages to the wall!"[142]

The politics of fear worked. In the March 5 elections, the Nazi Party won 43.9 percent of the vote. Despite the new government's use of terror to intimidate voters on the Left, the KPD still mustered 12.3 percent and the SPD 18.3 percent. The Nazis acted swiftly by outlawing the KPD on March 6. Against the opposition of only the SPD, parliament passed the Enabling Act on March 23, giving Hitler's cabinet the power to legislate without parliamentary interference. On May 1, the government outlawed all trade unions in Germany. On June 22, it was the SPD's turn. In a systematic reckoning with the Left, the Nazis detained at least 100,000 and perhaps as many as 200,000 "Marxists" by the end of 1933, most of them Communists.[143] SA pubs, sports grounds, and abandoned factories served as makeshift prisons and places of torture where the prisoners were pressured to give out the names and addresses of other comrades. In "Red Berlin" alone, SA and SS troops ran more than 170 "wild" camps, most of them in boroughs known for their opposition to Nazism. Already on March 13, Munich's new acting chief of police, Heinrich Himmler, had ordered the creation of Germany's first concentration camp in nearby Dachau. Prisoner number one was the young Communist Claus Bastian, a law student at the University of Munich.[144]

While German media publicized Dachau as a correctional facility that remade errant Communists into good Germans, the Nazis used the camp mostly for violent retribution against their political enemies. Hans Beimler, a prominent Communist and Reichstag deputy, was delivered to Dachau in April with a "Welcome!" sign strung around his neck. Dachau's commandant, Hilmar Wäckerle, a captain in the SS, awaited his trophy prisoner with glee. A former Freikorps soldier, Wäckerle had taken part in the storming of Munich in 1919. He passed around photographs of the murdered hostages to other SS officers at Dachau, telling them that now, fourteen years later, the time for a reckoning had come. Beimler had been a leading figure in the Munich Soviet Republic, but had played no role in the killing of the hostages. At Dachau, Beimler was cursed as "Bolshevik swine," tortured, and ordered to commit suicide or else face a brutal death at the hands of the officers. Miraculously, he survived, escaped from Dachau, and eventually made it to the Soviet Union.[145]

The delivery of two prominent Social Democrats, Friedrich Ebert, son of the former president of the republic, and Ernst Heilmann, a Reichstag deputy, to a wild camp in a defunct brewery in Oranienburg in June was widely reported in the national media as a reckoning with social democracy's "big racketeers," who had squandered the "workers' pennies." Heilmann was forced to introduce himself as a "super-scoundrel" who had

Concentration camp Oranienburg. SPD members and broadcast officials are admitted to the camp in August 1933. Ernst Heilmann stands to the right; Friedrich Ebert is next to him.[146]

"deceived the German people and betrayed the workers." One day, he and Ebert were sent into town, where they were made to scrape old SPD posters from the walls—in front of motion-picture cameras. The spectacle was meant to demonstrate how the Nazis would deal with the anti-German Left and restore order.[147]

Ebert was released after eight months, but Heilmann, who was Jewish, remained in the camp and would go on to endure the worst humiliations. Even though no German of Jewish faith was delivered to the early camps solely on the grounds of being Jewish, political opposition figures who were Jewish suffered more. Upon his arrival in Oranienburg, Heilmann was assigned to a "Jewish company" and ordered to clean the camp toilets with his bare hands. After years of abuse by guards in multiple camps, Heilmann's suffering came to an end in Buchenwald, where an SS guard gave him a lethal injection in April 1940.[148]

While any political oppositionist of Jewish background or even appearance counted as a sworn enemy of the Nazi state, the Nazis also proceeded to racialize Communists who were not Jewish. In Esterwegen, camp guards lumped "Jews, criminals, and functionaries" together into a single, unreformable pariah group. An August 1933 newspaper publication discussing the prospects for reeducation in the Oranienburg camp surveyed the facial features of the inmate population, concluding that many could not be salvaged.

> On some, one can see how years of incitement can transform a person's features into something brutal, mean, or also sly, false, and insidious. In other types, you can see, even if you are not an expert on skull dimensions or physiognomy, how the owner of this or that semianimal face cannot be anything other than an incorrigible Bolshevist. No instruction can help in these cases; even the most draconian education would be fruitless.[149]

Time and again, Nazi media touted the benefits of the forced labor camps, which "freed" former Communists and Social Democrats from erroneous convictions and redeemed them for the German *Volk*. (In 1936, the slogan "Arbeit macht frei" was inscribed on the iron gates of the Dachau and Sachsenhausen camps.) Those who held on to their beliefs ran the risk of being racialized as inveterate Bolsheviks and grouped with Jewish opposition figures, who maintained their status as racial enemies throughout.

The brutality of the Nazis' assault against the Communist opposition barely registered in the Western press at the time, lost among reports of escalating violence carried out against Jewish businessmen, lawyers, and intellectuals, and attacks on department stores, many of them owned by Jews. In response to these provocations, Jewish organizations in the United States and elsewhere called for a boycott against German goods. The boycott was eventually called off, but not before Hitler ordered a symbolic counter-boycott of Jewish stores on April 1. Foreign observers made no connection between the Nazi aggression against the Jews and their anti-Bolshevik campaign, even though German newspapers explicitly took aim at "Jewish-Marxist bigwigs" and emphasized the tranquility of their own "national uprising" compared to the Munich hostage shootings in 1919 or the "Bolshevik revolution, which cost Russia 3 million lives."[150] The boycott generated headlines across the world, which

"SA arrests communists in Berlin on March 6, 1933, the day after the Reichstag elections."

had the effect of obscuring the Nazis' much more sweeping and violent assault on Communism.[151]

The history of a photograph illustrates this transformation. It shows eight men facing an SA soldier with his firearm cocked, standing against a wall with their hands raised high. Taken in the "Blutburg," a notorious SA camp located off Berlin's Friedrichstasse, the picture was released to the press with the caption "SA arrests communists in Berlin on March 6, 1933, the day after the Reichstag elections."[152] Over the course of the month, it was reprinted in several international newspapers that reported on the Nazi crackdown on Communism. But in the wake of the April 1 boycott, the photograph began to serve instead as proof of the Nazis' brutal persecution of Jews, eliding the story of the Nazis' reckoning with Communism. On April 12, Winnipeg's *Evening Tribune* referred to the prisoners as Jews who were detained at the border and searched for money. Newspapers in Prague and China followed suit. Later that year, the picture featured in a brochure published by a "World Alliance for Combating Antisemitism."[153]

The larger reason behind why Western observers were not more vociferous in their condemnation of the mass incarceration of political oppositionists was their own anti-Communism. Papers that did correctly identify the victims in the "Blutburg" camp as Communists reported their detention with palpable satisfaction. A French magazine believed the photograph to show the captives being searched for weapons, while a Canadian newspaper alleged that they had been caught in an "underground labyrinth," apparently picking up on Göring's story of Communist weapons stashes and secret passageways. At the end of a long feature on Nazi terror that touched on the persecution of the SPD and the KPD, but that dedicated far more space to detailing the Nazis' brutal treatment of the Jews, *The New York Times* warned that Nazi violence would backfire, for "the remnants left of communism will only be steeled to sterner reprisals, should it be their turn that comes." A backlash against Nazi violence, the paper suggested, threatened to bring to power an even crueler Communist regime that would bring untold suffering to the "decent moderates of Germany."[154]

Many of these "decent moderates" jumped on the Nazi bandwagon in the spring and summer of 1933, swayed by Hitler's drastic actions, which appealed to their fears of the radical Left. In April, officials from Lower Bavaria recorded the satisfaction of the people that "the communist agitators have for the most part been rendered harmless."[155] Even among those Germans who loathed the Nazis for their uncouth appearance and brutal behavior, many ventured to say that the mass arrests served a good cause, as the violence and destruction coming from a triumphant Communist party would be infinitely worse.[156] From Rome, Pope Pius XI followed the persecution of the Communist opposition with relief: The chancellor's inaugural address to the German people had made the Vatican apprehensive about an imminent Communist takeover in Germany. Now, the pope praised Hitler as the first European state leader to join the Catholic Church in its long-standing fight against the godless Bolshevists.[157]

Hitler's most ardent backers celebrated the violent showdown with Bolshevism as evidence of Germany's recovery from a near-fatal disease. Virtually all of the Nazis who entered Theodore Abel's essay contest in 1934 described 1933 as a time of vindication: the year when their long struggle finally paid off. Rudolf Kahn, a schoolteacher and SA second lieutenant from Wolfsburg, recalled his state of alert in the days after January 30, 1933, convinced as he was that the "Bolshevists" were about to launch their murderous pogrom against the German people. As commander of a local SA company, he ordered his men to lie in wait night after night. "And then it came! Fire alarm in Berlin. Fire alarm everywhere in the country. Finally, the cathartic order. 'Take them!' And we took them!"

Kahn concluded his autobiography with an ode to the man "who, firmly and unbowed, has his hand on the helm of our ship of state" and "to whom we owe our strength as a united people: Hail our Führer! Hail our people and fatherland!"[158]

Chapter 2

SWASTIKA AND SOVIET STAR

Four days after he was appointed chancellor, Hitler met with the top generals of the German army. The occasion was a dinner at the apartment of the army's commander in chief, General Konstantin von Hammerstein-Equord, to celebrate the birthday of Foreign Minister Konstantin von Neurath. Hammerstein-Equord was no friend of the Nazis. He had referred to them as a "criminal gang" on more than one occasion, and as late as November 1932, he had told Hitler that should he attempt a coup d'état again, he would order his soldiers to fire on him and his followers. Many of the other party guests also arrived full of contempt for the grandstanding social upstart. But by the end of the evening, Hitler had won over most of the generals into his court with an after-dinner speech in which he promised the military a preeminent role in Germany's renewal.[1] Hitler's speech was to remain secret, as it totally contradicted his public pledges for peace and disarmament.[2]

Hitler began his talk, which ran longer than two hours, by extolling the centuries-old culture of Europe as the product of a minority "master race," which had harnessed the labor of millions of colonial subjects. But as he continued, he explained how the Great War and the "poisoning of the world by the Bolsheviks" (a reference to Soviet anti-colonialism) had eroded Europe's prominence, and Germany's within Europe. Hitler outlined two steps that would reinvigorate Germany. The first was to counter the dangerous creeds of pacifism, Marxism, and Bolshevism that had infiltrated German society. Once the army and the nation were remade in a spirit of "morality and nationalism," Germany could take the second step: an "active foreign policy" (read: war) to secure the "*Lebensraum*," or "living space," that Germany required to become a great power. A brutal fate awaited defeated territories. In Hitler's words, "A Germanization of the population of an annexed or conquered country is not possible. . . . We will have to ruthlessly evict several million people." With chilling precision, he announced the time he would need to "completely annihilate" Marxism in Germany and prepare the country for war: "six to eight years."[3] The land he then planned to take was in "the East."

Three days after the dinner party, female staffers in the intelligence division of the Comintern in Moscow received a coded radio message from Berlin containing Hitler's address to the generals. Two card-carrying Communist agents were operating in the closest proximity to General von Hammerstein-Equord—his daughters, Marie-Therese, twenty-four, and Helga, twenty. Marie-Therese, the only woman present during Hitler's address, assisted her father's aide de corps, who had been tasked with transcribing the chancellor's speech. Following the dinner, Marie-Therese handed the transcript to her sister, ostensibly for her to type it. Helga produced a copy and passed it to Leo Roth, a German Jewish Communist and Comintern agent, who then transmitted the document by radio to Moscow. Helga and Roth had been a couple since 1929, when they met on a socialist student association excursion. Included with the transcript, which bore the subject line "Fascism's Program," was a short characterization of Hitler's address, which must have been written by Marie-Therese. It noted that Hitler began his address "earnestly, then in ever greater ecstasy, he lay across the table, gesticulating. In the generals' opinion, it was all very logical and theoretically good. . . . As is his custom in agitational speeches, he repeated the most distinctive passages as many as ten times."[4]

Soviet observers took notice of Hitler's anti-Bolshevik vitriol early on. Writing in *Izvestiya*, the national newspaper, in March 1933, Karl Radek, who was in charge of foreign propaganda within the Central Committee and spoke German fluently, cited at length the Eastern policy chapter from *Mein Kampf*. He noted that sections laying out Germany's aggressive aims against Western Europe, which the Nazis feared might alienate Western readers, had been excised from the book's most recent German edition, published in 1932, but the lines about Germany's imperial destiny in the East had remained unchanged.[5] Just a few months later, in June 1933, Kremlin leaders would have the opportunity to read about the Nazi threat in full, thanks in part to an unabridged Russian translation of what Radek called "Hitler's autobiography," which was issued to Soviet government members in June 1933, a large swastika adorning its cover. (British officials had recourse only to a "polite" translation of *Mein Kampf* that had softened Hitler's vitriol to the point of falsification.)[6] Yet for all the anxiety among Soviet officials about the Nazis' plans in the East, the Soviet Union was dependent on good relations with Germany. German credit was bankrolling Soviet industrialization, and for the past decade the two countries had engaged in secret joint military operations, circumventing the Versailles Treaty.[7] Ultimately, Soviet leaders saw Nazism as only one of several threats to the Soviet Union. Two imperial powers appeared even more menacing to the Bolsheviks, who had faced the specter of foreign intervention since coming to power. Throughout the late 1920s and early '30s, Soviet papers had warned that Great Britain, which they considered Europe's leading power, was preparing an "imperialist" crusade against the USSR. And in 1931, Japan invaded Manchuria, seemingly positioning itself to expand into the Soviet Far East.[8]

Addressing a gathering of industrial managers in February 1931, Stalin had painted a dire picture of Russian weakness to justify his policy of breakneck industrialization. Russia's curse was its "backwardness, military backwardness, cultural backwardness, political backwardness, industrial backwardness, agricultural backwardness." Throughout its history, Russia had been beaten—"by the Mongol khans, the Turkish beys, the Swedish feudal lords, the Polish and Lithuanian gentry. She was beaten by the British and French capitalists. She was beaten by the

Japanese barons." But even as he emphasized the multitude of threats from abroad, Stalin pointedly omitted Germany.

Like Hitler would in his speech to the generals, Stalin presented the industrial leaders with a timeline: "We are fifty or a hundred years behind the advanced countries. We must make good this distance in ten years. Either we do it, or we shall be crushed."[9]

Also like Hitler, Stalin believed in the inevitability of a new world conflict and hastened to put his country on a war footing. Unlike Hitler, however, Stalin sought to keep the Soviet Union out of the coming war for as long as possible. While Hitler revolutionized Germany, Stalin turned his back on revolution: His program of "socialism in one country" reined in the Comintern, whose mission since its founding in 1919 had been to spark a global insurrection on behalf of Soviet state interests. Industrial strength and defense, rather than territorial expansion, were keys to Soviet survival. It was telling that Stalin gave his programmatic address to economic rather than military leaders. Defensive military spending in the USSR rose steadily in the aftermath of his address, consuming close to one-third of all state expenditures in 1940.[10]

Soviet defense needs also drove a ruthless collectivization campaign in the countryside intended to generate more grain for export and hard currency earnings. But the campaign met resistance in the villages and set the regime at odds with much of the Soviet population. As a result, millions of peasants were deported to Siberia and the Far North, and millions more died during a famine that began after government forces swept through starving villages to confiscate all remaining grain. In the end, Stalin's attempt to strengthen Soviet society in fact weakened its defenses and made him dependent on peaceful relations with Germany, despite the bellicosity of its new leaders.

COUNTERATTACK

Although Hitler's rise to power did not immediately alter the Kremlin's course, it galvanized grassroots activists in the Soviet Union and across

Book burning in Göttingen, May 10, 1933.
This photograph was sold as a postcard.

Europe who clamored for a broad anti-fascist alliance to fight Nazism.[11] Many of these anti-fascists were Communist writers who appeared on the arrest lists of the Nazi state and whose books fed bonfires outside German university libraries. Such authors portrayed their fight as a defense of the Enlightenment against fascist barbarism. Over time, the concerted actions of these activists propelled a reluctant Soviet leadership to the forefront of the global fight against Hitler.

Among the first to take up the fight was Willi Münzenberg, a German publisher and Communist member of the Reichstag, nominally on the payroll of the Comintern but acting largely on his own. Weeks after he was forced to flee from Germany to Paris, Münzenberg launched a weekly paper he called *Counterattack*, a rejoinder to Goebbels's daily *Attack*. Disregarding the Comintern's policy of excluding those on the moderate Left as "social fascist" defenders of the capitalist system that had supposedly spawned fascism, Münzenberg reached out to non-Communists as well.[12] In response to the Nazi book burnings, he joined forces with Heinrich Mann and other German writers exiled in France to call for the founding of a "German Freedom Library."[13] Münzenberg's most consequential action was the production in 1933 of *The Brown Book on the Reichstag Fire and Hitler Terror*.[14]

In the wake of the Reichstag fire, the Nazis had filed indictments against Marinus van der Lubbe, the arsonist arrested at the scene, as well as Ernst Torgler, the chairman of the German Communist Party's parliamentary group, and three Bulgarian Communists. Torgler had turned himself in after hearing of his arrest warrant. The three Bulgarians had been arrested by chance—a waiter in a Berlin café observed the group reading Communist papers and reported them as Russian spies. After some delay the police realized that one of the men was Georgi Dimitrov, the undercover head of the West European Bureau of the Comintern.[15] A trial was set in Leipzig, where the five would defend themselves against charges of preparing a Communist uprising.

The immediate purpose of *The Brown Book* was to prove that the Nazis themselves had set the fire in the Reichstag in order to finish off Communism—an idea popular at the time and still embraced by some historians today.[16] More fundamentally, the book provided the world with the first major indictment of Nazism. Using hundreds of documents, including scraps of survivor testimonies, letters, eyewitness reports, and photographs of mutilated bodies that had been smuggled out of Nazi concentration camps, the book painted a harrowing picture of the "great brown dungeon that calls itself the 'Third Reich.'"[17] Dozens of informants, including Helga von Hammerstein-Equord, contributed to the volume.[18] The German Communists who prepared *The Brown Book* from their place of exile in Paris remained anonymous, for fear that the Nazis would persecute family members still in Germany. The book's central section, which the editors were updating even as the publication went to press, was a "kill list of the 'Third Reich'"—250 documented murders extending over twenty-three pages. The list began with an epigraph quoting the daughter of a murdered German worker: "My father is dead. My mother is half insane. I'm also no longer entirely normal."[19]

In addition to the crimes perpetrated against Communists, *The Brown Book* also detailed the sufferings of Social Democrats, trade unionists, Jews, and the liberal intelligentsia—a decision that was remarkable for a Communist publication in 1933. The editors indicted Nazism as a "counter-historical" criminal movement. The "Brown inquisitors" thought they could "turn back the wheel of history to long before the French Revolution" and root out "everything Jewish or supposedly Marxist, everything that embodies the progress and enlightenment of the last hundred and fifty years." The Nazis' torturers operated at night, and the dungeons where they tormented and killed their victims were cloaked in darkness, thus concealing their deeds from millions of Germans: "Our book," the authors said, "will open their eyes."[20] Launched in summer and fall 1933 in multiple languages, *The Brown Book* marked the opening salvo in the struggle against Nazism.[21]

The next was single-handedly delivered by Georgi Dimitrov at the Reichstag trial. Ahead of the trial, Dimitrov spent six months in an isolation cell in Berlin's Moabit Prison, handcuffed for five of these six months. He kept a diary, in German, in which he sustained himself by recalling the deeds of literary freedom fighters. He also read up on German criminal law and the Code of Criminal Procedure.[22]

When Dimitrov was ushered into the courtroom of Leipzig's Imperial Court on September 21, he transformed the Nazi fixation on Bolshevism into a duel between Communist and fascist ideology. It would be carried out on a public stage set by the Nazis, who wanted to prove to Germany and the world that their fight against Communism was legitimate. For that reason, they held a fair trial, with open sessions and foreign correspondents in the courtroom. Van der Lubbe was listless throughout the trial, and Torgler agreed to let himself be represented by a court-appointed lawyer, but Dimitrov insisted on defending himself. A brilliant orator who spoke in impeccable, accented German, the Bulgarian earned the presiding judge's grudging respect by citing lines from Goethe—

> Learn in good time to be wiser:
> On the mighty scales of Fortune,
> The pointer is seldom at rest:
> You must rise or you must fall,
> You must win and be a master,
> Or you must lose and be a slave,
> You must suffer or triumph,
> Be the anvil or the hammer."[23]

John Heartfield, "The Judge and the Judged." Postcard, 1934.

The court case reached its climax on November 4, when Hermann Göring, the Prussian minister of the interior, was brought in as a witness for the prosecution. Wearing the brown uniform and top boots of an SA officer, Göring had come to denounce *The Brown Book*. "Every red rascal who needed money," Göring shouted, "had reports of atrocities at the ready to send to foreign agencies." When Dimitrov was accorded the right to cross-examine Göring and began to point out the inconsistencies in the prosecution's narrative, Göring lost all self-control: "I am not here to allow you to question me like a judge and to reprimand me! You are a scoundrel who should be directly hanged." Millions of Germans listened live on the radio as Dimitrov taunted Göring by reminding him that Communist ideology ruled a sixth of the planet. The daughter of the United States ambassador to Germany, present in the courtroom, noted Göring's choked voice and his face turning deep purple. Dimitrov, she noted by contrast, evinced "the most amazing vitality and courage in a person under stress." The wrangling between Dimitrov and Göring served as a symbolic expression of Soviet Marxist rationalism's triumph over Nazi irrationalism, of a brilliant intellect fearlessly dissecting primal aggression. A saying was heard across Europe: "There is only one brave man in Germany, and he is a Bulgarian."[24]

On December 23, 1933, the court found van der Lubbe guilty and sentenced him to death by guillotine. Torgler and the Bulgarians, including Dimitrov, were acquitted, despite Göring's raging protests. On Hitler's orders, Dimitrov was flown to Moscow. The sole reason he was released, a German policeman told Dimitrov at the airport, was that Germany wanted good relations with the Soviet Union. Once more, Dimitrov had the last word, saying that he looked forward to coming back as a guest of Soviet Germany.[25] In Moscow, Dimitrov was given a Soviet passport and praised for his performance as a Bolshevik role model.[26] John Heartfield's montage of photographs taken at the trial circulated widely in postcard form. It showed a dramatically shrunken Göring shouting epithets—"Red thug! Criminal! Riffraff! Crook! To the gallows!"—at a towering Dimitrov, dressed in a suit. In Paris, Münzenberg prepared *Brown Book II*, with the subtitle *Dimitrov Contra Göring*.[27]

When Stalin received Dimitrov in the Kremlin in early April 1934, he flattered the Bulgarian by recommending that he shake up the Comintern leadership. But when Dimitrov proposed abandoning the Comintern's sectarian fight against social democracy and forming a common front against fascism, Stalin withheld his approval. Nonetheless, in May 1934, Dimitrov was chosen to deliver the keynote address at the 1935 Comintern World Congress.[28]

THE PEN AS A BAYONET

A few months later, in August 1934, the Union of Soviet Writers convened for its first meeting in Moscow. The lavish gathering in the Pillar Hall of the House of Unions confirmed literature's standing as the preeminent Soviet art form. Soviet culture had been thoroughly textual from the start: It was from the "foundational" writings of Marx, Engels, Lenin, and later Stalin that Communist leaders inferred the "laws" of historical development. Persistent schooling campaigns that achieved near universal literacy throughout the USSR by the late 1930s further strengthened the authority of the country's writing profession. In May 1932, Stalin had famously addressed Soviet writers as "engineers of souls," tasking them with perfecting the psyche of their Soviet readership. Nazism's rise and the book burnings in Germany gave Soviet writers an additional mission that extended far beyond their country's borders. Now they began to portray the Soviet Union as a sanctuary for the world's "most progressive writers"—and for humanity writ large in the global standoff against fascism.[29] At the opening session of the union, Central Committee Secretary Andrei Zhdanov lectured the writers about the correct "socialist realist" style. He called on them to capture reality not "scholastically" or "objectively," but in its "revolutionary development." Since the imminent socialist paradise was not immediately visible to the uninformed eye, which registered only the grueling exertions and bare scaffoldings of the present, it fell to literature in particular to chart the course to the bright future. Pointedly, Zhdanov contrasted purposeful Soviet striving with Nazism's savage attacks on civilization.[30]

The writer's duty to help build the new world was the central theme in Ilya Ehrenburg's address at the Congress. With his checkered biography, the forty-three-year-old poet and writer made for an unusual presence there. Born into a wealthy Jewish family in Kiev, Ehrenburg had spent his childhood years in Moscow and enrolled in the city's First Classical High School, which only admitted Jewish applicants with exceptional scores. At the school, Ehrenburg befriended the future Communist Party leader Nikolai Bukharin, who was three years his senior. Both youths ardently supported the Bolshevik faction during the revolution of 1905, and both served prison terms in its aftermath. But while Bukharin joined Lenin's party, Ehrenburg did not and would not at any later point in his life. He was let out of prison on condition that he leave the country.

Ehrenburg settled in Paris, where he wrote poetry and prose in the cafés of Saint-Germain and Montparnasse. During the Great War, he worked as Paris correspondent for several Russian newspapers, before returning to Russia in 1917. The poet's attitude toward the Bolsheviks in power was, at best, ambivalent; his verses mocked the ambition to overhaul an entire society by decree and chided the Soviets for their destruction of Russian churches and other cultural relics. Arrested by the Cheka in 1920 on suspicion of being a foreign spy, Ehrenburg was freed in 1921 upon Bukharin's intervention. He left Russia with a Soviet passport later that year, settling first in Berlin and moving from there to Paris in 1924. Some of his best-known works appeared during this period, including *The Extraordinary Adventures of Julio Jurenito* (1922), a picaresque novel written in the mold of Voltaire's *Candide*, and *Trust D.E.* (1923), a fantastical take on the cultural pessimism that Ehrenburg encountered in postwar Europe.[31] *Trust D.E.*'s protagonist is the illegitimate young offspring of the Count of Monaco, who is so stung by an unrequited love that he marshals a group of American multimillionaires for a gigantic revenge operation. By the end of the book, his plan, "D.E.," which stood for Destruction of Europe, has been executed, and through a combination of ruthless economic and bacteriological warfare bankrolled by the American trust, all human life on the continent has been extinguished. One of Ehrenburg's aims in writing *Trust D.E.* was to parody European fears of the Soviet Union: The maligned Bolsheviks might not be Europe's principal threat.

That this fiercely independent critic would come to proclaim himself an emissary of the Soviet state at Moscow's First Congress of Writers testified to the seismic shift in European society and politics that Ehrenburg observed between the late 1920s and the early '30s. Ehrenburg's writings during those years focused in large part on the Great Depression's debilitating effects on ordinary working people and capitalist leaders' unwillingness to come to their aid. He wrote, with particular alarm, about the rise of Nazism. Shortly after the party's breakout success in the 1930 Reichstag elections, Ehrenburg also wrote ominously about "yesterday's pogromists and bandits" who now appeared as the "healthy movement of German youth." "There is nothing one can do: tomorrow the 'pogromists' will become councilors and ministers."[32]

Set against a Western civilization in crisis and the specter of Germany's descent into "medieval" barbarism, the Soviet Union's Five-Year Plan of purposeful construction appeared to Ehrenburg as the dawn of a new era. In 1932, the writer accepted the position of Paris correspondent for *Izvestiya*—an offer made by Bukharin, the paper's editor. That summer, he journeyed to the vast construction sites in the Urals and Siberia. The young workers there, who appeared to embody the Communist future, shared with him their diaries and letters as well as their thoughts about labor, education, motherhood, and love. Ehrenburg had the interviews transcribed so as to preserve them for his work. Upon his return from Siberia, he observed that "the revolution has truly created new people."[33] In words that earned him applause at the writers' congress in Moscow, Ehrenburg proclaimed his happiness and pride as a "rank-and-file Soviet writer," contrasting the intoxicating prospects of the emerging new socialist world with the despair of the dispossessed German writers he had met in Paris and Prague, and whose books the Nazis had destroyed. Ehrenburg also mentioned a female Chinese writer in attendance, who had told him that revolutionary writers in China were being buried alive. Never before, Ehrenburg said, had he heard such "simple and terrible" words.[34]

The speaker after Ehrenburg was People's Commissar for Defense Kliment Voroshilov. Voroshilov was introduced by a phalanx of Red Army soldiers from the Moscow garrison, who marched into the Pillar Hall and delivered "ardent Red Army greetings" to thunderous applause. Their commander reminded the audience that everyone in the room—soldier or writer—was a warrior; all would rise as one in defense of their country.[35] Ovations also greeted Willi Bredel, who had escaped from the Fuhlsbüttel concentration camp earlier in the year and made his way to the Soviet Union via Czechoslovakia. Writer and physician Friedrich Wolf described how he had escaped on skis while vacationing in Austria. "Like an old fighter, like an old German Red Guardist," Wolf declared to applause, he had broken through "four frontier cordons to get here and fight here for the USSR and for a red Germany." Wolf also remarked on a difference between Soviet and other anti-fascist writers: Whereas the former wrote novels heralding the new socialist age, writers in the West were fighting for their survival. Their existential struggle dictated the use of an overtly political, hard-hitting style. Once war broke out, Wolf predicted, Soviet writers would also write "inflammatory" prose.[36]

Wolf himself had been writing in this fashion for some time already, likely influenced by Vladimir Mayakovsky, who understood himself as a Communist propagandist more than a poet, and who famously proclaimed in 1925, "I want the pen to be on par with the bayonet."[37] When Wolf joined the German Communist Party in 1928, he exhorted fellow writers to brandish their pen as "a flag, a sword, a weapon!"[38] As early as the late 1920s, the Nazi press singled out Wolf as "one of the most dangerous representatives of Eastern Jewish Bolshevism."[39] After his dramatic escape in winter 1933, Wolf wasted no time in attacking the Nazi state with a new theatrical production. Entitled *Dr. Mamlock's Exit*, the play centered on a German Jewish chief surgeon who is persecuted in the wake of the Reichstag fire. Apolitical and bourgeois, Mamlock rejects Communist offers to join the resistance and sees no other way out but to commit suicide. Wolf wrote the play to expose liberal democracy's inability to combat fascism. Still, it ends on an optimistic note: The dying doctor beseeches his Communist son to keep fighting Nazism.[40]

After settling in the Soviet Union, Wolf prepared a screen version of his play. Less recognizably Jewish and more of a humanist, the Sovietized Mamlock is patterned on Georgi Dimitrov. Undeterred by the humiliations that the Nazis inflict upon him, the professor gives a public speech outside a bookstore denouncing Nazi Germany as a "barbaric country of torture, tears, and blood." An SA squadron opens fire on him mid-speech, signifying the death of the bibliophilic Germany the hero represents.[41]

In June 1935, less than a year after the Soviet writers' congress, two hundred and fifty authors from across Europe convened in Paris for a strikingly similar gathering. The International Congress of Writers for the Defense of Culture was a five-day event, with three thousand attendees filling the main hall of the Maison de la Mutualité. Many more followed the proceedings via loudspeakers outside the building.[42] Although no soldiers marched into the hall, as had happened during the Moscow congress, the members at the gathering in Paris also proclaimed themselves fighters against fascism. Writer after writer denounced French novelist Romain Rolland's exhortation during the Great War to remain "above the fray" as out of date.[43] In the words of the writer and philosopher Ludwig Marcuse, the essence of the anti-fascist creed was "the idea of humanitas; the idea of human solidarity . . . the idea of the right of all people to the fruits of the planet, which no more belong to *one* man or *one* group or *one* nation, nor to the white race or the yellow one more than to any other man or group or nation or race." Marcuse called this attitude a "militant" humanism, while Klaus Mann called it "socialist humanism," invoking the Soviet term for the USSR's civilizing mission, which had been making the rounds since the early 1930s.[44]

Soviet ideas and practices found a receptive audience in Paris in 1935. André Gide, the most highly regarded French writer at the time and the chair of the congress, extolled the Soviet Union as a society devoted to the "greatest possible development of every man" and went on to state that he embraced Communism as an individualist: "Precisely by preserving his uniqueness, every being serves his community best."[45] Unbeknownst to most people in the hall, the Paris gathering was bankrolled by the Comintern. The very idea for it had been Ehrenburg's. Disappointed with the lack of attention that the Moscow congress had received in the West, he had written to Stalin and received his approval to stage a similar event in Paris.[46] Ehrenburg wanted his two home cities—Paris and Moscow—to be twin capitals of a European-wide front against fascism. The project appealed to Stalin since it boosted Soviet culture and his own image as a doyen of world literature.

The newly forged French-Soviet literary axis formed part of a larger geopolitical realignment, bringing the USSR somewhat closer to anti-fascist Europe. After Japan and Germany departed the League of Nations in 1933, the Soviet Union had joined the league in September 1934, with the enthusiastic support of the French. In response to a riot staged by far-right groups in Paris earlier that year, the French Left had moved to create a "Popular Front" against fascism. On March 16, 1935, Hitler had openly defied a clause of the Treaty of Versailles by announcing the reintroduction of conscription and the enlargement of the German armed forces to a peacetime strength of eight hundred thousand soldiers. On March 31, *Pravda* had published a rebuke penned by the top Soviet military theoretician, Marshal Mikhail Tukhachevsky.[47] Two days later, *Pravda* and *The Times* published a joint communiqué in support of the "system of collective security in Europe" as stipulated by the League of Nations. On May 2, the Soviet Union and France signed a mutual assistance pact. Weeks later, a Czechoslovak-Soviet treaty completed the collective security design that was to contain Nazi aggression.[48]

One month after the Paris writers' congress, the Comintern proclaimed its support for the broad anti-fascist front that Dimitrov had been promoting for some time. At the 1935 7th World Congress in Moscow, which was attended by 513 delegates representing 65 Communist parties, Dimitrov singled out "fascism's offensive" as the chief political challenge of the day and indicted Nazism as fascism's most radical variant: "a government system of political banditry, a system of provocations and torture of the working class and the revolutionary elements of the peasantry, petit bourgeoisie, and intelligentsia. Nazism is medieval barbarism and atrocity. It is unbridled aggression against other nations and countries."[49] Dimitrov set wide parameters for a Comintern-led Popular Front; beyond workers and intellectuals, he offered to team up even with Catholics and anarchists, as long as all parties agreed on unity of action in the fight against fascism.[50] With prior approval from the Soviet Politburo, the congress elected Dimitrov secretary-general of the Comintern.

Stalin's absence at the congress was a clear indication of his lukewarm support for the new course. His foremost goal, after all, was to forestall the creation of a Europe united against Bolshevism—and too readily embracing the Popular Front risked being interpreted as a move for Communist domination, which might play into the imperialist-capitalists' hands.[51]

WORLD'S GREATEST DANGER

The Nazis countered the Comintern congress with a deliberate show of force at the party's annual rally held in the city of Nuremberg in.

Addressing 120,000 of his followers at the "Congress of Freedom," which was designated that year as a celebration of the country's emancipation from the fetters of Versailles, Hitler declared Germany healed from its internal struggles and ready to confront its greatest menace—the "storm of Bolshevik Jewry." "Here is the German response to Moscow," the *Völkischer Beobachter* intoned, quoting the Führer's words.[52] Speakers at the rally strove to outdo one another with shrill denunciations of the Soviet Union: "National Socialism sees nothing in Bolshevism but organized crime," declared Reich minister Hans Frank.[53] Bolshevism's deadly designs could be traced to the Jews, Joseph Goebbels explained, for "only in the brain of a nomad who is without nation, race, and country could this satanism have been hatched." Goebbels identified the progenitor of the Bolshevik faith as "a Jew named Karl Mordechai, alias Marx, the son of a Rabbi in Treves." Alfred Rosenberg proclaimed that Bolshevism was the creed of an alien bastard race—the Russian revolution of 1917 was "90 percent a Jewish matter," and even "those leaders of Bolshevism who were not Jews did not belong, and still do not belong, to the European family of peoples. Rather they are children of the steppe, such as Lenin, or sick, half-mad, unrestrained creatures."[54]

The racial opposition between Nazism and Jewish Bolshevism dominated the Nuremberg rally, culminating in the passage of three laws in a special session of the national parliament, which had traveled to Nuremberg to attend the gathering: the Flag Law, which adopted the swastika as the nation's official flag; the Law on the Protection of German Blood and German Honor, which forbade intermarriage and intercourse between Jews and Germans; and the Reich Citizenship Law, which effectively stripped Jews and other "undesirables" of their legal rights and their citizenship. The new Germany required a new national symbol, Göring told the members of parliament, to mark the conclusion of a fifteen-year-long battle over the nation's survival. This battle had been fought under the banner of two opposing flags, both of them made of the same bloodred cloth: One of them bore the Soviet star, the other "the shining sun sign of the swastika. If that red flag with the Soviet star had won, Germany would have perished from the bloodlust of Bolshevism. Let us thank

God and Providence that our standard was victorious, for with that a miracle occurred for Germany: it became one people and thus its salvation was assured for all time." The swastika, declared Göring, was an expression of Germany's continuing "fight for our own race," which was a "fight against the Jews as the destroyers of race."[55]

In his speech to parliament recommending acceptance of the three laws, Hitler described them as urgent measures to counter the Comintern's revolutionary zeal.[56] In a November 1935 interview with an American journalist, Hitler once again highlighted the fight against Bolshevism as the motive behind the Nuremberg Laws. Germans needed to be protected against "destructive Jewish influences." Nearly all "Bolshevik agitators" in Germany had been Jews, Hitler maintained. Moreover, Germany was separated from Soviet Russia by only a few miles. "For this reason, we must take steps to put a halt to this subversion and bring about a distinct and pure division between the two races."[57]

Hitler certainly heightened his anti-Bolshevik rhetoric in order to placate his American critics and gain approval for his foreign political ambitions. But the drive against "Moscow Bolshevism" was more than a tactical ploy.[58] No foreign observer attended the November 1935 congress of the German peasantry in the provincial town of Goslar, where Reichsführer-SS Heinrich Himmler presented the SS as "an anti-Bolshevik combat organization." Himmler painted a historical panorama of humans fighting Jewish-led subhumans that dated back to biblical times. The "Jewish-Bolshevik revolution" that the world was witnessing today represented merely the most recent—and, Himmler predicted, final—chapter in a ceaseless Jewish striving for world rule. The SS was ready to act as a "merciless executioner's sword" the minute Bolshevik aggression reared its head.[59] For political soldiers like Himmler, anti-Communist to the bone, this fight had begun in earnest with the killings and incarceration of thousands of German Communists in 1933. Now it was extending into a much wider campaign against global Bolshevism.[60]

The German military began openly discussing a future war against the Soviet Union in the fall of 1935. At a reception for Finnish intelligence officers on September 27, Commander in Chief of the Army Werner Freiherr von Fritsch assured his guests that in the "new Germany," "our work against Russia takes the very highest priority." The military began secretly drafting concrete plans. They included a defensive component, such as the construction of a fortified "Eastern Wall" modeled on the French Maginot Line, to deter a westward drive by the Red Army. But military thinking focused chiefly on offensive actions. The Army Weapons Agency, for instance, devised mechanisms to switch newly designed rail-mounted artillery onto the wider Russian gauge, and the Luftwaffe developed a strategic four-engined bomber aircraft, nicknamed "Uralbomber."[61]

Intelligence agencies prepared leaflets to be dropped over Soviet soil during a German invasion. Their propaganda took aim at the "commissars," the Communist officers in the Red Army, who had the task of leading by example and instructing soldiers on the political purpose of their fight. For German intelligence officers, the figure of the commissar summoned their darkest memories. Recalling the aftermath of the Great War, a memorandum composed by the head of the Foreign Armies East (*Fremde Heere Ost*, FHO) intelligence service cast the commissars as insidious and deceitful, adding that most of them were Jews. (The assertion was far off the mark: Jews comprised less than 9 percent of political officers in the Red Army in 1929.[62]) FHO leaflets sought to incite Red Army soldiers against their Bolshevik leaders: "You are not fighting for Russia, but for Messieurs Commissars and Party Functionaries, mostly filthy Jews. . . . Turn your bayonets around and fight with us against the cursed Jewish commissars."[63]

In August 1936, Hitler issued a plan to ready Germany's economy for a major showdown with Bolshevism in four years' time, explicitly modeling the program on the Soviet Five-Year Plan.[64] Earlier that year, Nazi propagandists had issued a five-hundred-page volume entitled *World Bolshevism*. Chapters detailed the activities of the Comintern in regions as far-flung as Latin America and Outer Mongolia, to bring to light the danger of a Jewish-Bolshevik ideology that "cunningly" concealed its imperialist designs behind a popular front. The only strategy left to prevent the world from succumbing to Bolshevik chaos was the formation of a "united front of anti-Communism."[65]

When Spanish Nationalist forces staged a military coup against the newly elected Popular Front government in Spain in July 1936 and turned to Germany for help, Hitler immediately dispatched fighter planes, along with a contingent of 6,500 military personnel. He explained his action as a last-ditch effort against the spread of Bolshevik terror rule. To Hitler, Spain had for all practical purposes turned Communist, and the "Bolshevization" of France was only a matter of time. This would leave Germany wedged between two powerful Communist blocs to its east and west, unable to meet a Soviet onslaught. Addressing the annual Nuremberg rally on September 9, Hitler warned that the "world's greatest danger" was swiftly becoming reality: Europe faced destruction at the hands of an "international Jewish revolutionary headquartered in Moscow." "We see, all around us, an era falling under the spell of evil."[66]

Soviet leaders, on the other hand, hesitated to provide military aid to the Spanish Republic, aware that such action would play into the Nazis' politics of anti-Bolshevik fear. It was not until mid-September that the Comintern called for the recruitment of volunteer International Brigades to fight in Spain. The first small-arms shipment to support the Spanish Republic left the Soviet Union on September 18.[67]

IMAGES FIGHTING WORDS

The 1936 rally enthralled spectators as no Nuremberg congress had before. The Nazi architect, Albert Speer, came up with the idea of holding the party's massive roll call after dark. The moment that Hitler's arrival was announced, 130 antiaircraft searchlights lit up, shooting spectral columns into the black sky above the heads of the 180,000 Nazi members in attendance. A participant recalled witnessing a "miracle" as the "milky blue columns" joined together to form a "dome of light" above the assembled crowd. British Ambassador Nevile Henderson felt as if he had been transported into a cathedral of ice. To the sound of great fanfare, Hitler walked through the center aisle and ascended a gigantic, illuminated stage. There, he was addressed by Robert Ley, leader of the

Hitler Youth: "We believe in Our Lord in heaven . . . who sent you to us, my Führer, so that you could liberate Germany. That is what we believe, my Führer!"[68]

Nazism invested in the power of images. Unlike the Soviet Union, where the leading art form was literature, the Nazis embraced the visual and performing arts above all, including painting, sculpture, architecture, film, and music. But the annual Nuremberg rallies were the purest form of Nazi artistic expression. To drum rolls, legions of Hitler Youth, Reich Labor Service men, and Wehrmacht soldiers paraded in military formation to showcase their regained collective strength. The sight of endless rows of physically fit young men filing past him appeared to Hitler as a "sublime demonstration of our people's eternal life."[69] The millions of Germans unable to come to Nuremberg for the rallies experienced the spectacle vicariously through Leni Riefenstahl's prizewinning documentary of the 1934 Party Congress, *Triumph of the Will*, which was Germany's most-watched film in 1935.[70]

The new Germany shaped itself as the antithesis of Bolshevism. At four consecutive Nazi rallies—from 1935 to 1938—speakers counterposed Communist chaos and disease to German order and health. The triple project of Germany's national unification, racial regeneration, and military expansion, they claimed, was a matter of utmost urgency because of the "pathological, criminal insanity" coming from the "'Jewish' Kremlin."[71] Hitler asserted at the 1936 Nuremberg rally that the first thing Communist rulers did after assuming power was to free "the asocial human scum concentrated in the workhouses, in order to then turn these animals loose on the frightened and stunned world around them."[72] But the fight against Bolshevism also presented an opportunity, he explained. As *The New York Times* quoted from Hitler's speech: "[The Russians] have eighteen times our territory, yet bolshevism cannot feed its people. What slops they are! We have to struggle for every acre reclaimed from swamp and sea. . . . If I had the Ural Mountains with their incalculable store of treasures in raw materials, Siberia with its vast forests and the Ukraine with its tremendous wheat fields, Germany and the National Socialist leadership would swim in plenty!"[73]

Nazi propagandists produced grotesque visual displays of the Soviet project. The 1936 rally saw the opening of an exhibition called "World Enemy No. 1—Bolshevism." The exhibition, which toured sixty-four German towns, depicted the Soviet Union as a country suffering unspeakable mass terror: "Innocent people were tormented to death by rats placed on them." A reviewer writing for a Munich newspaper described one photographic display: "The corpses of those slaughtered by the GPU [the Soviet security police] during mass executions are piled up into mountains. Above these frightful pictures of hunger and murder hangs the cynical saying of the red dictator Stalin: 'Life has become happier.'"[74] The exhibition, as a more critically minded spectator reported, featured blown-up portraits of Bolshevik leaders "with unshaven faces contorted with cynicism, the very image of murderous thieves." As the spectator noted, even the caricatures of Jews with exaggerated facial features and misshapen bodies that regularly appeared in *Der Stürmer* were "the faces of angels" compared with this representation of Bolsheviks.[75]

"Bolshevism: The Great Anti-Bolshevik Show." Exhibition in Karlsruhe, 1936.

A much larger exhibition, "Bolshevism: The Great Anti-Bolshevik Show," opened in Munich in November 1936. A reviewer described it as a "walk through hell." To amplify their oppressive impact, the display cases and walls of photographs documenting Soviet "terror, murder, and destruction" were placed in dark and poorly ventilated basement rooms with low ceilings and stone floors, presumably meant to look like secret

"Bolshevism Unmasked." Poster for "The Great Anti-Bolshevik Exhibition," Berlin, November 1937.

police torture chambers. A gigantic spider stared at visitors from a poster on one of the walls. Crowned with a Red Army helmet bearing a Soviet star, the bloodred spider sat atop a globe, its clawlike legs ripping into every continent.[76]

An inscription on one of the walls echoed the Book of Revelation: "The beast arose from the abyss and revealed itself in Russia. From its perch atop the Kremlin, it has sunk its talons into Spain's flesh and is preparing to trample mankind. The dragon is unchained, may he who stands with God take up the sword!" As viewers emerged from the vaults of terror, they were greeted by a brightly lit wall that spelled out renewed certainty: THE FÜHRER IS FIGHTING AND DESTROYING BOLSHEVISM! a headline intoned, above a barrage of text repeating Hitler's name.[77]

Yet another show, "The Great Anti-Bolshevik Exhibition," opened at the 1937 Nuremberg rally, before traveling to Berlin, Hamburg, and Vienna over the next year and a half and drawing nearly 1.5 million visitors. For added effect, the Berlin exhibition, which opened under the name "Bolshevism Unmasked," was housed in the burned-out shell of the Reichstag, vacant since the arson of 1933, to showcase the torched building as an example of Communist lawlessness in action.[78] Goebbels had issued instructions to the exhibition organizers: They were to observe a "particular primitiveness in representation." "Our specialists are becoming too much like scholars," Goebbels commented in his diary.

When the exhibition opened, Goebbels found it mostly to his liking: "Sometimes a bit too erudite, sometimes a bit too primitive. But I'll work it out."[79]

Another exhibition, "The Eternal Jew," opened in Munich in November 1937 before touring other major cities. Its centerpiece, "The Unleashing of Bolshevism by the Jews," featured two illuminated world maps covering the walls of one room. The first, a historical map, used neon light tubes to trace the phases of Jewish migration from ancient Palestine. The second, a present-day map, used the same light tubes to dramatize the Communist reach for world domination: From its center in Russia, Bolshevism had spread its tentacles across the globe.[80] Although the poster's "Eternal Jew" is marked as non-European, or "Asiatic," by his Mongolian-style beard, the chunk of Soviet-branded land that he holds under his arm is European Russia.[81]

Two other shows opened side by side in Munich earlier that year, to dramatize the contrast between a supposedly German aesthetic and a Jewish Bolshevik one. At the opening of the newly founded House of German Art on July 18, 1937, Hitler proclaimed his adherence to an "eternal" art form that was rooted in the ideals of classical Rome. As he extolled the healthy and strong bodies of Nazism's "new human type," Hitler lashed out against a modern art that he decried as a Jewish-Bolshevik invention aiming to corrupt the German spirit.[82] One day later, just a few blocks away,

Poster for the exhibition "The Eternal Jew," Munich, November 1937.

a strategic counter-exhibition opened in Munich's Archaeological Institute. It featured the very "Degenerate Art" that Hitler had derided in his speech: 650 paintings, sculptures, and prints by 112 modern and left-wing artists were crowded into the small storage rooms and dark corridors of the institute. Many of the paintings had been taken out of their frames and were nailed to the wall, to underscore their worthlessness. Graffiti-like comments on the walls lambasted the degeneracy and lunacy of the artists. The show, an official catalog explained, sought to expose "degenerate art as art-Bolshevism." An informant working for the German Social Democratic Party in exile noted that throngs of visitors, brought by Nazi organizations on chartered buses, crowded the exhibition. Most spectators, the report pointed out, responded to the pictures with horror and disgust.[83]

The exhibitions, in short, encouraged millions of Germans "to see contrasts, to make distinctions, to draw divisions." They taught them that Bolshevism was evil and bestial, that it disfigured and destroyed—and that it was the work of Jews who had become more monstrous and menacing than ever before. As they toured the exhibitions, spectators were encouraged to see themselves as members of a regenerated and superior Germanic race, pitted in an existential struggle against a murderous Eastern foe. "This or That?," the election poster from January 1933, had turned into a broad program that the Nazis now used to mobilize the population across Germany.[84]

Paradoxically, it was Nazi Germany that sponsored the first wave of Sovietology. German publishing houses in the 1930s issued more books on Soviet Communism than any other country outside the Soviet Union. Special bibliographies kept track of proliferating works on "Bolshevism and Jewry."[85] Many of these publications were sponsored by the "Anti-Comintern," a supposedly private organization that in reality was working under the direction of Goebbels's ministry to produce anti-Bolshevik propaganda. In 1934, the Anti-Comintern created its own publishing house, the Nibelungen Verlag. It was led by Eberhard Taubert, Goebbels's top specialist for anti-Bolshevik propaganda and later director of the Institute for the Study of the Jewish Question.[86] All the books brought out by Taubert's publishing house—ranging from reportage on Soviet famines and police terror to accounts of Soviet defectors and memoirs of German workers who had abandoned the Communist faith—sought to pierce the shiny veneer of Soviet propaganda and give an "unvarnished picture" of the reality of Bolshevism.[87] Another aim was to deliver proof to German readers that the Communist system was Jewish at its core.

A compilation of foreign reports from the Soviet Union published by Nibelungen Verlag in 1937 illustrated this strategy. The cover of the book, entitled *And You See the Soviets Correctly*, juxtaposed an image of a newly built Soviet hydroelectrical dam, as featured on a glossy Communist magazine, with a photograph of a starving child. Readers were to understand from this that the supposed creation of a "Soviet paradise" for workers and peasants was a lie: Soviet industrialization was a brutal affair that inflicted untold human suffering. Dozens of photographs inside the book, taken by visitors to the Soviet Union or by ethnic Germans who had managed to escape from Communist rule, provided further confirmation. The illustrations depicted victims of the 1932–33 famine and scenes of squalor in Soviet towns. People in "our cultural sphere" lacked the imagination to grasp the actual life conditions in the Soviet Union, the book's editor declared. It was the Jews, he explained, who bore responsibility for these Communist horrors. While the Soviet Union called itself a "dictatorship of the proletariat," it was in reality a "dictatorship of the Jews over the proletariat."[88]

Russian German émigrés eagerly shared their knowledge about the Soviet regime with the Nazis.[89] The personal contacts that they maintained with victims of Stalinist persecution lent their stories an aura of truth. The suffering of peasants who wrote letters from Siberia detailing the horrors of forced collectivization was undeniable. In the hands of émigré editors, many of them staunch backers of the Nazi Party, this suffering was forged into an indictment of Judeo-Bolshevism.[90]

One of Nibelungen Verlag's most popular titles was a booklet on Soviet forced labor by Hermann Greife, a Russian German who in the mid-1930s declared himself the doyen of Nazi Sovietology.[91] Greife's booklet came in response to a Soviet publication on the construction of the

Cover image of **U**nd **D**u **S**iehst die **S**owjets **R**ichtig (And **U** **S**ee the **S**oviets **R**ight), *1937. The German title forms the same acronym, UDSSR, as the name of the Soviet Union.*[93]

White Sea Canal, which extolled forced labor in the USSR as a means of remaking criminals into useful citizens.[92] Beyond charging Stalin's propagandists with disguising the "almost unbelievably gruesome" conditions in which Soviet penal laborers were kept, Greife made an even more alarming assertion about the Soviet concentration camps: They were the creation of Jews. Greife included in the booklet photographs of ten secret police, or NKVD, officials, all of them lifted from the earlier Soviet book. In the captions that accompanied the photos, he helpfully identified the men as Jewish and explained their involvement in the camps. "The Jew Jagoda (Hershel Jehuda), Chief of the Tscheka-G.P.U., now called 'Commissariat of the Interior.' All concentration camps are under his supervision." In another, "The Jew, Grigorij Davidsohn Afanasjew, Chief engineer of the concentration camps, a high G.P.U. official."[94] The visuals and captions aimed to strip Communism of its reputation as ethnically blind. Following Goebbels's mandate, they showed Bolshevism "unmasked." Within less than a year after its first publication, Greife's book had sold upward of 1.5 million copies.[95]

An English translation of Greife's booklet quickly followed the German edition. A foreword, "To Our American Readers," announced that the booklet would "dispel the clouds of doubt about the real nature of the U.S.S.R. and its Jewish leaders."[96]

Bolshevism was not only an oppressive presence among its own people, the Anti-Comintern stressed, it was also an aggressive force in international affairs. In January 1937, a representative of the organization spoke at the Technical University of Munich about Stalin's alleged war plans. The poster advertising the lecture showed two giant Soviet tanks standing on red-soaked Polish and Czechoslovakian soil, about to crush their way into Germany. A caption quantified the Red Army's fighting forces ("2,000,000 active soldiers, 11,000,000 reservists . . .") as well as the Soviet armaments expenditure since 1933. Another listed the flight times for warplanes taking off from Czech airfields: "to Munich: 30–35 minutes, to Dresden: 20–25 minutes, to Berlin: 42–45 minutes."

Propaganda of this nature informed and incited audiences around the globe. The Anti-Comintern staged exhibitions and distributed propaganda material for use across Europe as well as in Latin America and the United States. The agency created a photographic archive on the "Bolshevik horrors in Spain" for use by other anti-Communist organizations.[97] Its news bulletins on Communist activities in countries such as France, Portugal, Romania, Denmark, and Norway did double duty by supporting the work of German secret police agents, who compiled a detailed record of Communism's sympathizers.[98]

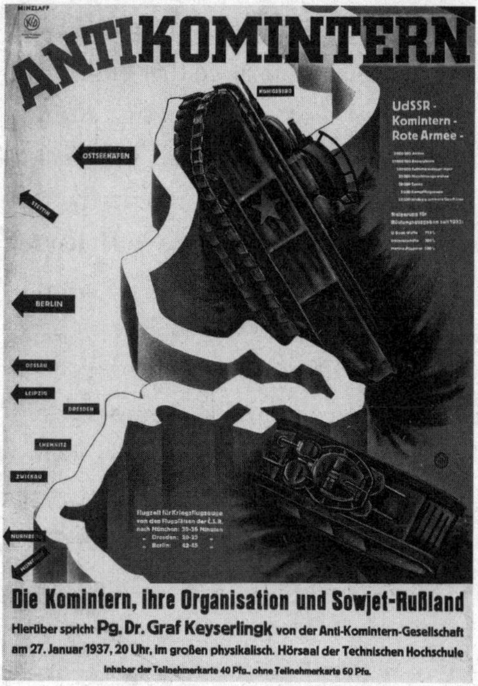

Poster featuring an Anti-Comintern talk in Munich, 1937.

The Nazi-led crusade

against Bolshevism also cemented the Axis. Germany and Italy, hitherto bitterly divided over competing imperial designs and dictatorial egos, began to join forces over the conflict in Spain. The Spanish Civil War served to link the Catholic Church and the Nazi regime in a common anti-Communist front.[99] In November 1936, Germany and Japan signed an Anti-Comintern Pact; the German side explained, "Two civilized states are thus openly defending themselves against the diabolical efforts of the Communist International."[100] Italy joined the pact on November 6, 1937. The opening of the exhibition "Bolshevism Unmasked" in the Berlin Reichstag on that day turned into a symbol of the enlarged pact against Soviet Communism: Several thousand soldiers and youth delegates from the Nazi and the Italian fascist movements assembled in front of the Reichstag as Nazi leaders called on the two nations to exterminate the "murderous Red plague."[101]

Anti-Bolshevism touched a nerve in Britain as well: Even as German and Italian forces stepped up their support of General Franco's Nationalist rebellion in Spain, culminating in the German Condor Legion's bombing of Guernica in April 1937, British policymakers insisted that Bolshevism was a greater threat to world peace than fascism. It was this attitude, "Better Franco Than Stalin," that made them cling to a policy of "malevolent neutrality" toward Republican Spain that would ultimately vault Franco to power.[102] This, it seems, was exactly as the Germans had intended. British anti-Bolshevik sentiment was fed by Francoist anti-Communist propaganda, which in turn made use of German anti-Bolshevik arguments.[103]

The 1936 Summer Olympics in Berlin had dazzled the world, complete with the newly invented torch relay from Greece to the Olympic venue, filmed to great effect by Leni Riefenstahl. Presiding over the Games, Hitler lauded their contribution to international cooperation and peace.[104] Germany won more Olympic medals than any other country. Then at the Paris World's Fair in 1937, Germany enthralled spectators with a visual demonstration of national unity and might. On the fairgrounds, the German and Soviet pavilions faced each other, dramatizing the competing global claims of their state ideologies. In response to the Soviet pavilion, which was crowned with a statue of two workers, a man and a woman, proudly brandishing a hammer and a sickle as they stride forward, chief architect Albert Speer designed the German pavilion to resemble an impregnable fortress.[105] Speer was inducted into the Légion d'Honneur.

When the Nazis convened the Nuremberg rally in September 1937, the number of participants attending the roll call had grown to 250,000; another 750,000 participants packed the neighboring squares. Popular demand to hear Hitler's speech was so great that event organizers outfitted public spaces with loudspeakers, including one in the lounge of a hotel that housed a large contingent of foreign journalists. The correspondent for *The New York Times* described what he saw: "As the cheers following the 'Sieg Heil' with which he concluded died away, the hotel audience to a man and woman rose to its feet with arms raised in the Nazi salute and joined in the emotional singing of 'Deutschland' followed by the 'Horst-Wessel-Lied.' It was typical for the end of eight days of steadily mounting excitement that words fail adequately to describe."[106]

CLOSING RANKS AGAINST FASCISM

In Spain, the Republican forces launched a surprise attack in early July 1937 to break Franco's siege of Madrid. The day after they conquered the town of Brunete, west of Madrid, soldiers from the victorious 11th Division marched into Valencia's city hall to display the captured fascist banners to a hundred international writers who had assembled for a Second International Congress of Writers in Defense of Culture. When "The Internationale" began, the delegates, many of them veterans of the Paris congress, erupted in ovations for the Soviet Union.[107]

Friedrich Wolf's prediction, sounded at the Moscow congress three years earlier, had become reality in Spain: War was transforming the writers and their craft. Some had taken his injunction to fight literally; they enrolled in the International Brigades and appeared at the Valencia congress wearing bandages and toting their rifles. Writers, César Vallejo declared, possessed the most formidable of all weapons: the written word. The time had come to wield it.[108] Ilya Ehrenburg, who was also in attendance, argued that the overriding need to destroy fascism dictated a propagandistic use of literature: "For years, if not for decades," he declared, "culture will be like a battlefield."[109]

Too impatient to wait for *Izvestiya* to send him, Ehrenburg had rushed to Barcelona when he heard of the revolt of the Nationalist rebels surrounding Franco in 1936. Shuttling between Paris and Spain over the next eighteen months, he produced a barrage of columns about the war. As ever, Ehrenburg's popular features agitated and incited, but they were factual at their core. In Spain, Ehrenburg talked with soldiers and civilians on the Republican side, probing their feelings so that he could convey their voices to readers at home.

He pointedly contrasted their voices with those of captured Germans and Italians, seeking to expose the latter as unthinking automatons, as creatures unresponsive to reason's power. Ehrenburg described Günther Löhning, a captured bomber pilot from the Condor Legion, as physically fit, but with "expressionless eyes." In response to a question from a Republican colonel—"Why are you waging a war against us?"—the German pilot said: "The Führer said that he wants peace, and the Führer is never wrong."

Ehrenburg continued:

> It is hard to believe that this is a living person, the son of a Hanoverian tailor, that he studied at a secondary school, that he has curly hair. . . . Günther Löhning is an ideal representative of that new fascist race that is now incubating in the breeding factories of the "Third Reich."[110] . . . The ruins of Madrid, Albacete, Cartagena, thousands of corpses—women, children. For what? "The German soldier never thinks."[111]

Two weeks after taking Brunete, the Republican forces were pushed out again. Franco's campaign proved overwhelming, in part because legions of Italian and German soldiers propped up his side, and in part because the defenders of the Republic descended into internecine strife.

Radicals on the left, many of them backers of Leon Trotsky, sought to use the war against fascism to turn Spain into a Communist dictatorship, or an anarchistic commune, in defiance of the broad Popular Front that was official Soviet policy. The conflict in some ways came to resemble a personal feud between Stalin and Trotsky. August 1936 saw a show trial directed at two of Stalin's political rivals, Grigory Zinoviev and Lev Kamenev, who were accused of conspiring with Trotsky to destroy the Soviet Union. That same month, Trotsky completed his manuscript for *The Revolution Betrayed*, which castigated Stalin's Popular Front policy as paving the way for a global bourgeois counterrevolution. In May 1937, Spanish Republican security services, firmly controlled by Soviet agents, squashed an anarchist insurgency in Barcelona that might have led to a victory for Trotskyism.[112]

In Moscow, the rifts that tore at the Popular Front prompted Stalin to unleash a terror campaign against "counterrevolutionaries" who he said had infiltrated the top ranks of the Soviet party and state. On June 2, he told a stunned group of military commanders that Marshal Mikhail Tukhachevsky and Jan Gamarnik, the head of the political directorate of the Red Army, had been exposed as leaders of a "German-Fascist financed military-political conspiracy against Soviet power." Their aim, allegedly, was to turn the USSR into a "second Spain."[113] Death sentences for treason were meted out to the suspected plotters. Over the next weeks and months, the NKVD would arrest another 9,500 officers in the Red Army. Though the accusations against them were patently false, several thousand would ultimately be executed.[114]

The fear of foreign spies pervaded Soviet society, and in 1937 led to the reappearance of the political commissar in the Red Army's command structure. Commissars had served in the Red Army during its founding years, tasked with inculcating soldiers in a Communist spirit and leading them as a "soldier-hero"—as well as watching over military commanders, most of whom had previously served in the Tsarist army. The reintroduction of the position, which had been abolished in 1925, testified to the sense of crisis that once again gripped Soviet leadership.[115] Arrests and executions on counterrevolution and treason charges spread beyond the Red Army to take the lives of hundreds of thousands, from industrial managers to members of the nobility, former kulaks, foreign residents, and Soviet nationals of German, Polish, Korean, or Latvian descent. Stalin personally drove the purge process, citing the need for unprecedented measures in the face of an imminent two-front attack by the Anti-Comintern powers, Germany and Japan.[116] The threat was not entirely invented: Japan had launched repeated military incursions into the Soviet Far East throughout the 1930s, and its July 1937 attack on China brought Japan and the USSR to the brink of war after the USSR signed a pact with Chiang Kai-shek's China the following month.[117]

The necessity of closing ranks in times of war was also the principal theme at the Valencia congress of writers that summer. In his address, Ehrenburg told the audience that their army of writers, which had seemed so powerful when assembled in Paris, was now suffering desertions when faced with an actual battle. The congress turned on one writer in particular who had chosen not to come to Spain: André Gide.[118] After Gide proclaimed himself a Communist-individualist at the 1935 congress, Ehrenburg had secured him an invitation to tour the USSR in June 1936. Gide returned to Paris that September, shocked by the adulation for Stalin and the lack of individual freedom he had observed during his extended Soviet visit. He was especially bitter about not being permitted to meet with Stalin in order to make his case for the suspension of the 1934 Soviet law banning homosexuality.[119] Gide resolved to write a scathing account of his trip. Ehrenburg learned about Gide's change of heart upon returning to Paris from the trenches of Spain and rushed to meet with him, imploring him to reconsider: "When Russia is making an immense effort to help Spain, this is really not the time to attack her."[120] His plea fell on deaf ears.

Gide's description of his time in the Soviet Union, published under the title *Return from the USSR* in November 1936, split the Left in Western Europe. The book's most incendiary sentence compared the Soviet Union, negatively, to Nazi Germany: "I doubt whether in any country in the world, even Hitler's Germany, thought be less free, more bowed down, more fearful (terrorized), more vassalized," Gide wrote.[121] Ensuing attacks from Communist critics were merciless, calling him a Trotskyite.[122] To them, Gide had committed a sin worse than desertion in turning his pen against his own side.

Another novelist immediately stepped in, intent on repairing the rift in the anti-fascist front. Acting on a long-standing official invitation, Gide's book in hand, Lion Feuchtwanger boarded a train to Moscow in late November 1936, eager to form his own impression and issue a rebuttal. In light of Gide's about-face, Soviet officials monitored Feuchtwanger's every step, making for a particularly well-documented visit.

Feuchtwanger harbored few illusions about the recent trial in Moscow of Grigory Zinoviev and Lev Kamenev. The sight of old Bolshevik Party leaders readily confessing to unimaginable crimes, he told his Soviet interpreter, had shaken Europe and cost the USSR two-thirds of its following.[123] While in Moscow, Feuchtwanger witnessed preparations for a second show trial. Alarmed by what he saw, the writer insisted on meeting with Dimitrov to address his doubts. Like Gide before him, Feuchtwanger was struck by the lack of freedom of opinion in the Soviet Union. Unlike Gide, however, he was determined not to discuss the matter upon his return to the West, not wanting to betray his anti-fascist commitments. The Nazis had chased Feuchtwanger into exile and burned his books on the pyre, and he had challenged them from the start, as one of the few openly named contributors to *The Brown Book II.* His contribution to that volume bore a title that said it all: "Murder in Hitler's Germany."[124] Feuchtwanger put all his trust in the unity of the Popular Front and saw the Soviet Union as the only power able to withstand fascism. Though Gide had the right to criticize what displeased him, the German writer said in *Pravda*, he was unserious, essentially an aesthete, unable to grasp the historical meaning of the Soviet project. But for all his ignorance, Feuchtwanger concluded, even Gide had to know that by offering such criticism during fascism's ascendancy in Europe, he was delivering a "blow against socialism and against global progress."[125]

By the time Feuchtwanger left the Soviet Union in early February

1937, the Moscow trial of the "Parallel Anti-Soviet Trotskyist Center" had just concluded. Most of the defendants had been found guilty of treason and sentenced to death. When his report appeared in March, Feuchtwanger's praise for the USSR as a bastion of human reason fighting against barbarism only deepened the rift within the Left. Some intellectuals were impressed: "A bit of a beacon of light for the errant" was Ernst Bloch's description. Others trashed the book. Unsure whether Feuchtwanger counted as friend or foe, the Communist press remained silent and waited for the Kremlin to signal its position.[126]

The waves of arrests and executions in the Soviet Union robbed many within the anti-fascist camp of their erstwhile convictions. Western socialists broke with the Soviet state en masse in 1937 and 1938.[127] Stalin's purges killed many of the USSR's most committed anti-fascists, including Tukhachevsky, Radek, and Bukharin. Some, like Tukhachevsky, never confessed to the fabricated charges that were leveled against them. Others pleaded guilty, in an effort to maintain the unified front against fascism. Bukharin, the most prominent defendant in the third show trial, used his prison time to write prolifically on the looming global showdown between socialism and fascism. As fate would have it, he entered his final guilty plea on March 13, 1938, the day after the Wehrmacht entered Austria in preparation for further conquests.[128]

Given the pervasive fear of foreign spies, the purges took particular aim at Communists who had foreign contacts. "All of you there in the Comintern are working your way into the hands of the enemy," Stalin ominously warned Dimitrov.[129] With Stalin breathing down his neck, Dimitrov ordered the maverick publisher Münzenberg back to Moscow so the NKVD could arrest him. Münzenberg opted to stay in Paris.[130] Leo Roth, the Comintern agent who had passed the transcript of Hitler's February 1933 speech to the generals and also secured vital documentation for *The Brown Book*, was executed on espionage charges in Moscow's Lubyanka prison, as was Mikhail Koltsov, the *Pravda* correspondent in Spain.[131] The NKVD prepared a file on Ehrenburg as well, but a warrant for his arrest was never issued. Ehrenburg, who had been recalled to Moscow from France in fall 1937, attended the third show trial, to witness the demise of his childhood friend Bukharin. He then sat down to write to Stalin, twice, to make the case that as a soldier in the fight against fascism, his place was in Paris and Madrid. Ehrenburg was allowed to leave the USSR.[132]

From Berlin, Goebbels followed the mass arrests with bewilderment. "Stalin is probably mentally ill. You cannot explain his bloody reign any other way. But Russia no longer knows anything other than Bolshevism. That is the threat we will have to put down one day," he noted in the wake of the Tukhachevsky case. Six months later, Goebbels recorded Hitler's thoughts: "Stalin and his eunuchs are sick. Mad! You cannot explain it otherwise. Must be eradicated."[133]

The purges wound down in late 1938. A report from the German embassy in Moscow covering the twenty-first anniversary of the October Revolution noted a marked decline of Soviet power. At the traditional parade, the report observed:

> There were fewer troops marching than in the past, and only about half as many planes flew over Red Square as in the previous year. . . . It was also unusual for individual commanders, after their troops had passed, to step down from the stands together with their assigned "political commissars," some of whom were even allowed to precede them. Even Marshal Budyonny, who commanded the parade, was constantly accompanied by a political commissar. His demeanor was submissive.[134]

"WOLVES"

In March 1938, Germany annexed Austria, an action the Nazis extolled as the unification of a people of common blood. In the same vein, they stepped up the persecution of "racial aliens," above all Jews.[135] In October 1938, the Gestapo began to round up Polish Jews residing in Germany and put them on trains headed for Poland.[136] Enraged over the deportations, which had affected his family in Hanover, a seventeen-year-old

Polish Jew shot a minor German embassy official in Paris on November 7. The official succumbed to his wounds on November 9, the anniversary of Germany's socialist revolution. Upon hearing of the diplomat's death, Hitler called for retribution against the Jews. That night, which history would come to know as Kristallnacht, SS and SA leaders launched a massive pogrom against Germany's Jewish community, setting synagogues ablaze, smashing the windows of Jewish stores, and ransacking Jewish homes. At least ninety-one Jews were murdered all over Germany, and hundreds committed suicide. Twenty-five thousand Jewish men were sent to concentration camps, where hundreds died from mistreatment.[137]

Anti-Nazi protests erupted throughout the Soviet Union in response to the pogroms. Thousands of demonstrators, Jews and non-Jews, marched in Moscow, Leningrad, Kiev, and Baku to express their indignation. A *Pravda* headline exclaimed FASCISTS, VANDALS, AND CANNIBALS![138] Writing in *Izvestiya*, Ehrenburg described how German storm troopers tore off the beards of old Jewish men and stuffed feces into women's mouths. Like packs of wolves, the Hitlerites burned, plundered, and killed with impunity, wrote Ehrenburg, in a dress rehearsal for the war on humanity that was fascism's aim and essence. As the "country of Goethe and Schiller" began to live by the fascist dictum that "man is a wolf to man," it jettisoned all that was left of its enlightened past.[139]

The Soviet protests were a matter of law and principle.[140] The Russian criminal code of the time stipulated harsh prison sentences for crimes against national communities, Jews in particular.[141] In 1931, Stalin had publicly condemned anti-Semitism—still rampant in some Soviet regions—as "the most dangerous survival of cannibalism" and a radical antithesis to Communist internationalism.[142] After the Nazis stripped German Jews of their citizenship, the Soviets doubled down. In response to the invectives directed at "Judeo-Bolshevism" during the 1936 Nuremberg party rally, Soviet Premier Viacheslav Molotov underscored the Soviet Union's "feelings of fraternity toward the Jewish people," who counted among their numbers Karl Marx, the "brilliant creator of the idea of the Communist emancipation of mankind," as well as other freedom fighters and some of the world's most renowned scientists and artists.[143] The USSR, Soviet spokespeople at the time maintained, had "solved the Jewish question"—through the assimilation of secular Jews to Russian-Soviet culture and the creation in Far Eastern Birobidzhan of an autonomous Jewish region for all those who still identified as Jews.[144]

Dr. Mamlock, the film based on Friedrich Wolf's play, premiered in Leningrad and Moscow in September 1938. By April 1939, sixteen million people in the Soviet Union had seen it. Released in U.S. theaters on the eve of Kristallnacht, the film became a media sensation, the first movie to inform Americans of the Nazis' violent persecution of the Jews.[145] Still, a *New York Times* critic took exception to the film's Communist orientation, complaining that the Soviet producers had "used the persecution of the Jews as a selfish political argument."[146] *Dr. Mamlock* was officially banned in Britain. The officials in charge were at pains not to antagonize Germany.[147]

Until early 1939, the British government identified the Soviet ideology of national liberation as a serious threat to their colonial empire. If Prime Minister Neville Chamberlain and Foreign Minister Viscount Halifax consistently appeased Hitler, they did so out of a shared anti-Bolshevik sentiment but also in an attempt to channel Nazi aggression into directions that suited British imperial interests.[148] Many European statesmen saw in Nazism a restorative force on a continent beset by socialist rebellion and responded favorably to the anti-Bolshevik refrains that German leaders sounded in advance of their annexation of the Sudetenland. When, on September 17, 1938, the Italian ambassador to Berlin asked Joachim von Ribbentrop about the precise nature of German aims in the current crisis, the German foreign minister informed him that Bolshevik chaos was spreading in Czechoslovakia, "just as in Spain," which necessitated an immediate intervention. A few days later, the French ambassador cabled Paris that Germany was increasingly portraying Czechoslovakia as a "red peril for Europe."[149] That same month, the Anti-Comintern issued a book indicting Czechoslovakia for tolerating Soviet power and "Bolshevik pestilence" in the heart of Europe.[150] Pointedly, the Munich conference, held on

September 30, at which Britain, France, and Italy accepted the German annexation of the Sudetenland, excluded representatives from Czechoslovakia and the Soviet Union.

The agreement that emerged from the conference spelled an end to collective security—the framework of agreements by which the European powers, including the Soviet Union, sought to stem Nazi aggression. The new, anti-Communist Europe excluded the Soviet Union and accommodated Nazi Germany. At Munich, Britain and Germany also signed a bilateral agreement pledging never to wage war against each other. In October, French Prime Minister Eduard Daladier dissolved the anti-fascist Popular Front government and announced a rapprochement with Nazi Germany.[151] In January 1939, Barcelona would fall to the Nationalists, effectively ending Spain's civil war. Two months later, Franco's Spain would join the Anti-Comintern Pact.

For some time after Munich, Soviet policy maintained its anti-fascist course. In November 1938, Dimitrov alerted Soviet readers to the discovery of German maps covered with markings that confirmed Nazi plans to attack Hungary and Poland in 1939; Yugoslavia, Romania, and Bulgaria in 1940; and France, Belgium, Holland, Denmark, and Switzerland in spring 1941. Finally, Dimitrov revealed the culmination of the Nazi plan: "Fascist Germany envisions its attack on the Soviet Union for the autumn of 1941."[152] As such warnings no longer served to mobilize anti-fascist sentiment across Europe, Soviet leaders adopted a new line. Speaking at a Party congress on March 10, 1939, Stalin reserved his greatest venom not for the fascist aggressor nations, but for Great Britain and France, which he described as conniving with fascism out of fear of a proletarian revolution. No longer would the Soviet Union "pull their chestnuts out of the fire"; Stalin signaled his openness to forging a pact with anyone who would respect Soviet security interests.[153]

On May 17, 1939, a memorandum, "The Future Plans of Aggression by Fascist Germany," reached Stalin's desk. It summarized a briefing given by Peter Kleist, the head of the Eastern Department in the German Foreign Ministry, to senior members of the German embassy in Warsaw earlier that month. Speaking behind closed doors, Kleist revealed Hitler's design to invade Poland during the summer and "mercilessly" crush all armed resistance "in 8 to 14 days." The point of this demonstration of overwhelming force, the emissary from Berlin explained, was to paralyze Britain and France, leaving them unable to fulfill their recent pledges to safeguard Poland's territorial integrity. After routing Poland, Germany would strike against France and Britain, before turning on the USSR. The "feasibility of the destruction of the Soviet Union," Kleist pointed out, hinged on Germany's ability to subjugate, politically or militarily, the two Western powers. For the moment, Germany required Soviet neutrality to rout Poland and then strike out against the West.

"Who is the 'source'?" Stalin wrote on the margins after reading the report. As with the intelligence report on Hitler's first address to his generals in 1933, the sources were German Communists working undercover for Moscow—in this case three staff members of the Warsaw embassy. The wife of one of them did additional secret work by photographing documents obtained from other spies.[154] Despite the bloodletting from the purges, Stalin could draw on the work of a dedicated network of anti-fascists who kept him abreast of Hitler's war plan.

The Soviet leader acted on the new intelligence: He began to put out feelers to the Nazis. If Hitler intended to turn against Poland, and if Great Britain and France were unable to prevent Polish defeat, a temporary rapprochement with the Führer made sense for the Kremlin. Such a strategy might allow the Soviets to secure some of the lands in Eastern Europe that Hitler would otherwise have kept for himself, and it would delay Germany's invasion of the USSR.[155] Stalin kept separate channels open to British and French leaders as he sought to gauge their interest in a mutual defense pact against Hitler. British interest was predictably low. Foreign Minister Viscount Halifax instructed his chief negotiator to draw out the talks with the Soviets as long as possible. Their sole purpose was to prevent a possible Polish-Soviet alliance and buy time for the British to find a settlement with Germany. There was no regular air service between London and Moscow, and the Anglo-French diplomats traveled by boat, a slow cargo and passenger ship rather than a fast cruiser. They arrived in Moscow on August 10. After fruitless talks, the

Soviet hosts suggested the visitors go back home and return with a clear commitment to a trilateral pact.[156]

At a meeting attended by Politburo members and Comintern leaders on August 19, Stalin laid out the two choices for his government. If the Soviet Union entered a treaty of mutual assistance with France and Great Britain, Germany would give up on Poland and seek to come to terms with the Western powers. "War will be prevented but in the future events can become dangerous for the USSR." If, on the other hand, the Soviets signed a nonaggression pact with the Nazis, Germany would "of course" attack Poland, rendering an intervention by the Western powers inevitable. "Western Europe will be exposed to serious unrest and disorder. Under these conditions we will be able to remain on the sidelines in the conflict and hope to enter the war from an advantageous position." Stalin named more benefits of this course of action: The pact with Germany would return to the Soviet Union territories lost by tsarist Russia during the Great War. Furthermore, a war of attrition in the West would weaken Germany, increasing the chances of a Communist revolution in the country. Even if Nazi Germany emerged victorious, it would be "too exhausted to begin an armed conflict with the USSR for at least ten years." These years would buy the Soviet Union critical time to further build up its armed forces ahead of the final battle. "We must," Stalin concluded, "agree to the pact."[157]

On August 23, two planes carried a delegation of German officials headed by Ribbentrop to Moscow. That day, Ribbentrop and Molotov signed a German-Soviet nonaggression pact for a duration of ten years, with the option of renewal. The text of the treaty spoke of the two countries' mutual desire for "strengthening the cause of peace." A top-secret additional protocol listed Germany's and the USSR's "respective spheres of influence" in Eastern Europe. It declared Poland divided and put Latvia, Estonia, Finland, and Bessarabia in the Soviet sphere of influence, while placing Lithuania in Germany's sphere.[158] By signing the pact, the Soviet leadership gave Hitler free rein to go on the attack and obtained from him license to forcibly annex much of Eastern Europe.

The publication of the nonaggression treaty left the world thunderstruck. Anti-fascists across the world responded with incomprehension to the widely publicized news of Ribbentrop arriving in Moscow while a Red Army orchestra played the "Horst-Wessel-Lied"—the Nazi Party song that had become Germany's co-anthem with the "Deutschlandlied." Many Communists who had remained loyal to the Soviet Union throughout previous crises now turned in their party cards.[159] As part of the agreement, the Soviets released hundreds of German Communists and Communist sympathizers who had been arrested as German spies. After crossing the border to Germany, they were once more detained and dispatched to concentration camps.[160] People in the streets and factories of Berlin were at a loss for words, an informant working for the German Social Democratic Party in exile reported. The pact put the Nazis in an awkward position "because their best agitational bit, Bolshevism, is now done for."[161] But most Germans appeared to care little. They overwhelmingly responded with relief that the specter of a war on two fronts was no more. Writing in her diary, a young female secretary in the Opel works in Rüsselheim hailed Hitler's "diplomatic victory" in Moscow, adding: "If both powers, Germany and Russia, don't butt heads over their *Weltanschauungen* [worldviews], that will be good."[162]

In the short run, the nonaggression pact altered the political lexicon in the two countries. Culture began to reflect the new political reality. The terms "Bolshevism" and "fascism" disappeared from the pages of German and Soviet newspapers. Soviet filmmaker Sergei Eisenstein's production of Wagner's *Die Walküre* premiered at Moscow's Bolshoi Theatre in the presence of German officials, suggesting a compatibility between Soviet and Nazi values.[163] But rather than glorifying German nationalism, Eisenstein presented the opera as a Communist allegory and Wagner as a visionary who anticipated the future rise of Soviet ideology. The Nazi officers in attendance complained that the production was full of "cultural Bolshevism" and "deliberate Jewish tricks." It closed after only six performances.[164]

Fundamentally, the Nazi-Soviet pact ran up against the adversarial nature of the two countries' ideologies, a hostility that both sides had nurtured over the past decade and that could not be ignored, even if it had been papered over temporarily. The internationalist creed and the militancy of Communist ideology had reflexively conditioned Soviet citizens to fight fascism as a barbaric foe of mankind. Writers still rushed to the literary front in the fight against fascism. Soviet readers continued to venerate the texts of Goethe and Schiller even though they understood that Germany had forsaken its humanist past, overrun as it was by "packs of wolves." It was for this reason that many Soviet citizens reacted with irritation when they learned about the nonaggression pact. "We had taught the youth to hate fascism," an NKVD informant recorded a Leningrad director as saying, "and suddenly, Stalin is standing side by side with inciters of pogroms."[165]

In Germany, Nazi-sponsored campaigns, ranging from book burnings to spectacular party rallies and traveling exhibits, had conditioned millions of ordinary people to view Bolshevism as Germany's radical, racialized opposite and greatest threat. The specter of unchecked Bolshevik violence transformed Nazi aggression into defensive and noble action. To the German public, however, the nonaggression pact was not a betrayal but evidence of the Führer's strategic plan to save his own people as well as Europe at large by avoiding a war on multiple fronts, at least for the time being. After all, the war against the USSR was unavoidable, its opening shot only a matter of time.

Earlier in 1939, and marking the anniversary of the Nazi seizure of power, the Führer addressed the Reichstag in a two-and-a-half-hour speech. Much of what he had promised the generals in von Hammerstein-Equord's apartment six years earlier had come true and could now be broadcast to the nation: Germany had banished "Bolshevik chaos," achieved national unification, and built up an army that would dominate Europe. Looking ahead, Hitler saw Germany confronted by a global coalition of warmongering Jews. His warning to his fellow politicians made clear how much he remained focused on the Soviet Communist state as his principal foe, despite the pact: "If international finance Jewry in and outside Europe should succeed in plunging the nations once more into a world war, then the result will not be the Bolshevization of the earth and thus the victory of Jewry, but the annihilation of the Jewish race in Europe.... A higher realization will triumph over the Jewish slogan 'Workers of the world unite!' namely: 'Members of all nations, recognize your common enemy!'"[166]

This vision remained unchanged through 1939. A few days after the signing of the pact, the Führer railed against commentators in Germany who regarded the German-Soviet understanding as the beginning of a new ideological era. The deal was in reality "a pact with Satan to drive out the devil."[167] Earlier in August, while the negotiations with Moscow were still under way, Hitler made a candid remark to Carl J. Burckhardt, the high commissioner of the League of Nations for the Free City of Danzig, to clarify his position:

> Everything I undertake is directed against Russia. If the West is too stupid and too blind to realize this, I will be forced to reach an understanding with the Russians, strike at the West, and then after its defeat turn with all my concerted forces against the Soviet Union.[168]

The German dictator returned to this theme in early June 1940. After cruising through Belgium and the Netherlands, the Wehrmacht had invaded France and was poised to crush the British Expeditionary Force at Dunkirk. France's imminent defeat presented an opportunity for Germany to claim vast colonial grounds in Africa, but the French colonies were not Hitler's primary concern. The end of the war in the West, the Führer explained privately to a group of Wehrmacht commanders, would free him to confront the "great and actual task" that awaited in the East: "the showdown with Bolshevism."[169]

Chapter 3

CROSSING THE RUBICON

A caring father and husband, forty-three-year-old Anton Roos started a brisk correspondence with his family in summer 1939, when he was summoned to Trier to help fortify Germany's western border. Roos would continue writing home throughout the war. In July 1940, his civil engineering unit was transferred to the French coast of the English Channel to prepare for Germany's invasion of Britain. France was to Roos's liking. As he told his wife, Elisabeth, he was avidly studying French and lived "like God."[1] But in May 1941, Roos was dispatched to the East. He took up quarters in a luxurious villa in Zakopane, a Polish mountain resort he compared to St. Moritz in the Alps. None of his comrades knew where they were headed. Roos speculated: Greece? The Caucasus? On June 20, news broke that the engineering unit was to be deployed. Many were certain that an attack on Russia was imminent, but Roos was skeptical: "I can't believe it and am still of the view that this is the greatest bluff in world history, and that our tour will lead right back to the Channel and then to England."[2]

Germany's surprise attack on the Soviet Union on June 22, 1941, transformed Roos's life. Following behind the attacking troops, he was thrust into an unfamiliar world that tested his limits. The scenes of destruction he witnessed made the wreckage of Dunkirk look like "child's play." On the road connecting Lemberg (Lvov/Lviv) and Tarnopol (Ternopil), the ruins of tanks, field guns, trucks, and planes stretched over

Anton Roos (center) in northern France, August 1940.

seventy-five miles. Strewn among them were dead "Russians" and horses, rotting in the heat. Roos commented with disgust on the miserable dwellings and the wretched-looking captured enemy soldiers he encountered in the destitute towns. The farther he marched into the Soviet Union, the darker his impressions became. "Desolate here are the days, and desolate the nights, desolate are the people and the cities, no shimmer of hope, no cheerfulness, only poverty and dreadful misery." Even good-size cities looked appalling—"conditions as in negro villages." Everyone in his unit, Roos wrote home, was pining for their days in France. Everyone was sick of the "Soviet paradise."[3]

Nothing aroused greater disgust in Roos than the Soviet Jews. Writing to his wife ("*Liebes Lieschen*," "dear little Liese"), he casually noted that "the worst thing here is the infestation of Jews and flies, but we'll manage both." All Jews in the Soviet Union, he wrote in another letter, served the Russian state; all of them belonged to the "Jewish-Marxist gang of Bolsheviks," and as such bore responsibility for the appalling conditions as well as the hostility the Germans encountered during their advance into Soviet lands.[4] Roos's letters were filled with a vitriol toward "Bolsheviks" and Jews that had been absent from his earlier writings. During his sojourn in Poland in early June, for example, Roos had visited the Cracow ghetto. His account of the "mugs" observed among the Jews there was not benign, but revealed aversion more than hatred.[5] As he and his fellow soldiers stepped onto Soviet soil, however, the specter of the demonic enemy in the East that had formed in their minds for many years appeared to become reality.[6] Primed as they were, Anton Roos and other Germans approached every Jewish Soviet citizen as a blood-lusting enemy of the German nation.[7] Justified as an "existential struggle" against Bolshevism, Germany's campaign against the Soviet Union unfolded as a war of racial annihilation against Soviet Jews and all other suspected "carriers" of Communism's "murderous plague."[8]

THE DESTRUCTION OF POLAND

Germany's war in the East was cruel from the outset. But its original plan was not the systematic murder of Jews. When the Wehrmacht crashed through the Polish defense lines on September 1, 1939, officially beginning World War II, its main goal was to eradicate any trace of the Polish army, the Polish state, and indeed Polishness itself. Large parts of Poland were to be claimed as German soil and turned over to the ethnic Germans who formed a minority in the Polish state. The invasion followed months of accusations by the Nazi press that Polish authorities were abusing the Germans living in Poland.[9]

German soldiers attacked with unsparing violence, carrying out the instructions Hitler had given to his commanders in August 1939: "Destruction of Poland a priority . . . Close hearts to sympathy. Act brutally." When Luftwaffe pilots raided the small Polish town of Wielun on the morning of September 1, their charge was to aim "directly at the market square!" The attack killed an estimated twelve hundred Polish civilians and destroyed most of the town. The order was given by General Alexander Löhr, commander of Air Fleet 4. Later in September, Löhr directed the bombing of Warsaw, the largest and most destructive series of air raids ever seen at the time. German soldiers on the ground displayed particular harshness toward Polish fighters who fell behind the quickly advancing Wehrmacht units. Regarded as unlawful combatants rather than regular soldiers, they were summarily shot. The Germans also executed hundreds of captured enemy fighters to avenge the killing of their own men.[10]

Five special task forces made up of men from the Security Police (Sipo) as well as the SS intelligence service (SD) followed the German army into Poland. Numbering about four hundred men each, these task forces had been assigned to track down and "render harmless" Polish nationalists, as Reinhard Heydrich, chief of both organizations, put it.[11] They worked with lists of names—some sixty-one thousand in all—that had been prepared in advance of the invasion.[12] The men chiefly targeted "priests and teachers," "chauvinists," and "German haters," as their reports from the field made clear.[13]

In the wake of the invasion, the Nazis started an enormous ethnic cleansing operation, personally overseen by Reichsführer-SS Heinrich Himmler in his new capacity as Germany's "settlement commissioner for the East." A broad swath of Western Poland was incorporated into the Reich and declared a settling ground for Germans, and ethnic Germans living throughout Eastern Europe were brought there by the thousands. "Racially valuable" Poles—those who could claim Germanic roots—were to remain in this newly created German province; all others, the vast majority, were to be driven into a protectorate farther east, called the General Government. This "inferior" human mass would be ruthlessly put to work. Under "strict, consistent, and just" German leadership, they would help Germany to realize its "everlasting cultural tasks and monuments." As Heydrich saw it, the "solution of the Polish problem" hinged on Germany's ability to make use of uneducated Polish laborers while eliminating the Polish intelligentsia. By spring of 1940, his commandos had killed more than sixty thousand suspected Polish nationalists.[14]

Ethnic Poles, not Jews, were the primary group targeted for execution by the German commandos. This, however, did not spare the 1.7 million Jews who fell into German hands from immediate violence and mounting misery.[15] As they came upon Jewish settlements, German soldiers loved to taunt the inhabitants by cutting off men's beards or forcing them to "clean" public places as though to atone for their polluting existence.[16]

Trailing the Wehrmacht, Heydrich's task forces proceeded even more brutally. In several towns, SS and SD commandos burned down synagogues and executed male Jews. Their deliberate use of "fear and terror" followed Heydrich's directives to encourage Jewish flight to regions in Eastern Poland that the Germans did not seek to occupy. German violence against Polish Jews in the early weeks of the campaign peaked in places close to the German-Soviet demarcation line. In the border town of Przemysl, two of Heydrich's commandos joined forces and arrested five hundred men from among the city's twenty thousand Jews. The men were herded to a nearby cemetery, ordered to dig their graves, and machine-gunned. Surviving Jews understood that the murders were a signal for them to pack up and leave. Many thousands were able to flee to the East, but the Soviets, who began to enter Poland on September 17, soon sealed the border.[17]

Jewish resettlement remained high on the agenda of SS officials through fall and winter 1939. On September 21, Hitler approved a plan worked out by Heydrich's Reich Central Office for Jewish Emigration to expel all Jews from the provinces of Poland that were to be Germanized and to herd them into a "Jewish reservation" along the eastern fringes of the General Government. In preparation for their deportation, Heydrich on the same day ordered that all of Poland's Jews be concentrated in cities.[18] Starting in October, the Jews were ghettoized—forced into specially designated quarters in the most destitute areas of town. In November, local authorities in Poland ordered all Jews under their control to wear a white armband with a blue Star of David. But the deportations kept being delayed, in part due to the fierce protests of Hans Frank, governor of the new protectorate in the East, who vehemently objected to his realm being turned into a dumping ground for Jews.[19]

Even as the SS officials in the Office for Jewish Emigration abandoned the idea of a single vast Jewish ghetto within the borders of the German empire, they came up with other ideas of forcible expulsion. In January 1940, the Berlin office contacted the Soviet government with a bold request: to accept all Jews presently under German rule, altogether more than two million people. The letter specifically mentioned Western Ukraine and the Autonomous Region of Birobidzhan as potential areas of Jewish resettlement. The Kremlin quickly turned down the proposal, fearing the expellees might become a fifth column.[20]

Germany's victory over France in June 1940 opened up the possibility of another destination for Poland's Jews: the French colony of Madagascar. The Madagascar Plan, also referred to at the time as the "final solution to the Jewish question," foresaw the resettlement to the distant island of one million Jews per year, for several years, from Poland and other parts of Nazi-occupied Europe. As one of the planners wrote: "The desirable solution is: all Jews out of Europe."[21] The project proved unviable because Great Britain, which controlled the seas in an ongoing naval blockade, refused to give its consent.

As the various plans were considered and dismissed, the plight of Poland's Jews became increasingly dire. The ghettos, created as holding pens for future deportees, trapped hundreds of thousands of people in undersupplied and unsanitary conditions. The German occupiers—Anton Roos among them—toured the ghettos, scornfully deriding the teeming streets and cramped quarters as characteristic of "Eastern Jews."[22] And yet German violence against Jews between 1939 and 1941 remained of a lesser scope compared to the mass murder of ethnic Poles. The mistreatment of Jews was fed by racial hatred, not a political calculus; expulsion, not annihilation, was its ultimate goal. Jews in the areas of Poland that had been annexed to Germany, a Nazi official noted in November 1949, posed "a less dangerous problem than the Poles themselves, since the Jews have no real political force such as the Poles have with their Greater Polish ideology."[23]

The German occupation of Poland, with its aim of crushing the Polish nation, differed radically from Nazi occupation policies elsewhere in Europe. In preparation for the conquest of Great Britain, the SS also drew up arrest lists, but those lists contained only 2,820 names—twenty times fewer than those created in Poland.[24] In the invasion of France and the Benelux countries, the Sipo/SD task forces were similarly limited in their scope of activity. France was allowed to conclude an honorable armistice with Germany, and Paris was not bombed. The Nazis felt a sense of racial and civilizational kinship toward the English, French, and Dutch, and respected their cultures. The East, by contrast, was marked as Germany's colonial ground, whose inhabitants were less civilized and rightfully subservient to German rule. As the occupation progressed, Joseph Goebbels recorded Hitler's "devastating" verdict on the Poles: "More like animals than human beings."[25]

Germany's subjugation of Western Poland was also distinct from the Soviet regime's repression in Eastern Poland. Under the terms of the Hitler-Stalin pact, Berlin and Moscow had agreed on dividing the Polish state. Like Hitler, Stalin was deeply suspicious of Polish nationalism and vigorously persecuted Poland's elites. In four major deportation waves, starting in January 1940 and ending in May 1941, the Soviets sent away to remote locations as many as 380,000 Polish citizens deemed "socially dangerous," on account of their class standing or political views.[26] Some 14,500 captured officers and policemen, largely reservists who belonged to Poland's educated elite and maintained careers as doctors, professors, and lawyers in their civilian life, were delivered to Soviet prison camps and then shot to death in April and May 1940, along with 7,300 Poles who had already been interned in Soviet prisons. One of the killing sites, not the largest but by far the most infamous, was a wooded area near Katyn, in Smolensk province, where 4,421 prisoners were executed.[27] Unlike the Nazis, who were primarily concerned with making room for Germans at the expense of everyone else, the Soviets styled themselves as liberators of oppressed peoples and nations. They gave the land expropriated from elites to poor peasants and granted new rights to minorities that had been persecuted under Polish rule, before clamping down on Ukrainians who "abused" these rights in pursuit of Ukrainian nationhood separate from the Soviet state.

Most Jews in Eastern Poland, except for some excitable youth who openly greeted the Soviet forces as liberators, met the Red Army with guarded relief. Anti-Semitism had been pervasive in Polish society, and Jews regularly faced humiliations that only worsened when a right-wing government began to introduce a growing number of anti-Jewish laws in

1936. But as avowed atheists, the Soviet authorities were not positively disposed to traditional Jewish culture. Under Soviet occupation, it became difficult to observe religious law, while ridicule of the Jewish faith appeared in anti-religious propaganda. The Soviets were also hostile to Zionism and forbade schooling in Hebrew. Still, they supported secular Jews on their path toward assimilation. The Soviet legal code that was imposed on Eastern Poland included a clause that made anti-Semitic speech and actions criminal offenses. While Poland had barred many young Jews from studying, the Soviets lifted such restrictions, paving the way for a sharp influx of Jews to the universities. Some joined the Soviet Communist Party or its youth organization, the Komsomol. The sudden presence of a few Jews in local administrative jobs—positions previously held only by Poles—struck ethnic Poles, Ukrainians, and Belorussians as a provocation, as more proof that Bolshevism was Jewish at its core and that Poland's Jews inherently supported Bolshevism.[28] Yet what these Gentiles regarded as the Soviets' preferential treatment of Jews was simply a reflection of their readiness to co-opt an ethnic group that appeared more open to the ideals of the October Revolution than Poles or Ukrainians. At the same time, Soviet officials arrested and deported a large number of Jews from Eastern Poland on charges of being bourgeois capitalists or harboring Zionist designs.[29]

Though some scholars have argued that Nazi rule and Soviet rule in Poland were similar in certain essential ways, citing comparable numbers of arrests, deportations, and killings, these arguments fail to capture the fundamental difference between the two occupying regimes.[30] In their attempt to make Eastern Poland socialist, the new Communist rulers opened Ukrainian and Belarusian schools and offered Soviet citizenship to all members of the population, with the exception of the former elites. In contrast, the Germans denied education and citizenship to Poles and Jews, seeing them as destined for hard labor in service of the Third Reich's aspirations. The Nazis' cruel abuse of the Jews has no equivalent on the Soviet side.[31]

DEATH TO THE COMMISSAR

For all its savagery, Germany's campaign in Poland was only a prelude to its assault on the Soviet Union. Against this implacable enemy, German military leaders believed, they would prevail only if they fought without the restraints imposed by civilization. In May 1940, Heinrich Himmler, SS-Reich Leader and Chief of Police, had presented Hitler with a plan to improve Germany's racial stock by separating racially valuable Polish children from their parents and bringing them to Germany for cultural assimilation. He described the project as "cruel and tragic" for the parents and their children, but "mild . . . when compared to the Bolshevik method of physical extermination of a people, a method that we reject in principle as non-Germanic and impossible."[32] A year later, about to come face-to-face with millions of "Bolsheviks," the Germans planned to act with the same ruthlessness they had ascribed to the enemy. In Poland, the German police and SS had carried out most of the shootings of civilians, drawing protests from some Wehrmacht commanders who invoked soldierly values, international law, or humanist traditions.[33] But for the invasion of the Soviet Union, the partition between the police and SS forces and the Wehrmacht would be dissolved. Every German in the field would be a fully empowered crusader against Bolshevism.

By 1941, Hitler had made good on his 1933 promise to the generals to clear Germany of Marxism within "six to eight years." Now the time had come to tackle the state that had given birth to the Communist menace. Hitler personally code-named Germany's invasion of the USSR "Operation Barbarossa," in reference to the medieval German emperor who had not only led the kingdom's expansion into Eastern Europe but also embarked on a crusade to the Holy Land.[34] On March 30, Hitler convened in his Reich Chancellery the top one hundred commanders and staff officers selected to lead "Barbarossa." The purpose of the gathering was to let them in on the campaign's true significance: The war against the Soviet Union was more than a mere military battle, or even a fight against an ancestral national enemy, as had been the case in Poland. This conflict would be nothing less than a showdown between the world's two competing *Weltanschauungen*—National Socialism and Bolshevism. Given the tremendous stakes, the imminent war would have to be fought to the finish. No mercy was to be shown to Communists, no regard for existing laws and soldierly conventions. Once more, Hitler secured his generals' enthusiastic backing. While the Führer spoke, Chief of Staff Franz Halder took detailed notes, under the heading "Colonial tasks!" On the margins Halder wrote down a sentence that appeared to hold special relevance: "The fighting will be very different from the fighting in the West. In the East, a stitch in time saves nine."[35]

Hitler's understanding of the German-Soviet war as a fundamentally ideological conflict helps to explain his fixation on a figure whom he viewed as Germany's principal nemesis on the battlefield: the Soviet commissar. In his address to the German commanders, he singled out for killing the political officers in the Red Army, since they were the standard-bearers of Bolshevism. Halder recorded Hitler calling for the "annihilation of the Bolshevik commissars," as did Colonel General Hermann Hoth. The commissars "don't deserve to be spared," Hoth cited Hitler in his diary. "They are not [to go] before courts-martial, instead to be eliminated immediately using the troops."[36]

Following his two-and-a-half-hour speech, Hitler quickly left the room, allowing no questions. There was little need for them. His speech had struck a chord with the commanders, many of whom had joined the right-wing militias of the Freikorps after the Great War to combat Bolshevism, domestically and in the Baltics. Colonel General Georg von Küchler, who had rebuked an SS combat regiment as a "stain" on the German army for killing Jews in Poland, now readily agreed with Hitler's call for the murder of the Soviet commissars. Even before an official decree was produced, Küchler instructed his officers to treat "political commissars and GPU agents" as criminals and kill them on the spot.[37]

In the weeks that followed Hitler's address, Halder and other senior officers within the Army High Command rushed to draft orders conveying Hitler's instructions to the troops. These officers may have been trying to ingratiate themselves with the Führer, but their actions demonstrated how deep-seated and widespread anti-Bolshevik sentiment was among the German military, and how much the German army's leaders contributed to the Nazis' plans to crush the USSR.[38] When the "Guidelines for the Treatment of Political Commissars" were finalized on June 6, 1941, they added specificity to the directive Hitler had laid out in his speech:

> When fighting Bolshevism, one cannot count on the enemy acting in accordance with the principles of humanity or International Law. In particular, it must be expected that the treatment of our prisoners by the political commissars of all types who are the true pillars of resistance, will be cruel, inhuman, and dictated by hate. . . . The political commissars are the originators of asiatic-barbaric methods of fighting. They must be dealt with *promptly* and with the utmost severity.[39]

Neither this official "Commissar Order" nor Hitler's earlier address mentioned Jews. The reason was simple: For the planners of Barbarossa, the commissar was so clearly marked as Jewish that no explicit identification was necessary. If "Jewish Bolshevism" were to be embodied in a single figure, it was the Soviet commissar, invariably coded as a cunning instigator of Asiatic forms of warfare, and as such the antithesis of the chivalrous German soldier.[40] Such depictions of the commissar had circulated in countless Freikorps memoirs and been translated into "fact" by Nazi "experts" such as Alfred Rosenberg, who had declared at the 1936 Nuremberg rally: "There is a Jewish spy attached to every commander, ready at any moment to turn an officer over to the murderous Jewish GPU."[41]

The stock image of the Jewish commissar went into mass production in June 1941 as the Nibelungen Verlag prepared its first new anti-Bolshevik title after the nearly two-year hiatus enforced by the nonaggression pact. The book's cover depicted a sinister-looking Red Army soldier with stereotypical Jewish traits. Dagger in hand, the soldier crawls apelike toward an unsuspecting German border guard, ready to stab him in the back. The book, entitled *Why Fight Stalin?*, portrayed Germany's war with its onetime ally as a last-ditch defense against a terror state that had already claimed millions of innocent victims—note the gallows crowding the background of the picture—and now stood to kill millions more.[42]

Cover image of Why Fight Stalin? *(1941)*

The commissar may have been seen as the tip of the spear, but to the planners of Barbarossa, the ideological threat of Bolshevism involved a much broader swath of Soviet society as well. They called on German soldiers to be especially wary of Asian-looking conscripts serving in the Red Army. Evoking earlier stories of Chinese soldiers acting as the Bolsheviks' executioners during the Russian civil war, German military leaders depicted Asiatic soldiers as exceptionally "treacherous," "unpredictable," and "unfeeling."[43] In addition, military planners warned of ambushes and sabotage actions by "carriers of the Jewish-Bolshevik worldview among the civilian population."[44] In response to this alleged threat, military lawyers devised a decree that absolved German soldiers of any guilt for crimes against enemy civilians. The Jurisdiction Decree delineated certain actions that counted as war crimes in other theaters of Germany's war but were permitted against the USSR as long as German soldiers did not "run wild."[45] Like the Commissar Order, the Jurisdiction Decree went through several drafts. The final version, presumably penned by a veteran of the Freikorps movement, came complete with a justification for the war crimes that German soldiers were expected to commit on Soviet soil: "In judging such deeds in any proceedings, consider that the collapse in 1918, the later period of suffering of the German people, the battle against National Socialism, and the movement's countless blood sacrifices were the result of Bolshevik influence, and that no German has forgotten this."[46] Together, the Jurisdiction Decree and the Commissar Order authorized German soldiers in the East to kill and destroy at will.

These two orders circulated only among top officers, and the Commissar Order was transmitted orally to commanders on the ground—an indication that those responsible for its issuance were aware of their breach of norms. For ordinary soldiers, the planners of Barbarossa prepared a set of guidelines that company leaders read out to the troops on June 21, 1941. The instructions summarized the impending campaign in plain language:

> 1. Bolshevism is the mortal enemy of the National-Socialist German people. Germany's struggle is directed against this subversive worldview and its bearers.
> 2. This struggle demands ruthless and energetic drastic action against Bolshevik agitators, irregulars, saboteurs, Jews and complete elimination of any active or passive resistance.[47]

Thus, the ground was prepared for a war of annihilation of unprecedented scale. More than three million soldiers massed along the western Soviet border. Unlike with the invasion of Poland, which followed an escalating propaganda war, German leaders readied the war against the Soviet Union with utmost secrecy, hoping to obliterate in a single strike the country with which Germany had signed a nonaggression pact. The Nazis even dispensed with a formal declaration of war.

In the early morning hours of June 22, an artillery barrage opened up over a front stretching 1,800 miles, while German bombers struck at targets deep in Soviet territory. Later in the morning, motorized formations pushed deep into enemy territory before encircling Soviet troops in choreographed pincer movements. Fighter planes strafed columns of civilian refugees.[48] With several million Soviet troops concentrated at the border and under strict orders not to retreat, the Germans captured

320,000 enemy soldiers during the first twenty days of the campaign. Hitler celebrated on July 9, believing that his side had destroyed up to two-thirds of the Soviet armed forces and five-sixths of all Soviet tanks and airplanes.[49]

The blows to the Soviet side were staggering, but they failed to knock out the Red Army. Part of the reason was that the Soviet Army Command was able to send new divisions, weapons, and supplies into battle, confounding German estimates about the enemy's available reserves.[50] But more significantly, the Red Army fought with a stubbornness and contempt for death that was unlike anything the Germans had seen during earlier campaigns in Western Europe, when they had cruised to victory with few losses of their own. German propagandists were quick to identify the reason for such behavior: the demonic Jewish commissar, who whipped dull Soviet soldiers into battle and shot recalcitrant recruits on the spot. In reality, this was rare. While some political officers did shoot men who disobeyed their orders, most others relied on verbal persuasion.[51] Several clear-eyed German intelligence specialists reported that not all political officers in the Red Army were Jews, and indeed cited captured Russian commanders who said that the share of Jewish commissars in the Red Army was negligible.[52] Yet these accounts did little to drown out a stream of reports that kept affirming the brutality of the Jewish commissars.[53]

Under orders to execute commissars, German troops were often at pains to recognize them. The indications given in the Commissar Order were sparse: "Political commissars as agents of the enemy troops are recognizable from their special insignia—a red star with a golden woven hammer and sickle on the sleeves," just below the elbow. Confused, Wehrmacht commanders filed many inquiries seeking assistance: Which Red Army units fielded commissars? (Correct answer: divisions and regiments.) Did a political instructor (*politruk*), as political officers on the battalion and company levels were called, count as a commissar? (Yes.) As the invasion progressed, German soldiers came upon fewer and fewer political officers who wore the special badge. News of their killing had passed to the Soviet side, prompting the Red Army Command to conceal their agitators. As a result, the Germans often "identified" Soviet political officers on the basis of their Jewish appearance, longer hair (as opposed to the shorn heads of ordinary recruits), educated looks, or clean hands.[54] What the Germans lacked in knowledge about the commissars they made up for with their strong convictions about who they were supposed to be. A first lieutenant claimed to recognize them by their "fanatical and strained" physiognomy. "The few we captured alive denied as a rule that they were commissars. They spoke with Jewish fluency and rhetoric. . . . They had grim, unforgiving, often surprisingly unintelligent faces."[55] Citing his personal experience, one intelligence officer defined the commissar as "the Asiatic mug of the whole red system" and decried the misfortune of any German soldier who would "fall into the hands of these red devils." His report used language from an information leaflet for German troops, issued earlier that month: "Anybody who has ever looked one of the red commissars in the eye knows what a Bolshevik is. . . . It would be an insult to animals to call the traits of these slave drivers, a high percentage of whom are Jewish, animal-like. They are the embodiment of the infernal, the personification of an insane hatred of all noble humanity."[56]

"A Jewish commissar digs his own grave."
(Original caption, 1941)

On July 3, 1941, Helmut Hartmann, an artillery soldier, wrote home to his parents: "The Russian leadership is totally Jewified. Even most of the lower-ranking commissars are Jews. What Hitler and Goebbels told us about Russia before the pact is correct." In a letter to an old friend from college, Hartmann displayed more swagger: "For a week, it was customary for us to shoot several political commissars every morning at breakfast time. An incredibly unfeeling people. They would dig their grave calmly, stand before it, and for the most part fall well enough into the pit that we only had to throw some dirt on top." Neither to his parents nor to his college friend did Hartmann expound on the bloodthirsty nature of the commissar. It was common knowledge.[57]

BOLSHEVISM UNMASKED

With the launch of Barbarossa, Goebbels once more sought to dramatize for millions of Germans the exceptional stakes of the war. At a press conference held on July 2, the propaganda minister instructed the entire German print media to focus their reporting on the "barbarity and squalor" of the "Jewish slave state." Their "task, in words and images," was to confirm the "terrible testimonies" of millions of soldiers who had seen Bolshevism's savagery firsthand.[58]

From the first days of the campaign, footage of ragged Soviet POWs being marched across a desolate landscape abounded in the Nazi newsreels. After Germany's invasion of Poland, the newsreels had shown Polish POWs, usually making them look inferior and defeated. But the Polish soldiers remained human; German officers were shown conversing with them or offering them a smoke. Polish soldiers were interviewed, in Polish, declaring their happiness about the war being over for them and confirming their good treatment by the Germans.[59] The newsreel footage from the Soviet Union, by contrast, sought to portray Red Army soldiers as brutal and mute, a bestial mass stripped of all vestiges of humanity.[60] The writer Edwin Erich Dwinger, who contributed to this portrayal through his war reporting from the Eastern Front, recorded in his diary the sight of a column of more than a thousand Soviet POWs passing him on the road: "An ocean of heads staggered toward me, an ocean of deep-set, expressionless eyes dully staring down at their feet, an ocean of mouths, roughly cut into faces, coarse lips, from which even now not a single word escaped."[61]

Vitriolic from the start, Germany's media campaign against Bolshevism reached a fever pitch once German soldiers entered the first cities in the Soviet Union's western borderlands. These were lands that the USSR had recently annexed as part of the pact with Hitler, and its rule there was already deeply contested. Two days into the German invasion, Ukrainian nationalists launched an insurgency in the Galician capital of Lvov (Lviv) in a bid for national independence. Soviet troops quelled the uprising, arresting thousands of nationalists. As local authorities scrambled to evacuate ahead of the advancing Germans, NKVD chief Lavrenti Beria ordered the killing of all political prisoners, lest they join forces with the Germans. The mass killings lasted for days, taking about twenty-one hundred lives in Lvov alone.[62] When the bulk of Soviet troops withdrew on June 28, the remaining Ukrainian separatists, who had long despised Lvov's large Jewish population, whom they considered sympathetic to the Soviet regime, stepped up their campaign of violence.[63]

The first German soldiers reached Lvov on June 30. Enraged residents brought them to see the prisons, where the cellars overflowed with the bodies of the political prisoners NKVD forces had killed before their retreat. Crowds of people thronged the prison gates, waiting to identify missing family members. Ukrainian militiamen dragged scores of local Jews to the cellars, ordering them to bring out the dead bodies, which had begun to decompose in the summer heat, and lay them out in rows in the prison courtyard. Voices in the crowd demanded that the Jews crawl through the prison gates on their knees to acknowledge their responsibility for the killings. Militiamen paraded a group of a hundred Jewish men through the city. With their hands raised, they were forced to shout: "We want Stalin!" Then they were killed. German soldiers mostly looked on and snapped photographs.[64] Similar scenes—of ethnic nationalists blaming Jews for Soviet actions, with deadly results—were reported from multiple other towns where the Soviets had killed political prisoners before retreating. At least thirty-five pogroms took place in Eastern Galicia alone, killing more than twelve thousand people.[65]

The Soviets had killed in great haste, using blunt objects along with submachine guns and grenades. Seeking to dramatize the sadism of the Bolshevik executioners, some of the locals took the violence further. They mutilated the corpses, using wire to sew their mouths shut, cutting off male genitals and female breasts, or nailing the bodies of children to doors. The skin that peeled off the decomposing bodies became "proof" that the Soviets had boiled their victims in kettles.[66] The Germans arrived at one such scene in Lvov with a small battalion of Ukrainian nationalist soldiers and dozens of Ukrainian interpreters, who often doubled as guides and scouts.[67] These Ukrainians conveyed the details of the sadistic Soviet killings to the Germans, and explained what was common knowledge among Lvov's non-Jewish population: that all of the city's Jews were ardent Bolsheviks, whether as active NKVD henchmen or profiteers of Soviet Communist rule.[68]

The killing grounds became tourist sites of sorts. In Lvov and elsewhere, German soldiers visited the prisons by the thousands, many taking photos.[69] One battalion commander stationed in the city required his soldiers to tour the prisons,

> so they would finally recognize the kind of beasts we face. A bloodbath was carried out here in such a horrific way that it can never be believed by people who have not seen it with their own eyes. . . . May every doubter confront these inhuman atrocities. Only then will he understand the need to struggle against the Jewish-Bolshevik gang and grasp that we must avenge a thousandfold every German soldier who lost blood or life in this decisive battle between order and chaos. This is, and shall remain, the oath of the 3rd Battalion until the total annihilation and eradication of the Bolshevik army.[70]

For many soldiers in the East, as well as the readers of their letters home, these horrific sights provided documentary proof of the warnings they had heard for years about Bolshevism. Addressing his pregnant wife, a soldier wrote that given her condition, he would not describe to her what he had seen in the GPU cellars but added that these scenes disproved his earlier belief that the "depictions of Bolshevik Russia were exaggerated, a primitive appeal to sensationalism. Today I know better."[71]

Anton Roos reached Lvov on July 8. Two days later he wrote to his wife: "In Lemberg [the German name for Lvov], I saw some of the ca. 5,000 slaughtered Ukrainians . . . it's impossible to describe the sadism, committed for the most part against women. A Ukrainian who was searching for and found his wife, killed one by one the eleven Jews who had been instructed to bury the bodies."[72]

What was found in the Soviet prisons proved a godsend for the German propagandists. "It seems doubtful that we will ever be able to capture images as useful for propaganda ends as those in Lemberg," a locally stationed intelligence officer wrote to the 17th Army Command, urging film crews and journalists to be sent over immediately. The same evening, Hitler gave orders for reporters to be flown out. Yet a plane could not be found, and the team took a day longer to get to Lvov by train. An officer with the 17th Army noted with regret that the late arrival "strongly diminished" the propagandistic value of the Lvov murders, as sanitary conditions on the ground had necessitated the removal of many of the bodies.[73] But the photographs and film footage obtained by the reporters proved stirring enough. On July 6, the *Völkischer Beobachter* carried gruesome pictures from Lvov, headlined: BLOOD FRENZY OF THE BOLSHEVIK BEASTS. More images of the murder scenes covered the front pages of the paper's July 7, 8, and 9 issues.[74]

Incorporated into a newsreel, the footage from Lvov sent Goebbels into ecstasy. Hitler, who watched the film prior to its release, rang the propaganda minister to say it was the best newsreel he had ever made.[75] Distributed on July 10, the film cut from rows of corpses and weeping women in the prison courtyard to portrait shots of individuals who were presented as "the murderous Jewish rabble that had worked hand in hand with the GPU agents." "Nothing eluded these monsters in human form," the narrator intoned. Brimming with "Bolshevik murderous lust,"

Wiener Ausgabe

Wiener Ausgabe

Wien, Mittwoch, 9. Juli 1941

VÖLKISCHER BEOBACHTER

Kampfblatt der nationalsozialistischen Bewegung Großdeutschlands

„...erkämpft das Menschenrecht“

Das ist das Paradies der Arbeiter, Bauern und Soldaten!

Völkischer Beobachter, *July 9, 1941.*

they had "tormented and slaughtered their innocent victims" in the most atrocious fashion.[76]

The graphic violence provoked revulsion and outrage. From movie theaters across Germany, Nazi informants reported that the "images of the victims of the Bolshevik terror in Lemberg are the most talked about part of the newsreel, since, in their horrific realism, they far surpass the effect of previous press and radio reports about Bolshevik atrocities." Moviegoers were heard saying that they finally understood the "true essence of Bolshevism and Jewry, in all its horror." While there were some, especially women, who found the images unbearable to watch, most viewers called for the inclusion of more brutal scenes, of more "sober facts," in newsreels going forward, in order to "convince even the most skeptical countrymen of the Jewish Bolshevik menace," and to emphasize "the profound necessity of the German struggle."[77] Spectators in the movie theaters reportedly expressed gratitude to Hitler, for "the Führer alone saw the Bolshevik danger from the start and has saved Europe from this danger."[78] On June 22, 1941, few Germans had showed any enthusiasm upon hearing of their country's surprise attack on the colossal

Soviet state. Coming two weeks later, the images from Lvov held tremendous mobilizing value, as they appeared to lend unassailable visual credibility to Hitler's claim that the invasion was a preventive strike against a ruthless "Jewish-Bolshevik" aggressor determined to "set not only Germany, but all of Europe, aflame."[79]

Goebbels made sure the Germans would remember Lvov, arranging for the graphic footage to be included in subsequent Nazi newsreels as well. He also prepared a book of letters from the Eastern Front, with a print run of three million copies, in which German soldiers gave their accounts as "witnesses against Bolshevism." Like earlier anti-Bolshevik publications, the heavily illustrated book, entitled *German Soldiers See the Soviet Union*, claimed to uncover the inner workings of the Communist system, hitherto shielded from view by Bolshevik propaganda, and to expose as lies the claims that the Soviet state was a workers' and peasants' paradise.[80] The soldier witnesses were especially appalled by the Lvov murders, and called for the "worst and harshest punishment" to be exacted upon for the Jewish-Bolshevik perpetrators. What other atrocities were being committed farther East? one wondered. Lvov had endured Soviet rule for only two years, but in the core areas of the Soviet Union, the Bolsheviks had terrorized the population for a generation. The soldier concluded: "It will be necessary to lance this pestilent boil" to break "Juda's domination of the world."[81]

As the publicity campaign surrounding the Lvov murders unfolded, Nazi propagandists exploded in unprecedented rage against Jews, arguing that the massacres were unmistakably their doing: "The Jewish desire to wade in flowing blood, which invented nauseating ritual slaughter, triumphed so long as no one was putting a stop to it."[82] The gruesome result, for Germany and for all of Europe, would have been even greater piles of "mutilated and defiled bodies"—had Hitler not had the prescience to wage a preemptive war against the Jewish-Bolshevik terror regime. Headshots of the alleged perpetrators, invariably grim and supposedly Jewish-looking Red Army men, ran alongside the horrific images, meant to evoke for all Germans the Jewish threat that had hung over humanity for a quarter century.

The German newsreels made no secret of the reckoning that lay in store for Soviet Jews. A film on the German seizure of the Bessarabian town of Balti again featured piles of corpses found in Soviet prisons. As the camera panned over the bodies, the narrator intoned: "After being tortured and tormented for hours on end, men, women, and children were bestially slaughtered by the executioners' Jewish minions." The film then cut to rows of despondent-looking men and women carrying bags and belongings. Among them were women with young children in their arms and an old, bearded man on crutches. "The Jewish population of Balti has been taken to collection camps," the speaker continued. "These Eastern Jews are the parasites that threaten to subvert their host countries and annihilate millenary cultures. Wherever they surface they bring crime, corruption, and chaos."[83] Nazi informants reported that moviegoers found the images of the Jews from Balti repulsive and wondered "what should be done with these hordes." Close-up shots of Soviet prisoners of war, invariably sorted into types—the "Jewish commissar," the "degenerate musket woman," the "dim Asiatic soldier"—provoked even stronger responses. Why should Germany even feed the captured Bolsheviks? one spectator asked. Others voiced horror that German soldiers had to fight against "beasts possessed of such cruelty," and still others called for the killing of female Soviet soldiers and commissars. Over and over again, everyday Germans were overheard saying that the military's treatment of Soviet prisoners, as represented on-screen, was "much too humane" and that this "Asiatic riffraff" should be eliminated as quickly as possible.[84]

These racially charged depictions recast Soviet Communists, soldiers, and Jews as criminals, degenerates, and subhumans. And they turned ordinary Germans, moviegoers and consumers of propaganda, into ruthless advocates of mass murder. The hatred of Bolshevism spanned political divides in Germany, taking root in Nazis as well as anti-Nazis. Clemens von Galen, the Catholic bishop of Münster, had earned fame across the country as the "Lion of Münster" when he held a series of sermons in July and August 1941, protesting against Hitler's "euthanasia" program to kill Germany's physically and mentally disabled. "Never,"

Galen declared from his pulpit, "under no circumstances, may a man kill an innocent, except in war and in legitimate self-defense." Galen's words resonated widely and forced Hitler to suspend the euthanasia program. Weeks later, Galen issued a public prayer, asking for God's intervention to protect German soldiers in their effort to defend Germany and Western Europe against the "pestilence of Bolshevism." Galen's passionate sermon repeated language he had used during the Spanish Civil War, when he called upon the faithful to fight and overcome "pestilent Communist infection."[85]

For Robert Ley, head of the German Labor Front and an early adherent of National Socialism, Germany's war against the Soviet Union conjured memories of the Nazis' confrontation with the "Bolshevik insanity" on the streets back in the 1920s. That clash, too, had been a struggle to the death. Even then, Ley wrote, it had been "clear to us that by far the strongest shock troop of Jewry was Bolshevism. . . . And that is how we understand today's struggle." While he saw Germany fighting a global Jewish conspiracy, singling out "intellectuals from London and New York" for special mention, he identified Soviet Communists as the greatest Jewish menace. "Bolshevism has opened the gates of hell, the Jewish hellhound has broken its restraints, and is being let loose on humanity,"[86] Ley continued, writing in the immediate aftermath of the Lvov murders. His language left no doubt about the stakes of the coming conflict:

> This war is Juda's war. Every German . . . must be clear about the grim nature of this struggle. It is a contest between life and death, being and nonbeing. There is no more compromise, no more point of return. We have crossed the Rubicon.[87]

SOVIET JEWS AS BOLSHEVIKS

In fact, the Rubicon had already been crossed in June. Outside the public eye, Einsatzgruppen, Nazi paramilitary death squads set up by the Sipo and SD and serving under the command of Reinhard Heydrich, had entered the Soviet Union soon after the Wehrmacht forces. Numbering some three thousand men, their assignment was to extinguish the Bolshevik "threat" with targeted assassinations.[88] On July 2, Heydrich reminded his men about their assignment:

> To be executed are all: functionaries of the Comintern (as in general professional Communist politicians); the higher, middle, and radical lower-level functionaries of the party, of the central committees, of the regional and district committees; people's commissars; Jews in party and state positions, miscellaneous radical elements (saboteurs, propagandists, snipers, assassins, agitators, etc.).[89]

Coming before the news from Lvov had shifted public sentiment, the instructions were in line with Hitler's speech on March 30, 1941, when he called for the destruction of all institutions and individuals embodying the Soviet system. Heydrich did not call for the extermination of all Jews, nor did he call for killing Jewish officials on racial grounds. Rather, the Jewish officials he targeted were singled out as representatives of Bolshevism.

As they reported back from the killing fields, SS officers listed not only the body count of political enemies they had "finished off," but also their identities. The reports often presented their targets in serial fashion, as "functionaries, agents, saboteurs, and Jews," or "Jews, Communist officials, saboteurs, Komsomol members, and Communist agitators," or "Bolsheviks, Jews, and asocial elements, etc.," or "Jews and other Communist tainted elements." With respect to "Communists" and "Jews," reports routinely provided alternating designations, talking about "Jewish Communists" in one place, "Jews and other Communist-tainted elements" in another, and "Communists and Jews" in a third.[90] All SS officers took it as self-evident that Soviet Communism was overwhelmingly Jewish and that Jews overwhelmingly supported Bolshevism.

The sight of killing grounds, in Lvov and many other cities in the Soviet borderlands, further radicalized the Sipo and SD units that followed on the heels of the advancing German forces.[91] Members of Einsatzgruppe

C, which was attached to Army Group South, reached Lvov just hours after German soldiers entered the city on June 30. With help from the local population, they sought to identify the corpses discovered in the local prisons. Some of the Einsatzgruppe's men participated in the Ukrainian-led mass lynching of Jews in the first days of July, but most simply watched or photographed the spectacle alongside the Wehrmacht troops, while applauding the locals for killing the "Jew-Bolsheviks." Their actions were in line with a pre-Barbarossa instruction Heydrich had given his SS men—to incite anti-Bolshevik actions in liberated Ukrainian and Baltic towns, but in discreet fashion so as to make them seem like acts of "self-cleansing."[92] As the pogrom came to an end, Einsatzgruppe C began to detain male Jews. An order had reportedly arrived from Hitler: the NKVD's murders were to be "avenged" using the harshest means, extending even to persons only remotely tied to the killings.[93] The men of Einsatzgruppe C confined some thousand Jewish men in a local athletic field, where they were abused at length. From there, they were loaded onto trucks, taken outside the city, and shot. As he ordered his men to line up facing the victims, a commanding officer read out an execution formula, stating the retaliatory nature of the killings.[94] Shortly thereafter, Einsatzgruppe C reported to Berlin that "approximately 7,000 Jews were rounded up and shot by the Security Police in retaliation for the inhuman atrocities [committed by the Communists]."[95] Upon leaving Lvov, the men of Einsatzgruppe C made stops in other towns where the NKVD had executed Ukrainian nationalists. Some of these towns held little strategic value for the German military, but the SS men were eager to punish the Jewish-Bolshevik perpetrators. Styling themselves as avengers of innocent Ukrainians, they went on a killing spree, murdering local Jews.[96]

Himmler, as both the head of the SS and the chief of the German police, encouraged this escalating violence, praising his policemen-soldiers and chiding their commanders for not detaining more Jews. On July 8, on a visit in Bialystok where he met with the heads of SS squads and police commanders, Himmler declared "that in principle every Jew is to be seen as a partisan." In the wake of this encounter, Arthur Nebe, chief of

Einsatzgruppe B (attached to Army Group Center), instructed his men "to immediately initiate actions against Jews upon moving into towns."[97] After Bialystok, Himmler visited Lvov, Dubno, Rovno, and Luck—all cities where hundreds of bodies had been retrieved from former NKVD prisons. While on the road, he ordered a massive increase in the ranks of the German political police in the East. Two SS brigades under the command of Higher SS and Police Führer Erich von dem Bach-Zelewski complemented the first Einsatzgruppen contingent and the eleven police battalions already stationed in the field, bringing the total German pacification force to more than sixteen thousand men, in addition to auxiliary police units that were drawn from the Ukrainian, Belarusian, and Baltic populations.[98] Writing to his wife on July 25, after reaching Hitler's headquarters in East Prussia, Himmler informed her that he was doing "very well under a heavy workload. I get treatments every day and sleep very well. The struggle goes well, but it is *unbelievably tough*. The enemy defends himself *tenaciously*. . . . Many sweet greetings and kisses, Your Pappi."[99]

As their forces expanded, the men of the Einsatzgruppen became ever more convinced that the enemy's treachery demanded harsh treatment. The same soldiers who had rarely acknowledged killings explicitly in their reports from Poland now described their participation in lethal violence on Soviet soil openly and as a matter of political duty, even pride.[100] Almost invariably, they saw their actions as a necessary response to ambushes and sabotage that they attributed to Soviet Jews. However, the SS and Sipo men were still distinguishing between Soviet Jews, who counted as Bolsheviks, and Jews elsewhere under German rule. When Hinrich Lohse, the newly installed chief administrator for Reich Commissariat Ostland (the Baltic lands and White Russia), informed the leadership of the SS and police in his jurisdiction of his plans to ghettoize the Jews who lived there, and put them to work as forced laborers, they were highly critical of his proposal, which they saw as too lenient. As Einsatzgruppen A chief Franz Walter Stahlecker wrote to Lohse, his suggested policy would have been appropriate for the General Government in Poland, where there was "no serious political danger in leaving

Public hanging in Zhitomir, August 8, 1941.[101]

the Jews in their living quarters and work places." But the Jews in the Ostland were "leading supporters of the Bolshevik idea," many of them Communist activists themselves. Citing recent experience gained on occupied Soviet soil, Stahlecker predicted sabotage and acts of terror from "the Jews who will use every opportunity to create disorder." This danger necessitated "radical treatment" by the German authorities in the East.[102]

The German security police regularly staged the mass murder of Soviet Jews as public retribution for alleged Bolshevik criminality. One such spectacle took place in Zhitomir, about sixty miles west of Kiev. Four weeks after capturing the town, agents of Einsatzgruppe C arrested two Jewish district judges, Wolf Kieper and Moshe Kogan. Under interrogation, Kieper, a Bolshevik since 1905, confessed to handing down a thousand death sentences since the establishment of the Soviet regime. The next day, an army propaganda truck outfitted with loudspeakers drove through Zhitomir, summoning all who heard it, in German and Ukrainian, to attend an execution in the city's market square the following day, August 8, 1941. More than four thousand people came to watch the hanging. A gallows was set up in the center of the square. Dozens of soldiers perched on the steep sloped roof of a public lavatory located behind the gallows. The malodorous fumes seeping from the windows and rafters did nothing to deter them from getting an unobscured view of the proceedings. Placards in German and Ukrainian affixed to the gallows proclaimed the identity of the victims. They read: "The Cheka Jew Wolf Kieper, murderer of 1,350 ethnic Germans and Ukrainians," and "The assistant of the Cheka Jew, henchman Mojsche Kogan."[103]

Members of Einsatzgruppe C forced several hundred Jewish men from Zhitomir to the market square. Ordered to cower on the ground and keep their hands clasped around their necks, the Jews had to watch the hangings. As soon as Kieper and Kogan were dead, the Germans turned their attention to these men. They were beaten, abused, loaded onto trucks, and driven to a nearby horse cemetery. Via loudspeakers, the Germans called on the crowd to follow. After further mistreatment, all the men were shot to death.[104]

Around the time of the hangings in Zhitomir, German mass killings in the occupied Soviet lands reached a new level of barbarity. Invoking the rationale that all Soviet Jews presented a security threat as "carriers of Bolshevism," SS officers in Ukraine and Belorussia expressed doubts that the killing of Jewish men alone could "bring about a fundamental solution to the Jewish problem." In late July 1941, the First SS Brigade searched towns and villages between Rovno and Zhitomir, shooting "800 male and female Jews aged 16–60 for favoring Bolshevism."[105] SS leaders directed and expanded these actions. After returning to Berlin from a three-day trip to Ukraine on July 23, Heydrich ordered a commando unit of Einsatzgruppe B to shoot all Jewish women and children in their area of operation in Belorussia, in addition to all the men.[106] On July 31, Himmler flew to Baranovichi in Belorussia, where he met with Bach-Zelewski to discuss ongoing operations to "comb and pacify" the nearby Pripyat Marshes. Impatient with the results, Himmler issued a terse radio order: "All Jews must be shot. Drive Jewish women into the swamps." The men followed his orders, only to discover that the swamps were too shallow to drown the women. They were subsequently shot.[107] Wehrmacht leaders agreed about the need to kill Soviet jews indiscriminately. A July 25 directive issued by the Army High Command warned against mounting partisan activity in the German rear. The decree ordered the maximal use of terror against civilians, designating all Jews as "pillars of the Jewish-Bolshevik system."[108]

Himmler's and Heydrich's orders to shoot all Jews—including women, children, and the elderly—soon became general policy. Among the first to carry out the new policy were SS units in the German-occupied Baltic republics. In town after town, ghetto after ghetto, they systematically killed all Jewish residents.[109] Lithuanians and Latvians who served the conquerors as auxiliary policemen enthusiastically participated in the killings.[110] By the end of 1941, 80 percent of all Jews in all these areas were dead. In those German-occupied Soviet territories that had formed part of the USSR before 1939, nearly 100 percent of detained Jews were killed by year's end. In contrast, in areas previously under Polish rule, the Germans murdered only between 15 and 25 percent of the Jewish population, and focused primarily on killing Jewish men.[111] The mass murder of all Jews—young and old, male and female—began with the murder of Soviet Jews. From inside the Soviet Union, it radiated out, first convulsing the occupied Western peripheries of the Soviet state, then spreading farther west.

Starting in late summer 1941, German security officials routinely portrayed Soviet Jews as partisans, as Himmler had done in Bialystok in early July. In fact, this connection was the subject of an officers' seminar on anti-partisan warfare, which took place in the town of Mogilev in late September. The theme was "Where there's a partisan, there's a Jew, and where there's a Jew, there's a partisan."[112] The course included the demonstration of a mass shooting in a nearby village of about thirty Jews and other suspicious people. The seminar's organizers warned that the enemy was using the elderly, women, and children for "reconnaissance" and encouraged divisional commanders to hang partisans and Communists. Those caught in violation of curfew—along with anybody else who aroused suspicion—should be shot.[113]

On October 2, thirty-six-year-old police administrator Walter Mattner wrote his wife from Mogilev, saying he had volunteered to take part in a punitive action against Jews. Mattner, who had left Vienna just twelve days earlier, had been detailed to the Higher SS and Police Führer with Army Group Center to work in supply and provisioning. The next day, he would have the opportunity to use his pistol for the first time. He had packed all twenty-eight bullets in his possession but sensed that this would not be enough and had asked to borrow another gun from a fellow policeman. "I don't know at all whether I am allowed to write you this, but of course, you've known for a long time that the Jews are our misfortune. . . . What we're doing is legitimate punishment for all the suffering that they have caused and still cause us Germans."[114] On October 5, he again wrote to his wife. His letter described the "enormous mass death" of October 3:

> For the first truckload my hand trembled slightly when shooting, but one gets used to it. By the time the tenth truck arrived I was aiming steadily and fired without hesitating at the many women, children and infants. I always bear in mind that I also have two babies at home, to whom these hordes would do the same, if not ten times worse. The death we gave them was a nice, fast death, compared to the hellish torture meted out to thousands upon thousands in the dungeons of the GPU. The infants flew in a wide arc through the air and we blew them away while still in flight, before they fell into the water in the pit. Let's get rid of this brood which has plunged all Europe into war, and is still warmongering in America until it drags them into the war as well.[115]

Mattner went on to quote Hitler's January 1939 prophecy that the Jews would be annihilated if they incited another world war. Most likely this line and the reference to the GPU prisons were bits of information that Mattner had picked up in lectures and courses that were offered to the soldiers to reinforce their hatred of "Jews and Bolsheviks." Such indoctrination became increasingly necessary as the enemies targeted for mass killing turned out to include scores of patently innocent women and children. On October 3, 1941, the German and Ukrainian police forces based in Mogilev—Mattner among them—murdered 2,208 local Jews. By the end of the month, Mogilev's Jewish population was wiped out.[116]

As delusional as the occupiers' fears of Jewish savagery were, events occasionally confirmed their sense of vulnerability in a hostile land run by "the Jews." As readers will remember, only five days after the German army marched into Kiev, several detonations destroyed a depot used to store captured equipment and ammunition located next to the main post office. Another explosion shattered the Grand Hotel, in which the Germans had set up their military headquarters, killing all the soldiers inside. Every few minutes, another building blew up, for hours on end. The explosions set off a huge fire that burned for days and reduced the city center to smoldering ruins. The attack was the work of the NKVD, which had placed mines before withdrawing from Kiev. Undercover Soviet agents remaining in the city detonated the mines in coordination with remote sabotage groups in an effort to cause maximum destruction. Altogether, the explosions killed between two hundred and three hundred German soldiers and many residents.[117]

The Germans instantly decided who was behind the attack. When the top security officials in the region—Higher SS and Police Führer for South Russia Friedrich Jeckeln, Einsatzgruppe C chief Otto Rasch, Sonderkommando 4a leader Paul Blobel, and Kiev's Wehrmacht commandant Generalmajor Kurt Eberhard—met on September 26, they quickly agreed on a mass reprisal against the Jews. "It has been proven that Jews participated significantly in the arson attacks," the SD reported on the outcome of the meeting. "Measures initiated for gathering of all Jews. Execution of at least 50,000 Jews envisioned."[118] The same day, posters went up in Russian, Ukrainian, and German announcing that all of Kiev's Jews (the city's prewar Jewish population numbered upward of 200,000) were to assemble at a certain point in the city's northwest.[119] They were to bring documents and valuables, as well as warm clothing. Anyone disobeying the order was to be shot. Rumors had it that the Jews were to be placed in a ghetto and put to work. Scores of Kievans—men, women, and children—made their way to the designated corner at

Melnikovskaya and Degtyaryovskaya streets on the morning of September 29. They walked into a trap. The area was cordoned off by armed German soldiers and policemen as well as Ukrainian militiamen. The people were forced to hand over their belongings and undress and then were taken to Kiev's Babi Yar ravine. Throughout that day and the next, the German police and SS, German soldiers, and Ukrainian auxiliaries killed 33,771 Jews.[120]

Wehrmacht soldiers and commanders stationed in Kiev condoned the actions of the SS and police. The propaganda unit attached to the Sixth Army had printed the posters ordering the Jews to assemble near Babi Yar. A corporal writing home on the eve of the Babi Yar massacre reported how "for eight days now the city is on fire and all of it is the Jews' doing. Therefore, all Jewish men aged 14 to 60 have been shot and the Jewish women will also be shot, otherwise there will be no end to it."[121] Ten days after the massacre, Sixth Army commander Walter von Reichenau issued an order, "On the Conduct of the Troops in the East," which asserted unequivocally that all acts of violence committed against Germans on occupied Soviet ground were "always instigated by Jews." Addressing his soldiers as "avengers of all the bestialities" inflicted upon the German nation, Reichenau ordered them to go beyond ordinary soldiering and accept the "necessity of a severe but just revenge on subhuman Jewry. . . . This is the only way to fulfill our historic task to liberate the German people once and forever from the Asiatic-Jewish danger."[122] Hitler was elated by Reichenau's words, and the Army High Command instructed all commanders on the Eastern Front to issue similar orders.[123]

AVENGING OUR DEAD

The belief in the need for a violent response to the alleged Jewish-Bolshevik threat was not Germany's alone. It was widely shared by Germany's allies, especially Romania. In 1940, Stalin had forced Romania to cede back to the USSR the provinces of Bessarabia and Northern

Bukovina, which had been under Russian imperial rule until 1917. Romania's dictator, Ion Antonescu, did not know that the secret protocol of the Hitler-Stalin pact had assigned these two provinces to the Soviet sphere of interest, but he could do nothing to prevent the Soviet land grab, especially after the Germans informed him that they were unable to come to his aid. As soon as Antonescu learned of Hitler's plan to attack the Soviet Union, he resolved to join the "holy war" against Judeo-Bolshevism.[124] As Romanian forces reclaimed the lost territories beginning on June 22, they incited pogroms against the country's Jews, vilifying them as supporters of Bolshevism. But Antonescu wanted more than Bessarabia and Northern Bukovina. From the start, his eyes had been set on the port city of Odessa, three hundred miles south of Kiev, the greatest prize in his design for a Greater Romania. By early August, Romanian forces had surrounded a heavily fortified Odessa, but the prolonged siege, lasting two months, cost them dearly in terms of manpower, leaving almost eighteen thousand dead and over eleven thousand missing. Venting his frustration in a letter to a fellow Romanian official on September 5, Antonescu blamed the "diabolical perseverance" of the "Jewish commissars" for Romania's losses. They "lead the slaves like a herd of cattle.... Had the Jewish commissars not been around, we would have taken Odessa long ago." The Romanians, Antonescu underscored, were not fighting against Russians or Slavs. They were enmeshed in a life-and-death struggle against the Jews—against "Satan himself."[125]

With some German support, the Romanians finally occupied Odessa on October 16. The city had a large prewar Jewish population, of whom up to ninety-five thousand remained at the time of the Romanian invasion.[126] Soldiers immediately went on a rampage, killing hundreds of Jews.[127] On the evening of October 22, mines were detonated in the city's former NKVD building, where the Romanians had set up their military headquarters. The blasts killed the commander, along with at least seventy-eight Romanian and German soldiers.[128] As in Kiev, NKVD agents had planted the explosives. Before their responsibility was even established, a Romanian general ordered the mass hanging of "Jews and Communists" in Odessa's squares. In the early morning hours of October 23, Antonescu followed suit with an order to hang at least one hundred Jews in each sector of the occupied city, and to execute a total of eighteen thousand Odessan Jews. The order spoke of "Jews" in one sentence and "Communist Jews" in another, making it clear that the phrases were interchangeable: every Jew counted as a Communist.[129] The mass killings began that day. Hundreds of gallows lined the streets.[130] Simultaneously, about sixty thousand more Jews were forced out of their homes and marched to holding pens outside of the city. Of this group, an estimated twenty-five thousand were machine-gunned and burned to death by Romanian soldiers in the coming days and weeks. The survivors were marched to the Bogdanovka concentration camp on the Bug River, from which the Romanians hoped to push them into the German-occupied military zone. The Germans, however, withheld their permission. As fears of a Soviet counterstrike on Odessa grew, Antonescu came to regard all Jews under his military rule as Bolsheviks and ordered their instant removal. All of Odessa's remaining Jews were to be forced from the city, he told his assembled ministers on December 16: "Pack them into the catacombs, throw them into the Black Sea, but get them out of Odessa. . . . I don't care if a hundred die, a thousand die, all of them die, but I don't want a single Romanian official or officer to die. . . . I am afraid that, on account of these Yids, a catastrophe might occur if the Russians land near Odessa."[131] On December 21, Romanian guards assisted by Ukrainian policemen proceeded to systematically murder the forty-eight thousand Jews detained in Bogdanovka. The men, women, and children were driven in groups to a nearby forest, forced to undress, and made to kneel at the edge of a ravine. Then they were shot in the neck. The killings were paused at Christmastime, resumed on December 28, and concluded the next day.[132] The remaining thirty-five thousand Odessan Jews were forced into a ghetto and shortly thereafter deported to concentration camps far from the front line. Almost none of them would survive the war.[133]

In the meantime, the Germans—like their Romanian allies—continued to encounter unforeseen Soviet resistance on the Eastern Front. Even though the Wehrmacht made significant advances throughout the summer and fall, the gains fell short of the ambitious goals spelled out in Barbarossa's battle plan. Gustav Roos, writing to his father Anton in August, described his fellow soldiers' frustration and anger:

> In the homeland, when you hear the word "deployment," you think of German troops storming forward, and Russians running backward, of Oak Leaves and Knight's Crosses. Our feelings now are very different. . . . Every attack is a fight to the finish. The Russian defends himself tenaciously and desperately. . . . And we all know we have to do our duty and obey. But we've had enough and long for an end to this shit. Again and again, you hear: "Man, can you believe that's what we have to fight against now!" The Poles, the Greek, and the French were at least still humans and even fair opponents for the most part. But these Russians, Asiatics, these semihumans, idiots, and cretins—fighting against them brings no pleasure.[134]

A newsletter for German troops published in September 1941 echoed Roos's thoughts: No longer promising soldiers a lightning victory, it summoned them instead to prepare for a grinding defense of everything they held dear. "This is not about measuring one's strength against a soldierly opponent man-to-man," the newsletter declared, "but about preventing savagery by these beasts. . . . Whenever the Bolshevik moves in, whenever these subhumans overrun a country, all noble blood is murdered, women are violated, monuments to culture are destroyed. Where life flourished, horror settles in."[135]

The German death toll after the first three months of Barbarossa stood at 200,000. The overall losses, including a further 196,000 wounded and sick, were staggering.[136] By comparison, all of Nazi Germany's pre-Barbarossa actions combined—the invasion of Poland, the war against Norway, the attacks in the West, and the operations in the Balkans—had resulted in the deaths of 134,000 Wehrmacht soldiers. Rumors circulated throughout Germany that the nation had lost up to a million men in the East. Nazi officials tried to counter the rumors by releasing their own falsified numbers, claiming that only 86,000 of their soldiers had died and 22,000 had gone missing in action. They also released inflated accounts of the enemy's losses: 1.8 million Red Army soldiers killed and as many taken prisoner. The actual losses for the Red Army at this time were colossal, but closer to 430,000 dead and 1.7 million imprisoned.[137] The key figure responsible for the Wehrmacht's losses, virtually all German observers agreed, was once again the commissar, whose presumed fanaticism, born from an Asiatic contempt for human life, had turned ordinary Russian soldiers into beasts. In September, army commanders fighting in the East submitted a bold request to the High Command: rescind the Commissar Order mandating that Germany execute all political officers in the Red Army. The order, they argued, contributed to Germany's losses, as it gave the commissars no option but to "use the most brutal means" to make Soviet soldiers fight to the finish. The Führer turned down the request.[138]

Hitler was determined to win the war as he had begun it, Blitzkrieg style. On October 2, he ordered an all-out attack on Moscow, calling it "the last great, decisive battle of this year." There was a shift though. During the launch of Barbarossa, German military commanders had fully expected to crush the Red Army in a single summer, by August at the latest. But in conversations behind closed doors during August and September, Hitler paid Soviet leaders grudging respect for their "fantastic war preparations" and praised the Red Army as a much fiercer opponent than any others Germany had encountered to date. By this time, the Führer appeared to have come around to believing the propaganda he had spread in June to justify his own aggression: The Soviet Union, as he saw it, was so strong that it would have easily overpowered Germany had he not launched a preventive surprise attack.[139] In an October 3 speech at the Berlin Sportpalast, his first public appearance in months, Hitler characterized the Red Army as "an enemy made up of animals or beasts, not humans." He had warned of the true nature of the so-called Soviet paradise: "After the end of this campaign, five or six million soldiers will confirm that I spoke the truth, they will be witnesses I can call upon.

They marched on those roads. They saw the miserable cottages—they could never live in them, they wouldn't even step into one unless it was absolutely necessary. They saw what this paradise is made up of. It is nothing but one huge arms factory at the expense of the people's standard of living, an arms factory against Europe."[140]

Hitler fumed about the death toll that the supposedly Jewish commissars and the Jews in general had inflicted on Germans in wars current and past: "This race of criminals," he exclaimed behind closed doors on October 25, with Himmler and Heydrich in the room, "carries the guilt of the two million dead of the [First] World War and now that of hundreds of thousands more. Let nobody tell me that we shouldn't drive them into the marshes in the East!"[141] Germany was fighting the world's only power "ruled by the Jewish spirit," Hitler declared in a public address on November 8. In the Soviet Union, he claimed, the Jews had succeeded in slaughtering the entire class of national elites and reducing the rest of the population to misery. Lording over these "proletarianized subhumans" was a "gigantic organization of Jewish commissars—that is, slaveholders."[142]

During the planning of Barbarossa, Hitler had believed that taking out the commissars would crush the Red Army's fighting spirit. Even though

Stalin's "New Organization of the Soviet Army"
(Preußische Zeitung, *July 21, 1941).*

German commandos detained and shot thousands of presumed political officers, their extreme actions did not diminish the tenacity of the Soviet troops. It was against this background that both Hitler and Antonescu came to conceive of their nations' mortal enemy in dramatically new ways, calling for what we today describe as genocide. All Soviet Jews had to be annihilated, lest a Jewish state on the model of the Bolshevik regime ever threaten the German or the Romanian nations again. Hitler and Antonescu had reached this conclusion in October and December 1941, respectively, and found little disagreement among SS and Wehrmacht commanders in the field and ordinary soldiers on the ground.

There was no single top-down order in summer 1941 that explains how the Shoah came to be; it erupted from the cumulative violence of Germany's attack on the Soviet system, the vicious anti-Bolshevik propaganda dating back to the 1920s, and the failure to win the quick victory Hitler had foretold. Reporting from occupied Soviet soil invariably cast Jews as perpetrators and beneficiaries of Soviet terror, and fused Jews, commissars, and secret police into a single and profoundly menacing figure. Increasingly, both ordinary soldiers and SS squads began to view all Soviet Jews, even women, children, and the elderly, as Bolshevik agents. Starting in late July 1941, this linkage triggered mass shootings.

It was a relatively simple task to organize the mass killing of Soviet Jews, due to their concentration in the Western borderlands, the former Pale of Settlement. The fact that the invading Germans had immediately issued orders to all Soviet Jews to wear markers identifying their presumed racial identity helped greatly.[143] Yet the occupiers had not initially mandated the wearing of yellow patches for the purpose of killing the Jews. Rather, their marking orders were in keeping with the logic of racial segregation and deportation that had taken shape during the Polish campaign. This logic shifted to genocide over the course of the summer and fall. Over this period, virtually every Soviet Jew came to be counted as a Bolshevik and thus had to be killed. In November 1941, Einsatzgruppe C, headquartered in Kiev, produced a report on political, economic, and cultural developments in Ukraine as well as on the mood of the population. Under the heading "ethnic questions," the report said:

> It need not be particularly stressed that Communist agitators received very warm support from the Jews. Under the prevailing conditions, it was important to stop the activity of the Jews in Volhynia and to remove thereby the most fertile soil from Bolshevism. The extermination of the Jews, who are, without any doubt, useless as workers and more harmful as the carriers of the bacillae of Communism, was necessary.[144]

A few weeks earlier, Anton Roos had expressed this same idea. Writing from Poltava, he informed his wife that "in the last few days, the Jewish question has been solved here in radical fashion":

> In Uman and Kirovograd, the most hideous crimes committed by Jews against Ukrainians and soldiers were discovered, crimes that would make your hair stand on end. Short work was made of all the Jews. Now that we're rid of these animals together with their offspring, they'll no longer be gobbling up anything, and we'll take over a territory free of Jews. Here in Poltava, something has also been happening in recent days. The Russian radio station announced that the town was about to be captured by the Soviet army. The Yitzhaks promptly got fresh and spread dishonest Jew propaganda. So, measures were taken to make such Jew-lies impossible. I watched as about a dozen Jews were knocked off. Oh, how they wailed, all of them innocent of course.[145]

Roos went on to underscore that by attacking the Soviet Union, Hitler had averted catastrophe. If not for this intervention, he wrote, countless Germans and Europeans would have shared the fate of the murdered people in the Soviet borderlands, where "the Bolsheviks' first actions consisted of slaughtering the entire intelligentsia. (In Riga, 30,117 people were shot by these beasts in the first week alone.)" Roos gave his wife "only one example" of what Bolshevik rule entailed in practice. It was the cliché of the Bolshevik nationalization of women that dated back to the Russian civil war:

> When one of these Jewish commissars liked a woman or a girl, he'd summon her to his office. If she didn't come, her husband or father would be arrested. If that didn't help, they'd have him exiled or shot. If the woman still remained steadfast, she herself would be arrested, and then the commissar would get what he wanted. Now, you can understand why no Jew remains alive here. Cold revenge is the order of the day. As the Jewish God Jehovah says in the Old Testament: "An eye for an eye, a tooth for a tooth."[146]

Walter Mattner, the policeman from Vienna and mass murderer in Mogilev, took Roos's logic one step further. "I'm already looking forward to this," he wrote to his wife in early October 1941: "Many here say that when we return to the homeland, it'll be the turn of our Jews at home."[147] Beyond identifying and killing any and all Soviet Jews as Bolsheviks, Mattner began to see Jews everywhere as a demonic enemy to be annihilated. He was among the first to Bolshevize Germany's Jews.

Chapter 4

A VIOLENCE SHAKING EUROPE

The invasion of the USSR inaugurated attacks on Communism across the continent. Within hours after the first German divisions set foot on Soviet soil on June 22, 1941, Gestapo agents detained over one thousand Communists in northern France and Belgium. In Zagreb, Croatian policemen preemptively arrested scores of Communists. In Belgrade, German military authorities ordered all Communists and former members of the International Brigades deported to a concentration camp.[1] The Germans expected Communists throughout Europe to rise up in response to their trampling of the nonaggression pact and saw these repressive actions as a preemptive measure. Soon enough, an outbreak of Communist activity proved them right. In Saloniki, leaflets from the local bureau of the Greek Communist Party called for rebellion and sabotage. A flyer announcing a "Proletarian Revolution" circulated in Bremen, a traditional stronghold of the left: "German workers, men and women, show your solidarity with the Red Army soldiers of the Soviet Union, the liberators of the world proletariat! Practice passive resistance!"[2] From virtually the moment the Germans marched into Belgrade in April of that year, they had faced guerrilla resistance, which intensified after June 22. As early as June 25, German observers in Belgrade noted, "Due to the outbreak of the war, strong communist propaganda activity is evident in Serbia. Well over half the population, especially in Belgrade, is pro-Soviet."[3] By contrast, in France, Belgium, and the Netherlands, where Communist movements were marginal and anti-Bolshevism enjoyed broad societal support, the German occupiers found it easy to maintain control.[4]

The war against the Soviet Union almost instantly changed how the Germans understood the enemies they were confronting in battle—not only in the USSR, but elsewhere as well. Most significantly, it transformed Jews into Bolsheviks. In addition to the arrests of Communists and International Brigades members, the military command in Belgrade ordered the detention of forty Jewish hostages per day, who were to be shot in the event of bodily harm being inflicted on Germans. A former SS officer standing trial in 1946 testified that he received orders in Belgrade that June to arrest "suspect persons who were marked as Communists."[5] In reality, the only marked individuals in Belgrade were Jews, who wore yellow armbands. But for this former official, Jews and Communists were interchangeable. Incidents described in Security Police reports from the field, such as the attempt by the "16-year-old Jew Haim Almuzlino to set fire to several German military vehicles in Belgrade," served as confirmation of the link between Jews and Communists. In reprisal for Almuzlino's attack, the SS killed "100 Jews and 22 Communists."[6]

Nazi leaders perceived Communist resistance across Europe as a single, Soviet-led front. Surveys of Communist activities in Western and Southern Europe formed an integral part of the reports from the occupied Soviet territories that were filed by the Security Police and the intelligence service, the SD. Edited in Heydrich's Berlin headquarters, the reports were distributed to a large number of Nazi officials.[7] In the words of the Chief of the Armed Forces High Command, Wilhelm Keitel, all Communist uprisings, including the "apparently trivial isolated incidents in areas which up to now have been otherwise quiet," were in fact a "*mass movement centrally directed by Moscow*."[8] In early July, with German troops advancing swiftly into the Soviet heartland, a Security Police unit based in Belgrade believed that local resistance would decline before long.[9] Such optimism was short-lived. Far from winding down, the guerrilla force led by Yugoslavia's Communist Party chief Josip Broz

Tito sharply increased its activities over the course of the summer. Irregular fighters, who proudly called themselves partisans, were capturing or killing scores of Germans, reducing an already small occupation force, and prompting the German military commander to doubt whether he could contain the insurgency.[10] In August and September, the representative of the German Foreign Office in Belgrade repeatedly urged his superiors in Berlin to pursue the deportation of Serbia's Jews, who were widely believed to be directing the partisan attacks. The Foreign Office ruled out deportation to Romania but consulted with officials in the Reich Security Main Office (RSHA) about possible deportation to Russia or the General Government. Ultimately, Adolf Eichmann, the RSHA's chief for Jewish affairs, deemed the deportation impractical. He instead suggested shooting all the Jews.[11] Eichmann's casual proposition was an ominous sign of the increasing admissibility of mass killings of Jews, which were also becoming commonplace in the occupied Soviet territories and setting a new standard for the treatment of Jews everywhere.

As the war raged on, anti-German actions intensified in other parts of Nazi-occupied Europe. On August 13, about seventy members of the French Communist Party's youth organization rallied in the north of Paris. They distributed flyers calling for a popular insurgency. The demonstration was quelled by policemen and soldiers, and six leaders were arrested, among them, the Germans pointed out, four Jews.[12] On August 19, two of the youths, Henri Gautherot and Samuel Tyszelman, were sentenced to death by a German military tribunal and executed. The following day, in a joint operation by the SS and Wehrmacht, an entire district of the French capital was searched for Jews. Unlike in Serbia, the Soviet Union, or Poland, the Jews of Paris did not yet have to wear a yellow or white armband, making it difficult to identify and arrest them. In the end, more than four thousand Jews were brought to Drancy, a newly established detention camp just outside the city. This was the second major roundup of Jews in France since the start of the occupation. The first one had taken place in May 1941, when the police arrested 3,733 Jewish immigrants from Poland, Austria, and Czechoslovakia and deported them to internment camps south of Paris. Nazi officials described those arrests as a "cleansing" operation against racial "parasites."[13] The August action, by contrast, was meant to target "Judeo-Bolshevik criminals," according to German Military Commander Otto von Stülpnagel's decree.[14] Jews and Bolsheviks were now interchangeable not only in the Soviet Union but in France as well.

On the evening of September 3, a German noncommissioned officer was shot and severely wounded in front of a hotel on the east side of Paris.[15] In response, the city's military commander ordered three Communist hostages to be shot. Hitler was incensed upon hearing of this order—a German soldier was worth significantly more than three French Communists! he told Keitel. In response to future terror acts, at least one hundred hostages were to be shot for each assassinated or wounded German. Only draconian action would ensure German rule in the occupied lands. At Hitler's urging, Keitel worked the Führer's tirade into a military order, issued on September 16. Distributed to top Wehrmacht commanders throughout Europe, the order stated that "in *every case* of resistance to the German occupying forces, no matter what the individual circumstances, *Communist origins* must be inferred," and called for the killing of fifty to one hundred Communists "as suitable atonement" for every German soldier's life lost to an act of resistance.[16]

Keitel's "Communist decree," as it was called at the time, was applied throughout Europe, though not to the occupied areas of the Soviet Union. The reason was simple: By September 1941, the Wehrmacht and the Security Police units operating on Soviet territory had already devised forms of retribution vastly more extreme than Keitel's. Instead of selecting hostages, they had resolved to kill *all* Jews and Communists, no matter how high the number.

To justify the disproportionate nature of the reprisal killings, Keitel explained that "human life in the countries concerned frequently counts for nothing."[17] Hence, the need for extreme deterrence. It soon became clear, however, that in some areas of the Nazi-designed political and racial map of Europe, lives counted far more than in others. In Serbia, Wehrmacht commander Franz Böhme, freshly appointed to quell the insurgency, adopted a severe reprisal policy. On October 2, Serbian partisans ambushed a truck convoy of German soldiers near the town of Topola. The twenty-two Germans who surrendered were shot at close range with machine guns. A search unit retrieved the bodies and reported that they had been mutilated in ghastly fashion. But when Böhme brought in forensic experts and photographers, evidently in order to confirm and exploit these crimes and document them for use as propaganda, no traces of mutilation were found. Nonetheless, Böhme proclaimed that Communist bandits had "bestially killed" the German soldiers and that one hundred Serbian hostages were to be shot for each murdered German. Böhme gave instructions to execute twenty-one hundred prisoners ("primarily Jews and Communists") from among the concentration camp population. He also ordered the mass detention of hostages and specified who should be arrested: "all Communists, male inhabitants suspected as such, Jews in their entirety, a certain number of nationalist and democratically minded inhabitants." Keitel's order had made no mention of Jews, but Böhme understood it to encompass Communists and Jews.[18]

The mass shootings were carried out by ordinary German soldiers. The task of the Security Police, an SS report noted, was "merely" to supply the necessary number of hostages. Work was under way, the report further noted, to increase the capacity of detention camps from fifty thousand to five hundred thousand.[19] By February 1942, more than twenty thousand inhabitants of Serbia, most of them Jewish, had been killed in "reprisal measures."[20] In a private letter sent to a high-ranking SS official in occupied Poland, Böhme's chief of staff explained why Jews bore the brunt of the drive against Serbian insurgents: "It's of course wrong, strictly speaking, that 100 Jews are being shot for every murdered German, when the ratio 1:100 really ought to come at the expense of the Serbs, but we had Jews in the camp, and ultimately they are Serbian citizens too, and also have to disappear."[21] As in the Soviet Union, German reprisals initially targeted only Jewish men, suggesting that the point was to suppress an armed Jewish insurgency. In Serbia, it took the invaders longer than in the Soviet Union, the heartland of Bolshevism, to identify every Jew, male and female, old and young, as an inveterate political enemy who should be killed. That stage would not be reached until early 1942, when the surviving women and children who had been herded together in camps were killed in gas vans. In June 1942, the head of the Security Police in Belgrade reported, "Serbia is free of Jews."[22]

In France and Belgium, German commanders challenged Keitel's Communist decree, claiming that mass shootings of Frenchmen and Belgians, far from deterring further violence, would only nurture hatred toward the occupiers and undermine their authority. Even after the assassination of the German field commander of Nantes on October 20, followed by another killing in Bordeaux the next day, Military Commander Otto von Stülpnagel ignored Keitel's order. While he had initially consented to shooting one hundred hostages in response to each attack on a German soldier, he subsequently lowered the number to fifty, insisting that "Polish methods" had no place in France and stood to spark public outcry. On October 22 and 24, ninety-eight hostages were shot in retribution for the two killings. Even this lower number set off a wave of protests in France and throughout the world. Over the following months, Stülpnagel continued to negotiate with the Wehrmacht command over the appropriate hostage rates. In January, he informed Keitel that mass shootings contradicted his conscience and sense of historical responsibility. Stülpnagel resigned in February 1942.[23]

Significantly, Stülpnagel had no such qualms punishing Jews for acts that were attributed to Communists. In December 1941, after another series of deadly attacks on German soldiers, Stülpnagel ordered 743 mostly wealthy Jewish men to be arrested and deported to the Compiègne concentration camp. These "criminal Jewish-Bolshevik elements," he announced, would be deported for forced labor in the East. Stülpnagel and other German authorities in Paris sought to portray the Communist resistance as non-French. The insurgents were Jewish and Bolshevik "mercenaries who seek to . . . sabotage German-French understanding."[24] As trains were unavailable to deport the Jews to the East, they were kept in Compiègne for the time being.

MARKING GERMANY'S JEWS

The designation of Jews as enemies also occurred within the Reich. Across Germany, informants for the SD overheard moviegoers who had just seen the July newsreels with accounts of Soviet atrocities in Lvov. Some of them reportedly believed that "the Jews are the real wire-pullers" and that "radical treatment of the Jews in the Reich" was therefore necessary.[25] In mid-August, after the mayor of Bielefeld prohibited Jews from shopping in the weekly open-air market, another informant reported that local residents claimed the measure would be ineffectual unless the Jews wore a special marking, "as is already common in the [General Government]." The informant continued: "Germans think it insufferable that in the streetcars, in buses, and elsewhere in public transport, they are forced to stand next to members of a race who bear the major guilt for the present war, and whose racial compatriots are trying in every way to destroy Germany."[26] On August 18, Goebbels noted a similar thought in his diary: "So we Germans have the honor of waging the war and, in the meantime, by dint of our people's strength, feeding the parasitic Jews, who are only waiting for our defeat in order to exploit it for themselves. This situation is downright outrageous! I will make sure that it is stopped."[27]

As head of the Nazi Party organization for the city of Berlin, Goebbels had been lobbying for some time for the city's Jews to be marked, in preparation for their deportation. With the setbacks in the military campaign in the East, the time had come to act. On August 15, Leopold Gutterer, Goebbels's state secretary in the Ministry of Propaganda, convened a meeting of party officials, including an Interior Ministry expert for racial affairs, to discuss a decree for marking local Jews. In his opening remarks, he said that Goebbels was constantly being approached by soldiers who had served on the Eastern Front. In view of their "horrid impressions of the war experience in the East"—including their memories of the mutilated bodies discovered in Lvov—they had trouble understanding why the Jews in Germany still enjoyed so many freedoms and could live their lives with impunity. Gutterer agreed: The Jews of Berlin formed an "agitational headquarter," clamoring for Germany's defeat. Only by marking them, Gutterer said, could Germany shield itself from their destructive efforts. Additionally, he claimed, the Jews did hardly any productive work; of the seventy thousand Jews of Berlin, only nineteen thousand were employed. Gutterer proposed to "cart off to Russia" all the nonworking Jews. Gutterer's reasoning: Germany's Jews acted in concert with their Soviet brethren. They were fellow Bolsheviks. As such, they needed to be deported to Russia, or better yet, killed on the spot: "It would be best to just beat them to death."[28]

Goebbels supplied Hitler with a memo detailing Gutterer's speech before seeing him on August 19. At their meeting, events on the Eastern Front drove the conversation. Hitler conceded that he had vastly underrated the capability of the Soviet war machine and that "the danger of Bolshevism cannot be overestimated."[29] Goebbels noted that Hitler then turned to the "Jewish problem":

> The Führer believes that his earlier prophecy in the Reichstag—if the Jews once again succeeded in provoking a world war, it will end with their annihilation—is being confirmed. It is coming true in these weeks and months with a certainty that seems almost uncanny. In the East, the Jews are paying the bill, in Germany they have already paid in part and will have to pay even more in the future. Their last refuge is North America; and there, they will sooner or later have to pay as well.
>
> Jewry is a foreign body among the cultured nations, and its activity over the last three decades has been so devastating that the popular reaction is absolutely understandable, necessary, indeed compelling. At any rate, in the world that is coming, the Jews will not have much reason to laugh. Already today, there is quite a united front against the Jews in Europe.[30]

Goebbels scored a partial success at the meeting. While Hitler objected to the immediate removal of Germany's Jews, citing transportation problems, he gave Goebbels a green light to deport the Jews of Berlin as soon as the campaign in the East was over. Hitler also consented to marking all the Reich's Jews immediately.[31] Heydrich, as eager as

Goebbels to deport the Jews, prepared a decree that was published in a government gazette on September 5. The decree stated that as of September 19, all Jews in Germany were to wear a yellow six-pointed star bearing the word *Jude*. The palm-size star had to be sewn onto clothes on the left side of the chest, at the height of the heart, to be fully visible when a Jew was in a public place. Jews were no longer allowed to leave their area of residence without police authorization or to wear medals and honorary decorations.[32] As it introduced the decree to the German public on September 13, the *Völkischer Beobachter* began by referring to the recently discovered "sadistic mass atrocities in the GPU prisons of Lvov, Dubno, and Lutsk, etc." The fact that these murders were "planned and carried out by Jewish men and women to the last bestial detail" explained the "absolute necessity" of marking Germany's Jews.[33] Goebbels's daily, *Der Angriff*, also wrote about the necessity of the decree:

> The German soldier has met in the Eastern Campaign the Jew in his most disgusting, most gruesome form. He has seen the aftermath of the GPU atrocities and the impoverishment of the masses—all the work of the Jews. This experience forces the German soldier and the German people as a whole to deprive the Jew of every means of camouflage in the homeland.[34]

Goebbels, who personally oversaw the release of this article, made sure it was kept short and placed inconspicuously, as he feared provoking open displays of solidarity with Jews.

Then, on September 18, Hitler reversed course and suddenly authorized the immediate deportation of Germany's Jews. Himmler reported the Führer's wish "that the Old Reich and Protectorate be emptied and freed of Jews from west to east as quickly as possible." As a first step, they were to be taken to the annexed Polish territories and then deported farther east in spring 1942.[35] The decision appeared intended in part to satisfy persistent demands from party leaders in Hamburg and Cologne to resettle bombed-out Germans in apartments currently owned by Jews. Hamburg had suffered a heavy British air raid on the night of September 15.[36] But in fact, Hitler's about-face was inspired mainly by the

Wehrmacht's recent triumph on the Eastern Front: On the evening of September 15, German panzer units had encircled four Soviet armies at Kiev, trapping the largest contingent of enemy forces in the history of warfare.[37] With victory in the East appearing imminent, vast areas inside the Soviet Union would become available as a place to deport Germany's—and subsequently Western Europe's—Jews.

On September 24, five days after the fall of Kiev, a large group of top Nazi officials gathered at Hitler's *Wolfschanze* headquarters in East Prussia. Goebbels noted the Führer's exalted mood and revitalized physical condition, following the strain of July and August. "The spell was broken," Goebbels wrote. Hitler predicted a rapid and conclusive victory in the East. All that was required of his soldiers was one further push into the industrial center of Kharkov (Kharkiv), and from there to Stalingrad. Once Russia's core industrial areas were in German hands, the Soviets would have to concede defeat. Hitler appraised his chances in personal terms. Of Stalin, who was sixty-seven, he said: "Even he is no longer able to withstand the final hardest test of nerves." (Hitler himself was fifty-two.) Stalin's defeat would in turn trigger the collapse of Winston Churchill, "an old man" who was showing signs of "the enormous nervous tension to which he has been exposed in the last two years."[38]

Preening as the preeminent leader in continental Europe, Hitler relished the thought of annihilating Bolshevism. Speaking with Goebbels, he described the fate that awaited Leningrad. Since September 8, the city had been encircled by German and Finnish troops. On September 21, Hitler had given orders not to storm Leningrad, as this would cost too many German lives, and the Germans had no desire, or means, to feed Leningrad's population, which they estimated at five million. Instead, the city would remain besieged and its residents starved to death. "Bolshevism," Goebbels recorded Hitler as saying, "began in this city, and it will be crushed in this city. . . . Bolshevism, which began with hunger, blood, and tears, will perish in hunger, blood, and tears. This is the harsh but nonetheless just nemesis of history." After all life in Leningrad had been extinguished, the city was to be blown to pieces and abandoned. Hitler prescribed the same fate for Moscow, Bolshevism's world capital.

If all went according to plan, Moscow would be surrounded by October 15.[39]

During this conversation, Goebbels learned of the about-face instruction Hitler had given to Himmler on September 18 and recorded it in his diary: "The Führer is of the opinion that the Jews must be removed from all of Germany. The first cities to be cleared of Jews are Berlin, Vienna, and Prague. Berlin is first in line, and I am hopeful that we will manage to deport a significant portion of Berlin Jews to the East in the course of this year."[40] Goebbels also complained to Heydrich that the Jews of Berlin were concealing their yellow stars. Deportation to the East would be an appropriate response to this provocation. "In the end," he noted in his diary, the Jews would be "transported to the camps created by the Bolsheviks. These camps were erected by the Jews; what could be more fitting than that they now also be populated by the Jews."[41] It was a curious revenge fantasy, in which Europe's Jews, as fellow Bolsheviks, would pay for the crimes of Russia's "Jew-Bolsheviks" in the Soviet Gulag. But for the time being, there were not yet enough Germans who shared Goebbels's and Heydrich's radical premise that all Jews were Bolsheviks at heart. Goebbels's ministry would have to work harder to fully establish this connection in the public mind.

To Jews in Germany, the introduction of the yellow star came as a shock. Victor Klemperer, a Jewish professor of literature in Dresden, noted in his diary how on September 8 a Jewish friend, "distraught and pale," appeared on the doorstep of his apartment. She had seen the decree in the government gazette. The fact that she followed this obscure publication at all suggests how much Jews lived in dread of what was to come. Failure to keep up with the ever-tightening restrictions could lead to public humiliation, a fine, a prison sentence, or worse. "This means upheaval and catastrophe for us," Klemperer tersely noted.[42] Upon reading about the decree in a local newspaper, one of Klemperer's Jewish neighbors suffered a heart attack. An astute observer, Klemperer noted that all Jews were now being incriminated for Soviet actions: "According to the newspaper, after the army had got to know, through Bolshevism, the cruelty, etc. of *the* Jew, all possibility of camouflage must be removed from the Jews here, to spare Germans all contact with them." Klemperer thought this was a fiction. The true reason for the decree, he believed, was that the campaign in the East was not going well, leaving Himmler's SS determined to consolidate their rule through sheer terror.[43] The day before the marking decree went into force, Klemperer picked up his yellow star, paying a ten-pfennig fee for the piece of cloth. That evening, he and his non-Jewish wife, Eva, celebrated their last day of relative freedom with a walk through their neighborhood. He expected a "long (how long?) imprisonment."[44] Over the next months, Klemperer would stay at home during the day, venturing out for brief walks only under cover of darkness. In his diary entry for December 31, 1941, he described the near-total isolation that the marking decree had inflicted on him as the past year's heaviest blow.[45]

Klemperer noticed how the decree changed the ways Jews and non-Jews in Germany understood themselves and one another. A young Jewish friend, assimilated like himself ("baptized, thoroughly European, and German-minded"), now talked about the "'Jewish nation.' It shook me. Hitler is the most important promoter of Zionism, Hitler has literally created the 'Jewish nation,' 'world Jewry,' *the* Jew."[46] The redefinition went both ways. "I always ask myself," Klemperer noted in late October, "who among the 'Aryan' Germans is really untouched by National Socialism? The contagion rages in all of them, perhaps it is not contagion, but basic German nature."[47] But he also recorded the limits of the Nazi attempt to remake Jews into the Germans' mortal enemies. While some Germans, especially juveniles and children, mocked and insulted Jews wearing the yellow star, others went out of their way to show them their respect: "An acquaintance, Frau Reichenbach, told us a gentleman had greeted her in a shop doorway. Had he not mistaken her for someone else?—'No, I do not know you, but you will now be greeted frequently. We are a group "who greet the Jew's star."'"[48] Other sources confirm that the yellow star met with disapproval in many German towns.[49] Those Germans who spoke out refused to accept Goebbels's assertion that

A Jewish family walking down a Berlin street wearing the Star of David on their lapels, September 27, 1941. Nazi propaganda photo.

German Jews were enemies on par with the Bolsheviks. While anti-Bolshevism was near universal across society, some Germans came out in defense of the Jews, whom they still recognized as compatriots.

Goebbels must have seen this, for he raged in his diary: "Our intellectual and social classes have suddenly once again discovered their feelings of humanity for the poor Jews. . . . The Jews need only to send an old lady with a Jewish star to walk on the Kurfürstendamm, and gullible Gunter on the street is already inclined to forget everything that the Jews have done to us in the past years and decades. But not us! We think more consistently about these things, and at least the German national flaw of forgetfulness is not to be found in our character."[50] To counteract any lingering sympathy, Goebbels proposed to launch a "new, grand campaign against the Jews that will be good for our petit-bourgeois, who are at the moment seeking to accept the dear Jews back into the human fold just because they have to wear a yellow star."[51]

For maximum mobilizing effect, Goebbels wrote a clamorous article titled "It's the Jews' Fault!" that he strategically placed in a seemingly respectable-looking newspaper so as to reach readers outside the Nazi

"Everybody knows: Whoever bears this mark is an enemy of our people." (1942)

Party. "What would happen if Germany lost the war in the East?" he asked. "The Jews would hurl themselves upon our people, our wives and children, to commit an act of revenge for which there is no precedent in history. That is what they did in Bessarabia and the Baltic states, when Bolshevism arrived there [in 1940]."[52]

TO THE POLAR SEA CAMPS

When Goebbels's article appeared, the deportations to the East were already under way. They had begun on October 15, in keeping with a schedule set by Heydrich and coinciding with the date that Hitler had set for the encirclement of Moscow. On that day, a trainload of a thousand Jews left Vienna for Lodz; transports from Prague, Luxembourg, and Berlin followed over the next few days. They were all to be brought to Lodz, but the sanitary crisis in the overcrowded ghetto led to the rerouting of several trains to Riga, Minsk, and Kaunas. To make room for the deportees from Germany, SS and police forces rounded up thousands of Jews in the Minsk Ghetto on November 7. Many were shot inside their dwellings; others were ordered onto trucks and driven off to a nearby camp. Two days later they were led to freshly dug trenches and machine-gunned. The date for this action—November 7, the anniversary of Lenin's party seizing power in Russia—was deliberately chosen to emphasize that the Jews were being killed as Bolsheviks.[53] On that same day, 990 Hamburg Jews learned of their imminent deportation to Minsk. When they arrived, after an arduous four-day journey, they were brought to a former school in the ghetto. Inside the building there were corpses everywhere—Jews killed to make room for the new arrivals. An SS officer ordered them to dispose of the bodies.[54]

In fall 1941, the objective of the "evacuation specialists" at Security Police headquarters in Berlin was not to kill the Jewish deportees upon arrival in the East, but to have them work as forced laborers for Germany's benefit.[55] Yet where exactly in the East the Jewish victims ended up mattered greatly. Those brought to Lodz could hope to live a little longer; many deportees to Soviet cities, by contrast, were immediately killed. Five transports of German Jews originally destined for Riga were rerouted to Kaunas in late November and shot shortly after their arrival.[56] On November 30, upon learning of these massacres, Himmler ordered that a transport of one thousand Jews from Berlin to Riga not be liquidated. But Himmler's message reached Riga too late. Friedrich Jeckeln, the Higher SS and Police Führer of North Russia, had chosen the day of the transport's arrival to begin a mass shooting of Riga's Jews, who had been cleared out of the ghetto. The Berlin Jews disembarked in Riga just when the mass murder operation was about to start. Rather than sending them to the ghetto, Jeckeln had them marched directly from the train station to the killing site where they would be shot alongside Riga's Jews.[57] In the wake of the mass shooting, Himmler reprimanded Jeckeln for acting on his own. At this juncture, it seems that Himmler still saw a significant distinction between German Jews and Soviet Jews. The latter were proven Bolsheviks and their liquidation a matter of no concern. The fate of the former, by contrast, had the potential to arouse public opinion worldwide. Jeckeln's problem was that he did not grasp the difference. For the time being, Himmler ordered a halt to the killing of Jews deported from Germany.[58]

Less than two weeks later, the clear line Himmler had drawn between

German and other Jews began to blur. After Japan's attack on Pearl Harbor and Germany's declaration of war on the United States, the U.S. Congress declared war on Germany. To Hitler, America joining the anti-Axis alliance proved beyond a doubt that Jews worldwide had taken up arms against Germany. The war against Jewish Bolshevism, which Germany had embarked on in June 1941, now turned into a broader war against world Jewry. The initial plan to annihilate all Soviet Jews was finally, fully extended to all Jews, no matter their country of residence or cultural home. Hitler announced this decision in a secret speech addressing top Nazi Party officials on December 12. Goebbels, who was in the room, recalled the speech in his diary:

> Regarding the Jewish question, the Führer is determined to clear the deck once and for all. He had predicted that if the Jews brought about a world war once again, they would be annihilated. This was no turn of phrase. The world war is here, the extermination of Jewry must be the necessary consequence. This question is to be considered without any sentimentality. We are not here to show compassion for the Jews, but rather to show compassion for our German people. If the German people have now once again sacrificed some 160,000 dead in the Eastern Campaign, the originators of this bloody conflict will have to pay for it with their lives.[59]

While the Führer's resolution to kill all Jews came on the heels of the United States' declaration of war against Germany, it was also prompted by unforeseen events on the Eastern Front. On December 5, Soviet forces launched a powerful counteroffensive near Moscow, pushing back the Germans and scrambling the whole design of Barbarossa. A week after his speech, Hitler met with Himmler. Less verbose than Goebbels, Himmler composed a pithy summary of the meeting: "Jewish question—exterminate as partisans."[60] Back in July, Himmler had cast Soviet Jews as partisans who had to be annihilated. He now used the same language to mark all of Europe's, indeed the world's, Jews for extermination.

Himmler's deputy Heydrich took charge of rounding up and dispatching the redefined Jewish enemy. At a conference of party and government officials convened on Berlin's Lake Wannsee on January 20, 1942, Heydrich declared that he had been appointed "delegate for the preparations for the final solution of the Jewish question in Europe." His Security Police had assumed "official central handling" of this process, "without regard to geographic borders." At stake were the lives of "approximately eleven million Jews."[61] Heydrich presented a detailed table listing their distribution by country. The largest share of Europe's Jews, according to the chart, was in the USSR: 5,000,000, with 2,994,684 of them living in Ukraine. The second-highest concentration of Jews was in the General Government: 2,284,000. Next to Estonia there was no number, but instead a remark: "free of Jews."

Heydrich offered a "short report" of the strategies Germany had used in the past, ranging from forced emigration to the "evacuation of the Jews to the East." In the future, such actions would be replaced by more effective methods. The solution Heydrich envisioned was a wholesale deportation of all eleven million Jews to the East, where they would form "large work columns, separated according to sex," building roads for the expanding German empire.

In conversations shortly before and after the Wannsee Conference, Heydrich was more specific, talking of the creation of massive concentration camps in the Polar Sea region of the USSR. The camps were to be formed within a newly created territorial entity, "North Russia/West Siberia," which the SS would run.[62] This plan was not new: Heydrich had discussed it with Goebbels during their September 24 meeting at *Wolfschanze*. But Hitler's December 12 decision had emboldened Heydrich to turn the Nazi vision of a historic revenge on Jewish Bolshevism into policy. Even though Heydrich talked about a Soviet-style Gulag as the final destination for Europe's Jews and extracting as much labor from them as possible, he made it sufficiently clear that the ultimate aim was to kill them. As he pointed out at Wannsee, under the harsh conditions of forced labor, "doubtless a large portion will be eliminated by natural causes." Only a "final remnant" would remain, consisting of "the most resistant portion." It would have to be "treated accordingly, because it is the product of natural selection and would, if released, act as the seed of a new Jewish revival (see the experience of history)."

HOW TO KILL BOLSHEVIKS

How the Jews were to be killed remained a matter of debate. Even Heydrich's Polar Sea camps were a suggestion rather than a fully conceived master plan. The Wannsee Conference concluded with discussions of "various kinds of means for a solution."[63] By January 1942, there was no shortage of ideas about how to murder efficiently and imaginatively. Many of these ideas were developed in the context of Germany's war against the Soviet Union. Modeled on supposed Bolshevik killing techniques, they were soon applied to Europe's Jews. The Bolsheviks, in the German imagination, maintained their terror regime through their aptitude for killing. They worked millions of prisoners to death in forced labor camps; they starved to death millions more, mostly peasants who refused to join the collective farms; and they conducted mass shootings of political enemies, often following sadistic acts of torture. Anti-Comintern-sponsored publications and exhibitions from the 1930s detailed gruesome accounts of GPU agents releasing famished rats to torment their victims.[64]

Among the methods of killing employed by Stalin's secret police, the most infamous was the shot in the nape of the neck. Like the alleged stab in the back with which the treacherous Marxists had brought down the valiant German army in 1918, this shot struck the unsuspecting victim from behind and was as cowardly and contemptible as it was deadly. It was the antithesis of the chivalry that the Germans believed characterized their own conduct of war—it was the criminal's way, discussed at length in German reporting on the Soviet Union in 1941. A July 1941 article in *Der Angriff* described in detail the "9-Millimeter Cure" that Red Army political commissars purportedly used. The cure was simple: Whenever a Soviet offensive wavered, a commissar would pull out his pistol and shoot from behind anybody caught falling back. The

"The 9-Millimeter Cure," Der Angriff, *July 20, 1941.*

illustration accompanying the article made it clear that the shot was aimed at the victim's neck. To leave no doubt that the commissar was Jewish, the author of the article asserted "the close connection between Jewry and the revolver shot from behind."[65]

Throughout the conflict, the Nazis employed specifically "Bolshevik" methods against the Bolshevik enemy. In advance of the German invasion, party and state officials in Berlin had worked out plans to starve to death tens of millions of Soviet citizens—not peasants, who were considered victims of Stalin's rule, but urban citizens.[66] Although not implemented to the extent originally envisioned, the plan to inflict starvation was realized in the besieged city of Leningrad, as well as the conquered cities of Kharkov and Kiev. Most of the two million Soviet POWs who perished in German captivity by early 1942 died of undernourishment, exposure, and disease.

The SS and police also expanded the scope and frequency of the mass shootings of Soviet Jews and other suspected Bolsheviks. In some documented instances, German units shot their victims in the nape of the neck to underscore their "Bolshevik" nature. Jeckeln, who took pride in the killing technique he'd devised, had the victims undress before they were marched through a gauntlet of guards and driven to the pits that had been designated as killing sites. The victims were ordered to lie face down on the ground, or on top of the bodies of the dying and the dead.

Then they were shot in the nape of the neck from a distance of less than six feet. Jeckeln instructed the killers to use Soviet machine pistols that could hold fifty rounds and were set to fire single shots. Jeckeln and many members of the SS and police may have felt especially righteous in applying a Bolshevik technique and Soviet weapons to kill what Nazi ideology claimed were Bolshevism's core agents.[67] After using this technique during the Babi Yar massacre, Jeckeln followed the same practice in the killing of fourteen thousand Jews from the Riga ghetto on November 30, 1941. In Riga, Jeckeln even invited prominent guests—SD and police officers, and civilian officials—to watch the shootings in the Rumbula forest.[68]

The same technique was also employed in German concentration camps. During the first weeks of the campaign, hundreds of thousands of captured Soviet military personnel had been transferred to camps inside Germany. SS leaders believed a great number of commissars were hiding among these masses and feared that these demonic figures would agitate among their own men and among German guards and workers with whom they came into contact. Heydrich ordered special police units to hunt through all POW camps in Germany to identify for interrogation and ultimately kill "fanatical Communists," members of the "Soviet-Russian intelligentsia," and "all Jews."[69] When they were captured on Soviet soil, suspected commissars could be shot in plain view of German troops. But in the German POW camps, the killings needed to be camouflaged, so as not to cause any public disturbance. Orders were given to remove the suspects from the POW camps and get rid of them "inconspicuously in the nearest concentration camp."[70] Several thousand "commissars" were to be brought to Sachsenhausen, less than thirty miles north of Berlin. At an August gathering held by the Concentration Camps Inspectorate in the nearby town of Oranienburg, Theodor Eicke, the founding director of the Inspectorate, solicited suggestions for how to kill the prisoners. Eicke told the assembled men that Hitler personally had given him approval to retaliate against the Bolsheviks for their shooting of German soldiers in Soviet captivity. That Eicke, by then commander of the SS-Death's Head Division, attended the meeting with bandaged limbs due to wounds received on the Eastern Front no doubt contributed to the vengeful mood in the room.[71]

Responding to Eicke's call, SS guards from Sachsenhausen and representatives of Heydrich's forensic science institute, which doubled as a laboratory for methods of mass murder and maintained a workshop in the camp, created a "nape-shot method" (*Genickschussanlage*).[72] They masked the killing site as a doctor's office. SS personnel dressed as physicians would have the prisoners undress and lead them one at a time into what looked like an examination room, equipped with a wall-mounted stadiometer, the familiar device for measuring height, with a headpiece set in a deep slot in the center of the measuring board. While the "doctor" pretended to note the height of the prisoner, a shooter concealed in a small room behind the measuring board took aim and fired through the slot. Loud music from a radio in the room helped muffle the sound of gunfire.[73]

The idea for the nape-shot method may have originated in popular descriptions of Soviet-style killing, such as the one found in this 1926 account by a Russian émigré: "In the Cheka prison on Lubianka Square in Moscow, it goes like this—a person who has secretly been found guilty is taken from his cell and told that he is to be interrogated again. He is ordered to walk ahead and enter a certain room. At the very moment he steps over the threshold of the room, he is shot dead from behind with a revolver."[74] Stories of GPU agents dispatching their victims with shots to the nape of the neck abounded in the Nazi press throughout the 1930s, and again in 1941. Thus, when concentration camp inspectors gathered once more in early September to see the new killing method in action, the reference to Bolshevism was so obvious as to need no explanation.[75] Seven Soviet prisoners were brought in and shot, one after the other. The presentation was a success. SS men were seen emerging from the killing site laughing and slapping their thighs. The method was approved for service.[76]

The nape-shot method proved popular, drawing in scores of shooters. All the camp's block leaders—the SS noncommissioned officers in charge of one or more rows of prisoners' barracks—were enlisted in the ruse, playing the doctor, firing the gun, or cleaning up after each killing. One

Holocaust scholar has surmised that this rotation system was set in place to share the burden of the killings, leaving as many of the camp SS men as possible with blood on their hands.[77] But in light of the sustained German losses on the Eastern Front, symbolized in the wounds of their beloved boss, "Papa Eicke," the SS men were likely already eager enough to participate in killing suspected commissars.[78]

The first mass transport of Soviet "commissars," consisting of almost five hundred soldiers, mostly from the Minsk area, reached Sachsenhausen on August 31. The trains arrived in nearby Oranienburg under cover of darkness, but the platforms of the train station were illuminated, and residents could observe how the prisoners, too weak to stand, fell out of the cars as the doors were pulled open. The camp authorities subsequently issued a special order that Soviet POWs on the verge of death should no longer be brought to Sachsenhausen. The dead bodies littering the road from the train station to the camp could not be concealed from the locals. Still, more than thirteen thousand Soviet POWs were brought to Sachsenhausen on at least twenty-five trains between late August and mid-November 1941. Three thousand were either dead on arrival or so exhausted by the conditions of their deportation that they died in the barracks. The remaining ten thousand were killed with the help of the nape-shot method.[79] Many of the prisoners were shot within hours of arrival. Even with blaring music muting the gunshots, the authorities could not hide what was happening inside the camp. For weeks, black smoke billowed from the crematorium and dirtied the laundry hung out to dry in gardens nearby. Children would ask passing SS men, "Are you burning Russians again today?"[80]

The news of the killings, which camp guards referred to as "the Russian action," reverberated among the camp inmates as well. On the premises of Sachsenhausen's brick factory, a message in a bottle prepared by an underground group of Communists was discovered after the war: "Today is September 19, 1941. Just now, we are learning that in the large camp another 400 Red Guards have been brought in. We are all distressed by these mass murders, which have already exceeded the number of 1,000. For the time being, we are not able to help."[81] Emil Büge, an anti-fascist activist who had been brought to Sachsenhausen in November 1939, worked as a clerk in the camp administration and had access to the registration documents. Aware of the immense crime unfolding around him, he produced meticulous copies of files about the Soviet POWs who arrived at the camp between September and November 1941 and smuggled them out of the camp upon his release in 1943. In October 1941, Büge noted the appearance of photographic equipment in the camp. Indeed, photographers took pictures of the Bolshevik prisoners to fuel the renewed anti-Bolshevik campaign.[82]

Among the SS officers invited to watch the demonstration of the Sachsenhausen nape-shot method was the commandant of the Mauthausen concentration camp Franz Ziereis. On his return to Mauthausen, Ziereis instructed his men to build a similar installation, which went into service killing Soviet soldiers in late October. An apparatus modeled on the Sachsenhausen prototype was built in Buchenwald. Eicke's successor, Chief Inspector Richard Glücks, authorized the method but appealed to camp commanders to be resourceful and come up with other methods as well.[83] The deadly experiments conducted by Mauthausen personnel included excessive hard labor, lethal injection, and

Soviet POWs brought to Sachsenhausen, 1941 (undated photograph).

starvation. In Flossenbürg, the SS favored mass shootings as their preferred form of dispatching Soviet "commissars." There, too, keeping the killings under wraps proved difficult. A nearby river swept blood and body parts into Flossenbürg village, provoking complaints from residents. In Gross-Rosen, where shootings originally took place in the open air, the guards forced prisoners to sing at the top of their voices to drown out the sound of gunfire, but people living nearby heard the shots anyway. In all three camps, the SS soon switched to lethal injections.[84]

Auschwitz was the first SS camp to test gassing on prisoners, though it was not the first use of gas to kill people. Since January 1940, the Nazis had been using carbon monoxide at special facilities to kill institutionalized patients and persons with disabilities. Most of these sites were repurposed psychiatric hospitals that had been outfitted with gas chambers. Starting in April 1941, concentration camp prisoners who were "unable to work" were selected for killing and transported to these facilities. In late July 1941, for example, a commission of doctors visited the Auschwitz camp and selected 573 prisoners, who were then sent to the Sonnenstein facility near Pirna and killed.[85]

Adopting this method of killing at Auschwitz seems to have originated with SS-Hauptsturmführer Karl Fritzsch, the deputy camp commandant. Rudolf Höss, the commandant, wrote that while he was away on official business in August 1941, Fritzsch came up with the idea of testing prussic acid, "which was used in the camp as an insecticide," to kill Soviet POWs who were suspected of being political officers.[86]

When Höss returned in early September, he had the next transport of Soviet POWs killed by the method Fritzsch had devised, observing the procedure from up close in a gas mask. Höss wrote that he did not retain a clear memory of this first gassing, as he had been preoccupied by the logistics. But the subsequent gassing of "900 Russians" in the camp's repurposed old crematorium remained etched in his memory:

> The Russians were ordered to undress in an anteroom; they then quietly entered the mortuary, for they had been told they were to be deloused. The whole transport exactly filled the

> mortuary to capacity. The doors were then sealed and the gas shaken down through the holes in the roof. . . . When the powder was thrown in, there were cries of "Gas!," then a great bellowing, and the trapped prisoners hurled themselves against both the doors. But the doors held. They were opened several hours later, so that the place might be aired. It was then that I saw, for the first time, gassed bodies in the mass.[87]

Also in September 1941, members of Heydrich's forensics institute came up with the idea of using mobile gas chambers for mass killing in the occupied Soviet territories. One gas van prototype was tested on mentally ill patients in Minsk; another model, developed in Sachsenhausen, used Soviet POWs for its first experiment. The van was fitted with a hose that diverted its poisonous carbon monoxide exhaust into the vehicle's cargo area, which had been made airtight. One of the designers of the gas van described how a group of naked men came out of a barrack and climbed into the truck. "The men got into the truck as one gets into a bus. They obviously had no idea what was going to happen. There must have been about thirty of them. Then the truck drove off. . . . I was told that the people . . . were Russians who would otherwise have had to be shot."[88] Gas vans began operating in the Soviet Union at the end of 1941, in Poltava in November and in Kharkov in December. By summer 1942, more than a dozen were in operation across occupied Soviet territory; several more had been sent to Serbia. Again and again, up to sixty people, overwhelmingly Jews, were crammed into the cargo area, before the hermetically sealing doors were closed and the motor started. The truck drove for fifteen minutes or longer until the victims' crying and screaming stopped. Then the vehicle was unloaded, usually at a mass grave, hosed out, and readied for the next assignment. Aside from the practical benefits of being able to move a gas chamber to where it was needed, the main consideration behind the vehicle's development was, in the words of the former head of the forensics institute, the "psychological stress" placed on the perpetrators who killed their victims in mass shootings. "This problem was overcome by the use of gas vans," he added.[89]

There was no shortage of Soviet prisoners in the autumn of 1941. The dizzying number of captured enemy soldiers inspired Himmler to fantasize about converting his camps into a slave empire. "Move one hundred thousand Russians into concentration camps," he noted on September 16. During a meeting with camp inspector Glücks a few days later, Himmler doubled the number—he wanted two hundred thousand or more Soviet prisoners.[90] Construction started on massive new camps: Majdanek, near Lublin, and Birkenau, the largest construction site, a short distance from the Auschwitz camp. Thousands of Soviet prisoners of war were brought to Auschwitz and Sachsenhausen, but most of them were too famished to work. SS men in Sachsenhausen asked: "So have these people come here to die or to work?" Their superiors in Berlin warned them not to confuse POWs arriving "for labor deployment" with those destined "for execution." The guards nonetheless found the designated workers just as threatening as the suspected commissars and abused and killed them at will, while occasionally snapping trophy photographs of their victims.[91] Indeed, a briefing issued by Gestapo officials to party functionaries called for extreme caution in dealing with all Russian prisoners, given that "since the start of the 1920s, the Russian has been systematically trained and indoctrinated in the Bolshevik spirit." The "Russian prisoners" did not count as "prisoners of war in the usual sense, but, as the Führer also emphasized, as animals and beasts. This is how you should treat them."[92]

By early 1942, two million Soviet soldiers in German captivity were dead. Many who survived were in poor shape. Those who were fit for labor had to be shared with industry and agriculture. Himmler would have to find workers for his slave empire elsewhere.

The Wannsee Conference in January 1942 gave a new lease to Himmler's designs. Now Jews were to replace the POWs as a source of forced labor to build up Germany's infrastructure in the East, as in the roadbuilding columns of Heydrich's imagination. Himmler indicated as much in a January 26 message to camp inspector Glücks. The inspector should not expect any further Soviet POWs, Himmler wrote. "Get ready to accommodate 100,000 male Jews and up to 50,000 Jewesses in the concentration camps

Cover photo of Die Wehrmacht, *November 5, 1941. The caption reads: "1,000 of 657,948! In the double battle of Bryansk and Vyazma, 657,948 prisoners were taken according to the OKW report of October 19. Our picture shows the transportation of prisoners from collection camps."*

within the next four weeks." The day before, Himmler had obtained permission from Hitler. "Why should I look at a Jew with different eyes than at a Russian prisoner?" Hitler asked.[93]

The fate of Europe's Jews was in important ways patterned on that of the Soviet POWs, which had in turn been prefigured by the Nazis' demonization of the "Jewish commissar." The systematic mass deportations of Jews to Auschwitz began in late March 1942. On March 30, a transport of eleven hundred men arrived from France, including more than five hundred detainees who had been arrested on December 12, 1941, and held in Compiègne.[94] Upon reaching the occupied town of Oswiecim, the newly arrived prisoners were directed first to Auschwitz Main Camp. They were outfitted with uniforms and wooden shoes, subjected to ferocious beatings, and issued a paltry meal before being marched double time to a complex under construction outside the adjacent town of Brzezinka—Birkenau in German. At the gates of this new camp, the Jews, bloodied, bruised, and breathless, had to run a gauntlet of guards who clubbed them as they passed. Several were bludgeoned to death on the spot. For those who survived, there could be no doubt that their lives would be nearly worthless here. This became even more apparent when the newcomers learned that the clothing they were given had belonged to murdered Soviet POWs. Rumors circulated that the original owners of these uniforms lay in the thousands beneath the barracks now inhabited by the arrivals from France.[95]

"BOLSHEVISM AGAINST EUROPE"

While Nazi propagandists cast the war against the Soviet Union as an existential struggle between the German race and Bolshevism, they were at pains to underscore its continent-wide significance. Invoking slogans that had been forged in the 1930s, they depicted Europe as under threat of devastation at the hands of "Asiatic hordes" doing the Jews' bidding. If Europe was to survive, it would need to accept German leadership and form a united front against Bolshevism. To convince European audiences of this danger, Nazi propaganda again combined anti-Semitism and anti-Bolshevism. When Goebbels learned about the NKVD murders in Lvov's prisons, he resolved to use the grisly images to "get Europe going" and mold public opinion not just in Germany, but everywhere—in allied Axis countries and German-occupied territories, in neutral states, and in enemy powers such as Great Britain.[96] In addition to producing newsreels in other European languages and adapting content for French, Spanish, and Romanian audiences, Nazi propagandists launched *Signal*, an illustrated magazine that was patterned on the American weekly *Life*. *Signal* appeared in more than twenty languages to sound the theme of Europe's standoff against Bolshevism.[97]

Anti-Comintern officials meanwhile set out to promote a new series of anti-Bolshevik exhibitions across Europe. One large show, patterned on the popular German exhibitions from the 1930s, opened in Budapest in December 1941. It featured images of Hungarian Communists who were marked explicitly as Jews as well as evidence of Soviet atrocities uncovered by the Germans in Lvov and elsewhere.[98] In Paris between March and June 1942, oversize placards on the city's avenues and boulevards exhorted passersby to visit the show "Bolshevism Against Europe." One poster posed a series of questions—"Why these massacres? Why such misery next to palaces? Why this monstrous army?" placing each question next to a photograph meant to represent the Soviet menace: a mutilated body, earthen huts against the backdrop of large Soviet office buildings, and Red Army formations parading on Moscow's Red Square. The poster added: "Find out by visiting the international exhibition, Bolshevism Against Europe." The photographs were made by André Zucca, a leading photographer for *Signal*. The exhibition next traveled to Lille, Bordeaux, Lyons, Marseille, and Toulouse. Close to a million French people attended the exhibition. Financing came from Germany, Hungary, Romania, Finland, Spain, and Portugal, as well as Vichy France.[99]

However, for all these efforts to sway the rest of Europe, the Nazi propaganda effort was largely directed inward. As early as August 1941, Goebbels registered that the rising German death toll in the stalled Eastern campaign had soured the popular mood. The German people, Goebbels reasoned, would pull themselves together instantly once they grasped the full extent of the menace. "Our German intellectuals do not know the danger of Bolshevism, because they have never dealt with it. We know it, because for years, we have crossed swords with Bolshevism in our domestic struggle." Goebbels proposed that writers, scholars, and

"Why these massacres? Why such misery next to palaces? Why this monstrous army?"

artists (people he believed were infatuated by Marxism) be taken to Soviet Gulag camps to convince them of the reality of the Soviet terror regime.[100] The propaganda minister also arranged for tours of camps housing "Bolshevik prisoners of war" near Berlin. The purpose of these trips, which were joined by camera crews, was to dramatize how Hitler and the Wehrmacht had saved Germany from the onslaught of such "subhumans." As Goebbels and his staff discussed how to use the images they obtained, they considered staging a traveling exhibition, the proceeds from which would be used to buy winter coats for German soldiers fighting in the East. In the spirit of ethnographic exhibitions popular at the time, they also suggested presenting live specimens of these Soviet "brutes," one or two at a time, at local meetings of the Nazi Party. One participant proposed having captured British officers and American reporters visit the camps to provide them with a better understanding of their Soviet ally.[101]

In the end, the Wehrmacht never reached the Russian Arctic, let alone Siberia, and no visitors from Germany were invited to tour the notorious Gulag, but the Nazis found a different solution. They re-created Soviet detention centers on German soil, to be explored by millions of viewers. "The Soviet Paradise" was the title of a lavish exhibition that opened in Vienna in December 1941 before touring through Berlin in May 1942, and multiple other German and European cities. Goebbels's ministry called it the most successful of all political exhibitions.[102]

Unlike earlier anti-Bolshevik shows, this one took place as German soldiers were deep inside the Soviet Union, making it possible, as the organizers stressed, to put a great amount of "original material" on display. This included captured Soviet weapons, which were shown both to evoke the strength of the Soviet military and to demonstrate that it could be defeated. A captured heavy Soviet tank rattled through the streets of Vienna and Berlin to advertise the exhibition, causing a stir. On the exhibition ground stood a decapitated Lenin statue that had been brought from Minsk to illustrate the transience of Bolshevik rule. In the style of a colonial show, the exhibition staged an ensemble of poorly furnished barracks and earthen dwellings, complete with life-size dolls clothed in

AUSSTELLUNG »DAS SOWJET-PARADIES«
BERLIN, LUSTGARTEN, 9. MAI BIS 21. JUNI 1942

Exhibition: "The Soviet Paradise," Berlin, May 9–June 21, 1942. The title at the top reads: "Bolshevism's Deceptive Façade."

rags, to expose the misery and oppressiveness of daily life in the Soviet state.[103]

The central part of the exhibition was devoted to Bolshevik terror. The organizers asked: "Why are the Bolsheviks putting up such tenacious resistance?" and answered: The brutal violence of the Soviet state, carried out by the GPU on orders of the Jews, had "created a gray and weak-willed mass that carried out every order with bovine dullness, because this alone offered a chance of living."[104] The exhibition evoked the labor camps in the "icy wasteland of Vorkuta" and other remote locations, where "millions of innocent people" die every year.[105] Visitors walked through the vaulted cellar of a former Soviet GPU prison. To the left and right of the corridor were prison cells containing instruments of torture. One room was presented as the "nape-shot cell." The small room had a tiled floor and walls, a hose to clean out the blood, and a puppet dressed as a dead victim, lying on its stomach after being shot in the back of the head. "According to the statements of a captured commissar," the exhibition catalog declared, "the GPU shot almost 5,000 people in 6 years behind the iron door of this death cell."[106]

More than three million people visited the exhibition during its extended tour. Nazi officials delighted in recording visitors' expressions of shock and disgust. The show vividly cast the monstrous conditions in the Soviet Union as the antithesis of German life. Its purpose, the lead-

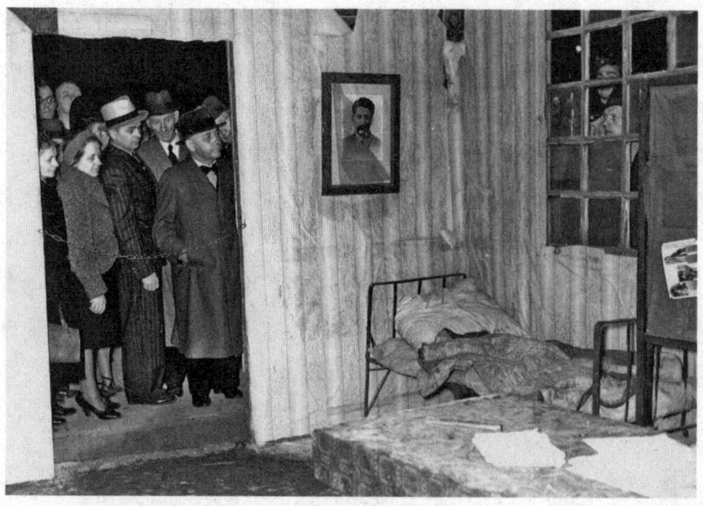

View of the exhibition "The Soviet Paradise" in Berlin. Viewers look into a dormitory with a portrait of Stalin.

ing Nazi newspaper commented, was "for men and women and our boys and girls to contemplate, as they stroll through the 'Soviet paradise,' how greatly divine providence, working through the genius of our Führer, has saved us, standing as we were on the edge of a seething crater, from being hurled out of the realm of the beautiful and good into death and destruction."[107] The campaign against the Soviet regime was so pervasive that even defunct office buildings in Berlin that had been part of the Soviet embassy were turned into anti-Bolshevik exhibition grounds. All the big embassies on Berlin's central boulevard, Unter den Linden—the Soviet, the American, and the French—were closed by late 1941. Alone among them, the Soviet embassy was cordoned off with white tape imprinted with black skulls and crossbones, as well as the words: "Beware! This building is being fumigated!" After closing the nearby Soviet tourism office, the Germans reopened it as an Anti-Comintern bookstore. In the window was a magic lantern that showed snapshots of Soviet soldiers all day long. Above the screen hung a sign that read "BEASTS are looking at you!"[108]

On May 18, 1942, activists belonging to the Communist underground Gruppe Baum set fire to the "Soviet Paradise" exhibition, damaging some of the objects. Four days later, the Gestapo arrested members of the group and discovered that several of them were Jewish. In retaliation, Himmler ordered the shooting of 250 Jewish hostages. They were murdered in Sachsenhausen on May 28 and 29. Ninety-six of them were already camp inmates; the others were taken from the 500 hostages seized in Berlin's Jewish community. Over the following weeks and months, more and more Jewish hostages were brought to Sachsenhausen and killed. For every Jew who was ordered deported to the East but eluded the authorities, scores of others were shot or gassed.[109]

In the evolving history of Nazi mass murder, Soviet soldiers held special trophy value. On Hitler's birthday, April 20, 1942, Mauthausen concentration camp commander Ziereis offered the Führer a special gift: the execution of 300 Soviet prisoners. The "present" was noted in the Death Book kept by the camp administration, along with the form the killing would take: a shot in the nape of the neck. The nape-shot method went into operation at 11:20 a.m. and continued in two-minute intervals 299 more times.[110]

On November 8, 1942, Hitler delivered his annual speech in Munich to the Nazi old guard in commemoration of the "Beer Hall Putsch" of 1923. It was broadcast over the radio and printed in the papers the following day. Once more, he repeated his prophecy about the extermination of the Jews. The enemies of 1942, Hitler declared, were the same as those of the Weimar era, except that they were now stretched across the globe, ranging from "the chief of this international Freemason lodge, the half-Jew Roosevelt and his Jewish Brain Trust, to Jewry in its purest expression in Marxist-Leninist Russia."[111] Jews in their purest expression, Soviet Bolsheviks, remained "World Enemy No. 1."

Chapter 5

JEWS AND BOLSHEVIKS, STEP FORWARD!

Maks Mints, a Jewish man from Vitebsk in Belorussia and a card-carrying member of the Communist Party, was a twenty-nine-year-old captain in the Red Army when the war broke out in June 1941. Within a week, his newly formed artillery regiment was deployed to the front, and Mints bade farewell to his wife. "Don't take up smoking, and don't let yourself be caught by the Germans" were her parting words.[1] A month later he wrote to his family: "Every day, they drop leaflets attacking the Communists and 'yids.' I have never seen such cynicism and disrespect." He vowed to annihilate the "fascist scum."[2]

During the Battle of Bryansk in early October, the Germans encircled Mints's regiment and the 50th Army to which it belonged. Panic broke out, and ordinary soldiers deserted by the hundreds. Mints was the sole senior officer left in his unit after the regimental commander, the commissar, and the head of the NKVD department took flight. With only a topographical map to guide him, he steered a small group of artillerists back toward Soviet-held territory. After a monthlong march, as Mints was crossing a frozen river, he was shot in the leg by a German soldier and fell into the icy water. The Germans, fighting with Soviets on the opposite bank, pulled him out and stripped off his soaked clothes, but did not notice the Communist Party ID in an inside pocket of his uniform. During his interrogation, Mints invented a Russian-sounding last name for himself, Minakov, to conceal his Jewish identity. When it seemed clear that he was just a straggler who could not give any insight on the operations of the Soviet unit across the river, his interrogators lost interest and locked him in a barn. The reason Mints was not searched more thoroughly was likely nothing more than the heat of combat. In any case, the captain's ordeal had only just begun.

A few days later, the Germans marched Mints and some two hundred other prisoners of war to a POW camp at Roslavl, about forty miles away. Mints described the march as more like a relentless run: "If anybody lagged three steps behind, a German would come up and shoot him. The entire way was strewn with corpses. Everybody was striving to keep up, for fear that if they fell behind, they'd be shot." Not having been fed for days on end, the soldiers reached the POW camp, where they spent the first night in a field. The wounded were shouting and moaning, imploring their comrades to put them out of their misery. The next morning, a German officer showed up, accompanied by a translator. His first order was for the Jews to step forward. No one moved. "No Jews?" the German sneered. "That can't be."[3]

The testimonies of Mints and other survivors of the German onslaught make clear how intensely the invaders scrutinized Soviet soldiers for their presumed racial (Jewish) and political (Bolshevik) traits. While Soviet Jews were viewed with the greatest suspicion as alleged ringleaders of Bolshevism, countless non-Jewish Soviet citizens were also considered Bolshevik agents. The two million Soviet soldiers who had already perished in German captivity by early 1942 died not from simple neglect but were deliberately starved or shot to death because they were widely believed to carry the Bolshevik virus spread by the "Jewish" commissars.

The Germans were wrong in attributing Soviet resistance to the vile designs of Jews; Jews were not instructing non-Jewish Bolsheviks how to act. If anything, it was the other way around: There was great mobilizing power in the Communist faith. Soviet ideology bestowed a heightened measure of civic obligation; it exhorted individuals—men and women—to rise above adverse circumstances and overcome their invader.[4] Even as many party officials responded to the invasion by retreating, abandoning millions of citizens to their fate, committed activists on the ground continued to engage the enemy. Their resistance rendered Germany's campaign against the USSR and Communist partisans elsewhere incomparably tougher than the warfare waged by Nazis on other fronts.[5] The Germans were right in one respect: Soviet Communism was a formidable opponent.

SORTING AND SIFTING SOVIET SOLDIERS

The Germans' search for their racial-political enemies began at the moment of capture. On the second day of the war, a Soviet civilian saw columns of Red Army men near the border town of Brest being marched off to the German rear, their heads bowed. German soldiers packed into trucks sped past them, yelling: "Bolshevik! Communist! Jew!" Some of the Germans trained their guns on the prisoners and fired.[6]

Major Suren Barutchev worked as the head surgeon in the 312th Division when his unit was encircled by the Germans near Orsha in Belorussia in early October 1941. During Barutchev's arrest, a German soldier pointed his rifle at him, shouting out: "*Jude*?" Barutchev, who spoke some German, answered that he was Armenian. The German lowered his rifle.[7]

Sofiya Anvaer, a nurse, described how the division in which she served had surrendered to the Germans that same month. Together with hundreds of soldiers, she was pushed into the flooded basement of a state-owned farm building, where the prisoners had to stand in frigid water, some of them waist-deep. German soldiers shot at anyone who scrambled to get out of the water. Scores of prisoners drowned. After a prolonged ordeal, the survivors were led out of the basement. They were met by Russian-speaking SS men. One of them, reading from a list, shouted out last names. The first three individuals who answered to their names were gunned down. As the SS soldier read out the next name, nobody responded. The name was repeated; again there was silence. Suddenly one of the prisoners pointed at a man, yelling, "That's him!" The German fired a volley in the man's direction, killing several prisoners. When the next name was called, a prisoner quickly rose up and was shot.[8]

In the Proskurov camp for captured Soviet officers, a call for all Jews to step out of line produced no results, so the camp commander ordered the first row of prisoners to lower their pants. With a German shepherd on a leash, he walked past the men. When he came upon a prisoner with circumcised genitals, the commander stopped, unleashed the dog, and ordered it to attack. "A frantic scream reverberated in the air. An ungainly lump rolled across the plaza, blackening the soil with patches of blood. Enjoying the spectacle, the first lieutenant pulled the dog back with effort. Another officer calmly shot the prisoner in the ear. 'Once again, I'm going to ask the Jews to step out of formation!' Three stepped out. Smirking with satisfaction, the commander gave a signal to his men. They led the Jews away."[9]

In several camps, the Germans resorted to a different type of physical profiling to expose the Jews. They led the prisoners of war one by one through the camp gates, past two SS officials. One SS man would look the prisoner straight in the face, the other would study his profile. Prisoners who passed the inspection walked on to be registered by the camp guards; those identified as Jews were led away. Taunting them as "Jewish pigs," the Germans would order the men to dig their own graves, undress, and get on their knees. Then they were shot.[10]

While soldiers who were suspected of being Jewish were often murdered on the spot, the Germans showed little regard for the lives of those captives who were not immediately killed. Mikhail Sviridovsky was captured during the encirclement of Kiev in September 1941. One of the first actions the Germans took was to march the prisoners—some fifteen thousand men—to a nearby airport, where they were arranged in an extended line formation and ordered to march back and forth across the airfield. Then they were allowed to sit down. Minutes later, German airplanes landed on the field. "That's when we understood that they had used our bodies to clear the airfield of mines," Sviridovsky recalled.[11]

Even if the soldiers survived the death marches to distant camps, their destinations promised no relief. Captured in September, Sergeant Aleksandr Kalimov was brought to a prison fortress in Tallinn, Estonia, where he watched a crowd of fellow inmates fight over crumbs of crackers strewn on the ground. Startled, he asked one of the prisoners what was going on. "This is what you'll be doing starting tomorrow," the prisoner responded, explaining that every day the Germans emptied three bags of crackers onto the ground for a population of three thousand soldiers. Despair among the captives ran so deep that some leapt to their deaths from the higher floors of the fortress. From Tallinn, Kalimov was transferred to the Viljandi camp, also in Estonia, where conditions were even worse: "Several thousand half-dead souls staggered around the camp. There was nowhere to sit or lie down. In the dark, when the guards couldn't see, we sat on corpses we had dragged together." Kalimov and another prisoner covered themselves with clothing stripped from the dead and staggered through the camp all night, fighting the urge to lie down for fear of freezing to death.[12]

These scenes were the result of an explicit Wehrmacht policy, worked out during the lead-up to Barbarossa, of treating captured Soviet soldiers more severely than other enemy combatants. General Hermann Reinecke had informed his staff in the Division for POWs that the camps to be built for Soviet prisoners could do without barracks. Rolls of barbed wire were all that was needed to set up and secure the sites.[13] At the time, no one but top Nazi and military officials knew of the secret plan to break the Hitler-Stalin Pact and invade the Soviet Union. Studying General Reinecke's instructions regarding the camps in May, one military official in Münster observed that they were meant for a population that was "not to be treated with the respect usually extended to prisoners of war." "Russians," he later noted, "as it turned out."[14]

In early June 1941, German military leaders projected the capture of one to two million enemy soldiers during the first weeks of the campaign. They made no provisions to feed them.[15] As convoys of prisoners were brought into the barren camps in summer and fall, the guards were ordered not to share food with them. The rare exceptions were often captured on film. A propaganda reel shows a lone German soldier standing

In an unidentified camp, Soviet prisoners of war beg for food, 1941.

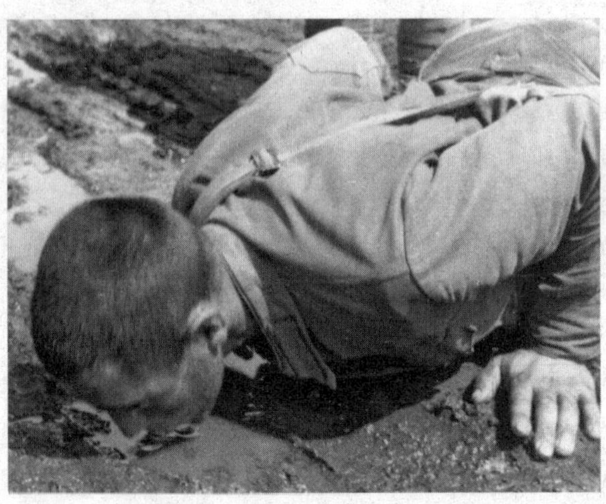

A Soviet POW drinking from a puddle.

on a mound and throwing morsels of food to the mass of prisoners in a ditch below. The camera slowly pans over the swarming bodies as they fight for the scraps.[16] A Soviet doctor who witnessed a similar scene described its demeaning purpose: "They threw breadcrumbs into the crowd. The prisoners fought over the crumbs, while the Germans photographed the melee. Here, look, this is how these primitive Russians devour our bread—and we even feed them!"[17]

In September 1941, Hermann Göring ordered that "Bolshevik prisoners" not be fed according to the requirements of international law.[18] Under his auspices, nutritional engineers developed a "Russian bread" (*Russenbrot*) that, in addition to its off-putting taste and extremely low nutritional value, included so much added sawdust that it caused violent diarrhea among the emaciated Soviet prisoners, killing even more of them.[19]

Also in September, General Reinecke distributed a leaflet to German military forces on how to treat the prisoners of war, which branded every Soviet soldier as a Bolshevik agent and "Nazi Germany's mortal enemy." Reinecke ordered guards to exercise utmost vigilance—"Never turn your back on a POW!"—and to immediately open fire in response to any form of active or passive resistance on the part of the captives. In every way, their treatment of prisoners, including those found to be docile, was to convey the "pride and superiority of the German soldier."[20] The leaflet drew criticism from the head of military intelligence, Admiral Wilhelm Canaris, who informed the Armed Forces High Command Chief Keitel that Reinecke's instructions contravened fundamental principles of international law that had been observed since the eighteenth century. In addition, as a signatory to the Geneva Convention on the treatment of prisoners of war, Germany was bound to treat Soviet prisoners humanely.[21] Canaris also questioned Reinecke's overall logic, which implicated ordinary Soviet soldiers in the murderous crimes committed by their government. Keitel was unmoved: "The objections are in accordance with a soldierly concept of chivalrous warfare! Here, however, we are dealing with Bolshevism, which must be annihilated! For this reason, I approve of the measures."[22] By fall 1941, many others in the German military had come to the same view: Service in the Red Army was a crime. And it would be on this basis that tens of thousands of Soviet soldiers were deported to concentration camps.

After being kept for a while in Orsha, near the site of his capture, where he was able to attend to his fellow POWs' wounds and injuries, the

Soviet surgeon Suren Barutchev was informed by a German doctor that he and the other prisoners would be evacuated to a "*prima Lazarett*," a first-rate field hospital. The severely wounded men, many of them missing arms or legs, were loaded onto freight trains and unloaded in Lublin seven days later. They were brought to a newly built camp that Barutchev remembered as looking unexpectedly inviting: "There were flowers everywhere: entire areas with pansies, wallflowers, stock. On the barrack walls, printed signs: hospital, out-patient clinic. Electric lighting everywhere. Everything was orderly and clean." But these were only Barutchev's first impressions, soon to change as the camp revealed its internal horrors. Its name was Majdanek.[23]

In addition to reserving the scarce food supplies in the East exclusively for Germans, the policy of starving the Soviets was beneficial in one other respect: It produced powerful images of savagery that abetted Germany's war effort. Mortality in camps holding Soviet POWs shot up in October 1941, reaching a monthly rate of 30 percent in the occupied Soviet Union and the General Government.[24] The extreme hunger induced cannibalism. Unsurprisingly, the fact that Soviet prisoners in their despair devoured the flesh, kidneys, and livers of the dead was exploited by the Germans. Camp commanders ordered the execution of transgressors to dramatize the divide between German decency and Soviet barbarism.[25] In the Salaspils camp near Riga, at roll call one morning, two prisoners with Asian features were paraded in front of the assembled men. They both had placards hung around their necks: "I am a cannibal." A translator read out the commander's order that prisoners were not allowed to eat fellow prisoners and should be content with their food rations. A photographer took pictures of the accused, before they were shot or strung up.[26]

In a letter to his wife from Mogilev, Walter Mattner reported a conversation over lunch with an SS officer who had just returned from a prisoner transport and described the inhuman practices of the "Asiatic prisoners": "They take those who died on the way, cut off their asses, put the flesh in a frying pan and eat it. . . . You can imagine the man-eaters we find ourselves among here. Tomorrow another group of gypsies will be dispatched (around 50). And that's how it goes every day. Human life is worth nothing to them. But it's a delight to be alive, and I'm still glad to be allowed to experience our people's fateful struggle and to take part in this fight."[27]

One contingent of Soviet soldiers delivered to a camp in the Latvian city of Jelgava was not given any food at all for four days. On the fifth day, the camp commander addressed the famished soldiers with the help of a translator: "No one will get anything to eat, as long as you refuse to tell us who among you is a Communist, a commissar, or a Jew." A former prisoner remembered the scene: "They brought biscuits and coffee into the camp. The commander stood there with his guard dog, a prisoner by his side. As the soldiers walked up to get a biscuit, the prisoner said, 'This one is a politruk.' The political officer was led around the corner and shot. The traitor was poured some coffee and given two biscuits. 'And this one is a Jew.' The Jew was taken away and shot, while the traitor got some more biscuits."[28]

How the Germans dealt with female Red Army soldiers who were captured remains largely undocumented. The lack of witness reports or memoirs detailing the plight of captured female machine gunners, tank drivers, political officers, or partisans suggests they were murdered out of sight.[29] A few days into Germany's attack on the USSR, the commander in chief of the Fourth Army, Günther von Kluge, issued an order: "Women in uniform are to be shot." That order was rescinded shortly thereafter—an intelligence officer had questioned the effectiveness of mass shootings of women—but other commanders followed suit with similar decrees.[30]

German photographs from summer and fall 1941 provide important context for Kluge's terse command. They suggest that Wehrmacht soldiers had appropriated the stereotype of the fiendish "riflewoman" that had been a staple of anti-Communist propaganda in the Russian and Spanish civil wars, using it to demonize Soviet women in uniform. The captions included with the photographs describe captured female Soviet soldiers as symbols of Bolshevism's moral depravity, bereft of "any feeling for womanhood or humanity."[31] A photograph taken in summer 1941 shows

A male German soldier leads a captured female Soviet soldier away, 1941.

a group of Red Army soldiers, arms raised in surrender, a woman among them. Standing nearby, a German soldier wearing a camouflage jacket looks the woman directly in the eye. The caption reads: "A riflewoman and female commissar in one, a dogged sniper, who presses Soviet soldiers to fight to the last breath."[32]

Guided by this logic, German commanders ordered the execution of scores of female Soviet soldiers. In October 1941, a divisional commander instructed his men to kill "female personages in Russian uniform on principle." That same month, the head of a panzer division declared that these "insidious, cruel partisans and riflewomen belong on the next bough, not in the POW camp."[33] Ordinary soldiers fighting in the East were issued grave warnings about these dangerous and violent women. During the battle for Kharkov, a German noncommissioned officer claimed to have seen a "bandit battalion" commanded by a red-haired woman wearing red boots. The fighting style of these "female beasts was extremely underhanded and dangerous." Anton Roos, writing to his wife from southern Ukraine in August 1941, had singled out female soldiers for special notice: "The Uman cauldron with 103,000 prisoners has surrendered. You should have seen the scum, all the types of Europe and Asia, and mostly children of 16–18 years who had been put into uniforms and turned loose on us. Yesterday, I saw a transport of riflewomen, lovely company, they won't get far."[34]

While the identification and punishment of Jews, commissars, and

"A riflewoman and female commissar in one . . ."
German propaganda photograph, 1941.[35]

female combatants were an integral part of the "sorting and sifting" of captured soldiers, the true purpose of the process was to establish which prisoners posed a political danger and which could be put to use as laborers. Camp commanders grouped their charges into ethnicities, separating Russians from ethnic Germans, Ukrainians, Baltic peoples, Asiatics, and Jews. In terms of their perceived political threat, Russians ranked alongside or immediately below Jews.[36] From early on, Russian soldiers were herded into "special camps," separated from other prisoners and surrounded by extra rows of barbed wire.[37]

Russian prisoners of war were initially not sent to Germany: The threat that they might "contaminate" fellow workers with "proletarian internationalism" was too great. The dire need for laborers on German farms softened this stance somewhat, but the sixty-five thousand Russian prisoners sent to Germany in July 1941 were kept under heavy guard and segregated from other prisoners and civilians.[38] A Nazi official who toured Soviet prisoner camps in Lithuania in October 1941 singled out the Russian soldiers as a "shapeless, dull mass hardly capable of any sensation beyond the need for the simplest necessities of life." He observed that while the Ukrainians in the camps joined choruses in the evenings to sing their national songs, the Russians remained silent, "like an aban-

Soviet POWs in a camp near Gzhatsk, Smolensk region, December 1941.

doned flock." It was misguided to think of these prisoners as Russians in a traditional sense, the Nazi visitor wrote. Bolshevism had transformed their souls, perhaps even their bodies. What faced him was a horde of mutants, primitive beings reduced to instinctual life and fully controlled by their Soviet Jewish rulers.[39]

Non-Russian Soviet citizens appeared to the Germans as less deformed by Communism.[40] Ethnic Germans, the so-called *Volksdeutsche*, enjoyed the greatest trust, followed by Ukrainians, Lithuanians, Latvians, and Estonians, with Turkic peoples and Caucasians, in that order, added later as well.[41] Captured soldiers hailing from these regions were thought to be possessed of good racial stock and healthy political views, and were often released from the camps or even recruited into newly formed "Eastern Legions."[42] Soviet soldiers of Slavic origin were quick to catch on to the German ethnic hierarchy. Surrendering Red Army men were often heard shouting that they were Ukrainian.[43] Their strategy paid off: Of the two hundred and eighty thousand Red Army soldiers that Germany had elected to free again by January 1942, two hundred and seventy thousand were listed as Ukrainians. No one who identified as Russian was freed.[44] A Wehrmacht official in the field summed up the difference between Ukrainians and Russians. The former were not to be "treated like negroes," he ordered. Russians apparently were.[45] German fighters in the East routinely referred to Russian soldiers as "negroes," as less than human. "There are hardly any people around," wrote Helmut Hartmann in July 1941. "The Russians are just a tribe of niggers. We live in order to destroy them. And to protect ourselves from being destroyed. Combat almost every day. Again and again."[46]

Wehrmacht commanders allowed ethnic German, Ukrainian, and Baltic POWs to be trained for police service, with few questions asked. As for Russians, only those who had been politically persecuted by the Soviets were readily admitted into the ranks of the German-led local auxiliary forces, or *politsai*.[47] Some German officials barred applicants who had previously belonged to the Communist Party or its youth organization.[48] Others enlisted former Communists on the condition that they publicly swore an oath of loyalty to Adolf Hitler and the "fight against Bolshevism—the enemy of my country and of the entire world." The Germans kept strict tabs on former Communists, expecting them to prove their loyalty over and over again.[49] But the need for a security force in the occupied territories was great, and thousands of Russians ended up serving with the *politsai*.[50] Many eagerly grasped at the opportunity to trade the dreadful conditions of the camps for a paid position and enthusiastically took up the Nazis' fight. Anti-Semitism among the auxiliary forces was rampant. In the Roslavl camp, where Maks Mints was held, the police consisted of two squads, one Ukrainian and one Cossack, both staffed with former prisoners. "They were walking about the barracks and looking at our faces—Jew or not? When they found a Jew, they'd pull him out and lead him away." Though Mints consistently presented himself as a Belorussian, the police frequently suspected that he was Jewish and questioned him repeatedly about his background.[51]

ESCAPE

While some POWs chose to work for the Germans, others saw flight as the only alternative to a slow and degrading death in the camps. The desire to escape was also spurred by feelings of military duty. Soviet soldiers knew that the Red Army regarded voluntary surrender as treason. During the early stages of the war, scores of POWs successfully fled the camps, which were then still poorly guarded.[52] No one knows their exact numbers, as the Germans did not keep track. But many were subsequently caught and brought back to the same camps, particularly in the Western territories, where local sentiment was staunchly anti-Soviet. Alexander Kalimov repeatedly escaped from his camp in Estonia, once with a fellow inmate. The men wandered through the countryside, wearing their coats inside out to conceal the SU sign—for "Soviet Union"—that was sown on the back. When they came upon a hut, they asked the woman inside for water. Communists and criminals, she answered, deserved only one thing: the gallows. The woman directed the exhausted men to a tub filled with dirty water. Kalimov and his comrade were still quenching their thirst when armed Estonians materialized and took them back to the camp.[53]

In the Soviet heartland, too, the odds were stacked against fugitives. Numerous German patrols and road checks watched for "Bolsheviks" and "partisans." Grigori Paniavin, a lieutenant in the Red Army, escaped from a camp in the Smolensk region in October 1941. As he recounted to a group of historians who interviewed him in 1944, he then headed east to rejoin the Red Army. While resting near a Soviet village, he saw a group of German soldiers approach. From his hiding place, Paniavin watched as the soldiers assembled all of the village's men and checked their documents. In consultation with the village elder, they chose a smaller group to work on the local collective farm. The others, twenty-eight men, were taken to the side and shot.[54] A few weeks later, Paniavin was caught and brought to a local prison. From there, an armored train took all the prisoners to the Dvinsk (Daugavpils) camp in Latvia. En route, the prisoners in Paniavin's car managed to twist apart the metal bars securing the skylight and six escaped. When the others arrived at their destination, they were astonished to see the six escapees already there, their attempt having failed. Paniavin described the camp, located inside the city's fortress, as hellish. The prisoners spent the night outside in subzero temperatures. At roll call the next morning, 150 men were missing—they had died overnight. The hundreds of captives who died every day in November were hastily buried in mass graves, each one large enough to hold three thousand bodies. Disposing of the bodies fell to Jewish prisoners, who were, at all times, fair game for the guards. Paniavin recalled: "The Russian policemen and the Germans formed a gauntlet. 'Faster! Faster!' they shouted as they beat [the Jews], some with a baton, some with a club, some with a bar. . . . If someone fell, a German would poke him with a bayonet and force another Jew to drag him away." Paniavin was shocked. It was the first time he had seen anyone abuse Jews. He hailed from the Urals, where few Jews lived, and moreover, he had been brought up in an "internationalist spirit, which did not recognize any differences between ethnicities."[55]

Paniavin's initial hope was to rejoin his army unit, but now, it seemed, the only road to salvation lay in linking up with the partisans—the irregular groups of Soviet soldiers who had been trapped on German-occupied soil and formed brigades to fight the enemy. Paniavin managed to escape from Dvinsk on November 26 but was apprehended again and delivered to another camp. He escaped from there, too, and was captured that time as well. He was then brought to the camp in the Glubokoe Monastery, north of Minsk, where he saw signs on the wall that read "For the eating of human corpses—execution on the spot. For the cutting out of entrails—execution on the spot." From there, Paniavin was taken to Minsk and put to work. It was now early 1942, and the German policy toward Soviet POWs had changed: They were to be used as forced laborers and given enough food to survive. Nevertheless, Paniavin—along with three other prisoners—plotted his next escape. One day at work digging peat, the four men threw themselves on a Ukrainian guard and strangled him to death. They managed to get away. Over time their group grew to about twenty escapees and stragglers. In October 1942, they joined a partisan brigade. Paniavin was made their chief of staff. "That's how my life in captivity ended, and a new life began, more cheerful and more useful."[56]

Maks Mints also sought to join the partisans. Together with several other inmates, he escaped from Roslavl with relative ease. After hiding in the forest for three days, the exhausted men entered a village and asked for help. Minutes later, they were arrested by the village elder and other armed men and brought back to the camp. Prior to escaping, Mints had scribbled a note inviting more prisoners to join in the escape, and an informant had passed the scrap of paper to camp guards. The guards, who were Russian, confronted Mints with the note, demanding to know why he had written it. "Thinking that I was talking to a comrade, I said that I considered it a duty of every Soviet citizen to escape from captivity." "Stalinist!" a guard shouted, punching him. "Jew," another exclaimed. The guards forced Mints to lower his pants. The sight of his circumcised genitals, in addition to his efforts to recruit others to join him, convinced his interrogators that they were dealing with a high-level commissar, the most dangerous of all Soviet Jews. The head of the camp was alarmed. He asked Mints through a translator whether he was a politruk. No, Mints said, he was an artillery captain. But how could he prove this? "At that moment, when death was staring me in the face, as they say, I felt a terrible calm. I was completely indifferent. I wasn't at all flustered. I was speaking as I'm speaking to you now. I was just not going to say that I was either a political leader or a Jew."[57] If he was a political officer, Mints replied, his knowledge of military affairs would be poor. He suggested that he be tested on the mathematical calculations involved in the deployment of artillery. The test was conducted to the Germans' satisfaction. There remained the fact of Mints's circumcision. Mints explained that it had resulted from a botched medical procedure when he was sixteen. Two German doctors were called in. They took Mints to the window to examine him. He heard them say, "Yes, indeed, *Operation*."

Mints knew perfectly well what awaited those who were recognized as Jews. Some who possessed vital skills for the Germans were spared execution, but their suffering was great nevertheless. Mints watched how the camp police abused a translator named Yefim, beating him on the head with an iron stick. When Yefim lost consciousness, the guards poured cold water over him until he came to, before continuing to taunt him: "You tried to destroy us for the last twenty-five years. It's going to take us just one year to destroy you! Do you understand, Yefim?"

"Yes, sir!"[58]

KNOCKING AT CIVILIANS' DOORS

Just as they hunted for "Bolsheviks" within the ranks of captured soldiers, the Germans searched out suspected political enemies among the ordinary citizens in conquered cities, towns, and villages. In the Baltic republics and Western Ukraine, German units could count on the active support of residents who were eager to punish anyone associated with the hated Soviet system.[59] Locals referred to Russians brought in after the Soviet annexation of these lands as "Easterners."[60] In Brest, which was located on the Soviet border and had been part of Poland until 1939, people took to the streets with flowers when the Germans arrived on June 22, 1941. Residents were quick to inform the Germans of the whereabouts of Jews and Communists. A German soldier came knocking at the door of Maks Sankshtein, a Jewish barber. Was Sankshtein a Jew? he asked. No, he was Polish, Sankshtein replied. The icon hanging on the wall persuaded the soldier that Sankshtein was telling the truth. The German checked his Soviet passport and then left. Evidently unable to read Russian, he had overlooked the line in the passport that identified Sankshtein as Jewish. In Brest alone, the Germans captured some seven thousand Jewish men during the first week of the occupation.[61]

In addition to Jews, hundreds of "Easterners" were hauled out of their apartments, lined up, and taken away, presumably to be shot. Many others went into hiding. The Germans planned to create a Communist ghetto, and at least one contingent of "Easterners" was forcibly resettled on Brest's "Soviet Street," where large families had to crowd into single rooms. The ghetto idea was later abandoned.[62] In Lvov, the wife of a factory director remembered being shouted at by Poles and Ukrainians: "Soviet! Communist! Go back to Stalin!"[63]

Throughout the Baltics, locals eagerly helped the Germans identify all remaining supporters of Soviet power. Just a week before the German invasion, the Soviet regime had deported around ten thousand Estonian officers, policemen, peasants, and criminals, whom it had classified as "anti-Soviet elements," to Siberia and the Russian North. In the opening days of the war, Estonian nationalists sought revenge, killing or delivering to the Germans anyone who had served the Soviet "occupants" in any capacity—even firefighters. "Active Communist" was the justification the Germans gave for executing these people.[64] From the interrogation cells in the central prison in Tartu, groups of Communist suspects were brought to a nearby POW camp, where they were made to undress, before being tied together by a long rope and forced to board a bus. Outside of town, they were shot at the edge of a ditch. The rope was then unstrung from the dead bodies and used to tie together the next group of prisoners. The blood-soaked rope made a terrifying impression on the camp prisoners.[65]

In Riga, a Latvian ship worker who was not a Communist described how he spent the first days of the war helping to load equipment from the shipyard onto trains bound for the East. Working day and night, he fell ill. Upon his return to work, he found the shipyard in German hands and was detained. His captors began the interrogation by punching him in the face and shouting, "You are a friend of the Jews!" The fact that the worker had a well-paying job under Soviet rule was reason enough to indict him as a Bolshevik. He was brought to Riga's central prison, where he remained for a year and a half.[66] Jean Bunka, a singer in Riga's Opera and Ballet Theater, was arrested by a fellow Latvian, in civilian dress, who came to search his apartment. Even though the search yielded nothing, Bunka was ordered to come to the prefecture and thrown into a cell that was so crowded that he had to be pressed inside. He recognized many of the cell's occupants—they were all members of the city's educated elite. Later, Bunka was interrogated by two policemen who appeared to be drunk. "Ah, you're a Chekist officer?" one of them yelled before punching Bunka in the face. Bunka believed he had been denounced by an informant, but the only possible reason he could think of was that under Soviet rule, he had headed the commission that oversaw the workings of the theater snack bar.[67]

In the western provinces, the German authorities had praised the zeal with which locals contributed to the hunt for Communists and Jews. An SS report noted, "The Ukrainian population showed laudable activity against the Jews during the first hours after the retreat of the Bolsheviks. In Dobromil the synagogue was set on fire. In Sambor, 50 Jews were clubbed to death by an enraged crowd."[68] Farther east, the picture was different. On traditionally Soviet ground, residents proved much less receptive to anti-Semitic propaganda.[69] German observers were baffled. In their understanding, the only reason why Russian civilians did not launch pogroms against local Jews as soon as the Germans took power was their fear that the Soviets would return and punish any anti-Semitic violence. Indeed, Soviet laws against anti-Semitic hate crimes were severe, including, for example, mandatory prison sentences for referring to Jews as "yids" rather than "Hebrews." To the Germans, these laws were yet another indication of how thoroughly the Judeo-Bolsheviks had bent the law to their own benefit. To handle insufficiently cooperative occupied areas, one analyst recommended the mass distribution of anti-Jewish visual propaganda of the kind featured in the Nazi press. Such stimuli, he suggested, would release dormant anti-Semitic sentiment among the population and incite pogroms.[70] In the meantime, however, the task would fall to the Germans themselves.

Minsk, the Belorussian capital, was the first large city in core Soviet territory to be conquered by the Germans. They arrived on June 28, before Soviet officials were able to mine office buildings and apartment complexes, as they would do elsewhere. Thus, it would be the invading forces that saw to Minsk's destruction themselves, conducting bombing raids that lasted several days and left the city "mostly in ashes," as an army report noted.[71] When the war came to Minsk, Khasya Pruslina, a forty-year-old teacher, had completed her research for a doctoral dissertation in history and written three chapters. All her documents were destroyed during the German attack. With her two small children, she joined a stream of refugees trying to escape, but German tanks were firing on the panicked people, killing hundreds, and German paratroopers were raining down from the sky. Pruslina sought cover in a ditch on the side of the road and survived. A member of the Communist Party and a Jew, she buried her party card and tried to remember the location since she hoped to retrieve it before long; she expected the Soviets to win the war in weeks. She and her children made it to a forested area where Red Army commanders were in hiding. Some of them recognized her as their children's history teacher.[72]

On July 2, four days after the first German units had entered Minsk, the city's commandant, Eckart von Tschammer und Osten, ordered all the city's male residents of fighting age to register at his office, the Kammandatur. "And everybody went there, like sheep," recalled the housewife Basya Levina—including her husband, a Jew like herself.[73] The men were herded into an open-air camp near Drozdy, three miles north of the city. They found themselves next to a huge camp for POWs, separated from it only by ropes. The area filled up with arrestees so quickly that by July 5 it was impossible to lie down, a survivor recalled. "There was fighting over space, bickering, jostling, swearing, and the entire time, the Germans were spraying us with bursts of machine gun fire." At one point the area held forty thousand civilians and one hundred thousand POWs. "For the purpose of tormenting the people, they gave out dried salted fish but nothing to drink."[74] There was a source of water in the camp—one survivor described it as a pond, another as a river—but those who drank from it were shot at. The men from Minsk were unprepared for their captivity and had arrived wearing light clothes. When some complained about the cold nights, Germans suggested they help themselves to the clothes worn by the Jewish men in their midst.

On July 10, all Jews were ordered to step aside. They were stripped of their boots and herded into a fenced-off section of the camp. On July 12 at 4:00 a.m., all the engineers, bookkeepers, teachers, lawyers, and other intellectuals in the Jewish section were ordered to register for special work assignments. Levina's husband, an engineer, was among them. In small batches, they were driven away in a truck. Every twenty minutes the truck returned empty, to depart with a new load. Nine hundred people were led away over the course of several days. Only gradually did it dawn on the survivors that they were witnessing a German "action" intended to destroy the Jewish intelligentsia, which they considered the mainstay of Bolshevism. The only educated professionals spared were medical doctors. The Germans needed them to fight the epidemics that would surely break out among the surviving Jews.[75]

In addition to targeting Soviet Jews, the Germans sought to separate all Communists—non-Jewish as well as Jewish—from the other detainees at Drozdy. They read out names from a list of members of the Belorussian Communist Party, which was found in a party office. Those who responded when called were shot.[76] The search yielded few card-carrying Communists. Most Communist officials had been able to clear out in time, and many of those who remained had the presence of mind, like Pruslina, to hide or destroy their party cards before falling into the enemy's hands.[77] Through that simple act, Communists could conceal their identity, an option not available to most Jews, whether they were party members or not.

On July 9, 1941, Commandant von Tschammer und Osten ordered all of Minsk's Jews to be marked with a yellow patch. As justification, he asserted that a Jewish organization of 120 men had sought to resist the Germans and been annihilated.[78] On the city streets, the Germans and their Lithuanian aides harassed Jewish-looking civilians not wearing the patch.[79] Dark-haired women were at risk of being beaten. One group of suspects was dragged to military headquarters, where buckets of yellow paint were emptied over their heads.[80] On July 19, the commandant ordered that a walled-in "yid sector" be set up in an impoverished section of town. "To heighten the humiliation," a Jewish survivor recalled, "the order said that the wall was to be built by the 'yids' themselves."[81] All Jewish women, children, and the elderly were to reside in the ghetto, as well as the Jewish men who had been released from the Drozdy camp and the Jews from the area surrounding Minsk. With more than one hundred thousand inhabitants at its height, the Minsk Ghetto became the largest population of "indigenous" Soviet Jews at the outset of the

Nazi occupation, followed by Kiev.[82] Both cities had been conquered too swiftly for Jews to evacuate in time.

Even after being fenced in—the wall decreed in the German order was never built—the Jews of Minsk still appeared menacing to the occupying Germans.[83] According to a September 1941 security report, saboteurs in the ghetto had repeatedly cut the German army's telephone cable. They had threatened members of the auxiliary police and even shot at them. In numerous cases, Jews were caught without the prescribed badge, and they commonly refused to work. For all of these reasons, the Germans believed the severest defense measures were necessary to check the aggressive behavior of the Jewish population. Over the course of three days, the auxiliary police, with the support of the German field police, carried out a major operation in the ghetto, arresting about 2,500 Jews, among them several women; 2,278 were executed. All were characterized as saboteurs and Jewish activists.[84]

Far greater violence lay in store. Some of the worst came on November 7, the anniversary of the October Revolution.* The Germans deliberately struck on that day to dramatize their retribution against Jewish-Bolshevik power. On the eve of the holiday, the police rounded up Jewish officials and their families, along with several hundred "specialists" and skilled workers, and took them to a concentration camp built on Shirokaya Street, outside the ghetto perimeter. They clearly wanted to exterminate someone, a survivor recalled, "But who? Those of us left in the ghetto, or the people over on Shirokaya?"[85]

Early in the morning on November 7, SS troops joined by Ukrainian and Lithuanian policemen marched into the ghetto and went from house to house, driving men, women, and children from their apartments and into a square, while barking at them: "Line up in rows of eight, as you always do on October Day!" The Lithuanians distributed large red flags bearing Soviet insignia. The men in the front row were forced to carry a banner that said "Long live the 24th anniversary of the Great Socialist

---

* While the Communists took power in Russia on November 7, 1917, according to the Gregorian calendar, the event is most commonly known as the October Revolution because at the time Russia still used the Julian calendar, which lagged the Gregorian calendar by thirteen days.

October Revolution!" As the Jews were ordered to march and sing revolutionary songs, men in civilian garb carrying movie cameras appeared on the scene to film the "demonstration." After marching for a few blocks, the demonstrators came upon a line of black trucks. They were ordered to climb into them and then were driven away.[86]

Tailor Mikhail Grichanik was one of the skilled workers who had been taken to the camp on Shirokaya Street the night before. That morning, he had been working his regular shift in the garment factory when he heard gunfire. All the workers in the factory immediately understood that a pogrom had begun. They begged their bosses to issue documents stating that their family members were related to skilled workers. They received the papers at midday and raced to the ghetto. Grichanik was stunned when he reached his apartment. His entire family was gone—his wife, their three children, his mother, sister, and the sister's two children. It looked like they had been pulled out of their beds. Minutes later, someone shouted that the Germans had detained a large group of Jews in a nearby barracks. The factory workers ran to the barracks. As they approached, they heard gunshots and saw trucks loaded with people drive out of the gates. The workers waved their documents, but the soldiers guarding the barracks were unmoved. "Get back to the camp!" they ordered.[87]

The November 7 "action" was not confined to the ghetto. Gallows went up on street corners, in parks, and at open-air markets throughout the city. Around one hundred people were hanged that day by the German Wehrmacht and their Lithuanian auxiliaries. Placards with the word "Communist" or "Partisan" were strung around their necks.[88] The violence continued for two weeks. Between November 7 and 11, at least 6,624 Minsk Jews were killed. Another 5,000 were executed on November 20.[89] The killings freed up space for the 7,000 Jews deported from Germany, who began to arrive on November 12.[90] The German-language newspaper in Minsk reported that the violence was a punishment inflicted on the Jews for attempting a Bolshevik uprising.[91]

"TO DIE AS A HUMAN BEING"

While the German fantasy of Soviet Communists, partisans, and Jews jointly conspiring against Nazi rule was generally far off the mark, in Minsk it contained a kernel of truth. Resistance there began as soon as the Germans arrived. Underground organizations sprang up across the city, not only in the ghetto but also in the "Russian sector," as the non-Jewish part of town came to be called. Cells composed of Jewish and non-Jewish Communists—men as well as women—created a united underground movement.[92]

The first groups were led by seasoned Communists and attracted young followers who had grown up reading tales of revolutionary heroism and thirsted for opportunities to prove their commitment. These early initiatives formed without official Soviet backing. Most Communists in Minsk did not know that their party leaders had been evacuated and waited for instructions from above. It took an outsider, the Polish Communist Hersh Smolar, to push them to independent action. Thirty-six years old, Jewish, and with rich experience in underground work, Smolar knew Minsk well—he had lived there for several years during the 1920s.[93] When the war broke out, he fled from his hometown of Bialystok. With the Germans close behind as he reached Minsk, he decided to stay there. He immediately formed a resistance group in the ghetto, complete with a printing press hidden in a cellar, and taught members how to forge documents that would give their bearers non-Jewish credentials. With the help of a stamp that bore the Nazi eagle, Smolar later recalled, his group "performed miracles in transforming Jewish faces into Aryan ones."[94]

Another underground cell worked from the Polytechnical Institute, which had become a makeshift hospital for Red Army soldiers. That group was led by a civil war veteran, Kirill Trusov, and a nurse, Olga Shcherbatsevich, both of them Communists, and included Olga's sixteen-year-old son, Vladlen (a contraction of Vladimir Lenin), her brother, and her sister's family, as well as Maria ("Masha") Bruskina, a seventeen-year–old Jewish girl who had begun volunteering in the hospital when

Execution of Kirill Trusov, Maria Bruskina, and Vladlen Shcherbatsevich, October 26, 1941.[95]

the war broke out.[96] The group provided wounded soldiers with medication and smuggled them out of the hospital into Olga's apartment. A seamstress, Elena Ostrovskaia, outfitted them with civilian clothes. Then the soldiers were spirited away to partisan groups hiding in the nearby forests. At least fifteen and perhaps as many as several dozen POWs were successfully brought to the forest before the Germans found out about the operation. Soon thereafter, all the cell members were arrested.[97] On October 26, Maria, Vladlen, his mother, Trusov, and eight other activists were taken from their prison cells and paraded through the streets in preparation for a public hanging, the first such event in Minsk. The prisoners were led in parties of three, comprised of two men and one woman. The Germans hung an identically worded placard around each woman's neck, asserting in Russian and German: "We are partisans and have shot at German soldiers."

To attract maximum attention, the four groups were strung up in different sections of town. Residents were herded to the execution spots, where German officers made threatening speeches that were translated into Russian. Maria, Vladlen, and Trusov were hanged at the gates of a yeast factory. Maria was the first to be executed, followed by Vladlen and Trusov.[98] According to witnesses, and confirmed by photographs, Maria

Close-up shot of the execution of Maria Bruskina.

turned her back to the spectators as the executioner placed a noose around her neck. He unsuccessfully tried to make her face the crowd. Only as she began to struggle in agony were they able to turn her body to the cameras.[99]

Maria Bruskina gave her brief life to the service of Communist ideals. She was the pioneer leader of her fifth-grade class and later headed the Komsomol organization of her middle school. When she was fourteen, the newspaper *Belorussian Pioneer* featured her photograph along with a caption: "Maria Bruskina, eighth grader in Minsk's 28th School. She has all good and excellent grades." As a member of the first generation born after the Revolution of 1917, and as a Jew who teamed up with non-Jews in the underground fight against the Germans, Maria embodied the spirit of Soviet internationalism.[100] She and her mother initially settled in the Jewish ghetto, but Maria moved to the Russian sector to continue her political work, bleaching her hair to conceal her Jewish background.[101] After her arrest, she managed to smuggle a note to her mother: "I am tormented by the thought that I have caused you great worry. Don't worry. Nothing bad has happened to me. . . . If you can, please send me my dress, my green blouse, and white socks. I want to be dressed decently when I leave here." Gallant to the end, Maria sent another note to a friend: "In any case, there is no chance I'll die of starvation."[102] Exceptional as her heroism may seem, Maria Bruskina was one of many young Soviet people who resolved to stand up to the German occupants no matter what the cost. They saw themselves as defenders of humanity against the depravity of the Germans. The occupiers made a point of singling out the female resisters, portraying them as callous Bolsheviks, bereft of femininity. Maria responded to these provocations by walking proudly to her death, her head held high. The photographs that were meant to taunt and vilify inadvertently became documentary proof of her dignity and equanimity in the face of death.

As the story of Maria Bruskina's death spread through Minsk, it spurred others to action. In the ghetto, twenty-one-year-old Emma Radova organized volunteers. In the Russian sector, many of Maria's former classmates joined the partisan movement.[103] To be Jewish was not a meaningful marker in Minsk's underground in 1941. What mattered were one's political credentials: "We Communists" was how Communist Jews from Minsk referred to themselves.[104] It was as Communists that the Jews from Minsk created the first ghetto combat organization in occupied Europe.[105] Communism furnished the imperative to act and join forces with fellow comrades. Apart from these groups, there was little else to counter the torrent of violence that came rushing down on Minsk's Jews.

The November 7 events were unfathomable even to seasoned Communists in the ghetto. "We couldn't imagine," remembered Etta Maizles, then forty-two years old and a member of Smolar's group, "that they would allow the extermination of thousands of people in the republic's capital." Maizles survived the pogrom in one of the many hiding spots, called *malinas*, that carpenters had built immediately after the creation of the ghetto. Some malinas, like camouflaged chimney openings or closets, provided space for only one or two people; others could shelter larger groups. Maizles and her four-year-old son were crowded in a secret room together with twenty-eight other people. "Hush, Vovochka," she kept whispering into his ear. The group was not discovered.[106]

Khasya Pruslina, the history teacher, was in another malina on November 7. After fleeing Minsk in July, she had sought to join a partisan unit, but as the weather turned cold and she could not locate the partisans, she returned to Minsk and moved into the ghetto with her eleven-year-old son. A Communist acquaintance living in the Russian sector had agreed to shelter Pruslina's younger daughter. Pruslina shuttled between underground organizations in the ghetto and the Russian sector, relaying Soviet broadcasts received from a radio hidden in a malina in the ghetto. In early November, her son came down with encephalitis, and when the pogrom started, she left him in his bed and crammed into the hiding spot with thirty other residents of her building. "I couldn't imagine that they would be so cruel as to take a sick child. Only after they had left did I see that he was no longer there. They had taken him."[107]

In the wake of the mass killings, the underground organizations in the ghetto and the Russian sector teamed up to rescue children from the ghetto. Female members of the Jewish underground would push children through the barbed wire. Women on the other side would take the children to orphanages or private households willing to provide shelter. An orphanage staff worker recalled taking in toddlers, complete with certificates attesting to their Russian-sounding names. Older children would come to the orphanage on their own, certificates in hand. Suspecting that many such certificates were false, the Germans sent inspectors to check on the children's nationality. In response, staff workers would hide all the Jewish-looking children when they arrived at the orphanage entrance.[108] Not all children were so fortunate, however. Etta Maizles also gave her son to an orphanage, where he was registered as Vova Lavrenkov. As his mother later learned, the Gestapo took Vova and thirty-four other children early in 1943. The deputy director of the orphanage had informed the Germans that they were sheltering children from the ghetto.[109]

March 2, 1942, eight months after the occupation began, was a watershed date in Minsk. Unlike the November 7 "action," when Jews were loaded onto trucks to be shot outside the city, this time the Germans staged a massacre in the ghetto. From her hiding spot, Etta Maizles observed what happened: "I had already seen my share of horrors, but when I saw them massacre the children, I couldn't bear it. I lost my mind. If you'd seen the piles of children, corpses with bent legs, you'd understand how it's possible to go mad from such horror." After that day, Maizles said, she felt unable to work, or live, any longer. For days, she could not say a word. "Everything inside me had turned to stone. Stoliarevych [a leader of the underground organization] summoned me and gave the order: 'Leave! There's been a decision from the underground committee. You and another woman are to leave.' They specified the place where I was to appear and sent us to a partisan detachment."[110] Maizles left on March 14, with twenty-three men and one other woman from the ghetto.

But joining the partisans was difficult. The problem was no longer finding them—by early 1942, the forests near Minsk were teeming with partisans, and since the previous fall some brigades had been sending emissaries to the ghetto, looking for weapons, medication, and warm clothes.[111] Rather, the problem was that most partisans did not want to take on the burden of women and children, and some were prejudiced against Jews. Pruslina knew how dependent the forest fighters were on ammunition, and she once struck a deal with one unit: In exchange for nineteen boxes of cartridges, which she had been able to acquire in the Russian sector, the partisans agreed to allow several women from the ghetto to join them.[112]

Passport photograph of Khasya Pruslina (Pelageia Petrovna Fediuk, pseud.), Minsk, 1942.

When Maizles and the twenty-four other Jews reached the forest, they were met with a cold welcome. A brigade leader grudgingly agreed to accept the refugees, all the while railing against "the Jews," who he said did not like to work or fight. In the eyes of the partisans, the Jews themselves were to blame for letting themselves be slaughtered. "If they'd at least hit the Germans with a brick!" a partisan leader commented. "But no, they obediently walk to their graves."[113] Soon, the brigade came under a German blockade, and conditions turned so dire that five Jews resolved to return to the ghetto. Maizles stayed on. Eventually, another brigade of partisans broke the blockade and took the Jews under its wing. Unlike the brigade they had initially joined, which was led by anti-Semites, this one was, according to Maizles, a truly "*Soviet* partisan detachment"—meaning it was faithful to the revolutionary movement's spirit of egalitarianism and internationalism. Under its auspices, she and her comrades "finally felt like human beings, not yids."[114]

Indeed, the prejudice among partisan groups was widespread. Hersh Smolar, the Polish Jewish leader of the resistance group in Minsk that Maizles had joined, became so exasperated by the partisans' rejection of Jews that in September 1942 he created several fighting units exclusively composed of Jews.[115] Upon hearing that some partisans did not just turn Jews down but in fact killed them, another partisan leader, of Belorussian background, also made a point of recruiting men from the ghetto.[116]

The effective, if frequently reluctant, alliance between the partisans and the Minsk underground saved thousands of lives.[117] It was the most successful rescue operation of ghettoized Jews anywhere in Eastern Europe. The work was particularly remarkable because it was self-directed and took place in the absence of any supporting state or central party structures. When Soviet officials retreated from Minsk less than a week into the war, activists on the ground proceeded to build ad hoc Soviet institutions—clandestine cells in the niches and crevices of the city, as well as in the dense forests that the Germans dared not enter. Some were dedicated Communists who acted from a personal sense of duty.[118] Others were stirred to action after watching the Germans abuse POWs and Jews and sensing they would be next. Still others simply could no longer endure their own degradation. Etta Maizles's testimony makes frequent reference to the Germans "taunting" her and other Soviet citizens. In describing the moment she joined the resistance effort, she later recounted the words of the printer Zinovy Okun upon his decision to join the underground. "I'll die like a human being, not like an animal."[119]

The Germans, meanwhile, extended their regime of violence throughout the region—rooting out Bolsheviks and confining or murdering millions of Jews, prisoners of war, and suspected partisans. But for all their efforts, they could not extinguish the sparks of resistance that lit up at the start of the occupation.

HAMBURG–MINSK

The rescue of Jews from Minsk was for the most part undertaken by men and women who were involved with Communist underground networks or shared in the Soviet faith. By contrast, those in the ghetto who lacked such contacts, or shunned the Communists, were doomed. This was the fate of the so-called Hamburg Jews. In October 1941, Himmler ordered twenty-five thousand German Jews deported to Minsk. General Walter Braemer, the Wehrmacht commander who would be responsible for receiving them, protested vigorously, warning that the Jews of Belorussia were the "driving force" behind the Bolshevik resistance. If they joined ranks with the German Jews, whom Braemer thought to be intellectually superior to their Belorussian brethren, security in the occupied lands would be further imperiled. In the end, Braemer's protests were partly successful; only seven of the planned twenty-five transports were sent to Minsk in November.[120] But the general's worry was unfounded: The German and the Soviet Jews would never team up.

The Hamburg Jews, as all Jewish arrivals from the Reich came to be called because the first transport had come from Hamburg, were settled in an enclosed area within the ghetto.[121] From the start, they were given preferential treatment in the form of larger food rations and less grueling work. As soon as officials on the ground learned that Ukrainian policemen in the ghetto were pilfering the possessions of the Reich Jews, they ordered the German section of the ghetto to be patrolled by German security.[122] Shortly after the delivery of a transport from Berlin, an SD officer showed up to greet the new ghetto residents. He asked where they came from and how they were feeling, before telling them with pride that his men had killed twenty-eight thousand local Jews to make room for the transports from Germany.[123] Wilhelm Kube, Commissar-General in White Ruthenia and the top German official in Minsk, repeatedly made a point of distinguishing between German and Soviet ghetto residents. The new arrivals from Germany were "human beings who come from our cultural sphere"; they had almost nothing in common with the "native bestial hordes."[124] Many Hamburg Jews appeared to share Kube's views. On the eve of their deportation, some had been told that they would become settlers in the Eastern colonies.[125] But when their train pulled into Minsk, the doors were yanked open, and SS men speaking Latvian and Russian cracked their whips as they proceeded to pull out the human freight. The sight of the poverty and squalor in the Russian ghetto was shocking.[126] Its effect was to reinforce existing stereotypes about the "Eastern Jews" that circulated among German Jews as well.

The authorities in Minsk tried to restrict all contact between the two populations, but German and Soviet Jews came together at workplaces outside the ghetto. It was there that Smolar and other underground workers attempted to draw the Hamburg Jews into their resistance efforts. They told the new arrivals about the November action and tried to explain that the Germans were planning to kill all the Jews. They also shared their plans for escape to the forest. But their overtures were rebuffed. The German Jews did not believe themselves to be in danger, and joining the resistance, they felt, would unnecessarily anger the authorities. "That's for the Eastern Jews, not for us," Smolar summarized their attitude.[127] The two groups were also marked differently. The Reich Jews wore yellow Stars of David with the word "Jude" inscribed onto the star, whereas the inmates of the Russian ghetto wore a yellow patch on their chests and backs.[128] But the differences between them extended far beyond these markings. The Jews from Minsk were stunned when they first saw the arrivals from the Reich dressed in elegant coats and dresses.[129] These newcomers, in their reading, were Germans and capitalists. The German Jews, for their part, looked down on the locals as "Easterners" and held them responsible for the German policy of mass murder. As the two sides appraised each other, neither of them recognized a fellow Jew. "They didn't like us, and we—we didn't like them much either," a Soviet survivor remembered.[130]

When the SS carried out the March 2, 1942, massacre, Kube shielded the Hamburg Jews, and they were left untouched. Days later, Heydrich flew to Minsk to reprimand Kube for his irresponsible behavior and force him back in line.[131] The reprimand was effective; the largest "action" in the Minsk Ghetto began on July 28, 1942, and continued for four days. Four gas trucks and thirty other trucks were in use nonstop. Except for a contingent of male workers, all the Hamburg Jews who had survived up to that point were ordered to pack their belongings and get ready for relocation. According to Soviet eyewitnesses, they wore Sunday clothes and carried umbrellas as they were led into the gas vans. Women entered first, followed by men, as was their custom in normal times.[132]

On July 31, the final day of the killings, Kube sent his superior, Reich Commissar Hinrich Lohse, a letter with the subject heading: "Struggle against partisans and Jewish action in General Region White Ruthenia." He had clearly taken to heart Heydrich's warning about the folly of differentiating between German and Eastern Jews. Kube informed Lohse that it was now evident to him that the partisan movement was composed of both types of Jews, along with Polish resistance fighters and Red Army soldiers. Thus, all the Jews in the region had to be treated according to political, rather than economic, considerations. In White Ruthenia, thanks to the "outstandingly diligent" work of the security forces, fifty-five thousand Jews had been killed in ten weeks, including ten thousand Jews in Minsk on July 28 and 29. The eighty-six hundred Jews who remained alive in the ghetto, Kube noted, did indispensable work for the railroad and arms factories.[133] Elsewhere in his domain, only seven thousand Jews would be left once the mass killings currently under way were completed: "The danger of the partisans being able to rely on Jewry in the future will then no longer exist. For me and the SD, it would naturally be most desirable to eliminate Jewry in General Region White Ruthenia altogether—once the Wehrmacht's economic claims have been satisfied."[134]

Mass killings in the ghetto were put on hold for more than a year following the July massacre, but the Germans continued to conduct targeted raids to disrupt the citywide resistance movement.[135] Khasya Pruslina described one such "political pogrom": "If they knew there was a Communist in a building, they would shoot not only everybody in the building but also everyone on the entire block. A Jewish woman lived at Kollektornaya Street 18. She was working as a doctor and under suspicion. Some Resistance people lived in an apartment in the same building. The Germans came to the building, read out a list, and demanded the handover of six people, Communists. Then they killed seventy-two people in that building and two others. They broke into the buildings using grenades, chased everyone out onto the street, made them lie down, and then killed them. When they shot at the female doctor, she pressed her child so tightly to her body that after they'd been killed they couldn't be separated, and so they were buried that way. The entire street was covered in blood. To the Germans, the ghetto was the 'breeding ground of the bandit contagion,' as they would say."[136]

Such actions wiped out almost the entire underground, but still the resistance did not let up, confounding the Germans.[137] On the night of September 22, 1943, Kube was killed in an explosion inside his heavily guarded private residence in Minsk. Soviet partisans had planted a bomb underneath his bed. In retaliation, Hitler ordered the killing of a thousand residents of Minsk.[138] The victims were taken from the camp on Shirokaya Street and shot. One month later, the SS and local police raided the ghetto one final time. This time, the goal was to kill all the remaining ghetto inhabitants. Only a handful survived.

Chapter 6

MOSCOW STRIKES BACK

A distraught letter reached the Moscow office of a Communist magazine in January 1941. Its author, a low-level propagandist in the Donbas region of Ukraine, was frustrated by the chilly reception he'd gotten since the USSR had signed the nonaggression pact with Germany over a year earlier. As an "agitator," it was his job to spread the party's political message to the masses. For the past twenty-nine years, he had burned with the "passion of a Bolshevik," lecturing to coal miners in the area. They had always been receptive to his views and eager to listen. But the carters he had recently been assigned to were of a different caliber: sly peasant folk who evaded his invitations to discuss current events. When he pressed them, they said they did not want to end up in an NKVD prison. For all his efforts, the most he was able to get them to do was to ask questions about current events. The questions they put to him, however, were so challenging that he forwarded seventy-seven of them to *Sputnik agitatora* (*The Agitator's Companion*), asking the editors for advice in responding. Many of the questions touched on international politics, and the Soviet Union's relations with Nazi Germany in particular:

- Why hasn't our press scolded the fascists since the autumn of 1939?

- Why don't the German Communists take Hitler and Goebbels by the throat, or are they licking Hitler's heels now?
- Why is there not enough food, fodder, and goods in the USSR? Or are they now sending Hitler everything?
- Does Hitler really love the USSR, or is he double-dealing? Tell us the truth!
- What if there's a war and all the countries attack the Bolsheviks? Who'll be in power in the USSR then, and will the Soviet Union still be around?[1]

The man from the Donbas was not alone. Propagandists across the country struggled for answers in the wake of the pact with Hitler. The writer and *Izvestiya* correspondent Ilya Ehrenburg was in Paris when he learned of it. The news threw him into a deep depression; he lost forty pounds. From Paris, Ehrenburg witnessed the German invasion of France in June 1940. Jewish, but with diplomatic immunity, he was able to pack up and leave. He crossed Germany by train, stopping in Berlin. The hotel where he spent the night had a sign on the door that read: "No Jews Allowed." Ehrenburg was sure that war was imminent. Back in Moscow, he was told not to mention this in print, but he was soon proven correct.[2]

The invasion of June 22, 1941, dealt the Soviet Union a devastating blow. More than three million Red Army soldiers were killed or captured by the end of the year. By 1942, an estimated sixty-five million Soviet people, almost a third of the prewar population, lived under German occupation. Soviet clothing production had fallen by half, and agricultural output by three-fifths since 1940. Most Soviet citizens worked eleven-hour shifts six days a week and lived below subsistence level. The war's impact on Soviet living standards was extreme, far exceeding that felt anywhere else in Europe.[3] But for all the deprivations and misery, the war breathed new life into the embattled Stalinist order.

The Nazis' stated aim was to wipe out Communism, which they believed was what millions of Soviet citizens wished for. Yet the ruthlessness of the Nazi onslaught had the unintended effect of strengthening support for the Bolshevik system. Soviet propagandists seized on the

German war of annihilation to build a moral case for their own war effort. Writers dispatched as war reporters to the front lines of the fight against the "barbaric" invaders sent back disturbing accounts of an enemy whose lethal designs were all too clear: Hitler was intent on exterminating everyone who backed the Soviet order. German military orders, diaries, and photographs, found by Red Army soldiers on the battlefield or in the pockets of captured or killed enemy soldiers, left no question about the Nazis' murderous aims. As shocking as they were credible, these documents circulated widely in the Soviet press, giving the mobilization effort tremendous support. Outraged Soviet readers vowed to defeat the hated invader. Recruits who had initially disliked Stalin or were reluctant to fight were stirred into action. Ilya Ehrenburg was one of the first to sense the war's moral calling. The minute he heard of Germany's attack, he wrote a column that predicted: "Our holy war, the war the invaders have thrust upon us, will be a war of liberation for enslaved Europe." The piece was published the next day.[4] Electrified, the insomniac Ehrenburg would not stop writing throughout the course of the war.

Stalin thought war with Hitler was inevitable. In March 1941, he ordered TASS, the central news agency, to compile a secret anti-Nazi propaganda dossier. It quickly filled up with reports of German atrocities pouring in from Poland and Yugoslavia, material that would prove useful once the gestures of false friendship had run their course.[5] In April, Stalin called up Ehrenburg, telling him to sharpen his anti-fascist pen.[6] Yet despite these preparations, Stalin failed to anticipate the actual attack on June 22. He did not think that Germany would go to war against the Soviet Union before finishing off Great Britain. And he believed that Britain, fighting alone against Germany, would do anything to provoke a conflict between Hitler and the Soviet Union. So, when Soviet undercover agents reported on Germany's invasion preparations, he dismissed their missives as British disinformation.[7]

When the assault began, Stalin was stunned. The task of informing the public fell to his deputy, Viacheslav Molotov. On the radio, he was introduced by the Soviet Jewish announcer Yuri Levitan, whose solemn and sonorous baritone would, over the course of the war, become the voice of the state for millions of Soviet listeners: "Attention, this is Moscow speaking! We are broadcasting an important government communiqué. Citizens of the Soviet Union! Today at four a.m., without any kind of declaration of war, the German armed forces attacked the borders of the Soviet Union." Molotov then spoke, invoking history and morality as the greatest weapons in the Soviet arsenal. This was not the first time that the peoples who made up the Soviet Union had been forced to repel an "arrogant foe." In Russia's Patriotic War of 1812, Napoleon had suffered defeat and met his doom. Likewise, the present "Patriotic War," fought "for our country, for honor, for liberty," would spell the demise of the fascist aggressor. "Our cause is just," Molotov proclaimed. "Victory will be ours."[8]

The following day, *Pravda* dubbed the new war the "Great Patriotic War of the Soviet People," to underscore its outsize order of magnitude. The term was coined by Bolshevik party historian Yemelyan Yaroslavsky, and it would quickly establish itself as the official name for the Soviet Union's war against Nazi Germany.[9]

Stalin did not speak to the nation until July 3. It was the first public radio address he had given in over two years. He spoke calmly but bluntly. He told the Soviet people that this was not an ordinary war between two armies, but a "life-and-death struggle for the Soviet state and the peoples of the USSR." To stop the Germans, everything of value that might fall into their hands—machines, fuel, food—"must be destroyed without fail." Soviet citizens whose land was overrun by the Nazis were to fight as partisans to render life "unbearable for the enemy."[10]

Stalin's address was also pleading and emotional, in ways that startled his listeners. A soldier stationed in the rear carefully recorded what he heard on the radio: "'Comrades, citizens, brothers and sisters, soldiers of the Red Army and sailors of the Red Navy, I am addressing you,' Com. Stalin began his speech this morning. He said 'comrades' as usual, 'citizens' more softly, and when he pronounced 'brothers and sisters' his voice trembled, it felt as if a spasm gripped his throat, his voice became tremulous, it seems tears had sprung from his eyes. A decanter clinked against a glass, and you could hear the pouring of water. There was a pause while he drank the water. Over the course of a ninety-minute speech, he drank four glasses of water."[11]

NKVD informants reported that most of the Soviet population felt invigorated by Stalin's words but noted exceptions: A lawyer was quoted as saying, "Our government missed the German offensive on the first day of the war, and that led to colossal losses in aviation and human resources." An office worker said, "Collapse is inevitable, the loss of Moscow is inevitable. Everything we built over the last twenty-five years, it has all turned out to be a myth. The collapse is obvious in Stalin's speech, in his desperate appeals."[12]

Overall, however, the NKVD report was accurate: Molotov's and Stalin's appeals fell on fertile ground. Even though June 22 was a Sunday, thousands of workers spontaneously went to their factories and offices to pledge loyalty to the government. Reservists reported for military service, alongside crowds of volunteers who had previously been exempted from military service because of age, gender, or occupation. In Leningrad alone, a hundred thousand volunteers reported to the city's military commissariats by the afternoon of June 23; the number more than doubled by week's end.

For more than a decade, the Soviet state had practiced a military-style industrialization campaign, dispatching "shock workers" to the "labor front." Using these established channels, after the attack officials ordered even larger armies of workers to prepare for war. One million Leningraders, more than one-third of the working-age population, dug trenches and built other defensive fortifications in July 1941. The Soviet Army Command formed a total of 109 new divisions that month, composed primarily of reservists and volunteers. Another 78 divisions were created in August. Though German troops wiped out or captured entire Soviet armies during their onslaught, the newly formed Committee of State Defense in Moscow was able to quickly mobilize yet more troops. On August 11, as fighting raged around Smolensk, Stalin, as head of the committee, set out a program to create an additional 85 rifle divisions and 25 cavalry divisions, mandating that the majority of these new troops enter the war by October, and the rest by mid-December.[13]

Stalin was the first leader in World War II to launch a "total war," though he never used the phrase: The quarter-century-long Soviet tradition of mobilizing the population in military style rendered it redundant. There was no "home front" that had to be built in the wartime Soviet Union. The Soviet people in their entirety formed a single army, differentiated only between "front" and "rear" units.

To keep this army inspired and focused, Soviet leaders ordered the media to conceal or minimize Soviet losses. When Minsk fell in late June, the Soviet news bureau (*Sovinformbiuro*) proclaimed victory instead. Readers could deduce the loss of Minsk only from the gradual shift in reporting to battlegrounds farther east. By mid-July, reports omitted city names altogether, replacing them with general locations: "northwestern," "western," "southwestern."[14] Throughout October, Soviet newspapers remained silent about the German attack on Moscow, which had begun early that month. They made no mention of the encirclement and destruction of army groups, let alone of instances of mass desertion or defection to the enemy. Stalin's draconian Order 270, issued in response to the retreat of the Soviet armed forces, denounced as cowards any Soviet soldier who gave himself up to the enemy. It was read out to all the troops but withheld from civilian readers.[15] In the initial months of the campaign, the Red Army lost twenty times as many soldiers as the Germans—a fact that would remain unmentionable long after the war's end.

COMPILING THE RECORD OF GERMAN ATROCITY

When it came to the civilian toll of Germany's war, however, the Soviet media spoke out loudly and for the most part truthfully. Beginning in July 1941, Soviet officials kept a record of the violence Germans perpetrated on Soviet soil. Starting with scraps of paper that preserved the testimony of refugees or the wording of German orders, this collection grew over time into a massive account of overwhelming power. *Red Star*, the daily newspaper of the People's Commissariat for Defense, was one of the first to publicize "German-fascist atrocities" against Soviet civilians. Dated August 10, 1941, the article cited multiple surviving witnesses, including a female member of the City Council of Brest. She described how the Germans rounded up all the city's "Easterners" and deported them with their families to a soccer stadium:

> When they brought me to the stadium, more than a thousand people were already there. They kept us in the open air without food and water. Hungry children were crying. Right in front of everyone who'd been arrested, a German soldier kicked a girl of three or four who'd been crying. Her mother rushed to protect the child, but the fascist hit her in the stomach with the stock of his gun. Several men protested the soldiers' mistreatment of children and women, and the soldiers beat them half to death. Every night drunken fascists burst into the stadium and took away young women by force. Over the course of two nights, German soldiers took away more than 70 women, who disappeared without a trace. The husbands and brothers of these unfortunate women tried to protect them, but the fascists made use of their pistols. Right then and there, the Germans shot about 20 men. On the third day, several officers arrived at the stadium. One of the officers called out names from a list. No fewer than 200 people in all were called out. The Germans lined them up on the north side of the football field and shot them with machine guns. The corpses of those who'd been shot lay in the stadium for three days. After that, the Gestapo men selected another 250–300 people from among the arrested citizens and took them away to an unknown location.[16]

On August 24, *Pravda* printed excerpts from a secret German order spelling out the ruthless terms of the occupation in the East. The order was dated June 15, 1941, proving that the invasion and the cruelty it brought had been carefully planned.[17] In response, Soviet journalists and writers immediately presented their readers with writings and statements from Nazi leaders that exposed them as "twentieth-century Barbarians." One week into the war, Ehrenburg ridiculed the hodgepodge essence of the Nazi race theory: "The fundamental idea of German fascism is the superiority of the German race over other races." But who among the Nazi leaders, Ehrenburg asked sarcastically, embodied the tall and athletic blond Aryan extolled by Germany's racial "experts"? The dark-haired Hitler? Fat Göring? Or Goebbels, who "on the whole barely resembles a human being—German or non-German—a monkey, diminutive in size, ugly and jumpy"? The Germans viewed the Slavs, wrote Ehrenburg, as a "second-rate race, created for toiling the land, for dances or choral songs, but ill-suited for urban culture and for a self-sufficient state existence. Russians, in the words of the fascist 'scientists,' were 'a cross between Mongols and Slavs created for life under the leadership of others.'"[18]

Writer Aleksei Tolstoi drew attention to Hitler's rabid anti-Communism, quoting a "hysterical" speech Hitler had given in a radio broadcast: "Either fascism or Communism . . . I alone am able to crush Communism in Soviet Russia and around the world. Follow me!"[19] Georgy Aleksandrov, head of the Central Committee's Propaganda and Agitation Department (Agitprop), set out to expose Hitler's agenda, citing the memoir of a former Nazi official turned anti-fascist: "War is the natural state of man. . . . If we want to create our great German empire, we must first displace and exterminate the Slavic peoples—Russians, Poles, Czechs, Slovaks, Bulgarians, Ukrainians, Belorussians. As for the Bohemian-Moravian basin, the territories that extend immediately to Germany's east, we will colonize them and expel their populations to Siberia. . . . In fulfilling this goal, my conscience will not suffer for a single second over the death of two or three million Germans. . . . We intend to establish and fortify our dominance so that it lasts at least a thousand years. . . . Our mission is to subjugate these peoples. We Germans are called to give the world a new class of masters."[20]

The granular detail in Soviet public reporting about Nazi Germany, and Ehrenburg's in particular, was remarkable. For instance, in an August 20, 1941, editorial, Ehrenburg cited an obscure article from the German newspaper *Völkischer Beobachter* about plans to reward German soldiers with large landholdings on occupied Soviet soil.[21] Soviet reporting on the enemy was also impressive for its insights into the true nature of the Nazi project. Nazi Germany, Ehrenburg and others concluded, sought global supremacy through an imperialist war. Its "new" or "eternal" order, formed in antithesis to the principles of humanism and international law, consisted of a social pyramid, with a small class of German rulers on the top. These would oversee armies of forced laborers, with those at the very bottom described as "human-machines, human-animals, or 'subhumans,' living in stalls . . . a silent, faceless toiling mass."[22] This was a discerning reading of Nazism, and exposed the ideology's racial animus against Slavs and its political animus against Communists. Yet it remained silent on a defining aspect of Nazi ideology, one that was central to Hitler's fixation on Soviet Communism in the first place.

It wasn't that Jews were left out of Soviet accounts of Germany's war. They did figure, from early on. On June 25, Belorussian party chief Panteleimon Ponomarenko informed Stalin that the German invasion had sparked panic among the Jews in his republic: "An animal fear of Hitler seized them, and instead of a fight, there was flight. All the Germans' agitation, oral and written, advances under the banner of the fight against Jews and Communists, which are synonymous."[23] The August 10 report in *Red Star* that included the account of the city council member from Brest also described the concentration camp that had been set up in Minsk:

> On July 21, the camp commandant forced a large group of Jews to dig foundation ditches. When these were ready, the fascists bound the Jews and threw them into a pit. Then, they ordered the Belorussians in the camp to cover the Jews with earth. All the Belorussians, to a man, flat-out refused to carry out the commandant's monstrous order. The infuriated fascists shot forty-five Jews and thirty Belorussians using machine guns. Every evening, the camp commandant selected people from lists, and in the morning, they shot them.[24]

Many more articles would soon appear in other newspapers, with detailed reports on the mass killing of Jews at Babi Yar, in Kharkov, and elsewhere.[25] But at no point during the war did the genocide of the Jews make nationwide headlines in the Soviet media, for two reasons.

The first had to do with Soviet fears of the power and reach of Nazi propaganda. If Soviet leaders openly acknowledged that the Nazis regarded the Soviet state as fundamentally Jewish, they risked activating scores of covert anti-Semites inside the Soviet Union who might throw their support behind the Nazis. Even though Soviet rulers had been combating anti-Semitism for years, the pressures of war began to pull at the Soviet social fabric and expose the limits of those efforts. Ponomarenko's remark that the Jews of Belorussia had chosen flight over fight was a milder variant of the harsh saying that made the rounds after the outbreak of the war: "Abraham is fighting the Germans from Tashkent," the city in far-flung Uzbekistan to which thousands of Soviet civilians had been relocated.[26] Given the surge of anti-Semitism among their own people, Soviet leaders chose to depict Nazism shorn of its Judeo-Bolshevik obsession. In January 1942, Soviet soldiers found Reichenau's directive, "On the Conduct of the Troops in the East," from October 1941. *Pravda* immediately presented the order in full, describing it as "so monstrous and cynical that all Soviet people and the entire civilized world must know about it."[27] The publication included a legible facsimile of the original order. But readers who knew German could compare the document with the translation prepared by the editors at *Pravda*. Where the German text described the principal aim of the German campaign as smashing the "Jewish Bolshevik system," *Pravda* took out the word "Jewish." On the other hand, the concluding phrase of the order, invoking the "historic task of liberating the German people from the Asiatic-Jewish menace once and for all," was left intact.[28]

The second and more important reason why the Nazis' preoccupation with the Jews did not receive more significant coverage in the Russian press was the Soviet belief in internationalism. The multinational Soviet republic was built on the principles of multiethnic unity. Reasons of state dictated that all Soviet peoples be shown as engaged in the same struggle, though even with this state of equality, there was a hierarchy: Russians, as "elder brothers," took the lead, followed by their Slavic siblings, and then all the others. As a nationality without a union republic bearing their name, Soviet Jews had no prominent place in this assemblage.* The Soviet internationalist creed explained why the *Pravda* editorial accompanying the publication of the Reichenau order described Hitler as seeking to "physically exterminate the Russian people, the Ukrainians, the Belorussians, and all the other peoples inhabiting the Soviet Union," erasing the Jews from the list. The Soviet Jewish tragedy had to be described as a Soviet tragedy.[29] This universalist framing had some justification: The Germans conflated Judaism and Bolshevism, and non-Jewish Communists and suspected partisans were often murdered alongside Jews. But it obscured the fact that Jewish civilians died in much greater numbers than other civilians, and that they were specifically targeted for elimination by the Germans.

Soviet Jewish activists themselves contributed to this obfuscation. For the most part highly urban and secularized, and not conversant with Yiddish or Hebrew, they were the most universalist of all Soviet peoples, since they had no particular republic to call home other than the Union of Soviet Socialist Republics. To rid themselves of negative ascriptions of Jewishness as parochial or self-interested, they sought to represent Soviet Jewish suffering as Soviet suffering writ large.[30] This universalizing thrust even took hold of Soviet Jews who embraced their Jewish identity in response to the German invasion. On August 24, 1941, a group of Soviet Jewish leaders, including Ehrenburg and theater director Solomon Mikhoels, gathered in Moscow to warn their fellow Jews about the mortal threat of Nazism. They proudly identified as Jews. As Ehrenburg declared: "Hitler hates us most of all. And that makes us look good." But they were also at pains to present themselves as Soviet citizens—politically engaged, combative, and ardently selfless—to counteract popular

---

* The Jewish Autonomous Region of Birobidzhan, founded in 1934, was an administrative unit on a much lesser scale than a Soviet Union republic. Moreover, it was officially meant to attract not all Jews living in the Soviet Union, but only those who chose not to assimilate to the Russian Soviet culture. At the peak of its growth, in the early 1940s, the Far Eastern region straddling the Chinese border had a population of fifty thousand. This was but a fraction of the overall Soviet Jewish population. E. R. Abdurazakova, N. V. Martynova, M. M. Udova, and V. V. Martynov, "The History of the Jewish Culture Formation in the Far East of Russia," *AmurCon 2021: International Scientific Conference* 126, *European Proceedings of Social and Behavioural Sciences* (2022): 1–10.

stereotypes of the self-interested and victimized Jew and cast fascism—"the bitterest enemy of all peoples, of all humanity"—as a universal challenge.[31]

Even as the Germans escalated their killing of Soviet Jews in the fall of 1941, others, namely Soviet POWs, who were for the most part non-Jewish, died in even greater numbers during this period. Their plight received ample coverage in the Soviet press from the very beginning of the war. Soldiers who had escaped from captivity reported on mass starvation, torture, and acts of "bestial murder." They described how the Germans used the Soviet prisoners to clear minefields.[32] In addition to documenting Soviet suffering, these press reports urged Red Army soldiers not to even consider surrendering to the Germans, warning that captivity inevitably meant unbearable suffering followed by a terrible death. DEATH IN BATTLE IS A THOUSAND TIMES BETTER THAN FASCIST CAPTIVITY! one headline roared.[33] On November 25, 1941, Molotov sent an official note about the fate of the Soviet POWs to all the governments with which the Soviet Union had diplomatic relations. The lengthy document listed dozens of cases of abuse and murder discovered along the entire Soviet-German front line. It referred to German decrees ordering that Soviet POWs be given less and lower-quality food than POWs from other nations, and cited harrowing reports of starvation from multiple camps. The Germans, Molotov concluded, are pursuing "the mass extermination of Soviet prisoners of war." Their behavior was a "Barbarian transgression" of the "elementary norms regulating international law," including the 1907 Hague Convention on Warfare, which was recognized by both Germany and the Soviet Union.[34]

Molotov's note barely registered in the countries to which it was addressed, but it was attentively studied by Joseph Goebbels.[35] As Goebbels saw it, the response had been so tepid because other governments knew the Bolsheviks had blood on their own hands, and so were not inclined to believe their accusations. Moreover, Goebbels in his diary cast doubt on the atrocities that Molotov had listed, suggesting that the Soviets were spreading lies in a desperate attempt to stem the flood of Red Army soldiers defecting to the Germans.[36] Goebbels had a trump card up his sleeve. On November 27, two days after Molotov's note had been dispatched, the propaganda minister presented "Georgy Molotov," the Soviet foreign minister's only son, to the international press corps in Berlin, to refute his father's claims. Molotov Jr., who had been captured near Vyazma in October, read a statement saying that he was being well treated. A German official then read passages from Molotov Sr.'s note describing acts of torture performed on Soviet prisoners and asked Georgy Molotov whether he had witnessed anything like that. Smiling, the prisoner shook his head: "I have not seen any such scenes, nor heard them reported by others."[37] *The New York Times* presented this story uncritically and at length, to Goebbels's great satisfaction.[38] The Kremlin issued a swift rebuttal, declaring that the Soviet foreign minister had no son and denouncing the revelations of the press conference as shameless fabrications, but their protests went largely unnoticed.[39] Well into fall 1941, Western commentators gave more coverage and credibility to Goebbels than to his Soviet opponents.

Molotov did not, in fact, have a son. The Germans had been deceived by a Red Army chauffeur fighting for his own survival. His name was Vasily Tarasov. When Tarasov was captured and saw how cruelly the Germans dealt with the prisoners, he presented himself to his captors as Lieutenant Georgy Vyacheslavovich Skriabin, son of Viacheslav Skriabin, otherwise known by his revolutionary pseudonym, Molotov, or "the hammer." Months later, after the Germans captured a Soviet officer who said he was Molotov's nephew, and after both alleged relatives of the foreign minister were submitted to a joint interrogation, Tarasov's cover was blown. But by that time, the photograph of "Georgy Molotov" had appeared on thousands of leaflets dropped over enemy trenches, with the impostor's inflammatory appeal to Red Army soldiers to defect to the German side. Tarasov also spoke on Germany's Russian language radio program, which aired throughout Eastern Europe, and his words were translated into Ukrainian as well. The note from his "father," he declared, was a desperate lie cooked up by a regime that knew no other way to motivate its soldiers. The Germans did not kill their Russian prisoners. "I am alive, you hear my voice . . . let me tell you how the workers and peasants really live in Germany. You don't know, because for the last twenty-four years the Jews and Bolsheviks have blinded you to the reality, just as I was blinded."[40]

ON THE BRINK

The Soviet war effort, and with it the survival of the Soviet state, hung in the balance in fall 1941. Vasily Tarasov was just one of 660,000 Soviet soldiers captured during the German advance on Moscow. The few German soldiers who fell into Soviet hands arrogantly predicted that the Wehrmacht would parade in Moscow in time for the Soviet revolutionary holiday in November.[41] On the night of October 14, the Germans broke through the defensive line protecting the western approach to Moscow. They were now less than sixty miles away from the capital's outskirts. The next morning, Soviet leaders ordered the immediate evacuation of most of the government to the rear, while preparing factories, offices, and warehouses for destruction. Thousands of desperate Muscovites thronged the train stations. Cordoned off from public view was a special train waiting to take Stalin and his retinue to the Urals. Ultimately, Stalin decided to stay. Against the advice of his generals, who feared German aerial attacks, he ordered his staff to proceed with preparations for the customary November 7 parade on Red Square.[42]

On the evening of November 6, Stalin addressed the Moscow City Council in Mayakovsky Station, the deepest of Moscow's new subway stations. The radio broadcast the address to millions of listeners. Speaking with what a witness described as a "strange mixture of black gloom and complete self-confidence," Stalin conceded that the enemy had reached the gates of Leningrad and Moscow. Nonetheless, he pointed out, Germany's Blitzkrieg had failed, for Hitler had banked on reaching the Urals by August.[43] The Germans had also failed to gauge the political strength of the Soviet system; the fighting power of the Red Army; and the ability of Great Britain, the United States, and the Soviet Union to form a united front. In its most probing sections, Stalin's speech denounced Nazism's moral depravity (though he did not speak of Nazism per se, instead using the terms "Hitlerism" and "fascism" interchangeably). "Hitler says, 'I liberate man from the degrading chimera called conscience. The conscience, as well as education, cripple man. I have the advantage of not being constrained by any theoretical or moral concerns whatsoever.'"[44] The moral degradation of the German invader, Stalin concluded, rendered their final defeat inevitable.

Stalin also quoted from a directive found on the body of a lieutenant from Frankfurt am Main: "You have no heart and nerves; they are not needed in war. Destroy the pity and compassion within you—kill every Russian, Soviet, don't hesitate if you have an old man or woman, girl or boy before you—kill, you will save yourself from death, ensure your family's future, and gain renown for the ages." The German invaders, Stalin explained, were waging a "war of annihilation against the peoples of the USSR." This, along with a pointed reference to the Nazis' "medieval pogroms against the Jews," was as close as Stalin came to acknowledging Germany's intent to eradicate the Jews. In turn, Stalin called on all people of the USSR to destroy the German occupiers and to remember: "Our cause is just—victory will be ours!"[45]

Stalin spoke again the next morning, standing atop the Lenin Mausoleum and addressing a parade of troops who either had come from the front or were on the way there. The time of the parade had been changed to deceive the Germans, but in any event, Stalin ordered that it not be halted should enemy planes attack.[46] Red Army fighter jets patrolled the skies, and the sound of artillery fire rolled in from the distance. Stalin's speech was broadcast over the radio and thus addressed to every participant in the Soviet war effort, including the "brothers and sisters in occupied territory, who have temporarily fallen under the yoke of the German bandits." He began by reminding everyone of the conflict's stakes: "The whole world is looking at you, for it is you who can destroy the marauding armies of the German invader. The enslaved peoples of Europe look upon you as their liberators. . . . Be worthy of your mission."[47] The Soviet war effort, he said, amounted to a defense of humanity against an invader with no moral compass. Stalin's rousing words and his display of fortitude within range of enemy fire had an effect comparable to that of Churchill's signature addresses.[48] Overall, Germany's brutal and unrestrained approach to war gave Stalin's rule broader legitimacy than it had ever enjoyed before. As the fight continued, millions of Soviet citizens ardently rallied behind a leader who had previously been more feared than loved. Throughout the war, Red Army soldiers went into combat shouting "For the Motherland, for Stalin!"—words that perfectly expressed how Soviet Communist values had blended with the new patriotic idiom.

Some listeners had questions about Stalin's speeches. On November 8, David Ortenberg, editor in chief of *Red Star,* received an urgent phone call from the Kremlin. Foreign journalists had asked to see the military directive found on the body of the officer from Frankfurt, which *Red Star* had published in its October 29 issue and Stalin had then cited.[49] The caller from the Kremlin ordered the newspaper to turn over the original document. As it turned out, the excerpts published in the paper had been wired by a reporter stationed near Leningrad. After a frantic search, the correspondent was located, but *sans* directive. He had returned it to the Political Department of the division with which he had been embedded, but the division could no longer be reached—it had perhaps been wiped out in the interim.[50]

The document has not been found to the present day, and it is widely believed to have been a forgery.[51] While possible, such an outright fabrication would not have been in keeping with the high standards the Soviet press generally adhered to in tracing the bloody trail of Germany's actions. The wording of the directive was consistent with many other German documents from summer and fall 1941, including Himmler's instruction to drive "Jew women" (*Judenweiber*) into the swamps, Keitel's Communist order, and the letters that Anton Roos and Walter Mattner sent to their wives. In any event, the botched case taught Soviet editors a lesson: It was imperative to preserve, and publish, the originals. This was likely why, two months later, *Pravda* featured the facsimile of Reichenau's order, along with the slightly altered Russian translation.

BATTLE FOR MOSCOW

The month of November saw a huge buildup of Soviet defenses. Many of the nearly one hundred divisions that had been formed after Stalin's August 11 order were consolidated into six new armies and tasked with repelling the German offensive against Moscow. Some of these divisions had been stationed in Eastern Siberia, but were ordered back to Moscow when Soviet agents stationed in Tokyo reported that Japan was preoccupied with preparations for an imminent attack on the U.S. Fleet in Pearl Harbor and therefore unlikely to strike out against the USSR in the near term. The scale of the deployment around Moscow amounted to the creation of a new Red Army. Despite the catastrophic losses suffered during the first months of Barbarossa, the Soviet military in November 1941 fielded 3.4 million soldiers and close to 2,000 tanks at the front. Soviet forces remained critically short of ammunition and armor—the war economy would not kick into full gear until early 1942—but the mobilization of manpower was extraordinary, far surpassing that of the Germans.[52]

The Soviet counteroffensive on December 5 delivered the Wehrmacht its first major defeat in World War II. Four Soviet armies combined forces to charge head-on against the enemy. Red Army ski and cavalry units advanced rapidly in the deep snow and surprised the exhausted German soldiers in positions that were not yet winter-proof. Hitler ordered his men to hold out "fanatically," but according to the German army leadership, the troops, who were accustomed to lightning-fast advances experienced a kind of "psychosis, almost a panic . . . Everywhere soldiers are retreating, without supplies, freezing, bewildered." By early January 1942, the German front line had been pushed back more than 150 miles from Moscow. Despite the chaos, Wehrmacht commanders found time to order that all settlements along the line of retreat be turned into "desert zones."[53] Villages recaptured by the Red Army presented scenes of utter destruction. Only groups of bare chimneys testified that humans had once lived there.

A team of cameramen headed by the Russian Jewish filmmaker Roman

Karmen was with the Red Army when it liberated the town of Volokolamsk, sixty miles west of Moscow, on December 21. The newsreel compiled from their footage shows trucks filled with Red Army men entering the town, past cheering residents. Soldiers distribute newspapers to the population, and posters go up on the building walls, celebrating Communist leaders and exhorting the population to join the partisan struggle. The silent film then cuts to the town square. A Red Army commander standing on a tank addresses a crowd of local people. Behind the commander is a crossbeam suspended between a birch tree and a telegraph pole. Dangling from the crossbeam are eight bodies, six men and two women—victims of the Nazis. People in the crowd look shaken, some cry.[54]

When David Ortenberg, along with several writers and photographer Aleksandr Kapustiansky, arrived in Volokolamsk later that day, the meeting was over, and the bodies had been taken down. Ortenberg remembered one of the two girls lying in the snow with her eyes wide open. "Having removed our hats, we honored the memory of these defenders of the Motherland. And right then and there, we decided to tell the entire world what we had seen here with our own eyes."[55] A week later, a *Pravda* correspondent reporting from Volokolamsk was able to

A Red Army commander addresses the townspeople of Volokolamsk, December 21, 1941.

identify three of the victims: Ivan Tikhonov, a cabinetmaker and card-carrying Communist, and two male agronomy students. One of the two young women was called Nina. Led by Tikhonov, the group had been caught as it sought to join the partisans. The Germans let their victims hang for multiple days as a deterrent to others. A placard was hung on one of the bodies: "This is what we do to everyone who gets in our way."[56]

Also in late December, *Pravda* reporter Pyotr Lidov was dispatched to the recently liberated town of Mozhaisk, forty miles south of Volokolamsk. Stopping at a peasant hut, Lidov heard an old man tell the story of a young female partisan who was executed by the Germans in the nearby village of Petrishchevo. "They hanged her, but she gave a speech!" he kept saying. Intrigued, Lidov ventured to Petrishchevo. He interviewed the villagers for days on end, and while they confirmed the hanging, no one could say anything about the girl beyond the fact that her name was Tanya. In Moscow, Lidov was able to consult the secret files of the Red Army's intelligence unit that trained Komsomol volunteers for sabotage missions behind enemy lines. He found several women by the name of Tanya, but no mention of Petrishchevo, and the women looked older than the descriptions given by the peasants. Back in Petrishchevo, Lidov asked to see "Tanya's" body. Locals directed him to a ditch. Snow and a thin layer of earth covered parts of her body. The rope was still strung around her neck. Tanya's shirt was torn, exposing her chest. One of her breasts had been cut off. Tanya's face did not match the photos that Lidov had been shown in Moscow. He decided to use *Pravda* as a platform to try to identify the young woman. Photographer Sergei Strunnikov, who had accompanied Lidov to Petrishchevo, took a close-up of "Tanya's" head and mutilated chest.[57]

In a departure from the Soviet tradition of not depicting nude bodies, *Pravda* published Strunnikov's photograph alongside Lidov's essay, which was simply entitled "Tanya." The essay presented Lidov's findings: One evening in early December 1941, German troops stationed in Petrishchevo had apprehended a partisan who was attempting to set houses and a stable on fire.[58] To their surprise, the arsonist turned out to be a young woman. Subjected to interrogation, she refused to divulge any

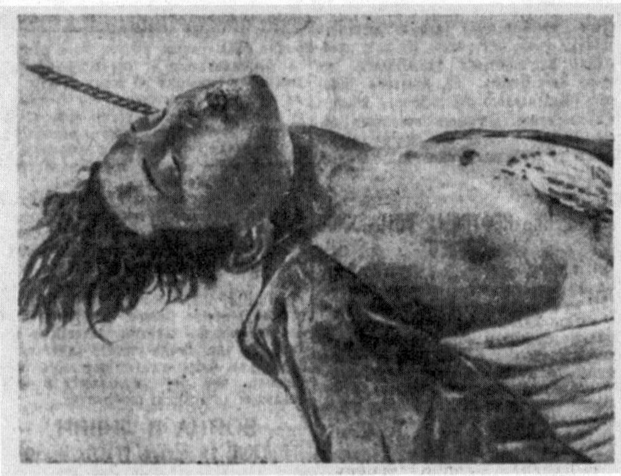

"The body of the Komsomolka Partisan Tatyana, who was bestially tortured and hanged by the Hitlerite bandits in the village of Petrishchevo, Vereisky district, Moscow region. Photograph: S. Strunnikov," Pravda, *January 27, 1942.*

information about who she was and who had sent her, bravely enduring thrashings with a belt. A German officer taunted her: "Tell me, where is Stalin?" "Stalin is at his post," she replied. The next morning, she was led to her death. A large group of German soldiers had gathered in front of a gallows erected in the village center. Residents were forced to watch the execution. The girl had to wear a sign saying "Partisan." In the final moments of her life, she addressed the Germans: "You'll hang me now, but I'm not alone. There are two hundred million of us, you're not going to be able to hang us all. Others will avenge me." Turning to the village residents, the girl exclaimed: "Farewell, comrades! Fight! Fear not! Stalin is with us! Stalin will come!" Her body was reportedly left hanging for weeks. On New Year's Eve, a group of drunken soldiers cut the rope and mutilated the girl's body. She lay there for a day before orders were given to take down the gallows and dispose of her remains in a ditch.[59]

Lidov's account was mostly accurate, but he altered some aspects of the young partisan's execution to make it fit the official requirements of unity and strength in the Soviet defense effort. During his interviews with the villagers of Petrishchevo, the journalist must have learned that

"Tanya" was actually apprehended by the Russian village elder, who had been put on guard after the young partisan had burned several houses in the same village the night before. The elder delivered her to the Germans and received a bottle of vodka in compensation. Lidov also left unmentioned that several of the villagers deeply resented the partisan for setting fire to their houses. One local woman was brought to the interrogation and given permission to beat "Tanya" and empty a bucket of dirty water over her head. The next day, when the partisan was brought to the gallows, another woman hit her with a stick. But for Lidov, it was imperative to present the entire village as victimized by the Germans. The residents of Petrishchevo were nevertheless interrogated by the NKVD in the following months, and two women were sentenced to death. Their story remained a secret throughout Soviet times.[60]

Lidov and his editors at *Pravda* also did not convey "Tanya's" final words with total accuracy. A fact-finding commission from the Moscow Komsomol organization, which had recruited and trained several thousand young saboteurs, visited Petrishchevo in early February in an effort to establish the girl's identity. Villagers who spoke with the commission confirmed that she had addressed her onlookers as she was being led to her execution. But their account of her speech was somewhat different: "Citizens! Don't stand around and watch, help us with the fight!" Even as a German officer threatened to hit her, she continued: "Comrades, victory will be ours! German soldiers, surrender before it's too late!" At the execution site, she reportedly stepped onto the box that stood below the gallows on her own. As the noose was laid around her neck she shouted: "You'll hang me now, but I'm not alone. There are one hundred seventy million of us, you're not going to be able to hang us all. Comrades will avenge me."[61] At that moment, a German kicked the box away, strangling her. Notably, her speech did not mention Stalin, although villagers confirmed she had said that Stalin was at his post, in response to the German officer. They also added one other salient detail that Lidov's report had not included: Scores of Germans formed a wide circle around the gallows and snapped pictures of the young woman. An officer turned her around several times to allow the photographers to get the best shot.

The Komsomol officials from Moscow had brought photos of a young female partisan who had disappeared in the Petrishchevo area. The villagers recognized her as the woman executed by the Germans. Her name, the commission informed the villagers, was not Tanya but Zoya Kosmodemyanskaya.[62] Even before the Komsomol commission was able to publicize its findings, the story of the young partisan spread like wildfire throughout Soviet society. Shortly after its publication in *Pravda*, Lidov's article was read out over the radio. The female announcer fought back tears as she told of the partisan girl who endured torture without divulging information and went to her death unbroken.[63] A listener called in and identified herself as Liubov Kosmodemyanskaya, "Tanya's" mother. On February 16, Zoya Kosmodemyanskaya was declared a Hero of the Soviet Union, the highest Soviet award. Her mother addressed Soviet youth over the radio, pleading with her listeners to avenge her daughter. She shared memories of the tram station where Zoya bid her farewell: "I still hear her proud and joyful voice: 'I'll come back a hero or die a hero. Don't you despair, mother.' And she smiled. I never saw her again."[64] On February 18, Lidov published a follow-up feature entitled, "Who Was Tanya?" It traced Zoya's path from a schoolgirl and Komsomol activist who kept a notebook in which she recorded aphorisms by Tolstoy and Kutuzov, Goethe and Mayakovsky, to a fighter behind enemy lines. "News of this brave girl-fighter," Lidov stated, "is spreading by word of mouth in villages liberated from the Nazis. Warriors on the front are dedicating their verses and the volleys they fire at the enemy to her. Memory of her instills new strength in the people."[65]

Lidov was not exaggerating: Letters poured in from everywhere. "We, the Soviet people," a history student wrote, "still have much to endure. And if it gets difficult, I'll read this sad story again and look at the beautiful, courageous face of this female partisan." Komsomol activists pledged to be "like Zoya": "I beg you to send me into the ranks of the Red Army, now that I've completed my nursing course," a twenty-year-old woman wrote to the Komsomol. "I just learned about 'Tanya' Kosmodemyanskaya the *partizanka* and how, like a true *komsomolka*, she showed her heroism. I, too, am a *komsomolka* prepared to sacrifice my life, and I cannot wait another minute." Mothers wrote to Liubov, expressing admiration for how she raised a heroine; soldiers on the front line shouted vows of revenge.[66]

Everywhere in the recently liberated villages and towns, Soviet activists set out to gather data on the German occupation. Some of the earliest reports were collected in an official "note about German atrocities against the Soviet civilian population" that Molotov sent to the Allies on January 6, 1942. While Molotov's 1941 note focused on the abuse of Soviet POWs, this document, almost seven thousand words long, listed multiple acts of assault on ordinary citizens—the multiple acts of humiliation, torture, and mass killings that had been discovered in liberated villages and towns. These deeds, Molotov emphasized, were not the excesses of individual soldiers or units; they represented a "deliberate strategy, devised beforehand and encouraged by the German Government and German Command. . . . No German is held responsible for the murder of a Soviet citizen, however senseless it may be." The note ended with a warning: "The Soviet people will never forget the brutalities, violence, devastation, and humiliation which the bestial German invaders inflicted and continue to inflict on the peaceful population of our country. They will not forget or forgive."

The most thorough documentary work during this first phase of the liberation was the oral history project mentioned in the early pages of this book. Headed by Professor Isaak Mints, a group of Moscow historians, accompanied by stenographers, traveled throughout the newly liberated areas to interview witnesses. By war's end, they would produce upward of a thousand transcripts, invaluable primary sources for a planned history of the Great Patriotic War.[67] Virtually every survivor they spoke to shared memories of the Germans' "beastly" deeds. The chairman of a kolkhoz, or collective farm, in the Tula region south of Moscow detailed the violence he had recorded:

> In the village of L'govo, thirty-five Red Army prisoners of war were burnt to death in a barn. At the Khrushchevo collective farm, Kolia Efremov was shot because he left his home after 4:00 p.m. They shot a thirteen-year-old boy! In the villages of

> Shakhovo, Isakovo, Rodionovo, and Lavrushkino, twenty-five people were hanged or shot. In the village of Glinishcha, two sisters were shot, Vera Sergeevna and Yevdokiya Sergeevna. The reason is unclear.[68]

A forty-year-old female kolkhoz worker described how the Germans entered her village on November 21, 1941, and arrested her son, believing him to be a partisan. Only after the rout of the Germans did she discover her son's body, near a village that the enemy had burned to the ground. The Germans also took her cow. The woman ended the interview with a vow to rebuild the kolkhoz, a task not made easier by the fact that the Red Army had helped itself to the few good horses that remained in the village. Though the woman mentioned the appropriated horses, the fight against the hated invaders was the overriding imperative: "We women like to say that if the German comes, we will take our pitchforks and confront him. I will tear any German to pieces after seeing how they stabbed my son eighteen times and left him there to die."[69]

Agitprop Chief Aleksandrov quickly grasped the stirring effect of survivor stories. He dispatched groups of peasant witnesses who had lived under occupation to participate in speaking tours that traveled to factories and mines in the Urals and Siberia. Their "simple, heartfelt

Residents of Istra (near Moscow) after liberation, 1941.

words" were particularly effective in "showing the beastly face of German fascism" and "reinforcing hatred toward the German invaders." Seized by loathing, audiences vowed to work tirelessly to contribute to the war effort, as did the speakers. One group of five individuals, for instance, was said to have given 316 speeches, reaching a total of seventy-one thousand listeners over twenty-two days.[70]

While remaining focused on deterring the German forces massed near Moscow, the Red Army also attacked in the south, liberating Rostov on December 2 and the Kerch peninsula on December 31, both places where there had been significant prewar Jewish populations before the war.[71] On January 2, 1942, a group of Soviet photographers landed on an airstrip in Kerch. Nearby they saw weeping residents wandering along rows of corpses that had been dug up from a trench and were now lying on the frozen ground. One of the photographers first thought these were the bodies of Red Army soldiers or POWs. But the dead were wearing civilian clothing, and they included many small children. He realized he was bearing witness to a crime even more damning than those that had been revealed during the liberation of the towns and villages around Moscow. The photographers had happened to land near a long anti-tank ditch at the outskirts of the village of Bagerovo, the very spot where the Germans had brought thousands of Jews from Kerch to be shot.[72] Twenty of the photographs taken on January 2 instantly found their way into wall newspapers ("TASS Windows") put up throughout Kerch. They were arranged below screaming headlines: "DEATH TO THE GERMAN OCCUPIERS!" "7,000 MURDERED, AND THEY DIDN'T SPARE OLD PEOPLE, WOMEN, OR CHILDREN." "TAKE REVENGE, PITILESS REVENGE, ON THE FASCIST MURDERERS!"

The Russian Jewish poet and war reporter Ilya Selvinsky, who fought with the 51st Army and took part in the liberation of Kerch, shared the shock of his discovery of the murders with readers of *Red Star*. His poem was entitled "I Saw It":

> You don't have to listen to folktales,
>   Or believe what you read in papers,
> I saw it myself. With my own eyes.

Residents of Kerch examine TASS Windows, 1942.

  Do you understand? I saw it. Myself.
The path's here. Over there is the hill.
  Between them,
           running like this,
                     the ditch.
And from out of this ditch anguish lifts.
Anguish without end.
. . .
Who are they? Soldiers? Not soldiers.
Partisans maybe? No.
Here lies lop-eared Kolya—
   Eleven years old.

And here's his whole family.

The poem then described other victims, including "a mutilated Jewess, / A child by her side," before concluding with an urgent appeal:

How terrible it is to write of this.
                   How strange.
  But I must write! I must!
. . .

The ditch . . . Can a poem tell of it?
Seven thousand corpses.
                    Jews . . . Slavs . . .
No! Words cannot tell this tale.
Fire! Only fire![73]

Some of the most striking evidence of German crimes came from photographs, diaries, and letters found on the bodies of captured or killed Germans. On February 4, *Izvestiya* correspondent Tatyana Tess reported on eight harrowing pictures discovered inside the camera of a German officer. Two days later, *Red Star* and *Pravda* followed suit, with articles by Ehrenburg and another writer, Valentin Kataev, both of which included the eight pictures. The photographs document the hanging of five men, presumably villagers suspected of being partisans. The Germans test the ropes, then arrange the men on a bench below the nooses, tighten the nooses around their necks, and kick away the bench. Three men dangle in the air, two fall to the ground, tearing the ropes. Using fresh rope, the Germans string them up once more. An avid photographer himself, Ehrenburg remarked on the significance of the images: "An eyewitness can forget, confuse, embellish the story. The camera lens has an unbiased eye, and no evidence is more terrifying than photographs." For Kataev, the photographs underscored the cold-bloodedness of the Germans. "Think about it! A man records an execution in this nonchalant, businesslike way. A man? Oh, no! Of course, not a man. This is a cold villain, a sadist, a son of a bitch. An animal? No. Even worse. This is a degenerate. Fascist." Studying the photographs, Tess was most struck by how stoically the five men were meeting their death. Ehrenburg echoed her insight:

> The five Russians met a terrifying death with courage. They knew they were stronger than the executioners. They knew they were stronger than death. . . . There is no death for a person who dies for others, he continues to live in the memory and in the

> flesh of his people. That is why the faces of the five radiate a lofty sentiment—contempt for death. Maybe the executioners thought that the Russians would scream, cry, beg for mercy. But they looked down upon their tormentors. They knew that life would triumph.

Ehrenburg's piece concluded with a call for vengeance:

> Anybody who has seen these photographs will not forget them. He will remember them in Vyazma. He will remember them in Kiev. He will remember them after crossing the border. There is truth in the world, there is retribution! There is no place in this world for hangmen. This is our oath. This is our final "farewell" to the five who were hanged.[74]

A month later, *Red Star* published two photographs found in the wallet of a dead German soldier. One was a self-portrait of German officers sitting behind a large sign with the motto that they had chosen for their campaign: "*The Russian Must Die, So That We Can Live.* The Stalwart 6th Company. Kersten, Captain and Company Commander." The other photograph showed a German commander and several soldiers standing

КРАСНАЯ ЗВЕЗДА

Мы не забудем эту виселицу. Не забудем и не простим!

"We shall not forget these gallows. We shall not forget and not forgive!" Red Star, *February 6, 1942.*[75]

next to rows of dead people, like hunters posing next to their prey. *Red Star* commented on the photographs:

> Hitler said he would free young Germans from their conscience. The operation was a success. Here they stand. They have hair, hands, fingernails. In their appearance, they resemble human beings. They have a backbone, liver, veins. The one thing they don't have is a conscience. Hair and nails can grow back. A conscience will not.

Soviet people were different, *Red Star* went on: "We have a conscience. . . . We want justice. Russian fighters will not respond to gallows with gallows and ignobility with ignobility." The article's unnamed author—in all likelihood, Ehrenburg—turned Captain Kersten's company slogan on its head, declaring: "The executioners must die so that people can live."[76]

READING THE GERMANS

Tess, Kataev, and Ehrenburg studied these photographs for clues about the state of the German soul. Outwardly, German soldiers looked like humans; they hailed from a nation of cultural luminaries—Goethe, Schiller, Heine, Beethoven. But the present-day Germans, the "Hitlerites," had renounced their humanity, flinging themselves from the heights of culture into the abyss of cold-blooded murder. Propagandists on both sides in the war, German as well as Soviet, denounced the other side as inhuman. But there was a crucial difference: The Germans viewed Soviet citizens as subhuman from the very start because they held them to be racially inferior. On the Soviet side, it was only the Germans' bestial deeds that led observers to question their humanity.

The Soviets' extensive press coverage of German atrocities pointed to another asymmetry: the Russian side's disproportionate use of professional writers as war reporters. Recognizing the written word's effectiveness in commanding attention, Soviet officials enlisted more than a

Ilya Ehrenburg in 1940.

thousand writers as military correspondents over the course of the war.[77] On the German side, by contrast, writers barely figured as propagandists. As discussed in earlier chapters, Nazi efforts to sway public opinion were much more focused on visual media, with the images of wretched villages serving to expose the "Soviet paradise" as a lie, and grotesque portraits of "Jews" and "Asiatic types" depicting the USSR's supposedly inferior racial essence.

No writer on the Soviet side studied German writings as fervently as Ilya Ehrenburg. And no one disseminated his findings with equal authority or reach. "I am very partial to the diaries of Fritzes and the letters of Gretchens," Ehrenburg commented sarcastically in January 1942, a half year into the war. "I have read at least a thousand letters."[78] Of the estimated fifteen hundred articles that he published over the course of the war in Soviet papers and in the Western media, many followed a similar pattern: excerpts of German sources interwoven with his commentary.[79] Ehrenburg's method worked exceptionally well to achieve his twin aims—documenting war crimes and indicting the perpetrators. For these articles to be effective, Ehrenburg knew, they had to be truthful beyond a doubt. In October 1941, he discovered that Sovinformbiuro had been using an altered version of a quotation from a German diary, which he had included in an article for *Red Star.* He wrote to Soviet propaganda leaders, imploring them to issue instructions not to edit German documents. Such interference, he explained, not only risked undermining the Soviet cause, it was also unnecessary: "The diaries of the Germans are so persuasive that, in my opinion, they do not require amendment."[80]

Ehrenburg's attempt to understand Germans' hearts and minds was also supported by a veritable army of ordinary Soviet readers who doubled as archivists, supplying him with a constant stream of fresh documents. Every day, letters arrived at the editorial offices of *Red Star* addressed directly to Ehrenburg. They were written by Soviet soldiers and civilians and included testimonials about life under Nazi rule. The senders often introduced themselves as devoted readers of Ehrenburg's editorials and voiced the hope that their evidence might prove useful to him.[81] He also received a vast amount of information about the Germans directly from the Red Army's Main Political Administration. Officers working there regularly wrote to *Red Star*, "to the attention of Comrade Ehrenburg." Sometimes they sent him parcels containing original German diaries, letters, and notebooks; more frequently, they sent Russian translations of documents.[82] In one case, the NKVD sent Ehrenburg the diary of Friedrich Schmidt, an officer in Germany's secret military police (*Geheime Feldpolizei*) who had been killed by Soviet agents working behind enemy lines in southeastern Ukraine, where the officer was stationed.[83]

Schmidt's diary covered February and March 1942, and principally dealt with the capture of suspected partisans who kept infiltrating the German-controlled town of Budyonnovka by skating over the frozen Taganrog Bay from the Soviet-held Rostov area.[84] Promptly after receiving the diary, Ehrenburg published long excerpts with minimal commentary in *Red Star* under the title: "A German."[85] Schmidt writes:

> February 25. . . . Around 4 pm, they brought me four eighteen-year-old girls who had crossed the ice from Yeisk . . . The whip made them more compliant. All four are students and beauties . . .
>
> February 26. Today's events surpass anything I ever experienced before. . . . They brought six more young men and one girl. No amount of persuasion helped, not even the cruelest beatings with a whip. They behaved appallingly! The girl didn't

shed a tear, she only clenched her teeth . . . After a merciless beating, my arm stopped working . . . I was given two bottles of cognac, one from Lieutenant Koch of Count von Förster's staff and the other from the Romanians.[86] I'm happy again. A southern breeze has set in and it is beginning to thaw.

March 2. I'm not feeling so well. I suddenly got diarrhea and have to lie in bed . . .

March 3. . . . In the evening, they again brought me five from Yeisk. As usual, these are adolescents. Using my simplified method, which has already proven itself, I forced them to confess—as always, I made use of the whip. The weather is getting milder.

March 9. The sun is out in all its glory, flooding the snow with a dazzling light, but even the golden sun cannot cheer me up. Today is a difficult day. I woke up at 3 o'clock, startled by a terrifying dream: I had been thinking about the thirty youngsters that I had to kill today. This morning, Maria prepared a savory tart for me . . . At 10 o'clock, two girls and six boys were brought in . . . I was forced to beat them mercilessly . . . Afterward, the mass shootings began: yesterday six, today thirty-three errant creatures. I can't eat. Woe, if they catch me. I don't feel secure in Budyonnovka anymore. Everybody here must hate me. If my family knew what a difficult day I've had! The ditch is almost full of corpses. And how heroically these young Bolsheviks go to their death! What is it, anyhow, that makes them so? Love of country? Or Communism that has entered their blood and suffused the whole system? Some of them, especially the girls, do not shed a tear. That's valor for you! They were ordered to strip naked (We must sell clothes) . . . Woe is me, if they catch me here!

March 11. The inferior race must be taught with the rod. Next to my house, I had a decent latrine built and hung out a big sign saying that civilians were forbidden to use it . . . Opposite my bedroom is the mayor's office, where workers engaged in excavation report in the morning. In spite of the warning they started to use the latrine. How I beat them for it! In the future I'll do some shooting.

March 19. I'm in bed. I had our army surgeon summoned. He examined my heart and found it all right. He diagnosed spiri-

> tual depression. He gave me pills for my constipation and some ointments for my itch . . . They delivered another fine pig. We ordered sausages.

Ehrenburg commented:

> I wrote down these terrifying lines with difficulty. In all of world literature, there is no villain so terrifying and despicable. . . . The pedantic little German, he writes down how many eggs he ate, how many girls he shot, and how his constipation alternates with diarrhea. . . . He writes with enthusiasm only about sausage, this executioner and sausage-maker.

The translated excerpt of Schmidt's diary that ran in *Red Star* came to about twenty-four hundred words.[87] Ehrenburg abridged some passages, but the only opinion he added—and one he felt entitled to, having read piles of enemy diaries and letters—was to declare Schmidt a typical German. Schmidt's diary was so valuable because it revealed "the German in all his greatness." "Read the diary of the German Friedrich Schmidt," Ehrenburg urged his readers. "Soldiers, my friends, remember that in front of you is Friedrich Schmidt. Don't say another word—just use your weapon. And fight to the death."

Ehrenburg preferred to refer to Wehrmacht soldiers as "Germans" rather than "fascists." He also avoided the compound "German fascists" used by other writers, to dispel the notion, widely held by Soviet propagandists in the early phases of the war, that ordinary German soldiers were fellow workers. Instead, Ehrenburg urged his readers to understand how fully the racial ideology of Nazism had poisoned the minds of Germans.[88]

"Methodical gunfire, sharp and purposeful" was how a fellow writer described Ehrenburg's editorials.[89] Ehrenburg himself found his articles wanting, certainly when compared to novels such as *War and Peace*. But he felt it inappropriate to write in times of war, when they could have a harmful effect: "Whoever takes it into his head to complicate the psyche of the invader," he wrote, "will knock the rifle out of the defender's hands." As a prolonged "exceptional emotional state," war knew only two literary genres: poetry ("the most emotional form of literature") and reportage. "These days, people open the newspaper before they open a letter from a close friend. The newspaper is a letter addressed to you. Your life depends on what's written in it."[90] Hundreds of letters preserved in Ehrenburg's archive make clear how much Red Army soldiers treasured his writings. "We read your articles and value them, like bombs, they help us smash our enemies. I would like to write you a lot—but I don't have enough time. We have to beat the German."[91] "In your writings," another soldier wrote, "we search for everything that we want to know."[92] In time, Ehrenburg became so important to the Soviet war effort that political officers forbade soldiers from using the paper on which his columns appeared for rolling tobacco; his articles had to be cut out and preserved for others to read.[93]

The public presentation of German letters and diaries by Ehrenburg and others heightened soldiers' feelings of hatred and fueled their desire for revenge, feelings further encouraged by the political officers' new policies. Before the war, only those soldiers who could prove their mastery of Marxist-Leninist texts were admitted into the Communist Party. During the war, a new criterion for admission was introduced. Red Army men and women received forms known as "vengeance accounts" to record the number of opponents they had killed and the number of enemy weapons they had destroyed. Soldiers with an empty account had no chance of being admitted to the party. Others, like the sniper Vasily Zaitsev, rose immediately to party member status—the number of Germans he had killed was recommendation enough. The vengeance accounts bore on their title pages words from Ehrenburg's 1942 editorial "Kill!": "Unless you've killed at least one German in a given day, your day has been wasted."[94] When Zaitsev was interviewed by Mints's team of Moscow historians, they asked what kept him going in the pursuit of his deadly work. It was the Germans' atrocities, Zaitsev explained: "You see young girls, children hanging from trees in the park. That has a tremendous impact."[95] Zaitsev had likely seen such hangings with his own eyes. But in a fundamental way, his understanding of the war's moral stakes bears the mark of Ehrenburg's influence. Ultimately, no other writer did more to help Soviet soldiers make sense of their own wartime experience and understand their obligations and responsibilities.[96]

A year into the fight against Germany, the meaning of the Soviet war had become crystal clear. Gone was the confusion of the prewar period that had plagued official agitators as they sought to explain to ordinary Soviet citizens why their country had made a pact with Hitler. This transformation was in great measure Ehrenburg's doing. His unceasing stream of daily columns filled countless Soviet readers with indignation and hatred. Writing to him in August 1942, one Red Army soldier foretold the task that would await the writer after the war's end: "When we try Hitler, we'll appoint Ehrenburg prosecutor: He'll tear him apart."[97]

ACTIVATING THE WEST

The Soviet documentation of Germany's war of annihilation reached Allied nations early on, contributing to a groundswell of popular sympathy for the Soviet Union. Histories of the making of the anti-Hitler alliance's formation typically emphasize the tanks, trucks, garments, and food that were shipped from West to East, courtesy of the United States Lend-Lease program. They often lose sight of a stream of other wartime commodities that flowed in reverse, from the USSR to the West, and proved no less important for Allied victory: the daily dispatches about the tenacity and valor of Red Army soldiers who fought back the Nazi invaders.[98]

Distrust between Soviet and Western leaders always ran deep. The morning after Hitler's attack of June 22, 1941, officials in Moscow believed that at any moment Britain would launch a simultaneous naval attack on the Soviet Union, in concert with the Germans. That fear was only relieved when Prime Minister Churchill's broadcast came over the air, pledging all-out aid to Russia.[99] But polls taken at the time of Germany's attack showed that many Britons and Americans viewed Nazi Germany and the USSR as identical evils. "The American people know," asserted *The Wall Street Journal*, "that the significant difference between Mr. Hitler and Mr. Stalin is the size of their respective moustaches."[100] In his June 22 address, Churchill called the Nazi regime "indistinguishable from the worst features of Communism," while insisting, nonetheless, that any alliance was useful as long as it served to combat Hitler, this "monster of wickedness, insatiable in his lust for blood and plunder."[101]

Other Britons were quicker to identify with the Soviet war effort. For many ordinary citizens, the fact that Britain was no longer fighting alone provided a significant degree of reassurance. Writing in her diary, Vere Hodgson, a social worker from London, felt her "morale rising" on June 22. A month later, she made a note about a report from Russia she had heard on the radio: "When the Germans entered the [town] the place was empty—except for seven men hiding under the bridge. They blew up the German tanks as they passed over the bridge—and themselves as well." The Russians, Hodgson concluded, seemed to "have guts which the Latins have not."[102] Hodgson was obviously thinking about France's ignominious fall. She and many Britons were under the spell of Sovinformbiuro, the Soviet war news agency that supplied the British media with much-in-demand accounts of the heroic Soviet defense against the Germans. "Whatever is relayed to England is reproduced by the English press. . . . Our popularity is at an incredibly high level," a Sovinformbiuro operative noted in early October.[103]

Churchill feared that the public enthusiasm would lead Britons to "forget the dangers of Communism."[104] Acting on his instructions, the Ministry of Information resolved to "steal the thunder from the left," by issuing pro-"Russian" propaganda of its own, while making sure to avoid any explicit mention of the "Soviet Union" or other Communist-sounding terms.[105] For instance, a 1941 poster asking British women to do war work drew on socialist realism and featured a female worker whose olive-colored dress looked vaguely Soviet. However, the ministry soon began to use the public support for Russia for mobilization purposes. Real Soviet women, as trade union delegates, were invited to visit British factories and mines to address British workers. A Cardiff newspaper quoted a visiting Madame Malkova as declaring: "Our people in

"Women of Britain: Come into the Factories. Ask at Any Employment Exchange for Advice and Full Details," 1941.

the Soviet Union are sacrificing themselves without rest but here we have seen that not everything is being done. Over the oceans and mountains and steppes, the call has come to the women of England."[106] In her diary, Hodgson extolled the "really formidable" feats of "Russian women."[107]

British Foreign Minister Anthony Eden was in Russia for talks with Stalin while the Red Army's winter offensive got under way. In earlier meetings with Moscow's ambassador, Eden had promised the dispatch of seventy thousand British troops to the Eastern Front. But as Eden readied himself to depart for Moscow in early December, Churchill ordered him to essentially retract the offer: There would be no British troops, just three hundred tanks and three hundred aircraft, diverted from America's Lend-Lease shipments to Britain. The strength of the Russian offensive, combined with the outbreak of war in the Pacific, where Japanese forces were sinking British warships and rushing to conquer British colonies, confirmed to Churchill that Britain could not afford to share its most vital human resources. Stalin was incensed.[108] Before leaving Moscow, Eden was taken on a tour of recently liberated towns northwest of Moscow. When he saw how the Tchaikovsky Museum in Klin had been vandalized by the Germans, Eden was furious.[109]

Vere Hodgson followed the campaign from Britain: "The Russians are doing marvels and have the Germans on the run in the snow." The contrasting fortunes of the British and the Soviet armies were not lost on her. After noting developments in the Pacific ("A bad lookout"), she went on: "But the Russians cheer us every day. They have recovered Tolstoy's estate—and found his grave desecrated. Village after village they are recovering."[110] The reception of Molotov's January 1942 note on German atrocities in the occupied territories signaled a shift in worldwide regard for the Soviets. While his note on the fate of Soviet POWs the previous fall had been largely ignored in the West, the 1942 report received prominent coverage. *The New York Times* called it "one of the most terrible indictments in the history of modern warfare."[111]

Scenes from Tolstoy's vandalized estate and the charred remains of the Tchaikovsky Museum, alongside shots of rape victims and women grieving the loss of relatives, featured in *The Defeat of the German Troops near Moscow*, a documentary released in Russia in February 1942 and brought to Western audiences as *Moscow Strikes Back*. It depicted scenes of murder and destruction discovered in the liberated regions and ended with a call for revenge. The film's stirring effect reverberated in the lines of reviews: "Here is a film to knot the fist and seize the heart with anger," *The New York Times* wrote, "a film that stings like a slap in the face of complacence, a scourge and lash against the delusion that there may still be an easy way out. Here is a film to lift the spirit with the courage of a people who have gone all-out."[112] Another reviewer observed the reaction of moviegoers: "While the film was shown, the theater hall, crowded with people, was completely silent. The people sat there holding their breath. But as the last images flickered over the screen, everybody erupted in applause and cheers."[113] The film won an Oscar for Best Documentary.

Moscow Strikes Back appeared in the West in August 1942, just as German forces pushed through the south of Russia to gain possession of the oil fields in the Caucasus and the prized city of Stalingrad. For the next six months, a battle raged for control of the city that bore Stalin's name. It would claim more lives than any battle before it in world history. From the very start, sympathetic observers the world over extolled Stalingrad as the defining event of the war. On the Allied side, the enthusiasm about the Red Army that had built up since the Moscow winter offensive led to identification with the defenders of Stalingrad. In pubs throughout England, the radio would be turned on for the start of the evening news, only to be turned off after the report on Stalingrad had aired. "Nobody wants to hear anything else," a British reporter noted. "All they talk about is Stalingrad, just Stalingrad." For some people in Britain, the Ministry of Information reported, "Stalingrad seems to be their own native town."[114] A Frenchman's diary repeated the same incredulous line across entries of September and October: "Stalingrad still holding out." A Polish Jew writing from the Vilnius Ghetto in September saw the battle as the "final defeat of Germany" and expected the "weary world" to "straighten its back."[115]

The British were, for the most part, acutely aware that the Soviets were putting forth a greater military effort than their own.[116] As early as September 1942, Churchill began receiving letters from Britons asking him to honor the valiant defenders of Stalingrad. In response, the prime minister had a special Stalingrad sword forged, inscribed with the words "To the Steel-hearted Citizens of Stalingrad, the Gift of King George VI, in Token of the Homage of the British People."[117] While receptive to such tokens of appreciation, Soviet commentators impatiently called on the British and Americans to keep the promises they had made in May 1942 and open a second front in Europe.[118] Ehrenburg, a fixture in the English-language publications of Sovinformbiuro and a regular contributor to U.S. papers, sounded the alarm in late July 1942: The Nazis were moving their divisions from France and Belgium and attacking the Caucasus and Stalingrad in full force. "The Russians are in perplexity. They ask: Where are our Allies?"[119]

The climax of the battle of Stalingrad came in November 1942, coinciding with the twenty-fifth anniversary of the Bolshevik revolution. Several months earlier, in August, Churchill had informed Stalin that the second front would not be formed that year.[120] In an address given November 7, the anniversary day, Stalin included an acerbic rejoinder to Churchill: "So, the main reason behind the Germans' tactical success at our front this year is the absence of the second front in Europe, which enables them to send all their free reserves to our front and ensures them of great numerical superiority."[121] Churchill was indeed responsible for postponing the projected Allied invasion on the Channel Coast. At his urging, American and British forces had instead launched a joint landing operation in French North Africa, which began on November 8. One of Churchill's main concerns in advocating an indirect route toward the liberation of Europe was to spare his own soldiers' lives. This objective was largely met: Only 574 British soldiers lost their lives during the landing in North Africa, which lasted nine days. By contrast, Soviet losses in the two-hundred-day-long Battle of Stalingrad averaged twenty-five hundred soldiers or more every day.[122]

In London, the anniversary of the Bolshevik revolution was marked with a lavish celebration. The main attraction was the visiting "Girl Sniper," Lieutenant Liudmila Pavlichenko, a former history student turned sharpshooter, with a kill score exceeding 300. Standing under a banner proclaiming "London's birthday card—anniversary greetings to the heroic people of the U.S.S.R.," Pavlichenko told the crowd of Londoners that the Soviet people were fighting not only for themselves but "for all progressive humanity. . . . We are grateful for the tanks made by British workers, but we are waiting and hoping for greater help, at least for such help that would divert from our front sixty to seventy German divisions." Like other Soviet visitors touring the West, Pavlichenko sought to shake up Western audiences and move them to action. As London volunteer firefighters executed drills under the sniper's watchful eyes, she held her watch in hand, timing the performances, and reminded the volunteers that in Moscow such drills took one-third of the time. Pavlichenko's remark spurred the volunteers to give it another try, a reporter noted: "The people . . . did their jobs with a feeling that it was an emergency."[123]

With assistance from the West unforthcoming, the Soviets took matters into their own hands. Between November 19 and 22, two Soviet army groups with a combined total of a million soldiers executed a pincer attack to surround the more than three hundred thousand Axis troops who sought to control Stalingrad and its surroundings. Within ten weeks, the Germans, Italians, and Romanians were routed. For the British, the encouragement provided by the Russian triumph was palpable. "Find myself getting far too pleased," Hodgson noted upon hearing of the enemy's defeat.[124]

In January 1943—as the Red Army prepared for a final attack on the sections of Stalingrad still in German hands—Ehrenburg was invited to opine on the conflict in the pages of *The New York Times Sunday Magazine.* Introduced by *Times* editors as "the most powerful Soviet writer today," Ehrenburg was to answer the question of questions: What had enabled the stupendous Soviet triumph over the seemingly invincible Germans? Ehrenburg began by recounting a conversation he recently had with a volunteer woman soldier, "a master sergeant and an excellent shot." When he asked her why she had joined the Red Army, she explained that she made the decision after her son had been killed. Thinking that she was around forty years old and that her son was a soldier, Ehrenburg asked her on what front he had been killed. He was just eight years old, she replied. "I had forgotten then that war changes people," Ehrenburg wrote, continuing:

> This woman was only 29. She told me everything. In the early months of the war, she tended the wounded. At that time, she looked upon the war as a "state affair." . . . In Rostov, she dressed the wound of a German lieutenant under fire, nursed him, sat by his bedside at night—"as though he were my own son," she said with a bitter smile. Her son was left behind in Kerch in the care of an old woman friend. When the Red Army recaptured Kerch, this woman was sent there with her ambulance unit. She did not find either the old woman or her son. They must have taken refuge in some village, she reassured herself.
>
> One morning, a horrible pit was reopened—a mass grave. Among the corpses this woman found her son. Near him lay his exercise book. The boy was on his way to school when the Germans killed him. And the woman said, in a quiet, muffled voice, with the calm beneath which one detects passion: "I don't dress wounds now—I shoot. Now the war is my own personal affair."[125]

For Ehrenburg, the woman's concluding sentence held the answer to the question he had set out to address. Americans pictured Russia as "something inhuman, made of iron." Yet Russia was "warm and genial. . . . If Russia has now become grim and incomprehensible, it is because the war is a 'personal affair' for every one of us. . . . We are settling accounts with death, and that is the meaning of our war."[126]

Ehrenburg made a point of using images that would connect with his Western audience. "I have never seen the Statue of Liberty," he concluded his essay for *The New York Times*, "but in my early youth, I often pictured it as a light amidst a dark ocean kindled by the will of free men. It was visible at the ends of the earth. Today, at the ends of the earth, is visible the little night light in the Russian dugout. It is a beacon torch in the hand of liberty; it is the hope of the world."

Soviet valor and sacrifice set the moral standard of the anti-Hitler coalition in early 1943. As the world fought against Nazi oppression, the Red Army's victory at Stalingrad shone to observers worldwide as freedom's brightest expression.

Chapter 7

ENSLAVEMENT

"Hitler the Liberator!" declared the poster. Above the words loomed an image of the German dictator, clad in a military-style brown tunic, hands on his hips, striking a visionary pose.[1] Such was the sight that greeted Kievans gathered at the notice board outside the city's Opera House in September 1941 looking for clues as to how the German occupation might affect their lives. The poster was only one of many similar proclamations distributed by the newly arrived Germans, all making the case that the Wehrmacht had come to deliver the Soviet people from a quarter century of Bolshevik oppression.

Hitler's true plans for the conquered Soviet lands were anything but liberation. Addressing his closest followers as the first German troops entered Kiev, he explained his views of "Russia" (as he habitually referred to the Soviet Union), "Russians," and "Slavs" in drastic terms: "The Russian expanse is our India, and as the English rule in India with a handful of people, so we shall govern this, our colonial expanse." Slavs, he continued, were a "mass of born slaves that cries out for a master." Russians were like rabbits, capable of copious reproduction, but unable to create and thus "not destined to a life of their own. They know this, and we shouldn't try to persuade them otherwise." Under no circumstances were Russians to be armed or educated, beyond being taught some rudimentary German words to ensure they could follow orders.[2] The Führer worried about the large Soviet population and its high birthrate,

In front of the Kiev Opera House, September 1941.[5]

which far surpassed Germany's. "What a dangerous reservoir of people Asia is!" Measures would have to be taken to increase Germany's birthrate and reduce births in the East.

Other top Nazi officials shared Hitler's views.[3] Propaganda Minister Joseph Goebbels believed that the Russians were "not a people, but an accumulation of dull animals. . . . Bolshevism has merely accentuated this racial propensity of the Russian people."[4] On the eve of Germany's attack, economists engaged by Hermann Göring worked out plans to plunder the Soviet Union of foodstuffs and other valuable resources. In their calculations, the population living outside the grain-producing regions was considered worthless. The plan to divert food produced on occupied Soviet soil to Germany, they readily admitted, would result in the annihilation of "tens of millions of people" through hunger, primarily in Russia.[6] In fact, two days after meeting with Göring's economic planners, Himmler gave a group of top SS officials a more precise figure: The purpose of the war against the Soviet Union, he said, was to "diminish the Slavic population by thirty million people." In a separate order, Himmler instructed SS leaders to reduce the population of "Russia Center"—the planned Reich Commissariat to be composed of Belorussia and Russian areas farther east up to the Urals—by twenty million people. The scale of the projected killing was so vast that it offended even Erich Koch, a Nazi official known for his brutality and chosen for that very reason to become the future Reichskommissar of "Russia Center." Koch turned down the job, saying it was "entirely negative," and opted instead to become Reichskommissar in Ukraine. The task of depopulating "Russia Center" would instead fall to Senior SS and Police Leader Erich von dem Bach-Zelewski.[7]

Throughout the first years of the war, Himmler solicited several drafts of a "Generalplan Ost" from various agencies under his purview. The plan envisioned the deportation of millions of inhabitants from the conquered eastern territories to Siberia and the introduction of Germanic settlers in their stead. To solve the "Polish problem," a draft produced in April 1942 recommended against "liquidating" all Poles, "in the way that is being done with the Jews," as this would have a negative impact on Germany's standing in the world. With respect to Soviet citizens, especially "Russians" who had spent a generation under Bolshevism, the plan had fewer scruples. Only practical considerations stood in the way of their annihilation: "The Russians" were too numerous to be killed off in their entirety, and the Germans would need some to support their rule over the vast territories. The strategic goal, however, remained "to weaken the Russian race in such ways so as to prevent it from choking us with the mass of its people."[8]

In every part of the continent under their rule, the Nazis extolled the creation of a "New Order" while actually pursuing narrow, chauvinistic German interests. Europe was being "enslaved" by the "Hitlerites," Ilya Ehrenburg wrote on June 22, 1941, when he appealed to Red Army soldiers to fight for the continent's liberation.[9] At the time, Ehrenburg was thinking of the fate of Poland, the Netherlands, Belgium, France, and Yugoslavia. He had no way of knowing that the Nazis' policies of despoliation would find their most sweeping and harshest expression in the occupied territories of the Soviet Union. No other land would be so completely stripped of its resources in the pursuit of conquest, no other population so thoroughly subjected to humiliation, hunger, physical abuse, and enslavement. The Soviet territories were, in the eyes of the Nazis, Germany's rightful colonies, and their inhabitants a dispensable mass of cheap laborers, considered barely human. Germany's colonial aims, of course, did not figure in the color prints that propagandists plastered throughout the occupied territories, but it would not be long before the locals who studied the images in Kiev and elsewhere would come to experience the stark reality of the New Order.[10]

HUNGER IN KHARKOV

The slogan "Hitler the Liberator!" was particularly popular in Western Ukraine, where the local population enthusiastically welcomed arriving German forces.[11] While the reception of the Germans in areas farther east was more subdued, there, too, many longed for deliverance from the hardships of life and work in the prewar Soviet Union.[12] Disaffection with Soviet power often became particularly pronounced just before the Germans captured a town, as the hurried retreat of the Soviets left the locals feeling betrayed and despairing. In Kharkov, Ukraine's second-largest city and a hub of industrial production, the equipment from 70 major factories was loaded onto 320 freight trains and shipped east as German troops approached the city. As much as possible, the Soviet state also took care to evacuate able-bodied men, senior party members, members of the political police, highly skilled workers, engineers, and the families of Red Army soldiers. Most of Kharkov's Jews were also able to flee. Altogether the Soviets managed to evacuate nearly half of Kharkov's prewar population. But many who wanted to leave could not. Scalpers exacted exorbitant prices for tickets to evacuation transports. Even some residents with tickets were unable to board the hopelessly overcrowded trains. But not all residents were eager to leave; some believed the assurances of Soviet propagandists that Kharkov would not surrender, while others did not want to abandon their homes or livestock.[13] The Red Army formations defended the city long enough for combat engineers to finish mining key buildings, bridges, and public works, in keeping with Stalin's order to prevent anything useful from falling into the enemy's hands. On October 20, Kharkov's power station and water main were blown up, leaving residents without heat and running water.[14]

Lev Nikolaev, forty-three, an ethnic Russian and professor of anatomy and anthropology, as well as a practicing doctor, was among those who were not evacuated. In September, he watched as trenches were dug in the city center as if to prepare for a prolonged defense. He heard of the mining of buildings, including the student dorm next to where he lived, and was incensed at the thought of the thousands of civilians who would die if the city became a combat zone. Deploring the fact that Kharkov was not declared an open city, as Paris, Athens, and Belgrade had been before, Nikolaev saw the prospect of urban warfare as another example of the Soviets' disregard for the people they ruled. In his diary, he professed not to be anti-Semitic yet also vented at Jewish local officials, who he believed were shirking military service. During the fight for the city, the Soviets unlocked granaries and other warehouses for residents to help themselves to the remaining supplies. Nikolaev denounced the marauders out on the streets, but he also profited from the power vacuum by moving his family into a larger vacant apartment in his building, which had belonged to a recently evacuated Jewish lawyer.[15]

One Soviet institution that Nikolaev was especially glad to see leave was the NKVD. Nikolaev had a history of brushes with the Soviet security police. In 1933, he was imprisoned for nearly three months after his work as a physical anthropologist was criticized as racist and anti-Soviet. The fact that Nikolaev had spent more than ten years of his childhood and youth in France, as the son of a Tolstoyan philosopher who had left Russia in 1904, made him even more suspect in the eyes of Soviet authorities. Upon his release from prison, Nikolaev publicly renounced his "incorrect" views, left his workplace, and abandoned his research in physical anthropology. Nonetheless, he continued to be denounced in the local press.[16]

With satisfaction, Nikolaev watched the Kharkov NKVD's central office go up in flames as part of the evacuation measures. A fellow doctor told him she wished to leave the city, against her supervisor's instructions to stay. She feared that if the Soviets returned the NKVD would arrest her for wanting to live under German rule. She confided to Nikolaev that the NKVD had interrogated her for an entire month in 1936: "By day, I worked, and at night, I was interrogated! Just imagine what I went through!" Reflecting on her account, Nikolaev wrote, "I shudder at the thought of how many people this cursed organization has ruined. If you talked openly with every citizen of the USSR, you'd find almost no one who hadn't, at one time or another, had some contact with the NKVD. Everyone remembers this with horror and revulsion! The NKVD is a symbol of Soviet power! Because of the NKVD's activities, many people resent this power, which under other conditions they might respect and appreciate!"[17]

As Nikolaev pondered what was in store for him, his city, and Ukraine as a whole, he remembered the German occupation of Kharkov in 1918. The regime had been harsh, but also well organized: "Peasants were flogged, workers were hanged. But there was enough food in the city. White rolls were sold at 1913 prices. It'll probably be the same thing now as well."[18] By contrast, Nikolaev wrote, Soviet rule had nearly destroyed his rich country: "Under the Bolsheviks, we found ourselves constantly on the verge of hunger, because all the foodstuffs were being sold abroad in exchange for machinery." He hoped that "under the Germans, the Ukrainian people will begin to breathe, and will start to live better."[19] Nikolaev fully grasped that the Germans were coming as conquerors, not liberators, but still felt that "the Germans are a cultured nation. It's certain that they won't rob the population and will try as soon as possible to restore cultural life in the city."[20]

The Germans entered Kharkov on October 24, finding the streets deserted and the townspeople huddled in their homes.[21] Their first actions startled residents: "They knock very quietly. You open," a female mathematics teacher reported after the war. "They walk in and open all the cupboards. I had a microscope—they took it, although I said that it wasn't mine. They took a gramophone, a gold chain, a silver cigarette case, everything they came across, and food. This went on for two, three days."[22] Another teacher, pregnant at the time, described the first day of occupation as "the first day of the looting committed by the German army." She had managed to store some oil, jam, and honey for the child she was expecting. They took it all.[23] The soldiers who entered the city were under orders to requisition food from the population to help feed the army. In keeping with preinvasion economic plans, the military commandant prohibited trade between the city and the surrounding village.[24] Two weeks into Kharkov's occupation, Nikolaev noted that the fields in the city's vicinity were covered with unharvested potatoes. City dwellers were eager to collect the potatoes on behalf of the Germans, hoping that perhaps they would be able to keep a small share for themselves, but soldiers shot at anyone who tried to get near the fields. "The thought stubbornly persists," Nikolaev wrote on November 5, "that the Germans want to cause starvation." The same day, he heard a story "that several days ago in Kiev there was a huge explosion, which was caused by delayed-action mines. Many civilians and German soldiers were said to have perished. In retaliation, the Germans shot tens of thousands of people (predominantly Jews)." Nikolaev exclaimed: "This is absurd!"[25] If the information was true, which he doubted, it would mean that the seemingly cultured Germans were in fact barbarians.

Terror soon hit home. On November 14, several buildings in the city center were blown up by radio-controlled land mines that had been planted before the Soviet retreat, killing a German division commander and part of his command staff. In response, the Germans took a thousand city residents as hostages and hanged two hundred of them.[26] Walking through central Kharkov on November 16, Nikolaev counted more than sixty bodies hanging from the second-floor balconies of buildings. "Their legs were only 1.5–2 meters above the ground, close enough for passers-by to touch them. The majority were men, but there were also women among those who were hanged. A dreadful spectacle!"[27] As it turned out, the hangings were only the beginning of the Germans' campaign of terror in Kharkov. As in Kiev, the occupiers soon responded to the explosions with massive reprisals against "the Jews."

On December 14, all of Kharkov's Jewish residents were ordered to march to a newly designated ghetto located on the grounds of a tractor factory on the city's outskirts. Nikolaev watched the "wretched scene" as the Jews assembled in the city center. "Thin, pale people in ragged clothes with packages, bags, baskets, suitcases were standing at the crossroads

Sumskaya Street, Kharkov, November 1941.[28]

and waiting for something. Several tried to hire movers, but the men pushed them roughly away from their wagons, scolded them, and showed their natural boorishness in full. They say that the wife of Professor Grishin threw herself from the third floor. I heard a story about a Jew who hanged himself. Of course, a lot of Jews have acutely negative traits, but this doesn't . . ." Nikolaev failed to complete the thought and later crossed out the incomplete sentence. He also struck out this observation: "The Jews have long mocked the Russians. All the GPU investigators who tortured me were Jews."[29]

With temperatures reaching –30 degrees C (–22 degrees F) at night, the Jews were held in the unheated barracks of the factory for two weeks before the killings began. A newly designed gas van had arrived from Berlin, but its small capacity made it of marginal use given the enormous number of those marked for execution. So the Jews were driven in trucks to Drobitsky Yar, a nearby ravine, forced to undress and lie face down on the frozen ground, and then shot in the nape of the neck. During the mass shooting, Soviet fighter planes attacked the ravine, wounding at least one member of the SS killing squad. Fearing that the planes marked the start of a rumored Soviet offensive, the Germans accelerated the shootings, as it was imperative in their view to kill the Jews of Kharkov before the Soviets attacked. Still, between the weather and the air raids, the mass shooting dragged on for a week. A total of about nine thousand Jews were killed. As at Babi Yar in Kiev, combat engineers were brought to Drobitsky Yar to blast the walls of the ravine to cover the corpses with earth.[30]

Anna Chernenko was one of a few Jews who managed to escape from the improvised ghetto at the tractor factory before the mass shooting. Earlier, as she was being marched to the factory, she sensed that she was going to her death. "But somehow, I was indifferent to it all, I was tired of starving."[31] Hunger was the predominant theme in the wartime accounts of virtually all Kharkovites, including Nikolaev. As prices soared to fifty to sixty times their prewar levels, Nikolaev did not know how he would possibly be able to feed himself, his wife, and their two children. Illegal trips to nearby villages, where he traded family jewelry for potatoes and flour, provided short-term respite. The mortality rate in Kharkov, Nikolaev noted in mid-December, had shot up so fast that gravediggers were unable to keep up. A woman from his building who had died of hunger ten days earlier was still lying in her room. Nikolaev was incredulous: "The Germans are behaving ridiculously," he wrote, still measuring them by the standards of a civilized nation despite all he had witnessed. "They are not attending to the needs of the population and are siphoning off everything from our starving country, to take it away to the west. Thus, they cannot play the role of culture bearers, but solely conquerors who are counting only on the strength of their arms."[32]

The closure of the city's academic and political institutions plunged many members of Kharkov's educated elite into misery.[33] A professor of Classics became destitute virtually overnight and was soon seen sitting on a street corner begging for food. Some of his former students gave him food, while others taunted the "Latin teacher who used to have a car under the Bolsheviks." German officials took notice and ordered the professor to stop posing as a beggar, suspecting him of agitating on behalf of the Bolsheviks. Only when the professor showed a Gestapo operative his empty apartment did the German understand that he was not acting.[34] Nikolaev himself was spared the worst: His specialized knowledge enabled him to take a job as head of the medical prosthetic workshops within his institution. This entitled him to a daily allowance of four hundred grams of bread for himself and an additional two hundred grams for each of his family members. At one point, he heard about a group of doctors who had left the starving city to work in Germany and be paid in German marks. It was a tempting prospect. In early March 1942, Nikolaev filed an application to join a transport carrying Soviet workers to the Reich. "A trip to Germany is very enticing to me. But for now, it's only a dream."[35] Nikolaev's mother still lived in Nice, France. A work assignment in Germany, he hoped, might enable him to visit her.

COME WORK IN GERMANY!

In early 1942, German authorities had started a massive labor recruitment drive throughout the occupied Soviet territories. By year's end, close to 1.5 million Soviet civilians had come to work in German factories and farms, comprising over half of all foreign workers in the country.[36] Always alert to potential security threats, Himmler ordered that all workers from the core areas of the Soviet Union wear a rectangular patch with the letters "OST" in white on a blue background so that they were immediately recognizable.[37] Himmler also insisted that the "Russians" be quartered in barracks enclosed by barbed wire, segregated from Germans and other foreign workers.[38]

In Kharkov and elsewhere, the authorities put up posters extolling Germany's splendor and calling on locals to register for work there.[39] "The wall is destroyed," one such poster announced, referring to the isolation and deceit Stalin had inflicted on his people. The figures in the illustration gaze with wonder through an opening in a brick wall at Germany's factory chimneys and cathedral spires rising through the mist in the morning sun. Their eyes opened, they can step into a happy future.

Trusting these images, and reacting to local conditions of deprivation, volunteers reported to the local labor offices in hopes of improving their lives in Germany. In Kiev, the first departures were accompanied by festive orchestral music at the train station.[40] The German demand

"The wall is destroyed." German propaganda poster, 1942.

for labor was so great that authorities did not wait for people to register and began to conscript by force. As early as February 1942, Kiev's mayor instructed city officials to meet a daily quota of at least fifty people from each district.[41] Tatiana Selinchuk, a Kievan waitress, was taken from her apartment at four in the morning. The building custodian forcibly delivered her to a crowded assembly point in the city. Everyone there was subjected to a medical inspection. Sick people were excluded from the transports, but no one found to be in good health was expected to decline an invitation to visit splendid Germany. They were told that by working in Germany they would assure victory for "their saviors" and help smash Judeo-Bolshevism. If such assurances did not convince, ominous questions ensued: "Who are you for? You don't want to go? Does that mean you're a Bolshevik?" Everyone was made to sign a form stating that they were leaving their country voluntarily.[42]

Selinchuk was detained at the assembly point for two days. Relatives and friends who came to say farewell or hand over personal items or food were not allowed to approach the people waiting to travel to the Reich. When they were put on the tram for the train station, people began to flee. At the station, those who remained were loaded onto dirty freight cars, and the doors were locked. The journey lasted eight days. For four days, no one received any food; later, they got a daily chunk of bread and watery soup.

"Voluntary Eastern workers are brought to Germany."
(Original caption, Kiev, 1942)

When the train stopped on the outskirts of Berlin, the detainees were taken to a compound of barracks surrounded by electrified barbed wire. Up to two hundred people were housed in each building. They slept on straw-covered bunks three tiers high. Selinchuk spent three days in this "distribution camp." Along with everyone else, she went through disin-

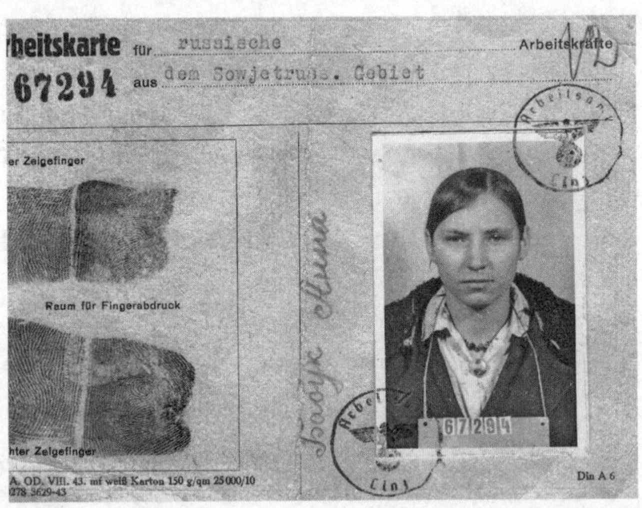

rbeitskarte für russische Arbeitskräfte
67294 aus dem Sowjetruss. Gebiet

er Zeigefinger

Raum für Fingerabdruck

hter Zeigefinger

A. OD. VIII. 43. mf weiß Karton 150 g/qm 25000/10
278 3629-43

67294

Din A 6

"Eastern worker" Anna Poleshchuk's labor card.

fection, passed another medical inspection, was photographed, and had her fingerprints taken. Then she received a little wooden plaque with a number printed on it. Eastern workers who were assigned to work in large factories were addressed not by their name, but by their identification number—one that they would remember for the rest of their lives.[43] "From that day on, I had neither surname nor first name. I was No. 1765 with the badge 'OST.'"[44]

Two hundred and seventy workers, including Selinchuk, were dispatched to a weapons factory in Wittenberg. Selinchuk had to scrub rust from used metal parts using a corrosive oil. Upon hearing from other workers that the toxic oil had destroyed the health of her predecessor, Selinchuk put her hands behind her back and refused to work. Her overseer screamed at her and beat her, but she would not yield. In the end, the infuriated foreman appeared with a mop and a brush and ordered her to clean the workshop. "From then on, I worked in that factory as a cleaning woman." Other workers were taken from the camp to labor offices, where they were offered for lease. Florisa Galetskaia, a twenty-two-year-old former medical student and children's home teacher from the Minsk region, described the scene at the Nuremberg labor office: "They undressed us and placed us in orderly fashion in a line of naked people. Customers were walking around us and tapping us in the back with a cane." Employers bid individually, depending on the laborer's age and health. A close inspection of their teeth and eyes was part of the routine. "We were a horrifying sight. The Germans looked at us as if we were animals," a female student from Mogilev remembered. Anastasia Kovalchuk, a twenty-six-year-old librarian from Simferopol, watched how farming couples began to squabble, with men seeking to buy younger girls, while their wives preferred older women: "They looked us over from all sides, like cattle. Remember Beecher Stowe's *Uncle Tom's Cabin*—they were buying slaves."[45]

In Germany, Soviet laborers occupied the bottom rung of the Nazi racial hierarchy. Their arrival pushed the groups that preceded them up a step. In May 1942, the German authorities stipulated that laborers from Western Europe be given German wages and working conditions.[46]

Another order entitled Polish laborers, hitherto the lowest of all workers, to German food rations.[47] As the new and inexperienced Soviet workers entered the workforce, the more experienced Polish laborers, who wore a badge marked "P," were entrusted with supervisory functions, a practice that often led to Poles abusing their subordinates.[48] Soviet workers received the worst diet: inedible soup and slices of the specially formulated "Russian bread," which made everyone sick and which one worker described as "baked from beet pulp, with an admixture of acorns and wooden sawdust."[49] Soviet laborers worked longer hours than others and received less pay.[50] A French worker writing to his mother in November 1942 remarked that the Russian prisoners were the most unfortunate of all. "The poor devils get nothing to eat. We can't complain, we're still the best off of all."[51]

In Kharkov, Lev Nikolaev's application was approved. In late March 1942, he learned that he had been assigned to join a transport of a thousand workers traveling to Berlin, which was to leave the next day. Nikolaev did not have to crowd into the same unheated freight cars as the regular workers—as a medical doctor, he was allowed to sit in the train's only passenger car—but the food given to him was still meager: four eight-ounce pieces of bread along with some soup and coffee for the eight-day journey. Soon after arriving in Berlin, Nikolaev fell ill and spent two weeks recovering in bed. He was then sent to examine the workers in the Gaubschat truck manufacturing plant at a labor camp in Neukölln. Unbeknownst to Nikolaev, the Gaubschat plant held particular significance for Germany's war in the East: On Himmler's orders, it assembled the "special vehicles," the gas vans, that were dispatched to Kharkov and elsewhere in the Soviet Union to kill ghetto and prison inhabitants.[52] While working at Gaubschat, Nikolaev established that of the three hundred workers who had been sent from Kharkov in the month of January, twenty-five had died of hunger before his arrival; four more would die over the eleven-day period that he spent in the camp. Nikolaev diagnosed more than half of the laborers as famished and unfit to work. When he prescribed the medications needed to treat the men, the camp commandant snapped at him: This is not a hospital! And besides, everyone in the camp had been declared healthy. Feeling unable to help, Nikolaev tendered his resignation and returned to Kharkov, but not before staying in Berlin for another two weeks to tour the city. While the trip to Nice to visit his mother would no longer be possible, Nikolaev was able to converse with French workers in the German capital. He was struck by their freedom of movement and decent living quarters, compared to the wretched conditions of his Ukrainian compatriots.

Sometime after his return to Kharkov, Nikolaev was summoned to the local Security Police headquarters, where a German official lectured him about the false and mistaken opinions he had expressed at the Gaubschat works. Nonetheless, he let Nikolaev leave as a free man. During a walk through the city in summer 1942, Nikolaev came upon a window displaying large photographs of Eastern workers in Germany. He drew closer and recognized in one of them a heavily sanitized image of the very clinic where he had examined the Gaubschat workers. Hidden from view were the barbed wire surrounding the camp, the bare bunks, and the meager portions of almost inedible food.

Posters and brochures that showed smiling workers singing of their new life in Germany appeared throughout the occupied Soviet territories in summer 1942. A young woman supposedly wrote to her relatives back home: "I'm feeling very well and send greetings to all my family members and acquaintances in Kharkov. We like it in Germany. Come here, too, we'll work together. Your Zina S." The cover page of the brochure containing Zina's message showed a worker destroying a red star with his jackhammer. Beneath the image was the caption: "Your work in Germany is a devastating blow to Bolshevism!"[53]

The happy stories told in these brochures, however, were at odds with a steady stream of much darker accounts arriving from Germany. Astonishingly, German officials initially encouraged Eastern workers in German factories to write home, expecting them to be full of praise and gratitude for their host country.[54] To this end, the workers were given preprinted postcards bearing slogans such as "Whoever has seen Germany must love it."[55] Their own words, recorded by employees of the various "foreign mail control offices" throughout the country, told a

"Your work in Germany is a devastating blow to Bolshevism!" Cover image and inside page of a German propaganda brochure, 1942.

different story. Eastern workers overwhelmingly experienced Germany as a vale of tears. Their desperate accounts showed that the supposedly voluntary work program was anything but. A woman from Belaya Tserkov described what happened when her village was ordered to provide twenty-five workers and nobody reported: "The German gendarmerie arrived and set fire to the houses of those who had run away. . . . The people who rushed to help were not allowed to put out the fires, they were beaten and arrested, so that six farms burned down. In the meantime, the gendarmes had set other houses ablaze. The people fell to their knees, kissing the hands of the gendarmes, but they beat them with rubber truncheons and threatened to burn down the entire village. . . . During the fire, the *politsai* went through the nearby villages, arresting and imprisoning people of working age. Wherever they failed to find a worker, they locked up the parents until their children showed up. They raged like this all night long. . . . Nowadays people catch people the way knackers used to snatch stray dogs."[56]

Understaffed and linguistically challenged, the officials at the foreign mail control offices censored only a fifth of the many letters heading to the occupied Soviet territories, letting most of them go on to reach their Soviet addressees. All the censors could do was to send alarming reports up the chain of command.[57]

RESETTING THE MORAL COMPASS

The trip to Berlin changed Lev Nikolaev. Forced to watch helplessly as Soviet workers died of hunger in the German capital, the disillusioned doctor revised his views of Nazi Germany. "We have been turned into colonial slaves," Nikolaev wrote in his diary in July 1942.[58] One month later, he sat down to write a detailed report, factual as well as accusatory, "On the situation of the Ukrainian workers in Germany." In it, he added a note asking that, in the event of his death, the document be submitted to the leadership of the Communist Party of Ukraine so it could serve as evidence of what the Germans had done.[59] Nikolaev wrote this report as German troops were nearing the Caucasus and the oil fields of Grozny. Whether Soviet power would return to Kharkov anytime soon, or at all, was uncertain.

Nikolaev's change of heart also affected how he saw the Soviet Union. "I am revaluating my values," he wrote. Stalin's violent industrialization drive of the 1930s, though it had inflicted death and misery on Ukraine, now appeared in a new light: "I don't know whether Stalin brilliantly foresaw all of this or there were several bright minds in the party, but the mere fact of the factories constructed beyond the Urals is amazing. It seemed an absurdity, but actually, it was very smart!" The diary entry concluded with an expression of ardent hope for the return of "our boys."[60] Earlier in the war, Nikolaev had observed events from a distance, writing about "the Reds" battling the Germans. Now he was taking sides.

Nikolaev was not alone. Everywhere on occupied Soviet soil, people were realizing that the "liberators" had come solely to take, and that almost everyone was worse off than before. When he was asked about German liberation, a teacher from Kharkov sarcastically responded, "The Germans 'liberated' us from water, and from food, and from work."[61] In rural villages, where the Germans had promised to allow the churches to reopen and to restore individual land ownership, Nazi rule remained popular—but only until the villagers understood that these were mostly empty promises.[62] Meanwhile, the Germans continued to tax and confiscate at will. Like the teacher from Kharkov, peasants in the Donbas region began to say that Hitler had liberated them of their cows and grain.[63] A joke made the rounds in Ukraine in summer 1942: "What did Hitler manage to accomplish in just one year that Stalin couldn't in twenty-four? Getting us to like Soviet rule."[64] "How the mood of the population has changed over the year," Nikolaev noted in October 1942: "A year ago, many saw the Germans as deliverers, but now, almost nobody can wait for the return of the Bolsheviks!"[65]

While the harsh conditions of occupation—hunger, skyrocketing prices, punitive taxes—came up time and again in the testimonies of Soviet survivors, disaffection with German rule sprang also from the occupiers' arrogance and utter disdain toward the local population. A professor from Stalino (now known as Donetsk) in Eastern Ukraine recalled the incredulous reaction of German visitors when they saw his large personal library: "Their astonishment perfectly expressed their general contempt for the Russian intelligentsia."[66] Women were incensed by the lewd behavior of German soldiers. As one of them recounted, "The soldiers would be standing around in their quarters, and as soon as a woman or a girl passed by,

Lev Nikolaev in Kharkov, undated photograph.

they'd talk shamelessly about bed, sexual intercourse. One day, I asked: 'Do you also act this way with your women in Germany?' Grinning brazenly, they answered: 'We're just joking.'"[67] For Soviet civilians sent to Germany, the degrading categorization as "Eastern workers" and the humiliations they had to endure were their biggest grievances, overshadowing even their coerced recruitment and wretched life behind barbed wire.[68]

German contempt for Soviet civilians found expression in countless acts of violence. Survivors were stunned by how frequently and easily the occupiers would resort to physical force.[69] The gratuitous beatings and shootings were essential to creating a sense of German superiority. A Polish woman from Lwów recalled the first beating she witnessed. One week into the city's occupation she saw a German on the street punching a Jewish woman in the face. "It was the order of the day. They treated all of us with great contempt. All of us equally. They felt like demigods. Everywhere, they were saying, 'Yes, yes, we've got this land to ourselves.'"[70] Scores of witnesses described brutal beatings that struck them as utterly senseless. A porter from Tarnopol recalled walking to a nearby village sometime in 1942, when he saw a peasant who had just delivered his grain quota and was on his way home: "He was riding a good horse and wanted to pass a few wagons that were traveling slowly ahead of him. He rode out into the middle of the road. Meanwhile, a car was coming. It signaled. While he was turning the horse back behind the wagons, the car was forced to stop. A German jumped out of the car and started to beat the peasant. The man was beaten up very severely. Some women helped him get home, but he died soon after." The porter went on, "The Germans never took responsibility, it was impossible to bring any charges against them. There was total impunity. Even people who worked for the Germans voluntarily dared not say anything to the Germans. For the slightest protest, they'd be murdered at once."[71]

The preferred German method of disciplining Soviet workers was to beat or flog them in public. In Stalino's factories, a doctor reported, "They started using sticks, straight to the face, right and left. They beat the workers with canes and fists, not only the rank-and-file laborers, but the engineers as well. Some acted so incredibly brutally that they even drew their revolvers. I had more than one wounded foreman lying here who had been beaten half to death and even shot."[72] The Germans would whip or beat workers for not saying a proper greeting, for failing to do so at once, or for keeping a hand in one's pocket.[73] In response to the unceasing beatings, Nikolaev heard in September 1942 that peasants in the Poltava region were turning against the Germans. "All of the higher-ups, anybody who felt like it, would hit the peasants right in the face. The slightest word—and straight to the teeth! The German commandant set the example of physical abuse, and then the village elder and members of the police, in a word, all the powers that be, followed suit."[74] Corporal punishment had been abolished in Russia in the early twentieth century and was described in Soviet textbooks as a sordid remnant of the country's feudal past. That the Germans wielded canes and whips signaled a return to serfdom.[75]

Even the hangings conducted by the Germans were administered with a twist, to accentuate their debasing cruelty. "I've never heard of any place in history that hanged people like the Germans did," a kolkhoz chairman from the Tula region said, describing the hanging of a woman who had been wrongly accused of being a partisan. "They hanged her like this: they undressed her, put a hook through her chin, and hung her up. She screamed for four days."[76] In 1942, a partisan who was flown to Moscow to update Communist officials confirmed that the German occupiers in Belorussia had set up gallows "on squares, in parks, and in front of theaters. Lately gallows were put up in every village district. They stick hooks into their jaws and pull them up, like fish."[77]

Civilians across the occupied regions witnessed the German policy of mass murder in action. Many watched Jews being led to their death and commented on their fate with more compassion than Lev Nikolaev. But the fact that Jews were often shot out of public view rendered their murder less immediate. In contrast, the suffering of the Soviet POWs unfolded for everyone to see. The sight of these wretched people being marched or worked to death invited near-total empathy, as nearly everyone had a father, brother, or son serving in the Red Army. An assistant professor of chemistry who found work as a teacher in a village near Stalino encountered a column of prisoners on her way to school:

> They looked pitiful, were barely walking. Many of them were in no condition to walk; they were put on wagons. Someone from among the Russians tried to throw them something. They rushed for a piece of bread, and the Germans began to beat them. I went on. A prisoner was lying in the field, his fingers broken off. It was such a dreadful scene that I couldn't look. When I approached the village, a dead man was lying there. In the village, the peasants told me that many of the POWs had been beaten outside the village or near the village. One was so exhausted that he could no longer walk. At their own risk, the peasants took him away, and he died ten minutes later, without even managing to say what had happened.

The prisoners were driven through the village in waves, one after another, and "class was disrupted each time because every one of the schoolchildren had a father, a brother at war. Once, the principal forbade us to go out and look at the prisoners, but the children cried so much that it was impossible to hold classes. They were crying, and I was crying."[78] In Stalino itself, another professor watched as sick and famished prisoners collapsed on the road and were shot by their guards. Trucks would then take the heaps of bodies away. "Even among the most indifferent Russian people, the suffering of our prisoners of war, the Germans' mockery of them, elicited hatred of the Germans."[79]

Some residents in Kharkov followed a group of captured Soviet sailors who were forced to march through the city center in October 1942. The prisoners, their hands tied, defiantly sang the "Internationale" and other Soviet songs, and when guards tried to stop them, the prisoner marching in front headbutted a German soldier. To the bystanders, it was clear that the men were being led to their deaths. Even though Nikolaev did not witness the scene firsthand, it stirred him: "For twenty-five years, I wavered and sat between two chairs. For twenty-five years, I prided myself on being neutral, on being 'above the fray,' 'au dessus de la mêlée.' And now—if I had the strength and a weapon, I would begin to beat the Germans (at least the officers). My patience has run out. These criminals have drenched all of Europe in blood in the name of *Deutschland über alles*."[80]

Almost without exception, Soviet men and women had been victimized by their own state throughout their prewar lives. Waves of deportations throughout the 1920s and '30s sentenced millions of people to distant exile or death. Virtually no family remained unaffected by the Stalinist purges. Despite this record of suffering, many Soviet witnesses characterized the violence inflicted by the German occupants as unprecedented. In theory, the Communist regime had been committed to reasoning with people and addressing them as citizens, even if Stalinism in practice did not live up to these ideals. The Germans communicated by barking orders or resorting to outright physical violence. The Germans' "cunning cruelty," as Nikolaev put it, led countless Ukrainians, Russians, and Belarusians to revise their sense of right and wrong. For this reason, a rediscovered—or, in Nikolaev's case, newly discovered—Soviet identity thrived in the occupied territories. Leaflets dropped behind enemy lines by Soviet planes and disseminated by partisans and a growing network of underground activists found a receptive audience, eager to heed their appeals to beat back the "the cursed enslavers of our homeland."[81] The changing military tide in winter 1942–43 reinforced this moral reorientation. In the wake of the Soviet victory at Stalingrad, scores of witnesses echoed what Nikolaev had noted in his diary the previous summer: They longed to be liberated by "our boys," and drew a sharp line between themselves and the German occupiers.

HELOTS OR HELPERS?

Some Germans objected to the mistreatment of the local population in the occupied Soviet regions. A Foreign Office representative with the

16th Army, headquartered near Pskov, criticized Wehrmacht military personnel in a report to his Berlin superiors in January 1942, noting how soldiers roughed up civilians, wantonly destroyed homes, and stole every "last hen and egg." When reproached for their behavior, soldiers would compare the Russians to savage dogs, who "deserved to be treated accordingly" or insist that "the bastards are to blame for our being here." Wehrmacht propaganda officials in Smolensk pointed out how shocked Russians were by German behavior. Worse than the plundering was the abuse and murder of captured Soviet soldiers, actions "which were frequently carried out in the middle of town right before the eyes of population." Civilians were "completely appalled." Among locals, these acts of cruelty coming from a "superior cultural nation" were the subject of animated discussions for weeks.[82]

Given the continual need for more recruits to replenish losses in the army and fill the ranks of the expanding armament works, German officials who had long been pushing for a more pragmatic approach in the East finally saw their opportunity. In December 1942, senior Wehrmacht officers and representatives of the Reich Ministry for the Occupied Territories met to discuss the future course of German policy in the East. They agreed on the need for a "radical change."[83] The occupation regime in the East had alienated the population. It was high time for a "grand political declaration" to integrate "the peoples of the East into the new Europe." Foremost on the minds of the participating military officers were the needs of the Wehrmacht: The losses in the Army of the East alone were estimated at eight hundred thousand—and this was before the Soviet offensive at Stalingrad, which would result in the loss of another three hundred thousand soldiers. The plan was to recruit, over the next four months, half a million eastern "auxiliaries" (*Hilfswillige*, or *Hiwis*)—who would be, for the most part, Russians.[84] For the new recruits to become Germany's loyal allies, conference participants agreed, they had to be allowed to fight for a free Russian state. They could not forever remain "helots." Germany's security alone dictated such a change.[85]

The Germans eventually found a willing confederate of some standing in the person of Andrei Vlasov, a lieutenant general who had distinguished himself during the Soviet counteroffensive at Moscow. After falling into German captivity in July 1942, Vlasov changed sides and proposed the formation of a Russian detachment to fight alongside the Wehrmacht. A flyer containing Vlasov's words led to an increase in defections from the Red Army in the second half of September. Wehrmacht propaganda officials then allowed the general to write another appeal addressed "to the soldiers and officers of the Red Army, to the entire Russian people and all the peoples of the Soviet Union," urging them to join Germany's fight against Bolshevism as "equal members in the family of peoples of the New Europe."[86] The second flyer was distributed in early 1943, around the time that the German Sixth Army was routed at Stalingrad.

That defeat further underscored the need for Germany to reorient its policy in the East. Gone was the Nazi dream of a German empire stretching to the Urals, driving Bolsheviks and "inferior races" into the depths of Asia. Now deprived of all its gains since the second half of 1942, Hitler's Germany was under ever-growing pressure from the "Asiatic hordes" that had outmanned and outfought the Wehrmacht at Stalingrad. In a public speech, Hitler called on all Europe to push against a cresting "inner-Asian, Bolshevik wave" that had already devastated Russia itself, signaling a renewed emphasis on Russians as victims of Bolshevism and potential allies against Stalin.[87] Behind closed doors, however, Hitler ruled out the idea of a Russian general fighting on his side. He also refused to make any public commitment about a future Russian state. Vlasov's sole purpose was to produce propaganda and convince Soviet citizens that the Nazi government had their interests in mind.[88]

Entrusted with launching a rousing post-Stalingrad propaganda campaign, Goebbels also felt the need to take a softer line with the Russians, directing the state's antipathy not at the civilians in the East but at the political enemy. He reminded his staff: "There is only one slogan which must be proclaimed again and again, and that is our fight against Bolshevism." Per Goebbels's instructions, they were to begin distinguishing between "Russians" and "Bolsheviks" so that Russians—hitherto considered Bolsheviks by default—could be recruited as fellow fighters against the "Judeo-Bolshevik terror regime." Goebbels also ordered his subordinates to stop referring to the occupied Soviet territories as "colonies" and the local population as "beasts and barbarians."[89] Graphic designers working under his direction produced Ukrainian- and Russian-language posters dramatizing the sharp contrast between "Bolshevism" and the "New Europe." Soviet citizens no longer gazed admiringly at Germany through a breached wall. Rather, they were invited to see themselves as part of a modern Europe that would triumph over Jewish-Bolshevik savagery. As he announced these directives, Goebbels made no secret of their duplicity. The plans for conquest in the East remained unchanged, he assured his inner circle, but the Russians needed to be convinced otherwise. Goebbels cited a surprisingly candid historical parallel: Before coming to power, he said, if the Nazis had talked openly about their intention to outlaw social democracy, jail all Communists, and fight the churches, "surely no one would have voted for us. Similarly, it is lunacy today to talk to the Russians about our intentions in the East."[90]

While much of the rhetoric about improving conditions for the Russians was indeed empty, the Nazis did enact some meaningful reforms. In the occupied Soviet lands, German officials began allowing to replace

Bolshevism—New Europe (1943).

the system of collective farms with one of private ownership. A June 3, 1943, directive mandated the privatization of agriculture for the entire "eastern" realm. Peasants would still have to deliver grain quotas, but they could keep any surplus.[91] However, any positive effect that this and other reforms might have had for the peasants was blunted by the fact that many German officials in the East were stubbornly committed to their self-image as colonial masters. One of them, Erich Koch, Reich commissar for Ukraine, had once declared that his subjects stood "far below us and should be grateful to God that we allow them to stay alive. We have liberated them; in return, they must know no other goal except to work for us. There can be no human companionship."[92] During a stopover in the city of Melitopol in summer 1943, Koch asserted in the presence of a large Ukrainian audience that "no German soldiers would die for these niggers." Later, in a village, a group of peasants welcomed the visitors with the traditional gift of bread and salt. Koch knocked the offering out of their hands, screaming that they should not dare offer gifts to a German dignitary.[93]

Nevertheless, many Wehrmacht commanders stationed in the East entreated their soldiers to view the *Hiwis* and Soviet civilians as vital allies in Europe's fight against Bolshevism. "The Russian is not our enemy, the Bolshevik is," a 1943 manual for German soldiers pointed out, before going on to describe "the Russian character." Despite all the suffering and deprivations under Bolshevik rule, the manual explained, the Russians had not lost their distinctive "racial traits." The Russian people were "childlike" and governed by emotions rather than reason, which required German soldiers to offer strong paternal guidance. While still affirming the Germans' innate cultural superiority and their destiny to lead, the manual also pleaded for "a friendly rapprochement with the population."[94] Russians recruited for labor in Germany were never to feel that they were being deported. They instead needed "to have the certainty of being appreciated and treated as a voluntary and valuable source of labor."[95]

Any attempts at moderation were undermined, however, by the entrenched racism of the Germans, as well as the country's overwhelming need for foreign workers, and for getting them fast. Fritz Sauckel, the government official in charge of labor deployment, aimed to mobilize 1.6 million new foreign workers over the course of 1943, one million of them from the occupied Soviet territories.[96] After a meeting with Hitler and Göring in July 1943, Sauckel flew to Minsk to implement their newest directives aimed at increasing Germany's steel production. In his talks with Wilhelm Kube, the general commissar for White Ruthenia, and other members of the German civil administration, Sauckel mixed new-style assurances with old-style coercion. He promised adequate food provisions for all Eastern workers who came to work for Germany. "Those who remain," he added, "can quietly starve." To meet the enormous requirements for manpower, Sauckel urged his subordinates not to bother recruiting on a voluntary basis.[97]

Soviet eyewitnesses described the labor recruitment efforts in 1943 as even more aggressive than those of the year before. Policemen would swoop into markets and churches and round up everyone inside. Those found to be suitable laborers were put on trucks and carted off to the train station.[98] Cinemas and dance halls were other favorite hunting spots. As a rule, young people in Kiev spent their lives in hiding.[99] A female technical drafter sent to Germany from Kiev in September 1943 described people dying on the train, as a woman nearby gave birth. "It was dark in the railcar, everyone was screaming and crying, while the soldiers outside were laughing, threatening to send us to the hardest jobs."[100] Another train, carrying a woman from Cherkassy, who had been a worker in a garment factory, made a stop in Lublin, where everyone underwent a medical examination. When the workers were put back on the train, several escaped. Upon establishing that ten workers were missing from one car, the Germans ordered the remaining forty people out of that car and made them stand to the side. Then everyone else on the train was also made to disembark so that they could watch as the forty people were shot. The train reached its destination, Königsberg, without further incident.[101]

On a sunny day in September 1943, Vasily Baranov, an eighteen-year-old villager from the Bryansk region, was unloaded from a freight train in Dresden along with other forced laborers and marched through the baroque inner city. He had never seen so many stately buildings, each adorned with carved figures and floral patterns: "I remembered that I had once read a book about old Germany, which called it a country of sculpture." He was also struck by the sight of Germans who gazed on the column of forced laborers from the sidewalks and the windows of their apartments. "They were muttering about something, pointing at us with their fingers. . . . They laughed at the one at the end, who was barely walking, dragging his broken leg, he was wearing traditional Russian clothes, but all in rags." Upon reaching the factory where they would work, the Soviet laborers were, in fact, given more to eat than previous workers had received. But their overseers still beat them regularly. "Swine" was the favorite word of the German and Polish foremen. "Now I understood," Baranov wrote in his diary days after arriving in Dresden, "that we—Russians—were actual slaves for the Germans."[102]

GANGS

The hunt for forced laborers in the East stoked the Soviet partisan movement. As police commandos became more and more unrestrained in their use of force, burning down villages and deporting laborers at gunpoint, locals began to reassess their views of the partisans. Initially seen as dangerous, self-serving marauders, the forest fighters now appeared as staunch defenders of the homeland. More and more young villagers joined them, not only because there was nowhere else to go, but to resist enslavement and to exact revenge. In September 1942, Stalin had declared the partisan war an "all-people's" struggle and called on all Soviet citizens living in the occupied territories to join the resistance effort.[103] German observers now noted local inhabitants "leaving the villages in droves" to join "the gangs" in response to "the incredible insensitivity" of the German labor recruitment drives.[104]

In response to the constant reports of resistance activity in the occupied eastern lands, Himmler, as Reichsführer-SS and chief of the German police, took on the responsibility for coordinating operations directed against the "so-called partisans." He immediately forbade the use of the ennobling term "partisan"; they were nothing but criminal gangs, he said. The heartland of the resistance movement lay in the heavily wooded areas of eastern Belorussia and western Russia. Himmler's representative in this sector of the front was Senior SS and Police Leader Erich von dem Bach-Zelewski, who had extensive experience in the mass killing of Soviet Jews and the conduct of anti-partisan warfare. Bach-Zelewski was particularly infamous for his frequent deployment of the notoriously sadistic Sonderkommando Dirlewanger, a Waffen-SS unit composed of around two hundred poachers and other criminals.[105]

In October 1942, Hitler followed Himmler's urging and gave Bach-Zelewski extensive powers to "fight the gangs" in the "entire eastern territory," including the areas close to the front.[106] Wehrmacht commanders in the field had long been cooperating with the SS to round up villagers suspected of harboring partisans and burning down their homesteads, often with the inhabitants locked inside.

General Gustav von Bechtolsheim, commander of the 707th Infantry Division, called all the residents of these villages guilty—"young and old, men and women." They were all products of Bolshevik "criminality, consciously grown and nurtured here for a quarter of a century."[107] Wehrmacht and SS commandos also compelled Soviet civilians to demine the access routes to partisan camps, intentionally enlisting women and children in the work. German documents recorded the number of children that were blown to pieces during these operations.[108] Soon, Hitler instructed his commanders to further intensify their anti-partisan warfare. In this "war of total annihilation of one side or the other," he said, scruples of any kind, including references to international law, constituted a "crime against the German people."[109]

Importantly, the counterinsurgency operations were motivated by economic as well as political concerns. So much arable land and produce were falling under partisan control that the German agronomists engaged by Göring to manage deliveries of livestock and produce saw their target figures imperiled. Henceforth, Göring dictated, anti-partisan operations should not only eradicate enemy fighters, but also seize any livestock and food from the villages and forcibly recruit all able-bodied adults (both male and female) for projects in the occupied East or in Germany.[110] Nevertheless, Himmler complained that Göring underestimated the partisan threat, and insisted that all Eastern workers would fall under the jurisdiction of the SS and, if needed, be treated to Gestapo methods.[111] By early 1943, the war against the partisans and the recruitment of Eastern workers became fused. In massive operations, code-named "Spring Festival," "Harvest Festival," or "Magic Flute," army and police troops cordoned off forest areas and settlements before proceeding to loot, deport, kill, and destroy.

The deadliest of all the raids, Operation Cottbus, began on May 20, 1943. It aimed to pacify the forest region northeast of Minsk and west of Vitebsk.[112] Led by Bach-Zelewski and Dirlewanger's brigade, now more than seven hundred strong, the operation likely took the lives of more than twenty thousand civilians; another six thousand were captured and sent to Germany. Upon reading these devastating results, Himmler

During an "anti-gang operation," SS men and members of the Order Police pose with women and children captured as "suspected partisans." Belorussia, undated (probably May 1943).

promoted Bach-Zelewski and recommended Dirlewanger for the German Gold Cross.[113]

Representatives of various German agencies took part in the raids and often worked at cross-purposes: While Wehrmacht commanders and representatives of Sauckel's labor deployment office competed for workers taken from the villages, Göring's men eyed the economic resources that they believed were most vital for Germany. A German agronomist entrusted with the seizure of foodstuffs in one county during Operation Cottbus reported entering villages that were empty of residents and livestock. Evidently, villagers had sought refuge in the forest. The agronomist and his men searched the houses and stripped them of everything of value. The action would have been more successful had it not been for the behavior of the Security Police. When some peasants returned from their hiding spots, members of this police force killed them all and set fire to the village, resulting in the loss of "a large quantity of hides and linen." The report went on to list in detail the livestock and materials that the county raid had yielded: "118 horses, 712 head of heavy, horned cattle, 595 sheep, more than 2,500 hides, 320 kg wool, several pieces of linen, grain and flaxseed."[114]

A village burned down during a "pacification campaign" directed against Soviet partisans by the SS, police, and Wehrmacht, northern Russia, 1943.

German propagandists could only watch helplessly as their plans for a New Order in the East forged on the illusion of cooperation went up in flames with the villages. A propagandist who accompanied Operation Cottbus complained bitterly to his boss, General Commissar Kube, in Minsk. What enraged him were not the mass killings of suspected partisans, but the sight of police commandos rummaging through peasant huts, throwing furnishings and bags of grain out on the streets. Slaughtered chickens were scattered about the villages. "The whole is a sorry picture of senseless destruction and, of course, makes the worst impression imaginable on the population . . . the senseless killing of livestock is highly objectionable and must be severely censured."[115] Under such conditions, the propagandist concluded, it was impossible for him to continue his work.[116] Kube in turn protested to Alfred Rosenberg, urging him to speak with Hitler. In August, Kube would go so far as to claim German commandos in the East were practicing "methods from the Thirty Years' War," which, if continued, would produce a mass uprising by next winter.[117] These entreaties proved successful to a certain extent. In the wake of Operation Cottbus, more villagers were deported and fewer murdered. But Nazi leaders would not accept the argument insistently made by officials on the ground that the brutal circumstances surrounding labor recruitment fed the partisan war. For Sauckel, the "gang question" was a separate issue, as he made clear during his visit to Minsk: Resistance fighters had always been in the forests, and they were fighting on Stalin's orders.[118]

Summer 1943 saw the onset of even more widespread violence against Soviet civilians as Nazi leaders adopted a new counterinsurgency tactic: the creation of "dead zones." On July 10, Himmler issued an order to clear all residents from the northern parts of Reich Commissariat Ukraine and the southern border of the zone of operations of Army Group Center, which the Reichsführer saw as "plagued by gang activity." They were to be murdered or deported to Germany, their property plundered, and their houses destroyed. Himmler's police force would manage the dead zones and shoot anyone who ventured into them. By July

1944, such zones comprised three-quarters of the arable land in military-occupied eastern Belorussia.[119]

The desertification of the partisan areas characterized Germany's retreat from the occupied Soviet lands, which picked up speed after a failed July offensive near Kursk. On September 7, 1943, two weeks after German troops gave up Kharkov, Himmler ordered his representative in the Reich Commissariat Ukraine to ensure that in the course of evacuation "no person, no head of livestock, no hundredweight of grain, no rail remains behind."[120] All along the Eastern Front, Wehrmacht commanders directed retreating troops to loot and destroy without restraint. Nothing of value was to fall into the hands of the advancing Red Army. Soldiers loaded movable goods onto trains that hurriedly departed west as engineers tore up the train tracks behind them. On its retreat, the German army burned down settlement after settlement. Soldiers blew up wells and dismantled the stone ovens that had survived the firestorms. Even hospitals counted as essential installations for the enemy's war effort were torched.[121] As for the civilian populations in these regions, the term "recruitment" disappeared from the German military lexicon: Every resident on occupied soil was to be "evacuated," to ensure that they would not work for the Soviet enemy. Those civilians who eluded the German dragnet counted as "losses." Taking stock in late 1943, Wehrmacht officials put this number at 9.4 million people. By contrast, 1.8 million civilians had left with the retreating German troops—1.2 million of whom were considered "evacuees," meaning that they were forced to leave against their will, and 600,000 of whom were "refugees," meaning that they joined the Germans of their own accord.[122]

Germany steadily filled up with foreigners as the war continued. By 1943, they made up 25 percent of the Reich's workforce. Volunteers from multiple nations, including Ukrainians from Galicia and Crimean Tatars, entered the Waffen-SS.[123] Over the course of the war, German officials invited nationalist leaders from India, Syria, and Central Asia to join Germany in a global campaign for colonial liberation.[124] Some also experimented again with the recruitment of ethnic Russians. In the

Bryansk area, the Second Tank Army sponsored a "Russian National Liberation Army," and the SD formed an ethnically Russian "Druzhina Brigade" under the command of Colonel Vladimir Gil. Both were used in anti-partisan operations.[125] But the idea of a larger Russian Liberation Army was still too extreme. "We will never build a Russian army," Hitler again declared behind closed doors in June 1943. "It is a complete illusion." Germany, he insisted, needed forced laborers, not a Russian army that risked turning its weapons on the Germans at any point.[126]

Though Hitler's words were not communicated to Andrei Vlasov, the general and his staff were painfully aware of their inferior standing, and they vented their frustration to the few Germans they trusted. "Apologies, he's a subhuman!" Vlasov quipped in the presence of a German when his orderly slammed a door behind him. An associate of Vlasov's once presented himself to a senior German staff officer as "*Untermensch* Captain Count Lamsdorff reporting!"[127] Colonel Gil went further. After visiting the Sachsenhausen camp in February 1943, where he saw the wretched POWs and talked with conscripted female workers from the East, Gil protested to an SS superior about the degradation of Russians at Germans' hands. In August 1943, following an insistent propaganda campaign from the Soviet partisans against whom Gil's Druzhina Brigade was fighting, Gil issued an order to his men to stop acting as Germany's "obedient tool for the enslavement of the Russian people." Of the 2,200 Druzhina men, 1,432 followed their commander's order and defected to the Soviet side. There they renamed themselves the "First Anti-Fascist Partisan Brigade."[128]

"ASIATICS"

Over the course of the war, Germans fought "Bolshevism" with ever more ruthless brutality. When German forces failed to take Stalingrad in fall 1942, a German newspaper provided this explanation: If Stalingrad had been defended by Britons or Americans, Germans would have conquered it in a matter of days. The Soviet troops, though, were

Waffen-SS tanks enter Kharkov, March 1943.

not fellow humans, but Bolsheviks—bestial creatures who fought to the death because they did not treasure life.[129] The claim was debatable. After defeating the Germans at Stalingrad, the Red Army pressed farther west and recaptured Kharkov in mid-February 1943. In response, the Wehrmacht command ordered in an SS Panzer Corps, which regained Kharkov on March 11. As they entered the city, soldiers of the Panzer Division Leibstandarte SS Adolf Hitler came upon four hundred severely wounded Soviet soldiers in an army hospital. The Waffen-SS men shot scores of the wounded before locking the building and setting it on fire.

Himmler visited the city a few weeks after its reconquest. On April 24, he addressed a gathering of SS men at Kharkov University to lay out the strategy for the further course of the war. Germany had been able to secure "the great fortress of Europe," he declared with pride, and Kharkov was destined to become a "fateful city in German history," in the "opposite sense of Stalingrad." It was "here in the East" that Europe's future would be decided. All Europeans had underestimated the Russians' ability to mobilize outsize armies. Based on "sober calculations," Himmler now reckoned that Soviet leaders still commanded over two hundred million people. This entire population would have to be "broken" if Germany was to prevail over the Soviet foe. A singular mission awaited the SS: "to bleed to death this people's body that is called Russia . . . Many people will get shaky at the knees. . . . We must stand firm and carry on the racial struggle without mercy." Himmler gave a timeline of twelve months to achieve this task.[130]

The German grip on Kharkov proved short-lived. In a series of offensives that began in early August 1943, the Red Army moved against Wehrmacht troops along a front line extending from Smolensk to Taganrog. Even as the Germans lost their position deep in Ukraine, Himmler reached the zenith of his power. On August 24, one day after German troops were conclusively driven out of Kharkov, the chief of the German Police and Reichsführer-SS added minister of the interior to his list of titles. As commander of the SS and of offices that included the Order Police, the Security Police and SD, the Waffen-SS, and the concentration camp administration, Himmler set the pace for the murder of the Jews, acted as top enforcer of German rule in civilian-run occupied territories, and coordinated the anti-partisan operations with the Wehrmacht. His latest promotion put him at the helm of one of the most important state ministries engaged in Germany's mission of fighting Bolshevism and defending the empire in the East.

Speaking to top SS leaders on October 4 in the city of Posen, Himmler returned to some of the themes of his Kharkov speech six months earlier, but presented them in even more chilling terms.[131] While the so-called Posen speech is best remembered for the sections in which Himmler spoke about the annihilation of the Jews, he referred to their killing as a largely settled matter. Most of the Jews in German-occupied Europe were dead, but the war in the East went on more implacably than ever. The face of Germany's most lethal enemy had morphed: It was now primarily "Russian," or "Asiatic," rather than Jewish. The current war, as well as the world's future, boiled down to a racial conflict between a German-led Europe, a citadel of culture, and Asiatic Russia, Bolshevism's bastion. Russians, Himmler made very clear, had no place in his concept of Europe.

Himmler began his address by asking the assembled officials to rise in honor of the memory of their fallen "old comrade and friend," SS Obergruppenführer Eicke, who had been killed on February 26, 1943, when his reconnaissance aircraft was shot down by Soviet flak near

Kharkov. As he proceeded to discuss the "situation in the fifth year of the war," Himmler mocked those Germans who clamored for the creation of a Russian Liberation Army to fight alongside the Wehrmacht. Germans like Alfred Rosenberg who had been born in the Russian Empire, Himmler continued, were not full-blooded Aryans, but "somehow of eastern provenance." For this reason, they failed to recognize that Russians, even those currently serving with the Germans, would always be Bolsheviks—beasts at heart. They were not to be trusted. "Make sure that these subhumans are always looking at you, that they always look their superior in the eye. It's like with an animal. So long as it looks its trainer in the eye, it won't do anything. But never forget you're dealing with a beast!" Auxiliary forces in the German army could be tolerated if they were outnumbered by Germans. But if a tank was handed to a commando unit of Russian soldiers, they would surely begin to conspire with the NKVD. Russians were not the victims of the Stalinist regime, but its agents.

As supposedly novice colonial masters, Germans still needed to learn how to control "the foreign-blooded masses." To do their job effectively, German rulers had to concentrate exclusively on "our people and our blood . . . and nothing else." Himmler exhorted his audience to always distinguish between "Germanic and Asiatic laws." The former, born from a sense of honor and civility, applied to Europeans alone, while the latter were appropriate for Russian and Slavic "subhumans."

Himmler then dwelled on past efforts to elevate the German race. Cardinal among them was the successful "annihilation of the Jewish people." The Reichsführer-SS extolled the executioners, many of them present in the room: "Most of you will know what it means when one hundred corpses are lying together, when five hundred are lying there, or one thousand are lying there. To have stood fast through this—and except for cases of human weakness—to have remained decent, that has hardened us. This is a glorious page of history that has never been written and must never be written." Through difficult work, the SS had purified Germany's blood and removed the naysayers, Jewish "saboteurs, agitators, and mongers"—the very group of people who had brought

Germany down in the Great War. For this reason, Germany in 1943 was a lot stronger than it had been in 1916 or 1917.

The Reichsführer-SS swore his listeners to secrecy: Even though Germans were morally duty bound to annihilate the Jews because the Jews had wanted to kill the Germans, this motivation could not be made public. Himmler knew that world public opinion would resoundingly condemn the Nazis for the mass murder of Germany's and Europe's Jews. The "Russians" were different. Not fully human to start with, their destruction did not have to remain a secret. "Whether or not ten thousand Russian females fall over during the construction of an anti-tank trench interests me only so far as it affects the completion of the trench. . . . If somebody comes to me and says: 'I cannot use women and children to construct an anti-tank trench. It's inhumane, they'll die'—then I'll have to say: 'You are the murderer of your own blood, for if the trench is not built, then German soldiers will die, and they are sons of German mothers. They are our blood.'"

Himmler concluded by looking ahead. For the coming winter and spring, he predicted intensifying onslaughts from the East, more partisan warfare, and additional aerial attacks and landings by British and American forces. With the SS in charge, Himmler was confident that German soldiers would fight their way back into the depths of Russia and build out an eastern border along the Ural Mountain range. Annual cohorts of young German men would soon begin to be dispatched into Russia's "ice cold winter" to defend Europe's frontier. Their fight against the Asiatic hordes would last for many generations, but it would ensure that the Germans would never grow soft. Shielded by the soldiers guarding the Urals, German colonists would settle the Eastern expanses. Alluding to the "General Plan East," Himmler foresaw German settlement proceeding "without any restraint, without concern for any traditions, with ardor and revolutionary zeal." Together, the settlers and the soldiers at the Eastern Front could not but succeed, Himmler explained, because in this huge struggle they embodied "the higher human values, the higher and stronger forces of nature." Ultimately, the Germanic people along with their fellow European countrymen would prevail over an

Asiatic enemy force, which Himmler believed would one day grow to a billion people or more.

The Reichsführer-SS did not enumerate how many million Soviet citizens the Germans had killed over the course of more than two years of fighting and mass murder, but he left no doubt that his goal was the total extinction of all "Russians," to the extent that they stood in the way of Germany's designs. By 1943, Nazi leaders were no longer content to eliminate all Soviet Jews, and in their wake, all Jews of Europe. Their vision of the tempering of the Germanic race foresaw the slaughtering of "Russian-Asiatic" soldiers and civilians for centuries to come.

Chapter 8

LIBERATION

Shortly after the Allied landing in North Africa, the U.S. president and the British prime minister convened in Casablanca on January 14, 1943, to discuss Allied operations for the upcoming year. The joint statement released by Roosevelt and Churchill after a week of deliberations saluted Stalin, who had been unable to join them "on account of the great offensive which he himself, as Commander-in-Chief, is directing." The Western Allies, the statement continued, were fully aware of "the enormous weight of the war which Russia is successfully bearing along her whole land front" and pledged to take on some of this burden themselves "by engaging the enemy as heavily as possible at the best selected points." Even though the opening of a second front in Europe, promised since the previous spring, had yet to take place, the two Western leaders declared that global peace required the "total elimination" of the Axis's war power and the "unconditional surrender" of Nazi Germany.[1] This statement, which came to be known as the Casablanca Declaration, revealed the deep impression made by the Red Army's triumph at Stalingrad. As Soviet forces completed the rout of the German troops still holed up in the ruined city, the rolling thunder of their massive artillery forces could be heard thousands of miles away.[2]

On January 22, the same day that Roosevelt and Churchill gave their first press conference in Casablanca, the High Command of the Wehrmacht released a communiqué on Stalingrad after weeks of virtual silence. It declared that the battle for the city had reached "a ferocity that has eclipsed all fighting on the Eastern Front to date." To underscore this point, the report included the account of a German artillery forward observer who had been posted at the battle's front line. Watching through his scissor scope at the crack of dawn, the observer saw that the enemy had assembled a huge array of fresh weapons during the night, including heavy artillery pieces, grenade launchers, and anti-tank guns. Minutes later, a terrible barrage began, lending cover to a first wave of Bolshevik infantry, who raced over the snow only to be cut down by German machine gunners. Then a second wave followed, assisted by Soviet tanks. German fire stopped the tanks, but only for a moment. "The situation became dangerous, when new tanks with mounted infantry suddenly appeared on the enemy side." These troops stormed the German dugouts. Fearless Wehrmacht soldiers jumped out of their trenches and assaulted the enemy with hand grenades and small arms. Several Soviet tanks blew up. "But it soon became clear that [the German defenders] would not be able to prevent the Bolsheviks from breaking through," the report noted ominously: "*They were too many.*"[3]

According to an SD report, the Wehrmacht communiqué transfixed the nation: All eyes turned to the "fate of Stalingrad." No other military bulletin since the outbreak of the Second World War had produced such a shattering effect.[4] That evening, a young woman in Bavaria quoted the Stalingrad communiqué in her diary before pondering the exceptional cruelty of the war, which had already killed six older brothers of her school friends. "After dinner, father and I sat in front of the map for hours. Suddenly, a dreadful thought came to me: what if the Russians come to us to murder, to devastate, to commit crimes that cry out to heaven?"[5]

Nazi officials cast the remaining German soldiers in Stalingrad as European freedom fighters. In a radio broadcast transmitted throughout the continent on January 30, Göring compared Germany's "Stalingraders" to the doomed Spartan warriors who held off the Persians at Thermopylae. In an address to the nation, which Goebbels delivered on his behalf, Hitler saluted his soldiers who were still fighting "in the vastness of the East to preserve Europe from annihilation." The same day, Hitler promoted Friedrich Paulus, "commander-in-chief of the glorious Sixth Army, heroic defender of Stalingrad," to the rank of Generalfeldmarschall.[6] Nazi newspapers detailed the last-ditch battle of Paulus and his men, who supposedly held out in the city's fortified GPU headquarters.[7] The truth was less edifying. The Sixth Army commander had in fact sought refuge in the basement of Stalingrad's Central Department Store. Upon learning of his promotion, Paulus refused to kill himself, as his new rank implicitly mandated, for tradition forbade a Generalfeldmarschall from submitting to captivity. In the early hours of January 31, German envoys brought a Soviet lieutenant colonel into the department store, where he found Paulus lying on a bed, listless and unshaven. Instead of the freshly minted Generalfeldmarschall, it would be a German divisional commander who negotiated with the Soviets. After the terms of the surrender were settled, a convoy of cars brought all of the German commanders left in the city, including Paulus, along with their retinue and suitcases, to the headquarters of the 64th Soviet Army outside the city. Cameramen filmed the tall Paulus stooping to enter a wooden house. Inside, he was interrogated by General Mikhail Shumilov, who treated his captive as aristocracy, addressing him as Generalfeldmarschall "von Paulus."[8]

In Germany, the authorities officially pronounced all German soldiers in Stalingrad dead. The German people were to believe that all German soldiers fought to their death and none had surrendered to the Soviets. They announced three days of national mourning, as photographs of Paulus's capture sped around the world. When Hitler saw them, he believed they were a Soviet forgery. After his personal photographer insisted that the images were genuine, Hitler blew up.[9] Paulus, he shouted, was a "weakling void of character" who had put his small existence above the life of his people! Hitler knew what would come next: "Paulus will go to Moscow. Just imagine the rat cage that awaits him there! He'll sign everything. He'll make confessions, issue proclamations. You'll see: He'll act like the lowest of the low."[10] (The "rat cage" was a horrific form of torture allegedly practiced by the Soviet secret police.)[11]

"VICTORY OR BOLSHEVISM"

The Red Army's triumph sent shock waves throughout Germany. While instilling in Germans a sense of impending doom, it filled millions of foreign forced laborers with hope that the hour of liberation was drawing closer. The SD remarked that the turning military tide in the East "increased the self-confidence of the alien peoples."[12] Workers were refusing to take orders and becoming pugnacious. Their attitude could be summarized in one sentence: "Tomorrow, we'll be the masters, and you the slaves."[13] Nazi authorities paid less attention to Western foreign workers, who did not have a reputation for challenging the Germans.[14] Even so, a government censor in Cologne remarked on how the news from Stalingrad had exploded like a "bombshell" among local Dutch workers, releasing "hidden hopes for liberation." Emboldened, the Dutch men began to complain about their meals, describing them as "pigswill" that even a dog would not touch. Even worse, they were forced to eat out of the same pan as Russian women.[15]

The foreign laborers that German intelligence reports tracked most closely were the very "Russians" from whom the Dutch workers recoiled. Nazi observers noticed a marked uptick in defiance among the Soviet Eastern workers.[16] Some were so sure of imminent liberation by the Red Army that they openly called for retribution, promising that "all Germans will have their throats slit."[17] In February 1943, a story about a Russian girl working for a local family circulated in Oldenburg. She allegedly said: "Mistress good. When Russkis come, I will make sure they shoot her dead right away and she is not tortured first."[18] That month, an unusual number of cows died in the Rhineland town of Altenkirchen. An SD agent smelled sabotage: The female Eastern workers in town were found to have large quantities of sewing needles, and it was suspected that they were putting them into animal feed. Faced with an enormous and largely untraceable menace, the Gestapo ordered preventive action. Police forces also searched labor camps; guards were told to be vigilant.[19]

Soviet forced laborers were, indeed, among the first to stage concerted resistance on German soil. Their actions began immediately after the Soviet victory at Stalingrad. In March, five Soviet officers in a prisoner of war camp for officers in Munich-Giesing founded the Fraternal Cooperation of Prisoners of War (*Bratskoe sotrudnichestvo voennoplennykh*, BSV). Invoking quintessentially Soviet ideals, the underground organization called on prisoners from all countries to join their antifascist fight. One of their earliest flyers proclaimed, "We are a force that can and will find the means to destroy Hitlerite Germany from within!" Over the next months, the BSV recruited four hundred members from camps across southern Germany, most of them fellow Red Army men, forming the largest non-German-led resistance organization in Germany. Members of the organization pledged to sabotage the German war industry, help prisoners escape from the camps, and punish Soviet captives who collaborated with the Germans.[20]

Florisa Galetskaia, a former medical student from the Minsk area, had been deported to Germany in winter 1943 and sold at the Nuremberg labor office for sixteen marks. She came into contact with the Soviet underground in the spring of 1943. Galetskaia was working as a housekeeper for a landlady in the town of Roth, near Nuremberg. One free Sunday, she joined a group of other young female forced laborers who were visiting a local POW camp. As they approached the high barbed-wire fence, a group of emaciated male prisoners on the other side, dressed in rags, ran toward them. After establishing that they all spoke Russian, the prisoners introduced the women to their leader, a man with thick black eyebrows and a "fiery gaze," whom they called Comrade Zheleznov ("Iron Man"). Zheleznov gave the visitors a short lecture on how a Soviet person was to comport herself while in fascist captivity. Before asking them to disperse so as not to draw the attention of the German guards, he asked Galetskaia for her address. A few days later, she received a letter from him. It was an acrostic poem; the first letters of each line spelled

"Stalin."[21] Later that year, Galetskaia was reassigned to work in a wire factory and moved into Zheleznov's POW camp, where she formally joined his underground organization, the Central Committee for the Liberation Struggle of the Enslaved Peoples in Fascist Germany. Zheleznov would communicate with her and other underground activists by way of coded messages that he wrote with lemon juice or milk. A note written with these liquids was invisible on a sheet of paper but revealed itself when the paper was held up to a light. Zheleznov's missives to "Russians, Ukrainians, and other enslaved people" were passed from hand to hand, both inside and outside the camps, urging prisoners to attempt escape en masse, and those working for Germans to sabotage machinery and blow up factories.[22]

In early March, while on a visit to Hitler's bunker in Vinnitsa, Goebbels was briefed about the unrest among the Eastern workers in Berlin, and he recorded in his diary Hitler's threat to send in the widely feared SS Division Leibstandarte, should those workers ever attempt a revolt: "That will make every lover of such excesses lose his appetite for them."[23] For Nazi leaders, the greatest danger posed by such disturbances on German soil was their potential to destroy the nation from within, as had happened in the closing months of the Great War. The specter of Germany's defeat was firmly on Goebbels's and Hitler's minds in March 1943, and their thoughts centered on the Jews: As long as there remained Jews in Berlin who would use their "semitic intellectualism" to incite the foreign workers, Germany was at risk of collapsing. Goebbels was adamant: "I shall see to it that there is no association between Berlin Jews and foreign workers. There will be no Spartacist tendencies in the Reich's capital in this war."[24]

A few weeks earlier, Goebbels had invoked the threat of Bolshevism to rouse his unnerved countrymen in the wake of Germany's defeat at Stalingrad. Addressing an audience of fourteen thousand in the packed arena of Berlin's Sports Palace on February 18, 1943, with wounded soldiers from the Eastern Front filling the first rows, Goebbels revived the themes of his prewar speeches at the Nuremberg rallies: "Behind the onrushing Soviet divisions, we already see the Jewish death squads, and behind them, complete anarchy and famine for millions," he declared.[25] Only through "swift and thorough" action could Germany avert certain extinction. "The hour has come to take off the kid gloves," Goebbels continued, vowing to eliminate the scourge of "Jewry" with a single, powerful blow, in spite of international protests. Germany's leaders, he shouted, would not be swayed by the foreign media's "crocodile tears" over the deserved fate of the Jewish "menace." To the contrary, Germany would now roll out "the most radical countermeasures." Goebbels's explicit call to step up the murder of Jews, broadcast live to a nationwide audience, earned frenetic applause from the crowd. "After these sentences," the stenogram recorded, "approving chants prevented the minister from speaking any further for several minutes."[26]

A poster that went into mass circulation after Goebbels's speech darkly summarized the stakes after Stalingrad: "Victory or Bolshevism." The poster pushed the duality common in Nazi propaganda to an existential extreme, setting a bright scene of Aryan family life against a nightmarish vision of German suffering. The villain, a murderous soldier whose facial features and Red Army cap mark him as a "Jew-Bolshevik," was modeled on a real soldier who was long dead—one of the thirteen thousand alleged Soviet commissars who had been executed in Sachsenhausen in fall 1941.[27]

"Victory or Bolshevism." German propaganda poster, February 1943.

In fact, the most "radical countermeasures" that Goebbels alluded to were already in place—the extermination camps. Treblinka, some fifty miles northeast of Warsaw, was ranked as the deadliest of them all. It had been outfitted in early 1942 with gas chambers large enough to kill five thousand people at a time. When Himmler ordered his SS commanders in July 1942 to annihilate the more than two million Jews in the General Government, he had Treblinka in mind as the primary site where the murders would take place.[28] Most of Treblinka's victims came from Warsaw, home to Europe's largest Jewish community. Every day, freight trains left the Warsaw Ghetto, each of their sealed cattle cars crammed with up to a hundred people. As they forced the Warsaw Jewish Council to select residents to send away, SS officials reassured ghetto administrators that the victims would be "resettled" to the East. The transports were so long—sometimes up to sixty cars—that after the short trip to the Treblinka village station they had to be divided into sections and pulled into the camp by a locomotive. Treblinka was camouflaged as a transit center, and the newly arrived were ordered to shower in a "bathhouse" to ready themselves for the rest of their journey. They were then marched through a cordon of heavily armed guards into the showers and asphyxiated within minutes.[29]

Soon after Goebbels's speech at the Sports Palace, Himmler traveled to Treblinka to observe the killing operations. Upon arriving, he was invited to watch the gassing of about one thousand young people who had been selected for the important visit. Over lunch in the camp dining facility, where prisoners had decorated the tables with flowers, the Reichsführer-SS learned from SS guards that the corpses of the more than seven hundred thousand Jews who had been killed at Treblinka since the previous summer had been buried rather than cremated. Later, a camp survivor saw Himmler walk up to a huge pit and silently peer into it. Before flying away in his personal plane that same day, he ordered the camp administrators to destroy any trace of the mass graves.[30] This was not the first time Himmler had issued such an order, but the Soviet victory at Stalingrad lent this one a particular sense of urgency. Now that the German grip over the Eastern territories was loosening, all evidence of Nazi crimes against the Jews had to be destroyed, lest it fall into Allied hands.[31] Within days of Himmler's visit, camp commanders had the mass graves reopened. A squad of able-bodied prisoners was ordered to retrieve the bodies and build pyres out of alternating layers of corpses and firewood. After burning the pyres to the ground, the prisoners were to collect any bones that would not burn and grind them in bone-crushing machines. The victims' ashes were then scattered over nearby fields or put into barrels and sent to Germany as fertilizer.[32]

The methodical killing and disposal of the Jews did not go as smoothly as Himmler had hoped. Knowledge of the Red Army's triumph inspired many Jews to rise up.[33] When SS troops entered the Warsaw Ghetto on April 19, 1943, to deport thousands more residents to Treblinka, they were attacked by young militants who had formed a combat organization patterned on the Communist underground in the Minsk Ghetto.[34] They were desperately short of weapons, which the Polish underground army had promised but did not send. Unable to overcome the Germans on military terms, the resisters sought symbolic victory as freedom fighters. In a report broadcast to Jewish organizations in the United States, they referred to their uprising as the "Battle of Ghettograd 1943." The name "Ghettograd," the report made clear, was to evoke the "stubbornness of Stalingrad" as well as the universalist aspirations of the Jewish fighters to "take revenge on Fascism, on the enemy of their people, the enemy of mankind."[35]

In a furious response, more than two thousand SS soldiers and policemen supported by armored vehicles stormed the ghetto, torched its buildings, and flooded the sewers where the ghetto fighters were hiding. The destruction of the ghetto, termed a "large-scale operation," concluded with the demolition of the Warsaw Synagogue on the evening of May 16, 1943. On that day, the commander of the task force, Jürgen Stroop, the senior-most regional SS and police official, told Himmler, "The Jewish Quarter of Warsaw Is No More!" Stroop filed his 125-page report in a leather-bound album. In it, he extolled Germany's heroic fight against an especially perfidious foe. Jewish men, Stroop wrote, assaulted the Germans from underground sewer lines, while Jewish women concealed pistols and grenades in their underwear for use against policemen and soldiers at the moment of capture.[36] Saturated with anti-Bolshevik imagery, the report included dozens of photographs showing burned dwellings and captured insurgents, the captions detailing how the Germans "smoked out the Jews and Bandits."[37] Stroop counted 631 destroyed bunkers and 7,000 Jews killed, in addition to an estimated 5,000 to 6,000 ghetto fighters who perished in the flames or bomb blasts. Close to 50,000 surviving Jews had been "seized," including 7,000 who had been deported to Treblinka and killed by the time the report was written.[38]

The courage of the ghetto fighters took Nazi leaders by surprise and prompted them to step up their killings of Jews, including those who up to then had previously been spared as useful laborers.[39] Throughout May and June, SS forces raided ghettos across Eastern Galicia. To ensure that their men would treat the Jews with an appropriate degree of fury, SS officials had them watch a propaganda film about the Soviet secret police before sending them into a ghetto. The discovery of a fortified bunker system in the ghetto of Rohatyn confirmed to the SS forces the reality of a unified Communist-Jewish enemy. Three of the bunkers bore the names of cities that had become symbols of Soviet resistance: "Stalingrad, Sevastopol, Leningrad."[40]

"EUROPE IS LIBERATING ITSELF FROM THE JEWS"

As the commanders of Treblinka and other camps sought to erase hundreds of thousands of their murder victims from their records, German soldiers stationed near Smolensk, five hundred miles to the northeast, unearthed a number of mass graves.[41] When they had first taken control of the city in summer 1941, they heard from locals that the Soviets had been shooting political prisoners in a nearby forest. But it was only in February 1943, after the German defeat at Stalingrad, that the military police began digging into the frozen soil in the village of Katyn. They immediately hit upon human remains. A forensic expert from the University of Breslau, head of a Wehrmacht task force on "Bolshevik Crimes," was called to the scene. By late March, temperatures had risen sufficiently to allow for more extensive excavations. These revealed several mass graves, each filled with hundreds of corpses, stacked twelve high. Most of the 4,143 dead could be identified as officers of the Polish army. The forensic specialist established that the officers had been murdered in April 1940. The last entries in the diaries and notebooks found on the bodies were from between April 6 and April 20. Holes in the men's skulls suggested that all had been killed by a shot to the nape of the neck.[42]

Overnight, the obscure village of Katyn morphed into a pilgrimage site. As they had done in the Soviet borderlands in July 1941, Wehrmacht commanders in Smolensk turned the exhumed mass graves into a "real-time" exhibition on the horrors of Bolshevism. Thousands of soldiers visited Katyn to observe the barbarity with their own eyes. Some arrived on trucks from the front more than fifty miles away. Soldiers guarding the area had to put up a barrier and a sign with operating hours in order to manage the rush of spectators, especially on weekends. Expert guides took groups of visitors past rows of exposed bodies, while holding forth on Jewish-Bolshevik criminality.[43] After initially allowing only German soldiers, the gruesome exhibit was opened to selected locals in late spring and summer 1943. Wehrmacht propaganda officers brought busloads of Russian and Belorussian collaborators to the killing grounds to provide them with dramatic proof of Bolshevism's murderous essence.[44]

In Berlin, Goebbels learned about Katyn one week into the exhumations. The propaganda minister could not believe his luck, gleefully anticipating the powerful effect that fresh pictures of mass graves would have on the German psyche.[45] Hitler personally urged Goebbels to dramatize Katyn as a Jewish crime. "Mass Murder at Katyn: The Work of Jewish Butchers," "Judah's Blood Guilt Exceeds All Bounds," "The GPU Murders 12,000 Polish Officers," screamed Nazi newspaper headlines.[46] The incident soon became so notorious that a new phrase entered the German lexicon in April 1943: "to Katynize." If the Soviet offensive could not be stopped, a drawing in the *Völkischer Beobachter* intimated, all Germans and Europeans would face the same fate. While mostly dire, the accompanying piece ended by assuring readers that the Jews would

"Bolshevik Dreams for the Future."
First Bolshevik: "With the help of our English-American friends, all of Germany and Europe will be in our hands!"
Second Bolshevik: "And what will we do with them, comrade?"
Jewish Commissar: "Katynize them, of course, you muttonheads!"
Völkischer Beobachter, *April 17, 1943.*

be called to account for their crimes, and that in the end Jewry, not Europe, would meet its demise.[47]

Goebbels's exploitation of the Katyn story had a clear foreign policy objective as well. For a while already, the propaganda minister had been seeking to counteract what he called the Western Allies' "attempts at whitewashing" Bolshevism. The newly discovered graves of Polish soldiers would furnish conclusive proof that the Soviet regime was "as black" as the propaganda minister had always claimed.[48] Goebbels's ultimate hope was to break up the anti-Hitler coalition by once again turning the West against Bolshevism. It was for this purpose that he formed a commission of forensic investigators from Axis-allied and neutral countries and flew them to Katyn to examine the graves. After studying the exhumed corpses for two days, the experts issued a "factual report" that confirmed the Nazis' earlier conclusion: The Soviet Union was responsible for the massacre.[49] The Soviet press shot back, charging the Germans for the murder of the Polish officers and smearing any party that upheld Goebbels's "foul fabrication" as fascist.[50]

Weeks after the news about Katyn broke, more murdered bodies attributed to the Soviet security forces came to light. In Vinnitsa, Wehrmacht soldiers dug up the remains of people shot by the NKVD during the purges of 1937–1938. The exhumations continued into the summer and fall of 1943, revealing a total of 9,432 corpses spread over multiple mass graves, including one in the city center, beneath a children's playground.[51] The Nazis dispatched German forensic experts to the graves of Vinnitsa before again bringing in a team of international investigators.[52] They also authorized reburials of the victims. A bishop of the Ukrainian Orthodox Church, who presided over a funeral ritual in Vinnitsa, likened Stalin's murder victims to Christ suffering torture at the hands of the Jews and called on the mourning crowd to rise at once against Soviet Bolshevik rule. "Europe is liberating itself from the Jews," a newspaper in Kiev proclaimed.[53]

These initiatives were part of an eleventh-hour effort by German occupation forces to regain the loyalty of the local population, which they had squandered in 1941. Fear of a renewed "Jewish Bolshevik" takeover, they hoped, would rally support for the embattled Nazi "New Order." A poster bathed in the color of fresh blood depicted a menacing Jewish commissar pointing his gun at the backs of unsuspecting women as they sought to identify missing loved ones at one of Vinnitsa's mass graves.

Throughout the occupied East, Germans issued ominous warnings about what Bolshevism's return would entail. They planted rumors that Kharkov residents who had left with the Red Army when the Germans retook the city in March 1943 had subsequently received harsh prison sentences solely for having lived under German rule.[54] Propaganda leaflets printed in Russian and Ukrainian asserted that Stalin's police forces were preparing a "new Vinnitsa" massacre.[55] In predominantly Polish Lwów, the German propaganda bore fruit. While initially skeptical about the stories and pictures from Katyn that filled the local press,

Poles became more credulous when they found the names of people they knew on the lists of victims compiled by the Germans.[56] Fear of Bolshevism prompted many of Lwów's residents to depart with the retreating Wehrmacht.[57] In core Soviet areas, however, German authorities had to resort to force to drag the population with them. Many locals disbelieved the German propaganda, as it contradicted their own painful experience of Nazi rule. A commissar with a Soviet partisan unit reported on the Germans' propaganda efforts to Nikita Khrushchev, first secretary of the Ukrainian Communist Party. The propaganda was not successful, the commissar noted: People were convinced that the purported victims of Soviet terror were in fact victims of crimes committed by the Germans.[59] In a similar vein, a member of the Communist underground in Odessa reported that the Romanian effort to discredit Soviet power had also backfired. On the city's outskirts, Romanian authorities had supervised the unearthing of bodies at a suspected Soviet killing site. Locals who were brought there to confirm the victims' identities recognized the neighbors who had been arrested by the Romanians in 1941 and accused the soldiers guarding the mass grave of being murderers themselves. The Romanians thereupon stopped the exhumations in Odessa, while continuing to sound the alarm about Katyn.[60]

"Vinnytsia." Ukrainian-language poster, 1943.[58]

For much the same reason, Goebbels's propaganda action failed to shatter the anti-Hitler alliance, even though in this case it contained a kernel of truth: Stalin was indeed responsible for the massacre at Katyn, which had taken place in 1940, predating the Germans' arrival. But Western officials for the most part found the Soviet denial more credible. Speaking with an adviser, Roosevelt refused to entertain the possibility that Stalin might have been behind the Katyn murder. The crime was "entirely German propaganda and a German plot," Roosevelt insisted. "I am absolutely convinced the Russians did not do this." The British ambassador in Russia was just as certain that the Polish officers had been murdered by the "Huns," "just to make propaganda pictures." Although Churchill believed the "Bolsheviks" entirely "capable of the worst atrocities," he declined the Polish appeals to denounce Stalin publicly, because he believed that the singularly barbaric nature of the Nazi system was the bigger threat.[61] In fact, the Soviet media had supplied the world with evidence of the barbarity of the Nazis. By 1943, the Western Allies had assimilated Soviet views that Nazism violated fundamental ideals of humanity, and they had agreed to a plan advanced by the Soviet Union to jointly hold a war crimes tribunal to punish Nazism's monstruous deeds.[62]

It was with such a reckoning in mind that Himmler's men swept through Ukraine in mid-1943 to conceal more of their mass killings from the advancing Soviet troops. Code-named Aktion 1005, the operation was led by SS-Standartenführer Paul Blobel, who now returned to the site of his greatest crime: the ravine of Babi Yar, where the men of his Sonderkommando 4a had killed 33,771 Jews over the course of two days in September 1941.[63] The murders at Babi Yar had gone on for two years, claiming more than 100,000 lives, Jewish and non-Jewish, POWs and civilians. Every day, residents from nearby districts heard the rattle of machine-gun fire. Gas vans kept arriving and discharging the bodies of Communists and suspected partisans.[64] For a time, the Germans had openly commemorated the killing ground. A Soviet underground informant reported on the existence of a plaque at Babi Yar informing visitors that 75,000 Jews had been executed here "at the request of the Ukrainians."[65] On a previous visit to Kiev in September 1942, Blobel had taken a higher-ranking SS official to Babi Yar and exclaimed: "Here lie my thirty thousand Jews." Blobel evidently did not seek to conceal his murders until after the Soviet victory at Stalingrad.[66]

During an inspection, Blobel realized the gigantic task that lay ahead. He had three hundred prisoners from the nearby Syrets labor camp brought in to unearth the bodies and burn them on gigantic pyres. Under heavy guard, prisoners walked the short distance from Syrets to Babi Yar. Upon entering the ravine, they passed a guardhouse that featured over its door a real human skull above two crossed bones. Inside the ravine, the prisoners, their hands and feet shackled, were driven with punches and kicks to take up their work. Some SS men visibly enjoyed their task: They forced the laborers who stacked the bodies on the pyres to wear caps with devil's horns.[67] The guards were all German, as Blobel feared that local policemen might divulge the secret operation. In their internal reports, SS leaders referred to Aktion 1005 as the "weather unit," and they recorded the number of corpses that were burned on a given day as the "cloud ceiling."[68] Back in Berlin, Himmler instituted a new system to disguise the killings across his entire empire of camps. Individual deaths in the camps were to be recorded on lists of 185. Once this number was reached, a new list began at 1. Any death list that might be stolen from a camp would only give away 185 executions. Only those few SS officials who were in possession of all the lists could keep track of the total number of murders.[69] Himmler's actions revealed two contradictory motives: on the one hand, a desire to escape accountability for his crimes in the world court of opinion, and on the other, an insistence on meticulously documenting the continued annihilation of Germany's racial-political foe.

At Babi Yar, the Nazi hopes for total secrecy were shattered in late September 1943. The prisoners noticed that the Germans were beginning to pack up. One prisoner who spoke German overheard guards saying that on September 29—the second anniversary of the first massacres—the operations in Babi Yar would conclude with the killing and incineration of all three hundred prisoners who had been brought in from the Syrets labor camp. The night before, a group of prisoners resolved to act. Using scissors and knives they had found on the bodies of the victims, they released dozens of their fellows from their shackles. The conspirators who prepared the mass escape knew the odds were stacked against them, but they hoped that at least two or three escapees might survive and inform the Soviet public what had taken place at Babi Yar.[70] When the signal was given, the prisoners emerged from their dugouts and ran. German guards opened fire, killing most of them, but fourteen managed to get away. The Gestapo promised a 10,000-ruble reward for the capture of every fugitive, but to no avail—the escapees were never recaptured.[71] Four weeks later, the advancing Red Army forced the Germans out of Kiev.

UNIVERSAL SUFFERING AND RAGE

As Soviet troops pursued the Germans through Ukraine and into the easternmost areas of Belorussia in fall 1943, evidence of the destruction inflicted on the land and its people was everywhere. Major Pyotr Zaionchkovsky, an intelligence officer in the 66th Army, wrote to his brother and sister on September 30: "Every day we are forced to behold horrifying tableaus of German atrocities: Villages burned, people burned, doused in gasoline. Poor, long-suffering Ukraine! What stirring encounters! I'll never forget how the people met us in Poltava. An elderly woman cried on my chest and then, upon parting ways, kept blessing me for a long time. On the square in Poltava, a little old woman walked with a bag of apples and silently gave each soldier a 'couple.' It's heartbreaking to see all this."[72] For Zaionchkovsky and countless other soldiers, the joy of liberating their native land and people was tempered by intense sorrow.

Ilya Ehrenburg was embedded with the Red Army during its westward advance and shared his impressions with millions of readers. "I drove a thousand kilometers—from Oryol to Sozh, from Ryl'sk to Kievskaya Slobodka," he reported in *Pravda* on October 29. "I have no words to describe the grief the enemy has brought to our country." Again and again, he came upon the same distressing scene: "ashes instead of villages, and a dozen distraught women hiding in the woods." "Ashes and the silence of death," he noted about the area around Buryn. "It seems to me that until the day I die, I will be haunted by that smell of burning, the shadows of the homeless under the autumn sky."[73] If, as in Taganrog, houses had remained intact and populated, this was because the enemy abandoned the town in haste and lacked the time to complete his destructive work. In Kozelets, forty miles north-northeast of Kiev, the Germans also failed to burn the houses before their retreat. But German bombers returned a day or two later and flattened the town.[74] "I have seen destruction before," Ehrenburg commented, "but in the present case, it is the magnitude of the thing that is staggering. You may drive in a car from morning until evening and not see a single town that has survived. The Germans have outdone themselves."[75]

Careful as always to ground his assessment in hard evidence, Ehrenburg cited German military orders that had been found on the battlefield instructing soldiers to destroy anything of value. The entire civilian population and all movable property were to be "evacuated" to the West, one order stated. "Anybody who heads in an easterly direction is to be fired upon."[76] Letters and diaries from captured German soldiers provided firsthand accounts of how the scorched-earth mandate was carried out: "The day before yesterday, we left Novgorod-Seversk," a soldier from the 12th Motorized Rifle Division wrote. "The entire city was burned. We also burn all the villages that we abandon. Today, we burned down a large village again. Residents are ordered to stand nearby and watch their houses burn." Another soldier, Johann Hauster, wrote to his "dear wife": "We are burning everything at night, as we retreat. Entire villages are in flames. Entire harvests in the fields must be burned as well."[77] The Germans even killed the cattle that they could not take with them, Ehrenburg noted with indignation. "Previously, they had just driven away the cows and eaten the pigs and geese. This time, the retreat was hasty, and the Germans shot the pigs and the cattle with machine guns. Dead cows with burst bellies were lying around in the fields. Can the killing of cows, sheep, pigs really delay the Red Army? After all, a cow is not a fuel tank. But it is milk for children." The German policy of destruction was not a military strategy, Ehrenburg intimated—it was meant to bring death, to kill as many Soviet people as possible.[78]

Ehrenburg was able to write as he saw fit, a rare freedom for a Soviet war reporter. No censor appears ever to have altered his wartime reports before publication.[79] Nonetheless, the heads of the propaganda apparatus in the Kremlin monitored which of Ehrenburg's articles appeared in which newspapers and how they were to be reconciled with Soviet state ideology. During his journey through Ukraine in fall 1943, the writer made the devastating discovery that the Germans had destroyed all the shtetls and murdered practically all the Jews in the historical areas of the Pale of Settlement. The areas through which he was passing, Ehrenburg pointed out in his report, had been home to Jewish life for centuries. They had produced Hasidic centers of learning, the playwright Sholem Aleichem, and the "new Soviet generation of Jews," a reference to assimilated secular Jews like Ehrenburg himself. All these communities were now extinct. "Who can imagine Ukrainian and Belorussian cities and towns without Jews? I saw this desert, these terrible ruins. Beneath them—a sea of blood. I am forced to utter terrible words. Let everyone read them. Let no one dare to ignore them. Let no one be able to forget them until their last breath: THERE IS NO LONGER A SINGLE JEW IN UKRAINE. The Germans did their job. There's no need to count the dead. I repeat: not a single Jew remains alive. I have heard many stories about how this happened. I couldn't bear to listen to them, but I listened." Ehrenburg's report on this tragedy did not make it into the pages of *Pravda* or *Red Star*; it appeared instead in Yiddish—a language that Ehrenburg did not speak—in a paper aimed solely at Soviet Jewish readers.[80] Ehrenburg was able to write about the German Judeocide as a premeditated and systematic project, but only if he was addressing Jewish readers exclusively.

On November 6, the Red Army entered Kiev, Ukraine's capital and home to the largest prewar community of Jews in the Soviet Union. Rows of murdered civilians lined the streets. In the days before, German commandos had combed the city quarter by quarter, forcing residents onto trucks, which left the city in a westward direction. Anyone who refused to board the trucks was shot.[81] To escape the dragnet, a group of Kievans had sought refuge in the botanical garden. Hiding in the gardener's office, they heard the huge detonations that destroyed the city's thermal power station on the eve of the Germans' departure. Gunfire erupted nearby, followed by the rattling sound of tanks. Suddenly, a man opened the door and said, "Come out, we are your people, don't be afraid." It was the Red Army. Another Kievan, Natalia Gubarkova, a nurse, sheltered in a dugout. On the morning of November 7, she learned that there were Soviet soldiers on the streets. She rushed outside. Interviewed three months later about the moment of Kiev's liberation, she was still at a loss for words: "I . . . you . . . me . . . I can't describe it. A soldier took my hands and kissed them, my dirty hands."[82]

Among the survivors were Olga Mukhortova-Pekker and her Jewish husband, Solomon Pekker. After the Gestapo agents stormed into their apartment in September 1941, the Pekkers escaped from the city and hid in a nearby forest. On September 29, Olga and Solomon returned to Kiev. Rumors were swirling about the mass shootings that had begun at Babi Yar. The massacre was not a secret at the time. Children had climbed trees in an adjacent park to observe the killings firsthand. That day, Olga vowed to fight against "cursed fascism" and its "cursed followers." After settling in a vacant apartment, she and her husband, who was a card-carrying Communist, contacted other Communists. They procured a typewriter and set about producing false identification cards and other documents to help the city's Jews evade the Nazis. The most effective type of document they fabricated was a note certifying that its bearer had been convicted of anti-Semitic hate speech, a punishable offense in Soviet law. This indemnification, made to look authoritative with the stamp from a local militia branch, was handed out to fellow Jews as a vital form of camouflage. To complete his disguise, Solomon dressed up as an Orthodox priest. Having grown a long beard, "just like Karl Marx," he would take up his station at the local market wearing a black robe and reading from a Bible. As bystanders walked up to hear him read his prayers, he would tell them that their miserable life was a punishment from God. God was angry because people did too little to prevent the murder of helpless victims. Solomon's listeners, mostly old men and women, would sigh, then offer him money, eggs, or bread. When one day a police agent in plain clothes threatened to arrest him for disturbing the peace, Solomon simply showed him the document certifying his past conviction for anti-Semitic propaganda. The note impressed the agent: "All right, grandfather, if you don't like the yids, you're free to go home."[83]

The Pekkers managed to survive in Kiev for years. When the Germans intensified their raids in October 1943, they fled the city again and camped out in an open field. They returned to Kiev in November, the day after the Red Army arrived. Speaking with Isaak Mints's team of historians in early 1944, Solomon tried to convey what liberation meant for a Soviet Jew like himself: "It is difficult for you to imagine what it means to say a person has the right to life."

Not everyone rushed to embrace the returning Soviet order. Local leaders returning from evacuation to their destroyed hometowns described a "sick" atmosphere. Many workers, wary of the Communists, evaded official calls for labor mobilization. They would use strange idioms, addressing returning officials as "Comrade Boss," or ask questions that revealed the deep influence of German propaganda had made on their minds: How were "the Bolsheviks" going to treat those who had remained under enemy occupation? Would everyone be shot? Was there widespread famine in the Soviet Union, and could Jews serve in the Red Army? Had Molotov's wife really left for the United States with all the Soviet gold reserves? The officials offered reassurances: No one who had been forced to serve the enemy should fear reprisals.[84]

To restore Soviet authority, in every liberated city or town political officers of the Red Army distributed pamphlets and hung posters explaining the Soviet war effort. Party leaders organized public lectures and film screenings on the horrors of Nazi occupation.[85] The galvanizing effect of these gatherings took even the organizers by surprise. In the southern Ukrainian city of Melitopol, the head of the municipal administration summoned all residents to a political rally six days after returning to his ravaged hometown in late October 1943. The official, Vassilii Filippovsky, initially distrusted his constituents, believing that they had all sold out to the German enemy. His stance softened somewhat when he saw people arrive with red flags and Stalin portraits that had been carefully stashed away during Nazi rule. Filippovsky opened the meeting and invited locals to share their traumatic experiences under German occupation. Several people recounted the horrors they had experienced. The last to speak were four partisans, two men and two women who had joined the partisan movement after the Germans shot their spouses, children, and parents. At this point, Filippovsky later recounted, the people in attendance were overcome by emotion. "What we witnessed was not a regular meeting—it was a single roaring and howling. The stories were so horrible, we all stood there, unable to move."[86] Through this cathartic outpouring of shared suffering, Soviet power was reconstituted in the hour of liberation. The very meaning of "liberation" acquired tangible significance in the sorrowful tales that aired in Melitopol and other towns retaken by the Red Army.[87]

The moment of liberation also produced a widespread reckoning with the Germans and their crimes. Everywhere in the destroyed villages and towns of Ukraine, a wartime correspondent observed, "people were seized with the spontaneous need to write, to bear witness. Stacks upon stacks of testimony were collected by the political sections of regiments and divisions. They were written on scraps of Gestapo forms, on the backs of idiotic Goebbels posters, and more frequently in school notebooks."[88] Before officials in charge of verifying and investigating German war crimes even appeared on the scene, residents in the ravaged localities had opened mass graves and taken up the work of documenting the murders. Often spearheaded by locals who had witnessed and experienced German violence close up—spouses of partisans who had been hanged by the Germans, mothers and sisters of young people who had been deported to Germany, nurses who had sought to care for POWs—these ground-level initiatives yielded thirty thousand accounts of German atrocities by November 1943.[89]

In Kiev, Jewish survivors took the lead in documenting the horrors of Nazi rule. After the city's liberation, an escapee from the Babi Yar prisoner squad, Vladimir Davydov, shared with the NKVD his account of the killings and burnings in the ravine.[90] Then Davydov led party chief Khrushchev on a tour of the site.[91] The testimony of another former member of the same squad, Iakov Steiuk, was deemed so important that the NKVD scheduled a repeat interview for November 15. It was conducted by Ukraine's newly appointed chief prosecutor, Roman Rudenko.[92] Rudenko sought to ascertain the number of corpses burned by the prisoner group. Steiuk informed him that there were ten gigantic pyres, each one resting on elevated cast-iron grates that had been ripped from a nearby cemetery. The prisoners stacked corpses four meters high atop wooden planks that covered the grates, then ignited them. Based on these calculations, he estimated the total number of incinerated bodies at forty-five thousand.[93] Rudenko put Steiuk in touch with a correspondent of the Second Ukrainian Front's army newspaper. On November 18, Steiuk's harrowing account of the incineration of the corpses in Babi Yar appeared in the newspaper.[94]

Within days after his interrogation by the NKVD, Steiuk asked to be mobilized into the Red Army. Fearless after living on the verge of death for almost two years, he enlisted as a sapper and was promoted to sergeant major before being transferred to a counterintelligence unit and charged with interrogating captured Germans. Born Yakov Shtein, Steiuk spoke German. He was the one who had overheard the German guards in Babi Yar discuss the planned execution of the prisoners.[95] Thirteen of the fourteen escapees from the prisoner squad joined the Red Army; four would be killed in battle. The fourteenth, Nikolai Panasik, was a former partisan who immediately rejoined the partisan movements after escaping from Babi Yar.[96] Countless other Soviet survivors of Nazi occupation streamed into the Red Army in 1943 and 1944, eager for revenge.[97]

Sergeant Major Iakov Steiuk, 1944.

Political officers in the Red Army, meanwhile, sought to exploit the stories of German atrocities to encourage the troops. "Meetings of vengeance" were held for frontline units to ensure they knew exactly what the Germans had done. Soldiers gathered in destroyed villages, at exposed mass graves, or in front of former Gestapo prisons, to bear witness to the horrors the Germans had inflicted on the Soviet people. The meetings resonated especially among new recruits. A battalion of Tatar soldiers described the bloodcurdling sight of "thousands of old men, children, and women torn to pieces and thrown in ditches and wells," of "mountains of rubble where wonderful Ukrainian cities and towns once stood." Vengeance meetings also took place in units stationed far from the front line. Civilian delegations from the ravaged war zones related the horrors they had personally suffered; letters from recently liberated towns and villages were read out to the troops.[98] Soldiers with relatives in regions still under German rule stepped up to share their anger and fear. Everywhere, the testimonials had one purpose: to make the war feel intensely personal for every soldier. Each meeting ended with the assembled unit taking a solemn vow to avenge Soviet suffering and destroy the enemy.[99] Red Army political officers described the gatherings as transformative: Soldiers emerged from them emboldened and more disciplined. By May 1943, more than a thousand such meetings had taken place and 80 percent of all Soviet soldiers had attended at least one.[100]

The meetings affected Soviet soldiers in profound ways, as their letters attested. Scores of servicemen, Jewish and non-Jewish, wrote to Ilya Ehrenburg, to provide their favorite war correspondent with still more evidence for his ongoing indictment of the Germans. A soldier named Gofman wrote upon learning that eighteen hundred Jews, including his entire family, had been murdered in his hometown near Mogilev. Gofman's letter ended with a vow that echoed those from the vengeance meetings: "I am a husband without a wife, a father without children, no longer young, and in my third year of fighting. . . . And I swear that I shall exact revenge as long as my hand can hold a weapon."[101] A soldier named Izbekov told Ehrenburg of his horror at the sight of an exhumed mass grave in Liady, a shtetl in eastern Belorussia. What shocked the soldier most were the "corpses of children with faces distorted by pain. Among the murdered there is even a six-month-old infant with a pacifier in its mouth, apparently buried alive, as there are no traces of murder." Izbekov, too, dwelled on vengeance as he described the reactions of the other soldiers: "Many were crying, but these were tears of rage, rage such as no one has ever experienced."[102]

Irrespective of ethnic background, Red Army soldiers expressed their fury in universal terms. Even those who were Jewish experienced the tragic fate of the Soviet Jews primarily as Soviet citizens. Few, if any, Jewish soldiers insisted on an exclusivity of Jewish suffering separate from the larger Soviet whole. One of Ehrenburg's correspondents suggested that the Soviet military form separate Jewish combat units because he believed that the particular furor animating such units would add to the Red Army's overall fighting power: "After all, there is not a single Jew who, in addition to the state's score with fascism in general, would not have a personal score to settle with the fascist monsters."[103] Veritable Soviet melting pots, the vengeance meetings fanned feelings of pain and rage across regions and republics. One letter, penned jointly by a group of soldiers, powerfully attested to this universal feeling of outrage: "Each of us has their score to settle with the Germans. I, for the destroyed city of Bryansk, for the tears of my mother and sister, who have already languished seventeen months in fascist captivity, and may no longer be among the living. Sergeant Major Pakhomov, for Rzhev. Dorozhenko, for Kharkov. And all of us together, for our Motherland, for our wives and children, for our brothers and sisters, fathers and mothers, factories and plants, for everything Russian, Soviet."[104]

As the Communists came back to power in non-Russian regions, they cast the process as a joyful return of oppressed nationalities into the Soviet family. At a public meeting attended by forty thousand residents of Kiev in late November 1943, the speakers emphasized Ukraine's suffering under Nazi rule, Ukraine's rescue by the Red Army, and Ukraine's special debt to the "Great Russian" soldiers who spearheaded the liberation effort. In keeping with this ethnic line, the two chosen witnesses who shared stories of their suffering were both Ukrainian nationals. The meeting ended with a vow to strengthen the brotherly union of Soviet nations.[105]

Jews did not rank among the fifteen titular nationalities that together formed the Union of Soviet Socialist Republics—yet another reason why it was difficult to articulate specifically Jewish sorrow within the Soviet experience. While Soviet newspapers reported on the German mass murder of Jews throughout the war, they covered isolated stories rather than casting them as part of a broader narrative. And they made sure to subsume Jewish suffering within that of Russians, Ukrainians, or Belorussians, who carried more weight in the multinational Soviet edifice.[106] Between December 1943 and February 1944, Russian and Ukrainian officials compiled and repeatedly revised an official Soviet government report about the toll of German destruction discovered in liberated Kiev. The report listed enormous cultural, economic, and human losses sustained by Soviet Ukraine. It described the Babi Yar massacre and cited Vladimir Davydov's and Iakov Steiuk's testimonies about the German exhumation and burning of the corpses in 1943. The line referring to the September 29, 1941, killings as "atrocious mass extermination of the Jewish population" was the only passage to raise objections by Georgy Aleksandrov, head of the Central Committee's Department of Agitation and Propaganda. Aleksandrov struck out all references to Jews. In his edit, "thousands of peaceful Soviet citizens" went to their deaths rather than "all of Kiev's Jews."[107]

The universality of sorrow remained a leitmotif of the Soviet narrative well after the liberation of Kiev. Soviet propagandists recognized its state-building power, especially in the Western borderlands where the Soviet regime's grasp had been shaky even before the German invasion. In all these regions, Red Army political officers and other officials marked local Nazi killing grounds as national sites of suffering in order to cast German fascism as the nation's principal enemy and Soviet power as its liberator.[108] When forensic experts traveling with the Red Army entered the Janowska Camp in Lvov in July 1944, they came upon a mill that had been repurposed for grinding bones during Aktion 1005, the German cover-up operation to destroy evidence of mass killings. Indeed, Paul Blobel's men had used this mill in Babi Yar. The Soviets immediately sensed that this tool in the German arsenal of death, which the SS

Former members of "Special Commando 1005" pose next to a bone-crushing machine, Janowska concentration camp, August 1, 1944.

had so far kept hidden, was itself a valuable piece of evidence. By publicizing the death mill, they joined the suffering of the people of Lvov to the plight shared by the Soviet family of nations.[109]

A "GERMAN SYSTEM" OF KILLING

The Nazi murder sites on Soviet soil strengthened Stalin's dictatorship. As the Communist regime returned to power in the liberated lands, it was buttressed by inspiring accounts of humanism repelling fascism, of good vanquishing evil. But not every opened grave supported this simple narrative. The landscape of liberation also contained evidence of Soviet crimes, including the mass graves at Katyn. Even as the Germans retreated, they continued to call attention to the Soviet murder of the Polish officers. One official government publication, 331 pages long, listed the identities of virtually all of the 4,143 exhumed bodies and contained photographs of fractured skulls, suggesting they had been pierced by bullets from behind.[110] The Soviet leadership, meanwhile, continued to blame the Germans for the slaughter. In a secret operation following the Red Army's liberation of Smolensk in September 1943, the same Politburo and NKVD officials who had ordered the 1940 mass killing of the Polish prisoners dispatched agents to Katyn to make the corpses appear to be victims of Nazism. NKVD agents cordoned off the execution grounds in the forest and went to work, preparing forged documents dated from summer 1941 and placing them in the pockets of the dead officers. They interrogated locals who had previously spoken with the German-led Katyn Commission and pressured them to produce witness accounts that contradicted the German record. After three months of work, the agents wrapped up their operation with a report containing seventeen detailed testimonies. It was sent to the Extraordinary State Commission for Establishing and Investigating Crimes Committed by the German Fascist Invaders (ChGK) along with instructions to the commission to investigate what had happened in Katyn for themselves.[111]

Fedor Burdenko, the Red Army's chief surgeon and a renowned brain specialist, knew nothing of the NKVD's evidence doctoring when he was appointed chair of the ChGK's special Katyn Commission in January 1944. The previous fall, Professor Burdenko had led the exhumation of five thousand civilians and prisoners of war buried at a camp near the prison of Oryol. While in Oryol, Burdenko came across a German newspaper that contained a detailed account of the German findings at Katyn. As he read the newspaper account side by side with his own forensic discoveries, Burdenko was stunned: The newspaper description of the "Bolshevik" killing method used in Katyn was in fact exactly what he had found in the Nazi victims he was examining in Oryol. Burdenko immediately informed the head of the ChGK, Nikolai Shvernik, of his discovery, which he saw as definitive proof that the Nazis had been the true perpetrators of the crimes at Katyn. It was on the strength of this report that Burdenko was appointed head of the Katyn Commission.[112]

For obvious reasons, Stalin did not want Burdenko's team to dig too deeply into the Katyn story. On his orders, the ChGK was given just one week to examine the site and present its findings. At the end of that week, the Kremlin staged a solemn reburial of the Poles killed at Katyn. To the sound of Chopin's funeral march, a Polish priest sprinkled holy water on the graves while Polish officers laid wreaths bearing the inscription "Glory to the memory of the victims of the Hitlerite terror in Katyn Forest."[113] Published in *Pravda* on January 26, 1944, Burdenko's report held no surprises; it established "irrefutable" proof that the Germans had shot the Polish prisoners.[114] For one thing, the decomposition of the bodies at Katyn matched that of victims found at other burial sites on formerly Nazi-occupied soil, suggesting that all the executions had taken place at around the same time, in fall 1941, after the German invasion. Dated documents found in the uniform pockets of the Polish prisoners (which had in fact been planted by the NKVD) provided further proof of this.[115] Burdenko concluded the report by once again stressing the congruence of the killing method in Katyn and other mass graves that he had personally inspected in Oryol, Voronezh, Krasnodar, and Smolensk. All the exhumed bodies were marked by pistol shots to the back of the neck; they all were part of the same "German system of killing." A professor of medicine with no direct ties to the NKVD, Burdenko had no way of knowing that Stalin's secret police had also killed their victims with shots to the back of the neck.[116]

Though the Germans may have adopted the nape shot from the Soviets, it became a German trademark in the early phase of the invasion, when it was used mostly on Jewish males. As the Germans extended their campaign of mass murder to include women and children, officials devised other methods of killing, such as gassing the victims, which were considered less traumatic for the killers and allowed them to quickly slaughter large groups all at once. But the executioners never stopped shooting throughout 1942 and 1943, and as their killing methods diversified, the number of their victims continued to climb ever higher.

The Nazis' increased pace of killing in these years was motivated in part by anxieties over the deteriorating military situation—with the Red Army's steady advance in the East, the American invasion of Italy, and the Allied bombings of German cities—as well as fears that the Reich's foreign worker population, which now numbered more than seven million, could soon stage a mass uprising. The rebellion, they feared, would be sparked by the Soviet workers who had become increasingly combative since Stalingrad. An October security report, one among many, noted that in a camp for Eastern workers "there is open talk of dates when a violent armed uprising must be attempted."[117] In anticipation of such uprisings, the Wehrmacht High Command had worked out a secret contingency plan, named "Valkyrie," to mobilize all military units stationed in Germany.[118] The Gestapo's feverish efforts to uncover the clandestine Fraternal Cooperation of Prisoners of War operating out of the POW camp for officers in Munich-Giesing paid off in November, when an undercover agent infiltrated the Soviet network. Almost four hundred activists were arrested, and scores were sent to their deaths.[119]

Nikolai Shevchenko's Central Committee for the Liberation Struggle of the Enslaved Peoples in Fascist Germany remained undetected. In her work for the organization, Florisa Galetskaia helped produce German-language flyers and post them in Nuremberg and Schwabach. The flyers informed readers about the advance of the Red Army and the Western Allies and called on the German population to join the fight against fascism. Policemen raided and searched Galetskaia's camp, while a local newspaper promised a 5,000-mark reward for information that led to the arrest of the "bandit worker" who had put up the flyers.[120]

The Warsaw Ghetto uprising had awoken SS leaders to the prospect of further Jewish-led insurgencies, and their fears were justified. Led by an underground organization, prisoners in Treblinka rose up on August 2, 1943. Armed with axes and knives, they confronted the guards and set buildings on fire. Throngs of prisoners broke through the fences, and a hundred managed to escape. In October, another uprising took place in Sobibor. It was organized by eighty Jewish Red Army men who had been brought from Minsk the month before. The arrival of these soldiers raised the morale of the camp prisoners. The Red Army men were led by Lieutenant Alexander Pechersky, who quickly reached out to the Jewish camp underground and took the lead in executing a preexisting escape plan. On October 14, the prisoners struck, nearly taking control of the entire camp. Eleven SS men and several non-German guards were killed,

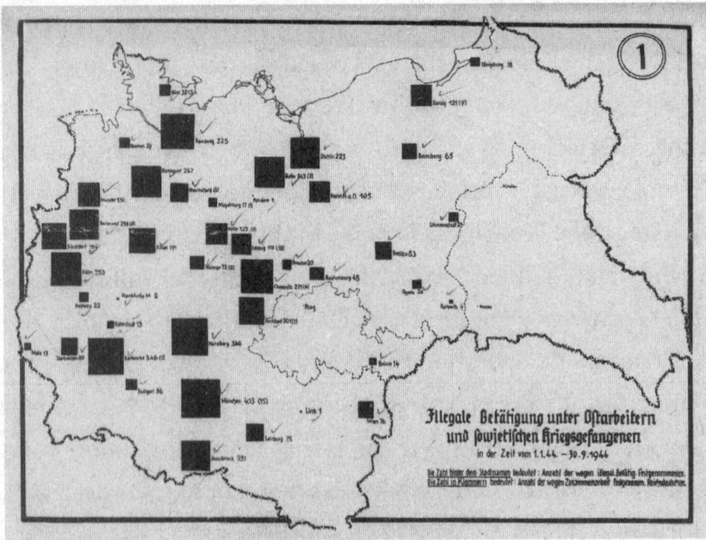

Map prepared at the Reich Security Main Office, showing illegal activities among Soviet forced laborers on German territory between January 1 and September 30, 1944. The figures provided after the names of cities refer to the number of forced laborers arrested there for illegal activities. More laborers were arrested in Munich and Nuremberg than in any other cities.

and three hundred Jews escaped.[121] The news from Sobibor was especially alarming to German authorities given that the camp held fewer than one thousand Jewish prisoners at the time, a small portion of the total population. A similar insurgency in a camp with more Jews, they reckoned, would have cost many more German lives. Himmler swiftly ordered the murder of all the remaining Jewish prisoners engaged in forced labor in the General Government. SS commanders dispatched a heavily armed force of several thousand men to the three major camps of Majdanek, Poniatowa, and Trawniki, where they were instructed to carry out a coordinated strike under the code-name Harvest Festival.

In the early hours of November 3, prisoners in Majdanek woke up to the sound of sirens. One of the prisoners, the Armenian military doctor Suren Barutchev, later recounted what happened next. Cordons of SS soldiers standing five feet apart surrounded the barracks. At the morning roll call, all Jews were ordered to step forward. They were brought to trenches on the outskirts of the camp and shot. As the morning wore on, Barutchev watched columns of Jews—including pregnant women and the severely ill, as well as some five hundred children—arriving from other nearby work camps. They, too, were marched to their death, silently, Barutchev emphasized, their will crushed by the Germans' overwhelming demonstration of force.[122]

More than eighteen thousand Jews were shot at Majdanek that day. Another twenty-four thousand were slaughtered in the Poniatowa and Trawniki camps on November 3 and 4. The SS left a few Jews alive for two weeks to burn the dead and remove traces of the killings. For those two weeks, the stench of burned flesh hung over Majdanek. Barutchev gave fellow prisoners "phenol to smell, chlorinated lime—whatever turned up," but the nauseating smell would not go away. Killing operations in Majdanek continued into 1944, but Sobibor was dismantled after the uprising and its grounds planted over with pine trees. The SS also closed Treblinka II. The extermination camp had been rendered obsolete after the recent outfitting of Auschwitz-Birkenau with a fifth crematorium that could burn 4,756 corpses every twenty-four hours. SS men and Ukrainian policemen erased the camp structures and built a farm on the site. The bricks from the gas chambers were used for the farmhouse. A Ukrainian who had formerly worked as a guard in Treblinka brought his family and farmed the ground.[123]

On July 21, 1944, the first Soviet troops crossed the Bug River into Poland. During the night of July 22–23, soldiers from the Eighth Guards Army, which had formerly defended Stalingrad, came upon Majdanek. They arrived just after the German camp commanders had departed, following frantic attempts to cover their tracks. Since April, the SS had been evacuating camp inmates to other death camps farther west, lest they fall into the hands of the Red Army. As Soviet troops closed in on Lublin in early July, German guards force-marched a last convoy of 1,250 disabled and wounded Russian prisoners to a town sixty miles away and put them on a train to Auschwitz; 600 prisoners collapsed during the march and were shot.[124] Before leaving Majdanek, the SS set the camp crematorium area on fire. However, the fire failed to destroy the ovens or the smokestack of the crematorium; gallows and other murder devices in the camp also remained intact, as did all of its 144 barracks. The Soviet liberators counted several hundred surviving prisoners.[125] A few days later, the first Soviet reporters arrived at the scene.

The sight of Majdanek jolted even seasoned correspondents who thought they knew all there was to know about the Nazis' murderous ways. When Konstantin Simonov, Russia's best-known war poet, set out to write his article, "Extermination Camp," which appeared in *Red Star*, he wrote haltingly, unable to fully comprehend a crime that felt novel, vast, and frightening.[126] All he could do at the moment, he noted, was to record what his own eyes and ears had registered.[127] Simonov took his readers through the gates and barbed wire of the camp entrance, past the neat houses with front gardens that had belonged to the SS guards, and into Majdanek's murderous core: a bare and empty concrete "crypt," its steel door fortified with iron clamps and lockable from the outside.[128] Simonov stepped into a small, adjacent room that was outfitted with a peephole to observe the interior of the gas chamber. Strewn on the floor were several cans marked "Zyklon B" in big letters, and in smaller print: "for special use in the eastern territories." Simonov walked the short distance to the crematorium, where heaps of yet uncremated corpses lay in front of the five furnaces. He learned from captured camp personnel that over the course of Majdanek's operation the Germans had doubled the speed of cremation by turning up the temperature in the ovens. The rush was due to "the Katyn affair," Simonov believed. Once their efforts to blame the Katyn massacre on the Soviets had been exposed as a lie by Burdenko's commission, he supposed, the Germans wanted to destroy the evidence of their crimes not just there, but throughout Europe—and as quickly as possible.

Simonov could not state with certainty how many people had been killed at Majdanek. But a camp barracks of about a hundred feet wide and a hundred feet long provided a clue. The "most terrible witness" of Majdanek's death machinery, the room was filled to the ceiling with shoes. Simonov saw every kind of footwear—coarse soldiers' boots, elegant women's slippers, rubber galoshes, "and what is the most terrible sight of all—tens of thousands of pairs of children's footwear: sandals, small slippers and shoes from ten-year-olds, from eight-year-olds, six-year-olds, one-year-olds. It is hard to imagine anything more terrible than this spectacle, this horrible silent testimony of the death of hundreds of thousands."

In a former camp office, Simonov came upon passports and certificates piled several feet high. As he leafed through the documents, he saw they had belonged to people from all over Europe. The passport of a female Ukrainian worker born in 1917 was the first document he looked at. Next were papers belonging to a French, a Bosnian, a Croat, a Dutch, an Italian, a Greek, a German, and a Pole. One document had Chinese characters that Simonov could not read. He noted that he'd picked the documents randomly, but his presentation followed the distinctly Soviet principle of nationalizing and universalizing the suffering of Nazism's victims. They represented the oppressed nations of Europe, and indeed, the world, with the Soviet Union figuring as their liberator. This claim had heightened importance now that the Red Army had entered Poland. Simonov's report listed Polish nationals as the largest victim group at Majdanek, followed by Russians and Ukrainians. Even though his essay spoke of transports of thousands of Jews who were brought to Majdanek to be killed, the destruction of the Jewish people paled, in his telling, beside the victimization of Europe itself. In poignant words, Simonov described the heap of documents in the camp office as a "burial mound for the whole of Europe, reduced to the confines of a single room." This way of looking at the victims of Nazi violence elided the great preponderance of Jews among them, for the passports of Europe's Jews, with the exception of Germany and the Soviet Union, did not list their Jewish identity.

Simonov's account was immediately translated into dozens of languages and sent around the world. It was also read on Soviet radio over three evenings.[129] Soviet cinemas showed moving images from the camp, the work of filmmaker Roman Karmen, who arrived in Majdanek after Simonov had penned his essay. His notes reveal how stunned he was by what he saw. The killing grounds at Babi Yar, which he had previously documented, were but a "country cemetery" compared to the "industrial complex of death" that was Majdanek. The gas vans that the Germans had operated in Russia were but an "artisanal form of murder" compared to the "conveyor belt method of human annihilation" practiced in this camp.[130] As he conveyed Majdanek's horrors on film, Karmen followed Simonov's lead, his camera stopping on the storage room overflowing with shoes, before zooming in on the passport photographs of murdered prisoners from all over Europe, as a voice-over identified them by name and nationality. The film added a "shocking detail" absent in Simonov's account: The Germans had used the ashes of the victims to fertilize the fields at Majdanek. The camera dwelled on thick heads of cabbage growing near the camp towers. Karmen's film concluded with a shot taken from outside the fortified fence. It tracked the emaciated and pained faces of the survivors, who still wore their striped prison garb and stood lined up behind the barbed wire.[131]

As these accounts of Majdanek spread throughout the world, Red Army political officers organized more vengeance meetings at the camp, along with special tours led by former prisoners, who explained every feature of the mass-murder facility.[132] Soldiers who could not come to Majdanek were shaken by the reports they read and the images they saw. A Polish Jewish Red Army soldier wrote to Ilya Ehrenburg from a hospital, where he lay with severe wounds to his head and arm, awaiting his discharge. He had just learned that his wife and small child, as well as his two brothers, had all been killed by the Germans. Where could he go now, a disabled man without a home? the soldier asked Ehrenburg. Only one road remained: "to the storage room of Majdanek, to look for my relatives' shoes among thousands of pairs of shoes." Overcome with grief and rage, but no longer able to fire a weapon, the soldier swore an oath of vengeance that he undoubtedly hoped Ehrenburg would convey to his millions of readers: "The bodies of my relatives are burned, but their blood boils and screams: 'Why were we deprived of life, why were we tortured, tormented, and then burned?! Our blood will not stop boiling until the seas and rivers run with the blood of the German bandits. Revenge!'"[133]

No vengeance meetings were held at Treblinka. The dismantled and overgrown former camp made it hard to imagine the human torment and industrial-style murder that had raged there through 1942 and 1943, claiming some nine hundred thousand lives.[134] It became the task of another Soviet war reporter, Ehrenburg's friend Vasily Grossman, to re-create the "Hell of Treblinka" through documents and interviews with survivors and captured camp guards. But not all evidence of the murders was gone. Walking across the "earth of Treblinka, bottomless earth, earth as unsteady as the sea," Grossman noticed trampled into the ground a mass of thick, wavy hair, gleaming like copper, and beside it, curls of blond hair and some heavy black plaits, "evidently the contents of a sack, a single sack that somehow got left behind." The writer, who had only recently found out that his own mother had perished in her hometown of Berdichev in September 1941, described experiencing "more sorrow" on his visit to Treblinka, "more grief, more anguish than any human being can endure."[135] He suffered a nervous breakdown after completing his assignment.

Grossman's essay noted another suggestive detail. Both the stern-looking Red Army soldier who guarded the room in which Grossman interviewed former camp officials, and the soldier who had transcribed their testimony, were "Stalingraders." They wore on their chests a medal with an olive-green silk ribbon that had been awarded to all Soviet defenders of the city. Grossman himself had reported from besieged Stalingrad and received a medal and an officer's rank for his services. His Treblinka piece cast Stalingrad as the first step in humanity's liberation from fascism. Treblinka, he pointed out, devoured most of its victims in fall 1942, when Hitler still controlled Europe and before that decisive turning point. "The whole world is silent, suppressed, enslaved by a gang of brown bandits that has seized power. London is silent and New York too. And only somewhere on a bank of the Volga, many thousands of kilometers away, the Soviet artillery is roaring."[136] From a captured guard, Grossman learned of Himmler's visit to Treblinka in early 1943 and his order to exhume and burn all the victims. What had made the SS chief do this? he wondered. "There could only be one explanation: the

Red Army's victory at Stalingrad." Had the Soviets not reversed Germany's eastward drive, at enormous human cost, no other force in the world would have interrupted the Nazi machinery of death.[137]

Stalingrad and Treblinka lay nearly a thousand miles apart. In between lay vast lands that the Germans had dominated for almost three years, sending millions of captured Soviet soldiers and civilians to their deaths. On their retreat, the occupiers methodically torched, destroyed, and killed even more, creating uninhabitable desert zones, all in the service of preventing the "Russian" enemy from reaching and destroying Germany. Fearing a possible postwar reckoning, Nazi officials set out to burn and pulverize the physical remains of their victims. They might have succeeded had the Red Army not seized the upper hand on the battlefield and advanced at a stunning pace, reaching some sites of Nazi mass murder before Blobel's SS men could begin their grisly work.[138] An army of Soviet civilians—from Babi Yar's survivors Davydov and Steiuk, to Ehrenburg and Grossman, and the countless people who assisted the ChGK from their devastated home villages and towns—documented every uncovered mass grave and painstakingly reconstructed the German record of violence in those places where the occupiers had sought to hide their crimes. Political officers in the Red Army took their soldiers to exposed murder sites, to educate and urge them on in their fight against Nazism. By 1944, the Soviets had assembled a vast chronicle of German crimes. How would this knowledge, and the deeply intertwined feelings of loss, sorrow, and revenge that it engendered, play out once the Red Army crossed over onto German soil?

Chapter 9

"HERE SHE IS, ACCURSED GERMANY!"[1]

In his message to the Soviet armed forces on May 1, 1944, International Workers Day, Joseph Stalin commended the Red Army: Three-quarters of the Soviet territories once occupied by Germans had been retaken, and four hundred kilometers of the USSR's western border restored.[2] But the enemy was not yet defeated, and more work lay ahead. Stalin compared Germany to "an injured beast that is forced to crawl away to lick its wounds." The Red Army's task was to chase the wounded animal to its lair and "finish it off." In the months to come, army newspapers printed Stalin's exhortation hundreds of times. By early 1945, the urge to kill the fascist beast was firmly planted in the minds of the Soviet soldiers, and their forces were poised to enter Germany. No matter when they had joined the war effort or where they had fought previously, virtually all who took part in the final operations had accumulated a wealth of knowledge about Nazi crimes in the East, drawn from propaganda, personal observations, and correspondence with loved ones back home. In their quest to avenge, many felt like this soldier from Kiev, who wrote to his wife from East Prussia in early February 1945: "You want to tell every German to his face: look, this is what you get for our suffering. This is for the suffering of my family and thousands of other families. And this is for the death of hundreds of thousands of Soviet people, for the death of our women and children whom you mercilessly murdered, whom you treated worse than animals."[3]

Stalin's message also addressed all Soviet citizens—including for the first time "the brothers and sisters who temporarily fell under the yoke of the German oppressors and were forcibly seized for fascist hard labor in Germany"—as well as the Western Allies. Germany, he reminded them, remained a formidable foe even in its weakened state; only a "combined blow" from East and West would successfully liberate Europe from Nazism. This was the latest in a series of appeals from Stalin to the Allies to honor their pledge, first made in 1942, to launch a cross-Channel invasion. In June 1943, when Churchill broke the news to Stalin that he was calling off the promised Normandy landing out of concern that it would end in a "great British defeat and slaughter," Stalin had indignantly reminded the prime minister of the larger stakes. A second front in Europe would save "millions of lives in the occupied regions of western Europe and Russia and reduce the colossal sacrifices of the Soviet armies, in comparison with which the losses of the Anglo-American troops could be considered as modest."[4] Indeed, by that time, the death toll in the Soviet armed forces had exceeded seven million.

The second front opened at the break of dawn on June 6, 1944, as a seaborne invasion force of over 150,000 Allied soldiers, braving ferocious fire from the Germans, established bridgeheads along fifty miles of Normandy's mined beaches.[5] Stalin had failed to congratulate Churchill on the risk-averse invasion of Sicily back in July 1943, an operation that the British prime minister referred to as the piercing of Axis Europe's "soft underbelly," but this time the Soviet leader offered effusive praise. The Western Allies had achieved what both "invincible Napoleon" and "hysterical Hitler" had failed to do—they had launched a successful invasion across the English Channel. "History will note this deed as an achievement of the highest order."[6]

"It has begun!" Ilya Ehrenburg exclaimed in *Red Star*. He hailed the gallantry of the ordinary Western conscripts—"weavers from Manchester, students from Oxford, metalworkers from Detroit"—who had risked their lives to join the gigantic battle against "fascist tyranny." D-Day was a proud day for the Soviet army, too, Ehrenburg continued. If Germany's vaunted Atlantic Wall crumbled so quickly, this was primarily owing to the Soviet war effort dating back to 1941: "For three long years, we have been destroying the Germans, their generals, their lieutenants, their Fritzes, their 'Tiger tanks,' their 'Messerschmidt planes,' their faith in victory. The blood of Russia has been eating away at the stones of the German fortress." Now, with the Allied powers fully committed, "the hunt for the beast" could start in earnest.[7]

On December 1, 1943, the final day of the Teheran Conference, Stalin had agreed to launch a Soviet offensive shortly after the cross-Channel invasion, to prevent Germany from diverting its forces from east to west.[8] Operation Bagration, named after a Russian general of the Napoleonic Wars, was launched in stages beginning on June 19, and timed to coincide with the third anniversary of Operation Barbarossa. Tens of thousands of Belorussian partisans began the offensive with strikes on German lines of communication. Partisans also helped coordinate massive bombing raids on German positions on June 21. On June 23, a ground force of nearly 1.7 million soldiers, 2,700 tanks, and 27,000 artillery pieces began a staggered attack across a 500-mile-long front, mangling the twenty-five German divisions that formed Army Group Center. Over the next two weeks, the Soviets killed, wounded, or captured at least 300,000 Wehrmacht soldiers.[9] To put this achievement on display, Stalin ordered the staging of a massive parade of German POWs in Moscow—the first of its kind. Back in 1941, when German forces appeared to be on the verge of taking Moscow, Hitler had ruled out a victory parade in Moscow, as he judged the soon-to-be destroyed city a poor backdrop and mused that rather than gathering "visible laurels," the objective was to "annihilate the enemy."[10] Now, defeated German soldiers were to be marched through the Soviet capital they had failed to conquer.

In all, twenty-six trains carrying fifty-seven thousand prisoners were brought to Moscow in mid-July from camps in Belorussia. The German soldiers were given extra food and water ahead of the march and, in accordance with the Geneva Convention, allowed to wear their uniforms and medals. Moscow residents learned only on the morning of July 17, a Monday, that the parade would be held that day. Public announcements called on spectators to maintain strict discipline.[11] Hundreds of

German prisoners of war in Moscow on the morning of July 17, 1944.

thousands of Muscovites rushed to the capital's Garden Ring, which served as a long parade ground, to catch a glimpse of the Germans. The prisoners marched in rows twenty men wide, flanked by NKVD guards on foot and horseback. A group of German officers and generals spearheaded the column, some with heads held high. Surviving film footage shows the encounter between the Germans and their Soviet spectators proceeding in almost total silence, the only sound the clanking of the tin bottles and bowls that the captives carried on their backs. Some photographs show spectators shaking their fists at the Germans. Later that day, Stalin received a report from the NKVD confirming that the march had proceeded without incident, and listing the slogans occasionally shouted by some of the spectators: "'Death to Hitler!' 'Death to fascism!' 'The bastards should bite the dust,' 'Why weren't you all wiped out on the front?' and others."[12]

The massive display of controlled Soviet rage was deemed so successful that Khrushchev secured Stalin's permission to hold another march of German prisoners through Kiev four weeks later. Unlike Moscow, Kiev had been under occupation and its residents had suffered at the hands of the Germans. Soviet Ukrainian authorities wanted to confront

German prisoners of war on the Moscow Garden Ring, July 17, 1944.

the Axis soldiers with the evidence of their crimes. The thirteen-mile route started near the Babi Yar ravine before proceeding through the ruined city center.[13] While onlookers were ordered to restrain themselves, the NKVD recorded agitation among the crowd. The march went past a hospital housing disabled war veterans, and several patients broke through the security cordon and hit prisoners with their crutches. "Shoot them all!" "Shame on the murderers!" were among the shouts recorded by the NKVD observer.

In his report to Stalin, Khrushchev peppered his account of the parade with emotional testimonies from spectators who had lived through the occupation. Many contrasted the humane Soviet treatment of the German prisoners with their own memories of the Germans' inhumane treatment of Soviet POWs over the past three years. A female bookkeeper remarked on the healthy appearance of "those cannibals," adding that she well remembered the terrible sight of the Red Army prisoners who had been forcibly marched through the streets of Kiev. "They drove our wounded at a trot, and we stuff their faces and let them walk at a gentle pace," a male worker asserted. "I wouldn't fuss over them like that. I'd repay them tenfold." To this, one woman responded: "We Russians forget offenses too quickly."[14]

The marches in Kiev and Moscow ended in almost exactly the same way. After the last prisoners were taken away, street-cleaning trucks brushed and sprayed the streets, symbolically cleansing them of German fascist filth. Some five thousand of the thirty-seven thousand prisoners who had been marched through Kiev were kept there to help rebuild the city. Others were sent as laborers to Ukraine's destroyed shipyards on the Black Sea and the flooded coal mines in the Donbas region. The Moscow prisoners, all recently captured, were marched to the city's two eastern train stations to board freight trains that took them to camps deep in the Soviet interior, where the process of assessing their guilt would begin.

THE FIRST NAZI WAR CRIMES TRIAL

As German soldiers poured into Soviet prison camps, their interrogators drew up an indictment that grew more comprehensive every day. Operatives from the NKVD and SMERSH (an acronym for "Death to Spies" used to denote a collection of military counterintelligence units) strove to document every single Nazi crime. They proceeded methodically by linking evidence of specific atrocities to Axis units that could be proven to have been present at the time, and then charging the members of these units.[15] The fact that German soldiers often took photographs documenting their participation in the mass shootings of Jews and suspected partisans helped Soviet prosecutors significantly in assembling a case-by-case record of the offenses.

Pravda shared some of this record with Soviet readers in an October 1943 report that featured five photographs retrieved from the body of a German officer killed near Smolensk. The pictures showed the hanging of the female partisan Zoya Kosmodemyanskaya (initially identified as "Tanya") on November 29, 1941. Soviet readers remembered well the photograph of Zoya's dead and mutilated body that Sergei Strunnikov had taken when he and *Pravda* reporter Pyotr Lidov covered her story in the January 1942 article entitled "Tanya." The newly discovered

ПРАВДА 3

Проклятие и смерть гитлеровским палачам!

Убийство Зои Космодемьянской

Смотрите, люди!

Пять немецких фотографий

Page from Pravda, *October 24, 1943.*

photos revealed how the Germans had treated the partisan as she was being put to death. One image, the first of the five, shows the gallows in an empty village square, with two soldiers standing guard. Another focuses on Zoya wearing a placard around her neck with the word "Partisan" written on it, as German officers and soldiers, some of them smiling, lead her to her execution. A third depicts a crowd of German soldiers and Russian villagers surrounding the gallows. Zoya, her head turned away from the gallows, appears to speak to the spectators. Two Germans fit the noose around her neck in the fourth photograph. In the fifth, they pose for a final shot next to Zoya's lifeless body.[16]

Once more tasked with writing about Zoya, Lidov voiced outrage about the "Hitlerites" who did not merely "torture and hang" but celebrated these acts as spectacles. Lidov noted that the soldiers in the photographs had been identified as members of the 332nd Regiment, part of the 197th Infantry Division. A captured NCO from the regiment had confessed to witnessing the execution. The soldier who had taken the photographs was dead. Remaining at large was the main culprit, Lieutenant-Colonel Ludwig Ruederer, who had interrogated Zoya and was one of the two German officers who hanged her. "Everything that was hidden is becoming clear," Lidov commented; none of the German perpetrators would escape Soviet judgment.[17]

Soviet efforts to prosecute German war crimes predated those of their Western Allies and proceeded with greater zeal. Planning for the Extraordinary State Commission for Establishing and Investigating Crimes Committed by the German Fascist Invaders (ChGK) had begun in early 1942, shortly after the Red Army first regained control of towns and villages that had been ravaged by the Nazis.[18] The ChGK took up its work in November 1942, and within a year had accumulated a dossier of thirty-two thousand serious crimes.[19] By contrast, the UN War Crimes Commission (UNWCC), which was founded in the West, did not begin its work until October 1943, and within its first year assembled a much smaller volume of cases.[20]

As early as October 1942, Soviet leaders proposed the formation of an international tribunal to try Nazi perpetrators.[21] The idea initially found no support among Western Allied leaders, who believed such a forum was impractical for dealing with an entire criminal regime and favored summary executions performed out of the public eye.[22] There was the additional fear that wartime prosecutions of German POWs would provoke German reprisals against captured British or American soldiers. The Soviet side had nothing to lose on this score, as millions of Soviet POWs and civilians had already died at the hands of their German captors.[23] Allied delegations patched over some of their differences at the Moscow Conference in November 1943 by agreeing that all major Nazi perpetrators whose crimes transcended a particular geographic location would face a joint Allied tribunal after the end of hostilities. Lesser war criminals would be returned to the scene of their crimes to be judged "by the peoples whom they have outraged." No effort would be spared to pursue the accused "to the uttermost ends of the earth."[24]

The ink on the Moscow Declaration had barely dried when the Soviet government began preparations for the first Nazi war crimes tribunal held by any Allied power. The Kharkov trial opened on December 14, 1943—two years to the day after the mass shooting of the city's Jews.[25]

Kharkov's Drama Theatre served as the venue for the four-day public hearings. To allow as many members of the public to attend as possible, different spectators were brought into the auditorium each day; cameras also filmed the proceedings for millions of Soviet viewers to witness. *The Christian Science Monitor* correspondent, Edmund Stevens, was among the journalists who followed the trial in person, and he described the atmosphere in the theater as one of concentrated silence: "The faces of these Kharkov civilians who had lived through two years of Nazi occupation—mostly young girls and older men and women—were charged with a breathless tenseness that never once relaxed through the long hours of the interrogation." Stevens had reported from Moscow for many years, and his first impressions in Kharkov brought back memories of the 1930s show trials. He pointedly noted that two of the defense lawyers had participated in the infamous Moscow trials. Noting this "element of direct continuity," Stevens had questions about the validity of the Soviet charges. By the time the Kharkov court had reached its verdict, however, Stevens's doubts had vanished. The evidence that had been brought against the German defendants was overwhelming.[26]

Three of the four men standing trial were Germans: a noncommissioned officer from the German military's Secret Field Police, a captain from the Wehrmacht's espionage service, and an SS second lieutenant from a special commando unit of the Security Police. The fourth defendant was a Russian who had worked for the commando unit as a driver.[27] The men were indicted for the mass killing of Soviet POWs and civilians, including by asphyxiation in gas vans. The gas van drew particular attention from the court. As the SS had been at pains not to let any of their "special vans" fall into Soviet hands, prosecutors in Kharkov questioned the defendants at length about how they were operated. Several of the men confirmed that they had seen how victims were loaded onto the vans and then removed after suffocating to death. The Russian defendant, Mikhail Bulanov, testified that his job was to maintain a gas van that had been brought from Germany in early 1942. While cleaning the cargo area, he frequently saw children's knit caps or shoes on the floor. He declared that he had never personally operated the van.[28]

The three Germans confessed to having killed scores of Soviet POWs and civilians. But they all sought to relativize their personal responsibility for these deeds. The defendant from the special commando unit, Hans Ritz, testified that after his transfer to Kharkov in late May 1943 he learned that three thousand residents who had welcomed the Red Army during its brief occupation of the city earlier that year were to be shot. Ritz volunteered to attend the shooting. At the killing site, an SS major who knew Ritz from before the war turned to him and said: "Show us what you're made of." "And I," Ritz stated, "as a military man, an officer, did not refuse. I took a submachine gun from one of the SS soldiers and fired a burst at the prisoners." Though the Soviet state procurator extracted an acknowledgment from Ritz that he had carried out the killings of his own free will, Ritz blamed the "systematic" culture of lawlessness on the Eastern Front, where individual German soldiers were under express orders to transgress international conventions of war. Wilhelm Langheld, the captain from the Wehrmacht's espionage service, went even further, characterizing himself as a "victim" of orders issued by the German government.[29]

On December 18, the court found the defendants guilty of all charges

The defendants at the Kharkov trial. From left to right: Mikhail Bulanov, Hans Ritz, Reinhard Retzlaff, and Wilhelm Langheld.

brought against them and sentenced all four to death by hanging. Death on the gallows had been outlawed in revolutionary Russia as an inhumane form of execution, but it was reintroduced in April 1943 to deal specifically with Axis perpetrators of "unheard-of atrocities and monstrous violence" on occupied Soviet soil.[30] The public execution that took place in Kharkov's City Square on December 19 resembled the well-documented German execution of Wolf Kieper and Moshe Kogan in Zhitomir in August 1941: The defendants were hoisted onto the back of open trucks, where nooses were fastened around their necks. At a signal, the trucks pulled away, leaving the four men kicking in midair.[31] The similarities between the executions stopped there though: Unlike in Zhitomir, where the German show trial served as the prelude to a massacre of hundreds of local Jews, no Soviet official incited the many thousands of spectators to rampage and kill. An observer described the execution as proceeding "in a somehow very businesslike, mundane way. Little boys whistled, the public applauded." Only one woman was heard shouting: "It's not enough to hang these bastards! Burn them!" The observer learned that Germans had shot or hanged the woman's daughter on the same city square.[32]

Every reporter who covered the Kharkov trial came to watch the executions, save for Ilya Ehrenburg, who reportedly called hanging morally debasing.[33] From his earliest articles, even when calling on Red Army men to kill German soldiers, Ehrenburg had stressed the importance of keeping the moral high ground.[34] Under no circumstances were Soviet citizens to act on a desire for "total revenge." To allow instinct to guide their actions would ultimately lead to the murder of German children or the destruction of Goethe's house in Weimar. "Revenge and payback speak the same language. We, however, don't share a language with the fascists."[35] The significance of the Kharkov trial to Ehrenburg was its affirmation of justice, rather than blind vengeance, as the way to deal with fascism. The Soviet exercise of justice would force the Germans to account for deeds they thought would go unpunished.[36]

Or would it? As he listened to the German defendants, Ehrenburg had doubts about the power of trials to confront the evil at the heart of

Nazism. The men's words revealed a human deformation that was far more troubling than their individual criminal records. For the past ten years, Nazism had encouraged millions of Germans to abandon their sense of right and wrong. "If you cut off a man's hair, the hair will grow back," Ehrenburg wrote. "But if you cut out his conscience, it will not grow back." Without a moral compass, these Germans had become hardened criminals. While pretending to fight a defensive war, in reality they had launched a "gigantic raid on Europe," which would ultimately lead to "the destruction of everything sacred to humanity." Could justice prevail against such deep wickedness? And was there, Ehrenburg wondered, a courthouse sufficiently large to accommodate all German war criminals?[37]

In the aftermath of the trial, when further evidence of the Nazis' crimes reached his desk, Ehrenburg's perspective on the enemy grew darker still. In a January 1944 article, the writer presented testimony from four rank-and-file German soldiers. A combat engineer (Lothar Franke, private first class of the 751st Army Sapper Battalion) detailed under interrogation how his unit and others had methodically torched and destroyed entire villages. An infantryman (Hermann Scholz, Sixth Infantry Division) described in a letter to his brother how he had carried out a superior's order to "liquidate" a "small bunch of women" found hiding in the forest: "My machine gunners were not hard to persuade, everything was resolved in three or four minutes." The third man in this sample was a German tanker (Paul Vogt, 23rd Panzer Division) who wrote in a personal letter: "We tied these girls up, and then we gradually flattened them with our tracks in such a way that was pleasant to look at." The fourth was a former bank employee assigned as a waiter to an officers' mess. Under interrogation, he confessed to raiding a village near Gatchina and returning with a truckload of local girls to please the "gentlemen officers." The next morning, the girls were handed over to the waiter and other soldiers, who raped them in turn. These documents demonstrated to Ehrenburg that German criminality was not confined to the SS, the Secret Field Police, and other security organs. All Germans deployed to the East were implicated.[38]

Days later, another German document fell into Ehrenburg's hands. Writing to his brother, a technical sergeant named Günther Zessner recalled the eighteen months he had spent as a member of the occupation forces in Kiev, Ehrenburg's city of origin: "Sometimes, I was forced to resort to harsh measures, but frankly speaking, I'm not sentimental, and my nerves are strong. On the other hand, for a year and a half, my life was one of complete pleasure: the cooking was good, vodka, beer, girls, walks, and so, I took what I could get out of life." At this time, Ehrenburg was feverishly at work preparing a compendium of documents detailing the Nazi murder of Soviet Jews, provisionally entitled *The Black Book*. He read Zessner's letter side by side with a letter he received from a Jewish survivor of the Babi Yar massacre.[39] The witness recorded the last words of a little girl whom the Germans had thrown into the ravine to bury alive. "Why are you throwing sand in my eyes?" the little girl screamed. "I hear this child's scream at night," Ehrenburg wrote, "and I think: Günther Zessner has left Kiev. He's alive. . . . Will Zessner really escape punishment? . . . Will thousands and thousands of child killers really escape punishment?" Overcome with rage, Ehrenburg suggested a new way of reckoning with the Germans before they were able to get away. Eschewing his earlier differentiation between moral justice and revenge, he appealed directly to his Red Army soldier readers to act as avenging judges:

> If you've seen the ashes of the villages, you will not forget. If you've seen a mother's tears, you will not forgive. You will not relinquish your rights to anyone: you are the judge. . . . Find the executioners now. . . . Track down the cursed Günther, and Kurt, and Karl. All of them! Remember the little girl screaming "Why are you throwing sand in my eyes?" Do not let her executioners get away. Hurry! They want to slip away, worm their way out, hide. They came to our country, but they will not leave.[40]

Never before had Ehrenburg called on Red Army soldiers to take justice into their own hands, and never would he repeat this raw appeal. Even after this article, he would continue to advocate for justice through courts and trials. And yet the writer's momentary lapse of judgment would prove momentous. Propagandists in the Red Army deemed the piece so important that after its first publication in the army newspaper *Defeat the Enemy!* it was reprinted in twenty-three other army papers and scores of brochures. Millions of Red Army soldiers read or heard Ehrenburg's plea.[41]

CHANGING THE GERMANS?

Influential as it was, Ehrenburg's indictment of all German soldiers differed from other official Soviet views. As early as February 1942, Stalin had made a principled distinction between "Hitler's clique" and Germany as a whole, concluding: "The experience of history indicates that Hitlers come and go, but the German people and the German state remain."[42] Citing this dictum, a leading Red Army propagandist said, "We know no racial hatred toward the Germans and do not intend to destroy Germany and its people."[43] According to this line, even Germans who had joined Hitler's party or fought in his army could redeem themselves if they were receptive to Marxist-Leninist political education. Also in early 1942, sixty German writers and politicians in Soviet exile called on their compatriots "to wash the shame whose name is Hitler from the German homeland" and to reclaim its erstwhile standing as the nation of "Goethe and Schiller, Bach and Beethoven . . . Hegel, Marx, and Engels."[44]

Among the authors of the declaration was Friedrich Wolf, the German Communist writer who had advocated literature as a weapon at the Moscow Congress of Writers in 1934. Wolf stood at the forefront of the fight to reclaim Germany from the Nazis. Over the course of the war, he wrote and broadcast hundreds of appeals to Nazi soldiers to denounce Hitler.[45] When Soviet victory at Stalingrad brought the prospect of Nazism's defeat into view in early 1943, the Kremlin approved the creation of a German national committee on Soviet soil, which Wolf and other German Communists in exile had lobbied for.[46] Weeks later, Stalin abolished the Comintern to signal that the USSR had abandoned its prior commitment to world revolution and would instead work with Allied leaders to defeat German fascism.[47]

The National Committee for a Free Germany (NKFD), a state-sponsored organization, was formed in July 1943 in a prisoner camp near Moscow. Two-thirds of its founding members were captured Wehrmacht officers and soldiers, and the other third was comprised of German Communists in Soviet exile, including Wolf.[48] "Germany must not perish!" the committee's founding manifesto proclaimed, urging all other Germans to break with Hitler to rescue their "freedom and honor."[49] NKFD leaders sought to do their part by assisting Soviet efforts to spiritually transform former fascist soldiers. Prisoners in some camps attended "anti-fascist schools," where the Soviet instructors sought to inculcate in them a sense of personal responsibility for their past actions. In addition to taking mandatory courses in Marxism-Leninism, prisoners were encouraged to compose autobiographies that traced their emerging awareness of the "Hitlerite" regime's depravity and their own complicity in it. In doing so, the NKFD's organizers hoped, captured Nazi soldiers might be able to regain their conscience.[50]

Some of the efforts bore fruits. Lieutenant Bernd von Kügelgen, who had fallen into Soviet hands in July 1942 and gone through anti-fascist schooling, traveled to the front lines in Ukraine in fall 1943 as an NKFD spokesman. Under Soviet supervision, Kügelgen summoned newly captured German soldiers to Babi Yar to exhume the dead. He observed them as they set out to work in the ravine:

> They are silent. They have no words to express what moves them. Only now and then do they speak up, denounce Hitler, denounce his murderous troops. But they know that merely saying "I didn't do it," or "Down with Hitler!" isn't enough. For we are all to blame. And it must be our business to bring these criminals to justice, for the sole way to overcome our guilt is through action.[51]

In the evenings, after the POWs had returned to the barracks and cleansed themselves with disinfectant, Kügelgen organized group meetings to encourage joint reflection. Without prompting, soldier after soldier stepped up to break with Hitler and join the anti-fascist fight.[52]

While Kügelgen saw seeds of redemption sprouting from the site of a horrific crime, other NKFD emissaries felt overwhelmed as they came face-to-face with what the Germans had done. Upon seeing the razed city of Mariupol and talking with pained survivors, Wolf understood that such systematic brutality, which included the mass shootings of civilians, could not have been carried out by just a few SS commandos. The trail of violence indicted the Wehrmacht as a whole.[53] To Wolf's dismay, hardly any of the captured German soldiers he talked with expressed contrition for their deeds. In addition, the younger recruits revealed themselves to be severely undereducated: They lacked basic math skills and had trouble identifying leading German writers and statesmen. From the start of the war, Wolf had intentionally struck a colloquial tone in his leaflets addressed to Wehrmacht soldiers in order to reach average Germans fighting for Nazism.[54] He now came to the bitter realization that the words and values of a German writer in exile no longer spoke to his young countrymen who had been groomed by Hitler. "I'm often distressed when I see these 'Germans,'" Wolf wrote to his wife from southern Ukraine.[55]

In February 1944, the Red Army trapped sixty thousand enemy soldiers west of the Dniepr River. The highest-ranking NKFD officers rushed to the pocket between Korsun and Cherkasy to convince the trapped German commanders to lay down their arms. Their appeals fell on deaf ears. In anticipation of such encounters, Wehrmacht propagandists had produced leaflets denouncing "the Jew Friedrich Wolf" and other national committee members: One leaflet noted that the NKFD, in their "jabberings" over loudspeakers, addressed the German soldiers as "countrymen," and indignantly protested that the soldiers were not from Palestine, and while they were indeed fighting for a free Germany, they understood it as a Germany free of Jews.[56] Ruling out capitulation, Hitler ordered other troops to the rescue. As the encircled divisions fled through a narrow opening cut into the pocket, Red Army tanks and cavalry units gave chase, killing at least twenty thousand Germans.[57]

For General Walther von Seydlitz, the highest-ranking NKFD general to negotiate in the Korsun-Cherkasy pocket, the failed disarmament attempt served as a reminder of the enduring power of the "Bolshevik scare." If German soldiers could not be dissuaded from fighting Soviet troops to their death, this was owing to the deep-seated fear of all things Bolshevik that the Nazis had been inculcating for years.[58] Seydlitz also attributed the NKFD's poor performance to their dependence on Moscow; the organization could easily be dismissed as a Bolshevik front organization. As Seydlitz reported to Soviet officials about the fruitless journey to the Korsun pocket, he pleaded with them to free the National Committee from Communist oversight, but his appeal went unanswered.[59] The Bolshevik stain also hampered the work of the NKFD inside the German prison camps. In the end, only a relatively small number of captured Wehrmacht soldiers became committed anti-fascists. Most remained loyal to their officers, who as a rule remained ardent anti-Communists.[60]

For as long as he possibly could, General Field Marshal Friedrich Paulus, the German military leader who had been captured at Stalingrad, avoided taking on a public role in the NKFD. He feared entering history as the perpetrator of a new "stab in the back" against the German army. In the wake of the failed assassination attempt against Hitler on July 20, 1944, sixteen Wehrmacht generals who had been captured during Operation Bagration publicly called for Hitler's overthrow. Soviet political officers now pressured Paulus to take a stand: Would he come out as a "marshal of the German people" or as "Hitler's marshal"? If he chose the latter, the Soviets predicted an "ignominious death" for Paulus—a veiled allusion to death by hanging at a future tribunal.[61] Time was of the essence: Operation Bagration's stunning success had brought the Red Army to the border of East Prussia in summer 1944.

On August 8, Paulus broke his silence on the "Free Germany" radio station, calling on his countrymen to renounce Hitler and demand peace.[62] His appeal appeared in the NKFD's newspaper next to a picture of him and General Seydlitz shaking hands. In the photograph, Paulus's eyes are closed; he looks lifeless.[63] Nazi leaders responded to Paulus's action by incarcerating his wife and children. The High Command in Berlin had already punished Seydlitz in absentia the previous spring, dismissing him from the army and condemning him to death for cutting a deal with the Bolsheviks, thereby "stabbing his fellow soldiers in the back."[64]

INTO GERMANY

Massive artillery strikes pounded East Prussia's border regions on the morning of October 16, 1944. The attack on Germany had begun. In preparation for the Soviet onslaught, the Germans had built up three defensive rings, mined the land, and turned villages into fortresses. Fighting was so intense it took three days before the first soldiers of the Third Belorussian Front stepped onto German soil. Their advance was short-lived: Within days, German reinforcements beat back the Soviets, at terrific human cost to the Red Army.[65] Only in January 1945 did the Soviet High Command gather enough reserves to launch a second, far larger offensive against East Prussia. That strike, which began on January 13, involved 1.6 million soldiers, four times the number that had taken part in the operation in October. In less than two weeks, the Red Army had encircled East Prussia and laid siege to the capital city of Königsberg. This second offensive was part of a larger campaign involving nearly 6.5 million Soviet troops, double the number that the Germans had mobilized for their invasion of the Soviet Union. On January 12, an army more than 2 million strong had attacked along the Vistula River, bypassing the well-defended "fortress" of Warsaw and forcing the Germans to abandon the Polish capital. On January 18, the Red Army took Cracow, which the Germans had made the capital of the General Government. Nine days later, on January 27, Soviet troops liberated Auschwitz.

Ehrenburg wrote of the incursion into Germany in *Red Star*. The reckoning awaited by the Soviet people had arrived. He scoffed at the vow made by Erich Koch, East Prussia's gauleiter and formerly Reich commissar for Ukraine, not to cede an inch of Prussian soil. Soviet soldiers

A truck with Soviet soldiers passing over a bridge in the East Prussian town of Eydtkuhnen. The poster to the right announces: "Forward into the lair of the fascist beast!" December 1944.

knew Koch all too well, Ehrenburg wrote; they remembered his crimes and those of innumerable other Germans in the East. "We are going into their country, our hearts filled with the grief for . . . the torn bodies of the children of Babi Yar, the ravaged villages they left behind . . . the many who starved during the siege of Leningrad . . . grief for the gallows in Volokolamsk . . . and the 'ghettos' where millions of defenseless people were brutally murdered." Ehrenburg ended: "Woe to those who have murdered children, woe to the instigators, perpetrators, and accomplices. They will not escape retribution."[66]

Ehrenburg had become the voice of Russia's war: In addition to appearing in multiple newspapers, the writer's flaming words filled frontline military directives, were featured on flyers and posters, and infused the personal writings of Red Army soldiers as they crossed into Germany. An order from Marshal Georgy Zhukov, commander of the First Belorussian Front, to the soldiers fighting in the second East Prussian operation liberally borrowed from Ehrenburg's writings as it invoked the memory of those "burned in the hellish ovens," those "put to death in the gas chambers," and those "shot and hanged," before declaring: "We are going to Germany, yet behind us lie Stalingrad, Ukraine, and Belorussia. We are walking through the ashes of our cities and villages, along the trails of blood left by our Soviet people who were tortured to death and torn to pieces by the fascist jackals. Let the land of the murderers tremble with terror!" The last line was Ehrenburg's.[67] But the order continued with a declaration that unquestionably contradicted Ehrenburg's thinking: "We will exact cruel revenge for everything."

In the hands of military commanders and political officers, Ehrenburg's prose was reworked to maximally condition Soviet soldiers for combat. In the process, the writer's critical distinction between justice and vengeance got lost and appeals to retributive rage that he generally rejected won the upper hand. "Exact merciless revenge on the fascist child murderers and henchmen!" wrote Colonel-General Vasily Glagolev to the soldiers under his command.[68] The military council of the 20th Army demanded that soldiers "mercilessly exterminate" the "fascist, bloody murderers." In winter 1944, a battalion of former deserters who were meant to redeem themselves in battle marched past a poster bearing the words: "Soldier, you are the judge!—Ilya Ehrenburg." During an interview with a historian, the battalion's commander refused to discuss in detail how his soldiers interpreted Ehrenburg's truncated message. Their behavior on German soil, he said, spoke for itself.[69]

The Soviet winter campaign into Germany's eastern provinces unleashed a rampage that had no precedent in the history of the Red Army. No region between the Memel River and Upper Silesia remained untouched by Soviet soldiers marauding, raping, and murdering. Their violent deeds were extensively documented—not only by German survivors, but by Soviet observers as well.[70] But as the Red Army marched through Europe, their destruction was greater in some areas than in others. The 300,000 Soviet soldiers who took part in the liberation of Belgrade in late 1944 committed 1,219 rapes during that campaign, according to Yugoslav authorities. The real number may have been much higher, but even so, it was significantly less than the possibly hundreds of thousands of rapes committed by Soviets in East Prussia.[71] The vast difference in the scale of violence owed to the sharp distinction Soviet soldiers made between friendly soil and enemy soil. No place was more reviled than Germany.[72]

Soviet soldiers articulated this hatred in their letters and diaries. At pains to justify their actions, authors emphasized the death and destruction that Germany had dealt to the Soviet people since 1941. "We are retaliating for everything, for our wounds, for Leningrad, for Moscow, for the children and the elderly, for our girls," a soldier wrote to his friend on the eve of the first invasion of East Prussia. "If you knew what I saw as I walked across the fields of our dear Belorussia and Lithuania, you'd understand what I am thinking now," a Jewish sergeant wrote to his sister prior to the January offensive. A month later, he wrote to her again from inside Germany. "You know very well that we came here to take revenge, and if you knew how we took revenge, you'd agree that the Germans will never dare to invade us again."[73] A soldier from the Moldovan town of Tiraspol after entering East Prussia wrote: "Let the German mother now curse the day she gave birth to a son! Let the German women now feel the horrors of war! Let the Germans now experience what they inflicted on other peoples."[74]

Artillery officer Yuri Uspensky (39th Guard Army), a veteran soldier who had fought since 1941, kept a diary detailing his activity in East Prussia. "The war has been raging for more than three years," he wrote in January 1945. "Millions of people have lost their lives and millions must bear monstrous torments." His mother was dead, Uspensky noted, his father had died in battle, his sister did not respond to his letters, and his wife was so ill that he feared for her life.[75] Uspensky entered East Prussian cities that were already in Soviet hands. The sight of truckloads of Soviet soldiers filing through Insterburg elated the officer, even as he acknowledged its ominous meaning for the Germans. "This is revenge for everything the Germans have done to us. Now their cities are being destroyed and their people are learning what war means!" The German slogan "Death to Bolshevism," painted on the walls of buildings in Gumbinnen, reminded Uspensky of the identically worded flyers the

Germans had showered over Soviet front lines in 1941. "You reap what you sow!" he wrote as he watched fellow Red Army soldiers set local buildings on fire.[76]

How was the quest for vengeance to be squared with the Red Army's mission as a liberating army? Was violence against German civilians justified in light of the horrors that the Germans had perpetrated on Soviet soil? How far should retributive violence go? Most of the Soviet soldiers who struggled with these questions in their diaries were highly educated officers and party members, believers in Marxism and Communist ethics. Some worked in intelligence, others were artillerists—both military sectors known for their high educational standards. They looked down on "backward" peasant recruits who often fought in the infantry, the branch of the Soviet military with the lowest percentage of Communists and highest incidence of disciplinary breaches.[77]

When Uspensky heard of the murder of a German woman and two children in a recently occupied village, his initial reaction was to justify the killings:

> The Germans deserved the atrocities, which they committed first. One need only remember Majdanek to understand why our soldiers take pleasure in destroying East Prussia. It is very cruel to kill children, but the Germans' cold-bloodedness at Majdanek was a hundred times worse. And the Germans celebrated their actions. . . . It's especially criminal that they're continuing with the war when there is no doubt about its outcome: Because of this, Germany will have to suffer.[78]

But every day, Uspensky learned of more crimes, some of them committed by soldiers from his own unit. The house in which the divisional staff had taken quarter was filled with German refugees—mostly women and children. Groups of drunken Red Army men had reportedly entered the house and raped the women and girls. One woman was dragged outside, forced to lie down on a slaughtered cow, and raped atop the animal's frozen intestines. Such "orgies" went on all night, Uspensky wrote: "You can't say this is good. One should take revenge, but with a weapon, not the penis." Soviet acts of violence against enemy civilians, especially children, threatened to obliterate the distinction, essential to Uspensky, between the Red Army as a force fighting for humanist values and the Wehrmacht, which fought against everything humanism stood for. "We are not Germans," another officer wrote in a letter to his family, as he described why it was wrong to give soldiers free rein in their treatment of German civilians.[79]

As commander of a reconnaissance team that crisscrossed East Prussia, Sergeant Major Nikolai Inozemtsev witnessed a trail of Soviet destruction that left no part of the province unscathed: "Burning German cities," he wrote in his diary, "traces of hit-and-run battles on the roads, groups of captured Germans (they surrender in groups, afraid to do so individually—for fear they'll be shot), corpses of men, women, and children in apartments, processions of carts with refugees, . . . raped women . . . devastated villages, hundreds and thousands of abandoned bicycles on the roads, a huge number of cattle bellowing with all their might (there's no one to milk and water the cows)." Inozemtsev then took note of his own activities: "dozens and hundreds of kilometers ridden daily, a changing landscape, stops in rich manor houses, rushed meals, meetings with liberated Russians, French, Americans, who will certainly be remembered for a lifetime, sleeping at night for three–four hours, trophies—all this flickers as if in a kaleidoscope, filling the cup of life to the brim."[80]

The kaleidoscope was an apt analogy. Inozemtsev's invocations of conquest and liberation, violence and exuberance, were too conflicting to fit into a single frame. And yet a frame had to be found. Like Uspensky and other Soviet soldier-diarists, Inozemtsev objected to Red Army atrocities committed against German civilians, as they offended his identity as a Soviet citizen and officer. A conversation with an officer friend provided some clarity. Both men readily agreed that German suffering was not the issue. What concerned them was how the brutes among the Red Army's rank and file undercut the "dignity of the army as a whole and of each soldier individually." There remained one reassuring thought: No matter how shameful, the violence perpetrated by

Soviet soldiers running wild took place in violation of the laws and stated principles of the Soviet state. By contrast, the mass murders performed by the Germans "were organized and led by the government."[81]

In fact, the Soviet military had been struggling to stem the lawlessness among their own ranks since the beginning of the winter campaign. A January 20 order signed by Stalin threatened with execution any soldier who raped women or committed other acts of unjustified violence on conquered soil.[82] Army group leaders and army commanders subsequently passed similar decrees invoking Stalin's words.[83] An order by the 48th Army Command described a case in which inebriated servicemen had shot German women and elderly people. The shooting was "caused by no necessity of any kind whatsoever and was done only out of mischief." The order instructed military prosecutors to shoot selected culprits in the presence of their unit and urged political officers to explain to soldiers that burning down German houses and killing enemy civilians were criminal infractions.[84] A *Red Star* editorial reminded readers that "if the Germans marauded and publicly raped our women, it does not mean that we must do the same. . . . Our revenge is not blind."[85]

In response to these instructions, some officers executed perpetrators. In occupied Allenstein, a colonel shot a lieutenant who had lined up his men in a passageway and ordered them to gang-rape a German woman who was lying on the ground.[86] Other commanders chose to ignore such violations. Sometimes soldiers shot the officers who sought to discipline them.[87] Even though Red Army prosecutors handed down more than four thousand criminal sentences to officers alone between January and March 1945, the NKVD reported the ongoing rape of women of every age, including girls.[88] A woman from East Prussia told NKVD interrogators that she had been gang-raped by Soviet soldiers the very first day they entered her town. Later, after suffering multiple additional serial rapes, sometimes in the presence of her children, she slit her wrists and her children's. The report does not say whether any of them survived.[89] Multiple NKVD operatives came upon groups of German civilians bleeding from attempted suicides. Some of them refused medical help. Expecting even worse violence, they considered a quick death preferable.[90]

Red Army soldiers also directed their fury against German-owned houses and apartments. "There is no mercy for any house. No mercy for furniture, for clocks, for mirrors" was how a serviceman from Novgorod described the destruction in a letter to his parents.[91] A feeling of retribution was evident in these outbursts. As the soldier continued: "Let their wives, mothers, and others shed tears for everything, just as you shed them." The vast material gap between Germany and the USSR reinforced Red Army soldiers' resentment. They were baffled when they saw the comparable luxury of German life, even in the sixth year of war. The varied and well-stocked stores, the richly furnished dwellings, and the soft bedding like something out of a fairy tale prompted outrage: Why did the Germans, who had everything, attack a country that had so little?[92] The gap seemed to demean the poor victors in the rich conquered land. As a female Red Army soldier wrote to a friend back home in the Urals:

> Nina, if there was a way, one could send wonderful packages of loot. There are a lot of good things here. Something to cheer each of our barefooted ones, our ragged ones. The cities I have seen, the men and women! When I see them, I am overcome with such hatred! They go for walks, love one another, they are simply living their lives, and we liberate them while they laugh at us and call us "*Schwein*."[93]

Even those Soviet soldiers who refrained from assaulting enemy civilians and burning down their houses felt a simmering rage toward the Germans, who continued to project their feeling of racial supremacy even in defeat.[94]

In February 1945, Ehrenburg traveled to East Prussia to see firsthand the country that had occupied his attention for the past twelve years. His subsequent feature for *Red Star*, entitled "In Germany," dealt with two interrelated issues.[95] The first was the German denial of guilt. Ehrenburg spoke with Germans in numerous conquered villages and towns. Few confessed to having backed Hitler; no one admitted to knowing anything about German crimes in the East. A villager from near Elbing mumbled he was an "anti-fascist" and raised his fist, shouting the communist greeting "Rot Front." But Red Army soldiers searching his house found a photo album the man had failed to burn in time. Along with pictures of picnics, newlyweds, and children, the album featured two photographs of hanged Russians with placards attached to their chests that said: "I am a partisan accomplice. I wanted to set fire to the sawmill." A third picture showed a group of women with yellow stars sewn on the backs of their coats. They were standing in a fenced-off area, awaiting execution.[96]

The second issue addressed in Ehrenburg's report was the Soviet treatment of the Germans. He introduced this topic through the story of Major Rozenfeld, the Red Army commandant in Rastenburg whose entire family had been murdered by the Germans, but who nevertheless refrained from doing to the Germans what they had done to him.[97] Rather than imposing a violent punitive regime, Rozenfeld simply commanded German women and elderly men to clean the streets of the destroyed town. The Germans "eagerly wait for instructions," Ehrenburg contemptuously added. At pains to uphold a principled contrast between fascist inhumanity and Soviet humanity, he only featured idealized Soviet soldiers in his reporting, such as a column of Red Army men who on a dark and icy day "quietly" passed a group of fleeing German women and their children. Ehrenburg knew he could not possibly put in print that Red Army men drank, pillaged, and raped; he could only reiterate how Soviet soldiers *should* behave. But the reminders in his text—"I've written more than once that the concept of revenge is inconsistent with the role of the Red Army"—suggested that he had witnessed troubling scenes in East Prussia.

Ehrenburg raised the alarm with political and military authorities upon his return to Moscow. At a meeting with the editorial staff of *Red Star* in early March, he described whole swaths of the Soviet army as "on the verge of disintegration. They engage in looting, destroy and steal valuables, get drunk, and don't refuse the 'favors' of German women." This was as explicit as Ehrenburg felt he could be in addressing the topic of rape. Later that month, Ehrenburg used a presentation at the Frunze Military Academy to castigate the low "culture" among Soviet rank-and-file soldiers: "In the occupied cities and counties, the destruction of property, food, and livestock could be summed up as 'beat, break, smash.'" The political command of the Red Army also came in for criticism. While army propagandists had succeeded in filling Soviet soldiers with rage for the enemy, Ehrenburg remarked, they had failed to raise their own soldiers above the level of the Germans.[98]

Ehrenburg's words confounded his listeners. None of the 150 officers at the military academy who had listened to his blistering talk dared to challenge the famous writer in the moment. But subsequently, four political officers teamed up to denounce him. Three journalists jointly wrote a separate denunciation in response to Ehrenburg's earlier visit to *Red Star*'s office. On March 29, 1945, the head of Soviet military counterespionage notified Stalin: "Lately, the writer I. Ehrenburg, lecturing in public places about his impressions of his trip to East Prussia, has slandered the Red Army."[99]

FEAR AND LOATHING

As the Red Army made its way across East Prussia, Nazi warnings about an impending apocalypse, which had been circulating for twenty-five years, appeared to come true for millions of Germans. Ever since the founding of his movement, Hitler had preached that Bolshevism was organized criminality and that the Jews who controlled the Kremlin sought nothing less than the destruction of Germany. Such rhetoric grew increasingly brutal as the prospect of German victory faded away. One month after the defeat at Stalingrad, the Führer described the threat of Bolshevism as "burned cities . . . destroyed cultural monuments . . . brutally slaughtered masses of people, victims of the hordes from inner Asia, just as in the time of the Hun and Mongol invasions."[100] In early 1944, he called on Germans and their allies to fight even harder, lest they all be killed by a shot to the nape of the neck or "waste away in the woods or swamps of Siberia."[101] Each successive call for resistance cast Germany as a victim of Jewish-Asiatic bloodlust. None mentioned the Nazis' attack on the Soviet state, which had brought the Red Army to Germany's borders in the first place.

Every remaining resource was to be thrown into the fight to stop the Soviet onslaught. Against the backdrop of images of boys from the Hitler Youth fervently digging trenches alongside older male and female workers, a Nazi newsreel from August 1944 elaborated on the effort to build a "defensive wall against the approaching storm of Bolshevism." According to the voice-over, the East Prussian defenses showed "that total war is not just a catchphrase for us, and that the German people are unbeatable when their strengths are fully deployed."[102] In September, Hitler ordered the call-up of all civilian men aged sixteen to sixty. This "total deployment," or *Volkssturm*, was an effort to thwart the enemy's "final design—the extermination of the German race."[103] In this national militia, newly introduced National Socialist Leadership Officers, explicitly modeled on the Soviet political commissar, were tasked with making recruits understand and "fanatically" embrace the existential stakes of Germany's war against Bolshevism.[104] Alongside these propaganda efforts, the military handed out an unprecedented number of death sentences for cowardice, defeatism, and desertion. One army commander ordered that the condemned be hanged the same way the Germans had punished "Bolsheviks," with demeaning placards affixed to them attesting to their "dishonorable" crime.[105]

Nazi leaders also rushed to provide documentary footage that would confirm their predictions of unspeakable Bolshevik terror. During a counterattack, German forces recaptured the village of Nemmersdorf, where they discovered the bodies of twenty-six German civilians—thirteen mostly elderly women, eight men, and five children. Army commanders dispatched officials from the Secret Field Police to Nemmersdorf, where, together with an army doctor, they produced a detailed report. The police inspected the victims who had been laid out in an open grave by local members of the *Volkssturm*. Most had been shot at point-blank range, some in the chest, others in the back of the skull. One woman had been raped before she was murdered. While in Nemmersdorf, the investigators also interviewed refugees from areas farther east. A twenty-three-year-old woman told of her first encounter with Soviet troops in front of her farmhouse. The soldiers fired shots in the air and asked, "You Hitler?" After she said no and was let go, she rushed into the house to burn all her swastika flags and portraits of Hitler. Meanwhile, several Soviet tanks arrived. The tank crews then talked with the Polish laborers at the farm. A short while later, the entire German family—the woman, her parents, and her brother—were brought outside and ordered to stand in front of the barn, where soldiers had set up a machine gun. An officer ordered them to feed the soldiers. After the men had eaten, they left, and the family was spared. The next day, "friendly" Russians stopped at the farmhouse. They shook hands with the young woman after receiving two geese they had demanded. A group of "not particularly friendly" soldiers then followed. They implored an officer to have the family shot. The Germans were spared again when the Polish laborers described their employers as good people. The woman added to her account that on the day of her first encounter with the Red Army, she had been raped by two Soviet soldiers, who took her to a room, pistols drawn, under pretext of an interrogation, and abused her.[106]

Nazi censors did not publish this complex account of Soviet soldiers' alternately savage and more restrained behavior. The story that Nazi leaders highlighted instead was unambiguous and extreme: A BLOODY SIGNAL EVENT—NEMMERSDORF. MOSCOW HAS UNLEASHED ITS MURDEROUS BEASTS screamed the front page of the *Völkischer Beobachter* when the story broke. The paper claimed that Soviet soldiers in Nemmersdorf had acted on orders to terrorize and kill German civilians. The report furnished gory eyewitness accounts of girls and mothers who had been raped and of young children who'd been shot in the head before rising to a passionate peroration:

> Who was it who believed that the Bolsheviks were not so bad? Who thought Katyn and Vinnitsa were fairy tales? . . . Who dismissed the nape shot and the mass grave as inflammatory

> fables? Where is the fool, no, the criminal, who dared to see the Bolsheviks as even a little more human, when we have for years tirelessly shown the world their bloodthirsty countenance? Let him go to Nemmersdorf, and his blood will freeze with horror at the sight of these atrocities, which have never been seen on German soil.

The Nazi paper demanded revenge and the annihilation of Bolshevism "so that the decent people of our continent get the satisfaction they deserve." Days later, photographs and film footage from Nemmersdorf filled the Nazi media, causing panic in towns near the eastern border.[107]

Around the same time, Nazi military propagandists distributed a flyer in German that purported to have come from the Soviets. The flyer called on Red Army soldiers to "break by force the racial arrogance of Germanic women! Take them as your rightful prey!" The exhortation was accompanied by a signature: Ilya Ehrenburg. The Soviet writer had never written these words.[108] This was not the first time that the Germans had put words in his mouth or twisted his statements.[109] By the time the Wehrmacht circulated the falsified flyer, Ehrenburg had become the most widely recognized face of the Jewish Bolshevik enemy. Hitler himself, on January 1, 1945, took aim at him in a warning to Wehrmacht soldiers that "Stalin's house-Jew Ehrenburg" wanted the German nation "smashed" and "eradicated."[110]

In early February 1945, German military intelligence learned about the existence of "strict" orders for Red Army soldiers "to treat German civilians with lenience." One-on-one interrogations of captured Soviet soldiers confirmed that the "beastly behavior" of individuals was in violation of official policy. To the surprise of the German interrogators, there was no order from Stalin decreeing that Soviet soldiers should rape and kill.[111] These findings circulated among party and SS leaders, but did not alter the Nazi claim that the Soviet regime sought the wholesale extermination of the German people. In a February 28 radio address to the nation, Propaganda Minister Goebbels invoked the "agonized cries of millions of tortured people, raped both in body and soul, whom Bolshevism has taken into its pitiless arms in Europe's north, east, and southeast, and now in the east of our own fatherland." Goebbels spoke of German women "begging for their children's lives as lecherous soldiers from the steppes fell upon them, treating them as wild game, subjecting them to indescribably shameful physical and spiritual mistreatment, laughing devilishly as murdered babies lay at their feet." Goebbels summoned his audience for a final decisive fight against the monstrosities of Bolshevism: "Resistance at all costs!"[112]

An undated German poster, likely designed after the start of the Soviet offensive, depicted a gun-toting skeleton in a revolutionary-era Red Army cap and heavy felt boots treading on a heap of skulls. The barrel of his gun protruding at waist-level like a phallus, the skeleton uses it to push a curtain to the side, as if invading the privacy of a bedroom, an association the caption confirmed: "Bolshevism is slavery, rape, mass murder, destruction! Defend yourselves! Fight until victory! Never surrender!"

Another poster, produced in February 1945, warned of a Jewish revenge campaign if the Germans gave up their fight. The face of the Soviet political officer on the poster had a real-life precedent—it was one of the "mug shots" of captured "Jewish Bolsheviks" that the Nazis had published in July 1941 after their discovery of the murdered Ukrainians in

German propaganda poster on a wall in Vienna, 1945.

"This threatens us should we fail—Therefore fight to victory!" German propaganda poster, February 1945.

Lvov's prisons. The Bolshevik enemy, this poster made clear, remained a Jewish enemy until the end, even though he had increasingly assumed Russian traits as the war wore on.

Such terrifying portraits of Bolshevism succeeded in forging intense communal bonds among war-weary Germans, who had long stopped believing in Nazi slogans of victory. Existential fear of the enemy from the East galvanized Germans in the hour of defeat. Never did Germans feel more unified than in their shared fear of imminent extinction at the hands of bloodthirsty Soviet soldiers.[113] Extreme dread pushed ever greater numbers of German recruits to do as the poster demanded and fight rather than surrender. The death rate in the military rose sharply in 1945, with at least two hundred thousand soldiers dying on the Eastern Front every month between January and April.[114] At the same time, scores of civilians took their own lives, often collectively, a final expression of Germany's "community of fate."[115] Suicide rates increased everywhere in Germany in early 1945, but nowhere as dramatically as they had in the eastern provinces ahead of the Soviet troops' arrival.[116]

Those Germans who wanted to live usually fled. Millions hastily loaded their families and a few belongings onto horse carts and joined wagon trains that moved entire communities westward to safety. At times, retreating German forces overtook refugee treks, leaving the fleeing civilians trapped between the lines, which led to horrific carnage. Thousands of civilians lost their lives as they crossed lagoons that were only partially frozen or boarded ships in Baltic ports that were later torpedoed by Soviet submarines. Refugees received little if any help from Wehrmacht soldiers, who, concerned with their own survival, broke into abandoned German homes in the hope of finding civilian garb.[117]

During their flight, the refugees often came face-to-face with Nazi prisoners who were moved around to feed the German war engine until the end. A ten-year-old evacuee from East Prussia remembered seeing large dark "objects" in the roadside ditch. He jumped from the wagon to get a closer look, only to realize with horror that these were human beings who had frozen to death. Stars were sown onto their jackets. When the boy asked the adults on the trek who they were, he was told, "Those are Jews."[118] For Lore Ehrich, an East Prussian housewife, the "most shocking" part of her journey came after she had crossed the frozen Vistula lagoon together with her two children and the larger group they were traveling with. As the party halted to repair damaged wheels and adjust shifting cargo, thousands of "Russian" prisoners passed the refugees on the narrow road. Ehrich described the prisoners as dressed in rags and "looking utterly miserable, many of them were Mongols, and each had two turnips hung on his uniform for food." A dead horse lay nearby, and the prisoners tore pieces of flesh off the carcass, ravenously devouring the raw meat. "Be careful, young lady," a German guard shouted out to Ehrich, "they are hungry, one never knows what can happen." The encounter with the prisoners, Ehrich wrote in 1946, made her shake with fear.[119]

These wretched people were only one of innumerable convoys of concentration camp prisoners on the move in the final months of the war. Acting on Himmler's order that no captive was to fall into Russian hands, camp commanders sent their human charges on forced marches toward central Germany.[120] On roads westward from Auschwitz, armies of ghostlike figures staggered along in their wooden clogs, giving off a strong stench. Camp guards, sometimes on bicycles, pushed the weakened captives on, beating them viciously. Anyone who fell behind was shot. A tailor from Minsk recalled that the highway was strewn with the bodies of his compatriots. A schoolteacher from Dnepropetrovsk described how her convoy was pushed off the road by German civilians and soldiers driving past on carriages and carts. While their guards fed some of the prisoners, "Russians" and Jews received no food and were kept under special watch.[121] In February 1945, a large number of female prisoners from Auschwitz reached the Ravensbrück women's camp located some sixty miles north of Berlin, only to be driven on a few weeks later. The SS at Ravensbrück was attempting to empty the camp and destroy the evidence of its crimes before the Red Army arrived, but they only managed to dismantle the main gas chamber before retreating in haste. Gas vans, meanwhile, continued their murderous work. As they abandoned the camp, nervous guards force-marched thousands of prisoners toward Hamburg, in a desperate bid to get away from the Soviets.[122]

Even in areas that appeared safe from the advancing Red Army, Germans were terrified by the specter of "Russians." When the U.S. Army crossed into Germany in November 1944 and intelligence officers assessed the popular sentiment west of the Rhine, they were startled to find all levels of society, everyone apart from old Marxists, filled with a "phobia of the Russians." Everywhere they went, the Americans heard Germans refer to Soviet people with hatred and contempt, calling them "uncultivated," "barbarous," "greasy."[123] They were not referring to the Red Army soldiers fighting on the Eastern Front, but rather the "Eastern" forced laborers who made up the bulk of the foreign workers in Germany—7.7 million strong in early 1945.[124]

Soviet slave laborers were hardest hit by the Allied bombings that struck German industrial centers with increasing frequency in the late phase of the war. Unlike forced laborers from Western Europe, Soviet workers and POWs were not allowed into municipal bomb shelters, and whenever the barracks of Eastern workers burned down during a bombing, the surviving workers were left without shelter.[125] By late 1944, thousands roamed the ruins of bombed-out industrial areas. The local police authorized the summary execution of any foreigner who appeared to pose a threat. Vigilante militias comprised of men from the SA and

Volkssturm confronted suspected looters. German records meticulously recorded the infractions that justified a given vagrant's death sentence: a stolen jar of jam, a package of margarine, a wool blanket.[126]

Violence toward Soviet prisoners and workers increased in the closing months of the war and implicated ever broader segments of German society. In early February 1945, when more than four hundred Red Army officers escaped from the so-called Death Block in the Mauthausen concentration camp in Upper Austria—an amazing feat, as this detention block for Soviet prisoners was isolated from the rest of the camp by a granite wall, topped by a high-voltage electrified fence—Mauthausen's commander, Franz Zieries, went on local radio to order a manhunt for the escaped "Russian criminals." He called on *Volkssturm* men and the population at large to immediately kill every captured prisoner and promised a reward to anyone who could produce evidence that he had done so. Witnesses described the men and women who took up the chase and proceeded to comb nearby forests and villages as being in the throes of "bloodlust." The escapees, for their part, did not threaten the locals, the Mauthausen police reported. But that did not stop the locals from mercilessly killing them. In the end, only eleven survived.[127]

Killing sprees like this swept across Germany. Vigilantes comprising local *Volkssturm* men and Hitler Youth banded together to shoot "red pigs" or go hunting for "Zebras," as they called the escapees in their striped camp rags. Many witnesses testified that they saw captured prisoners pleading for their lives before being shot by German boys in cold blood. The killers stated that they needed to protect their communities from a demonic threat.[128]

As U.S. troops neared the Rhine, Gestapo agents in the industrial Ruhr region organized mass shootings of foreign workers thought capable of organizing uprisings, the overwhelming majority of whom were from the Soviet Union.[129] Other local authorities rounded up vagrant foreign workers and directed them, under armed escort, to towns farther from the front. A large contingent was taken into the nearby Sauerland Forest, where an SS general, Hans Kammler, oversaw a V-2 rocket launchpad. Annoyed by a column of foreign workers blocking the road,

Kammler was heard to remark, "This riffraff ought to be eliminated." During a walk a short time later, Kammler came upon a group of Soviet workers preparing chickens to cook. A veteran of the Freikorps and a member of the Nazi Party since 1931, Kammler assessed the situation as a security threat. As he explained to his men, the peaceful appearance of the Eastern workers was a cover. With the war ending, these workers were facing pressure to engage in sabotage in order to earn their honorable return to the USSR. Preventive action was necessary to save German lives. That evening, March 20, 1945, German troops entered the workers' makeshift camp in Warstein. A soldier announced that anyone wishing to transfer to another camp should step forward. In all, 71 Eastern workers volunteered, including 56 women and a 6-year-old child. They were put on trucks, taken to the forest a few miles away, and shot. Two more mass shootings were conducted over the course of the following days, taking 157 more Soviet lives. A week later, on April 7, 1945, the U.S Army liberated Warstein.[130]

U.S. and British journalists eager to glean first impressions of Germany followed in the wake of the American forces. A journalist with the Ninth Army told of German residents who approached his jeep. "Can you do something to help us?" they asked. "Escaped Russian prisoners have got hold of weapons and are looting our village. People who don't have any food to give them are being shot." The reporter and a group of GIs drove to the village to find the escaped prisoners, who were indeed in possession of rifles. "But all they had destroyed, except for the cellar of the local liquor store, was five cows, which they had picked pretty clean." The reporter established that the prisoners were survivors of a POW camp in Gelsenkirchen, which had also held French and Belgian soldiers. When the Germans disbanded the camp, they forced the prisoners to march to the rear. While the French and Belgians were given food rations, the Russians received nothing. The German guards shot at least ten Russians when they attempted to grab some turnips from a silo. "The complaint about released Russians' behavior is pretty common," the reporter concluded. "It is not a question of their being bad soldiers. They have just been systematically starved by the Germans."[131]

In a small town some forty miles northwest of Warstein, another reporter came upon a famous critic of the Nazi regime—Count Clemens von Galen, the Catholic bishop of Münster whose fearless public denunciations of the Nazis' "euthanasia" program had made headlines around the world. Less well known were the bishop's sermons against the "Jewish-Bolshevik" rulers in Moscow and his enthusiastic endorsement of Hitler's "crusade" against Bolshevik "pestilence." In April 1945, von Galen told the stunned American correspondent that he remained loyal to his fatherland in defeat and therefore had to consider the Allies as enemies. He then went on to complain about the thousands of liberated "Russians" who were plundering German homes in full view of the U.S. Army. When asked about the future, von Galen declared that it would largely depend on the Americans. If they let the Russians into Germany, "then we will have communism."[132]

One of the "plundering Russians" was Aleksandr Kalimov, the sergeant who had been captured by the Germans in September 1941 and nearly starved to death in several Estonian prison camps. After a succession of escape attempts and recaptures, Kalimov and several other escapees made it to Homburg, where about twenty thousand liberated Soviet prisoners had gathered in a former POW camp, setting up bonfires, cooking and drinking, and riding around on stolen bicycles. The freed prisoners had no intention of terrorizing Germans. Foremost on their minds was settling accounts with their countrymen who had helped the Germans run the camp: "Policeman Nikolai Balamut was thrown from a third-floor window, cook Alexei was killed using knives, policeman Volodya was hanged, the interpreter [a woman] was drowned in the restroom. The lynching went on for a week, but then they calmed down."[133]

"THE LAST ACT"[134]

After crossing the Rhine River in late March 1945, the U.S. Ninth Army moved east, north of the Ruhr region. The First Army, meanwhile, approached from the south. The two armies then joined in a pincer movement that encircled the entire region. Trapped inside was Germany's Army Group B, which over the winter had mounted a last-ditch offensive in the Ardennes forest to stop the advancing Western forces. The ring surrounding the Germans grew tighter every day, finally leading to the surrender of 320,000 Germans on April 18. British forces, meanwhile, pushed northeast toward Bremen and Hamburg. Altogether the Western Allies moved much more swiftly through Germany than had been expected and took relatively few losses. Some 10,000 U.S. troops were killed in Germany between the crossing of the Rhine on March 23 and the war's end.[135] Berlin, the war's ultimate trophy, was within reach. In repeated cables to Supreme Allied Commander Dwight Eisenhower in late March and early April, Churchill urged the American general to take the German capital. Eisenhower refused, citing the U.S.-British-Soviet agreement reached in the Crimean resort town of Yalta in February: Berlin and all German territories east of the Elbe River were to fall to the Soviets.

After the failure of the Ardennes offensive, Hitler was left with limited forces to face the Western Allies. The bulk of Germany's remaining military strength—an estimated eighty-five divisions and numerous smaller, separate units—was thrown into the final struggle on the Eastern Front.[136] Fierce fighting between Germans and Soviets raged in East Prussia, the Baltic states, and Silesia. While Soviet troops had reached the Oder River as early as February and were within forty miles of Berlin, they needed reinforcements and fresh supplies to deliver the final blow, which was planned for May.

From Moscow, Ehrenburg followed the unfolding battle for Germany with alarm. While he dutifully praised American and British successes, the asymmetric developments on the Western and Eastern fronts gave Ehrenburg pause. What was the rationale for deploying such an outsize portion of the remaining German forces against the Red Army? And why weren't German soldiers in the West fighting as hard as they were in the East? Among the best-informed Soviet war observers, Ehrenburg regularly received recent issues of newspapers from Germany, the Allies, and neutral countries such as Sweden. He laced his writings with references to the international press. Citing a report that had aired on a London radio station, Ehrenburg informed his Soviet readers on April 4 that German soldiers were surrendering to the Americans in droves. "Where is the nearest POW camp?" German grenadiers were asking the perplexed GIs.[137] The city of Mannheim, Ehrenburg wrote on April 7, had capitulated "via telephone," and the surrender of Heidelberg had been handled by eight German officers, who crossed the front line in a car outfitted with a huge Red Cross flag, handed the Americans a city map, and offered their services as interlocutors.[138]

In an April 9 feature in *Pravda* entitled "Enough!" Ehrenburg compared the peaceful surrender of these cities to the bloody conflict at Königsberg, which Soviet troops had just conquered after a two-month-long siege.[139] The reason for the imbalance was clear to Ehrenburg: The Germans had incomparably more blood on their hands in the East than in the West. German soldiers' fear of a reckoning for their war of annihilation against the Soviet people ruled out the possibility of their surrendering to the Red Army, Ehrenburg believed.

The article dwelled on the wounds the Germans had inflicted on the Soviet people—wounds, the writer commented ominously, "that many people do not want to know about, and that many people want to forget." This was a reference to the Western Allies, who were indeed focused on their own much lighter losses. Ehrenburg mentioned General Charles de Gaulle's recent visit to the "martyred" village of Oradour, where an SS commando had killed all 642 villagers in June 1944.[140] There were just four villages on record in France, Ehrenburg noted, where the Germans had done something similar in response to partisan raids—whereas in Soviet Belorussia, countless villages had been burned.[141] "I try to restrain myself," Ehrenburg wrote with palpable emotion, "I try to speak as quietly as possible, as sternly as possible, but I have no words. I have no words to remind the world once again of what the Germans did to my land." How could this suffering be adequately conveyed? Through the invocation of places of mass murder—Babi Yar, Maly Trostinets, Kerch, Ponary, Belzec?[142] Or through numbers? Ehrenburg provided a survey conducted among 2,103 soldiers from a single Red Army unit:

Relatives who perished on the front: 1,288.

Wives, children, relatives who were shot and hanged: 532.

Number forcibly sent to Germany: 393.

Relatives who were beaten: 222.

Farms that were looted and destroyed: 314.

Homes that were burned down: 502.

Cows, horses, and small livestock that were taken away: 630.

Relatives who returned from the front as invalids: 201.

Number personally subjected to beating in the occupied territories: 161.

Number wounded on the front: 1,268.

That the Germans would seek to evade accountability for their staggering record of violence was something Ehrenburg had predicted all along. Still, he was stunned by the impudence of the enemy in their hour of defeat. In British press reports filed from occupied Germany, Ehrenburg read of their imperious appeals to Allied soldiers to capture escaped Soviet POWs so they could finish sowing the crops.[143] Incidentally, he noted, the Western troops were at least occasionally receptive to such requests: A *Daily Telegraph* reporter found the position of the "slave owners" reasonable, and the Allied military had already produced flyers in five languages asking the liberated foreign laborers to return to their former place of work.[144] Ehrenburg also chided American reporters for "conversing with" rather than interrogating the Germans. The interview with Bishop von Galen was a case in point. Why, he asked, was the bishop given free rein to express his disgust for Russian forced laborers and his fear of Communism? Ehrenburg furnished the answer: The bishop's anti-Communism was entirely in line with the views of the American and British papers that carried his words.

Ever suspicious of collusion between the Nazis and the Western Allies, Ehrenburg placed his trust in the Soviet Union's staunchest allies: the outraged countries and populations that had also experienced Nazi racial arrogance and mass murder. To the peoples of Poland and Yugoslavia, Czechoslovakia and France, Belgium and Norway, Ehrenburg emphatically added the American and British soldiers who had liberated Nazi concentration camps and seen with their own eyes how Germans tortured "Russian POWs and Jewish girls." He relayed the angry words of a U.S. colonel who had marched German townspeople to a nearby former camp to confront them with Nazi atrocities: "For this, we will hate you to the end of our days!" Ehrenburg ended on a note of confidence: All the people who had witnessed the worst of Nazi-German rule knew that Hitler's Germany was a gangster state, and their shared determination would ensure that the country would not rebound as it had after the First World War. "This isn't 1918. Enough!"[145]

Ehrenburg's reporting was closely studied in the Kremlin, where the first days of April saw a strategic reshuffling. In response to the Western Allies' unexpectedly rapid push into central Germany, Stalin ordered his generals to accelerate the Berlin operation to ensure that the German capital would fall to the Red Army. Stalin knew from his network of foreign spies about Churchill's cables to Eisenhower.[146] He had also learned of plans by German commanders to surrender their troops in northern Italy to the Western Allies. The deeply suspicious Soviet leader read the German-American negotiations over the terms of the surrender as incipient moves toward a separate peace and the formation of a joint front against Communism. Stalin indignantly wrote Roosevelt on April 7, expressing thoughts that appeared to be lifted from Ehrenburg's most recent articles:

> The Germans have on the Eastern front 147 divisions. They could without harm to their cause take from the Eastern front

> 15–20 divisions and shift them to the aid of their troops on the Western front.[147] However, the Germans did not do it and are not doing it. They continue to fight savagely with the Russians for some unknown junction Zemlianitsa in Czechoslovakia, which they need as much as a dead man needs poultices, but surrender without any resistance such important towns in Central Germany as Osnabrück, Mannheim, Kassel. Don't you agree that such a behavior of the Germans is more than strange and incomprehensible?[148]

Careful not to antagonize the Soviet ally whose cooperation he needed to realize his vision of the postwar world order, Roosevelt assured Stalin that the Western powers together with the Red Army would complete the rout of Nazi Germany. It would be Roosevelt's final cable before his death from a cerebral hemorrhage a few hours later.[149]

The preservation of the anti-Hitler alliance held paramount importance for Stalin as well. A German rapprochement with the Western powers risked snatching the spoils of victory from the Soviet Union and prolonging the war indefinitely. It was therefore in the Kremlin's interest to soothe German fears of the Bolshevik enemy, both to forestall further German overtures to the West and to ease the Soviet advance toward Berlin. There was one other reason for a softer political line: Unlike Silesia and East Prussia, which would fall to Poland and the Soviet Union after the war, and from which ethnic Germans would be expelled, the battlefield on which the upcoming Berlin offensive would be fought was to remain German. Germans residing west of the Oder and Neisse rivers had to be reassured that they need not flee.

The new line first appeared in *Pravda* on April 14. Its announcement was couched as a rebuttal to Ehrenburg's April 9 feature and titled "Comrade Ehrenburg Oversimplifies." The author was the Soviet Union's chief propaganda official, Georgy Aleksandrov. While praising Ehrenburg for his "truthful and forceful" description of German atrocities on "sacred" Soviet soil, Aleksandrov faulted the writer for asserting that the Germans in the East fought so desperately because they feared Soviet retribution.[150] Most Germans in 1945 no longer wanted to fight for Hitler and his "clique," Aleksandrov countered, and they should not become targets of Soviet rage. Referring to the recent Yalta resolution and citing Stalin's 1942 dictum of the coming and going of Hitlers, Aleksandrov declared that the Soviet government was committed to preserving the German nation and state. Aleksandrov undoubtedly knew that Ehrenburg had opposed the wholesale extermination of all Germans and indeed had called for revenge only fleetingly—but that was beside the point. The purpose of his article was to publicly break with the retributive line that Soviet soldiers and the Germans identified with Ehrenburg.

The Berlin offensive began on April 16, with an all-out attack by the Soviet troops. After days of intense fighting, the 1st Ukrainian Front under the command of Marshal Ivan Konev neared Berlin's southern suburbs, while Marshal Zhukov's 1st Belorussian Front started shelling Berlin's city center from the north. On that day, Stalin ordered both marshals to "improve" the Red Army's treatment of German civilians and POWs: "Harsh treatment of the Germans arouses their fear and drives the soldiers to fight to the death. The civilian population fears revenge and is organizing into gangs. Such a situation is disadvantageous for us."[151]

The day Soviet shells began falling on Berlin, April 20, Hitler was marking his last birthday. The Führer observed the day by emerging from his bunker eight meters below ground to decorate the boy soldiers in his youth movement with the Iron Cross. Several days earlier, on April 15, in anticipation of the Soviet offensive, Hitler had issued a final decree to his soldiers, exhorting them to fight with "steadfastness and zeal," to stop the Eastern enemy from massacring old men and children, turning German women and girls into "barrack whores," and deporting everyone else "to Siberia." The Bolshevik enemy, Hitler proclaimed, would "suffocate in a bloodbath." Berlin would remain German, and Europe would never become Russian.[152]

The prospect of dealing the death blow to Hitler's hated regime stirred the exhausted Soviet troops. Soldiers used oil paint and chalk to inscribe their feelings on tanks, horse-drawn carts, and artillery shells: "You'll deliver Berlin!" "Hurry to the enemy's lair!" "Death to the cannibal Hitler!" "Death to fascism!" "The war will be over really soon!" One soldier wrote from Wandlitz, just north of the German capital: "I had the honor of storming the final lair of the beast—fascist Berlin. Soon, we will parade through the city."[153] Soviet war correspondents noted a "special elation" among the troops; wounded soldiers would not let themselves be evacuated to the rear, insisting that they first had to conquer Berlin.[154] Crossing the Spree River under fire on April 24, Lieutenant Vladimir Stezhensky, a member of military intelligence, paused long enough to look down at the "foul little river" and spit three times into its "cursed water."[155]

Amid heavy fighting that involved house-to-house and hand-to-hand combat, Red Army formations advancing from the southeast, south, and north reached the center of Berlin on April 28. The soldiers spearheading the final offensive had their eyes set on the Reichstag, the building with the greatest symbolic value in Soviet eyes. Millions of Soviet spectators knew from films, books, and lectures about the Reichstag burning and Georgi Dimitrov's trial. Soldiers competed in a race to take the burned-out building. Nine Soviet flags flown in from Moscow were handed out to nine different teams. Late in the evening of April 30, soldiers of the 150th Rifle Division planted the "banner of victory" high up on the roof.[156] On May 1, one year after calling on the Red Army to "finish off" the fascist beast, Stalin proclaimed: "The fascist beast is mortally wounded and near his last breath. Only one task remains—putting an end to him."[157] The following day, the commandant of Berlin surrendered to the Soviets. More than eighty thousand Red Army soldiers lost their lives storming the city, the last chapter in the war against Germany, a war that claimed the lives of at least eleven million men and women in the Soviet military.[158] Writing in his diary on May 2, Lieutenant Stezhensky acknowledged that the "historic event we have been waiting for, for four years" had finally come to pass. There were rumors, he noted, "that Hitler, Goebbels, and their henchmen committed suicide, but I don't think this is the case. They probably went underground or ran away somewhere. We'll definitely catch them."[159]

Hitler ensured that he would not have to face the enemy's wrath. Before swallowing cyanide and shooting himself on April 30, he dictated a political testament in which he explained his suicide: He would not be used for a spectacle arranged by Jews for the purpose of "amusing their agitated masses." He had never wanted war, Hitler claimed. In his view, every act of aggression since 1939 had been the work of the Jews alone. To fight the "poisoner of all of the peoples of the world," Germany's duty after his death was to "meticulously" enforce racial laws and continue with its "merciless resistance." To succeed him, Hitler appointed Commander of the Navy Karl Dönitz as Reichspräsident and Goebbels as Reichskanzler.[160] Goebbels and his wife, who occupied a neighboring bunker, committed suicide the following day, after killing their six children. From the northern port city of Flensburg, Dönitz informed the nation via radio on May 1 that the "Führer" had died a hero's death fighting Bolshevism to his last breath: "He had recognized the terrible danger of Bolshevism early on and dedicated his life to this struggle. . . . His life was one sustained act of service to Germany, and beyond. He struggled against the Bolshevik storm on behalf of Europe and the entire civilized world." The newly appointed president's priority was saving Germans from the advancing Bolshevik enemy. It was for this reason only that he continued to fight.[161]

The Dönitz government, along with other Nazi leaders and military commanders acting on their own, did as Ehrenburg and Stalin had predicted: They attempted to make a deal with the Western Allies to escape the reach of Soviet justice. On May 2, General Kurt von Tippelskirch, commander of the 21st Army on the collapsing Eastern Front, ordered his soldiers to march west to the Ludwigslust headquarters of the U.S. 82nd Airborne Division. There, he surrendered his army—144,000 men, two-fifths of what had been Army Group Vistula. The next day, the Red Army's Eighth Mechanized Corps arrived in Ludwigslust.[162] On Dönitz's orders, the commanders of German forces in northwestern Germany, the Netherlands, and Denmark surrendered to Great Britain's Field Marshal Bernard L. Montgomery and his forces on May 4. During the ceremony, a German admiral explained to Montgomery that it was out of the question to surrender to the Russians, as they were "uncivilized people."[163] Two days later, representatives of the German High Command met with Western officials at the Allied Supreme Headquarters in Reims to propose Germany's capitulation on the Western Front. Eisenhower insisted on Germany's immediate capitulation on all fronts and pointedly refused to meet with the Germans until after they had signed an act of surrender. The Reims accord that was prepared by Eisenhower and signed in the early morning hours of May 7 provided a tacit concession though: The document stipulated that the surrender would take effect on May 8 at 11:01 p.m., giving the Germans extra time to evacuate more troops and refugees from the east.

Soviet Military Liaison Mission Commander General Ivan Susloparov cosigned the Reims accord after unsuccessfully seeking guidance from the Kremlin. Stalin was asleep. As soon as the Soviet dictator learned of the accord, he ordered his liaison not to sign, but it was too late. After meeting with a furious Stalin, Soviet Chief of Staff General Alexei Antonov wrote to Eisenhower expressing concern that the continued fighting at the Eastern Front made the Reims accord look like a separate peace between the Western powers and Germany. Indeed, on May 7, the day Eisenhower signed the Reims accord, the commander of German Army Group Center, active in the Czech lands, ordered his soldiers to redouble their efforts in fighting the Red Army. Commenting on the accord, he declared, German forces had capitulated to the Western Allies only. The German forces would absolutely not "surrender to the Bolsheviks."[164]

Fortunately, Susloparov had inserted a clause into the Reims accord allowing it to be superseded by a "general" act of German surrender imposed by the United Nations, should any of the Allied powers so desire.[165] Stalin latched onto this clause to override the Reims accord, which in his eyes signified a German capitulation principally to the Western Allies. He additionally insisted that the final capitulation act be signed not on liberated foreign soil, but in the capital of the Nazi aggressor state, and by representatives of each of the three German armed services.[166] Eisenhower agreed to Stalin's demands. The representatives, with Field Marshal Wilhelm Keitel the most senior among them, were flown from Flensburg to Berlin early on May 8 and taken to the former officers' mess

Field Marshal Keitel, waiting to sign the unconditional surrender of the German Wehrmacht at Soviet headquarters in Berlin. Photographer: Georgi Petrusov.

hall in Karlshorst, which was serving as Soviet headquarters. Late in the evening, they were called into the main hall, where members of the Allied Expeditionary Force had gathered with the Supreme High Command of the Red Army, headed by Marshal Zhukov. After Keitel sat down, Zhukov called him over to the area where the Soviet delegation was gathered. There the field marshal, surrounded by reporters from the world over, signed the final terms of Germany's unconditional surrender.[167]

The formal ceremony in Karlshorst belied the dramatic acts of violence and rescue that continued in nearby districts and towns until the very last hours of the Nazi regime. Thousands of concentration camp prisoners were dragged over roads and through forests north of Berlin. Many fell prey to roaming SS commandos and armed villagers who considered the captives a murderous threat.[168] The prisoners in one convoy understood that their guards were debating whether to surrender to the Red Army. A guard came up to a group of women that included Elena Budayeva, the tailor from Minsk, and said, "My children, I feel very sorry for you, but I am afraid that the Russians will hang me." A woman in the group said he need not be afraid, as they would vouch for him. "We understood that our Russian forces were nearby, otherwise this German would not have talked to us so kindly," Budayeva told a historian who interviewed her in August 1945. The German seemed to trust the women. But the next morning, the guards forced the prisoners on, hoping to reach American forces. Budayeva and other prisoners took advantage of an aerial attack to escape into the forest. Soon they were surrounded by soldiers. At first, they believed they had been recaptured. But the men spoke Russian, and they gave the women a warm welcome.[169] A group including Yevdokiya Ustyanova, the schoolteacher from Dnepropetrovsk, also escaped from their convoy. On a hillock they spotted a Red Army man armed with a submachine gun. They walked up to the Soviet soldier to kiss his hands and feet. "Who on earth are you?" asked the flustered soldier. They were prisoners, they explained. When the soldier brought them to his unit, Ustyanova cried from joy.[170] Two Ukrainian women who had been deported to Neubrandenburg to work in an airplane factory hid in a basement as the other workers were force-marched, "like cattle," out of the factory gates. They left their hiding spot only when they heard Russian spoken in the building. Their first encounter with a Soviet soldier filled one of them with "such happiness as no words can describe." "The day of my liberation," the other declared, "will remain etched in my memory for the rest of my life."[171]

These stories of deliverance contrasted dramatically with the experiences of German civilians at the hands of the Red Army, even though the Soviet soldiers were more restrained during the storming of Berlin than they had been during the invasion of East Prussia.[172] As he drove through the German capital's western suburbs in early May, Lieutenant Stezhensky commented on the "continued rampaging" of the troops "despite the most threatening orders and warnings. Now, in all the boroughs occupied by us, there is not a single house that has not been plundered and not a single woman aged 15 to 60 who has not experienced a Russian. And not just once."[173] In the town of Schwerin an der Warthe (Skwierzyna), war correspondent Vasily Grossman sympathetically noted the "horror in the eyes of women and girls." Grossman spoke with residents who had suffered serial sexual assaults by Soviet troops, and he noticed how children of four and five stood up in silence and raised their hands when a member of the Red Army entered their house. Stories of marauding and raping Red Army soldiers scandalized many observers. In Berlin, a freed French laborer came up to Grossman to declare, "Monsieur, I love your army and that's why it is painful for me to see its attitude to girls and women. This is going to be very harmful for your propaganda."[174]

No contemporary observer compared Soviet infractions against German civilians to similar assaults committed by Western Allied soldiers. Yet parish records in southern Germany recorded countless cases.[175] Like their Soviet counterparts, Western soldiers did not uniformly steal or rape as they advanced through Europe. Rather, they specifically targeted Germans who represented in some way the despised Nazi system. The desire for retribution among Western soldiers increased significantly whenever they came face-to-face with Nazi atrocities. Amid fierce fighting against SS forces on April 29, American soldiers freed forty thousand prisoners from a POW camp on the outskirts of Moosburg, northeast of Munich. The intensity of combat, combined with the sight of the emaciated survivors, enraged the soldiers. After taking the town, they ransacked buildings and assaulted female residents.[176] In some cases, liberated forced laborers led GIs to the homes of local oppressors, pleading for their suffering to be avenged.[177]

If Soviet acts of violence against German civilians were more frequent and severe than those committed by other Allied soldiers, this imbalance undoubtedly owed to the disproportionate Soviet losses. As they pressed toward Germany, U.S. troops had not passed through the ruins of American towns or villages that had been destroyed under German occupation. American GIs had not received letters from loved ones informing them that the Germans had killed family members or wiped out their community. Liberated American and British prisoners of war generally emerged from captivity much better off than surviving Soviet prisoners, who were often so weak that they could barely walk. Unlike the Soviets, the Western Allies lacked correspondents such as Ehrenburg, who catalyzed the grief of his millions of readers into burning rage. Enormous doses of suffering and hatred fed the Soviet explosion of violence in Germany, even though such suffering and hatred could not justify the pain and devastation that Red Army fighters visited upon hundreds of thousands of German civilians. Ehrenburg regularly reminded his soldier readers to act in the name of justice, not revenge—though his own anger about German cruelty could at times overwhelm him. Ultimately, Ehrenburg and other Soviet leaders fell short of their aim to conquer Berlin with the same restraint that Soviet spectators had displayed during the Moscow march of the German POWs in 1944.

Still, the most notable outcome of the Soviet conquest of Germany was that Germans' worst fears did not come to pass. Hitler had envisioned "immense columns of [German] men treading their way to the Siberian tundra" and predicted the wholesale rape, enslavement, and annihilation of the German population at the hands of the Red Army.[178] Goebbels had foreseen Germany's "Katynization"—the execution of thousands of Germans by shots to the nape of the neck. In contrast to these prophecies, the triumphant Communist state coupled the celebration of Soviet victory with affirmations of German cultural value, thus renewing a long-standing Russian-Soviet tradition of admiring their Western neighbor. Even Ehrenburg, who had judged Germans with unsparing harshness throughout the war, changed his tune not long after Aleksandrov's scolding. As he celebrated the first days of peace, Ehrenburg respectfully wrote about Goethe as a poet who inspired Pushkin, while not forgetting to point out that the veneration of great poets no matter their country of origin distinguished Soviet soldiers from their Nazi counterparts. Unlike the Wehrmacht, which had inculcated its soldiers with a love of weaponry and conquest, he noted, Soviet culture relied on the enlightening power of the book.[179]

In his first proclamation, signed on April 28, 1945, Colonel-General Nikolai Berzarin, the Soviet commandant in Berlin, ordered the repair of Berlin's destroyed power plants and water mains.[180] Berzarin worked in tandem with German Communist leaders and "Free Germany" committee members, who emphasized two goals: dispatching Communists and other trusted "anti-fascists" from Moscow to help build a new German state, and explaining to the local population "the cause of the catastrophe, Germany's war guilt, the crimes of the Nazi system, and the joint responsibility of the German people."[181]

On May 7 and 8, *Pravda* published the Extraordinary State Commission's findings on the extermination camp at Auschwitz. The voluminous report, which drew on forensic research, documents found on site, and medical examinations of more than two thousand former prisoners, was undoubtedly rushed to publication to add to the indictment of Nazi Germany: "In terms of forethought, technical organization, in terms of mass scale and cruelty in the extermination of human beings, the Auschwitz camp far surpasses everything hitherto known about the German 'death camps,'" the report stated.[182] In mid-May, Soviet occupation forces distributed a summary of the Auschwitz report in German translation.[183]

The physician Anne-Marie Durand-Wever noted in her diary: "In the *Tägliche Rundschau*, big reports about the death camp in Auschwitz. Even if only a small part is true, and I fear it is all true, then the rage of the entire world against the Nazis is understandable. Poor Germany!"[184] Durand-Wever was a respected doctor from the Weimar era, who held progressive views. The fact that she read the Soviet report and did not deny the Nazi horrors set her apart from most other Germans. Nonetheless, the devastating indictment of German sadism and mass murder filled her with pity only for "poor Germany"—not for the victims. Observers from several Allied countries remarked on the striking insularity of German thought in the aftermath of defeat. The mental universe of the vanquished nation appeared to an American reporter like "an island of thought completely segregated from the outside world."[185] "The Germans you meet seem to have no idea of their enormous load of guilt," another reporter noted.[186] As they presented themselves to Soviet officials, German residents exhibited a striking lack of remorse. The fate that awaited them consumed their thoughts.[187]

Some interlocutors who spent time listening to Germans did detect pangs of conscience. The U.S. intelligence officer who had produced the first November 1944 survey of German sentiment in the Rhineland and picked up on the universal revulsion expressed for "Russians" noted to his surprise—he was Jewish himself—a "strange sense of guilt about the Jews, an uneasy feeling, and frequently an open admission that a great wrong has been committed." A year earlier, the SD reported that some Germans saw the Allied bombing of German cities as "retaliation for our actions against the Jews in November 1938."[188] In autumn 1944, several German women in Berlin reportedly defended an Italian worker who had been refused a seat on a streetcar. One of the women was quoted as saying that one had to remain humane, "because we have already incurred enough guilt through the treatment of the Jews and Poles, and they will get back at us."[189] In Berlin-Spandau on March 19, 1945, an SD informant recorded a conversation between two workers. The workers agreed "that we ourselves were to blame for this war because we treated the Jews so badly. We shouldn't be surprised if they do the same to us now." The informant went on to say: "Similar remarks are often heard now."[190]

Some Germans admitted their responsibility for the fate of the Jews, especially those whom they remembered as former fellow citizens. Sometimes they also regretted what had been done to Poles. But hardly any Germans talked in this way about the "Russians." The reason was a fundamental German reluctance to concede to Soviets a degree of humanity, to recognize them as people who had been wronged and deserved justice. Ehrenburg, who pored over German letters and diaries more than any other observer at the time, was wrong on one count: Germans had been so frantic to flee Soviet troops not because they feared a reckoning for their crimes in the East. What they feared (and what they believed had led them to declare war on the USSR in the first place) was the menace of a subhuman primal aggressor attacking from the East. Feelings of guilt had no place in a life-or-death scenario where Germans invariably cast themselves as the Red Army's ultimate victims.[191]

Chapter 10

ERASURE

The Soviets at the Nuremberg International Military Tribunal were the last of the four powers to present their case, following the Americans, British, and French. Roman Karmen filmed the crowded courtroom on the morning of February 8, 1946, as Lieutenant General Roman Rudenko began his eight-hour indictment. In a speech given weeks later in Moscow, Karmen marked this day as the "triumph of justice," the day on which the Russian language resonated through the Nuremberg courtroom. "Which people, if not our Soviet people," he asked, "have the sacred right to speak to the fascist executioners who brought us so much suffering and grief? . . . If not for the Soviet Army, if not for the heroic Soviet people, who played a decisive role in the victory over Germany, there would be no Nuremberg, there would be no trial of the war criminals."[1]

The indictment of the top twenty-two Nazi defendants, including Hermann Göring, Joachim von Ribbentrop, Karl Dönitz, Wilhelm Keitel, Hans Frank, and Fritz Sauckel, was jointly worked out by the four powers, but the tone and substance of the charges brought by each country differed markedly. U.S. Chief Prosecutor Robert Jackson, who opened the proceedings, soberly dressed in a dark civilian suit, invoked the judgment of the law rather than "the hand of vengeance" as the tribunal's defining contribution to history. Of all four accusing powers, Jackson declared, the United States was in the best position to assure a fair outcome, because "having sustained the least injury, it is perhaps the least animated by vengeance. Our American cities have not been bombed by day and by night, by humans, and by robots. It is not our temples that have been laid in ruins. Our countrymen have not had their homes destroyed over their heads."[2] While Jackson and his British colleague Sir Hartley Shawcross dwelled on the dispassionate workings of the law, the prosecutors from the two countries that had been invaded by Germany—France and the Soviet Union—spoke with palpable emotion as they demanded harsh reckonings for their violated peoples. Alone among the four delegations, the Soviet prosecutors and judges donned military attire, accentuating their role in the defeat of Nazi Germany.[3] Reporting from Nuremberg for *The New Yorker*, Janet Flanner observed how the Soviet delegation's "militant attitude" dominated the court proceedings, even when each of the Western Allies made their case and the Soviet side sat "watchfully" silent: "Of the judges, only the Russians are in khaki; of the prosecuting lawyers, only the Russians wear a kind of regimental dress—chocolate brown uniforms with green trimmings. Even the Russian female interpreters and typists can easily be identified, in court or out of it, if only by a rear view of their military-looking frocks. Each of the four Allied prosecutions has brought to this international tribunal its special flavor. The Russian contribution has been mostly emotional—a swift heartbeat of anger and anguish which Chief Prosecutor Rudenko has made audible to the listening Court, as if his microphone were a sort of stethoscope."[4]

Jackson targeted the top Nazis in the dock exclusively, taking care not to incriminate the "whole German people." Had the Germans freely backed Hitler, he argued, there would have been no need for the Nazis to set up concentration camps in 1933. Rudenko went in the opposite direction, accusing all officers of the German armed forces in addition to the police and other pillars of the Nazi state. Ultimately, he arraigned an "entire generation" of Germans whose "conscience and mind" had been "poisoned" by Nazi propaganda. Rudenko identified Nazism's theory of racial supremacy as the driver of Germany's war of annihilation: "This theory proclaimed that German fascist usurpers are not bound by any

Chief Soviet prosecutor Roman Rudenko speaks at the Nuremberg Tribunal.

laws or commonly accepted rules of human morality." As members of a "master race," Germans felt entitled to "build their own welfare on the bones of other races and nations." Rudenko cited excerpts from *Mein Kampf*, SS reports, and Nazi youth songs ("The world may lie in ruins / Why the devil should we care / We'll keep on marching forward / Even if everything falls apart / For today, Germany is ours / And tomorrow, the world") to illustrate how German fascism "set loose the wildest and lowest instincts," turning ordinary Germans into mass murderers. "No matter how revolting and shameless, cruel, and monstrous," their actions "were based on the idea of the superiority of this race."[5]

Race figured more prominently in Rudenko's speech than in the indictments brought forth by the other Allied prosecutors. The contrast he drew between the Nazi theory of the "master race" and "ideas of freedom, the ideas of enlightenment, and the demands of humanity" was perhaps to be expected from an official of a socialist state premised on an anti-racist creed. But even as he stressed the defendants' "indescribable and blasphemous crimes . . . against the principles of human ethics and of international law," Rudenko also spoke as a representative of a country that had experienced firsthand the fires of racial hatred.[6] The Soviet prosecutor described the scope of Germany's murderous designs, citing the "thirty million Slavs" who were meant to be killed during Germany's colonial conquest, as per Himmler's orders to his top operatives in the East. Rudenko also cited a pre-Barbarossa instruction by Heydrich ordering the destruction of the entire Soviet political and cultural elite, including "all prominent Government and party officials, particularly professional revolutionaries, persons working for the Comintern . . . all former political commissars in the Red Army . . . the Soviet Russian intelligentsia, and all Jews." In closing, Rudenko referred to a planned "extermination to the last man of the Jewish population of the world." The Nazis "carried out this extermination throughout the whole of their conspiratorial activity from 1933 onward," he continued. "The bestial annihilation of the Jewish population took place in Ukraine, in Belorussia, and in the Baltic states. Some 80,000 Jews lived in the town of Riga before the German occupation. At the moment of the liberation of Riga by the Red Army, there were only 140 Jews left."

The British and the American prosecutions based their cases almost entirely on written documentation (such as military orders). Shawcross's only two witnesses were German naval officers who accused Dönitz of war crimes. Jackson summoned six witnesses, four of them SS officers, including Göring and Albert Speer.[7] Another was SS Einsatzgruppen leader Otto Ohlendorf, who claimed that he had simply been following orders as he coldly related how his men murdered ninety thousand Jews, including women and children. Jackson also showed a compilation of American and British footage taken during the liberation of Nazi concentration camps in April 1945, bringing into the courtroom disturbing images of charred and mutilated bodies, and emaciated survivors displaying their wounds. The narrator of the hour-long film referred to the victims by nationality (Russians, Czechs, Poles, French, Belgians, etc.), obscuring the fact that most of them were Jewish.

The French prosecution was the first of the accusing parties to summon witnesses who had suffered under the Nazi regime—eleven of them. Each of the nine camp survivors among them detailed the hellish conditions they had witnessed and personally endured. Marie-Claude Vaillant-Couturier, a Communist member of the Résistance, spoke about her experience at Auschwitz and Ravensbrück:

> It is difficult to convey an exact idea of the concentration camps to anybody, unless one has been in the camp oneself. . . . If asked what was the worst of all, it is impossible to answer, since everything was atrocious. It is atrocious to die of hunger, to die of thirst, to be ill, to see all one's companions dying around one and being unable to help them. It is atrocious to think of one's children, of one's country, which one will never see again, and there were times when we asked whether our life was not a living nightmare, so unreal did this life appear in all its horror.
>
> For months, for years we had one wish only: The wish that some of us would escape alive, in order to tell the world what the Nazi convict prisons were like everywhere, at Auschwitz as at Ravensbrück.[8]

Several of the witnesses called by the French prosecution focused on the exceptional mistreatment of Soviet prisoners in the camps. Paul Roser, a former POW, asked for permission to describe the "terrible picture" of the arrival of a transport of "Russian" prisoners into the Rawa-Ruska Stalag in November 1941:

> The Russians arrived in rows, five by five, holding each other by the arms, as none of them could walk by themselves. "Walking skeletons" was really the only fitting expression. Since then we have seen photographs of those camps of deportation and death. Our unfortunate Russian comrades had been in that condition since 1941. The color of their faces was not even yellow, it was green. Almost all squinted, as they had not strength enough to focus their sight. They fell by rows, five men at a time. The Germans rushed on them and beat them with rifle butts and whips.[9]

The French prisoners were allowed to move about freely within the camp that day, Roser added, as it was a Sunday, and upon seeing the beatings they began to shout in protest, prompting the Germans to send them back to their barracks. Roser stated that out of the ten thousand Soviet POWs who had arrived in November 1941, only twenty-five hundred were alive two months later. "The dead and the dying were piled up between the barracks and thrown into carts. The first few days we could see the corpses in the carts, but as the German camp commandant did not like to see French soldiers salute their fallen Russian comrades, he had them covered with canvas after that."[10] Many of the sick Russians were thrown into a common grave, even before they were dead. Maurice Lampe, a member of the Résistance and former Mauthausen prisoner, asked the court's permission to share an example of German atrocity that he could not forget. An evening roll call in September 1944 took longer than usual because someone was missing: "After a long wait and searches of the various blocks, they found a Russian, a Soviet prisoner, who perhaps had fallen asleep and had forgotten to answer roll call. . . . Immediately the dogs and the SS went up to the poor wretch, and before the whole camp—I was in the front row, not because I wanted to be but because we were arranged like that—we witnessed the fury of the dogs let loose upon this unfortunate Russian. He was torn to pieces in the presence of the whole camp. I must add that this man, in spite of his suffering, faced his death in a particularly noble manner."

"I would like to say more about the Russians, because they have gone through so much," declared Francesc (Francisco) Boix, a Catalan Communist who had fought in the Spanish Civil War as a youth and subsequently joined the French army before being deported to Mauthausen. According to Boix, the Soviet prisoners of war who arrived in Mauthausen were worked to their deaths more relentlessly than prisoners from any other nation. Out of a group of seven thousand Soviet prisoners, only thirty remained alive three months later, following nonstop abuse and torture in the camp's quarry. When Rudenko asked Boix what he knew of the extermination of Soviet prisoners, Boix responded that not even a month would suffice for him to tell the court everything he had witnessed. A trained photojournalist, Boix had been assigned to Mauthausen's photo lab, where he developed—and secretly stashed away—photographs taken by SS guards, including trophy shots of their captives.[11] As supporting evidence for his testimony, Boix showed the court several of these pictures, including one depicting Soviet POWs—rows of emaciated naked bodies—during a roll call in fall 1944. The men in the front row look directly at the German photographer as they stand upright, their fists clenched.

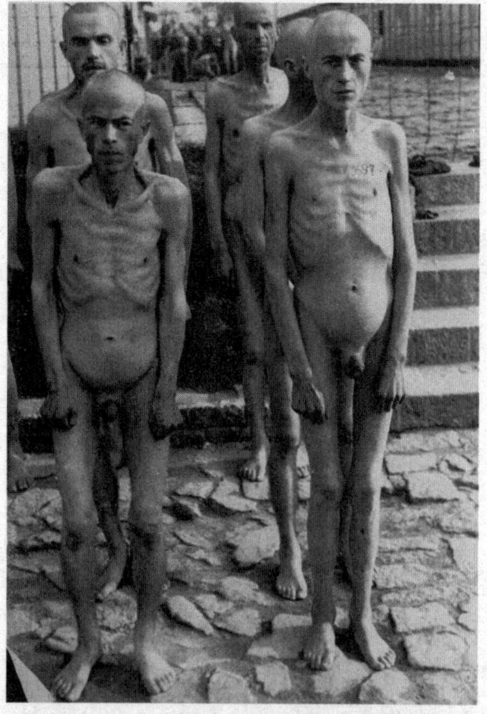

Soviet POWs during a roll call in the Mauthausen camp, September 1944.

After the French, it was the Soviet prosecution's turn to present its case. The USSR contributed by far the largest amount of evidence to the Allied indictment. In addition to presenting five hundred folders of written documents, Soviet prosecutors initially sought to bring thirty-five witnesses to Nuremberg before ultimately settling on ten.[12] Among them were three Jews: an escaped member of the Babi Yar prisoner squad that had been forced to burn the bodies of those massacred; a former prisoner from Treblinka, who had taken part in the August 1943 uprising and escaped from the camp; and the Yiddish poet, Communist, and partisan fighter Abraham Sutzkever, who recounted in detail the extermination of the Jews of Vilna, including his own mother and child. Ehrenburg, who had known Sutzkever since 1944, had pushed for the poet's inclusion on the witness list. He idealized the partisan fighter as a distinctly Soviet Jew—someone who had not only suffered but also fought back. In fact, Sutzkever was more committed to fighting back than anyone could have guessed: He planned to smuggle a revolver into the courtroom to kill Göring. In the end, Ehrenburg talked him out of it.[13] Significantly, the Soviet Union was the only power to bring Jews to the stand in Nuremberg. The French prosecution settled on Vaillant-Couturier as their star witness, in order to play up the heroic French resistance against Nazi rule and to downplay the country's complicity in the murder of Jews.[14] The British decision to bring only two naval officers signaled that their focus would be on military matters. Robert Jackson decided against inviting Jewish witnesses as he feared they would be overly emotional and vengeful, undercutting their evidentiary usefulness."[15]

In addition to the formal witnesses for the Soviet prosecution, the Soviet delegation also included Ehrenburg, who joined the court proceedings in December 1945, and Karmen, who helped prepare an hour-long documentary that was shown on February 19, 1946, capping the Soviet case. In introducing the film, Soviet Assistant Prosecutor Colonel Yuri Pokrovsky declared that it would bring into the courtroom "tens of thousands of witnesses": "I cannot name them, and you will not swear them in," he said, "but it is impossible not to believe their testimony, for the dead never lie. . . . The mute testimony of those burned alive in hospitals, mutilated beyond recognition by torture,

Abraham Sutzkever in Vilna after the city's liberation, summer 1944.

ground down by hunger will be stronger than any of my words—of this, I am sure."

The chronologically arranged film displayed a panorama of suffering extending over more than three years and spanning vast territories, from the liberation of Rostov in late 1941, to Kerch, Kharkov, Babi Yar, Majdanek, Auschwitz, and finally the Sonnenburg prison in Germany, where the eight hundred inmates who remained were shot just ahead of the Red Army's arrival. Unlike the American film, the Soviet documentary identified victims by name and featured interviews with survivors. The film overwhelmed many of the courtroom spectators. A reporter for *The New York Times* described the compilation as a "tale of broken bodies, strangled women, mutilated prisoners, death camps and burned villages," and observed how "war-hardened Army guards gasped and swore under their breath and the defendants fidgeted or averted their eyes."[16] The screening marked the culmination of a specific form of witness justice that the Soviets pioneered at Nuremberg.[17] Its impact would prove short-lived.

CURTAIN FALLS

On March 5, 1946, two weeks after the showing of the film, with the Nuremberg trials still ongoing, Winston Churchill gave a speech at Westminster College in Fulton, Missouri. Voted out of office the year before, Churchill minimized the importance of his appearance, stating that he had not come on an official mission and spoke only for himself. But with U.S. President Harry Truman introducing the British guest and thanking him for visiting his home state, every word of Churchill's carried great weight. The former prime minister used the occasion to warn of "war and tyranny" as the two great dangers facing the world. While professing his "strong admiration and regard for the valiant Russian people" and their leader Marshal Stalin, he decried the tyrannical regimes that were forming everywhere the Red Army had set foot. An "iron curtain" had descended, he said, separating Warsaw, Berlin,

Prague, and other Soviet-occupied capitals in Central and Eastern Europe from the rest of the continent. Invoking the specter of further Communist expansion and likening it to the past forms of Nazi aggression, Churchill called on the "fraternal association of the English-speaking peoples" to defend their distinct traditions of freedom against Communism's onslaught.[18]

In a sharp rebuttal published in *Pravda*, Stalin turned the tables, comparing Churchill to Hitler. The Nazi Führer, Stalin declared, had invoked a theory of German racial supremacy to unleash the Second World War. Churchill was now "agitating" for a war against the Soviet Union based on a similar racial theory that asserted the global preeminence of the Anglo-Saxon nations. With respect to the Red Army's presence in Eastern Europe, Stalin pointed out that Germany's invasion had cost the Soviet Union the lives of many more soldiers than all British and American casualties put together. "Some may want to consign to oblivion the colossal sacrifices of the Soviet people, which delivered Europe from Hitler's yoke," he wrote. "But the Soviet Union cannot forget them. How can anyone be surprised that the Soviet Union wants to ensure its security in the future, to make certain that these countries have governments committed to loyal relations with the Soviet Union?" If Churchill and his allies were to start a military campaign against "Eastern Europe," which Stalin rendered in quotation marks, they would be beaten, "as they were beaten . . . twenty-six years ago"—a reference to the failed Allied intervention against the Bolsheviks in the Russian Civil War, which Churchill, then Secretary of State for War, had supported.[19] *Pravda* also charged Churchill with plagiarism: The term "iron curtain" was not his own, but lifted from an essay penned by Goebbels in early 1945. *Pravda* printed side by side the nearly identical phrasings from Churchill's Fulton speech and Goebbels's essay, to highlight that the British statesman had embraced the typical fascist slander of the Soviet order. In this instance, *Pravda* was right: The iron curtain was an important metaphor in Goebbels's text; he used it twice. Should Germany be defeated, an iron curtain would descend over all the East and Central European lands held by the

Red Army, after which another surge of Bolshevik aggression would bring the iron curtain down on Great Britain.[20]

The duel between Churchill and Stalin shook the Nuremberg courtroom. The two leaders traded shots in the media just as the Allied prosecutors ended their indictment and the court prepared to listen to the defense. On the day after Churchill's address, a Soviet lawyer saw the faces of the defendants shining with expectation. That morning an American army newspaper had printed a headline: UNITE TO STOP RUSSIANS, CHURCHILL WARNS AT FULTON. German defense attorneys pretended to be reading the paper, but in fact enabled their clients to read Churchill's speech over their shoulders.[21] The German defendants sought to exploit the rift in the wartime coalition, offering themselves to the Western powers as allies against Bolshevism. Since they came to power in 1933, said Göring, the first of the defendants to speak, the Nazis had been acting in self-defense against a Communist menace: "We wanted to finish off the Communists as quickly as possible," he said, by way of explaining the creation of the Gestapo and the concentration camps.[22] The presiding British judge did not interrupt Göring when he asserted, with a glance at the Soviet judges, that he had copied the idea of camps from abroad. Speaking after Göring, former foreign minister Joachim von Ribbentrop cast the Soviet Union as a fellow aggressor nation as he shared details about the top-secret protocol of the Hitler-Stalin pact.[23] He and Hitler had broken the pact with deep regret, he said, and invaded the Soviet Union only to ward off an imminent Bolshevik onslaught. Once more, the presiding judge did not cut Ribbentrop short, even though weeks earlier the Soviet prosecution had disproven the Nazi line that their war had been preventive.[24] Fritz Sauckel insisted that he had never relied on forced labor and suggested that the "Eastern workers" had come to Germany of their own free will to fight Bolshevism.[25]

The defense centered their efforts on debunking a Soviet accusation that they knew to be a lie—that the Katyn murders were committed by the Germans. At Stalin's insistence, the Katyn dossier, with its falsified evidence pointing to German culpability, had been included among the

Soviet documents submitted at Nuremberg. The point was to cast the Soviet Union entirely as a victim of Nazi aggression rather than a rival regime with its own violent history. Speaking as witnesses for the German side, three Wehrmacht officers who had been stationed near the Katyn forest in fall 1941 denied any German involvement in the mass shootings. A forensic expert summoned by the Soviet prosecution then compared the specifics of the Katyn massacre to other Nazi atrocities, noting that the same cause of death had been identified in multiple mass graves that had been exhumed across German-occupied regions: "a shot in the nape of the neck, at point-blank range."[26] In the end, the Germans failed to expose the Soviet cover-up. While some Western observers once more raised suspicions about Soviet wrongdoing at Katyn, the London *Times* concluded that there was no merit to the German claims of innocence.[27] The falsity of the Katyn folder did not imperil the trustworthiness of the Soviet indictment.

But the Allied front cracked nonetheless. The split opened over diverging assessments of the nature of Nazism and the severity of the verdict. During the judges' final deliberations, Soviet Judge Iona Nikitchenko succeeded in amending the British-produced draft, reworking passages that struck him as overly soft. Rather than calling Auschwitz and Treblinka "forced labor camps," as the British had proposed, the final draft designated them sites of "mass extermination." Nikitchenko also managed to persuade his colleagues to place more emphasis in the verdict on Nazi race theory as an essential part of "the overall policy of German fascism." The British draft, he said, was mistaken in blaming only "Hitler's confused brain" for the "blind and ruthless hatred toward Jews." Rather, this hatred had a systemic character.[28] Yet the most important Soviet demands went unheeded. Nikitchenko vehemently objected to the three other judges' decision not to indict the German government, the SA, and the Armed Forces High Command as criminal organizations. When the Western judges voted to sentence seven defendants to prison terms and to acquit another three, Nikitchenko wrote an angry dissenting opinion that insisted on death by hanging for every defendant. Standing trial, he argued, were not twenty-two men with a discrete record of individual crimes, but the most prominent representatives of a state that had preached mass murder as its mission.[29]

At the end of his time in Nuremberg, Roman Karmen rushed back to Moscow to produce a documentary film on the trial. Titled *Judgment of the Nations*, the film unequivocally supported the dissenting Soviet opinion, calling it the voice of "all of progressive mankind." Over close-ups of the ten hanged defendants, the nooses still around their necks, the narrator intoned: "The righteous gallows fulfilled the peoples' will." After its release in the Soviet Union, Karmen's film was also shown in a New York movie theater. *The New York Times* praised it as "a display of human justice," while the *New York Herald Tribune* disparaged the film as tendentious, commenting that the Soviet "propaganda line" that the Nazi menace was about to engulf the world until halted by the Red Army was "not likely to win friends." "There is nothing new in the current film, an elongated newsreel," the paper's reviewer wrote. "Strange as it seems, the pictures of the Nazi atrocities have somehow lost their steam through constant repetition. This moviegoer has developed a defense mechanism where a flat picture having no depth or color is only a bad dream to be forgotten as quickly as possible." The reviewer instead recommended another documentary, which highlighted the extreme oppressiveness of Soviet life, depicting eight-year-old boys inducted into the military. "These little potential officers are an eye-opener."[30]

Indeed, public sentiment in the United States was turning staunchly anti-Soviet. As early as April 1945, while U.S. and Soviet troops were shaking hands at the Elbe River, American journalists were warning against Russian expansion and describing the Soviet domination of Eastern Europe as a first step toward further conquests. Few observers in the United States were sympathetic to Soviet security interests, even after Nazi Germany's devastating invasion, nor was there any interest in helping the postwar Soviet Union recover from its wartime losses.[31] Most began to describe the Soviet Union in terms that decidedly portrayed it as an enemy. A new expression made the rounds in 1946, "Red Fascism," which American officials used to cast the Soviet Union as another, potentially even more sinister, variation of Nazi Germany. That year,

Congresswoman Clare Boothe Luce declared that "18 million people" languished in Soviet "concentration and forced labor camps," vastly inflating the numbers of the Soviet prison population, and comparing the Gulag to Auschwitz.[32] In March 1947, President Truman spoke to both houses of Congress to marshal support for a movement against "totalitarian" aggression. Unlike Churchill's address the year before, Truman's speech, soon dubbed the Truman Doctrine, made no mention of the West's "valiant" Russian ally, instead describing the Soviet Union as a global menace. Political currents within the United States contributed to Truman's choice of words: The Democratic Party had lost both houses of Congress to the Republican Party in November 1946, with Americans of Eastern European descent deserting the Democrats in huge numbers, angry over the party's handling of domestic issues. To win them back, Truman ran on a strongly anti-Communist platform during the 1948 election, ultimately prevailing by a relatively wide margin.[33]

The rhetoric of the early Cold War revived fears of Communism that had been rising in the United States throughout much of the interwar period. It reduced the wartime alliance with the Soviet Union to a mere interlude in a longer history of American anti-Communism. Truman was surrounded by advisers who had launched America's first "Red Scare" in 1919. Two of them especially, CIA Director Allen Dulles and FBI Director J. Edgar Hoover, would be instrumental in discrediting the political Left for many years to come.[34] This new view of the U.S.-Soviet alliance as an outlier reached into every aspect of American life. In fall 1947, the Congressional House Committee on Un-American Activities conducted prolonged hearings into alleged Communist influence in the American film industry, targeting among others the scriptwriter and the narrator of the Oscar-winning 1942 documentary *Moscow Strikes Back*. It and other Soviet films that had shown Americans the horrors of the Nazi occupation in the East were consigned to oblivion.[35] In response to the House investigations, motion-picture executives produced anti-Communist and anti-Soviet propaganda films, including *The Red Menace* (1949) and *I Was a Communist for the FBI* (1951)—the latter based on the true story of an FBI undercover agent of Eastern European descent who denounced American Communists as Soviet agents and cynical racists.[36]

Ilya Ehrenburg traveled to the United States in spring 1946, just as the East-West rift was deepening. Taking part in an American-Soviet cultural exchange program that had been hatched in 1945, the Russian writer spent two months touring the United States, his first visit to the country.[37] On the eve of his departure for Russia, Ehrenburg summarized his impressions for *The New York Times*. Understanding America was difficult, Ehrenburg wrote, as the country appeared to lack a middle ground. France, which he knew well, was full of color, he explained; in America, by contrast, "everything is black or white." While extolling the country's magnificent universities and museums, as well as the many Americans he had met who dreamed of the "happiness of the whole of humanity," Ehrenburg chided media pundits who sought to mobilize ordinary Americans for a "crusade against Moscow." It would be absurd for the two former allies to go to war against each other. Americans and Soviets were duty bound to remember "the soldiers of the Rhine and the soldiers of the Elbe, the heroes who fell in Stalingrad and the heroes who gave their lives in Normandy." Yet fascism was not dead and buried, Ehrenburg remarked. It lived on in the agitation for war and in the belief in racial supremacy.[38]

During his trip, Ehrenburg had insisted on visiting the Deep South. In Alabama and Mississippi, he sat down to interview local Black newspaper editors and tenant farmers, puzzling his official hosts.[39] Ehrenburg's piece for the *Times* castigated the racial oppression that he had observed firsthand, and he took the opportunity to lash out at American reporters who decried life under Communism as a form of enslavement: "I remember how the American newspapers were roused to indignation at the fact that, in the elections in Yugoslavia, people who had compromised themselves by collaboration with the occupants were deprived of their right to vote. I have been in the State of Mississippi, where half of the population were deprived of their right to vote. What is better: To deprive of the right to vote a man who has a black conscience or one who has a black complexion?" The Soviet visitor ended his piece on a hopeful note, describing the United States and the Soviet Union as "two great and noble peoples." Nothing, he insisted, separated these peoples "but the curtain of fog drawn by the slanderers who are preparing the Third World War."[40]

Churchill saw the capitals of Eastern Europe receding behind an iron curtain; Ehrenburg concentrated his efforts on preventing the continent's breakup into East-West compartments. In 1948, he helped organize the World Congress of Intellectuals for Peace in Wrocław, which brought together hundreds of luminaries, including Pablo Picasso, Anna Seghers, W. E. B. Du Bois, and Aimé Césaire. Like the writers' congresses of the 1930s, this and other "peace congresses" elsewhere in Europe failed to thwart the growing East-West conflict. But they did earn Ehrenburg a spot on the State Department's blacklist. Concerned over his sharp criticism of racial fascism American style, U.S. consular officials in Europe sought to banish the Soviet writer from Western Europe. Ehrenburg was denied visas to France and Italy, though he did manage to address a peace conference in Brussels, which U.S. officials monitored with evident concern. The event was attended by eighteen hundred people, they noted, not "the usual wild-eyed and ragged Communist run-of-the-mill," but mostly "white collar classes." The Dowager Queen of Belgium sat in the Royal Box throughout Ehrenburg's almost two-hour speech and became friendly with him afterward.[41]

With the deepening of the Cold War, Ehrenburg increasingly accused ordinary Americans of being militant anti-Communists, echoing his earlier comments about the involvement of ordinary Germans in Nazi crimes. He wrote with sardonic horror about U.S. newspapers that praised the atomic bomb as they advertised the "fifty-seven sauces of Heinz." That fantasies about a Third World War could so easily take hold of American minds Ehrenburg attributed to the fact that most Americans had not been exposed to the brutal reality of modern warfare. They had not been slaughtered by the millions and their cities had not been pulverized. Ehrenburg contrasted the United States with the

Soviet Union, where the war had cut deeply into the bodies and the souls of the people. Soviet men and women knew war intimately; that was why they hated it so much.[42] Ehrenburg's observation was confirmed by Communist agitators who reported back from peace rallies staged in Soviet villages and towns. They remarked on the many local women at the meetings who shared moving stories about loss and grief. "We do not want war" was their resounding refrain.[43]

JEWISH AND SOVIET

Inside the Soviet Union, Communist authorities staged numerous reckonings with fascism around the time of the Nuremberg trial. A few days before the opening of the tribunal, the Politburo ordered the convening of eight domestic war crimes trials. Soviet papers emphasized that these trials, while small in scale and locally focused, were part of a broader and concerted global court of justice.[44] Following the model of the 1943 Kharkov trial, the proceedings were open to the public and took place in theater halls. In an effort to expose the systemic nature of German crimes during the war, the defendants included not only SS officials but policemen and simple soldiers as well. Spectators in attendance often knew the victims personally, and sometimes the accused; this made for a charged atmosphere. The audience in the Victory cinema in the town of Velikie Luki gasped and cursed while listening to the testimony of surviving witnesses; several people fainted.[45] More than one hundred thousand people came to watch the hangings that concluded the trial in Minsk.[46] The trials galvanized the Soviet nation.

In line with the Soviet approach at Nuremberg, the prosecutors in the provincial trials focused on German crimes against humanity and on Nazi race theory as the driver of the mass killings in the East. This once more propelled the suffering of Soviet Jews to center stage. In the trials in Riga, Minsk, and Kiev, cities with large prewar Jewish populations, twenty-six of forty-one defendants were charged with the murder of Jews. In Riga, Higher SS and Police Commander Friedrich Jeckeln was accused of directing the "complete extermination" of three hundred thousand "Soviet citizens of Jewish nationality" in the Baltic area and two hundred thousand in Belorussia. At the Minsk trial, a general of the Order Police described receiving orders from the Generalkommissar of Belorussia, Wilhelm Kube, to liquidate the Minsk Ghetto. A former ghetto inmate recounted how the executions proceeded in waves beginning in August 1941. In Kiev, Order Police Commander Paul Albert Scheer admitted to participating in the Babi Yar massacre, together with the Einsatzkommandos and the Security Police. The mass killing did not "complete the task," however, and his men continued hunting down Jews. As justification, Scheer referred to Himmler's 1942 verbal order to kill every single surviving Jew in his jurisdiction.[47]

A lone survivor of the Babi Yar massacre appeared at the Kiev trial: the actress Dina Pronicheva, who recounted how she joined thousands of other unsuspecting Kievan Jews who followed German orders to report for resettlement. When she grasped that she was being led to her death, Pronicheva threw away the passport that identified her as Jewish and addressed a local guard in Ukrainian, imploring him to spare her. She was Ukrainian, she said, and had been mixed up with the deportees by mistake. She was led to the side and watched how victims who had been forced to undress cried in despair and lost their minds. That evening, a German officer came upon Pronicheva and others who had been spared for the moment, and ordered all of them to be shot, even if they were not Jewish, in order to eliminate any witnesses to the mass murder. Pronicheva jumped into the ravine just before the shots rang out and fell onto a heap of bodies. Her training as an actress may have saved her. When Germans stepped into the ravine to kill off survivors, one soldier stomped on Pronicheva's wrist with his hobnailed boot to check for a reaction.[48] She did not flinch. Hours later, she crawled out of the ravine under the cover of darkness.

Soviet readers and spectators in 1946 were presented with more detailed knowledge about the German mass murder of Jews than audiences anywhere else in the world.[49] The Jewish witnesses spoke in a distinctly Communist idiom, stressing their active resistance to fascism, to avoid appearing as helpless victims. At some point in her testimony, Pronicheva described how the soldiers and auxiliary policemen had arranged themselves in two rows at the entrance to the execution area. From both sides, they attacked the prisoners with clubs and guard dogs. In recounting this, Pronicheva emphasized her bravery: "I walked proudly, I did not fall," she declared. A recording of her testimony was edited to remove any hints of weakness, such as the moments when she became overwhelmed by the telling of her painful memories. An observer at the trial remembered her repeatedly falling to her knees and fainting, and how two people came to her assistance after she had finished testifying to carry her from the room.[50]

Though Jewish voices were specifically brought to the fore on the Soviet public stage during the early postwar years, they would soon be drowned out. Once again, the exceptional fate of Soviet Jews came into conflict with the Soviet political mandate of equal suffering, a tension that grew over time. The Germans had murdered 2.6 million Soviet Jews in their effort to eradicate the Jewish people. This genocidal thrust distinguished the fate of Soviet Jews from the ordeals suffered by countless Russians, Ukrainians, or Belorussians. Many Soviet Jews recognized the difference early on; it prompted them to recover a hitherto disavowed Jewish identity. In his August 1941 radio address to Jews around the world, Ehrenburg voiced this feeling himself: The Nazis had reminded him that in addition to being a Russian writer born in a "Russian city" (he meant Kiev, which was mostly Russian-speaking at the time), he was also something else: "My mother's name was Hannah. I am a Jew. I say this proudly. Hitler hates us more than anything, and this makes us proud."[51]

For a time, Soviet leaders approved of such declarations as long as they did not disrupt the broader Soviet order. In fall 1941, the Kremlin encouraged the formation of a Soviet Jewish Anti-Fascist Committee (JAC), which it tasked with placing articles about Nazi atrocities in the American and British press, in order to solicit the support of foreign Jews for the Soviet war effort. After Ehrenburg joined the committee in 1942, he and several other writers on the JAC set out to work on a so-called Black Book indicting the Nazi regime for its annihilation of the Jews. But the editors soon began to disagree about the materials that were to fill the Black Book. All of them, with the exception of Ehrenburg, envisioned it as a collaborative venture pursued together with Jewish organizations in the United States and Palestine. From Princeton, New Jersey, Albert Einstein had signaled enthusiastic support for a joint Black Book that would document the Nazi mass murder of the Jewish people. Ehrenburg, who chaired the Writers' Commission within the JAC, vigorously objected. His vision of the Black Book was centered on the Soviet Union, and he insisted that if Einstein and other Jews abroad went ahead with their plan, the JAC would produce a separate Black Book devoted solely to the fate of the Jews in the USSR. He also sought to foreground evidence of Jewish resistance and Soviet interethnic solidarity in the fight against fascism. His concerns were an expression of his personal desire to align his newly asserted Jewish identity with his deep loyalty to the Soviet state. But it also reflected his shrewd political mind. Ehrenburg sensed that any collaboration with Jews abroad would expose the JAC to charges of Zionism and risk a violent crackdown by the Kremlin.

In the end, Stalin's stance on the Jewish question turned out to be just as Ehrenburg predicted. The Soviet leader supported Jewish efforts for statehood in Palestine, but with respect to Jews living in the USSR, he insisted on their overriding allegiance to the Soviet state. Soviet Jews who identified primarily as Jews were denounced as subversive Zionists. Sometime in 1944, a government informant in Kiev overheard the writer Dovid Hofshteyn remarking that perhaps the suffering of the Jews would prompt them to see themselves as a distinct national group: "What the Jews are now enduring is good. It will restore their national consciousness, which had been lost." The informant reported this remark to Ukrainian Communist leaders, who subsequently established that Hofshteyn had also organized a meeting of Kievan Jews in September 1944 to mark the third anniversary of the Babi Yar massacre, and chided the local secret service for failing to prevent this meeting.[52]

In early 1945, after learning that members of the JAC had sent some of their draft chapters to American colleagues for inclusion in what would now be an American-published volume, Ehrenburg angrily quit the Writers' Commission. His friend, the writer and war correspondent Vasily Grossman, stepped in to take his place. Shortly thereafter, the writers on the JAC received Einstein's proposed preface to the Black Book. To their dismay, Einstein had cast the book not as an indictment of German fascism but as a justification for establishing a Jewish state in Palestine. In response to protests from the Soviet Jewish editors, Einstein withdrew the preface. *The Black Book: The Nazi Crime Against the Jewish People* appeared in 1946 and included numerous documents submitted by the JAC.[53]

In Moscow, the JAC editors working under Grossman's supervision ended up yielding to Ehrenburg's desire for a separate and specifically Soviet Black Book. Yet the venture was doomed. The secret police raided the printing press in 1948 and destroyed all copies of the manuscript along with the printing plates. Despite the editors' efforts to preempt government concerns that the project would encourage Jewish nationalism in the Soviet Union, it was nevertheless deemed subversive. A new purge was under way, targeting overtly Jewish activists and even assimilated Soviet Jews as crypto-Zionists. The fallout between the USSR and Israel after fierce initial Soviet backing of the first Jewish state made matters worse. The JAC was closed down and most of its leaders were executed.[54] Ehrenburg tried to stem the rising tide of anti-Semitism, risking his own arrest. When colleagues pressured him to sign an open letter denouncing arrested Jews as foreign spies, he refused.[55] Ehrenburg never renounced his Jewish identity, and by the time of Stalin's death in 1953, he was the only public figure in the USSR still trying to reconcile what now seemed irreconcilable: Soviet and Jewish. Ehrenburg managed by always foregrounding his faith in Soviet universalism. This delicate balancing act may have saved his life. [56]

The Kremlin's shrill anti-Zionism silenced the memory of Soviet Jewish suffering that had brought Jewish survivors into the witness stands of postwar Soviet courts. Stalin's death in 1953 was followed by a period of political liberalization, which came to be known by the title of Ehrenburg's novella published that same year: *The Thaw.* Under rising pressure, party officials encouraged public debate over numerous issues, but not the Judeocide. When the question of a Babi Yar memorial came up in the Ukrainian Central Committee in 1957, its leaders refused to discuss the possibility, doubling down on their denial by ordering the construction of a sports stadium near the killing grounds. The ravine was to be dammed up and filled with mud and water pumped in from nearby brick quarries. Construction proceeded even as workers uncovered the remains of corpses. When the dam collapsed after a period of heavy rain in early 1961, killing more than one hundred people, Kievans spoke about the victims of Babi Yar taking their revenge.[57] Upon hearing of the broken dam, the young Moscow rebel poet Yevgeny Yevtushenko visited Kiev and wrote a poem titled "Babi Yar." It was published in the largest Soviet literary newspaper on the twentieth anniversary of the massacre. The paper sold out at once.

Yevtushenko wrote the poem to castigate the Soviet government's anti-Semitism, which he blamed for the silencing of the Jewish tragedy. The poem begins:

> No monument stands over Babi Yar.
> A steep cliff only, like the rudest headstone.
> I am afraid.
> Today, I am as old
> As the entire Jewish race itself.[58]

The speaker then casts himself in rapid succession as a Hebrew in ancient Egypt, Jesus Christ, Alfred Dreyfus, a young victim of pogrom violence in Bialystok, Anne Frank, and every old man and every child murdered at Babi Yar, explaining that his identification with the Jewish people is based on consciousness rather than blood: As a devoted internationalist, a Soviet Russian poet had no choice but to fight anti-Semitism. Yevtushenko received enthusiastic praise as well as damning criticism, including from party chief Nikita Khrushchev, who chided him for political immaturity and historical ignorance: "The poem represents things as if only Jews were the victims of the fascist atrocities,"

Khrushchev wrote, "whereas, of course, the Hitlerite butchers murdered many Russians, Ukrainians, and Soviet people of other nationalities." As for Yevtushenko's accusation of official anti-Semitism, Khrushchev asserted that Jews had enjoyed equal rights since 1917 and that there was "no Jewish question" in the USSR. Ehrenburg, too, came under fire for supposedly having inspired Yevtushenko's "irresponsible" writings.[59]

Following more outcries by more Russian artists, Communist leaders reversed course and held a competition for a Babi Yar memorial. They made two stipulations: that the monument not honor Jews exclusively, but all the people who had died at Babi Yar; and that it express the "courage and the fearlessness of Soviet citizens in the face of death." The prize-winning monument was unveiled in 1976. A huge bronze composition, it featured several muscular men—including a partisan fighter, a Red Army soldier with clenched fist, and a sailor—who stand at the edge of a precipice shielding distraught women and their children. The competition had been limited to Ukrainian artists, to mark the memory project as local in origin. A terse sentence in Ukrainian engraved on a plaque read: "Here in 1941–43, the German Fascist invaders executed more than 100,000 citizens from Kiev and prisoners of war."[60] The information was not exactly inaccurate: After their massacre of Jews on September 29 and 30, 1941, German commandos used the execution site for two more years, shooting tens of thousands of victims: Jews and non-Jews, Soviet POWs, Roma, mentally ill patients, and suspected partisans.[61] Nonetheless, the wording on the plaque erased Nazism's targeted assault on Soviet Jews and, along with it, the ideological rationale for Germany's invasion of the Soviet Union.

The Babi Yar monument formed a late addition to a memorial landscape devoted to the Great Patriotic War.[62] Many of these memorials that sprang up across the Soviet Union after 1945 depicted in one way or another the family of Soviet nations joining forces in the fight against fascism. Membership in the family was extended to the fifteen Union republics; Soviet Jews who did not have a Soviet republic to call their home received no special mention.[63] Memorial grounds in the outer zones of Soviet influence offered a similar picture. The Communist memorials at Auschwitz in Poland and Buchenwald in East Germany invoked the suffering of prisoners from multiple European nations but said nothing about Jews. But while they silenced the particularity of Jewish suffering, Communist governments were more determined than Western states to document Nazi atrocities. The Auschwitz memorial was unveiled in 1947, and East German plans to commemorate Buchenwald dated back to at least 1950. The first concentration camp memorial at Dachau, located in West Germany, did not open until 1965, after years of lobbying by surviving prisoners.

In contrast, Western remembrance of Nazi crimes focused on the exceptional suffering of the Jews. At the Nuremberg trial, the Judeocide had not been understood as a crime distinct from the other horrors of the Second World War; that insight came only later in Israel, the United States, and Western Europe, with the Eichmann trial in Jerusalem, the Civil Rights Movement in the United States, and transatlantic student radicalism in 1968. Over time, the invocation of the Holocaust as a singular crime, and with it an obligation to defend human rights, turned into a Western liberal credo. In 1978, President Jimmy Carter asked Auschwitz survivor Elie Wiesel to chair a commission that would gather ideas for a national Holocaust memorial. As part of its mission, the commission explored how other countries, including Poland, Israel, Denmark, and the Soviet Union, commemorated the Holocaust. When members of the Presidential Commission arrived in Kiev in August 1979 to tour the Babi Yar memorial, American and Soviet memories of the Nazi past collided head-on. A reporter for *The New York Times* accompanied the Presidential Commission on its visit to the killing grounds, where, he noted, the Nazis had machine-gunned "more than 70,000 Jews over a 10-day period in 1941." As the visitors gathered in front of the monument, a Ukrainian guide read out in English the information given on the memorial plaque. The American reporter recorded the "exclamations of disbelief" that came from the stunned visitors: "'Not a word about the Jews!'"[64]

FORGED IN ANTI-FASCISM

The experience of fighting Nazi Germany shaped the postwar Soviet order in fundamental ways. Fascism, and German fascism in particular, remained a defining enemy of the Soviet state for many years to come. In dealing with the peoples and regions that had formerly been under Nazi rule, postwar Soviet officials judged them according to their history: Only those with a proven record of resisting Nazism could join the Soviet community.[65]

The first to feel the exclusionary thrust of this postwar stance were the millions of Ukrainians, Russians, and Belorussians who had been deported to Germany as forced laborers or prisoners of war. Exhausted from years of mistreatment, most of them were eager to return to their former homes.[66] But Soviet repatriation officials offered them an icy greeting. The NKVD in conjunction with military counterintelligence detained all returnees in "filtration camps," where they were subjected to repeated interrogations, sometimes lasting weeks or months. The purpose was to weed out traitors and opportunists, including auxiliary policemen and Red Army personnel who had surrendered to the Germans rather than fighting to the death. Every Soviet person who had come into prolonged contact with the Germans was suspect—and there were no simple ways of proving one's loyalty. Even the documentation that certain returnees provided attesting to their anti-fascist credentials could hurt rather than help, as some secret service operatives assumed these documents must be fabrications intended to conceal a history of collaboration.[67]

Filtration led to the arrest and subsequent deportation to labor camps (or "special settlements") of three hundred and fifty thousand people, 6.5 percent of the total number of Soviet repatriates.[68] While most other returnees were initially cleared, they remained under a cloud of suspicion. The onset of the Cold War triggered another wave of persecution aimed at the repatriates, this time targeting anyone who had interacted with the former Western Allies.[69] Maks Mints, the captain who had been captured by the Germans and exposed as a Jew, fell victim to this wave of arrests. Mints had led an extraordinary life: Beyond staging numerous escapes from German prisons, he had founded an underground antifascist committee in the Fallingbostel camp and established ties to underground organizations across Germany. As the Third Reich collapsed, Mints's committee at Fallingbostel seized control of the camp and handed it over to British and American troops.[70] Mints went through two rounds of filtrations and was cleared for residence in Moscow, where he settled with his wife and son, working as an engineer. His arrest in 1947 came out of the blue. Prosecutors brushed aside Mints's anti-fascist record. They posed just one question to him: How had he as a Jew managed to survive German captivity? Mints's request that witnesses be called in who could testify to his wartime activities was denied. He was tried on charges of treason and sentenced to fifteen years of hard labor.[71]

Mints was rehabilitated in 1955 and publicly recognized as a committed anti-fascist. Many others were not. All Soviet citizens who had lived on occupied soil or been deported to Germany received a notation in their identification papers, flagging them as potential traitors or spies. Women who ventured to talk about what they had endured in Germany were routinely slandered as "Nazi whores."[72] Countless survivors of Nazi occupation thus found themselves ostracized from the Soviet anti-fascist community. There was no place for their memories in the national pantheon of self-sacrificing struggle. Among them was Aleksandr Kalimov, who returned to his hometown in the Komi Republic following his release from German captivity. In his diary Kalimov recorded the insinuations he faced at his workplace. Former POWs like himself were widely believed to have surrendered to the enemy to save their skin. "I'm often asked how I remained among the living. It's very hard to respond. After all, I never thought about staying alive." While his colleagues marched together on November 7, the anniversary of the Bolshevik revolution, Kalimov sat at home, alone, listening to the radio coverage of the parade on Red Square. "I felt sad," he wrote. "There is no one to whom I can confide my grief."[73] Instead, Kalimov entrusted it to his memoir, which was discovered only after his death.[74]

The remembrance of the devastating war began as a populist initiative. Looking to the future and impatient to rebuild the state's strength, government leaders wished to treat May 9, the anniversary of the war's end, as an ordinary workday. But Soviet veterans began celebrating it informally, taking time off to mourn and drink. In regions that had fallen under German occupation, bereaved survivors would gather at local mass graves to commemorate the dead. "Officers in the reserves kissed soldiers in service," a war veteran remembered celebrations in Vinnitsa in the 1950s. "Everyone recalled memories from the war and expressed amazement at still being alive."[75] The Communist state, however, was slow to understand how commemorating the day could be a means of inspiring patriotism. At the behest of Ukraine's Communist leader, Petro Shelest, the Politburo in 1965 finally decreed Victory Day a national holiday and marked it with an annual military parade on Red Square. Such celebrations, he argued, would "immortalize the people's heroic feat," mobilize workers, contribute to the military patriotic education of Soviet youth, and offer a powerful rejoinder to West German "revanchist saber-rattling."[76] Soviet party leaders followed Shelest's recommendation and called for the building of more war memorials across the USSR. The expanding war cult soon became a powerful force in society. Younger generations greeted with veneration and gratitude the aging war veterans who marched during parades and were invited into schools to recount their experiences. A popular song from 1975 called May 9 a "holiday observed with tears in the eyes." As part of the renewed commemoration of the war, the Kremlin also became more forthcoming about the scale of Soviet losses. In his 1946 response to Churchill, Stalin had put the USSR's military losses at seven million, leaving aside civilian casualties.[77] In 1965, Party Secretary Leonid Brezhnev announced a dramatically higher estimate: "More than twenty million" Soviet people, he said, had lost their lives in the war against fascism, approximately half of them civilians.[78]

ACCUSING FASCISM

On the national and international stage, the legacy of the Second World War pushed Soviet postwar politics in two directions at once. On the one hand, it sharpened Soviet prosecutors' investigations of Germany's genocidal war, spurring them to hunt down former Nazis.[79] But it also prompted Communist leaders to lodge blunt accusations of "fascism" against a host of perceived enemies with few or no actual ties to Nazism. The divergence between Soviet policies toward West Germany and Eastern Europe exemplified this tension.

In 1949 the Kremlin freed most of the four hundred thousand Wehrmacht soldiers and other German operatives still in captivity. But it held on to those who had been sentenced as war criminals or who remained under investigation: former SA, SS, SD, and Gestapo members, former camp guards, and Wehrmacht soldiers accused of having taken part in reprisals against Soviet citizens—a total of thirty-seven thousand men.[80] Six years later, in a gesture of goodwill toward the new West German state, Khrushchev repatriated these last German prisoners, on condition that the worst offenders continue to serve time in German prisons. (Chancellor Konrad Adenauer agreed to indict proven war criminals in West German courts. But when the thousands of prisoners arrived back home, they were greeted as martyrs and no one was tried.[81]) In the USSR, the 1960s brought a new wave of trials against fascist collaborators.[82] Soviet journalists at the time wrote of justice being delivered, methodically and inexorably, contrasting the Soviet dedication to uprooting fascism with West Germany's widespread rehabilitation of former Nazis. They also publicized trial materials containing specific information about Nazi perpetrators still at large in Germany, to push West German authorities into action.[83]

In their search for justice, Soviet law enforcement officials lifted a corner of the Iron Curtain. In 1963, Roman Rudenko, who had become Soviet Prosecutor-General, supplied his counterparts in West Germany with newly obtained documentation about former Einsatzkommando leaders.[84]

Soviet prosecutors also furnished the State Criminal Police Office of Baden-Württemberg with a copy of the diary of secret military police officer Friedrich Schmidt, in which Schmidt described the torture and killing of young female Soviet partisans. Schmidt's journal, which Ehrenburg had publicized in 1942 as the musings of a "typical German," was now to be used as evidence against members of Schmidt's military police unit, GFP 626.[85] Soviet officials additionally agreed to send dozens of Soviet survivors of wartime atrocities to serve as witnesses in West Germany's first trials against former Nazis.[86] Some of the witnesses refused to go; others asked for police protection for the duration of their stay in Germany.[87] Dina Pronicheva traveled to Darmstadt in 1967 to attend a trial of former members of the Einsatzgruppe that was responsible for the Babi Yar massacre. Pronicheva made the journey reluctantly, fearing that Nazis would attempt to kill her.[88] In West Germany, Soviet witnesses also had to contend with defense lawyers and reporters who automatically dismissed any Soviet testimony as untruthful. One Soviet Auschwitz survivor who spoke at a trial in Frankfurt felt treated "almost like a defendant."[89]

The Auschwitz survivor ended up criticizing the West German justice system for treating former Nazis with kid gloves.[90] He had a point. The paucity of convictions of war criminals in West Germany was a direct consequence of the predominance of ex-Nazis in the West German police and justice systems. As late as 1966, two-thirds of the leading officials in the Ministry of Justice were former Nazis. In the Federal Criminal Police Office, the equivalent of the FBI, they comprised three-quarters of the force, and more than half of those were former SS men.[91] Unsurprisingly, perhaps, the charges that the State Criminal Police Office of Baden-Württemberg had brought against the former unit GFP 626 members were ultimately dropped.[92] Former Nazis were also able to sway West German public opinion. When the Kindler publishing house announced a translation of Ehrenburg's multivolume memoirs in 1960—publisher Helmut Kindler had befriended Communist writers during the 1930s and fought in the anti-Nazi resistance movement—German veteran organizations instigated a campaign against Ehrenburg as "one of the worst anti-German agitators." They repeated false claims made by Wehrmacht propagandists in the final phase of the war that Ehrenburg had signed a flyer calling for the raping of German women. The intervention by the veterans prompted Kindler to halt the publication and launch an inquiry into the existence of the flyer. When no corroborating evidence was found and the memoir was shipped to vendors, the veterans printed overtly anti-Semitic posters and hung them at the entrances of stores selling the book. The posters read: "This bookshop is ignoble and tasteless enough to make a profit off the memoirs of the greatest murderer in world history on the principle that 'money doesn't stink.'" The campaign was effective; sales of the initially popular work ground to a halt.[93]

Most West Germans during this period refused to acknowledge German war crimes in the Soviet Union; their first impulse was to blame the Soviet side instead. Rather than focus on Nazi criminals, law enforcement officials pursued trials against former German POWs who had served as "anti-fascist" activists in Soviet camps and denounced fellow soldiers to the Soviet authorities.[94] The West German government sponsored the publication of a multivolume oral history, including an abridged English translation, of expellees from Germany's eastern provinces who told about their suffering at Soviet hands, regularly racializing Soviet soldiers as "Asiatics" and "Mongols." A Prussian doctor of aristocratic descent compared the advance of the Red Army in 1945 to "a flood of rats that exceeded all of the Egyptian plagues."[95] When West German Chancellor Konrad Adenauer visited Moscow in 1955 to renew diplomatic relations between the two countries, severed in 1941, he offended his Soviet hosts by indicting the Red Army for its "terrible" crimes against Germans in 1944 and 1945, while hardly making any mention of Germany's invasion of the Soviet Union. A furious Khrushchev reportedly jumped up and shook his fist at Adenauer, prompting the aged chancellor to get up and shake his fist too. In the end, Adenauer sought to placate the Soviet side by stressing that the war had brought equal suffering to Germans and Soviets. He returned from Moscow believing the visit to have been a success. As Adenauer declared at a press conference, with the resumption of formal ties between the Soviet Union and West Germany, "this war thing is disposed of once and for all."[96] But the past continued to haunt Adenauer's government. His Minister for Expellees in the late 1950s was a former Nazi known for his public tirades against "Judeo-Bolshevism"; he had been charged by Soviet as well as East German and Israeli prosecutors with the mass killing of Jews and the abuse of Soviet POWs. But although the minister was forced to step down when these charges came to light, he was never brought before a West German court.[97]

Within its own borders and those of other Eastern bloc nations, the Soviet Union wielded the threat of fascism more indiscriminately and primarily to preserve its own power. This was particularly the case in the Western borderlands of the Soviet Union, where Communist power remained contested. For several years after their reconquest of Western Ukraine in 1944, Soviet security forces remained embroiled in heavy fighting against Ukrainian nationalists, killing an estimated 153,000 insurgents and deporting hundreds of thousands to forced labor camps. To these Soviet troops, the separatist militants they were fighting were fascists. At summary trials, hundreds of captured insurgents were indicted as former Nazi collaborators and hanged, Nazi style, wearing signs reading "Traitor."[98] Even after the region's pacification, Soviet authorities kept staging such show trials to defuse separatist unrest.[99] For the same purpose, Communist leaders in the Baltic republics published wartime records highlighting Latvian, Estonian, and Lithuanian participation in German-led massacres. Allegations of Nazi collaboration also served to discredit anti-Soviet émigré groups.[100] Political purposes aside, such allegations also indicated real Soviet fears of a renewed Nazi crusade against the USSR.

Throughout the Eastern European lands that the Soviet Union annexed or occupied between 1939 and 1945, anti-fascism conveyed both a deeply felt memory of suffering and a claim to imperial rule. One of the first memorials to go up outside Soviet borders was the monument to Soviet tank crews erected in Prague in July 1945. It featured a heavy tank on a stone pedestal, its barrel pointing westward.[101] In 1947, a bronze statue of a soldier was erected in central Tallinn. Standing above a Red Army burial site, the Estonian-designed memorial commemorated the soldiers as Soviet Estonia's "liberators." In 1949, a memorial park in Berlin's Treptow district was unveiled, built over the mass graves of thousands of Red Army troops who had fallen during the Battle of Berlin. At its center, a twelve-meter-tall Soviet soldier stood, holding a child atop a crushed swastika, his sword resting at his side. To Soviet observers, the blood shed by Red Army soldiers in the war against fascism justified their dominance in postwar East Central Europe. On a visit to Prague in 1946, the Soviet poet Konstantin Simonov pointed out that Czechs and Slovaks had done little to stop Hitler. While Eastern European nations were more affluent and made their Soviet visitors look poor by comparison, Simonov and other Red Army veterans insisted on their nation's moral preeminence, derived from their sacrifices in the fight against fascism.[102]

Whenever their rule was challenged, Communist Party leaders in the Soviet Union and elsewhere in Eastern Europe responded by lashing out against opponents, calling them fascists. In this fashion, Communist officials labeled the East German workers' uprising in June 1953 a "fascist putsch" and had it crushed. In Hungary, Communists invoked the Soviet Thaw to enact reforms of their own, but the movement spun out of control, as large parts of the population turned against the "Russian occupiers." In response, the new hard-line Communist government, put in place with the help of Soviet tank divisions, pronounced the Hungarian Revolution a fascist-led "counterrevolution" and proceeded to label even socialist reformists with impeccable anti-fascist credentials as Nazis.[103] In 1961, East German leaders walled up the GDR's western borders to stem the westward drain of cheap labor that threatened to destroy the socialist economy. East German leaders soon began to refer to the Wall as their "anti-fascist protection bulwark." The suppression of the 1968 Prague Spring by Warsaw Pact troops under Moscow's command was yet another "anti-fascist" action.

As time passed, these repressive measures only served to tarnish the Soviet Union's standing. For many Czechoslovaks in the wake of 1968, the heavy tank on the pedestal in Prague emblematized "Russian" totalitarian rule, eclipsing earlier memories of the Soviet Union's role in liberating the country from Nazism. Across the socialist bloc, decades of state repression devalued the anti-fascist claims of government leaders and engendered a broad sense of victimization under Communism. A workers' strike in Poland, supported by the Catholic Church and the United States, catalyzed a broad national liberation movement that succeeded in securing the first pluralistic elections since 1947. The anti-Communist national movement won in a landslide. In response, Soviet leaders announced a wave of reforms and disclosures intended to preserve state socialism. In August 1989, the Kremlin conceded for the first time that it had signed a secret protocol with Nazi Germany in 1939 that paved the way for Soviet annexation of the Baltic states. The admission came days before the fiftieth anniversary of the pact and was meant to placate nationalist opposition in the Baltic states.[104] It did nothing to stop the wave of secession, however. On August 23, 1989, two million Lithuanians, Estonians, and Latvians joined hands in a human chain running through the three republics, chanting patriotic songs and denouncing the 1939 pact. The Baltic states won independence in 1990, ushering in the collapse of the Soviet Union. In Prague, Soviet power was stripped of its remaining legitimacy on April 28, 1991. Early that morning, a group of rebel artists covered the Monument to Soviet Tank Crews with pink paint. On the turret, they affixed a huge erect finger. Czechoslovak soldiers covered the tank with a tarp and repainted it in its original color. After further artistic assaults, the government moved the tank to a military museum outside Prague.[105]

AN OCEAN OF GRIEF

As state socialism disintegrated, monuments that had come to symbolize Communist oppression came tumbling down across the Eastern bloc, including in Russia and other core areas of the Soviet state. But there was a revealing difference when it came to the personal remembrance of the Great Patriotic War. In the borderlands and on the fringes of the Soviet empire, where nationalist currents were at their strongest, claims about the Red Army as a liberating force had always rung hollow, and memorials dedicated to Soviet war heroes were increasingly perceived as a provocation.[106] Inside the Soviet Union's core areas, by contrast, memories of the war against fascism retained an intense hold on society even after Communism's demise. The writer Ales Adamovich, who had fought as a young partisan in the Belorussian forests and seen with his own eyes how German soldiers burned down entire "partisan villages" together with their inhabitants, interviewed the few survivors from the burned villages in the aftermath of the war and collected their grief-filled testimonies into a book. The eyewitness accounts gathered by Adamovich subsequently informed Russian filmmaker Elem Klimov's *Come and See*, perhaps the most harrowing anti-war film ever produced. It appeared in 1985, marking the fortieth anniversary of the end of the war. That same year, the Belorussian writer Svetlana Alexievich published *The Unwomanly Face of War*, a book of interviews with Soviet women veterans of the Second World War. Alexievich had worked as a student volunteer in Adamovich's project and inherited his passion as a documentarian of the wounds of war that refused to heal.[107]

Five years later, Soviet President Mikhail Gorbachev saluted the anniversary of the end of World War II in Europe by declaring that the time had come to reveal the full extent of Soviet losses. Relying on the findings of a commission of historians, statisticians, and demographers that he had formed the year before, he presented a colossal figure: "nearly 27 million" Soviets had been killed, not counting the millions more who had been severely wounded or permanently disfigured.[108] Gorbachev spoke of "an ocean of grief" formed from the blood and tears of the Soviet people, and he identified Nazi Germany's vicious way of war as the main cause: "The blow of the aggressor was inflicted on the entire people, on the very foundations of its existence." Gorbachev also took aim at the callousness of the Stalinist regime: "Nobody is forgotten, and nothing is forgotten," he declared, a nod to the Soviet soldiers and civilians who had been doubly victimized, first by fascism and then by the Stalinist state. Importantly, the Soviet government also admitted in 1990 that the Katyn massacre had been the work of the NKVD, issuing a candid statement: "The Soviet side expresses deep regret over the tragedy, and assesses it as one of the worst Stalinist outrages."[109]

Gorbachev invoked the memory of the war to call for a new international order promoting peace and universal human values. He eulogized the Soviet people ("A people that won this war can overcome any kind of difficulty and solve any kind of problem. A people that has endured such a war cannot but yearn for peace with all its soul.").[110] But who exactly comprised the Soviet people in May 1990 was subject to debate. Earlier that month, the Soviet republics of Latvia and Estonia had declared their independence from the USSR, following Lithuania's example. Nationalist parties in Western Ukraine were scoring victories. More unrest elsewhere was tearing the Soviet Union apart.

The last anti-fascist memorial to be revealed in the Soviet Union was the Black Book. After Ilya Ehrenburg's death in 1967, his daughter, Irina, discovered a surviving copy of the manuscript in her father's archive. Following a circuitous journey, the book of Soviet Jewish suffering and resistance was published in its original Russian in Kiev in 1991, just months before the breakup of the USSR. Jewish communities greeted the publication, but it failed to shake the world as Ehrenburg had hoped.[111]

THE PERILS OF ERASURE

As the Soviet order and Soviet memories of the war against Nazi Germany receded from the world stage, a different memory regime rose to prominence. In April 1993, the United States Holocaust Memorial Museum (USHMM) opened in Washington, D.C., capping years of work undertaken by the Presidential Commission on the Holocaust. The Nazis had carried out their murderous campaign far from U.S. shores, but the commission nonetheless called for a national memorial in the center of the U.S. capital casting American political ideals as the antithesis to Nazi racism and genocide. The Holocaust, it declared, was "an event of universal significance" with special meaning for Americans: "In act and word the Nazis denied the deepest tenets of the American people."[112]

The USHMM rapidly established itself as the most visited Holocaust memorial in the world.[113] Its permanent exhibition, entitled "The Holocaust," takes visitors on an unsettling journey through Nazism's rise to power and Nazi Germany's systematic persecution and annihilation of Europe's Jews and other minorities. In contrast to Soviet memorials, which focused primarily on the civic duty to fight fascism, viewers of the new exhibit in Washington were asked to identify with the victims of Nazism; upon admission, each visitor received a randomly chosen ID card printed with the photograph and personal history of a victim—for example, a Jew, a homosexual, a Jehovah's Witness, or a Gentile. Some of the victims survived the Holocaust, many others perished. In another departure from Soviet memorials, the USHMM emphasizes Americans as liberators. The very first hall that visitors enter after stepping out of an elevator is a dark room where light shines only on two flanking walls: The wall to the left is covered with a black-and-white photograph depicting American soldiers in a liberated camp. The soldiers stand around the charred remains of a huge pyre formed from the bodies of prisoners. The letters of the exhibition title imprinted on the wall to the right look like they were seared into the metal surface by the flames of the pyre.

After an opening section covering events in Germany from 1933 to the outbreak of the war in September 1939, the exhibition proceeds to the "Final Solution—1940–1945."[114] As they enter this part of the exhibit, visitors pass through a tower whose three-story-high walls are covered with photographs of residents of a single Jewish community in Lithuania, massacred in September 1941 by SS Einsatzgruppen and their Lithuanian auxiliaries. Visitors walk on cobblestones brought from the Warsaw Ghetto, and they see other surviving artifacts from the ghetto: a baby carriage, a workbench that concealed the entrance to a hiding place for Jews, and a metal milk can in which resistance fighters stored for posterity testimonies of Jewish life, fully aware of its imminent extinction. Also on display are an authentic railcar that was used to transport victims to a killing center and portions of an actual barrack from Birkenau. There are pellets

Entrance to the permanent exhibition in the United States Holocaust Memorial Museum, Washington, D.C.

of Zyklon B that were found at Majdanek, and a metal casting of the camp's gas chamber door, complete with a peephole through which guards could view the killings. These objects were deliberately chosen by museum planners to refute the lies of Holocaust denialists.[115]

The artifacts account for the exhibition's emotional power. One room contains a huge mound of shoes; they were brought from Majdanek, where the Germans had piled up the clothing and the passports of hundreds of thousands of their victims. Many visitors describe this room as the exhibition's most moving place.[116] "The smell of the shoes of so many people . . . I will never forget that smell. This can never be allowed to happen in any form again," a visitor from California said after seeing the room.[117] Profoundly affecting, the artifacts are at times presented without important historical context. Viewers of the mound of shoes are not informed that Majdanek was the first death camp to be freed by Allied troops, specifically, by the Red Army. While the museum offers the testimony of multiple Americans who freed the camps in 1945, it does not cite the voices of the Soviet soldiers who were the first liberators. The Nazi invasion of the USSR and the Red Army's liberation of the camps are strangely understated throughout the exhibition and do not register as two of the most momentous events in the war.[118]

To be fair, the permanent exhibition acknowledges, beyond the Nazi murder of six million Jews, the fate of "millions" of other victims of the war, naming, in this order: "Roma and Sinti," "Germans with Disabilities," "Poles Targeted as a Racial and Political Threat," "Soviet Prisoners of War Targeted as a Racial and Political Threat," and "Political and Other Prisoners of Nazi Concentration Camps."[119] But other than the Soviet prisoners of war, the exhibition remains silent about the German killings of Soviet citizens and it does not engage with Soviet estimates of their own dead—whether Stalin's seven million, Brezhnev's twenty million, or Gorbachev's twenty-seven million. To produce the ID cards handed to visitors, museum workers collected the personal histories of six hundred victims of Nazism from all over Europe. Of this collection, a mere nine cards tell the stories of Soviet citizens.[120]

The exhibition's greatest omission is subtler, but more consequential. The Germans carried out their war of extermination in the belief that they were fighting a Jewish-Communist foe. The exhibition in the USHMM largely omits the political component of this composite in favor of the racial dimension, which ostensibly speaks for itself: "The leaders of Nazi Germany, a modern, educated society, aimed to destroy millions of men, women, and children because of their Jewish identity."[121] In the process, the fact that the Nazis rose to power and generated enormous backing across Germany and throughout Europe on the strength of their stridently anti-Communist politics and their ability to fuse Communists and Jews into a single monstrous threat is lost. The omission is perhaps convenient: Imagine a U.S. government institution having to explain to millions of Americans and visitors from all over the world that the Soviet Communist order was Nazi Germany's defining target and that the Holocaust was the culmination of a policy that persecuted Communists as subhumans. But if the USHMM's mission is to prevent the Holocaust from happening again, as President Bill Clinton pointed out during the museum's opening, it is important to depict the full history of Nazism's rise and demise without regard for ideological preferences.[122]

In the history of the Second World War, the Soviet Union was Germany's "World Enemy No. 1." It was chiefly for this reason that twenty-six million Soviet citizens, roughly half of them civilians, lost their lives after Germany's invasion in June 1941. Hitler and his followers began by burning mountains of books before proceeding to annihilate millions of people, a campaign undertaken out of rage against the Soviet ideology of universalism, which they had called Jewish Bolshevism. Even as he lashed out against the Red Army's "Asiatic hordes," Hitler got the nature of his opponent right when he identified the Bolsheviks as the Enlightenment's most radical offspring. With this statement, Hitler acknowledged the struggle between Nazi Germany and the Soviet Union as a global struggle with European roots: a tribal rebellion against the forces of universalism.

For three years, from June 1941 to June 1944, Soviet men and women bore the full brunt of Germany's war. They offered the earliest resistance to Nazism's global conquest, and they inflicted decisive defeats on the enemy long before the Western Allies landed in Normandy. Even after D-Day, and right up to Keitel's capitulation in Berlin, the war remained principally a fight between Germany and the Soviet Union—as the death rates along the Eastern Front demonstrate. Soviet cultural producers, often Jewish—such as the radio announcer Yuri Levitan, the filmmaker Roman Karmen, the reporters Vassily Grossman and Ilya Ehrenburg, and many others—were among the first to formulate a response to the Nazi onslaught. Their call to arms dramatized the stakes of this war. In May 1942, three long years before Hitler's empire was crushed, Ehrenburg penned a sentence that succinctly presented his sense of the Nazi threat: "The world is too small a place to hold both us and the fascists," he wrote.[123] In Ehrenburg's wartime writings, "us" never denoted just the Soviet people; it extended to any and all of the nations threatened by Nazism and beyond. "Us" meant humanity writ large. In the hour of Germany's defeat, the Red Army was widely viewed as the decisive victorious power.[124] Even as the Cold War was beginning to set in, the French witnesses in the Nuremberg courtroom saluted the Soviet prisoners of war who had been murdered in front of their eyes.

Today, sentiment has shifted markedly. A rift runs through Europe's East, with nations on either side remembering the Second World War in starkly different terms. On the one side, Russia and Belarus enthusiastically cultivate the memory of Soviet victory, while their neighbors to the West stress a history of suffering under Soviet rule. One side casts the Red Army as humanity's liberator, the other as an occupier and oppressor. Clashing head-on, these memory wars have fueled political and, more recently, military strife. Their explosive charges carry far beyond Eastern Europe: At stake is how people around the world will remember one of the most violent chapters in human history, and how that memory will guide their actions.

Accounts of past oppression are foundational to histories of many states in the former socialist camp. They describe the experience of Nazi and Soviet rule as a "double occupation" by two totalitarian powers, unfolding in three stages: Soviet, 1939–1941; National Socialist, 1941–1944; and Soviet again, 1944–1991. Of the two, the Soviet Union ranks as the much greater enemy, not only because its rule lasted longer, but also because Soviet Communism, unlike Nazism, rejected ethnonationalism.[125]

One year after the fall of the Soviet Union, the Lithuanian government opened the Museum of Genocide Victims in Vilnius. The museum, situated in a building that formerly housed the NKVD, the Gestapo, and the KGB, made virtually no mention of the plight of Lithuania's Jews. In its exhibits, the term "genocide" referred exclusively to Soviet deportations and executions of Lithuanian freedom fighters. This erasure was especially remarkable, given that Vilnius was once Europe's preeminent center of Jewish learning. After criticism from Jewish organizations, in 2011 the museum turned one of the former interrogation cells in the basement, which had previously been used to evoke the Soviet terror, into an exhibit space devoted to the mass murder of Lithuania's Jews. In response to further outcry from international observers, the Lithuanian Parliament in 2018 had the term "genocide" removed from the museum. The building was renamed the Museum of Occupations and Freedom Fights.[126] The permanent exhibit, spanning three large floors, remained largely unchanged. To this day, it tells a story of Lithuanian suffering and resistance under Soviet rule. The text and photographs in the basement show nothing about the pogroms that Lithuanian activists had carried out against "Jew-Bolsheviks," in some instances even before the arrival of the invading German troops.

After the three Baltic republics and five other Eastern European states joined the European Union in 2004, they began to press for European-wide recognition of the crimes committed by the Communist regimes. The EU at the time recognized the Holocaust as the continent's defining crime. The Memorial to the Murdered Jews of Europe was unveiled in Berlin's center in 2005. That same year, the European Parliament proclaimed January 27—the anniversary of the Red Army's liberation of Auschwitz-Birkenau—European Holocaust Remembrance Day. Eastern European delegates had challenged the choice of date as inappropriate, arguing that the act of freeing captives from one prison only to lock them up in another could hardly be called liberation.[127] In the end, January 27 was the chosen date, but these protests reflected a shift in the prevailing political sentiment: "Never again Auschwitz!" became "Never again totalitarianism!"[128]

In short order, European institutions began to treat Nazism and Soviet Communism as equally abhorrent. In July 2009, the Parliamentary Assembly of the Organization for Security and Cooperation in Europe (OSCE) meeting in Vilnius passed this resolution: "In the twentieth century, European countries experienced two major totalitarian regimes, Nazi and Stalinist, which brought about genocide, violations of human rights and freedoms, war crimes and crimes against humanity." The Vilnius Declaration urged all fifty-seven member states to take a "united stand against all totalitarian rule from whatever ideological background." Following an earlier proclamation by the European Parliament, the declaration also officially designated August 23, the day of the signing of the Hitler-Stalin pact, as a "Europe-wide Day of Remembrance for Victims of Stalinism and Nazism."[129] Russia criticized the draft declaration as an attempt to distort and politicize history, but the Russian delegates in Vilnius could not prevent its passage, given the near-unanimous support.

In subsequent years, the European Union undertook further steps to obscure the Soviet contribution to the anti-Hitler alliance. A 2019 European Parliament resolution, passed on the eightieth anniversary of the outbreak of the Second World War, indicted both the Soviet Union and Nazi Germany for "crimes committed on a scale never before seen in history against millions of human beings." The resolution called for a second Nuremberg Tribunal—this one to investigate the historical crimes of the Soviet Union. And it voiced deep concerns "about the efforts of the current Russian leadership to distort historical facts and whitewash crimes committed by the Soviet totalitarian regime."[130] The outraged Russian president responded to the resolution with an hour-long lecture. Wielding archival documents, he sought to prove that the Soviet government was more committed to the anti-Hitler coalition than any other countries at the time, and that those other countries shouldered more blame than the Soviet Union for the outbreak of war in Europe.[131]

These more recent clashes should not obscure the fact that in earlier years Russian political leaders had been seeking inclusion in a European politics of remembrance. In September 2009, President Putin attended commemorations in Poland marking the seventieth anniversary of the start of World War II, and the following year, he and Polish Prime Minister Donald Tusk gathered in the Katyn forest to pay respect to the Polish victims of the massacre that Stalin had ordered in 1940. "There can be no justification for these crimes," Putin declared, while Tusk pointed out that "a word of truth can mobilize two peoples looking for the road to reconciliation. Are we capable of transforming a lie into reconciliation? We must believe we can."[132]

But the move by leading European organizations to equate the Communist regimes imposed on Eastern Europe with Nazi rule unleashed a strong reaction. In 2009, Putin appointed a Presidential Commission to Counter Attempts to Falsify History to the Detriment of Russia's Interests. Its task, a commission member explained, was to advise the president on how to counter historical falsifications aimed at tarnishing Russia's international reputation.[133] Another member, the Duma deputy

Natalya Narochnitskaya, expressed the central grievance that motivated the commission in an interview with a Latvian journalist: "Russia is accused of spreading Communism, which is described as worse than Hitler's project. But for God's sakes, people! Today you are fine folk, gentlemen and ladies, whereas Hitler wanted to turn you into illiterate maids and pig herders. The Poles, the Czechs, the Romanians, the Hungarians, the Baltic peoples—they were all backward agrarian nations, and they all ended up with violinists, professors, engineers, academies of sciences, institutes, factories, movie studios. . . . And the main thing is, they all remained nations. Which would never have happened under Hitler."[134]

As Russia continued to be denied recognition for its historical role as liberator, its officials dug in their heels, insisting on a defiant celebration of the Great Patriotic War. Even before Putin, President Boris Yeltsin—an avowed democrat and anti-Communist—had revived what was originally a Soviet tradition and turned it into state policy. Celebrating May 9 with an annual parade of heavy tanks, rocket launchers, and medal-bedecked veterans marching through Red Square was his innovation.[135] But while the Yeltsin government separated the cherished memory of the people's war from Stalin's brutal regime, Putin reverted to the Soviet practice of declaring the people and their leaders indivisible, a single whole. Unlike Soviet commemorations of the war, which expressed sorrow alongside pride, commemorations in the Putin era have sounded a more triumphalist note. In 2014, the government passed a law making it a criminal offense to claim Soviet responsibility for the outbreak of World War II. The law likewise banned any public attempt to equate the ideologies and actions of the Soviet Union and Nazi Germany during the war, or to question the narrative of Soviet victory in World War II.[136] Official historians vehemently deny crimes perpetrated by Soviet soldiers, such as the mass rapes of German women. The government has been building military theme parks that glorify the Red Army. One such venue, Patriot Park near Moscow, features a miniature mock-up of the Berlin Reichstag, which is regularly used for reenactments of the Red Army's 1945 storming of the building. The replica made international headlines because it was modeled on the present-day German federal parliament rather than the historic Reichstag building.[137]

The Russian state has deployed this massive memory culture to project political influence throughout the territories of the former Soviet empire. Just as Soviet culpability has been used to bind the enlarged European Union, so too has Russia sought to hold together the Commonwealth of Independent States (CIS) with joint commemorations of Soviet victory in World War II. "We Have Fought Against Fascism Together" was the title of an exhibit in a Moscow Museum in 2015, to which all CIS states were invited to contribute historical artifacts.[138]

By this time, parts of the CIS had already turned into a battleground. The war in Ukraine's Donbas region, which over time turned into an overt Russian-Ukrainian conflict, was fought in large measure as a contest over the memory of the Second World War. After a wave of pro-European public protests ousted Ukraine's pro-Russian President Viktor Yanukovych in February 2014, replacing him with a pro-European successor, Eastern Ukrainian insurgents supported by Russia seized government buildings in Donetsk and Luhansk, proclaiming their independence from Kyiv. Insurgent leaders proclaimed the defense of the memory of Soviet victory to be one of their main reasons for fighting.[139] For his part, Ukraine's new president, Petro Poroshenko, promoted a national memory of Ukrainians who throughout their history had fought Russian and Soviet domination. At his initiative, Ukraine's parliament passed a law that hailed Stepan Bandera and other World War II–era Ukrainian insurgents—many of them known for atrocities against communists and Jews—as national freedom fighters. Poroshenko also introduced a new May 8 holiday in an effort to "Europeanize" Ukraine's calendar and shift Ukrainians' memory away from the traditional Day of Victory, May 9.[140]

For the Donbas insurgents and many Russians, these measures only reinforced their conviction that "Bandera fascists" were ruling Kyiv. When Russia launched its full-scale invasion of Ukraine in 2022, Ukraine's "denazification" was one of its key stated goals. With his decision to go to war, Vladimir Putin weaponized historical memory in a new manner. As the Russian president called for all Ukrainian "Nazis" to be delivered to a Nuremberg-style court, the Russian army set out to kill thousands of Ukrainian soldiers and civilians, bomb Ukraine's cities into ashes, and terrorize their residents.[141]

As of this writing, how the current war will end is anyone's guess, but what's clear is that political invocations of history have fueled its flames. As a result, history itself has become a casualty on the battlefield of historical memory. More than ever at risk of being forgotten today is how the most systematically lethal actions in the history of human violence actually came to form, and how they were brought to an end. It was the German crusade against "Judeo-Bolshevism" that drove the Nazis' most extreme violence and turned Soviet territories into a laboratory for the German politics of mass murder. And it was the Soviet Union that contributed the lion's share to Nazism's defeat.

That the Soviet Union figured so centrally in Germany's deadly designs is an inconvenient truth in today's world. It runs up against the desire by Western leaders to portray their countries as the leading victors; it challenges tenets of Holocaust history, which is tied to the invocation of liberal democratic values and therefore belittles the central place of communists, alongside Jews, as Nazism's chief victims; and it appears to play into the hands of Russia's president, who is invoking the Soviet contribution to victory over Nazism as a justification for his current war against Ukraine. But none of these objections are valid. Historical truth is not subject to negotiation. Historians must not yield to political pressures of the present day. Only then can the writing of history become a basis for meaningful discussion and dialogue in tomorrow's world.

Acknowledgments

This book came into being through the support and generosity of many individuals and institutions. The History Department at Rutgers University has, over the years, provided a dynamic and intellectually generous environment for developing and refining new ideas. I am deeply grateful to my colleagues and to my graduate and undergraduate students whose insights, questions, and critiques have enriched this project at every stage.

From the outset, the Fritz Thyssen Foundation provided vital support, enabling the team of researchers I led to access and prepare for publication hundreds of interviews with Soviet survivors of the German occupation, drawn from archives in Russia, Ukraine, and Belarus. My special thanks go to Frank Suder and Thomas Suermann at the foundation in Cologne. I am also indebted to the late Bernd Bonwetsch, to Nikolaus Katzer, and to Sandra Dahlke—intrepid captains at the helm of the German Historical Institute Moscow (2005–2024)—for their steadfast leadership in steering this international research project through darkening skies and turbulent seas, holding a steady course even as the winds turned against us. For their collegiality, trust, and shared belief in the enduring value of the historian's craft, I thank our partners Sergei Zhuravlev, Nikolai Petrov, and Konstantin Drozdov at the Institute of Russian History of the Russian Academy of Sciences, Olga Bazhan at the Central State Archives of Public Organizations of Ukraine, and the directors and staff of the National Archives of the Republic of Belarus. I also want to acknowledge Aliaksandr Pustavitau for his invaluable hands-on assistance.

My long-standing collaboration with Viktoria Naumenko (Kharkiv, currently Berlin) and Darya Lotareva (Moscow) has been essential to this book's development. Our sustained engagement with the historical records generated by the Isaak Mints commission in Moscow and its counterparts in Kiev and Minsk has been both intellectually enriching and personally rewarding.

This project has been sustained by the generous support of multiple distinguished institutions, including the American Academy in Berlin, the John Simon Guggenheim Memorial Foundation, the Princeton University Davis International Center, and the Internationales Kolleg Morphomata at the University of Cologne. Most recently, the Dorothy and Lewis B. Cullman Center for Scholars and Writers at the New York Public Library has provided an ideal setting in which to bring the manuscript to completion. In this treasure house of books that is also a city palace and a sanctuary for intellectual exchange, I have had the privilege to reside as the John and Constance Birkelund Fellow—a title I am pleased to spell out in full, in keeping with one of the few formal requirements of this unique fellowship.

Don Fehr, my literary agent, has been a guiding force behind this book. When we first met, I was still envisioning a more narrowly focused study of the Soviet experience of Nazi Germany's war of annihilation. But as I ranged across topics and timelines, Don listened carefully and urged me to consider something bolder—a sweeping history of the Nazi-Soviet standoff, culminating in the Second World War. That pivotal conversation set the course for what this book has ultimately become. I am also deeply thankful to Michael Geyer, Joyce Seltzer, Peter Fritzsche, and Philip Dwyer, whose encouragement to think beyond disciplinary and geographic confines helped me push the conceptual boundaries of the project.

From its earliest drafts, the manuscript has grown through the equally generous and rigorous feedback of many readers. Above all, I am indebted to two friends whose contributions are woven into the fabric of the book. Jan Plamper (March 23, 1970–November 30, 2023) was my first and most consistent reader. He offered sharp critiques and unwavering support, even annotating the final chapter while battling a grave illness. If Jan raised a concern, I knew I had to return to the text and rethink my approach. His clarity of mind and intellectual passion are so fully present in these pages that this book is, in a profound sense, also his.

Paul Hanebrink brought equal dedication to every chapter draft, reading with care and offering pointed reflections in our ongoing conversations—whether over lunch in Long Island City or cold drinks in Riverside Park. Paul has a rare gift for identifying conceptual gaps and gently pressing for deeper clarity. His groundbreaking monograph on the myth of Judeo-Bolshevism did more than inform my own thinking—it carved a path for this project to follow.

I am also grateful to the many colleagues and friends whose readings of the manuscript, in whole or in part, left a lasting mark on its development. My thanks go to Yarden Avital, Omer Bartov, Belinda Davis, Victoria de Grazia, Dina Fainberg, Tanja Hommen, Ekaterina Makhotina, Anna Nath, Brandon Schechter, and Yuri Slezkine for their thoughtful comments and probing questions. For their insights on specific sections of the book, I thank Yulia Cherniavskaia, Melissa Feinberg, Peter Holquist, Seth Koven, Jackson and Karen Lears, Yan Mann, Paul Mercandetti, Jennifer Mittelstadt, Susan Neiman, Philip Nord, Kristin O'Brassill-Kulfan, and Judith Surkis.

Ulrich Bach and Ray Brandon deserve special thanks for their extensive research assistance—from combing through editions of the *Völkischer Beobachter* to tracking down historical maps that helped reconstruct the movements of Soviet partisans across the frozen bay of Taganrog. I am also indebted to the meticulous fact-checking performed by Henrik Halbleib and Karin Hielscher.

Few writers get to work with an editor like Sara Bershtel. I was lucky enough to do so. What I thought was a finished draft, she approached with clarity and insight, turning it into writing that's crisper, more coherent, and more compelling. The book's conclusion found its lasting form—on the fourth attempt—thanks to her patient, incisive feedback. Sara's unwavering belief in this project sustained me at every stage.

As this book nears the end of the production process, I want to extend special thanks to the team at Penguin working under Scott Moyers's brilliant direction: Mia Council, Michael Brown, Jane Cavolina, Mollie Reid, and Jessie Stratton. With an added note of appreciation to Connor Guy.

Finally, I owe a debt of gratitude that exceeds words to Katinka, Jakob, and Antonia. For years—indeed, in some cases since birth—they have lived with this book and its demands, bearing its weight with unfailing love along with varying degrees of patience, and a steady supply of humor. To them, I offer my deepest thanks.

New York Public Library, June 9, 2025

Notes

Abbreviations

BArch: Bundesarchiv—German Federal Archives.

ChGK: Chrezvychainaia Gosudarstvennaia Komissiia—Extraordinary State Commission for Establishing and Investigating Crimes Committed by the German Fascist Invaders, a Soviet state committee created in 1942 to investigate and document Nazi war crimes.

Comintern: The Communist International (1919–1943), an international organization founded with the purpose of promoting world revolution and coordinating the activities of communist parties worldwide.

FHO: Fremde Heere Ost (Foreign Armies East), a military-intelligence organization of the Oberkommando des Heeres.

GARF: Gosudarstvennyi arkhiv Rossiiskoi Federatsii—State Archive of the Russian Federation.

Gestapo: Geheime Staatspolizei, the Nazi German secret police. See also SiPo.

GFP: Geheime Feldpolizei, the secret military police of the German Wehrmacht during World War II.

GPU: Glavnoe politicheskoe upravlenie, the Soviet secret police between 1922 and 1934, then renamed into NKVD. Prior to 1922, the secret police was named the Cheka.

Gulag: Main Directorate of Correctional Labour Camps, the Soviet system of forced labor camps.

HSSPF: Höherer SS- und Polizeiführer (higher SS and police leader), a senior Nazi Party official who commanded an SS component.

JAC: The Soviet "Jewish Anti-Fascist Committee" (1942–1948).

KGB: Komitet gosudarstvennoi bezopasnosti (Committee for State Security)—Soviet secret police from from 1954 until the collapse of the USSR in 1991.

KPD: Die Kommunistische Partei Deutschlands—the Communist Party of Germany.

NA IRI RAN: Nauchnyi arkhiv Instituta Rossiiskoi istorii Rossiiskoi Akademii nauk—Scientific Archive of the Institute of Russian History of the Russian Academy of Sciences.

NARA: National Archives and Records Administration.

NARB: Natsional'nyi arkhiv Respubliki Belarus'—National Archive of the Republic of Belarus.

NKVD: Narodnyi komissariat vnutrennykh del—Soviet Secret Police between 1934 and 1941; successor organization to the GPU.

OKH: Oberkommando des Heeres, the Supreme High Command of the German Army before and during World War II.

OKW: Oberkommando der Wehrmacht—High Command of Nazi Germany's Armed Forces.

RGAKFD: Rossiiskii gosudarstvennyi arkhiv kinofotodokumentov—Russian State Film and Photo Archive.

RGALI: Rossiiskii gosudarstvennyi arkhiv literatury i iskusstva—Russian State Archive for Literature and the Arts.

RGASPI: Rossiiskii gosudarstvennyi arkhiv sotsial'no-politicheskoi istorii—Russian State Archive for Social and Political History.

SA: Sturmabteilung ("Storm division")—the Nazi Party's paramilitary wing, known for its brown uniforms, hence also referred to as "Brownshirts."

SD: Sicherheitsdienst—SS intelligence agency.

SiPo: Sicherheitspolizei, an organization created in 1936 by SS leader Heinrich Himmler to combine the Gestapo (responsible for investigating political and racial threats to the Nazi regime) and the Criminal Police, and to bring both under SS control.

SPD: Die Sozialdemokratische Partei Deutschlands—the Social Democratic Party of Germany.

SS: Schutzstaffel ("Protection squadron")—Nazi paramilitary organization that rose to become the foremost agency of security, mass surveillance, and state terrorism within Germany and German-occupied Europe.

TsDAHOU: Tsentralnyi Derzhavnyi Arkhiv Hromadskykh Obiednan ta Ukrainiky—Central State Archives of Public Organizations of Ukraine.

Introduction

1. *Die "Ereignismeldungen UdSSR" 1941: Dokumente der Einsatzgruppen in der Sowjetunion I*, ed. Klaus-Michael Mallmann, Andrej Angrick, Jürgen Matthäus, Martin Cüppers (2011), 740 (report of October 31, 1941); whenever available, the English translation follows *The Einsatzgruppen Reports: Selections from the Dispatches of the Nazi Death Squads' Campaign Against the Jews, July 1941—January 1943*, ed. Yitzhak Arad et al. (New York, 1989), 216. Report by Olga Mukhortova-Pekker (January 15, 1944): NA IRI RAN, f. 2, razd. 6, op. 10, d. 15V.
2. Alfred Rosenberg, *Pest in Russland! Der Bolschewismus, seine Häupter, Handlanger und Opfer* (Munich, 1922), 95.
3. Carl J. Burckhardt, *Meine Danziger Mission 1937–1939*, 3rd. ed. (Munich, 1980), 346.
4. Paul Hanebrink, *A Specter Haunting Europe: The Myth of Judeo-Bolshevism* (Cambridge, MA, 2018), 84.
5. "Hitlers Denkschrift zum Vierjahresplan 1936," *Vierteljahrshefte für Zeitgeschichte* 3, no. 2 (1955), 204–5.
6. "Der Fall Budenko: Bolschewismus und jüdische Verheißungen," *Der Stürmer* 18, Mai 1939: 1–3 (3).

7. Helmut Hartmann, Letter of September 14, 1941 (Deutsches Tagebuch-Archiv, Emmendingen).
8. Johannes Hürter, *Hitlers Heerführer. Die deutschen Oberbefehlshaber im Krieg gegen die Sowjetunion 1941/42*, 2nd. ed. (Munich, 2007), 7.
9. According to recent German calculations, 2,775,000 civilian laborers were deported to Germany from the Soviet Union. See https://www.zwangsarbeit-archiv.de/pictures/lernsoftware/ze-karte-herkunftslaender.swf. Pavel Polian's careful calculations put the actual number at 3,200,000; Pavel M. Polian, *Zhertvy dvukh diktatur. Zhizn', trud, unizheniia, smert' sovetskikh voennoplennykh i ostarbaiterov na chuzhbine i na rodine*, 2nd rev. ed. (Moscow, 2002), 131–32.
10. Alex Kay, *Empire of Destruction: A History of Nazi Mass Killing* (New Haven, 2021), 6–7, 98, 127–28, 169, 283–84, 294; Mark Harrison, "Counting the Soviet Union's War Dead: Still 26–27 Million," *Europe-Asia Studies* 71, no. 6 (2019): 1036–47. Some scholars believe that up to 42 million Soviet citizens died as a result of the war. S. N. Mikhalev, *Liudskie poteri v Velikoi Otechestvennoi voine 1941–1945 gg. Statisticheskoe issledovanie*, 2nd ed. (Krasnoiarsk, 2000), 26–28; B. V. Sokolov, "The Cost of War: Human Losses for the USSR and Germany, 1939–1945," *Journal of Slavic Military Studies* 9, no. 1 (March 1996): 152–93. For the official figure, see: G. F. Krivosheev, *Soviet Casualties and Combat Losses in the Twentieth Century* (Barnsley, 1997), 157.
11. Hans-Heinrich Wilhelm, "Die Prognosen der Abteilung Fremde Heere Ost 1942–1945," in *Zwei Legenden aus dem Dritten Reich* (Stuttgart, 1974), 7–75. David Glantz and Jonathan House, *When Titans Clashed* (Lawrence, KS, 1995), 67–68.
12. *Krasnaia zvezda*, January 10, 1945.
13. While many scholars have analyzed how Nazis and other Germans viewed Russians, Slavs, or the non-European peoples of the Soviet Union, the German racialization of the Soviet enemy as "subhuman," "Asiatic," and supposedly steered by Jews remains poorly explored. Most Holocaust scholars studying Nazi propaganda and policies toward the Soviet Union focus on Nazi anti-Semitism at the expense of anti-Bolshevism. As a result, they lose sight of important context. For instance, Jeffrey Herf contends that "Hitler and his leading propagandists were able to entertain completely contradictory versions of events simultaneously, one rooted in the grandiose idea of a master race and world domination, the other in the self-pitying paranoia of the innocent, beleaguered victim." Jeffrey Herf, *The Jewish Enemy: Nazi Propaganda During World War II and the Holocaust* (Cambridge, MA, 2006), 5. But when we consider how the Nazis described the Soviet Union as both non-European and monstrous, the two strands of thinking that Herf views as incompatible come together perfectly.

    Jewish-Bolshevism, in the understanding of many Germans, was an ideology that was hatched on the steppes of Asia and threatened to obliterate Europe. Jews formed an innate part of this menace. Some Nazi race experts, Alfred Rosenberg among them, believed that Jews constituted an "Asiatic counter-race" to German "Aryans." Others maintained that Jews were not a race among races, as their defining activity was the destruction of race, the very "substance of human existence." Both positions concurred that the Jews as Bolsheviks had "fully eradicated" all European elements in Russian society, rendering the Soviet Communist order Asiatic in essence. With regard to Russia, Nazi publications presented it as a "land between Europe and Asia," historically populated by Slavs, who in principle counted as an "Indo-Germanic race" but had "racially degenerated" long before the advent of Bolshevism, due to racial "mixing" with "Mongols." Curt Rosten, *Das ABC des Nationalsozialismus* (Berlin, 1933), 232; Theodor Fritsch, *Handbuch der Judenfrage. Die wichtigsten Tatsachen zur Beurteilung des jüdischen Volkes*, 41st ed. (Leipzig, 1937), 21; Reinhard Bollmus, *Das Amt Rosenberg und seine Gegner: Studien zum Machtkampf im nationalsozialistischen Herrschaftssystem* (Stuttgart, 1970), 22; John Connelly, "Nazis and Slavs: From Racial Theory to Racist Practice," *Central European History* 32, no. 1 (1999): 1–33 (32); Johannes Dafinger, "Speaking Nazi-European," in *A New Nationalist Europe under Hitler: Concepts of Europe and*

Transnational Networks in the National Socialist Sphere of Influence, 1933–1945, ed. Johannes Dafinger and Dieter Pohl (New York, 2019), 43–56 (46).

14. *Geheime Welten. Deutsche Tagebücher aus den Jahren 1939 bis 1947*, ed. Heinrich Breloer (Frankfurt, 1999), 94–95.
15. Ilya Ehrenburg, "Khvatit!," *Pravda*, April 7, 1945. The death rate of British soldiers in German captivity during World War II was 3.5 percent; for Soviet soldiers it was 57.5 percent or more. Niall Ferguson, "Prisoner Taking and Prisoner Killing in the Age of Total War: Towards a Political Economy of Military Defeat," *War in History* 11, no. 2 (2004): 148–92 (186).
16. Drew Middleton, "Films Back Charge of German Crimes," *New York Times*, February 20, 1946.
17. The website of the USHMM justifies its version of Niemöller's confession by pointing out that the confession was recorded in multiple different versions. This is true, but every recorded began with the "Communists." See Harold Marcuse, "The Origin and Reception of Martin Niemöller's Quotation 'First they came for the communists . . . ,'" (July 31, 2014), https://marcuse.faculty.history.ucsb.edu/projects/niem/articles/Marcuse2014NiemoellerQuote147gWeb.pdf; website of the U.S. Holocaust Museum, https://encyclopedia.ushmm.org/content/en/article/martin-niemoeller-first-they-came-for-the-socialists; for the references to U.S. politicians and the encyclopedia of the Holocaust, see Peter Novick, *The Holocaust in American Life* (New York, 1999), 221.
18. Recent scholarship has analyzed the intricate dynamic between ethnic prejudice and war, shifting the focus of Holocaust Studies toward the war period, see e.g., Omer Bartov, *Anatomy of a Genocide: The Life and Death of a Town Called Buczacz* (New York, 2018). "Without the war," Doris Bergen writes, "the Holocaust would not—and could not—have happened." Warfare extended the framework of what the Nazis thought possible, beginning with Germany's ruthless invasion of Poland, which delivered into German hands large Jewish populations who were being treated in progressively more brutal ways, in line with the further brutalization of Germany's conduct of war. Bergen tells of the attack on the Soviet Union as part of a chapter that starts in 1940 with the Nazi invasion of Denmark, Norway, the Low Countries, and France. This cumulative reading of German acts of violence in the course of the war is revealing insofar in that it shows the near simultaneity of "euthanasia" killings with the shootings of French Senegalese tirailleurs and Polish and Soviet citizens; however, it fails to recognize the new quality of violence that the Germans applied at the Eastern Front starting in June 1941. Doris Bergen, *War and Genocide: A Concise History of the Holocaust*, 3rd. ed. (London, 2016), 3, 167–206.
19. Words from a speech by Hitler, February 26, 1943, quoted in Herf, *The Jewish Enemy*, 196.
20. For a long time, Holocaust scholars focused on Nazi death camps in Poland as Germany's essential murder sites for Jews. The more recent attention to the mass killing of Jews on the Nazi-occupied territories of the Soviet Union has extended this picture, but not unsettled the idea that the Holocaust was centered on the gas chambers of Auschwitz. The "Holocaust by bullets" in this reading figures alternatively as a Soviet chapter or a prologue in the history of the Shoah, but not as the site where the idea of killing all Jews was first conceived and implemented. For documentations of the mass murder of Soviet Jews, see the "Untold Stories—Murder Sites of Jews in Occupied Territories of the USSR" project created by Israel's Yad Vashem World Holocaust Remembrance Center, at https://collections.yadvashem.org/en/untold-stories; and Yitzhak Arad, *The Holocaust in the Soviet Union* (Lincoln, NE, and Jerusalem, 2009).
21. A salient example: The Nazis killed off or starved to death innumerable Soviet POWs before they even began to compile records of Soviet soldiers in their captivity. Noting how the sparse documentation of the plight of the captured Soviet soldiers contradicted the overall habit of meticulous recordkeeping within the German Army, Christian Streit regards this documentary void as an intentional omission: Army officials sought

to cover up the mass murder of captured enemy soldiers. Only in early 1942, after Nazi leaders decreed that Soviet POWs should be better fed and used as laborers, did the Army Command begin to compile detailed statistics. Christian Streit, *Keine Kameraden. Die Wehrmacht und die sowjetischen Kriegsgefangenen, 1941–1945*, new ed. (Bonn, 1991), 129–30; Ulrich Herbert, *Hitler's Foreign Workers* (Cambridge, 1997), 155–57.

22. François Furet famously described Nazi Germany and the Stalinist Soviet Union as totalitarian twins enjoined in "belligerent complicity." François Furet, *The Passing of an Illusion: The Idea of Communism in the Twentieth Century* (Chicago, 1999), 161. In *Bloodlands: Europe Between Hitler and Stalin* (New York, 2010), Timothy Snyder casts the USSR and Nazi Germany as rival evils, jointly responsible for the suffering of millions. Michael Burleigh refers to the two nations as "brotherly enemies," each the common foe of decent humankind, in *Moral Combat: A History of World War II* (London, 2010), 76. Mark Edele and Michael Geyer's coauthored exploration of the German-Soviet war oscillates between such neototalitarian framings and an insistence on the singularity of Nazi violence—a reflection perhaps of disagreements among the two contributing authors; Mark Edele and Michael Geyer, "States of Exception: The Nazi-Soviet War as a System of Violence, 1939–1945" in *Beyond Totalitarianism: Stalinism and Nazism Compared*, ed. Michael Geyer and Sheila Fitzpatrick (Cambridge, 2009).
23. Most recently, Sean McMeekin, *Stalin's War: A New History of World War II* (New York, 2022). While the history of anti-fascism has attracted much scholarly attention over the past decade, this scholarship either brackets out Soviet contributions to this transnational history or limits itself to the study of Soviet anti-fascism as official state policy. See Joseph Fronczak, *Everything Is Possible: Antifascism and the Left in the Age of Fascism* (New Haven, 2023); José María Faraldo, "An Antifascist Political Identity? On the Cult of Antifascism in the Soviet Union and Post-Socialist Russia," in *Rethinking Antifascism: History, Memory, and Politics, 1922 to the Present*, ed., Hugo García (New York, 2016), 202–27.
24. Antony Beevor, *The Fall of Berlin 1945* (New York, 2002); Manfred Zeidler, "Die Rote Armee auf deutschem Boden," in *Der Zusammenbruch des Deutschen Reiches 1945: Die militärische Niederwerfung der Wehrmacht*, ed. Rolf-Dieter Müller (Stuttgart, 2008), 681–775.
25. Mallmann et al., ed., *Die "Ereignismeldungen UdSSR" 1941*, 28–29. See also Ronald Headland, *Messages of Murder: A Study of the Reports of the Einsatzgruppen of the Security Police and the Security Service, 1941–1943* (1992), 78; Jeffrey Veidlinger, *In the Midst of Civilized Europe: The Pogroms of 1918–1921 and the Onset of the Holocaust* (New York, 2021), 366–67.
26. Arno Mayer, *Why Did the Heavens Not Darken? The "Final Solution" in History* (London, 1988); Ernst Nolte, *Der europäische Bürgerkrieg, 1917–1945* (Munich, 1997); *Nationalsozialismus und Bolschewismus* (Berlin, 1987); idem, "From the Gulag to Auschwitz," in François Furet and Ernst Nolte, *Fascism & Communism* (Lincoln, NE, 2001), 23–30. Pioneering work on Nazi anti-Bolshevism also includes: Omer Bartov, *Hitler's Army: Soldiers, Nazis, and War in the Third Reich* (Oxford, 1992); Klaus-Michael Mallmann, "Die Türöffner der 'Endlösung': Zur Genesis des Genozids," in *Die Gestapo im Zweiten Weltkrieg: 'Heimatfront' und besetztes Europa*, ed. Gerhard Paul et al. (Darmstadt, 2000), 437–63; Hanebrink, *A Specter Haunting Europe.*

That the Eastern Front and the Nazi-occupied territories of the Soviet Union formed an area of unrestrained German terror was forcefully shown for the first time in the travel exhibition "War of Annihilation: The Crimes of the Wehrmacht, 1941 to 1944," conceived by the Hamburg Institute for Social Research. After its opening in March 1995, the exhibition toured thirty-five German and Austrian cities. At the center of the exhibition were hundreds of small-format photographs showing the mistreatment and executions of Jews and other Soviet citizens. Arranged in the form of an Iron Cross (a military decoration in Nazi Germany), the images indicted the Wehrmacht as a criminal army. The photographs also made abundantly clear the extent to which ordinary soldier-photographers had internalized the Nazi image of the Bolshevik enemy. The exhibit was contested by right-wing critics, and some found out that a small number of photographs (including photographs taken in Lvov in July 1941, more on this in chapter 3) in fact depicted victims of Soviet rather than German terror. They also pointed out that the perpetrators in other photos were not members of the Wehrmacht but were soldiers of the allied Axis powers and local collaborators. The criticism led to the closure of the exhibition and the cancellation of a planned world tour. A revised exhibition, which opened once more in Hamburg in 2001, shifted its depiction of the war from visual to written sources, such as military orders, which were deemed more reliable. The exhibition's social focus shifted accordingly from simple German soldiers to their commanders. Hannes Heer und Birgit Otte, eds., (Hamburg, 1996); *Eine Ausstellung und ihre Folgen. Zur Rezeption der Ausstellung Vernichtungskrieg: Verbrechen der Wehrmacht 1941 bis 1944* ed. Hamburger Institut für Sozialforschung (Hamburg, 1999); Ulrike Jureit, ed., *Verbrechen der Wehrmacht: Dimensionen des Vernichtungskrieges 1941–1944, Ausstellungskatalog*, 4th ed. (Hamburg, 2021).

27. In Ilya Ehrenburg's archive in the Russian State Archive for Literature and the Arts (RGALI, f. 1204), I also discovered some of the original German letters and diaries that the writer quoted in the editorials that he published in *Red Star* or *Pravda*. Ehrenburg's quotations from the original sources were invariably accurate. His archive additionally reveals how the personal documents of German soldiers that were found on the battlefield made their way to the desk of the Soviet Union's preeminent war reporter. The conduits included political departments of Red Army divisions at the front, as well as ordinary Red Army soldiers who corresponded with Ehrenburg throughout the war.
28. On the work of the Mints Commission, see Jochen Hellbeck, *Stalingrad: The City That Defeated the Third Reich* (New York, 2015), 68–82; idem, "The Antifascist Pact: Forging a First Experience of Nazi Occupation in the Wartime Soviet Union," in *Slavonic & East European Review* 96, no. 1 (2018): 117–43; Sergei V. Zhuravlev, ed., *Vklad uchenykh-istorikov v sokhranenie istoricheskoi pamiati o voine. Na materialakh Komissii po istorii Velikoi Otechestvennoi voiny AN SSSR, 1941–1945 gg.* (Moscow, 2015), 77–129; D. D. Lotareva, "Komissiia po istorii Velikoi Otechestvennoi voiny i ee arkhiv: rekonstruktsiia deiatel'nosti i metodov raboty," *Arkheograficheskii ezhegodnik za 2011 g.* (Moscow, 2014): 123–66.
29. Remarkably, the NKVD or other Soviet security agencies took no interest in the work of the Mints Commission, or the work of several sister commissions that were formed in the image of the "Central" Moscow commission. Today, most of their documentation is stored in NA IRI RAN (Moscow), TsDAHOU (Kyiv), and NARB (Minsk). A team of Russian and Ukrainian scholars under my direction is preparing for publication a documentary monograph featuring the voices of Soviet survivors of Nazi occupation.
30. The stenographic transcripts of more than seven hundred interviews with Soviet survivors of Nazi occupation—the joint work of the Mints Commission and partner commissions created in Kiev and Minsk—are presented in fully searchable form on the internet portal at https://qed.perspectivia.net/soviet-survivors/.
31. Willi Alfred Boelcke, *Wollt ihr den totalen Krieg? Die geheimen Goebbels-Konferenzen 1939–1943* (Stuttgart, 1967), 257; Ortwin Buchbender, *Das tönende Erz. Deutsche Propaganda gegen die Rote Armee im Zweiten Weltkrieg* (Stuttgart, 1978), 157. Goebbels also penned an essay on the subject, which he placed in a German weekly with international circulation: Joseph Goebbels, "Die sogenannte russische Seele," *Das Reich*, July 19, 1942.
32. See e.g., Timothy Snyder, *Bloodlands: Europe Between Hitler and Stalin* (New York, 2010); Catherine Merridale, *Ivan's War: Life and Death in the Red Army, 1939–1945* (London, 2006); Antony Beevor, *Stalingrad: The Fateful Siege, 1942–1943* (New York, 1999). Studies that do foreground Soviet Communist institutions and values include Lisa Kirschenbaum, *The Legacy of the Siege of Leningrad: 1941–1995: Myths, Memories,*

and Monuments (Cambridge, 2006); Wendy Goldman and Donald Filtzer, *Fortress Dark and Stern: The Soviet Home Front During World War II* (Oxford, 2021); Kristen Ghodsee, *The Left Side of History: World War II and the Unfulfilled Promise of Communism in Eastern Europe* (Durham, NC, 2015).

33. See e.g., Brandon M. Schechter, *The Stuff of Soldiers: A History of the Red Army in World War II Through Objects* (Ithaca, NY, 2019); idem, "'The People's Instructions': Indigenizing the Great Patriotic War Among 'Non-Russians,'" *Ab Imperio*, no. 3 (2012): 109–33; Serhy Yekelchyk, *Stalin's Empire of Memory: Russian-Ukrainian Relations in the Soviet Historical Imagination* (Toronto, 2004); Charles D. Shaw, "Making Ivan-Uzbek: War, Friendship of the Peoples, and the Creation of Soviet Uzbekistan, 1941–1945" (PhD diss., UC Berkeley, 2015).
34. In *Bloodlands*, Timothy Snyder consistently casts Ukrainians and Belarusians in ethnic terms, rather than as Soviet citizens. Regrettably, he does not draw on Amir Weiner's pioneering work on the Second World War, even though this work is listed in the book's bibliography. Weiner argues that the war against Nazi Germany forged a new Soviet identity. A person's place in the social order was no longer determined by class origins, but what and how this person had contributed to the Soviet war effort. Focusing on the Ukrainian province of Vinnytsia, Weiner makes clear how this new Soviet identity took hold of a region where Soviet institutions and values had been in short supply prior to the war. Amir Weiner, *Making Sense of War: The Second World War and the Fate of the Bolshevik Revolution* (Princeton, 2000).

Chapter 1: A Front Against Bolshevism

1. Theodore Abel, *Journal of Thoughts and Events, Appendix to vol. 1: European Trip, June to September 1933*, entries for June 30, July 5 and 29, September 7 and 9, 1933, Theodore Abel Papers, Box 16, Folder 15, Hoover Institution.
2. Theodore Abel, *Why Hitler Came into Power* (1938; Cambridge, MA, 1986), 3–5.
3. Full digital scans of 615 autobiographies, or "biograms," are available at the Online Archive of California, https://oac.cdlib.org/findaid/ark:/13030/tf3489n5vz/dsc/#ref31. A selection is reprinted in *"Warum ich Nazi wurde," Biogramme früher Nationalsozialisten, Die einzigartige Sammlung des Theodore Abel*, ed. Wieland Giebel (Berlin, 2018).
4. Inventory of the Theodore Fred Abel papers (Hoover Institution), biogram #263 Max Hausmann, #286 Karl Bennewitz, #171 Gerhard Ullein.
5. Inventory of the Theodore Fred Abel papers, biogram #220 Egon Rehmer.
6. Abel, *Why Hitler Came into Power*, 160; inventory of the Theodore Fred Abel papers, biograms #291 Robert Reinecke, #31 Rudolf Kahn, #263 Max Hausmann, #184 Karl Schlee.
7. Inventory of the Theodore Fred Abel papers, biogram #46 Grete Kircher (incorrectly referred to as Kirchner in the archive inventory).
8. Inventory of the Theodore Fred Abel papers, biogram #291 Robert Reinecke, #582 Margarete Schrimpff, #162 Alfred Kotz, #278 Richard Weber, #253 Armin Franz.
9. Inventory of the Theodore Fred Abel papers, biogram #31 Rudolf Kahn; Abel, *Why Hitler Came into Power*, 139.
10. Inventory of the Theodore Fred Abel papers, biogram #199 Hans Schönherr.
11. Peter H. Merkl, *Political Violence under the Swastika: 581 Early Nazis* (Princeton, 1975), 517.
12. Inventory of the Theodore Fred Abel papers, biogram #31 Rudolf Kahn. Anti-Communist observers at the time referred to the Bolsheviks often as "Bolshevists." This book preserves the name they used, as it carries a distinct accusatory charge. In contrast, the book uses the term "Bolsheviks" when speaking about Soviet Communists in a value-neutral way.
13. For an outstanding recent history of anti-Jewish inflected anti-Bolshevism, see Paul Hanebrink, *A Specter Haunting Europe: The Myth of Judeo-Bolshevism* (Cambridge, MA, 2018). See also *Der Antikommunismus in seiner Epoche: Weltanschauung und Politik in Deutschland, Europa und den USA*, ed. Norbert Frei and Dominik Rigoll (Göttingen, 2017).

14. While Nazis often referred to the entire left spectrum as "Marxism," the term was often code for Social Democrats and socialists (whether SPD, USPD, or SAPD), while "Communism" also had general applications but meant primarily the KPD. Similarly, Bolshevism had at least three different connotations: It could refer to any party to the political Left, or to the German Communist Party, or to Soviet Communists specifically. Often, terms and targets were used interchangeably so as to blur distinctions and thus smear the entire Left. Common to all these variations, in the eyes of the propagandists, were the Jews.
15. Nikolaus Wachsmann, *KL: A History of the Nazi Concentration Camps* (New York, 2015), 70–73.
16. The Russian term "Bolshevism" translates as "majority faction," the name Lenin chose for the radical members of the Russian Marxist party in order to belittle their ostensibly outnumbered moderate rivals: "Everyone by now knows," an anti-Communist brochure published in 1920 noted, "that the origin of the term 'Bolshevik' was merely the accidental fact that at the Brussels-London Conference of the Left Social Democratic Party in 1903, the extreme left wing had a majority (Bol'shinstvo)." George Pitt-Rivers, *The World Significance of the Russian Revolution* (Oxford, 1920), 18.
17. Mark D. Steinberg, *Voices of Revolution, 1917* (New Haven, 2001), 283–86, 299.
18. Robert Gerwarth, *The Vanquished: Why the First World War Failed to End, 1917–1923* (New York, 2016), 97; Anthony Read, *The World on Fire: 1919 and the Battle with Bolshevism* (New York, 2008), 23.
19. Read, *The World on Fire*, 23.
20. Ivan Bunin, *Okaiannye dni* (Moscow, 2012), 38–39 (entry for February 25, 1918, old style). Sakhalin is a penal colony on the eponymous island, north of Japan.
21. A Collection of Reports on Bolshevism in Russia, London 1919, https://archive.org/details/collectionofrepo00grea/page/6/mode/2up. Over the course of the year 1919, the "horrors of Bolshevism" featured in thirty-one articles of *The Times*.
22. *Bolshevik Propaganda. Hearings before a Subcommittee of the Committee on the Judiciary, United States Senate, February 11, 1919, to March 10, 1919* (Washington, DC, 1919), 65, 128, 341, 458, 992.
23. *Bolshevik Propaganda*, 14.
24. Othmar Plöckinger, *Unter Soldaten und Agitatoren: Hitlers prägende Jahre im deutschen Militär 1918–1920* (Paderborn, 2013), 273, with multiple further examples.
25. The declaration on equal rights that benefited Jews and other minorities was passed on March 22, 1917, before the Bolsheviks' coming to power. See also Yuri Slezkine, *The Jewish Century* (Princeton, 2004), chap. 3.
26. Oleg Budnitskii, *Russian Jews Between the Reds and the Whites, 1917–1920* (Philadelphia, 2012), 53.
27. *A Collection of Reports on Bolshevism in Russia* (London, 1919), 6.
28. Budnitskii, *Russian Jews*, 173–74.
29. Michael Hagemeister, "The Protocols of the Elders of Zion: Between History and Fiction," *New German Critique* 35 (2008): 83–95.
30. Armin Pfahl-Traugber, "Die Protokolle der Weisen von Zion. Der Nachweis der Fälschung und die tatsächliche Entstehungsgeschichte," *Judaica (Basel)* 46, no. 1 (1990): 22–31; Budnitskii, *Russian Jews*, 187–88; Michael Kellogg, *The Russian Roots of Nazism: White Émigrés and the Making of National Socialism, 1917–1945* (Cambridge, 2005), 60.
31. Christoph Dieckmann, "'Jüdischer Bolschewismus' 1917 bis 1921," in *Holocaust und Völkermorde. Die Reichweite des Vergleichs*, ed. Sybille Steinbacher (Frankfurt am Main, 2012), 55–81 (59–60); Budnitskii, *Russian Jews*, 195; Jeffrey Veidlinger, *In the Midst of Civilized Europe: The 1918–1921 Pogroms in Ukraine and the Onset of the Holocaust* (New York, 2022).
32. Karl Graf von Bothmer, *Mit Graf Mirbach in Moskau* (Tübingen, 1922), 12, 93.
33. Kai-Uwe Merz, *Das Schreckbild: Deutschland und der Bolschewismus, 1917–1921* (Berlin, 1995), 392.

34. Laura Spinney, *Pale Rider: The Spanish Flu of 1918 and How It Changed the World* (New York, 2018), 58. The influenza pandemic was referred to as the Spanish flu because Spanish newspapers, unconstrained by war censorship, were the first to report on it. It probably originated in the United States.
35. Jan Christoph Elfert, *Konzeptionen eines "dritten Reiches": Staat und Wirtschaft im jungkonservativen Denken 1918–1933* (Berlin, 2018), 62.
36. Gerwarth, *The Vanquished*, 109.
37. Russell F. Weighley, "Strategy and Total War in the United States: Pershing and the American Military Tradition," in *Great War, Total War: Combat and Mobilization on the Western Front, 1914–1918*, ed. Roger Chickering et al. (Washington, DC, 2000), 327–45.
38. *War in Peace: Paramilitary Violence in Europe after the Great War*, ed. Robert Gerwarth and John Horne (Oxford, 2012), 41.
39. Merz, *Das Schreckbild*, 219; Björn Laser, *Kulturbolschewismus! Zur Diskurssemantik der "totalen Krise" 1929–1933* (Frankfurt am Main, 2010), 60–65.
40. Boris Barth, *Dolchstoßlegenden und politische Desintegration. Das Trauma der deutschen Niederlage im Ersten Weltkrieg 1914–1933* (Düsseldorf, 2003), 230.
41. Read, *World on Fire*, 25.
42. Read, *World on Fire*, 166. The Paris peace agreements installed a safeguard against the spread of Communism in the form of a "sanitary cordon" of buffer states hemming in Soviet Russia's western borders.
43. "Armistice with Germany" (Article XII), https://www.loc.gov/law/help/us-treaties/bevans/m-ust000002-0009.pdf.
44. Gerwarth, *The Vanquished*, 70; Barth, *Dolchstoßlegenden*, 261.
45. Vejas Gabriel Liulevicius, *War Land on the Eastern Front* (Cambridge, 2000), 231–32; see also Gerwarth, *The Vanquished*, 72–73; and idem, "The Central European Counter-Revolution: Paramilitary Violence in Germany, Austria and Hungary after the Great War," *Past & Present* 200, no. 1 (2008): 175–209.
46. Barth, *Dolchstoßlegenden*, 261–65. Alongside inveighing against "Asiatics," at least one German commander in the Baltic republics referred to Soviet rule in Russia as "pure Jewish rule. Of 480 people's commissars, 13 Russians, 12 Armenians, even a negro, all of the rest Jews." Barth, *Dolchstoßlegenden*, 273.
47. "Die Heimat ist in Gefahr!," illustrator, V. Arnaud, https://www.loc.gov/resource/cph.3g11608/.
48. E.g., "Germany's ideal future under the rule of the Bolshevist," 1919, https://www.loc.gov/item/2004665972/; "The Bolshevik Is Coming!," 1919, https://www.loc.gov/resource/cph.3g11909/; "Join the Antibolshevik League!," https://www.iwm.org.uk/collections/item/object/15643.
49. Merz, *Das Schreckbild*, 173, 266–67; Plöckinger, *Unter Soldaten und Agitatoren*, 278–82. For all their variation, including depictions of wolves and monsters, none of the German anti-Bolshevik posters in 1918 or 1919 employed overt anti-Semitic messaging.
50. Gerwarth, *The Vanquished*, 74–75.
51. Vejas Gabriel Liulevicius, *The German Myth of the East: 1800 to the Present* (Oxford, 2009), 154–60; Gerd Koenen, *Der Russland-Komplex. Die Deutschen und der Osten, 1900–1945* (München, 2005).
52. Kellogg, *The Russian Roots of Nazism*, 85–86.
53. Klaus Theweleit, *Male Fantasies, vol. 1: Women, Floods, Bodies* (Minneapolis, 1987), 74–79. Many of the veterans of Grenzschutz Ost—Heinz Guderian, Gotthard Heinrici, Erich Hoepner, Erich von Manstein, Friedrich Paulus, and Walter von Reichenau—would resume their fight against Bolshevism leading commanders Wehrmacht commanders in 1941. Hürter, *Hitlers Heerführer*, 89, fn86.
54. Liulevicius, *The German Myth of the East*, 156.
55. Hürter, *Hitlers Heerführer*, 87–89; Barth, *Dolchstoßlegenden*, 231.
56. Gerwarth, *The Vanquished*, 126–27.

57. Volker Ullrich, "Mord in München," *Die Zeit*, no. 9 (2009): 92.
58. Hermann Gilbhard, "Thule-Gesellschaft, 1918–1933," in *Historisches Lexikon Bayerns*, http://www.historisches-lexikon-bayerns.de/Lexikon/Thule-Gesellschaft, 1918–1933.
59. Barth, *Dolchstoßlegenden*, 227.
60. Josef Karl, *Die Schreckensherrschaft in München und Spartakus im bayrischen Oberland. Nach amtlichen Quellen aufgezeichnet* (Munich, 1919), 192.
61. Gilbhard, "Thule-Gesellschaft, 1918–1933"; Thomas Weber, *Becoming Hitler: The Making of a Nazi* (Oxford, 2017), 54.
62. Volker Ullrich, *Die Revolution von 1918/19* (Munich, 2009), 99; Ian Kershaw, *Hitler: 1889–1936: Hubris* (New York, 1998), 113–16; Thomas Weber, *Hitler's First War: Adolf Hitler, the Men of the List Regiment, and the First World War* (Oxford, 2010), 246; Theweleit, *Male Fantasies*, vol. 1, 229.
63. Adolf Hitler, Mein Kampf, trans. Ralph Manheim (Boston, 1943), 205–6.
64. Weber, *Hitler's First War*, 250–51.
65. For a differing view, see Weber, *Hitler's First War*.
66. Brigitte Hamann, *Hitlers Wien: Lehrjahre eines Diktators* (Munich, 1996), 239–41, 499–500; Thomas Weber, "The Pre-1914 Origins of Hitler's Antisemitism Revisited," *Journal of Holocaust Research* 34, no.1 (2020): 70–86.
67. Plöckinger, *Unter Soldaten und Agitatoren*, 185–87.
68. Plöckinger, *Unter Soldaten und Agitatoren*, 186 (the chairman, Eugen Fuchs, spoke in mid-October 1919); Hanebrink, *A Specter Haunting Europe*, 16.
69. The police report was filed under the rubric "Incitement Against Jews" (*Judenhetze*). Adolf Hitler, *Sämtliche Aufzeichnungen, 1905–1924*, ed. Eberhard Jäckel (Stuttgart, 1980), 138–39.
70. Hitler, *Sämtliche Aufzeichnungen*, 219.
71. The political literature given to Hitler as an army agitator included Ernst Lindenau's popular brochure, "What One Needs to Know about Bolshevism," which contained gory descriptions of the Red Terror and the alleged nationalization of women by the Soviets. See Plöckinger, *Unter Soldaten und Agitatoren*, 231–33.
72. "*Der Münchener Geiselmord: Wer trägt die Schuld? Special Geiselnummer*," *Münchener Neue Illustrierte*, September 29, 1919; *Der Geiselmord in München: Ausführliche Darstellung der Schreckenstage im Luitpold-Gymnasium nach amtlichen Quellen* (Munich, 1919); *Ein Jahr bayerische Revolution im Bild. Photobericht [Heinrich] Hoffmann* (Munich, 1919).
73. The introduction happened through the writer Dietrich Eckart, who was active in the Thule Society and first met Hitler in fall 1919. Kellogg, *The Russian Roots of Nazism*, 70–72.
74. Kellogg, *The Russian Roots of Nazism*, 227–28.
75. Alfred Rosenberg *Pest in Russland! Der Bolschewismus, seine Häupter, Handlanger und Opfer. Mit 75 Originallichtbildern aus Sowjetrussland* (Munich, 1922). Similar torture methods are described in S. P. Melgunov, *Red Terror in Russia*, 162–200; I. N. Steinberg, *In the Workshop of the Revolution* (New York, 1953), 145.
76. Alfred Rosenberg, "*Der Pogrom am deutschen und am russischen Volke*," *Völkischer Beobachter*, August 4, 1921, 3. Rosenberg revised his fantastical victim count even higher for a 1923 publication in which he claimed "over 40 million" Russian deaths as a result of Jewish terror. Kellogg, *The Russian Roots of Nazism*, 230.
77. Hitler and Rosenberg held each other in high esteem at this time. Impressed by Hitler's energy and rhetorical skills, Rosenberg joined his party, where he soon began to take on editorial duties at the *Völkischer Beobachter*. Speaking of Rosenberg, Hitler in turn said that he was the only man whose ideas he would always listen to. Kellogg, *The Russian Roots of Nazism*, 72–73; Hanebrink, *A Specter Haunting Europe*, 35–36.
78. Kellogg, *The Russian Roots of Nazism*, 232. The original source is *Völkischer Beobachter*, August 16, 1922, 6.
79. Kellogg, *The Russian Roots of Nazism*, 48–49.

80. Alfred Rosenberg, *Die Protokolle der Weisen von Zion und die jüdische Weltpolitik* (Munich, 1923), 5.
81. Hitler, *Mein Kampf*, 51, 60, 326 (on page 326, the German "Schleier" is rendered as "cloaks").
82. Hitler, *Sämtliche Aufzeichungen*, 558–60. Hitler's anti-Bolshevism became pronounced after Soviet Russia's resurgence after the civil war. Until 1921, few observers in the West believed that the Soviet regime would survive the turmoil; most saw it as another short-lived experiment, on par with the Soviet republics in Munich and Hungary.
83. Hitler, *Sämtliche Aufzeichungen*, 767.
84. Hitler, *Sämtliche Aufzeichungen*, 833–34.
85. Hitler, *Sämtliche Aufzeichungen*, 955–56.
86. Bernhard H. Bayerlein, "The Abortive 'German October,' 1923: New Light on the Revolutionary Plans of the Russian Communist Party, the Comintem and the German Communist Party," in *Politics and Society Under the Bolsheviks* (London, 1999), 251–62.
87. Ulrich Bach, "'Bei Euch, ihr Männer von der Ruhr, liegt die Last der Abwehr, aber auch ihre Kraft!': Die politische Rolle der Bergarbeitergewerkschaften während des Ruhrkampfes 1923," *Geschichte in Köln*, 20, no. 1 (1986)," 91–120 (108).
88. Gerhard Paul, "Der Sturm auf die Republik und der Mythos vom 'Dritten Reich': Die Nationalsozialisten," in *Politische ldentität und nationale Gedenktage*, ed. Aleida Assmann (Opladen, 1989), 255–79 (271).
89. Gerhard Paul, *Aufstand der Bilder: Die NS-Propaganda vor 1933* (Bonn, 1990), 131.
90. Paul, "*Der Sturm auf die Republik*," 271.
91. Decree on the Exercise of Martial Law in District Barbarossa, in Frans Coetzee and Marilyn Shevin-Coetzee, *The World in Flames: A World War II Sourcebook* (New York and Oxford, 2011), 94–95.
92. The book had two parts. Volume 1 focused on Hitler's biography and the early years of the Nazi movement. It was completed while Hitler was in prison and appeared in July 1925. Volume 2 expounded on political theory, party tactics, and foreign political goals and was published in December 1926. Later editions presented both parts in a single volume.
93. Hitler, *Mein Kampf*, 384.
94. Hitler, *Mein Kampf*, 622–23. In a related key, Rosenberg wrote in 1923, "Nowadays the red and golden Internationals have openly become the Jewish National as they earlier secretly were." Kellogg, *The Russian Roots of Nazism*, 224. Events in the Soviet Union appeared to validate Hitler and Rosenberg's diagnosis: Starting in 1921, the Soviet leadership adopted the New Economic Policy (NEP) and reintroduced small-scale capitalist elements. But while the Nazis viewed the policy as an expression of global Jewish Bolshevism and Jewish capitalism working in concert with each other, Soviet leaders regarded NEP as a tactical retreat before a renewed assault on capitalism.
95. Hitler, *Mein Kampf*, 505.
96. Hitler, *Mein Kampf*, 652–53, 666.
97. Adolf Hitler, *Reden, Schriften, Anordnungen: Februar 1925 bis Januar 1933, Bd. 1: Die Wiedergründung der NSDAP*, ed. Clemens Vollnhals (Munich, 1992), 325.
98. Boaz Neumann, "The Phenomenology of the German People's Body (*Volkskörper*) and the Extermination of the Jewish Body," *New German Critique*, 106 (2009): 149–81.
99. See illustration on page 42. Already in 1923 Hitler remarked to an American journalist, "Our German workers . . . have two souls. One is German, the other is Marxian. We must arouse the German soul. We must root out the taint of Marxism. Marxism and Germanism, like German and Jew, are antipodes." Hitler, *Sämtliche Aufzeichnungen*, 1,025.
100. Martin Broszat, "Die Anfänge der Berliner NSDAP 1926/27," *Vierteljahrshefte für Zeitgeschichte*, 8/1 (1960): 85–118 (98).
101. Timothy Scott Brown, *Weimar Radicals: Nazis and Communists Between* Authenticity and Performance (New York, 2009), 50. The illustration first appeared in *Der Angriff*, 32, August 6, 1928. It is illustrated in Brown, *Weimar Radicals*, but incorrectly dated.
102. Hitler, *Mein Kampf*, 492.

103. Paul, *Aufstand der Bilder*, 38.
104. Communist meetings in Berlin saw banners demanding: READ THE "RED BANNER," KARL AND ROSA'S NEWSPAPER! Demonstrators carried images of Lenin, Liebknecht, and Luxemburg, with slogans like "Complete their work!" and "This is how red Berlin honors its dead!" See *Die Rote Fahne*, January 17, 1933. For the important distinction Communists made between agitation and propaganda, see chapter 2.
105. Richard H. Bodek, "'We Are the Red Megaphone!': Political Music, Agitprop Theater, Everyday Life and Communist Politics in Berlin During the Weimar Republic" (PhD diss, University of Michigan, 1990), 309–15.
106. Hitler, *Mein Kampf*, 470 (emphasis in the original). Hitler was contemptuous of the written word: "The greatest revolutions in this world have never been directed by a goose-quill!," Hitler, *Mein Kampf*, 106; Paul, *Aufstand der Bilder*, 39.
107. Hitler, *Mein Kampf*, 543 (emphasis in the original).
108. Paul, *Aufstand der Bilder*, 135, citing SA leader Ernst Röhm. The propaganda marches were first devised by Benito Mussolini's Fascist movement. Sven Reichardt, *Faschistische Kampfbünde: Gewalt und Gemeinschaft im italienischen Squadrismus und in der deutschen SA* (Cologne, 2009), 104.
109. Eve Rosenhaft, "Working-Class Life and Working-Class Politics: Communists, Nazis and the State in the Battle for the Streets, Berlin 1928–1932," in *Social Change and Political Development in Weimar Germany*, ed. Richard J. Bessel and Edgar J. Feuchtwanger (London, 1981), 207–40 (213).
110. Broszat, "Die Anfänge der Berliner NSDAP," 92.
111. Inventory of the Theodore Fred Abel papers, biogram #588 Clara Petersson; Broszat, "Die Anfänge der Berliner NSDAP," 111; Giebel, "*Warum ich Nazi wurde*," 883–92.
112. Broszat, "Die Anfänge der Berliner NSDAP," 111.
113. Broszat, "Die Anfänge der Berliner NSDAP," 623.
114. Broszat, "Die Anfänge der Berliner NSDAP," 118–19. Reichardt charges those historians who describe the Communists as the principal aggressor in the street fights of the Weimar Republic with taking the Nazis' defensive pose at face value, and with not studying the sources with sufficient care. The attitude among the German police and judiciary was staunchly anti-Communist; this made them disproportionately record and persecute Communist violence while often turning a blind eye to Nazi aggression. Broszat, "Die Anfänge der Berliner NSDAP," 54–75.
115. *Völkischer Beobachter*, May 28, 1930, cited in Ernst Gumbel, *Lasst Köpfe rollen: Faschistische Morde 1924–1931* (Berlin, 1931), 67, and in Giebel, "*Warum ich Nazi wurde*," 618.
116. Broszat, "Die Anfänge der Berliner NSDAP," 91.
117. David Irving, *Göring: A Biography* (New York, 1989), 93–94; for Carin Göring's letter in the original German language, see David Irving, *Göring. Eine Biographie* (Kiel, 1986), 77.
118. Eve Rosenhaft, *Beating the Fascists? The German Communists and Political Violence 1929–1933* (Cambridge, 1983), 63–64; Reichardt, *Faschistische Kampfbünde*, 112.
119. Inventory of the Theodore Fred Abel papers, biogram #259 G. Hilger (born 1884, not identical with the well-known German diplomat, who was born in 1886).
120. Inventory of the Theodore Fred Abel papers, biogram #199 Hans Schönherr.
121. "Hitlerites in Riots, Stone Jewish Shops as Reichstag Opens," *New York Times*, October 14, 1930, 1.
122. Paul, *Aufstand der Bilder*, 71.
123. The rally was in part meant to substitute for the two last scheduled party meetings in Nuremberg, which had to be canceled after protests from Nuremberg's mayor. The police force in Braunschweig, by contrast, was controlled by a Nazi minister.
124. Reichardt, *Faschistische Kampfbünde*, 110–11; *Daily Mail*, September 24, 1930, quoted by *Völkischer Beobachter*, September 25, 1930.
125. Harold Callender, "Herr Hitler Replies to Some Fundamental Questions," *New York Times*, December 20, 1931.

126. In May 1930, a parliamentary commission in the Reichstag resolved to fight "cultural Bolshevism," by which it understood "efforts aimed at the subversion and destruction of religion, custom, order, and the state in the fields of education, broadcasting, film, theater, music, and other performances." See Laser, *Kulturbolschewismus!*, 113–14.
127. Georg Bollenbeck, "German Kultur, the Bildungsbürgertum, and its Susceptibility to National Socialism," *German Quarterly* 73, no. 1 (2000): 67–83 (76). Some of the latter charges had an anti-Semitic ring: Laser, *Kulturbolschewismus!*, 161, 189–91.
128. Laser, *Kulturbolschewismus!*, 209; Bollenbeck, "German Kultur," 78 (Walter Dirks).
129. Dirk Gerhardt, "Die Lüge von den Heckenschützen," *Der Spiegel*, July 13, 2012. After the Nazis assumed power, four Communists allegedly responsible for the killings of the two SA men were tried and sentenced to execution by axe in August 1933. In March 1932, police authorities in Germany's southwest discovered that a series of bomb attacks that had plagued the region since the previous summer was not the work of Communists, as was initially assumed, but of Nazis. The lead organizer was regional SS leader Theodor Eicke, soon to become the first commander of the Dachau concentration camp. Hitler was quick to excuse the "excessive" incidents as a legitimate defense against Communist aggression. Daniel Siemens, *Stormtroopers: A New History of Hitler's Brownshirts* (New Haven, 2017), 51–52.
130. "Ordinance of the Reich President on the Restoration of Public Security and Order in the Territory of the State of Prussia," July 20, 1932, https://www.1000dokumente.de/Dokumente/Verordnung_des_Reichspr%C3%A4sidenten,_betreffend_die_Wiederherstellung_der_%C3%B6ffentlichen_Sicherheit_und_Ordnung_(%E2%80%9EPreu%C3%9Fenschlag%E2%80%9C).
131. Paul, *Aufstand der Bilder*, 235.
132. While the man on the left could not be identified, the photograph on the right featured the well-known German-Jewish gallerist Alfred Flechtheim, whose promotion of modernist art made him a prominent target in the campaign against "cultural Bolshevism." Ottfried Dascher, *"Es ist was Wahnsinniges mit der Kunst." Alfred Flechtheim: Sammler, Kunsthändler und Verleger* (Wädenswil, 2011), 291–326. I thank Andres Zervigon for identifying Flechtheim on the poster.
133. Jutta Ciolek-Kümper, *Wahlkampf in Lippe: Die Wahlkampfpropaganda der NSDAP zur Landtagswahl am 15.01.1933 = Kommunikation und Politik*, Bd. 8 (München, 1976).
134. *Völkischer Beobachter*, February 2, 1933.
135. See illustration at https://commons.wikimedia.org/wiki/File:Hitler_na_wiecu_(Historia_str.238).jpg.
136. Heinrich August Winkler, *Der Weg in die Katastrophe. Arbeiter und Arbeiterbewegung in der Weimarer Republik* (Bonn, 1990), 877.
137. Peter Fritzsche, *Hitler's First Hundred Days: When Germans Embraced the Third Reich* (Oxford, 2021), 138.
138. Kershaw, *Hitler*, 456–57; Benjamin Carter Hett, *Burning the Reichstag: An Investigation into the Third Reich's Enduring Mystery* (Oxford, 2014), 14.
139. To this day, historians debate whether a single person was able to set the Reichstag on fire, and whether the Communists or the Nazis were behind the fire. There is as of yet no compelling evidence to prove van der Lubbe was not the perpetrator. "Der Kronzeuge war ein Psychopath. Neue Forschung zum Reichstagsbrand 1933," *Der Spiegel*, November 29, 2019; Sven Felix Kellerhoff, *The Reichstag Fire: The Case Against the Nazi Conspiracy* (Barnsley, 2023).
140. Hett, *Burning the Reichstag*, 16.
141. Wachsmann, *KL*, 29.
142. "Der Reichstag in Flammen!," https://www.europeana.eu/en/item/08547/sgml_eu_php_obj_p0008107.
143. The KPD leadership reported the arrest of 130,000 and the murder of 2,500 of its members by the end of 1933. Conservative accounts note 100,000 arrests and 600 deaths. Richard

Evans, *The Coming of the Third Reich* (New York, 2004), 348; Nikolaus Wachsmann, who also includes Social Democrats, gives a far higher estimate: Wachsmann, "The Dynamics of Destruction: The Development of the Concentration Camps, 1933–45," in *Concentration Camps in Nazi Germany: The New Histories*, ed. Nikolaus Wachsmann and Jane Caplan (Oxford, 2009), 17–43 (18). The KPD had 330,000 members in early 1933. Siegfried Bahne, *Die Kommunistische Partei Deutschlands* (1960), 662.

144. Wachsmann, *KL*, 52–56; Anna Andlauer, "Claus Bastian—Der Häftling mit der Nummer 1," in *Lebensläufe: Schicksale von Menschen, die im KZ Dachau waren*, vol. 2, ed. Hans-Günter Richardi (Dachau, 2001), 27–28; *Die Linke im Visier: Zur Errichtung der Konzentrationslager 1933*, ed. Nikolaus Wachsmann and Sybille Steinbacher (Göttingen, 2014).
145. Wachsmann, *KL*, 23–26; Timothy W. Ryback, *Hitler's First Victims: The Quest for Justice* (New York, 2015), 93; Hans Beimler, *Im Mörderlager Dachau*, ed. Friedbert Mühldorfer (Cologne, 2012).
146. From right to left: Ernst Heilmann (member of the Reichstag, SPD), Friedrich Ebert (member of the Reichstag and SPD, and a newspaper editor), Alfred Braun (broadcast announcer), Heinrich Giesecke (ministerial counsel, ret., director, Reichs-Rundfunk-Gesellschaft), Dr. Hans Flesch (broadcast intendent), and Dr. Kurt Magnus (director, Reichs-Rundfunk-Gesellschaft).
147. Fritzsche, *Hitler's First Hundred Days*, 171; Wachsmann, *KL*, 42–43.
148. Wachsmann, *KL*, 189, 221.
149. *The Nazi Concentration Camps, 1933–1939: A Documentary History*, ed. Christian Goeschel and Nikolaus Wachsmann (Lincoln, NE, 2012), 57–59.
150. See "Aufruf der Reichsleitung der N.S.D.A.P.," *Völkischer Beobachter*, March 30, 1933, 1–2, trans. in *The Persecution and Murder of the European Jews by Nazi Germany, 1933–1945, vol. 1: German Reich, 1933–1937* (2019), 117–21 (117–18).
151. Christoph Kreutzmüller, "'Augen im Sturm': britische und amerikanische Zeitungsberichte über die Judenverfolgung in Berlin 1918–1938," *Zeitschrift für Geschichtswissenschaft* 62, no. 1 (2014): 25–48 (35–38); Kershaw, *Hitler*, 471–72.
152. The picture, which shows traces of violence (the face of one prisoner is bruised, and another is unable to raise his right arm), was taken by Georg Pahl, a well-known freelance photographer at the time. The SA commanders who allowed Pahl into the *Blutburg* did so with satisfaction, as they wanted the outside world, including political opposition, to know what kind of reckoning awaited enemies of the state. Only with the founding of the Ministry of Propaganda on March 13, and in response to foreign protests against Nazi brutality, Propaganda Minister Goebbels stepped in to stem the dissemination of images from the camps. Irene von Götz and Christoph Kreutzmüller, "Spiegel des frühen NS-Terrors. Zwei Foto-Ikonen und ihre Geschichte," *Fotogeschichte* 131 (2014): 73–75; on Georg Pahl, see: Charles W. Sydnor, Jr., The Bildarchiv of the Bundesarchiv," *Central European History* 7, no. 3 (September, 1974): 281–85 (283).
153. Whether Jews were among the eight Communists on the photograph could not be established. Von Götz and Kreutzmüller, "Spiegel des frühen NS-Terrors."
154. "German Fugitives Tell of Atrocities at Hands of Nazis," *New York Times*, March 20, 1933, 1, 5. For an exception to the rule, see "The Terror in Germany," *Manchester Guardian*, March 28, 1933.
155. Ian Kershaw, The "Hitler Myth": Image and Reality in the Third Reich (Oxford, 1987), 56; see also Robert Gellately, *Backing Hitler: Consent and Coercion in Nazi Germany.* (Oxford, 2001), 60, 257.
156. Paul Moore, "'Man hat es sich viel schlimmer vorgestellt': German Concentration Camps in Nazi Propaganda, 1933–1939," in *Kontinuitäten und Brüche: Neue Perspektiven auf die Geschichte der NS-Konzentrationslager*, ed. Christiane Hess et al. (Berlin, 2011), 99–114 (111–12).
157. Thies Schulze, "Antikommunismus als politischer Leitfaden des Vatikans?," *Vierteljahrshefte für Zeitgeschichte* 3 (2012): 353–79 (361–62); Klaus Grosse Kracht, "Campaigning

Against Bolshevism: Catholic Action in Late Weimar Germany," *Journal of Contemporary History* 53, no. 3 (2018): 550–73.

158. Inventory of the Theodore Fred Abel papers, biogram #31 Rudolf Kahn.

Chapter 2: Swastika and Soviet Star

1. Never before had the German army been "identified more with the tasks of the new state than today," wrote Colonel Walther von Reichenau, a top Defense Ministry official, in a news brief published a few days later. "Die Armee Schulter an Schulter mit dem neuen Kanzler," *Völkischer Beobachter* 36/37, February 5–6, 1933, 1. Even before Hitler came to power, Reichswehr leaders were intent on shaking off the constraints of the Versailles Treaty; the new chancellor was a "willing partner, not the initial instigator, of rearmament. Ian Ona Johnson, *Faustian Bargain: The Soviet-German Partnership and the Origins of the Second World War* (Oxford, 2022). Hammerstein-Equord was one of the few men in the room not to bend to Hitler. He resigned in early 1934.
2. Domarus, *Hitler, Reden und Proklamationen*, vol. 1 (Würtzburg, 1962), 193.
3. Andreas Wirsching, "'Man kann nur Boden germanisieren.' Eine neue Quelle zu Hitlers Rede vor den Spitzen der Reichswehr am 3. Februar 1933," *Vierteljahreshefte für Zeitgeschichte* 49/3 (2001): 517–50 (525–26).
4. Wirsching, "'Man kann nur Boden germanisieren,'" 522–24; Hans Magnus Enzensberger, *Hammerstein oder der Eigensinn* (Frankfurt, 2010), 115–24. Wirsching and Enzensberger doubt the claims of von Hammerstein's two daughters who said they had helped produce the protocol. Wirsching and Enzensberger cite two male witnesses at the dinner who said that Hitler's speech was attended only by men. But the aide de camp taking notes was following the proceedings from behind a curtain, shielding the daughter assisting him from view. More important, the reference to Hitler's "agitational speeches" points to Communist authorship, which in turn supports the daughters' claims.
5. K. Radek, "Kuda idet Germaniia?" *Izvestiia*, March 22, 1933, 2; Sabine Dullin, "Le role de l'Allemagne dans le rapprochement franco-sovietique 1932–1935," in *Deutschland-Frankreich-Russland*, ed. Il'ia Mieck and Pierre Guillen (Munich, 2000), 245–62; Iu.V. Galaktionov, *Otechestvennaia istoriografiia germanskogo fashizma* (Kemerovo, 2007), 63–66.
6. Galaktionov, *Otechestvennaia istoriografiia germanskogo fashizma*, 90–91; Otto D. Tolischuss, "The German Book of Destiny: Mein Kampf," *New York Times*, October 18, 1936, 43, 153, 172 (172); James Barnes and Patience Barnes, *Hitler's Mein Kampf in Britain and America: A Publishing History, 1930–39* (Cambridge, 1980), 3.
7. The German-Soviet military partnership dated back to 1919, the year of the Versailles Treaty. Top secret, it enabled the Germans to develop and test new military technology on Soviet soil, in exchange for German specialists training and modernizing the Red Army. Germany would dissolve the partnership in 1933. Johnson, *Faustian Bargain*.
8. Jonathan Haslam, *Soviet Foreign Policy, 1930–33. The Impact of the Depression* (London, 1983).
9. J. V. Stalin, *Problems of Leninism* (Moscow, 1953), 454–58. Given the economic and clandestine military ties between the Soviet Union and Germany at the time, Stalin's address made no reference to Germany as a foreign aggressor.
10. Mark Harrison and R. W. Davies, "The Soviet Military-Economic Effort During the Second Five-Year Plan (1933–1937)," *Europe-Asia Studies* 49, no. 3 (1997): 369–406.
11. While Hitler's rise to power galvanized a global Left movement and self-consciousness, the rise of a popular anti-fascism, often in defiance of left-wing party doctrines, dates back to the early 1920s. The appeal for the founding of an International Antifascist League, signed by artists, intellectuals, socialists, and Communists from across Europe, was signed on November 7, 1923, two days before Hitler's putsch in Munich. Beyond seeking to mobilize for a united fight against fascism, the proclamation called for "educational work on the nature and culturally destructive consequences of the fascist reign." Kasper Braskén, "Making Anti-Fascism Transnational: The Origins of

Communist and Socialist Articulations of Resistance in Europe, 1923–1924," *Contemporary European History* 25, no. 4 (November 2016): 573–96 (573–74).

12. Babette Gross, *Willi Münzenberg. Eine politische Biographie* (Stuttgart, 1967), 255; Sean McMeekin, *The Red Millionaire: A Political Biography of Willy Münzenberg, Moscow's Secret Propaganda Tsar in the West* (New Haven, 2008), 261–64.
13. Gross, *Willi Münzenberg*, 253–54. McMeekin, *The Red Millionaire*, 263.
14. *Braunbuch über Reichstagsbrand und Hitlerterror. Faksimile-Nachdruck der Originalausgabe von 1933* (Frankfurt, 1979); Gross, *Willi Münzenberg*, 257–60; Anson Rabinbach, "Staging Antifascism: The Brown Book of the Reichstag Fire and Hitler Terror," *New German Critique*, 103 (2008): 97–126.
15. Hett, *Burning the Reichstag*, 109–10.
16. On the controversy, see Hett, *Burning the Reichstag*.
17. *Braunbuch*, 1 (editors' preface, unpaginated).
18. Enzensberger, *Hammerstein*, 126–27.
19. *Braunbuch*, 332–54.
20. *Braunbuch*, 146, 183, 367; English translation: *The Brown Book of the Hitler Terror and the Burning of the Reichstag* (New York, 1933), 152. The sentence, "Our book will open their eyes," is omitted from the English translation (page 190). Missing, too, is the reference to fascism's "counter-historical" direction, part of an open letter written by the French writer Romain Rolland.
21. Rabinbach, "Staging Antifascism," 101; Gross, *Willi Münzenberg*, 260.
22. Georgi Dimitroff, *Tagebücher 1933–1943*, ed. Bernhard H. Bayerlein (Berlin, 2000), 22–23, 710; Marietta Stankova, *Georgi Dimitrov: A Biography* (London, 2010), 105; Georgi Dimitroff, "Die revolutionäre Literatur im Kampfe gegen den Faschismus," *Internationale Literatur*, no. 5 (1935), 10–11.
23. *Dimitrov protiv Geringa. Po materialam Georgiia Dimitrova o Leiptsigskom protsesse 1933 goda* (Moscow, 1966), 299. Translation of Goethe's lines: Richard Stokes, *The Book of Lieder* (Faber, 2005).
24. Kellerhoff, *The Reichstag Fire*, 92–93; Stankova, *Georgi Dimitrov*, 109–10; *Braunbuch II: Dimitroff Contra Goering: Enthüllungen über die wahren Brandstifter* (Paris, 1934), 228, 245; John D. Bell, *The Bulgarian Communist Party from Blagoev to Zhivkov* (Stanford, CA, 1985), 47.
25. Dimitroff, *Tagebücher*, February 27, 1934; Hett, *Burning the Reichstag*, 172.
26. Mikhail Kol'tsov, *Izbrannoe*, ed. B. E. Efimova (Moscow, 1985), 403; Stephen Kotkin, *Stalin, vol. 2: Waiting for Hitler, 1929–1941* (New York, 2017), 170–71.
27. *Braunbuch II*. The book cover featured Heartfield's photo montage.
28. Kotkin, *Stalin*, vol. 2, 175–76, 189–90, 259.
29. Katerina Clark, *Moscow, the Fourth Rome: Stalinism, Cosmopolitanism, and the Evolution of Soviet Culture, 1931–1941* (Cambridge, MA, 2011), 11–15, 27.
30. *Pervyi vsesoiuznyi s"ezd sovetskikh pisatelei 1934. Stenograficheskii otchet* (Moscow, 1934), 4.
31. Ilya Ehrenburg, *The Extraordinary Adventures of Julio Jurenito and His Disciples*, trans. Usick Vanzler (New York, 1930); idem, *Trest D.E. Istoriia gibeli Evropy* (Berlin, 1923). A German translation appeared in 1925 and was republished in 1932: Ilja Ehrenburg, *Trust D.E. Die Geschichte der Zerstörung Europas*, trans. Lia Calmann (Berlin, 1925).
32. Il'ia Erenburg, *Sobranie sochinenii v deviati tomakh*, vol. 5 (Moscow, 1962), 215–16; see also Julian Laychuk, "The Evolution of I. G. Ehrenburg's Weltanschauung [*sic*] During the Period 1928–1934," *Canadian Slavonic Papers* 12, no. 4 (1970), 395–416; Boris Fresinskij, "Ilja Ehrenburg und Deutschland," in *Stürmische Aufbrüche und enttäuschte Hoffnungen. Russen und Deutsche in der Zwischenkriegszeit*, ed. Karl Eimermacher et al. (Munich, 2006), 291–327 (313).
33. llya Ehrenbourg, "Jeunesse Russe," *La Nouvelle Revue Francaise* 232 (1933), 5–35 (6). Older workers, who included numerous exiled kulak peasants, were noticeably absent from these transcribed conversations.

34. *Peryi vsesoiuznyi s"ezd*, 182.
35. *Peryi vsesoiuznyi s"ezd*, 186–87.
36. *Peryi vsesoiuznyi s"ezd*, 331–32.
37. Victor Erlich, "The Dead Hand of the Future: The Predicament of Vladimir Mayakovsky," *Slavic Review* 21, no. 3 (September 1962), 433–40 (437).
38. Friedrich Wolf, "Art Is a Weapon! (Kunst ist Waffe!)," in *The Weimar Republic Sourcebook*, ed. Anton Kaes et al. (Berkeley, 1994), 230–31; Herrmann Haarmann, "Friedrich Wolfs literarischer Kampf gegen Faschisierungstendenzen in der Endphase der Weimarer Republik," in *Friedrich Wolfs Auseinandersetzung mit dem Faschismus und seiner Ideologie.* (Berlin, 1987), 20–23 (22).
39. "Der Jude als Verführer," *Völkischer Beobachter*, February 27, 1931.
40. On the genesis and the evolving versions of the famous play, which Wolf originally titled "Dr. Mamlock's Exit," see Maria Teresa Sciacca, "'Mamlock'—Variationen—Ein Drama und seine verschiedenen Fassungen," in *Exil. Forschung, Erkenntnisse, Ergebnisse* 26, no. 1 (2006): 37–51.
41. The film was produced in 1936 (director, Herbert Rappaport). The premiere in 1938 is discussed on page 504, note 186. On Wolf's rewriting of the play in Soviet exile, see Christoph Hesse, *Filmexil Sowjetunion. Deutsche Emigranten in der sowjetischen Filmproduktion der 1930er und 1940er Jahre* (Munich, 2017), 476–508 (492–99).
42. A few months earlier, left-wing writers convened a First American Writers' Congress in New York. Among the speakers was Friedrich Wolf, who called on his audience to abandon neutrality and take up a political stance. As every German writer knew, he declared, there were only two ways: for or against Hitler. *American Writers' Congress*, ed. Henry Hart (New York, 1935), 19–21.
43. *Paris 1935. Erster Internationaler Schriftstellerkongress zur Verteidigung der Kultur*, ed. W. Klein (Berlin, 1982), 317–18. See also Jacob Boas, *Writers' Block: The Paris Antifascist Congress of 1935* (Cambridge, 2016).
44. Klein, ed., *Paris 1935*, 155–56, 395–400, quotes from 398. Klaus Mann said that fascism, "as paradoxical as it sounds—makes it easier for us to clarify and define the nature and appearance of what we want." Mann called this "socialist humanism," "actually a European task," see 155–56.
45. Klein, ed., *Paris 1935*, 124, 129. An indication of his anti-fascist commitment, Gide traveled to Berlin with André Malraux in January 1934 to petition Goebbels for Dimitrov's release from prison. Julian Jackson, *The Popular Front in France: Defending Democracy, 1934–38* (Cambridge, 1990), 119, 157.
46. Ehrenburg's childhood friend Nikolai Bukharin, who was then editor in chief at *Izvestiya*, encouraged the writer to reach out to Stalin. Boris Frezinskii, *Pisateli i sovetskie vozhdi. Izbrannye siuzhety 1919–1960 godov* (Moscow, 2008), 279–90.
47. Kotkin, *Stalin*, vol. 2, 245.
48. Jonathan Haslam, *The Soviet Union and the Struggle for Collective Security in Europe* (London, 1984).
49. Kotkin, *Stalin*, vol. 2, 259; Stankova, *Georgi Dimitrov*, 127–28.
50. Katerina Clark, "Germanophone Intellectuals in Stalin's Russia: Diaspora and Cultural Identity in the 1930s," *Kritika: Explorations in Russian and Eurasian History* 2, no. 3 (2001): 529–51 (531).
51. Haslam, *Collective Security*, 29–30; Kotkin, *Stalin*, vol. 2, 259.
52. "Der Führer vor seiner SA: 'Hier steht die deutsche Antwort auf Moskau,'" *Völkischer Beobachter*, September 16, 1935 (Berliner Ausgabe); "Die Schlussansprache des Führers auf dem Kongress," *Völkischer Beobachter*, September 17, 1935, 1–3.
53. *Der Bolschewismus. Seine Entstehung und Auswirkung*, ed. Wulf Bley (Munich, 1938), 283.
54. Joseph Goebbels, *Communism with the Mask Off* (Berlin, 1935), 22. Alfred Rosenberg, "Der Bolschewismus als Aktion einer fremden Rasse," *Nationalsozialistische Monatshefte* 6, no. 67 (October 1935), 866–73 (869). Indignant Soviet diplomats cabled excerpts from Rosenberg's remarks to Moscow. Stalin advised them to ignore such invectives:

"Nuremberg is their response to the Congress of the C[ommunist] I[nternational]. The Hitlerites cannot help but indulge in insults, if one considers that the Congress of the CI heaped rubbish on them and dragged them through the mud. *Pravda* is supposed to criticize them on principle and politically but without insults." *Deutschland, Russland, Komintern, II. Dokumente (1918–1943)*, ed. Hermann Weber et al. (Berlin, 2015), 1,131–32. At the 1936 Nuremberg rally, Rosenberg made specific references to the present-day role of Jews in the Soviet Union. With an air of scientific precision, he made the far-fetched claim that the Soviet leadership was "95–98 percent" Jewish. Rosenberg differentiated between the secret police (100 percent Jewish), Soviet domestic policymakers (98 percent), and industrial managers (95–98 percent). *Dokumente der deutschen Politik, Bd. 4: Deutschlands Aufstieg zur Großmacht* (Berlin, 1939), 82–85.

55. The swastika in fact succeeded the traditional black-white-red horizontal stripes of the national flag of the Kaiser era, which the Nazis had reintroduced in early 1933, thereby abolishing the hated black-red-gold of the Weimar Republic, *Dokumente der Deutschen Politik*, Bd. 3, 24–29. The key passage on the battle between the Soviet flag and the swastika is missing in Max Domarus's summary of Göring's speech, Domarus, *Hitler, Reden und Proklamationen*, 537–38.
56. Domarus, *Hitler, Reden und Proklamationen*, 536.
57. Domarus, *Hitler, Reden und Proklamationen*, 555.
58. Domarus, *Hitler, Reden und Proklamationen*, 536.
59. Heinrich Himmler, *Die Schutzstaffel als antibolschewistische Kampforganisation*, 3rd ed. (Munich, 1937).
60. See also: "Bolschewisten unter uns?" *Das Schwarze Korps*, October 10, 1935.
61. Rolf-Dieter Müller, *Enemy in the East: Hitler's Secret Plans to Invade the Soviet Union* (London, 2014), 57–58; R. J. Overy, "From 'Uralbomber' to 'Amerikabomber': The Luftwaffe and Strategic Bombing," *Journal of Strategic Studies* 1/2 (1978): 154–78 (155).
62. Alec Nove and J. A. Newth, "The Jewish Population: Demographic Trends and Occupational Patterns," in *The Jews in Soviet Russia since 1917*, ed. Lionel Kochan (Oxford, 1978), 125–59 (158).
63. Babette Quinkert, *Propaganda und Terror in Weissrussland, 1941–1944* (Paderborn, 2009), 47; Hürter, *Hitlers Heerführer*, 261.
64. "Hitlers Denkschrift zum Vierjahresplan 1936," *Vierteljahrshefte für Zeitgeschichte* 3/2 (1955): 204–10 (204); Waddington, *Hitler's Crusade*, 89–90.
65. *Der Weltbolschewismus. Ein internationales Gemeinschaftswerk über die bolschewistische Wühlarbeit und die Umsturzversuche der Komintern in allen Ländern. Herausgegeben von der Anti-Komintern. In Verbindung mit den Sachkennern der ganzen Welt bearbeitet von Dr. Adolf Ehrt* (Berlin, 1936), 7, 505.
66. Domarus, *Hitler, Reden und Proklamationen*, 638.
67. Michael Jabara Carley, "Caught in a Cleft Stick: Soviet Diplomacy and the Spanish Civil War," in *The International Context of the Spanish Civil War*, ed. Gaynor Johnson (Cambridge, 2009), 151–81 (160–62); Kotkin, *Stalin*, vol. 2, 343.
68. "Nuremberg Rally," *The Times*, September 12, 1936, 12; Ullrich, *Hitler: Ascent, 1889–1939* (New York, 2016), 526.
69. "Die Schlussansprache des Führers auf dem Kongress," *Völkischer Beobachter*, September 17, 1935.
70. Ullrich, *Hitler*, 534.
71. All citations from Joseph Goebbels, "Die Weltgefahr des Bolschewismus" (September 10, 1936), in *Dokumente der Deutschen Politik, Bd. 4: Deutschlands Aufstieg zur Großmacht 1936*, ed. Paul Meier-Benneckenstein, 3rd ed. (Berlin, 1939), 53–77.
72. Domarus, *Hitler: Reden und Proklamationen, Band I/2*, 645–46.
73. Frederick T. Birchall, "Hitler Tells Reich It Would Prosper with Soviet Lands," *New York Times*, September 13, 1936, 1, 33; incomplete rendering of Hitler's original speech: Domarus, *Hitler: Reden und Proklamationen*, 642–43.

74. Christoph Kivelitz, *Die Propagandaausstellung in europäischen Diktaturen: Konfrontation und Vergleich: Nationalsozialismus, italienischer Faschismus und UdSSR der Stalinzeit* (Bochum, 1999), 214–15, 545; Rosemarie Burgstaller, *Inszenierung des Hasses. Feindbildausstellungen im Nationalsozialismus* (Frankfurt, 2022), 199–200.
75. *Deutschland-Berichte der Sozialdemokratischen Partei Deutschlands (Sopade): 1937* (Frankfurt, 1980), 21 (January 1937).
76. Kivelitz, *Die Propagandaausstellung*, 218–19, 547; Burgstaller, *Inszenierung des Hasses*, 202–42.
77. Kivelitz, *Die Propagandaausstellung*, 217–19.
78. Michael S. Cullen, *Der Reichstag. Im Spannungsfeld deutscher Geschichte*, 2nd ed. (Berlin, 2004), 54. In Berlin, the exhibition ran as "Bolshevism Unmasked."
79. Kivelitz, *Die Propagandaausstellung*, 554; Jutta Sywottek, *Mobilmachung für den totalen Krieg. Die propagandistische Vorbereitung der deutschen Bevölkerung auf den Zweiten Weltkrieg* (Wiesbaden, 2013), 113; *Die Tagebücher von Joseph Goebbels* I/3, 245, 260 (August 24 and September 9, 1937).
80. Kivelitz, *Die Propagandaausstellung*, 226, 558.
81. Jürgen Bernatzky, "Der nationalsozialistische Antisemitismus im Spiegel des politischen Plakates. 'Juden—Läuse—Flecktyphus,'" in Günther Ginzel, ed., *Antisemitismus: Erscheinungsformen der Judenfeindschaft gestern und heute* (Bielefeld, 1991), 389–417 (404–5); Burgstaller, *Inszenierung des Hasses*, 252–90.
82. David Welch, *The Third Reich: Politics and Propaganda*, 2nd ed. (London and New York, 2002), 204–8.
83. *Führer durch die Ausstellung Entartete Kunst* (Berlin, 1937), 4; Ursula A. Ginder, "Degenerate Art Exhibition: Kunststadt München 1937" (PhD diss., University of California, Santa Barbara, 2011), 211–17; *Deutschland-Berichte der Sozialdemokratischen Partei Deutschlands (Sopade). Vierter Jahrgang 1937*, 1,534. The Sopade informant noted the presence of "discreet visitors who, with serious faces, walk silently through the rooms," while making clear that their numbers were few (1,535). An April 1933 exhibition of "Cultural Bolshevik images" that was on display in Mannheim and included a counter-exhibition of exemplary German art may have served as precedent for the better known Munich art shows: Christoph Zuschlag, "Die Ausstellung 'Kulturbolschewistische Bilder' in Mannheim 1933—Inszenierung und Presseberichterstellung," in *Überbrückt: Ästhetische Moderne und Nationalsozialismus. Kunsthistoriker und Künstler 1925–1937*, ed. Eugen Blume and Dieter Scholz (Cologne, 1999), 224–36.
84. Peter Fritzsche, *Life and Death in the Third Reich* (Cambridge, MA, 2008), 92.
85. *Kampf dem Bolschewismus. Ein Bücherverzeichnis über Bolschewismus, Marxismus, Judentum* (Freiburg, 1936); *Bolschewismus—Judentum. Eine Zusammenstellung einschlägigen Schrifttums* (Leipzig, 1939).
86. Hanebrink, *A Specter Haunting Europe*, 90; Taubert's first publication was a "Red Book" on the Reichstag fire, a rejoinder to Münzenberg's publication. Klaus Körner," Eberhard Taubert und der Nibelungen-Verlag," *Berlinische Monatsschrift (Luisenstädtischer Bildungsverein)* 12 (1997): 44–52 (45).
87. Jan C. Behrends, "Back from the USSR: The Anti-Comintern's Publications on Soviet Russia in Nazi Germany (1935–41)," *Kritika: Explorations in Russian and Eurasian History* 10, no. 3 (2009): 527–56.
88. *Und du siehst die Sowjets richtig. Berichte von deutschen u. ausländischen "Spezialisten" aus der Sowjet-Union*, ed. Alfred Laubenheimer, 2nd ed. (Leipzig and Berlin, 1937), 47, 351 (emphasis in the original). Alfred Laubenheimer was a German engineer who had worked and resided in the Soviet Union for two years. See Dr. Ing. A. Laubenheimer, *Die Sowjetunion am Abgrund! Mit zahlreichen Originalaufnahmen des Verfassers u.a.* (Berlin, 1933), 4.
89. James Casteel, "The Politics of Diaspora Russian German Émigré Activists in Interwar Germany," in *German Diasporic Experiences: Identity, Migration, and Loss*, ed. Sebastian Siebel-Achenbach et al. (Waterloo, 2008), 117–29.

90. E.g., *Ein deutscher Todesweg: Authentische Dokumente der wirtschaftlichen, kulturellen und seelischen Vernichtung des Deutschtums in der Sowjet-Union* (Berlin, 1930), which begins with a letter from Siberia, 7. See also *Brüder in Not! Dokumente der Hungersnot unter den deutschen Volksgenossen in Russland*, ed. Adolf Ehrt (Berlin, 1933). Even as Anti-Comintern publishers sounded the alarm about a Bolshevik genocide of the German people, their main objective was not to rescue starving peasants but to expose the Soviet state as a world-destroying Jewish conspiracy. Burgstaller, *Inszenierung des Hasses*, 148–57.
91. Hermann Greife, *Zwangsarbeit in der Sowjetunion*, 16th ed. (Berlin, 1936). Greife, whose doctoral dissertation was proclaimed a "scientific investigation of Marxism and Bolshevism," began to enact a purge among German Sovietologists starting in 1936, nazifying research institutions in the field of *Ostforschung*. A "Soviet researcher," Greife noted, "can only be someone who not only knows the country's general conditions . . . but who is furthermore thoroughly acquainted with the goals and tactics of Marxism-Bolshevism, and who clearly recognizes the particular situation of the Soviet Union as a country conquered by international Jewry." Hermann Greife, *Sowjetforschung: Versuch einer nationalsozialistischen Grundlegung der Erforschung des Marxismus und der Sowjetunion* (Berlin, 1936), 70. See also Fleischhauer, *Das Dritte Reich und die Deutschen in der Sowjetunion*, 51–52.
92. *Belomor: An Account of the Construction of the New Canal Between the White Sea and the Baltic Sea*, ed. Maxim Gorky, L. Auerbach, and S. G. Firin (New York, 1935).
93. The cover image reproduces the cover page of the Soviet journal *USSR in Construction* 1 (1934). The journal was published in five languages.
94. Hermann Greife, *Slave Labor in Soviet Russia*, trans. B. Warkentin (Kitchener, 1937), 10, 26, 33. The photographs were taken from the Soviet *Belomor* edition (see previous note). Whereas the Soviet volume only gave the initials of NKVD officials' first names and patronyms, Greife provided the names in full in order to reveal their alleged Jewish identity.
95. Greife, *Sowjetforschung*, 72.
96. Greife, *Slave Labor in Soviet Russia*, 6.
97. The Anti-Comintern also published a *Red Book on Spain*: *Das Rotbuch über Spanien: Bilder, Dokumente, Zeugenaussagen. Gesammelt und herausgegeben von der Anti-Komitern* (Berlin, 1937). Lorna Waddington, "The Anti-Komintern and Nazi Anti-Bolshevik Propaganda in the 1930s," *Journal of Contemporary History* 42, no. 4 (2007): 573–54 (585).
98. Their lists were thorough. With respect to Norway, they included the members of the Bund norwegischer Frauen [Association of Norwegian Women], and all Norwegians who had studied in the Soviet Union, Russisch-deutsches Projekt zur Digitalisierung deutscher Dokumente, https://wwii.germandocsinrussia.org, see "Dokumente der deutschen Geheimpolizei," Akte Nr. 215 = Russian State Archive of Socio-Political History (RGASPI), f. 458, op. 9, d. 215.
99. Beth A. Griech-Polelle, "The Impact of the Spanish Civil War upon Roman Catholic Clergy in Nazi Germany," in *Antisemitism, Christian Ambivalence, and the Holocaust*, ed. Kevin Spicer (Bloomington, 2007), 121–35; John Cornwell, *Hitler's Pope: The Secret History of Pius XII* (New York, 1999), 180–81.
100. *Dokumente der deutschen Politik, Bd. 4: Deutschlands Aufstieg zur Großmacht* (Berlin, 1939), 171; Waddington, *Hitler's Crusade*, 83–85, 90–96. Italy joined the pact a year later.
101. *Völkischer Beobachter* (Munich edition), November 7, 1937, 1; November 8, 1937, 5.
102. Douglas Little, "Red Scare, 1936: Anti-Bolshevism and the Origins of British Non-Intervention in the Spanish Civil War," *Journal of Contemporary History* 23, no. 2 (1988): 291–314 (306–7); Douglas Little, *Malevolent Neutrality: The United States, Great Britain, and the Origins of the Spanish Civil War* (Ithaca, 1985), esp. 221–65; Jonathan

Haslam, *The Spectre of War: International Communism and the Origins of World War II* (Princeton, 2021).

103. Waddington, "The Anti-Komintern and Nazi Anti-Bolshevik Propaganda," 584.
104. *The Nazi Olympics: Sport, Politics and Appeasement in the 1930s*, ed. Arnd Krüger and William Murray (Champaign, IL, 2003).
105. Prior to the exhibition, Speer had secured the Soviet blueprints from the Paris organizers. Karen Fiss, *Grand Illusion: The Third Reich, the Paris Exposition, and the Cultural Seduction of France* (Chicago, 2009), 55–58, 103–4.
106. Frederick T. Birchall, "Third Reich Builds on Colossal Scale," *New York Times*, September 15, 1937; idem, "Hitler's Own Men March Before Him," *New York Times*, September 13, 1937, 10. See also the report by the British Consul General, cited in *Fremde Blicke auf das "Dritte Reich": Berichte ausländischer Diplomaten über Herrschaft and Gesellschaft in Deutschland 1933–1945*, ed. Frank Bajohr and Christoph Strupp (Göttingen, 2011), 472.
107. To allow as many delegates as possible to attend the congress, it opened in Valencia (the Spanish Republic's provisional capital), before moving to Madrid and Barcelona and concluding in Paris. Manuel Aznar Soler, "Le deuxième Congrès international des écrivains pour la défense de la culture (1937)," *La contemporaine: "Matériaux pour l'histoire de notre temps"* 1, nos. 123–24 (2017): 8–15.
108. Soler, "Le deuxième Congrès international," 11; Willi Bredel, "Vorwort," *Das Wort*, no. 9 (1937): 3, 6.
109. I. G. Erenburg, *Ispanskie reportazhi 1931–1939*, ed. V. V. Popov and B. Ia. Frezinskii (Moscow, 1986), 217.
110. Il'ia Erenburg, "Geroi 'tret'ei imperii,'" *Izvestiia*, February 28, 1937. For more on Günther Löhning, see Stefanie Schüler-Springorum, *Krieg und Fliegen. Die Legion Condor im Spanischen Bürgerkrieg* (Paderborn, 2010), 201.
111. Erenburg, "Geroi 'tret'ei imperii.'"
112. Kotkin, *Stalin*, vol. 2, 408.
113. Kotkin, *Stalin*, vol. 2, 417–20; Earl F. Ziemke, *The Red Army, 1918–1941: From Vanguard of World Revolution to America's Ally* (London, 2004), 202. On the foreign political background to the Great Purges, see Oleg Khlevniuk, "The Reasons for the 'Great Terror': The Foreign Political Aspect," in *Russia in the Age of Wars, 1914–1945*, ed. Silvio Pons and Andrea Romano (Milan, 2000), 159–69.
114. Reese, *The Soviet Military Experience: A History of the Soviet Army, 1917–1991* (London and New York, 2000), 86.
115. Dale R. Herspring, *Soldiers, Commissars, and Chaplains: Civil-Military Relations Since Cromwell* (Lanham, 2001), 103–24; *Russkii arkhiv: Velikaia Otechestvennaia, Prikazy Narodnogo komissara oborony SSSR (1937–21 iiunia 1941gg.) T. 13 (2–1)* (Moscow, 1994), 11, 19, 24–25.
116. William J. Chase, *Enemies Within the Gates? The Comintern and the Stalinist Repression, 1934–1939* (New Haven, 2008), 8; Khlevniuk, "The Reasons for the 'Great Terror,'" 159.
117. Anastasia S. Lozhkina et al., "Soviet-Japanese Relations after the Manchurian Incident, 1931–1939," in *A History of Russo-Japanese Relations: Over Two Centuries of Cooperation and Competition*, ed. Dmitry V. Streltsov and Shimotomai Nobuo (Leiden and Boston, 2019), 218–37.
118. Soler, "Le deuxième Congrès international," 13; Erenburg, *Ispanskie reportazhi, 1931–1939*, 215.
119. Michael David-Fox, *Showcasing the Great Experiment: Cultural Diplomacy and Western Visitors to the Soviet Union, 1921–1941* (Oxford, 2011), 263–66; W. J. Marshall, "André Gide and the U.S.S.R: A Reappraisal," *Australian Journal of French Studies* 20 (1983): 37–49.
120. Joshua Rubenstein, *Tangled Loyalties: The Life and Times of Ilya Ehrenburg* (London, 1996), 161.

121. André Gide, *Return from the U.S.S.R.*, trans. Dorothy Bussy (New York, 1937), 62–63. Within a year, the book had been reprinted ten times and translated into fourteen languages. David-Fox, *Showcasing the Great Experiment*, 263.
122. The accusation was not entirely unfounded. By this time, Gide had openly proclaimed his sympathies for Trotsky: Marshall, "André Gide and the U.S.S.R," 46.
123. Anne Hartmann, *"Ich kam, ich sah, ich werde schreiben": Lion Feuchtwanger in Moskau 1937. Eine Dokumentation* (Göttingen, 2017), 12.
124. Lion Feuchtwanger, "Der Mord in Hitler-Deutschland," in *Braunbuch II*, 402–4.
125. Hartmann, *"Ich kam, ich sah, ich werde schreiben,"* 287.
126. Hartmann, *"Ich kam, ich sah, ich werde schreiben,"* 72; Claudie Villard, "Die Rezeption von Lion Feuchtwangers Moskau 37 in den Exilzeitschriften," in *Autour du 'Front Populaire Allemand' Einheitsfront—Volksfront*, ed. Michael Grunewald and Frithjof Trapp (Bern, 1990), 289–313.
127. "The latest events in Russia are making it increasingly difficult for every honest socialist to maintain his positive attitude toward the Soviet Union," *Sopade* reported from Germany. "The impetus given anti-Bolshevik propaganda by these incidents cannot be ignored." *Deutschland-Berichte der Sozialdemokratischen Partei Deutschlands (Sopade). Vierter Jahrgang 1937*, 769–70.
128. Jochen Hellbeck, "With Hegel to Salvation: Bukharin's Other Trial," *Representations* 107, no. 1 (2009): 56–90.
129. Dimitroff, *Tagebücher*, February 11, 1937, 149.
130. Münzenberg died in France in December 1940 under circumstances that indicate he was murdered. It remains unclear whether he was murdered by NKVD or Gestapo agents. See Kasper Braskén, "'Hauptgefahr jetzt nicht Trotzkismus, sondern Münzenberg'—East German Uses of Remembrance and the Contentious Case of Willi Münzenberg," *Comintern Working Paper* 22 (2011).
131. Roth's partner, Helga von Hammerstein, never received a visa to enter the Soviet Union. She remained in Germany and obtained a PhD in chemistry in 1939. Playwright and physician Friedrich Wolf escaped the maelstrom of the Great Terror by joining the International Brigades. En route to Spain in early 1938, he was arrested in France. A Soviet passport issued to the doctor in early 1941 enabled his return to Moscow, by which point the immediate danger had passed. Enzensberger, *Hammerstein*, 240. Reinhard Müller, "'Was ist ein Mensch?' Aus der Moskauer Kaderakte Friedrich Wolfs," in *Einspruch: Schriftenreihe der Friedrich-Wolf-Gesellschaft: Exil in der Sowjetunion, 1933–1945* (Berlin, 2010), 23–52; *Deutschland, Russland, Komintern, II. Dokumente (1918–1943)*, ed. Hermann Weber et al. (Berlin, 2015), 1,635n51.
132. Rubenstein, *Tangled Loyalties*, 174.
133. *Die Tagebücher von Joseph Goebbels*, I/3, 198–99 (July 10, 1937); I/5, 65 (December 22, 1937).
134. "Moskauer Feier des Revolutionstages," Deutsche Botschaft Moskau, November 11, 1938, 3–4, Russisch-deutsches Projekt, https://rgaspi-458-9.germandocsinrussia.org/de/nodes/226-akte-nr-223-dokumente-aus-dem-dossier-des-gestapa-jahrestag-der-oktoberrevolution-weisungen-des-gestapa-an-alle-gestapo-stellen-und-grenzstellen-zur-sonderkontrolle-von-personen-die-im-transit-durch-deutschland-in-die-sowjetunion-zu-den-feiern-des#page/219/mode/inspect/zoom/5.
135. *Deutschland-Berichte der Sozialdemokratischen Partei Deutschlands (Sopade). Vierter Jahrgang 1937*, 931–32; Saul Friedländer, *Nazi Germany and the Jews: The Years of Persecution, 1933–1939*, vol. 1 (New York, 1997), 241–48.
136. The action came in response to a Polish decree stripping Polish Jews living abroad of their citizenship.
137. Friedländer, *Nazi Germany and the Jews*, 275–76; Christian Goeschel, *Suicide in Nazi Germany* (New York, 2009), 101–3.

138. *Pravda* editorial, November 18, 1938; Olga Gershenson, *The Phantom Holocaust: Soviet Cinema and Jewish Catastrophe* (New Brunswick, NJ, 2013), 13–14.
139. Ehrenburg's diagnosis was "fascism," and his piece covered the wolf packs hounding Italy as well. "Writers no longer write long books," Ehrenburg commented with the coming war in view. "You won't finish them anyway." I. G. Erenburg, *Ispanskie reportazhi* 1931–1939 (Moscow, 1986), 341–45.
140. Western studies mostly stress instrumental uses: Gerschenson, *The Phantom Holocaust*, 13; Jeremy Hicks, *First Films of the Holocaust: Soviet Cinema and the Genocide of the Jews, 1938–1946* (Pittsburgh, 2012), 21–22.
141. Already in 1918, Lenin signed a decree on the "Struggle Against Anti-Semitism and Jewish Pogroms." Yuri Luryi and Alexander Lyubechansky, "Soviet/Russian Legislation Against National or Racial Hatred and Discrimination," *Review of Central and East European Law* 20, no. 2 (1994): 217–31 (217–21).
142. Anne Hartmann, "Lion Feuchtwanger and the Question of Jewish Identity in Stalinist Russia," in *Feuchtwanger and Judaism: History, Imagination, Exile*, ed. Paul Lerner and Frank Stern (Oxford, 2019), 165–87 (166–67).
143. V. M. Molotov, *The Constitution of Socialism. Speech Delivered at the Extraordinary Eighty Congress of Soviets of the U.S.S.R., November 29, 1936* (Moscow, 1937), 11, 23–24; see also "Uvekovechenie Kholokosta v SSSR," Yad Vashem, https://www.yadvashem.org/ru/education/educational-materials/learning-environments/families/additional-materials/memory.html.
144. Hartmann, "*Ich kam, ich sah, ich werde schreiben*," 324–29 (325). The Jewish Autonomous Region in Birobidzhan (Eastern Siberia) was officially founded in 1934 to attract Soviet Jews as settlers. Officials encouraged the practice of the Yiddish language as well as Jewish songs and dances but forbade the building of synagogues and the celebration of religious holidays. E. R. Abdurazakova, N. V. Martynova, M. M. Udova, and V. V. Martynov, "The History of The Jewish Culture Formation in the Far East of Russia," *AmurCon 2021: International Scientific Conference* 126, *European Proceedings of Social and Behavioural Sciences* (2022): 1–10.
145. Hicks, *First Films of the Holocaust*, 18–19, 28–29; *Kremlevskii Kinoteatr. 1928–1953: Dokumenty*, ed. K. M. Anderson and L. V. Maksimenkov (Moscow, 2005), 539.
146. Frank S. Nugent, "Russia Grasps a Nettle," *New York Times*, November 13, 1938.
147. Hicks, *First Films of the Holocaust*, 40.
148. Haslam, *The Spectre of War*, 62–63, 176.
149. Waddington, *Hitler's Crusade*, 150.
150. Karl Vietz, *Verrat an Europa. Ein Rotbuch über die Bolschewisierung der Tschecho-Slowakei. Herausgegeben von der Anti-Komintern* (Berlin, 1938).
151. Franz Knipping, "Die Deutsch-französische Erklärung vom 6. Dezember 1938," *Beihefte der Francia*, vol. 10 (1981).
152. G. Dimitroff, "*Einheitsfront gegen den Faschismus. Nach der Münchener Verschwörung*," *Deutsche Zeitung*, November 11, 1938.
153. Kotkin, *Stalin*, vol. 2, 608. Stalin's declaration predated the German invasion of the Czech lands by a few days. Great Britain and France responded to Hitler's aggression by pledging the inviolability of Poland's territory.
154. David Edmund Murphy, *What Stalin Knew: The Enigma of Barbarossa* (New Haven, 2005), 14–15, 19.
155. Murphy, *What Stalin Knew*, 15–18. Haslam, *The Spectre of War*, 309–10.
156. Murphy, *What Stalin Knew*, 20. Upon learning of the Anglo-French expedition to Moscow, German diplomats sprang into action and invited the Soviets to discuss their mutual interests in Poland. Haslam, *The Spectre of War*, 319–20.
157. Murphy, *What Stalin Knew*, 24–26. The Red Army would in fact increase its manpower by three million men between 1939 and 1941. Vast amounts of new equipment were ad-

ditionally fed into the armed forces. Roger Reese, *The Soviet Military Experience: A History of the Soviet Army, 1917–1991* (London and New York, 2000), 93–95; Mark Harrison, *Soviet Planning in Peace and War, 1938–1945* (Cambridge, 2002), 115–21.

158. "Treaty of Nonaggression Between Germany and the Union of Soviet Socialist Republics," The Avalon Project, n.d., https://avalon.law.yale.edu/20th_century/nonagres.asp; "Secret Additional Protocol," The Avalon Project, n.d., https://avalon.law.yale.edu/20th_century/addsepro.asp.
159. Bernhard H. Bayerlein, "Deutscher Kommunismus und transnationaler Stalinismus, 1929–1943," in *Deutschland, Russland, Komintern I: Überblicke, Analysen, Diskussionen*, ed. Herrmann Weber et al. (Berlin, 2014), 388–90.
160. Hans Schafranek, *Zwischen NKWD und Gestapo. Die Auslieferung deutscher und österreichischer Antifaschisten aus der Sowjetunion an Nazideutschand, 1937–1941* (Frankfurt, 1990), 57–59.
161. *Deutschland-Berichte der Sozialdemokratischen Partei Deutschlands (Sopade) 1934–1940. Sechster Jahrhang 1939*, ed. Klaus Behnken (Frankfurt, 1982), 985–89.
162. Lore Walb, *Ich, die Alte—ich, die Junge: Konfrontation mit meinen Tagebüchern 1933–1945* (Berlin, 1997), 130 (September 3, 1939); Nicholas Stargardt, *The German War: A Nation Under Arms, 1939–1945* (London, 2016), 41–74; Ian Kershaw, *Hitler, 1936–1945: Nemesis* (New York and London, 2000), 205.
163. See Wladimir Neweshin, "Die Reaktion der sowjetischen Öffentlichkeit auf den Hitler-Stalin-Paktund die Wandlung des Bildes von Nazi-Deutschland in der UdSSR (1939–1941)," in *Stürmische Aufbrüche und enttäuschte Hoffnungen, Russen und Deutsche in der Zwischenkriegszeit*, ed. Karl Eimermacher and Astrid Volpert (Paderborn, 2005), 1071–99 (1085–86); *Eisenstein und Deutschland*, ed. Oksana Bulgakowa (Berlin, 1998), 55–64.
164. Tahirih Motazedian, "The Communist Walküre: Eisenstein's Vision for Marrying German Wagnerism with Soviet Communism," *Journal of Musicological Research* 40, no. 3 (2021): 183–213.
165. These words were recorded by an informant for the NKVD. Neweshin, "Die Reaktion der sowjetischen Öffentlichkeit auf den Hitler-Stalin-Pakt," 1,079.
166. Domarus, *Hitler: Reden und Proklamationen*, 1,047–67 (1,058).
167. Klaus Hildebrand, *Das Dritte Reich* (Munich, 2009), 48.
168. Burckhardt found Hitler's admission so improbable that he failed to report it to the French and British diplomats with whom he secretly met after talking with Hitler. (He would recall the words only in June 1941.) Burckhardt did convey to the French and British what Hitler had to say about the military preparedness of the Soviet Union: "The Russians, and we know them better than do most other people; hundreds of our officers have trained in Russia, have no offensive strength and will not haul the chestnuts of others out of the fire. A nation does not murder its officers if it plans to wage a war. We defeated the Russians in Spain. The Japanese have also defeated them. (Hitler states scornfully.) One cannot give us goose pimples by talking about the Russians." See annotated transcript of exchange between Hitler and Burckhardt, World Future Fund, http://www.worldfuturefund.org/wffmaster/Reading/Germany/Burckhardt.htm; Carl J. Burckhardt, *Meine Danziger Mission 1937–1939*, 3rd ed. (Munich, 1980), 346; Waddington, *Hitler's Crusade*, 156–57.
169. Andreas Hillgruber, *Hitlers Strategie: Politik und Kriegführung, 1940–1941*, 2nd ed. (Munich, 1982), 145, 724–25.

Chapter 3: Crossing the Rubicon

1. Anton Roos to Elisabeth Roos, second half of July and September 20, 1940, https://jugend1918-1945.de/portal/ARCHIV/thema.aspx?bereich=archiv&root=9898&id=9898&redir.
2. Anton Roos to Elisabeth Roos, June 8 and 20, 1941.
3. Anton Roos to Elisabeth Roos, August 22 and 25, 1941.
4. Anton Roos to Elisabeth Roos, August 25 and October 12, 1941.

5. Anton Roos to Elisabeth Roos, June 8, 1941. "We were in Cracow for a day, lovely city. Also looked at the ghetto, I've never seen so many Jews packed together in one place. Behind the border, we drove through a village in which only Jews and German police live. The mugs you could see there."
6. Omer Bartov, *Hitler's Army* (Oxford, 1992), 152–59.
7. The extent to which Roos's thoughts about the Soviet Union were patterned on Nazi propaganda is demonstrated by the fact that passages from his letters to his wife corresponded verbatim to formulations found in an army newsletter that was distributed to every Wehrmacht company, underscoring the circularity of ideas between Nazi propaganda offices and German soldiers on the ground. The newsletter noted: "One word recurs again and again in the field post from the East to convey an impression, the word 'desolate.' The villages and the cities are desolate, the poverty of the people is desolate, the people themselves are desolate. A well-traveled man, who had spent many months in Africa getting to know the most primitive of peoples, said that their miserable living conditions were golden compared to the average way of life of the people in the Soviet state." "Die Rettung Deutschlands vor dem Ansturm des Untermenschentums," *Mitteilungen für die Truppe*, no. 136 (September 1941): 1.
8. "Existential struggle": Hitler's words in a meeting with top German generals, March 30, 1941. Johannes Hürter, *Hitlers Heerführer. Die deutschen Oberbefehlshaber im Krieg gegen die Sowjetunion 1941/42* (Munich, 2007), 7–8; "Bakterienträger": *Die "Ereignismeldungen UdSSR" 1941: Dokumente der Einsatzgruppen in der Sowjetunion* I, ed. Klaus-Michael Mallmann, Andrej Angrick, Jürgen Matthäus, Martin Cüppers (2011), report no. 133 (November 14, 1941), 792; "murderous plague" (mordplage): "Der Kampf gegen den Bolschewismus ist wirklich ein 'Kreuzzug,'" *Mitteilungen für die Truppe*, no. 123 (July 1941): 1–2.
9. Jochen Boehler, *Auftakt zum Vernichtungskrieg: Die Wehrmacht in Polen 1939* (Frankfurt, 2006), 36–41.
10. Boehler, *Auftakt zum Vernichtungskrieg*, 32; Bogumił Rudawski, "Nalot bombowy na Wieluń 1 wrze-śnia 1939 r.," *Z Archiwum Instytutu Zachodniego*, 2016, no. 7.
11. *Nazism, 1919–1945: A Documentary Reader, vol. 3: Foreign Policy, War and Racial Extermination*, ed. J. Noakes and G. Pridham (Exeter, 1983), 930. In the course of the campaign, the number of Einsatzgruppen was raised from five to seven. *Die Berichte der Einsatzgruppen aus Polen 1939, Vollständige Edition*, ed. Stephan Lehnstaedt and Jochen Böhler (Berlin, 2013), 7–9. Einsatzgruppen first formed in preparation of the annexation of Austria, and they also worked during subsequent annexations of Sudetenland and Czechoslovakia, but in the Polish campaign, they were allowed to act with greater brutality.
12. Peter Longerich, *Holocaust: The Nazi Persecution and Murder of the Jews* (Oxford, 2010), 144; Alexander B. Rossino, *Hitler Strikes Poland: Blitzkrieg, Ideology, and Atrocity* (Lawrence, KS, 2003), 16. A list available online features more than ten thousand names, many of them Jewish-sounding last names. Yet only a few of these names are specifically identified as "Jews," which suggests that at this stage of the campaign, Jews were not targeted solely on account of their racial ascription. "Szczegóły obiektu: Sonderfahndungsbuch Polen," Śląska Biblioteka Cyfrowa, last updated February 11, 2020, https://www.sbc.org.pl/dlibra/publication/edition/24330?id=24330.
13. *Die Berichte der Einsatzgruppen aus Polen 1939*, 360, 420.
14. *Nazism, 1919–1945*, 929–34; Longerich, *Holocaust*, 146.
15. A week into the invasion, Heydrich reprimanded Army commanders that the killings were proceeding too haltingly, and he clarified the stakes of the campaign: "We intend to spare the little people, but the nobles, the popes, and the Jews must be killed." Michael Wildt, *An Uncompromising Generation: The Nazi Leadership of the Reich Security Main Office* (Madison, WI, 2009), 230. The context suggests that Heydrich urged the killing of Jewish leaders, not Poland's entire Jewish population. Of the 54,500 Poles that German security forces shot between September and December 1939, seven thousand were Jews. Włodzimierz Borodziej, *Geschichte Polens im 20. Jahrhundert* (Munich, 2010), 193.
16. Mazower, *Hitler's Empire*, 82.

17. Boehler, *Auftakt zum Vernichtungskrieg*, 211–16; Frank Golczewski, "Polen," in *Dimension des Völkermords. Die Zahl der jüdischen Opfer des Nationalsozialismus*, ed. Wolfgang Benz (Munich, 1991), 411–98 (421–25); *Jews in Eastern Poland and the USSR, 1939–46*, ed. Antony Polonsky and Norman Davies (New York, 1991), 312.
18. Christopher Browning, "Nazi Resettlement Policy and the Search for a Solution to the Jewish Question, 1939–1941," *German Studies Review* 9, no. 3 (October 1986): 497–519 (502); Dan Michman, *The Emergence of Jewish Ghettos During the Holocaust* (Cambridge, 2011), 77–79; *The Persecution and Murder of the European Jews by Nazi Germany, 1933–1945, Volume 4: Poland, September 1939–July 1941*, ed. Klaus-Peter Friedrich (Munich, 2023), 183.
19. Browning, "Nazi Resettlement Policy and the Search for a Solution to the Jewish Question," 504–5; Mark Mazower, *Hitler's Empire: How the Nazis Ruled* Europe (New York, 2009), 86–87.
20. Ilya Altman and Claudio Ingerflom, "Le Kremlin et L'Holocauste, 1933–2001," in Vassili Petrenko, *Avant et après Auschwitz* (Paris, 2002), 217–81 (232–40). Nonetheless, the USSR did allow about three hundred thousand Jews from German-occupied regions to settle in the Soviet Union between 1939 and 1941. *Dimension des Völkermords*, 425.
21. Peter Longerich, *Heinrich Himmler* (Oxford, 2012), 508. The conquest of France also led to an increase of German violence against Poles, as it nurtured the fantasy of Germanizing all of Germany's conquered territories in the East, including the General Government.
22. Michman, *The Emergence of Jewish Ghettos During the Holocaust*, 82.
23. Ian Kershaw, "Improvised Genocide? The Emergence of the 'Final Solution' in the 'Warthegau,'" *Transactions of the Royal Historical Society* 2 (1992): 51–78 (56).
24. *The Black Book (Sonderfahndungsliste G.B.). Facsimile Reprint Series, Number 2*, ed. Imperial War Museum (London, 1989).
25. Stephen Fritz, *Ostkrieg: Hitler's War of Extermination in the East* (Lexington, KY, 2011), 20. These views carried long-standing stereotypes about a German cultural mission in the "barbaric East." See Vejas Gabriel Liulevicius, *The German Myth of the East: 1800 to the Present* (Oxford, 2009).
26. Bogdan Musial, "*Konterrevolutionäre Elemente sind zu erschießen*" (Berlin, 2000), 35–36. Gregorz Hryciuk, "Victims 1939–1941: The Soviet Repressions in Eastern Poland," in *Shared History, Divided Memory: Jews and Others in Soviet-Occupied Poland, 1939–1941*, ed. Elazar Barkan et al. (Leipzig, 2007), 173–200.
27. *Katyn: A Crime Without Punishment*, ed. Anna M. Cienciala, Natalia S. Lebedeva, Wojciech Materski (New Haven, 2007), 1, 30–31, 332; George Sanford, *Katyn and the Soviet Massacre of 1940: Truth, Justice, and* Memory (London and New York, 2005), 94.
28. Christopher Mick, *Lemberg, Lwow, and Lviv, 1914–1947: Violence and Ethnicity in a Contested City* (West Lafayette, IN, 2016), 283–87.
29. Szymon Rudnicki, "Anti-Jewish Legislation in Interwar Poland," in *Antisemitism and Its Opponents in Modern Poland*, ed. Robert Blobaum (Ithaca, 2005), 148–70 (165–68); Dov Levin, *The Lesser of the Two Evils: Eastern European Jewry Under Soviet Rule, 1939–1941* (Philadelphia-Jerusalem, 1995); Sheila Fitzpatrick, "Annexation, Evacuation, and Anti-Semitism in the Soviet Union, 1939–1946," in *Shelter from the Holocaust: Rethinking Jewish Survival in the Soviet Union*, ed. Mark Edele et al. (Detroit, 2017), 133–60 (136–37); Tarik Cyril Amar, *The Paradox of Ukrainian Lviv: A Borderland City Between Stalinists, Nazis, and Nationalists* (Ithaca, NY, 2015), 66–87.
30. Timothy Snyder, *Bloodlands: Europe Between Hitler and Stalin* (New York, 2010).
31. Jan Gross, *Revolution from Abroad* (Princeton, 2002), especially chaps, 2 and 4; Mick, *Lemberg, Lwow, and Lviv*, 279–80.
32. Christopher Browning, *The Origins of the Final Solution: The Evolution of Nazi Jewish Policy, September 1939—March 1942* (Lincoln, NE, and Jerusalem, 2004), 69–70. Making a similar distinction, Hitler, in his address to the 1936 Nuremberg rally, contrasted German "decency" and Nazism's "more humane approach to fellow human beings"

with Bolshevism's inherent "cruelty" and "repulsiveness." Domarus, *Hitler, Reden und Proklamationen*, vol. 1 (Würtzburg, 1962), 645–46.

33. Manfred Messerschmitt, "'Harte Sühne am Judentum': Befehlswege und Wissen in der deutschen Wehrmacht," in *"Niemand war dabei und keiner hat's gewußt": Die deutsche Öffentlichkeit und die Judenverfolgung 1933–1945*, ed. Jörg Wollenberg (Munich, 1989), 115; Martyn Housden, *Hans Frank. Lebensraum and the Holocaust* (New York, 2003), 77–78; Alexander B. Rossino, "The Case of the Einsatzgruppe von Woyrsch," *German Studies Review* 24, no. 1 (2001): 35–53 (42–44).
34. Arno J. Mayer, *Why Did the Heavens Not Darken? The "Final Solution" in History* (New York, 1988), 34.
35. Hürter, *Hitlers Heerführer*, 9.
36. Hürter, *Hitlers Heerführer*, 6–8.
37. Hürter, *Hitlers Heerführer*, 260–61.
38. Currying favors: Hürter, *Hitlers Heerführer*, 258.
39. "Commissar Order," https://germanhistorydocs.ghi-dc.org/pdf/eng/English58.pdf; emphasis in the original. For detailed discussions of how the order came about, see Christian Streit, *Keine Kameraden. Die Wehrmacht und die sowjetischen Kriegsgefangenen*, 1941–1945, new ed. (Bonn, 1991), 44–49; Felix Römer, *Der Kommissarbefehl: Wehrmacht und NS-Verbrechen an der Ostfront 1941/42* (Paderborn, 2008), 75–85.
40. One Wehrmacht general who explicitly remarked on the commissar's supposedly Jewish nature was Colonel General Erich Hoepner, commander of Panzergruppe 4. In a May 1941 instruction to his subordinate commanders, Hoepner described Germany's imminent invasion of the Soviet Union as the "defense of European culture against a Muscovite-Asiatic flood, and a fight against Jewish Bolshevism." Römer, *Der Kommissarbefehl*, 165.
41. *Dokumente der deutschen Politik, Bd. 4: Deutschlands Aufstieg zur Großmacht* (Berlin, 1939), 85. Beyond overestimating by a drastic margin the presence of Jews in the Red Army Command, the authors of the Commissar Order appeared unaware that, strictly speaking, no political commissars existed in the Red Army in early 1941. The office had been abolished in August 1940, as part of the military reforms in the wake of the purges of 1937, and former commissars were demoted to chiefs of "sections for political propaganda" under military command. It was not until July 16, 1941, that the commissar was reintroduced into the Red Army in order to counter the German onslaught with increased political agitation. See Ziemke, *The Red Army*, 239, 281. On the percentage of Jews in the political command of the Red Army, see page 447, note 62.
42. *Warum Krieg mit Stalin? Das Rotbuch der Anti-Komintern* (Berlin and Leipzig), 1941. The book was available in print as early as June 27, 1941, and soon surpassed a circulation of five hundred thousand copies. Herf, *The Jewish Enemy*, 96; *Die Verfolgung und Ermordung der europäischen Juden durch das nationalsozialistische Deutschland 1933–1945. Bd. 7: Sowjetunion mit annektierten Gebieten I*, ed. Jens Hoppe (Berlin, 2018), 226n3.
43. "Richtlinien für das Verhalten der Truppe in Rußland," in *"Unternehmen Barbarossa." Der deutsche Überfall auf die Sowjetunion 1941*, ed. Gerd Ueberschär and Wolfram Wette (Paderborn, 1984), 312. On the strength of these images, German soldiers entering the Soviet Union "saw" Mongolian sharpshooters—nowhere evidenced in Soviet archival records—who were placed in trees to kill German soldiers in the head. *Die "Ereignismeldungen UdSSR" 1941*, report no. 3 (June 25, 1941), 47. In fact, few non-Slavic soldiers fought in the Red Army in 1941. Only in spring 1942 did the Kremlin order the frontline mobilization of recruits from Soviet Central Asia. At this point, too, women were allowed to join the Red Army as soldiers. The Red Army's catastrophic bloodletting in 1941 mandated these moves. Brandon Schechter, "'The People's Instructions': Indigenizing the Great Patriotic War Among 'Non-Russians,'" *Ab Imperio* 3 (2012): 109–33.
44. Streit, *Keine Kameraden*, 39.

45. "The Barbarossa Decrees (1941)," trans. Geoffrey Giles, https://pages.uoregon.edu/dluebke/NaziGermany443/Kommissarbefehl.htm.
46. "The Barbarossa Decrees (1941)," trans. Geoffrey Giles.
47. Ueberschär and Wette, "*Unternehmen Barbarossa*," 312. On the distribution of the Guidelines to the troops, see Felix Römer, "The Wehrmacht in the War of Ideologies: The Army and Hitler's Criminal Orders on the Eastern Front," in *Nazi Policy on the Eastern Front, 1941: Total War, Genocide, and Radicalization*, ed. Alex J. Kay et al. (Rochester, 2012), 73–100 (78).
48. NA IRI RAN, f. 2, razd. VI, op. 17, d. 7.
49. Streit, *Keine Kameraden*, 83; *Die Tagebücher von Joseph Goebbels*, 2, vol. 1, 30–31 (July 9, 1941).
50. See the FHO's assessments, "Personelle Wehrleistung und Menschenreserven in der Sowjet-Union (Entwicklung seit Kriegsbeginn)," spanning the period 1941–1943, in NARA, T78, Roll 493.
51. For a detailed discussion of the German fantasy image of the commissar in relation to available evidence, see Christian Hartmann, *Wehrmacht im Ostkrieg: Front und militärisches Hinterland, 1941–42* (Munich, 2009), 501–15.
52. Römer, *Der Kommissarbefehl*, 300.
53. Römer, *Der Kommissarbefehl*, 290–306.
54. Testimony by Stepan Prokofievich Baranov, kolkhoz chairman in the Tula region: "The Germans stop, ask whether or not you're a Russian soldier. They look whether your hair is shorn, they take off your cap. Or they ask whether you're a commissar, ask you to show your hands. If your hands are white, then they say you're commissar." NA IRI RAN, f. 2, razd. 6, op. 3, d. 1.
55. Römer, *Der Kommissarbefehl*, 305.
56. *Rotarmisten in deutscher Hand: Dokumente zu Gefangenschaft, Repatriierung und Rehabilitierung sowjetischer Soldaten des Zweiten Weltkrieges*, ed. Rüdinger Overmans, Andreas Hilger, and Pavel Polian (Paderborn, 2012), 322–23; Römer, *Der Kommissarbefehl*, 309–10.
57. Helmut Hartmann, letter to Konrad Henkel, August 9, 1941. Helmut Hartmann's letter collection (Signatur 1614) is preserved at the Deutsches Tagebucharchiv, Emmendingen.
58. Rolf Sachsse, *Die Erziehung zum Wegsehen. Fotografie im NS-Staat* (Dresden, 2003), 316–17; *Die Tagebücher von Joseph Goebbels*, part 1, vol. 9, 400 (June 24, 1941).
59. *Die Deutsche Wochenschau* #471, September 14, 1939.
60. *Die Deutsche Wochenschau* #564, June 25, 1941; #565, July 4, 1941.
61. Erich Edwin Dwinger, *Wiedersehen mit Sowjetrussland. Tagebuch vom Ostfeldzug* (Leipzig, 1942), 73.
62. Estimates from Kai Struve, *Deutsche Herrschaft, ukrainischer Nationalismus, antijüdische Gewalt. Der Sommer 1941 in der Westukraine* (Berlin, 2015), 252. Tarik Amar puts the number of the murdered prisoners at 2,500. Amar, *The Paradox of Ukrainian Lviv*, 95. For much higher estimates, see Musial, *Konterrevolutionäre Elemente sind zu erschießen*, 138. Mass killings of the prisoner population took place in many other cities across the Soviet borderlands. On the territory of former Eastern Galicia alone, the NKVD murdered between 7,500 and 10,000 people (Struve, *Deutsche Herrschaft*, 215–16).
63. Musial, *Konterrevolutionäre Elemente sind zu erschießen*, 175; Amar, *The Paradox of Ukrainian Lviv*, 94.
64. Musial, *Konterrevolutionäre Elemente sind zu erschießen*, 154, 176–77. This account of the pogroms departs from Struve's, who downplays the anti-Jewish violence in Lvov predating the arrival of the Germans to argue for the latter's instrumental role in catalyzing the pogrom, which ostensibly began only on July 1, Struve, *Deutsche Herrschaft*, 360–77.
65. Amar, *The Paradox of Ukrainian Lviv*, 97. Dieter Pohl believes the number of victims to have been much higher. Dieter Pohl, *Nationalsozialistische Judenverfolgung in*

Ostgalizien 1941–1944: Organisation und Durchführung eines staatlichen Massenverbrechens (Munich, 1996), 64, 67n159.

66. For detailed evidence of such mutilations, see Alexander V. Prusin, *The Lands Between: Conflict in the East European Borderlands, 1870–1992* (New York, 2010), 157; and Musial, "*Konterrevolutionäre Elemente sind zu erschießen*," 262–69. Struve disparages the possibility that enraged nationalists prepared the corpses of the victims; he instead interprets the sightings of mutilated bodies as indications of a religious fervor that had gripped the population of Lvov in the wake of liberation from Soviet oppression. Struve, *Deutsche Herrschaft*, 278–88. Mick dismisses the sightings of tortured and crucified prisoners as "false rumors." Mick, *Lemberg, Lwow, and Lviv*, 291.
67. Amar, *The Paradox of Ukrainian Lviv*, 95.
68. These "facts" entered the SS reports from the ground: *Die "Ereignismeldungen UdSSR" 1941*, report no. 24 (July 16, 1941), 131. Starting in fall 1939, the German Einsatzgruppe stationed in Warsaw relied on local Ukrainian allies to gather "information" on the role that Jews allegedly played in the Soviet system. A November 1939 report from Warsaw cited a "credible agent" stating that "all leading administrative positions" in Soviet-occupied Poland were said to be "being filled by Jews brought from inside the Soviet Union." *Die Berichte der Einsatzgruppen aus Polen*, 436; see also Hanebrink, *A Specter Haunting Europe*, 141–42.
69. Musial, *Konterrevolutionäre Elemente sind zu erschießen*, 210–12; *"Schöne Zeiten": Judenmord aus der Sicht der Täter und Gaffer*, ed. Ernst Klee et al. (Frankfurt, 1988).
70. Struve, *Deutsche Herrschaft*, 374–75.
71. Stargardt, *The German War*, 163 (June 30, 1941).
72. Anton Roos to Elisabeth, July 10, 1941.
73. Struve, *Deutsche Herrschaft*, 392–93.
74. See the front pages of *Völkischer Beobachter*, July 6, 7, 8, 9, 1941.
75. *Die Tagebücher von Joseph Goebbels*, Teil 1, Bd. 9, 433 (July 8, 1941).
76. *Die Deutsche Wochenschau* #566 (July 10, 1941); Pietrow-Ennker, "*Die Sowjetunion in der Propaganda des Dritten Reiches*," 93–96.
77. *Meldungen aus dem Reich. Die geheimen Lageberichte des Sicherheitsdienstes der SS, 1938–1945*, vol. 7, ed. Heinz Boberach (Herrsching, 1984), 2,536.
78. *Meldungen aus dem Reich*, 2,537.
79. Domarus, *Hitler: Reden und Proklamationen*, 1726–32 (1727).
80. *Deutsche Soldaten sehen die Sowjet-Union. Feldpostbriefe aus dem Osten*, ed. Wolfgang Diewerge (Berlin, 1941).
81. *Deutsche Soldaten sehen die Sowjet-Union*, 39–47 (43, 45).
82. "'. . . erkämpft das Menschenrecht.' Das ist das Paradies der Arbeiter, Bauern und Soldaten!," *Völkischer Beobachter*, July 9, 1941, 1.
83. *Die Deutsche Wochenschau* #570 (August 6, 1941). The speaker may have intentionally avoided the term "concentration camp," a term too well known in Germany.
84. *Meldungen aus dem Reich*, vol. 6, 2473, 2507–8, 2515, 2563–64, 2632, 2650.
85. *Bischof Clemens August Graf von Galen. Akten, Briefe und Predigten, Bd. 2: 1939–1946*, ed. Peter Löffler (Mainz, 1988); Beth A. Griech-Polelle, *Bishop von Galen: German Catholicism and National Socialism* (New Haven, 2002), 113–14.
86. Dr. Robert Ley, "Der bolschewistische Höllenhund!," *Der Angriff*, August 9, 1941, 1–2. Ley ended his prophecy on an optimistic note: "*The Bolshevik hellhound will be defeated*" (emphasis in original).
87. Dr. Robert Ley, "Das ist der Plan der Juden, jedoch der Führer der Deutschen vereitelte ihn," *Der Angriff*, July 9, 1941.
88. Longerich, *Holocaust*, 184–85. In Poland, such task forces received support solely from ethnic Germans among the Polish population; in the Soviet borderlands, support from the local population was widespread. Locals willingly assisted the Germans in identifying and killing political enemies.

89. Ralf Ogorreck, *Die Einsatzgruppen und die "Genesis der Endlösung"* (Berlin, 1996), 102–3.
90. *Die "Ereignismeldungen UdSSR" 1941*, reports no. 24 (July 16, 1941), 132; no. 38 (July 30, 1941), 207; no. 59 (August 21, 1941), 327; no. 73 (September 4, 1941), 404. See also no. 19 (July 11, 1941), 104, for "Bolshevik, predominantly Jewish functionaries, agents, etc."; no. 30 (July 22, 1941), 163, for "communists and Jews"; no. 32 (July 24, 1941), 171, for "Jews and other Communist-tainted elements"; no. 36 (July 28, 1941), 195, for "Bolshevik functionaries, criminals, Asiatics, etc."; no. 86 (September 9, 1941), 471, for "Bolsheviks, Jews, and asocial elements."
91. Mass killings of Jews predated the first discoveries of Soviet murders in the Western borderlands, but they were isolated. In Bialystok on June 27, a police battalion operating within a security division under Wehrmacht command went on a killing spree, murdering at least two thousand Jews, including women and children. Members of the battalion locked an estimated five hundred people into the synagogue before setting it on fire. Longerich, *Holocaust*, 203.
92. Longerich, *Holocaust*, 190.
93. Ogorreck, *Die Einsatzgruppen und die "Genesis der Endlösung,"* 145. Struve doubts whether there was a formal Hitler order, as no such command is preserved in the archives, and the former SS men standing trial in postwar courts, on whose testimony Ogorreck builds his case, were likely to exculpate themselves through reference to a *Führerbefehl*. Either way, the Soviet murders had the same radicalizing effect on the SS men, whether on orders by Hitler or self-generated on the ground. Struve, *Deutsche Herrschaft*, 394–402 (400–401).
94. Ogorreck, *Die Einsatzgruppen und die "Genesis der Endlösung,"* 146.
95. *The Einsatzgruppen Reports*, 31 (July 16, 1941).
96. Ogorreck, *Die Einsatzgruppen und die "Genesis der Endlösung,"* 146; Musial, *Konterrevolutionäre Elemente sind zu erschießen*, 250–51; *Die "Ereignismeldungen UdSSR" 1941*, report no 50 (August 12, 1941).
97. Ogorreck, *Die Einsatzgruppen und die "Genesis der Endlösung,"* 178.
98. Browning, *The Origins of the Final Solution*, 310; on the SS brigades, see Martin Cüppers, *Wegbereiter der Shoah. Die Waffen-SS, der Kommandostab Reichsführer-SS und die Judenvernichtung, 1939–1945* (Darmstadt, 2005).
99. *The Private Heinrich Himmler: Letters of a Mass Murderer*, ed. Katrin Himmler and Michael Wildt (New York, 2016), 200, emphasis in the original.
100. For instance, the SD reports from occupied Poland made no mention of the Przemysl massacre carried out between September 16 and 19, 1939. See *Die Berichte der Einsatzgruppen aus Polen*.
101. Several sources date the hanging August 7, 1941, even though the date given in the SD report is August 8.
102. Letter of August 6, 1941, in Andrew Ezergailis, *The Holocaust in Latvia, 1941–1944: The Missing Center* (Riga, 1996), 378–79. Browning infers from Stahlecker's proposed "radical treatment" an intention to murder all Soviet Jews. This seems far-fetched. Stahlecker's recommendation was to remove Soviet Jews from their settlements and expel them into the Soviet East. He also advocated sterilization. Nonetheless, his insistence that Soviet Jews posed a political danger would ultimately lead to the decision to murder them in their entirety. Browning, *The Origins of the Final Solution*, 310; Longerich, *Holocaust*, 232.
103. *Die "Ereignismeldungen UdSSR" 1941*, report no. 47 (August 9, 1941), 266. For recollections of German eyewitnesses and photographs of the hangings, see "*Schöne Zeiten*," 105–14. Identification of the public restroom, https://waralbum.ru/369843/#comment-130879.
104. The SD reported that four hundred Jews from Zhitomir, most of them "saboteurs and political functionaries," had been "liquidated" during this action (*The Einsatzgruppen Reports*, 79 [August 9, 1941]). See also "'Die Organisation kann als vorbildlich bezeichnet werden,'" https://archivtag.hypotheses.org/637.
105. Cüppers, *Wegbereiter der Shoah*, 137–38.

106. Kay, *Empire of Destruction*, 77–81.
107. Browning and Matthäus, *The Origins of the Final Solution*, 281; Henning Pieper, *Fegelein's Horsemen and Genocidal Warfare: The SS Cavalry Brigade in the Soviet Union* (New York, 2015), 88.
108. Kay, *Empire of Destruction*, 75–77.
109. Mazower, *Hitler's Empire*, 175.
110. Richard Breitman, "Himmler's Police Auxiliaries in the Occupied Soviet Territories," *Simon Wiesenthal Center Annual* 7 (1990), 23–39. Unlike Lithuania and Latvia, two countries counting large Jewish communities, very few Jews lived in Estonia in 1939. For this reason, the German occupants did not immediately coopt Estonian auxiliary policemen (25).
111. Christian Gerlach, *Kalkulierte Morde: Die Deutsche Wirtschafts-und Vernichtungspolitik in Weissrussland, 1941 bis 1944* (Hamburg, 1999), 606; Yitzak Arad, "The Holocaust of Soviet Jewry," in Yad Vashem Studies, vol. XXI (Jerusalem, 1991–95), 18–22.
112. Walter Manoschek, "'Wo der Partisan ist, ist der Jude, und wo der Jude ist, ist der Partisan.' Die Wehrmacht und die Shoah," in *Die Täter der Shoah. Fanatische Nationalsozialisten oder ganz normale Deutsche?*, ed. Gerhard Paul (Göttingen, 2002), 167–85.
113. Gerlach, *Kalkulierte Morde*, 643–44; Waitman Wade Beorn, *Marching into Darkness: The Wehrmacht and the Holocaust in Belarus* (Cambridge, MA, 2014), 102–3.
114. *Befehle und Erklärungen der Nazi-Kriegsverbrecher über die Erschießungen der Juden in Russland in 1941–43*, ed. Tuviah Friedman (Haifa, 1959), Mattner file, 7.
115. *Befehle und Erklärungen der Nazi-Kriegsverbrecher*. trans., EHRI Online Course in *Holocaust Studies*, http://training.ehri-project.eu/d05-excerpts-letters-police-secretary-mogilev-his-wife; on Police Battalion 322, see Wolfgang Curilla, *Die deutsche Ordnungspolizei und der Holocaust im Baltikum und in Weißrussland* (Paderborn, 2005), 532–65.
116. Gerlach, *Kalkulierte Morde*, 588.
117. Karel Berkhoff, *Harvest of Despair: Life and Death in Ukraine, 1941–1944* (Cambridge, MA, 2004), 30–33; David Stahel, *Kiev 1941: Hitler's Battle for Supremacy in the East* (Cambridge, 2012), 258.
118. Hürter, *Hitlers Heerführer*, 580–81.
119. For Kiev's population in 1939, broken down by ethnicities, see http://www.demoscope.ru/weekly/ssp/ussr_nac_39_ra.php?reg=216.
120. *Die "Ereignismeldungen UdSSR" 1941*, reports no. 101 (October 2, 1941), 105, and 106 (October 7, 1941), 640–41. For German eyewitness accounts of the shootings, see *"Schöne Zeiten,"* 66–70.
121. Saul Friedländer, *The Years of Extermination: Nazi Germany and the Jews, 1939–1945* (New York, 2006), 293, letter dated September 28, 1941.
122. *Trial of the Major War Criminals Before the International Military Tribunal* (Blue Set), vol. 4 (Nuremberg, 1947), 458–60, https://avalon.law.yale.edu/imt/01-07-46.asp#zelewski.
123. Hürter, *Hitlers Heerführer*, 579; Ueberschär and Wette, *"Unternehmen Barbarossa,"* 339–44.
124. Dennis Deletant, *Hitler's Forgotten Ally: Ion Antonescu and His Regime, Romania 1940–44* (London and New York, 2006), 79–83; Hanebrink, *A Specter Haunting Europe*, 136–38.
125. Deletant, *Hitler's Forgotten Ally*, 116–17. The Romanian Conducător reiterated these points in a public response to a Romanian-Jewish community leader who had implored him to stop the pogroms against Romania's Jews: "Your Jews, who have become Soviet commissars, are driving Soviet soldiers in the Odessa region into a futile bloodbath, through horrendous terror techniques as the Russian prisoners themselves have admitted, simply to cause us heavy losses." The entire Jewish community of Romania, Antonescu insisted, bore responsibility for the Romanian deaths near Odessa. Jean Ancel, *The History of the Holocaust in Romania* (Lincoln, NE, 2011), 335.
126. According to date given in A. A. Kruglov et al., *Kholokost v Ukraine: Reikhskomissariat "Ukraina," gubernatorstvo "Transnistriia"* (Dnipro, 2016), 442, 95,000 Jews remained in

Odessa. Radu Ioanid estimates that one third of the three hundred thousand Jews who lived in the Odessa region on the eve of the Axis invasion were able to evacuate. Ioanid, *The Holocaust in Romania: The Destruction of Jews and Roma under the Antonescu Regime, 1940–1944* (London, 2022), 330–31.

127. Jean Ancel, *Transnistria, 1941–1942: The Romanian Mass Murder Campaigns*, vol. 1 (Tel Aviv, 2003), 217; Kruglov et al., *Kholokost v Ukraine*, 387–82.
128. Kruglov et al., *Kholokost v Ukraine*, 382, counts seventy-nine soldiers killed and thirteen missing.
129. Kruglov et al., *Kholokost v Ukraine*, 382–84; see also Deletant, *Hitler's Forgotten Ally*, 171–72.
130. Ancel, *Transnistria, 1941–1942*, vol. 1, 189–90, 193–94, 200–203.
131. Deletant, *Hitler's Forgotten Ally*, 176–77.
132. Deletant, *Hitler's Forgotten Ally*, 181; Ancel, *Transnistria, 1941–1942*, vol. 1, 133–34.
133. Ioanid, *The Holocaust in Romania*, 349–50; "Odessa," Holocaust Encyclopedia, https://encyclopedia.ushmm.org/content/en/article/odessa.
134. Gustav Roos, letter to Anton Roos, August 6, 1941, https://jugend1918-1945.de/portal/ARCHIV/thema.aspx?bereich=archiv&root=9898&id=9898&redir.
135. "Die Rettung Deutschlands vor dem Ansturm des Untermenschentums," *Mitteilungen für die Truppe*, no. 136 (September 1941): 1.
136. Rüdiger Overmans, *Deutsche militärische Verluste im Zweiten Weltkrieg* (Munich, 1999), 238–39, 279; idem, Menschenverluste der Wehrmacht an der "Ostfront," http://www.dokst.de/main/sites/default/files/dateien/texte/Overmans.pdf, 3–4, 8. The losses at the Eastern Front made up 99 percent of Germany's overall military casualties.
137. *Meldungen aus dem Reich*, vol. 8, 2,787–88; G. F. Krivosheev, *Velikaia Otechestvennaia bez grifa sekretnosti* (Moscow, 2010), 60.
138. Martin Broszat, Hans Buchheim, Hans-Adolf Jacobsen, and Helmut Krausnick, *Anatomie des SS-Staates* (Munich, 1967), 509. Earlier in September, the Wehrmacht had undertaken the unprecedented step of dropping 160 million flyers over enemy trenches. The leaflets appealed to Red Army soldiers, in Russian, to "Strike the Yid-Commisar, His mug shouts out for a brick!" The campaign's disappointing results were one reason why commanders asked to rescind the commissar order. Hartmann, *Wehrmacht im Ostkrieg*, 511; Buchbender, *Das tönende Erz*, 98, 100 (with an illustration of the flyer).
139. *Hitler: Monologe im Führerhauptquartier* 61 (September 17, 1941); *Die Tagebücher von Joseph Goebbels*, Teil 2, *Diktate 1941–1945, Bd. 1. Juli–September 1941*, ed. Elke Fröhlich (Munich, 1998), 260–61 (entry for August 19, 1941).
140. Domarus, *Hitler: Reden und Proklamationen*, 1,764–65.
141. Jochmann, *Monologe*, 106–8. Hitler made this declaration as he recalled Himmler's August 1 order to pacify the Pripyat area by driving Jewish women into the swamps.
142. Adolf Hitler, "Ansprache im Münchener Löwenbräukeller zur Erinnerung an den Marsch auf die Feldherrnhalle 1923," in *Judenverfolgung und jüdisches Leben unter den Bedingungen der nationalsozialistischen Gewaltherrschaft, vol. 1: Tondokumente und Rundfunksendungen, 1930–1946*, ed. Walter Roller and Susanne Höschel (Potsdam, 1996), 199–200.
143. On the marking and registering of Jews on orders of Wehrmacht administrative commands, see Yitzhak Arad, *The Holocaust in the Soviet Union* (Lincoln, NE, and Jerusalem, 2009), 96–97.
144. *The Einsatzgruppen Reports*, 236 (November 14, 1941).
145. Anton Roos, letter to Elisabeth Roos, October 12, 1941, https://jugend1918-1945.de/portal/ARCHIV/thema.aspx?bereich=archiv&root=9898&id=9898&redir.
146. Anton Roos, letter to Elisabeth Roos, October 12, 1941. Roos's letters were pedagogical in part: as he lectured his wife and sons about Germany's world historical struggle against "Jewish Bolshevism," he sought to combat the war-weariness that he felt had taken grip of parts of German society, including his wife. As he wrote to her on September 13, 1941, "for woe unto Europe if this rabble of plutocrats and Bolsheviks were to

win. This constant whining certainly doesn't make our life on the front easier, and I don't want to hear any more of this nonsense from you."

147. Mattner's reference to the collective sentiment among his police unit further suggests that his lethal fantasies were widely shared among members of Police Battalion 322. Gerlach, *Kalkulierte Morde*, 589.

Chapter 4: A Violence Shaking Europe

1. *Die "Ereignismeldungen UdSSR" 1941: Dokumente der Einsatzgruppen in der Sowjel*, ed. Klaus-Michael Mallmann, Andrej Angrick, Jürgen Matthäus, Martin Cüp (2011), 43, 52, 55.
2. Mallmann et al., ed., *Die "Ereignismeldungen UdSSR" 1941*, 50 (June 26, 1941), 64 (July 2, 1941). A Sipo-SD report noted: "Increased communist agitation in the industrial centers. At the steel plant in Hayingen, alongside the hammer and sickle symbol, the slogans 'Cheers for Moscow!' 'Down with Germany!' and 'Moscow must triumph!' were added in red print." *Meldungen aus dem Reich. Die geheimen Lageberichte des Sicherheitsdienstes der SS, 1938–1945*, vol. 8, ed. Heinz Boberach (Herrsching, 1984), 2,706–7.
3. Mallmann et al., ed., *Die "Ereignismeldungen UdSSR" 1941*, 48.
4. Ahlrich Meyer, ". . . dass französische Verhältnisse anders sind als polnische." Die Bekämpfung des Widerstands durch die deutsche Militärverwaltung in Frankreich 1941," in *Repression and Kriegsverbrechen. Die Bekämpfung von Widerstands- and Partisanenbewegungen gegen die deutsche Besatzung in West- und Südeuropa*, eds. Guus Mershoeck, et al. (Berlin, 1997), 43–91 (53). On anti-Semitism in Belgium, see Saul Friedländer, *The Years of Extermination: Nazi Germany and the Jews, 1939–1945* (New York, 2006), 259.
5. Walter Manoschek, "*Serbien ist judenfrei." Militärische Besatzungspolitik und Judenvernichtung in Serbien, 1941–42* (Munich, 1993), 46.
6. Manoschek, "*Serbien ist judenfrei*," 44; Mallmann et al., ed., *Die "Ereignismeldungen UdSSR" 1941*, 200 (July 29, 1941).
7. Browning, *The Origins of the Final Solution*, 263.
8. *Nazi Conspiracy and Aggression*, ed. Office of United States Chief of Counsel for Prosecution of Axis Criminality, vol. 6 (Washington, DC, 1946), 961 (emphasis in the original). Ulrich Herbert, "Die deutsche Militärverwaltung in Paris und die Deportation der französischen Juden," in *Von der Aufgabe der Freiheit: Politische Verantwortung und bürgerliche Gesellschaft im 19. und 20. Jahrhundert*, eds. Christian Jansen et al. (Berlin, 1995), 427–50 (437).
9. Mallmann et al., ed., *Die "Ereignismeldungen UdSSR" 1941*, 92 (July 8, 1941).
10. Mallmann et al., ed., *Die "Ereignismeldungen UdSSR" 1941*, 421 (September 9, 1941); Browning, *The Origins of the Final Solution*, 334–37.
11. Browning, *The Origins of the Final Solution*, 323; Manoschek, "*Serbien ist judenfrei*," 103.
12. Mallmann et al., ed., *Die "Ereignismeldungen UdSSR" 1941*, 317 (August 20, 1941). The report blamed "Jewish incitement" for the demonstration.
13. Friedländer, *The Years of Extermination*, 174–75, 257.
14. Christopher Neumaier, "The Escalation of German Reprisal Policy in Occupied France, 1941–42," *Journal of Contemporary History* 41, no. 1 (2006): 113–31 (116–17).
15. The assassination attempt was likely carried out by Communist youth, many of them sons and daughters of immigrants from Poland and Russia. Their actions formed an important but rarely acknowledged early chapter of the French Resistance. Meyer, ". . . dass französische Verhältnisse anders sind als polnische," 44, 50.
16. *Nazi Conspiracy and Aggression*, vol. 6, 961–63 (Document C-148), emphasis in the original. Today, Keitel's order is mostly known under the name *Sühnebefehl* ("Reprisal Order").

17. As much as the entire order, this sentence was squarely aimed at the Balkans. "Life in the Balkans counts for nothing" appears to have been a popular saying among Germans serving in Serbia. Browning, *The Origins of the Final Solution*, 335–36.
18. Manoschek, "*Serbien ist judenfrei*," 84–86.
19. Mallmann et al., ed., *Die "Ereignismeldungen UdSSR" 1941*, 656 (October 9, 1941).
20. Christopher Browning, "Wehrmacht Reprisal Policy and the Mass Murder of Jews in Serbia," *Militärgeschichtliche Mitteilungen* 31 (1983), 31–47.
21. Mallmann et al., ed., *Die "Ereignismeldungen UdSSR" 1941*, 666n1. The letter was dated October 17, 1941.
22. Browning, "Wehrmacht Reprisal Policy."
23. Meyer, ". . . dass französische Verhältnisse anders sind als polnische," 52–53, 60–61, 73; Herbert, Die deutsche Militärverwaltung in Paris, 430, 438–39, 446.
24. Meyer, ". . . dass französische Verhältnisse anders sind als polnische," 60–61; Neumaier, "The Escalation of German Reprisal Policy in Occupied France," 123–24.
25. *Meldungen aus dem Reich*, vol. 7, 2,505 (July 10, 1941).
26. *The Jews in the Secret Nazi Reports on Popular Opinion in Germany, 1933–1945*, eds. Otto Dov Kulka and Eberhard Jäckel (New Haven, 2010), 533–34.
27. *Die Tagebücher von Joseph Goebbels*, part 2, vol. 1, 254 (August 18, 1941).
28. Bernhard Lösener, "Das Reichsministerium des Innern und die Judengesetzgebung," *Vierteljahreshefte für Zeitgeschichte* 9/3 (1961): 262–313 (302–3). Lösener was the Interior Ministry expert in question; he recalled the meeting after the war.
29. *Die Tagebücher von Joseph Goebbels*, part 2, vol. 1, 260–61 (entry for August 19, 1941).
30. *Die Tagebücher von Joseph Goebbels*, part 2, vol. 1, 269 (entry for August 19, 1941).
31. *Die Tagebücher von Joseph Goebbels*, part 2, vol. 1, 265–66 (entry for August 19, 1941).
32. "Polizeiverordnung über die Kennzeichnung der Juden vom 1. September 1941," *Reichsgesetzblatt* (government gazette), http://www.verfassungen.de/de33-45/juden41.htm.
33. "Juden nur mit Judenstern!," *Völkischer Beobachter*, September 13, 1941, 1–2.
34. "Juden jetzt mit Judenstern!," *Der Angriff*, September 14, 1941, 2. The article appeared at the bottom of the page. Neither *Der Angriff* nor *Völkischer Beobachter* mentioned the marking decree in subsequent issues.
35. Browning, *The Origins of the Final Solution*, 325–26.
36. Browning, *The Origins of the Final Solution*, 324; Friedländer, *The Years of Extermination*, 264.
37. David Stahel, *Kiev 1941: Hitler's Battle for Supremacy in the East* (Cambridge, 2012), 229.
38. *Die Tagebücher von Joseph Goebbels*, part 2, vol. 1, 481. Hitler evidently did not take into account the effectiveness of the Soviet evacuation effort in those areas deep inside the Soviet Union where officials had had time to prepare the retreat. By the time German troops reached Kharkov and the coal mines of the Donbas, most of the industrial assets there were gone or destroyed.
39. *Die Tagebücher von Joseph Goebbels*, part 2, vol. 1, 481–82. Hitler had talked about erasing Moscow and Leningrad from the face of the earth already in July 1941. See Ueberschär and Wette, "*Unternehmen Barbarossa*," 332–33.
40. *Die Tagebücher von Joseph Goebbels*, part 2, vol. 1, 485 (September 24, 1941). Browning, *The Origins of the Final Solution*, 326.
41. *Die Tagebücher von Joseph Goebbels*, part 2, vol. 1, 480–81 (September 24, 1941).
42. Victor Klemperer, *I Shall Bear Witness: The Diaries of Victor Klemperer, 1933–41. Abridged and Translated from the German Edition by Martin Chalmers* (London, 1998), 410 (September 8, 1941). A cousin of the conductor Otto Klemperer, Victor Klemperer was born into a Jewish family in 1881 but converted to Protestantism as an adult. Nonetheless, the Nazis stamped him a Jew.
43. Klemperer, *I Shall Bear Witness*, 410–11 (September 15, 1941), emphasis in the original. The passage on Himmler and the SS is not in the abridged English edition of the diary. See Victor Klemperer, "*Ich will Zeugnis ablegen bis zum letzten*," *Tagebücher 1933–1945*, vol. 1, ed. Walter Nowojski (Berlin, 1995), 663–64. It is true that Klemperer and many

other Jews throughout German-occupied Europe understood that Nazi victory would entail their demise and secretly, or not so secretly, wished for Germany's war effort to falter. On July 14, 1941, Klemperer wrote: "The dreaded Sunday special announcement came and exceeded all expectations. Stalin Line [i.e., fortifications along the prewar Soviet border with Poland] taken, in the south considerable forward advance from Romania. . . . Emphasis, and rightly so, evidently, that the war against Russia has been decided, that Hitler can carry on the war for years, that he is invincible master of the whole continent. Asia will be added to Europe. For us in a personal sense that means slavery until the end of our lives. Very depressed evening." Klemperer, *I Shall Bear Witness*, 401. See also *Die Verfolgung und Ermordung der europäischen Juden durch das nationalsozialistische Deutschland, 1933–1945, Bd. 4: Polen, September 1939–Juli 1941*, ed. Klaus-Peter Friedrich (Munich, 2011), 55–56.

44. Klemperer, *I Shall Bear Witness*, 414–15 (September 18, 1941).
45. Klemperer, *I Shall Bear Witness*, 435–36 (December 31, 1941).
46. Klemperer, *I Shall Bear Witness*, 430 (December 17, 1941), emphasis in the original.
47. Klemperer, *I Shall Bear Witness*, 421 (October 25, 1941).
48. Klemperer, *I Shall Bear Witness*, 426 (November 24, 1941).
49. Friedländer, *The Years of Extermination*, 252–55; Howard K. Smith, *Last Train from Berlin* (London, 1942), 143–44, 196–98.
50. *Die Tagebücher von Joseph Goebbels*, part 2, vol. 2, 194 (October 28, 1941).
51. *Die Tagebücher von Joseph Goebbels*, part 2, vol. 2, 188 (October 27, 1941).
52. *Die Tagebücher von Joseph Goebbels*, part 2, vol. 2, 188 (October 27, 1941).
53. Yitzhak Arad, *The Holocaust in the Soviet Union* (Lincoln, NE, and Jerusalem, 2009), 153–54; Friedländer, *The Years of Extermination*, 266–67. The killings in the Minsk Ghetto are described in greater detail in chapter 5.
54. *"Existiert das Ghetto noch?" Weißrussland: Jüdisches Überleben gegen nationalsozialistische Herrschaft*, ed. Projektgruppe Belarus im Jugendclub Courage Köln e.V. (Berlin, 2003), 214; NA IRI RAN, f. 2, razd. VI, op. 15, d. 13, Maizles, 174.
55. Michael Wildt, *An Uncompromising Generation: The Nazi Leadership of the Reich Security Main Office* (Madison, WI, 2009), 312.
56. Christoph Dieckmann, *Deutsche Besatzungspolitik in Litauen, 1941–1944*, vol. 2 (Göttingen, 2011), 959–64.
57. Andrew Ezergailis, *The Holocaust in Latvia, 1941–1944: The Missing Center* (Riga and Washington, DC, 1996), 255; Andrej Angrick and Peter Klein, *Die "Endlösung" in Riga: Ausbeutung und Vernichtung, 1941–1944* (Darmstadt, 2006), 146–47. These Jews from Berlin were the first to die in the Rumbula forest massacre, where SS commandos killed twenty-five thousand Jews over the course of two days.
58. Peter Longerich, *Heinrich Himmler* (Oxford, year), 550.
59. *Die Tagebücher von Joseph Goebbels*, part 2, vol. 2, 498–99 (December 13, 1941).
60. Christian Gerlach, "Die Wannsee-Konferenz, das Schicksal der deutschen Juden und Hitlers politische Grundsatzentscheidung, alle Juden Europas zu ermorden," in idem, *Krieg, Ernährung, Völkermord. Forschungen zur deutschen Vernichtungspolitik im Zweiten Weltkrieg* (Hamburg, 1998), 85–166 (117); Friedländer, *The Years of Extermination*, 280. The vertical drawn by Himmler seems to have functioned as a hyphen or equal sign.
61. For this and further references to the conference, see the facsimile of surviving conference protocol, https://www.ghwk.de/fileadmin/user_upload/pdf-wannsee/dokumente/protokoll-januar1942_barrierefrei.pdf. English translation from Wannsee Protocol, The Avalon Project, January 20, 1942, https://avalon.law.yale.edu/imt/wannsee.asp.
62. *Protektoratni politika Reinharda Heydricha*, eds. Miroslav Karny et al. (Prague, 1991), 220 (Document 61); *Tagesordnung: Judenmord. Die Wannsee-Konferenz am 20. Januar 1942; eine Dokumentation zur Organisation der "Endlösung,"* ed. Kurt Pätzold and Erika Schwarz (Berlin, 1992), 131; *Der "Generalplan Ost." Hauptlinien der nationalsozialistischen Planungs- und Vernichtungspolitik*, ed. Mechthild Rössler et al. (Berlin, 1993), 38n116, 40n130.

63. Several attendees suggested dispensing with deportations and killing Jews directly in the areas of their present settlement but doing so discreetly to avoid "disquiet among the population." *Tagesordnung: Judenmord*, 92–93; see also Gerlach, *Wannsee*, 132, 145.
64. Christoph Kivelitz, *Die Propagandaausstellung in europäischen Diktaturen* (Bochum, 1999), 214–15.
65. "Die 9 Millimeter-Kur," *Der Angriff*, July 20, 1941, 1–2; see also "Stalin lässt die Bluthunde los" ("Stalin Lets Loose the Bloodhounds"), *Der Angriff*, July 18, 1941, 2.
66. These plans included "Operation Hunger," composed by Herbert Backe, state secretary in the Reich Ministry of Food and Agriculture, as well as "Plan Oldenburg," also known as the Green Folder, which was worked out under Göring's aegis. Wigbert Benz, *Der Hungerplan im "Unternehmen Barbarossa" 1941* (Berlin, 2011); Der "Generalplan Ost."
67. Ezergailis, *The Holocaust in Latvia*, 241. In Soviet captivity und under interrogation, Jeckeln stated in December 1945 that the campaign against Bolshevism was essential to the political training of his SS men. *Verhört. Die Befragungen deutscher Generale und Offiziere durch die sowjetischen Geheimdienste 1945–1952*, ed. Vasilij Stepanowitsch Christoforow et al. (Berlin, 2015), 237. The exhibition catalogue of the Hamburg exhibition on the "Crimes of the Wehrmacht" contains eighty German amateur photographs that make references to the "shot in the nape of the neck," suggesting that the supposed Bolshevik killing method was a cliché in German thinking at the time. *Verbrechen der Wehrmacht. Dimensionen des Vernichtungskrieges 1941 bis 1944* (Hamburg, 2021), 202–10.
68. Ezergailis, *The Holocaust in Latvia*, 240–45, 249–56. Friedländer, *The Years of Extermination*, 261–62; Angrick and Klein, *Die "Endlösung" in Riga*, 140.
69. These were Heydrich's *Einsatzbefehle* 8 and 9, passed on July 17 and 21, 1941, and reprinted in Overmans, Hilger, and Polian, ed., *Rotarmisten in deutscher Hand*, 33–34. At least 38,000 Soviet soldiers were selected for killing over the course of summer and fall 1941. Reinhard Otto, *Wehrmacht, Gestapo und sowjetische Kriegsgefangene im deutschen Reichsgebiet, 1941–42* (Munich, 1998), 268. Alfred Streim gives a documented minimum number of 140,000 by 1945, adding that the real figures were probably much higher, Alfred Streim, *Die Behandlung sowjetischer Kriegsgefangener im "Fall Barbarossa." Eine Dokumentation* (Heidelberg, 1981), 244. Using much more restrictive search criteria, Felix Römer concludes that not more than 10,000 Soviet political commissars had been executed under the terms of the Commissar Order. His calculation is based on the discovery of 3,430 confirmed executions, and extrapolation from other areas where German military records were less detailed and complete. See Felix Römer, *Der Kommissarbefehl: Wehrmacht und NS-Verbrechen an der Ostfront 1941/42* (Paderborn, 2008), 359, 367.
70. Nikolaus Wachsmann, *KL: A History of the Nazi Concentration Camps* (New York, 2015), 261.
71. Wachsmann, *KL*, 262.
72. The apparatus is described in many studies, but none of them remark on its intended nod to the "Bolshevik commissar." *Mord und Massenmord im Konzentrationslager Sachsenhausen, 1936–1945*, ed. Günter Morsch (Berlin, 2005), 55–57; Wachsmann, *KL*, 262–65; Stefanie Endlich, Heike Ponwitz, *Der Massenmord an sowjetischen Kriegsgefangenen im Konzentrationslager Sachsenhausen. Ein Kunstwerk erinnert* (Berlin, 2012).
73. Description of apparatus taken from deposition by former camp commander Anton Kaidl at the Sachsenhausen trial in 1947, http://isurvived.org/Lustig_Oliver-CCDictionary/CCD-05_FG.html#B4.
74. Alexander Elfenbein's account, cited in Donal O'Sullivan, *Furcht und Faszination. Deutsche und britische Russlandbilder, 1921–1933* (Cologne, 1996), 71.
75. Goebbels's diaries for fall 1941 are replete with references to the "Bolshevik shot in the neck." His use of the term was not only to demonize the Soviet regime, but clearly also a matter of belief. *Die Tagebücher von Joseph Goebbels*, part 2, vol. 1, 432, 436, 462, 489.
76. Endlich and Ponwitz, *Der Massenmord*, 31, 40.
77. Wachsmann, *KL*, 272.

78. As prosecutors at the postwar trial of former Sachsenhausen camp guards established, participants in the shootings received decorations and were sent to Italy for a vacation, *Todeslager Sachsenhausen. Ein Dokumentarbericht vom Sachsenhausen-Prozeß* (Berlin, 1948), 31.
79. Overmans, Hilger, and Polian, ed., *Rotarmisten in deutscher Hand*, 359; Alfred Streim, *Die Behandlung sowjetischer Kriegsgefangener im "Fall Barbarossa." Eine Dokumentation* (Heidelberg, 1981), 232–33.
80. Endlich and Ponwitz, *Der Massenmord*, 9, 38, 41.
81. Endlich and Ponwitz, *Der Massenmord*, 47. "Russian Action," *Todeslager Sachsenhausen*, 31.
82. Endlich and Ponwitz, *Der Massenmord*, 48–57, with excerpts from: Emil Büge, *1470 KZ-Geheimnisse. Heimliche Aufzeichnungen aus der Politischen Abteilung des KZ Sachsenhausen, Dezember 1939 bis April 1943* (Berlin, 2010).
83. Wachsmann, *KL*, 265.
84. Wachsmann, *KL*, 265–67; Christian Streit, *Keine Kameraden. Die Wehrmacht und die sowjetischen Kriegsgefangenen*, 1941–1945, new ed. (Bonn, 1991), 94.
85. *Nazi Mass Murder: A Documentary History of the Use of Poison Gas*, ed. Eugen Kogon et al. (New Haven, 1993), 26, 40–51; Danuta Czech, *Kalendarium der Ereignisse im Konzentrationslager Auschwitz-Birkenau, 1939–1945* (Reinbek, 1989), 105–6.
86. Rudolf Hoess, *Commandant of Auschwitz: The Autobiography of Rudolf Hoess* (Cleveland and New York, 1959), 162
87. Hoess, *Commandant of Auschwitz*, 162. According to German records, 8,320 Soviet POWs died or were executed in Auschwitz between October 7, 1941, and February 28, 1942. Streim, *Die Behandlung sowjetischer Kriegsgefangener*, 226.
88. Kogon et al., ed., *Nazi Mass Murder*, 54.
89. Kogon et al., ed., *Nazi Mass Murder*, 52–72.
90. Wachsmann, *KL*, 278. In October, the Reichsführer-SS received a letter from a retired army doctor who offered his unprompted thoughts about what to do with the Soviet POWs in German captivity. The doctor extolled the "bright perspectives opening up by the possibility alone that three million Bolsheviks, at present prisoners of war in German hands, could be sterilized and thus be at our disposal as workers, without any possibility to multiply." He suggested a drug extracted from a South American plant that had been tested on mice and rats and could sterilize humans without their knowledge. See Irena Strzelecka, "Experiments," in *Auschwitz, 1940–1945: Central Issues in the History of the Camp*, vol. 2, eds. Wacław Długoborski and Franciszek Piper (Oświęcim, 2000), 347–69 (348). See also Raul Hilberg, *The Destruction of the European Jews* (New Haven, 2003), 1,006–7. The physician's name was Dr. Adolf Pokorny.
91. Strzelecka, "Experiments," 284.
92. Streit, *Keine Kameraden*, 95.
93. Wachsmann, *KL*, 295.
94. "Vichy," in *Enzyklopädie jüdischer Geschichte und Kultur*, Bd 6: Te–Z (2015), 286.
95. Wachsmann, *KL*, 298.
96. *Die Tagebücher von Joseph Goebbels*, Teil 1, Bd. 9, 430; Hanebrink, *A Specter Haunting Europe*, 147–48; Lorna Waddington, *Hitler's Crusade: Bolshevism and the Myth of the International Jewish Conspiracy* (London, 2007), 187–93.
97. Waddington, *Hitler's Crusade*, 201–2; Rainer Rutz: *Signal. Eine deutsche Auslandsillustrierte als Propagandainstrument im Zweiten Weltkrieg* (Essen, 2007), 10.
98. Hanebrink, *A Specter Haunting Europe*, 149.
99. Dominique Rossignol, *Histoire de la propagande en France de 1940 à 1944* (1991), 279. The Nazi campaign to draw Europe into a common front against Bolshevism met with an enthusiastic response: By December 1941 more than forty-three thousand volunteers from across Europe were fighting in the Soviet Union on the side of the Wehrmacht. Waddington, *Hitler's Crusade*, 201–2; Rolf-Dieter Müller, *The Unknown Eastern Front: The Wehrmacht and Hitler's Foreign Soldiers* (London, 2014), 255.

100. *Die Tagebücher von Joseph Goebbels*, part 2, vol. 1, 267 (August 19, 1941).
101. Overmans, Hilger, and Polian, ed., *Rotarmisten in deutscher Hand*, 664–65; *Die Tagebücher von Joseph Goebbels*, part 2, vol. 1, 315 (entry for August 27, 1941). For Wochenschau footage of one of the tours, see www.youtube.com/watch?v=qVjgdkouZt8.
102. Rosemarie Burgstaller, *Inszenierung des Hasses. Feindbildausstellungen im Nationalsozialismus* (Frankfurt, 2022), 412–63; Kivelitz, *Die Propagandaausstellung in europäischen Diktaturen*, 228–29; *Das Sowjetparadies* (dir. Friedrich Albat), an eponymous propaganda film with footage from the Eastern Front, was also released in 1942 and shown at the Berlin exhibition. Burgstaller, *Inszenierung des Hasses*, 437–38.
103. The dugouts on display at the exhibition were likely shelters that had been built by bombed-out Minsk residents after the German attack.
104. *Das Sowjetparadies: Ausstellung der Reichspropagandaleitung der NSDAP. Ein Bericht in Wort und Bild* (Berlin, 1942), 29. Kivelitz, *Die Propagandaaustellung*, 228–33.
105. *Das Sowjetparadies*, 32.
106. *Das Sowjetparadies*, 29. A 1942 book publication complemented the exhibition: *In den Kerkern der G.P.U. Tatsachenberichte aus der Sowjetunion*, ed. Karl Baumböck (Berlin, 1942).
107. Burgstaller, *Inszenierung des Hasses*, 456.
108. Smith, *Last Train from Berlin*, 107–8.
109. Günter Morsch, ed., *Mord und Massenmord im Konzentrationslager Sachsenhausen*, 191–200.
110. Tony Paterson, "Archive Reveals Full Horror of Hitler's Executioners," *The Independent*, May 18, 2006, https://www.independent.co.uk/news/world/europe/archive-reveals-full-horror-of-hitlers-executioners-478602.html.
111. Herf, *The Jewish Enemy*, 169.

Chapter 5: Jews and Bolsheviks, Step Forward!

1. NA IRI RAN, f. 2, razd. VI, op. 22, d. 2, Mints. Maks Mints was interviewed by members of the [Isaak] Mints Commission in Moscow in November 1945.
2. Maks Mints: "Ochen' trudno nesti bremia, mnogo prevoskhodiashchee tvoi sily," https://memorial.krsk.ru/memuar/K/Kasabova/08/07.htm.
3. NA IRI RAN, f. 2, razd. VI, op. 22, d. 2, Mints.
4. Jochen Hellbeck, *Revolution on My Mind: Writing a Diary Under Stalin* (Cambridge, MA, 2006), 13–14.
5. Even amid the catastrophic conditions of fall 1941, the Red Army performed counterstrikes that proved vital in stopping the German drive toward Moscow. David Stahel, *Operation Barbarossa and Germany's Defeat in the East* (Cambridge, 2010), 159, 170, 205, 209, and passim; David M. Glantz and Jonathan M. House, *When Titans Clashed: How the Red Army Stopped Hitler* (Lawrence, KS, 2015), 85.
6. NARB, 750-P-1-112, Berestovskii.
7. NA IRI RAN, f. 2, razd. VI, op. 8, d. 9, Barutchev.
8. S. Anvaer, *Krovotochit moia pamiat': Iz zapisok studentki medichki* (Moscow, 2005), 13–18.
9. Aron Shneer, *Plen. Sovetskie voennoplennye v Germanii 1941–1945* (Moscow, 2005), 439.
10. Shneer, *Plen*, 430–32.
11. NA IRI RAN, f. 2, razd. VI, op. 10, d. 13, Sviridovskii.
12. *Tsena pobedy. Rossiiskie shkol'niki o voine* (Moscow, 2005), 348–50. Kalimov wrote his memoir in 1946.
13. Gerlach, *Kalkulierte Morde*, 781–88 (782); Shneer cites a camp commander who prescribed mildness toward the Soviet prisoners because he had two sons who were fighting at the Eastern Front and feared Soviet reprisals for how the Germans mistreated captured Red Army soldiers. Shneer, *Plen*, 176.
14. *Rotarmisten in deutscher Hand: Dokumente zu Gefangenschaft, Repatriierung und Rehabilitierung sowjetischer Soldaten des Zweiten Weltkrieges*, ed. Rüdinger Overmans, Andreas Hilger, and Pavel Polian (Paderborn, 2012), 497.

15. Christian Streit, *Keine Kameraden. Die Wehrmacht und die sowjetischen Kriegsgefangenen*, 1941–1945, new ed. (Bonn, 1991), 79.
16. Laurence Rees, director, *War of the Century: When Hitler Fought Stalin* (BBC, 1999), ep. 1, 1999.
17. NA IRI RAN, f. 2, razd. VI, op. 15, d. 23, Taits.
18. Streit, *Keine Kameraden*, 143–44.
19. A German camp commander complained in January 1942 about the detrimental quality of the food given to Soviet POWs. What drove him were not humanitarian motives, but considerations of efficiency: "the Russians" had to be better fed to perform the grueling work expected of them. Overmans, Hilger, and Polian, ed., *Rotarmisten in deutscher Hand*, 511, 557.
20. Ueberschär and Wette, "*Unternehmen Barbarossa*," 351–54.
21. At the time of the German invasion the Soviet Government had not officially acceded to the Hague Conventions of 1899 and 1907 on the rules of warfare. But, as Soviet lawyers and politicians had pointed out already before the war, these legal acts merely codified laws and customs that were universally recognized, including by the Soviet Union. Four weeks into the war, the Soviet government proclaimed its adherence, effective immediately, to the letter of the Hague Convention. Germany declared the Soviet note invalid. Molotov's note of November 25, 1941 (discussed in chapter 6) reiterated the Soviet commitment to treating captured Axis soldiers in accordance with the principles of the Hague Convention. George Ginsburgs, "Laws of War and War Crimes on the Russian Front During World War II: The Soviet View," *Soviet Studies* 11, no. 3 (1960): 253–85; Shneer, *Plen*, 173–74.
22. Reinecke's instructions and the exchange between Canaris and Keitel are reprinted in Wette and Ueberschär, "*Unternehmen Barbarossa*," 355–57.
23. NA IRI RAN, f. 2, razd. VI, op. 8, d. 9, Barutchev.
24. Streit, *Keine Kameraden*, 130–37, 244–49, 268–72.
25. Shneer, *Plen*, 194–96.
26. B. N. Sokolov, *V plenu* (St. Petersburg, 2000), 49. Such racializing shots of accused "cannibals" had a long colonial prehistory. Already in the First World War, German propaganda featured mug shots of captured colonial French soldiers, indicting them of cannibalism and seeking to expose as a lie French and British claims that they were fighting Germany "in the name of culture." Paul Schreckenbach, *Der Weltbrand. Illustrierte Geschichte aus großer Zeit mit zusammenhängendem Text*, vol. 1 (Leipzig, 1919), 159.
27. Letter of October 9, 1941, cited in *Befehle und Erklärungen der Nazi-Kriegsverbrecher über die Erschießungen der Juden in Russland in 1941–43*, ed. Tuviah Friedman (Haifa, 1959), Mattner file, 2.
28. Shneer, *Plen*, 434.
29. On Soviet women serving with the Red Army, see Roger Markwick and Euridice Cardona, *Soviet Women on the Frontline in the Second World War* (London and New York, 2012); *Mascha, Nina und Katjuscha: Frauen in der Roten Armee, 1941–1945*, ed. Claudia Freytag and Peter Jahn (Berlin, 2002).
30. Felix Römer, "Gewaltsame Geschlechterordnung. Wehrmacht und 'Flintenweiber' an der Ostfront 1941–42," in *Soldatinnen: Gewalt und Geschlecht im Krieg vom Mittelalter bis heute*, ed. Klaus Latzel, Franka Maubach, and Silke Satjukow (Paderborn, 2011), 331–51 (335).
31. From the caption of a propaganda photograph of captured female Soviet soldiers dated September 15, 1941, BArch, Bild 183-L20140, https://www.bild.bundesarchiv.de. *Flintenweib* made it into an edition of *Meyers Lexikon* where they were described as "contradicting the task ordained by nature to women to be mothers and keeper of the nation, and leading to such a moral coarsening and to atrocities such as were previously considered impossible among cultured nations." *Mascha, Nina und Katjuscha*, 53; *Meyers Lexikon*, Bd. 4, 1938.
32. Cited in *Mascha, Nina und Katjuscha*, 52 (with illustration), 59.

33. Ground level reports issued by the troops confirm that these orders were enacted. Römer, "Gewaltsame Geschlechterordnung," 336–37. Walther von Reichenau's infamous October 10, 1941, order spelled out the immediate shooting of "degenerate women" found among Soviet POWs, https://phdn.org/archives/www.ess.uwe.ac.uk/genocide/USSR2.htm.
34. Anton Roos, letter to Elisabeth Roos, August 11, 1941; see also *Mascha, Nina und Katjuscha*, 56, 63.
35. A portrait shot of the captured woman was published in the 1942 SS picture book, *Der Untermensch*, where it was used as a contrasting foil to a smiling young blond woman dressed in folkloric garb. The captions to the two photos read: "May fate spare us this type!" and "Women of this kind shall become the mothers of Europe," *Der Untermensch*, ed. Der Reichsführer-SS, SS-Hauptamt (Berlin, 1942), 15–16.
36. Overmans, Hilger, and Polian, ed., *Rotarmisten in deutscher Hand*, 341–43 ("Sichtung, Aussonderung"). An OKH order of July 24, 1941, grouped "Asiatics (racially defined), Jews, and German-speaking Russians" in the same category. Russians who spoke German were presumed to be Bolshevik activists and emissaries of the Comintern. *Rotarmisten in deutscher Hand*, 343.
37. Solveig Grothe, "Unter dem Gras," *Spiegel Geschichte* 3-2022 (May 23, 2022), https://www.spiegel.de/geschichte/kriegsgefangenenlager-in-sandbostel-archaeologen-suchen-nach-spuren-von-damals-a-5617e885-0002-0001-0000-000204216454.
38. Overmans, Hilger, and Polian, ed., *Rotarmisten in deutscher Hand*, 393, 404.
39. The analysis was stereotypical: to confirm his observations, the author cited a recent publication from *Völkischer Beobachter*. In conclusion to his report, the Nazi visitor gleefully expounded on the unique possibilities that the Soviet prisoner population held for advancing scholarship in race, ethnology, and Bolshevism. He recommended that researchers spend 10 days per camp, along with the requisite tools—"measuring instruments, cameras, etc." Overmans, Hilger, and Polian, ed., *Rotarmisten in deutscher Hand*, 676–81. Early Soviet culture had indeed marginalized Russian national culture, to mitigate minorities' fears of Russian "chauvinism." Ethnic Russians were to identify as Soviet citizens and sing Soviet songs, while member of minority nations, including Ukrainians, were encouraged to express themselves in ethnic terms. Germany's invasion catalyzed a countertrend: Soviet Russians' proud identification with Russian history and culture.
40. A German official expressed preference for prisoners of war from the Western areas of the Soviet Union, "as it is to assume that their Bolshevik contamination is low." Overmans, Hilger, and Polian, ed., *Rotarmisten in deutscher Hand*, 397. Such territorial distinctions were not consistent though. Many German observers kept referring to "the Bolshevik soldier" when speaking of any member of the Soviet armed forces, 352.
41. Overmans, Hilger, and Polian, ed., *Rotarmisten in deutscher Hand*, 341.
42. Joachim Hoffmann, *Die Ostlegionen, 1941–1943. Turkotartaren, Kaukasier, Wolgafinnen im deutschen Heer* (Freiburg, 1976); Rolf-Dieter Müller, *The Unknown Eastern Front: The Wehrmacht and Hitler's Foreign Soldiers* (London, 2014), 227–41.
43. See Weiner, *Making Sense of War*, 157; Mark Edele, *Stalin's Defectors: How Red Army Soldiers Became Hitler's Collaborators* (Oxford, 2017), 79–80.
44. Sergei Kudryashov, "The Hidden Dimension: Wartime Collaboration in the Soviet Union," in *Barbarossa. The Axis and the Allies*, ed. John Erickson (Edinburgh, 1994), 238–54 (242); Katrin Boeckh, *Stalinismus in der Ukraine. Die Rekonstruktion des sowjetischen Systems nach dem Zweiten Weltkrieg* (Wiesbaden, 2007), 76.
45. The full original quotation reads: "Nicht Negerstandpunkt, sondern vernünftige Behandlung nach Richtlinien Reichsminister Rosenberg." Truman Anderson, "Incident at Baranivka:German Reprisals and the Soviet Partisan Movement in Ukraine, October– December 1941," *Journal of Modern History* 71, no. 3 (September 1999), 585–623 (605n42).
46. Helmut Hartmann, letter to Konrad Henkel, July 20, 1941, Deutsches Tagebuch Archiv Emmerdingen.

47. Such narratives catapulted even ethnic Russians into the SS, even though the SS stopped short of creating Russian units. D. Zhukov and I. Kovtun, *Russkie esesovtsy* (Moscow, 2010). An exception obtained for Cossacks, ethnic Russians renowned for their warrior features and anti-Soviet stance, and allowed to form a distinct SS cavalry corps.
48. Overmans, Hilger, and Polian, ed., *Rotarmisten in deutscher Hand*, 657–58, 668; Sergei Kudryashov, "Ordinary Collaborators: The Case of the Trawniki Guards," in *Russia: War, Peace, and Diplomacy. Essays in Honour of John Erickson* (London, 2005), 230.
49. Jeffrey Burds, "'Turncoats, Traitors and Provocateurs': Communist Collaborators, the German Occupation and Stalin's NKVD, 1941–1943," *East European Politics & Societies* 32, no. 3 (August 2018): 606–38 (630).
50. By the end of 1941, the auxiliary police force in the occupied Soviet territories numbered thirty-three thousand men. Browning, *The Origins of the Final Solution*, 310; Overmans, Hilger, and Polian, ed., *Rotarmisten in deutscher Hand*, 657–58, 668. The first cohort of five thousand so-called *Trawniki* men who were trained by the SS for service in Nazi labor camps and killing centers was recruited from among Soviet POWs. They were trained in an abandoned sugar factory in the Polish village of Trawniki. Sergey Kudryashov, "Ordinary Collaborators"; Peter Black, "Foot Soldiers of the Final Solution: The Trawniki Training Camp and Operation Reinhard," *Holocaust and Genocide Studies* 25, no. 1 (2011): 1–99.
51. NA IRI RAN, f. 2, razd. VI, op. 22, d. 2, Mints.
52. See for example, NARB, f. 750-P, op. 1, d. 111, Paniavin; NA IRI RAN, f. 2, razd. VI, op. 22, d. 2, Mints. The harsh stance on surrender in the Red Army predated the German invasion but was further reinforced in decrees issued in July and August 1941, respectively. Mark Edele, *Stalin's Defectors: How Red Army Soldiers Became Hitler's Collaborators, 1941–1945* (Oxford, 2017), 41.
53. Irina Kalimova, "'Ia ne smeiu govorit . . .' Vospominaniia moego deda A. A. Kalimova o fashistskom plene (1941–1945)," in *Tsena pobedy. Rossiiskie shkol'niki o voine* (Moscow, 2005), 343–63 (355).
54. German records mention 24,668 people who were shot for lack of documents until September 1941. Babette Quinkert, *Propaganda und Terror in Weissrussland, 1941–1944* (Paderborn, 2009), 153; see also Overmans, Hilger, and Polian, ed., *Rotarmisten in deutscher Hand*, 344–45, 358.
55. NARB, f. 750-P, op. 1, d. 111, Paniavin.
56. NARB, f. 750-P, op. 1, d. 111, Paniavin. With their military skills and experience as commanders, Red Army officers—both stragglers and escapees—were predestined to take on leadership roles in the emerging partisan movement. The records of the Soviet partisan movement list 56,000 Red Army personnel as having fought among their ranks. Some historians believe the actual number to be many times higher. V.A. Perezhogin, "Iz okruzheniia i plena—v partizany," *Otechestvennaia istoriia*, no. 3 (2000): 25–33 (31–32); Christian Streit, "Partisans—Resistance—Prisoners of War," *Soviet Union/Union Soviétique* 18, nos. 1–3 (1991): 259–76 (275).
57. Mints appeared to cite lines from the soldiers' chorus in Friedrich Schiller's drama *Wallenstein*: "He who can look death in the eye / is truly the free man."
58. NA IRI RAN, f. 2, razd. VI, op. 22, d. 2, Mints.
59. Leonid Rein, "Local Collaboration in the Execution of the 'Final Solution' in Nazi-Occupied Belorussia," *Holocaust and Genocide Studies* 20, no. 3 (2006): 381–409.
60. The political reality was more complex, as Soviet power extended far beyond "Eastern" officeholders. Many formerly dispossessed and disenfranchised Baltic people supported the Soviet state and took to arms or fled east in the immediate aftermath of the German invasion. Konstantin Fuks, "The Soviet Latvian War Effort: Experiencing, Remembering, and Narrating the History of the Second World War" (PhD diss., University of Toronto, 2023), chap. 3.
61. NA IRI RAN, f. 2, razd. VI, op. 16, d. 3, Sankshtei; f. 2, razd. VI, op. 16, d. 6B: Dokladnaia o sostoianii g. Bresta vo vremia voiny. Axis soldiers frequently checked apartments they

entered for the presence of icons, to ensure that the residents were not Jewish. See, e.g., NA IRI RAN, f. 2, razd. VI, op. 12, d. 11, Gaivoronskaia.

62. NA IRI RAN, f. 2, razd. VI, op. 16, d. 5, Khromova; d. 7, Spiridonova; Martin Dean, *Collaboration in the Holocaust: Crimes of the Local Police in Belorussia and Ukraine, 1941–1944* (London, 2003), 21–22.
63. NA IRI RAN, f. 2, razd. VI, razd. VI, op. 18, d. 2, Zhur.
64. NA IRI RAN, f. 2, razd. VI, op. 20, d. 3, Andrezen; d. 12, Shtamm.
65. NA IRI RAN, f. 2, razd. VI, op. 20, d. 15, Tarvel'.
66. NA IRI RAN, f. 2, razd. VI, op. 19, d. 14, Sheibergs.
67. NA IRI RAN, f. 2, razd. VI, op. 19, d. 7, Bunka.
68. *Die "Ereignismeldungen UdSSR" 1941: Dokumente der Einsatzgruppen in der SowjeI*, ed. Klaus-Michael Mallmann, Andrej Angrick, Jürgen Matthäus, Martin Cüp (2011), 132 (July 16, 1941). Elsewhere, the praise was mixed with criticism. In Latvia, so many people were denounced to the authorities as Communists and Jews that the Germans soon issued public warnings not to issue baseless denunciations. Fuks, "The Soviet Latvian War Effort," chap. 3.
69. Recent research has confirmed that the Soviet policy of interethnic solidarity significantly curbed everyday anti-Semitism within Soviet society: Diana Dumitru, *The State, Antisemitism, and Collaboration in the Holocaust: The Borderlands of Romania and the Soviet Union* (Cambridge, 2016); Anika Walke, *Pioneers and Partisans: An Oral History of Nazi Genocide in Belorussia* (Oxford, 2015).
70. Mallmann et al., ed., *Die "Ereignismeldungen UdSSR" 1941,* 233 (August 5, 1941), 677 (October 12, 1941); see also Gerlach, *Kalkulierte Morde*, 536–37.
71. Quinkert, *Propaganda und Terror in Weißrussland*, 157.
72. NA IRI RAN, f. 2, razd. VI, op. 15, d. 26, Pruslina.
73. NA IRI RAN, f. 2, razd. VI, op. 17, d. 4a, Levina.
74. NA IRI RAN, f. 2, razd. VI, op. 15, d. 30a, Bas'ko; Paul Kohl, *Der Krieg der deutschen Wehrmacht und der Polizei, 1941–1944. Sowjetische Überlebende berichten* (Frankfurt, 1995), 247; Barbara Epstein, *The Minsk Ghetto 1941–1943: Jewish Resistance and Soviet Internationalism* (Berkeley, 2008), 80–81.
75. NA IRI RAN, f. 2, razd. VI, op.17-4a, Levina; f. 2, razd. VI, op. 15, d. 23, Taits (Minsk). Slightly different dates: *The Unknown Black Book: The Holocaust in the German-Occupied Soviet Territories*, ed. Joshua Rubenstein and Ilya Altman (Bloomington, IN, 2010), 235–36; Hersh Smolar, *The Minsk Ghetto: Soviet-Jewish Partisans Against the Nazis* (New York, 1989), 15. Smolar writes of three hundred killed members of the Jewish intelligentsia and describes the "action" as having taken place on July 12 only. The different numbers given in different sources could add up.
76. Barbara Epstein, *The Minsk Ghetto*, 81–82; NA IRI RAN, f. 2, razd. VI, op. 15, d. 26, Pruslina. Scattered evidence indicates that many Soviet officials (Jewish or non-Jewish) were murdered on the spot within days after the Germans' arrival. A brigade leader from a railroad factory was among the three hundred to four hundred suspected Soviet "leaders" rounded up in Baranovichi. He managed to hide and watched as all the others were shot to death. NA IRI RAN, f. 2, razd. VI, op. 17, d. 15, Kaminka (Baranovichi). The murder of suspected Soviet officials is poorly researched.
77. NA IRI RAN, f. 2, razd. VI, op. 16, d. 9, Gribakina (Brest); op. 17, d. 7, Ignatovich (Slonim).
78. NA IRI RAN, f. 2, razd. VI, op. 15, d. 13, Maizles; d. 35, Pylilo.
79. NA IRI RAN, f. 2, razd. VI, op. 15, d. 35, Pylilo.
80. G. Smoliar, *Mstiteli getto* (Moscow, 1947), 8.
81. *"Existiert das Ghetto noch?" Weißrussland: Jüdisches Überleben gegen nationalsozialistische Herrschaft*, 214; NA IRI RAN, f. 2, razd. VI, op. 15, d. 13, Maizles.
82. "Indigenous" is meant in opposition to ghettos further West, such as in Bialystok, Vilnius, or Lvov, that held Jews who had lived under Soviet rule for less than two years.

Hersh Smolar, *The Minsk Ghetto*, 1. For the ghetto population, see Epstein, *The Minsk Ghetto*, 42, 90 (with references to Smolar).

83. Epstein, *The Minsk Ghetto*, 14. The Jews who built the fences were given three hundred grams of bread. NA IRI RAN, f. 2, razd. VI, op. 15, d. 26, Pruslina.
84. Mallmann et al., ed., *Die "Ereignismeldungen UdSSR" 1941*, 547 (September 23, 1941).
85. Smolar, *The Minsk Ghetto*, 40–41; NA IRI RAN, f. 2, razd. VI, op. 15, d. 13, Maizles.
86. Smolar, *The Minsk Ghetto*, 41; Ilya Ehrenburg and Vasily Grossman, *The Complete Black Book of Russian Jewry* (New Brunswick and London, 2002), 118; *The Unknown Black Book*, 237–38, 245, 251. One witness remembered that during their march the "demonstrators" were fired upon with machine guns. *"Existiert das Ghetto noch?,"* 216.
87. *The Unknown Black Book*, 238–39. The following day, the Jewish council and professionals were returned to the ghetto with their families from the Shirokaya camp. Yitzhak Arad, *The Holocaust in the Soviet Union* (Lincoln, NE, and Jerusalem, 2009), 154; Smolar, *The Minsk Ghetto*, 42.
88. *The Unknown Black Book*, 237–38
89. Browning, *The Origins of the Final Solution*, 393 (citing these numbers from German reports).
90. *"Existiert das Ghetto noch?,"* 173–76; Browning, *The Origins of the Final Solution*, 376.
91. *"Existiert das Ghetto noch?,"* 216.
92. Epstein, *The Minsk Ghetto*, 12.
93. Epstein, *The Minsk Ghetto*, 113.
94. The underground workers in the Russian sector did not believe Smolar when he told them how the resistance organization in the ghetto had been built from the ground up. They were convinced he was a Comintern official operating on Stalin's orders and gave him the nome de guerre "Skromny," the modest one. Smolar, *The Minsk Ghetto*, 37, 43–44; *"Existiert das Ghetto noch?,"* 228–29.
95. This and many other illustrations of the execution can be found at https://commons.wikimedia.org/wiki/Category:Masha_Bruskina; the hangings of the nurse Olga Shcherbatsevich and the seamstress Elena Ostrovskaia were also photographed, see https://collections.ushmm.org/search/catalog/pa1050369 (Shcherbasevich), and https://waralbum.ru/175736/ and https://myagkayasila.ru/26-oktyabrya-1941-goda-kazneny-belorusskie-partizany/ (Ostrovskaia).
96. Maria's name at her birth was Merke, a Yiddish name that has the same meaning ("bitter") as the Hebrew name Miriam, https://www.jewishheroes.live/heroes/bruskina.
97. Lev Arkadiev and Ada Dikhtiar, "The Unknown Girl: A Documentary Story," *Yiddish Writers' Almanac* 1 (1987): 161–204.
98. Lev Arkadiev and Ada Dikhtiar, "The Unknown Girl: A Documentary Story," 186.
99. See *Verbrechen der Wehrmacht. Dimensionen des Vernichtungskrieges 1941 bis 1944* (Hamburg, 2021), 144–45; BArch, Bild 231-052. Avid hobby photographers, German soldiers stationed in Minsk had their films developed in local photo studios. When a young Soviet photographer by the name of Aleksei Kozlovskii, who worked in one of these studios, developed the shocking images of Maria Bruskina's hanging, he made extra prints for himself and stashed them away. After the liberation of Minsk in 1944, Kozlovskii handed his collection, which by then had grown to 287 photographs of German crimes, to the Red Army Command. "'Neizvestnaia' Masha Bruskina."
100. The Soviet ideology of the friendship of peoples was a lived experience for many Soviet Jews at this time. Walke, *Pioneers and Partisans*; and Epstein, *The Minsk Ghetto*.
101. The site contains a 1938 photo of Bruskina as well as a picture of her parents, https://dnevniki.ykt.ru/%D0%94%D0%B8%D0%BD%D0%B0_%D1%80%D0%B0/1069094.
102. Arkadiev and Dikhtiar, "The Unknown Girl," 177, 202.
103. Smolar later entrusted Radova with performing as liaison operative between the ghetto and city underground organizations. She was arrested in September 1942, interrogated, and tortured, but did not give the Germans any information. Radova was executed on

January 9, 1943. Smolar, *The Minsk Ghetto*, 33; Epstein, *The Minsk Ghetto*, 127–28; Arkadiev and Dikhtiar, "The Unknown Girl," 194.

104. NA IRI RAN, f. 2, razd. VI, op.15, d. 13, Maizles; d. 26, Pruslina. The leader of the Communist underground organization in the Russian sector was Isai Kazinets, a Jewish officer in the Red Army who remained in Minsk after retreating from Bialystok. Reuben Ainsztein, *Jewish Resistance in Nazi-Occupied Eastern Europe* (London 1974), 483. Arrested and hanged by the Germans in January 1942, Kazinets was posthumously declared a Hero of the Soviet Union. See "Kazinets Isai Pavlovich (Pinkhusovich)" at: http://www.warheroes.ru/hero/hero.asp?Hero_id=2664.
105. Smolar, *The Minsk Ghetto*, 1.
106. NA IRI RAN, f. 2, razd. VI, op. 15, d. 13.
107. NA IRI RAN, f. 2, razd. VI, op. 15, d. 26, Pruslina.
108. NA IRI RAN, f. 2, razd. VI, op. 15, d. 2, Dubovik.
109. Speaking with the historians who visited Minsk in August 1944, six weeks after the city's liberation, Maizles had no information about when or where her son died. NA IRI RAN, f. 2, razd. VI, op. 15-13. Hundreds of Jewish children from Minsk were saved by orphanage workers who concealed them at enormous risks to their own lives. Epstein, *The Minsk Ghetto*, 171–80.
110. NA IRI RAN, f. 2, razd. VI, op. 15, d. 13, Maizles.
111. Thirty thousand partisans fought in Belorussia in late 1941, Gerlach, *Kalkulierte Morde*, 861.
112. NA IRI RAN, f. 2, razd. VI, op. 15, d. 26, Pruslina.
113. NARB, f. 750-P, op. 1, d. 111, Bulat.
114. Emphasis added. This was the well-known Avenger Brigade ("Mstitel"), headed by Major Voronzhanskii, nicknamed "Uncle Vasya." Masha Cerovic, *Les enfants de Staline. La guerre des partisans soviétiques, 1941–1944* (Paris, 2018), 52.
115. "*Existiert das Ghetto noch?*," 231. Khasya Pruslina and Basya Levina also escaped into the forest to fight with the partisans. Like Etta Maizles, Levina also encountered strong antisemitic feelings in the brigades that she joined. NA IRI RAN, f. 2, razd. VI, op. 17, d. 4a, Levina.
116. The partisan leader, Kirill Prokof'evich Orlovskii, was previously a lieutenant colonel in the NKVD. As he welcomed the Jews into his unit, he found them unarmed, barefoot, and hungry. They told him: "We want to take revenge on Hitler, but we don't have the means to do so." NARB, f. 750-P, op. 1, d. 111.
117. Epstein, *The Minsk Ghetto*, 13.
118. This of course is not to suggest that all—or even most—Communists became resistance fighters. This was far from the case. See Burds, "'Turncoats' Traitors, and Provocateurs.'"
119. NA IRI RAN, f. 2, razd. VI, op. 15-13, Maizles.
120. Browning, *The Origins of the Final Solution*, 333.
121. As more transports arrived from different parts of the Reich, the ghetto for Reich Jews was divided into five distinct camps: the Hamburg, Berlin, Rhineland, Bremen, and Vienna camps. Shalom Cholavsky, "The German Jews in the Minsk Ghetto," *Yad Vashem Studies* XVII (Jerusalem, 1986): 219–45 (230).
122. Epstein, *The Minsk Ghetto*, 103–4; "*Existiert das Ghetto noch?*," 177.
123. Cholavsky, "The German Jews," 225.
124. Browning, *The Origins of the Final Solution*, 394.
125. Christopher Browning, *Ordinary Men* (New York, 1998), 43.
126. Cholavsky, "The German Jews," 222–24.
127. Only on a few occasions did the underground use the services of some Germans to write leaflets in German addressed to the German Army. Cholavsky, "The German Jews," 236–38; Epstein, *The Minsk Ghetto*, 104.
128. Cholavsky, "The German Jews," 232, NA IRI RAN, f. 2, razd. VI, op. 15, d. 35, Pylilo.
129. Cholavsky, "The German Jews," 237. As a Soviet survivor exclaimed: "How was it possible for Hitler to kill [the German Jews]? To kill us—that was understandable. We are

Soviet people, Jewish communists. But they? Not even externally did they look any different from the Germans," 227.

130. "*Existiert das Ghetto noch?*," 226.
131. Gerald Fleming, *Hitler and the Final Solution* (Berkeley, 1987), 116–19.
132. Cholavsky, "The German Jews," 237.
133. According to postwar estimates from Soviet survivors, Epstein notes, between eighteen thousand and thirty thousand Jews were murdered during the July massacre. Epstein writes that twelve thousand Jews were spared. Epstein, *The Minsk Ghetto*, 105–6.
134. Kohl, *Der Krieg der deutschen Wehrmacht und Polizei*, 235–36.
135. Epstein, *The Minsk Ghetto*, 314n6, citing a March 1942 report that provides a picture of the underground organization "on the basis of arrests made thus far." On the decimation of the city's underground organizations, see 133–38.
136. NA IRI RAN, f. 2, razd. VI, op. 15, d. 26, Pruslina.
137. Epstein, *The Minsk Ghetto*, 137.
138. *The Holocaust: An Encyclopedia and Document Collection, vol. 3: Holocaust Testimonies*, ed. Paul R. Bartrop and Michael Dickerman (Santa Barbara, CA, 2017), 902. Christian Gerlach writes that several hundred residents of a district in Minsk were killed in reprisal for Kube's assassination. Gerlach, *Kalkulierte Morde*, 865. Still resentful at how Kube had meddled with his design to murder all German Jews, Himmler reacted to the news of Kube's murder, calling it a stroke of luck for Germany. Raul Hilberg, *The Destruction of the European Jews*, vol. 2 (New York, 1985), 151.

Chapter 6: Moscow Strikes Back

1. An editor at *Sputnik agitatora* promptly forwarded the letter to the NKVD, recommending that the security police investigate the obviously "anti-Soviet"-minded drivers. How the NKVD reacted to this request, and whether the agitator received the advice he sought, are not clear. *Sovetskaia propaganda v gody Velikoi Otechestvennoi voiny: "kommunikatsiia ubezhdeniia" i mobilizatsionnye mekhanizmy*, ed. A. Ia. Livshin and I. B. Orlov (Moscow, 2007), 74–78, 79n2.
2. Il'ia Erenburg, *Liudi, gody, zhizn'. Vospominaniia v trekh tomakh. Tom vtoroi* (Moscow, 1990), 221.
3. John Barber and Mark Harrison, *The Soviet Home Front, 1941–1945: A Social and Economic History of the USSR in World War II* (London: Longman, 1991), 77–78; Wendy Z. Goldman and Donald Filtzer, *Fortress Dark and Stern: The Soviet Home Front During World War II* (Oxford, 2021), 167, 275. Dieter Pohl estimates that 55 to 65 million Soviet people fell under Axis rule in 1941 and 1942. Dieter Pohl, *Die Herrschaft der Wehrmacht*, 124; a Russian publication puts this number at between 65 and 68 million Soviet citizens. *Liudskie poteri SSSR v period Vtoroi Mirovoi voiny. Sbornik statei* (St. Petersburg, 1995), 145.
4. Il'ia Ehrenburg, "V pervyi den'," in *Ot sovetskogo informbiuro . . . 1941–1945. Publitsistika i ocherki voennykh let*, vol. 1, (Moscow, 1984), 21–23.
5. D. F. Kraminov, *V orbite voiny. Zapiski sovetskogo korrespondenta za rubezhom, 1939–1945* (Moscow, 1986), 169.
6. Erenburg, *Liudi, gody, zhizn'. Tom vtoroi*, 228.
7. Gabriel Gorodetsky, *Grand Delusion: Stalin and the German Invasion of Russia* (New Haven, 1999), 222–23, 277–79, 296–97; Erik Van Ree, *The Political Thought of Joseph Stalin: A Study in Twentieth Century Revolutionary Patriotism* (London, 2003), 6.
8. Text of Molotov's address in English, https://sourcebooks.fordham.edu/mod/1941molotov.asp; audio, https://www.youtube.com/watch?v=KewkPactF2M. Audio of Levitan's address at https://www.youtube.com/watch?v=ZAtRykr2vkg.
9. Em. Iaroslavskii, "Velikaia Otechestvennaia voina sovetskogo naroda," *Pravda*, June 23, 1941, 4.
10. *Organy gosudarstvennoi bezopasnosti SSSR v Velikoi Otechestvennoi voine. Sbornik dokumentov. T. 2, kn. 1: Nachalo. 22 iiunia—31 avgusta 1941 goda* (Moscow, 2000), 161–65.

11. Diary of Stepan Podlubny, Tsentr dokumentatsii "Narodnyi arkhiv," f. 30. op. 1. ed. khr. 19, l. 13. This archive has been incorporated into Rossiiskii Gosudarstvennyi Arkhiv Noveishei Istorii (RGANI), and there is no information about the archival call number of Podlubny's diary.
12. *Organy gosudarstvennoi bezopasnosti*, t. 2, kn. 1, 168–69.
13. Evan Mawdsley, *Thunder in the East: The Nazi–Soviet War, 1941–1945* (London, 2015), 108–9; Walter S. Dunn, *Stalin's Keys to Victory: The Rebirth of the Red Army* (Westport, CT, 2006), 73–74. To illustrate the enormity of this mobilization effort, Dunn points out that the United States formed a total of ninety divisions during the entire war.
14. Jeffrey Brooks, *Thank You, Comrade Stalin!: Soviet Public Culture from Revolution to Cold War* (Princeton, NJ, 2021), 161.
15. The order is reprinted in *Organy gosudarstvennoi bezopasnosti*, t. 2, kn. 1, 482–86.
16. "Nemetsko-fashistskie zverstva v Breste i Minske," *Krasnaia zvezda*, August 10, 1941.
17. A. Piterskii, "Varvary XX veka," *Pravda*, August 24, 1941.
18. I. Erenburg, "Fashistskie mrakobesy," *Krasnaia zvezda*, June 29, 1941.
19. Aleksei Tolstoi, "Kto takoi Gitler i chego on dobivaetsia," *Izvestiia*, July 17, 1941.
20. G. Aleksandrov, "Bibliia liudoedov," *Pravda*, July 16, 1941. In a single departure, where Rauschning cited Hitler as seeking to "wipe out" Czechs and Bohemians only, and only alluding to the need for German Lebensraum at the expense of all Slavs, Aleksandrov edited the quotation by bringing it up to date to where fascism stood in 1941. Hermann Rauschning. *Gespräche mit Hitler*, reprint of the first, 1940 edition (Zurich, 2005), 42–44. Many historians today caution against accepting the "Conversations with Hitler" at face value, as Rauschning took great liberties in quoting or paraphrasing Hitler. Irrespective of this debate, the book played a pivotal role in the history of anti-fascism. After the war, Rauschning conceded that he had devised "Conversations with Hitler" as a "weapon against Hitler's politics" and an attempt to "shed light on his person and political intentions." Albrecht Hagemann, *Hermann Rauschning. Ein deutsches Leben zwischen NS-Ruhm und Exil* (Cologne and Weimar, 2018), 242. The book became an immediate bestseller. Stalin also read it, see further below.
21. Il'ia Erenburg, "Po dva arshina," *Krasnaia zvezda*, August 20, 1942. Ehrenburg did not give a date, but the article could be identified: it was a small piece on page 6 of *Völkischer Beobachter*'s July 12 issue. Ehrenburg's quotations from the German source were accurate. See "Soldaten bevorzugt. Der Einsatz in den Ostgebieten," *Völkischer Beobachter* (Wiener Ausgabe), July 12, 1941.
22. Tolstoi, "Kto takoi Gitler"; Il'ia Erenburg, "Kto oni?," *Pravda*, July 13, 1941; K. Demidov, "Izverg Gitler—liutyi vrag russkogo naroda," Pravda, July 13, 1941; G. Aleksandrov, "Propoved' chelovekonenavistnichestva i zverstv (Mif XX stoletiia)," *Pravda*, July 31, 1941.
23. Il'ia Al'tman, *Zhertva nenavisti. Kholokost v SSSR: 1941–1945 gg.* (Moscow, 2002), 385; Sheila Fitzpatrick, "Annexation, Evacuation, and Antisemitism in the Soviet Union, 1939–1946," in *Shelter from the Holocaust: Rethinking Jewish Survival in the Soviet Union*, ed Mark Edele et al. (Detroit, 2017), 133–60 (139).
24. "Nemetsko-fashistskie zverstva v Breste i Minske."
25. Mordechai Altshuler, "The Holocaust in the Soviet Mass Media during the War and in the First Postwar Years Re-examined," *Yad Vashem Studies* 39, no. 2 (2011): 121–68; Karel C. Berkhoff, "Total Annihilation of the Jewish Population": The Holocaust in the Soviet Media, 1941–45," *Kritika: Explorations in Russian and Eurasian History* 10, no. 1 (2009): 61–105.
26. Rebecca Manley, *To the Tashkent Station: Evacuation and Survival in the Soviet Union at War* (2009), 111–15; *The Unknown Black Book*, 21.
27. Sovinformbiuro, "Chudovishchnyi prikaz gitlerovskogo generala ob unichtozhenii vsekh istoricheskikh i khudozhestvennykh tsennostei i ob istreblenii muzhskogo naseleniia v zakhvachennykh nemtsami sovetskikh raionakh," *Pravda*, January 15, 1942, 2.
28. *Pravda* removed the references in the order that talked about soldiers in the East as "avengers for all of the bestialities that have been inflicted on German and related cul-

tures and traditions" and "to fulfill the historic task of liberating the German people from the Asian-Jewish danger once and for all."

29. "Chudovishchnyi prikaz gitlerovskogo komandovaniia," *Pravda*, January 15, 1942, 1; Yarden Avital, "The Jewish Anti-Fascist Committee Between Universal Being and Particular Suffering" (PhD diss., Rutgers University, 2022).
30. Yuri Slezkine, *The Jewish Century* (Princeton, 2004); David Shneer, *Through Soviet Jewish Eyes: Photography, War, and the Holocaust* (New Brunswick, NJ, 2010), 169–70. Jews in wartime France and the United States—two other republics with powerful universalizing ideas—also sought to stress their credentials as French or U.S. citizens. Peter Novick, *The Holocaust in American Life* (New York, 1999), 35–36, 115–16; Jacques Semelin, *The Survival of the Jews in France, 1940–1944* (Oxford, 2018), 90.
31. *Izvestiya* the next day carried not only transcripts of the speeches, including Ehrenburg's words, but also the text of an open letter, "To Brothers Jews of the Whole World." "Brat'ia evrei vsego mira!," *Izvestiia*, August 26, 1941.
32. "Luchshe smert' v boiu, chem fashistskii plen," *Krasnaia zvezda*, July 10, 1941. In the first year of the war with Germany, well over two hundred items about Soviet prisoners of war appeared in the central papers. Karel Berkhoff, *Motherland in Danger: Soviet Propaganda During World War II* (Cambridge, MA, 2012), 123, referring to a bibliography, *Zverstva fashistskikh varvarov: Ukazatel' faktov, opublikovannykh v pechati* (Moscow, 1943), 29–69.
33. "Uzhasy fashistskogo plena," *Krasnaia zvezda*, October 16, 1941.
34. "Nota Narodnogo Komissara Inostrannykh Del tov. V. M. Molotova," *Izvestiia*, November 26, 1941, 1. The German mistreatment of Soviet POWs had the effect of softening the official Soviet stance toward their own captured soldiers. Until Molotov issued the note, the act of giving oneself up into captivity was described as a shameful crime (see "Bessmertnyi podvig trekh russkikh voinov," *Krasnaia zvezda*, September 6, 1941. Evidence of fascist criminality in turn victimized the Soviet POWs and rendered them into martyrs.
35. Neither the London *Times* nor *The New York Times* reported on the note, nor is it mentioned in the memoirs of the then British Foreign Secretary Anthony Eden (see below, note 110).
36. *Die Tagebücher von Joseph Goebbels, Teil II: Diktate 1941–1945. Band 2: Oktober-Dezember 1941*, 371–72 (November 27, 1941).
37. For a transcript of portions of the press conference, see "Gitlerovskaia propaganda 1941-go: fal'shivyj syn Molotova," Radio Svoboda, December 5, 2009, https://www.svoboda.org/a/1896844.html.
38. "Nazis Show Captive as Molotoff's Son," *New York Times*, November 28, 1941, 3. In his diary, Goebbels exulted about the "sensational" coverage of Molotov's son in the U.S. media. *Die Tagebücher von Joseph Goebbels, Teil II, Band 2*, 388 (November 29, 1941).
39. Goebbels registered them, of course. *Die Tagebücher von Joseph Goebbels, Teil II, Band 2*, 407 (December 1, 1941). See also "Gitlerovskaia propaganda 1941-go."
40. Tarasov had rendered the Germans a service and was not punished for his deceit. He spent the rest of the war in a Berlin prison for captured officers. "Gitlerovskaia propaganda 1941-go."
41. Rodric M. Braithwaite, *Moscow 1941: A City and Its People at War* (New York, 2006), 233–34, 252.
42. Braithwaite, *Moscow 1941*, 278–79.
43. Alexander Werth, *Russia at War, 1941–1945* (New York, 2017), 244.
44. I. V. Stalin, *Sochineniia. Tom 15* (Moscow, 1997). Stalin's citation is a recognizable though not verbatim quotation from Rauschning's 1940 book, which he did not reference.
45. I. V. Stalin, "Doklad na torzhestvennom zasedanii Moskovskogo Soveta," *Pravda*, November 7, 1941. The slogan "Death to the German occupiers!" soon adorned every

Soviet newspaper every day of the war. See N. P. Popov and N. A. Gorokhov, *Sovetskaia voennaia pechat' v gody velikoi otechestvennoi voiny, 1941–1945* (Moscow, 1981), 74.

46. Braithwaite, *Moscow 1941*, 255
47. For a detailed description of both speeches, see Werth, *Russia at War*, 244–49.
48. Barber and Harrison, *The Soviet Home Front*, 72; Werth, *Russia at War*, 249–51.
49. "Dokumenty o krovozhadnosti fashistskikh merzavtsev," *Krasnaia zvezda*, October 29, 1942.
50. D. I. Ortenberg, *Iiun'—dekabr' sorok pervogo* (Moscow, 1984), 248.
51. Manfred Zeidler, "Der Minsker Kriegsverbrecherprozeß vom Januar 1946. Kritische Anmerkungen zu einem sowjetischen Schauprozeß gegen deutsche Kriegsgefangene," *Vierteljahrshefte für Zeitgeschichte*, 2004/2, 211–44 (227); Yitzhak Arad, *The Holocaust in the Soviet Union* (Lincoln, NE, and Jerusalem, 2009), 540–41. The name of the German lieutenant has been rendered inconsistently. *Krasnaia zvezda* first rendered it as "Schiegel" (Shchigel'). Stalin referred to him as "Tigl."
52. Dunn, *Stalin's Keys to Victory*, 79–83, 90; Mawdsley, *Thunder in the East*, 112.
53. *Organy gosudarstvennoi bezopasnosti SSSR*, T. 2, kn. 2, 595–96; details at David M. Glantz and Jonathan M. House, *When Titans Clashed: How the Red Army Stopped Hitler* (Lawrence, KS, 2015), 87–91.
54. This scene entered the film *The Rout of the German Troops Near Moscow*, dirs., Leonid Varlamov and Ilya Kopalin (1942), released in the United States as *Moscow Strikes Back* and discussed further below. Some visual editing was performed for the American production; in the process, the scene with the gallows in Volokolamsk was inserted into the film's last segment depicting the liberation of Mozhaisk, perhaps in order to impart a climactic ending. See https://www.youtube.com/watch?v=YFd3cYr2X60 (at 9:30).
55. Ortenberg, *Iiun'—dekabr' sorok pervogo*, 328–30.
56. O. Kurganov, "Vosem' poveshennykh," *Pravda*, December 27, 1941.
57. Lidov, "Tania," *Pravda*, January 27, 1942.
58. It was later established that the partisan was captured on November 28 and executed the following day. M. M. Gorinov, "Zoia Kosmodem'ianskaia: pravda i vymysel," *Otechestvennaia istoriia* 1 (2003): 77–92.
59. Lidov, "Tania."
60. Gorinov, "Zoia Kosmodem'ianskaia," 83. It is of course possible that the villagers did not talk with Lidov about their hatred toward the young arsonist. This inconvenient truth may have surfaced only in the NKVD's interrogation transcripts.
61. Zoya remembered the Soviet population as comprising 170 million people, a number widely reported in the wake of the 1939 Soviet census. The number of 200 million Soviet citizens cited in Lidov's article additionally comprised the residents of the territories that the Soviet Union had annexed in 1939 and 1940.
62. *Moskva prifrontovaia, 1941–1942. Arkhivnye dokumenty i materialy* ed. M. M. Gorinov et al. (Moscow, 2001), 564–66.
63. To read the text was unbearable, the speaker, Olga Vysotskaia, later remembered, see https://www.youtube.com/watch?v=fkmjoM6Y-l4.
64. "Vystuplenie po radio L.T. Kosmodem'ianskoi—materi Geroia Sovetskogo Soiuza Z.A. Kosmodem'ianskoi (Radioperedacha dlia molodezhi)." Text at https://0gnev.livejournal.com/449906.html; audio file at http://www.staroeradio.ru/audio/10981.
65. Lidov, "Kto byla Tania," *Pravda*, February 18, 1942. The circumstances of Zoya's recruitment as a partisan were not known to Lidov at the time. She was one of several thousand young Muscovites to respond to a Komsomol recruitment drive during the critical October days. Addressing the young men and women, the head of the Moscow Komsomol organization warned them that the fascists were "merciless with partisans" and that "95 percent of you may die." Any of the volunteers was free to reconsider their decision and step back. No one did. From among the volunteers, about two thousand were chosen to receive training from a reconnaissance and sabotage unit of the Red Army. Gorinov, "Zoia Kosmodem'ianskaia," 73. Zoya's mission followed Stalin's No-

vember 17, 1941, order to burn down villages in which the Germans had found shelter. *Moskva prifrontovaia, 1941–1942*, 156.

66. Roger D. Markwick and Euridice Charon Cardona, *Soviet Women on the Frontline in the Second World War* (Basingstoke and New York, 2012), 117; Lidov, "Kto byla Tania." The "Zoya" campaign peaked with the eponymous film directed by Lev Arnshtam that appeared in mid-1944. A recipient of a 1946 Stalin Prize, the film drew twenty-two million spectators in 1944 alone. Markwick and Cardona, *Soviet Women on the Frontline*, 124–25.
67. On the commission's work, see this book's introduction.
68. NA IRI RAN, f. 2, razd. VI, op.3, d. 1 (Baranov).
69. NA IRI RAN, f. 2, razd. VI, op. 3, d. 1 (Kozyreva).
70. *Sovetskaia propaganda v gody Velikoi Otechestvennoi voiny*, 347–48.
71. Rostov had been under German occupation for eight days only; this accounts for the relatively small number of victims who numbered in the hundreds, rather than thousands. "Ne zabudem, ne prostim: Fotodokumenty o krovavykh zverstvakh fashistskikh merzavtsev v Rostove-na-donu," *Krasnaia zvezda*, December 11, 1941. The mass murder of the city's Jewish residents did not start until after the Germans took Rostov again in July 1942.
72. The photographers included David Baltermants, Evgenii Khaldei, Lev Borodulin, and Israel Ozerskii—all of them Jewish. Shneer, *Through Soviet Jewish Eyes*, 100–101. *Besatzungspolitik und Massenmord: Die Einsatzgruppe D in der südlichen Sowjetunion, 1941–1943* (Hamburg, 2003), 356.
73. Ilya Selvinsky, "I Saw This," trans. Daniel Weissbort, in *Twentieth Century Russian Poetry: Silver and Steel. An Anthology*, ed. Albert C. Todd and Max Hayward with Daniel Weissbort (New York, 1993), 362–65.
74. Tat'iana Tess, "Vosem' nemetskikh fotosnimkov," *Izvestiia*, February 4, 1942; Il'ia Erenburg, "My ne zabudem etu viselitsu, ne zabudem i ne prostym!," *Krasnaia zvezda*, February 6, 1942; Valentin Kataev, "Poklianemsia nikogda ne zabyvat' etogo!," *Pravda*, February 6, 1942. Tess's initial report that the German soldier was captured and that his photographs showed six victims was corrected by the other writers to five victims and that the German was found dead on the battlefield.
75. As was custom in Soviet media publications at the time, *Red Star* heavily retouched the photographs of the hangings. Several of the original photographs are preserved in Yad Vashem's archive: https://collections.yadvashem.org/en/photos/71084; https://collections.yadvashem.org/en/photos/71658. For a larger collection, see https://waralbum.ru/3360/comment-page-2/#comments. The photographs are housed in the State Archive of the Russian Federation (GARF).
76. "My ne zabudem, otomstim!," *Krasnaia zvezda*, March 19, 1942. Ilya Ehrenburg likely wrote this piece. In a signed article that he wrote for *Red Star* in December 1943, the writer described the Germans who had been freed from their conscience using the exact same words. Il'ia Erenburg, "Iz zala suda," *Krasnaia zvezda*, December 19, 1943. See chapter 9, below. Picture source: https://0gnev.livejournal.com/236462.html.
77. *Muzy v shineli. Sovetskaia intelligentsiia v gody Velikoi Otechestvennoi voiny. Dokumenty, teksty, vospominaniia* (Moscow, 2006), 9. Soviet writers were not alone in joining the war against fascism as propagandists and political educators. This call registered with left-wing writers from many countries, including Anna Seghers, Ernest Hemingway, and Pablo Neruda.
78. Ilya Ehrenburg, *Russia at War* (London, 1943), 107 (January 25, 1942). Even though Ehrenburg also embraced photography as a documentary method, he was more partial to reading personal texts. As he explained in his memoirs, he took up photography to compensate for the scarcity of diaries and personal letters in modern society. And yet, Ehrenburg added, the photographer's voyeuristic gaze could not penetrate the human psyche as effectively as writing in a self-reflexive vein. See Katherine M. H. Reischl, *Photographic Literacy: Cameras in the Hands of Russian Authors* (Ithaca, NY, 2018), 167. Recall Ehrenburg's collection in 1932 of the diaries and letters of the young workers he

met in the Urals and Siberia, and his insistence on having his meetings with the workers stenographed (see chapter 2).

79. Ehrenburg developed this method during the Spanish Civil War, see chapter 2. In the absence of a complete bibliography, the total of Ehrenburg's wartime writings is impossible to calculate. Ehrenburg's biographers, Boris Frezinskii and Joshua Rubenstein, believe the number to range between 1,500 and 2,000. Erenburg, *Voina, 1941–1945*, ed., B. Ia. Frezinskii (Moscow, 2004), 8; Rubenstein, *Tangled Loyalties*, 191.
80. *Sovetskaia propaganda v gody Velikoi Otechestvennoi voiny*, 309–10. A month before, a high official in the Red Army's Main Political Administration wrote to the administration's office for war propaganda with a similar complaint. The official's memorandum detailed several cases in which the diaries of German soldiers had been altered in Soviet publications. He demanded to stop the production of such "unfortunate texts," which would only impede Soviet counterpropaganda efforts among captured enemy soldiers. *Die Verfolgung und Ermordung der europäischen Juden durch das nationalsozialistische Deutschland. Band 7: Sowjetunion mit annektierten Gebieten I*, ed. Bert Hoppe and Hildrun Glass (Munich, 2011), 292–95 (Dok. 83).
81. D. Ortenberg, *1942* (Moscow, 1988), 356. While the archive of *Red Star* remains off limits to researchers, a portion of the letters that Ehrenburg received via *Red Star*'s offices survives in his personal archive in the Russian State Archive for Literature and the Arts: RGALI, f. 1204, op. 2, d. 3449: *Materialy o zverstvakh nemetskikh voisk na okkupirovannoi territorii: dnevniki i vospominaniia grazhdan*; d. 3453: *Vospominaniia, rasskazy i ocherki uchastnikov Velikoi Otechestvennoi voiny*; d. 3454: *Perepiska uchastnikov Velikoi Otechestvennoi voiny s rodnymi i znakomymi.*
82. These documents are inventoried in two separate folders: See RGALI, f. 1204, op. 2, ed. 3452. *Dnevniki nemetskikh soldat. Na nemetskom iazyk*, op. 2, ed. 3444: *Pis'ma, dnevnikovye zapisi i protokoly doprosov i dr. nemetskikh soldat, vziatykh v plen chastiami Sovetskoi Armii. 1941–1945.*
83. Along with their report to the head of the NKVD's counterintelligence department, Viktor Abakumov, the operatives submitted Schmidt's diary, complete with a Russian translation. Abakumov received the materials on October 8, 1942, and circulated them among top NKVD officials. One reader noted: "I think it may be expedient to . . . forward the diary to I. Ehrenburg and have him write an article." Abakumov had Schmidt's diary delivered to Ehrenburg on October 10. The next day, *Red Star* published Ehrenburg's piece. V. V. Pavlov, "Dnevniki gestapovtsa," *Lubianka* 2 (2005): 91–112 (104).
84. For a German military map depicting the Bay of Taganrog in early 1942, with references to the variable thickness of its ice, see: http://www.lexikon-der-wehrmacht.de/Gliederungen/Korps/Karte/XI0142.jpg.
85. I. Erenburg, "Nemets," *Krasnaia zvezda*, October 11, 1942; reprinted in *Pravda*, October 12, 1942, and dozens of other newspapers. The article appeared in eleven collections of Ehrenburg's wartime writings (see Erenburg, *Voina*, 100). English translation at *True to Type: A Selection from Letters and Diaries of German Soldiers and Civilians Collected on the Soviet-German Front* (London, 1945), 48–56. Friedrich Schmidt (born 1897 in Wanne-Eickel, "killed" on August 10, 1942) formed part of Geheime Feldpolizeigruppe (GFP) 626, see Eberhard Stegerer, *Die Geheime Feldpolizei im Dritten Reich, 1939–1945, Sicherheits- und Abwehrpolizei der Wehrmacht und deren Kriegsverbrechen und Verbrechen gegen die Menschlichkeit 1941–1944 in der Sowjetunion u. a.* (Göttingen, 2022), 331–33. Friedrich Schmidt's original diary is held in the "Politburo Archive" of the Archive of the President of the Russian Federation, AP RF, F. 3, Op. 58, D. 453 ("*Nemetskie dokumenty*" [1942 god]), ll. 56–172. I thank Sergei Kudryashov for obtaining this information.
86. Sigismund von Förster (1887–1959), commandant Rear Army Area 550, 17 AOK, starting October 1, 1941; Wolf Keilig, *Die Generale des Heeres* (Friedberg, 1983), 92.
87. V. V. Pavlov, "*Dnevniki gestapovtsa*," in *Lubianka* 2 (2005): 91–112 (104–12).
88. As early as March 1933, Ehrenburg had written about the new Hitler regime: "They have started with shootings. They will end with arson, pogroms, and murder. They feel

no guilt: they do everything that they are capable of." I. Erenburg, "Ikh Geroi. O Khorste Vessele," *Izvestiia*, March 20, 1933, cited in Boris Fresinskij, "Ilja Ehrenburg und Deutschland," in *Stürmische Aufbrüche und enttäuschte Hoffnungen. Russen und Deutsche in der Zwischenkriegszeit*, ed. Karl Eimermacher et al. (Munich, 2006), 291–327 (315). Before 1933, Ehrenburg wrote about Germans with much greater complexity. These writings qualify the charge that Ehrenburg was a Germanophobe at heart, and that his views of Germans bordered on racism. This said, his wartime writings contain anti-German clichés, some of them markedly French in provenance. While the "pedantic" German was a stock figure of the Russian imagination as early as the nineteenth century, the brutish and unrefined qualities of the German resonate with the French image of the German *boche*. Given Ehrenburg's decades-long socialization in France and his known penchant for French culture, this view of the Germans through an unstated French lens may not come as a surprise. Fresinskij, "Ilja Ehrenburg und Deutschland"; on charges of racism, see Berkhoff, *Motherland in Danger*, 183.

89. Vsevolod Vishnevsky writing to Ehrenburg on February 27, 1942, in *Pochta Il'i Erenburga: Ia slyshu vse . . . 1916–1967*, ed. B. Ia. Frezinskii (Moscow, 2006), 82.
90. Erenburg, *Voina*, 445–49.
91. Letter by F. Golub, October 1941, in *Pochta Il'i Erenburga*, 73.
92. Letter by Moisei Aizenberg, June 1, 1944, in *To Pour Out My Bitter Soul: Letters of Jews from the USSR, 1941–1945*, ed. Arkadi Zeltser (Jerusalem, 2016), 94. See also *Sovetskie evrei pishut Il'e Erenburgu. 1943–1966*, ed. Mordechai Al'tshuler et al. (Jerusalem, 1993).
93. Rubinstein, *Tangled Loyalties*, 193
94. Quoted from Jochen Hellbeck, *Stalingrad: The City That Defeated the Third Reich* (New York, 2015), 357. Original source: Il'ia Erenburg, "Ubei!," *Krasnaia zvezda*, July 24, 1942.
95. Hellbeck, *Stalingrad*, 371.
96. The Prozhito database of Soviet diaries and memoirs lists 101 authors who referred to Ehrenburg between June 1941 and May 1945, https://prozhito.org.
97. Letter of August 5, 1942, in *Pochta Il'i Erenburga*, 97.
98. Richard Overy observes that the deep sense of moral superiority over Nazi Germany was a key binding agent that held the anti-Hitler coalition together and ultimately accounted for Allied victory in 1945, but his preconceived notion that morality resided in the West and was defined by it reduces this important insight. "The moral coalition," he writes, "worked only to the extent that the West was able to suppress or at least lighten their [Soviet] ally's dark image." Richard Overy, *Why the Allies Won* (New York, 1995), 296. Ralph Levering traces the intensely pro-Russian mood that took hold of public opinion in the United States starting in 1941 and peaked during the Battle of Stalingrad but also disparages this sentiment as misguided. Ralph Levering, *American Opinion and the Russian Alliance* (Chapel Hill, NC, 1976), 89–107.
99. "The Soviets and the Post-War. A Former Ambassador to Moscow Answers Some Perplexing Problems," *Life*, Special issue USSR, March 29, 1943, 49–66 (50); Mikhail N. Narinsky, Lydia V Pozdeeva, et al., "Mutual Perceptions, Ideals, and Illusions," in *Allies at War: The Soviet, American, and British Experience, 1939–1945*, ed. David Reynolds, Warren F. Kimball, and Aleksandr O. Chubar'ian (New York, 1993), 307–32 (308).
100. Peter H. Buckingham, *America Sees Red: Anti-Communism in America, 1870s—1980s* (Saskatchewan, 1988), 49; Elliott West, "The Roots of Conflict: Soviet Images in the American Press, 1941–1947," in *Essays on American Foreign Policy*, ed. M. F. Morris and S. L. Myres (Austin, 1974).
101. Minister Winston Churchill's Broadcast on the Soviet–German War, London, June 22, 1941, at http://www.ibiblio.org/pha/policy/1941/410622d.html.
102. Vere Hodgson, *Few Eggs and No Oranges: A Diary Showing How Unimportant People in London and Birmingham Lived Through the War Years, 1940–1945* (London, 1976), 166–67 (July 27, 1941).
103. L. V. Pozdeeva, "Sovetskaia propaganda na Angliiu v 1941–1945 godakh," *Voprosy istorii*, 1998, no. 7, 63–74 (65; report dated October 2, 1941). As of July 11, 1941, the Soviet

embassy in London published a daily bulletin, "Soviet War News," with a circulation of 11,000–12,000 copies, 64.

104. Narinsky and Pozdeeva, "Mutual Perceptions, Ideals, and Illusions," 315.
105. Ian McLaine, *Ministry of Morale: Home Front Morale and the Ministry of Information in World War II* (London, 1979), 197–216.
106. Sonya Rose, *Which People's War? National Identity and Citizenship in Wartime Britain, 1939–1945* (New York, 2004), 114.
107. Hodgson, *Few Eggs and No Oranges*, 223.
108. Evan Mawdsley, *December 1941: Twelve Days That Began a World War* (Yale, 2011), 112–14, 274–78.
109. Anthony Eden, *The Reckoning: The Eden Memoirs* (London, 1965), 298–99; *Moskva prifrontovaia*, 391–92.
110. Hodgson, *Few Eggs and No Oranges*, 196, 199–200 (December 7 and 17, 1941).
111. "More Nazi Crimes Listed by Soviet," *New York Times*, January 8, 1942, 7.
112. "The Screen: 'Moscow Strikes Back,' Front-Line Camera Men's Story of Russian Attack, Is Seen at the Globe," *New York Times*, August 17, 1942, 19.
113. *New York Post Meridian*, December 2, 1942; *Motion Picture Herald*, December 1942, cited in *Tsena kadra*, 1009–10 (reverse translations from Russian).
114. Narinsky and Pozdeeva, "Mutual Perceptions, Ideals, and Illusions," 316.
115. Jochen Hellbeck, "La flamme de Stalingrad s'est éteinte," in *Une histoire de la guerre. Du XIXe siècle à nos jours*, ed. Bruno Cabanes et al. (Paris, 2018), 672–79.
116. Narinsky and Pozdeeva, "Mutual Perceptions," 316; Philip M. H. Bell, "Großbritannien und die Schlacht von Stalingrad," in *Stalingrad. Ereignis-Wirkung-Symbol*, ed. Jürgen Förster (Munich, 1992), 350–72 (355).
117. Bell, "Großbritannien," 356–57.
118. Derek Watson, "Molotov, the Making of the Grand Alliance and the Second Front, 1939–1942," *Europe-Asia Studies* 54, no. 1 (January 2002): 51–85.
119. "Nazis Strip West, Russian Declares," *New York Times*, July 30, 1942.
120. W. S. L. Churchill, *The Second World War. Vol. 4: The Hinge of Fate* (Boston, 1950), 477–80. Ehrenburg renewed this plea in an article published on August 22, 1942, the day the Germans began to carpet-bomb Stalingrad: Ilya Ehrenburg, "Red Army Awaits Allies," *New York Times*, August 22, 1942, 4.
121. Narinsky and Pozdeeva, "Mutual Perceptions," 310.
122. "H-013-3 Operation Torch—The Naval Battle of Casablanca," Naval History and Heritage Command, https://www.history.navy.mil/about-us/leadership/director/directors-corner/h-grams/h-gram-013/h-013-3.html. Conservative estimates place the number of Soviet dead at 479,000. G. F. Krivosheev, *Soviet Casualties and Combat Losses in the Twentieth Century* (London, 1997), 125, 127; S. N. Michalev, *Liudskie poteri v Velikoi Otechestvennoi voine 1941–1945 gg. Statisticheskoe issledovanie* (Krasnoiarsk, 2000), 17–41. For much higher estimates, see B. V. Sokolov, "The Cost of War: Human Losses for the USSR and Germany, 1939–1945," *Journal of Slavic Military Studies* 9 (March 1996): 152–93.
123. "Red Anniversary Hailed in London," *New York Times*, November 8, 1942, 38. The Soviet visitors, who had been sent by the Soviet Komsomol, toured factories across Britain and were received exuberantly. Even the police, called up to contain the crowds, joined in the cheers. Rose, *Which People's War?*, 49–50.
124. Hodgson, *Few Eggs and No Oranges*, 263, 293. A poll conducted in March and April 1943 revealed widespread British awareness of the superiority of the Soviet military effort as compared to the British one. Narinsky and Pozdeeva, "Mutual perceptions, Ideals, and Illusions," 316; Bell, "Großbritannien," 355.
125. Attentive readers of Ehrenburg's article could gather that the woman Ehrenburg talked about was Jewish. Almost all the civilians killed by the Germans in Kerch were Jewish.
126. Ilya Ehrenburg, "Hate Is Russian Ammunition," *New York Times*, January 3, 1943.

Chapter 7: Enslavement

1. This was the first poster printed by the Eastern Expanse Department of the German propaganda ministry. It was printed in a large run, showing Hitler in a varying attire, though always with the same gaze. The text was published on adhesive strips in a range of languages: Russian, Ukrainian, Belarusian, Lithuanian, Latvian, Estonian, Georgian, Armenian, Azerbaijani, and Kalmyk. See Ortwin Buchbender, *Das tönende Erz. Deutsche Propaganda gegen die Rote Armee im Zweiten Weltkrieg* (Stuttgart, 1978), 36–37, 264.
2. *Adolf Hitler: Monologe im Führerhauptquartier, 1941–1944. Die Aufzeichnungen Heinrich Heims*, ed. Werner Jochmann (Munich, 1980), 62–66, entries for September 17 (first quotes) and 25 (last two quotes), 1941.
3. Alexander Dallin and other historians have underscored heterogeneity and strife in German political engagement toward the people of the Soviet Union during the Second World War. Alexander Dallin, *German Rule in Russia, 1941–1945: A Study of Occupation Policies* (New York, 1957). While this is not incorrect, what gets lost is a clear sense of whose views held sway and when. Less Russophobe officials had no influence in the early stages of Barbarossa, and even when their views received a hearing in late 1942 this proved to be of little consequence. For an excellent overview, see Manfred Wessbecker, "'Wenn hier Deutsche wohnten . . .' Beharrung und Veränderung im Russlandbild Hitlers und der NSDAP" in *Das Russlandbild im Dritten Reich*, ed. Hans-Erich Volkmann (Cologne, 1994), 9–54.
4. *Die Tagebücher von Joseph Goebbels*, part 2, vol. 3, 198–99 (January 27, 1942).
5. The poster was glued straight onto a theater poster that had not long ago announced the operatic performance of *A Zaporozhian Beyond the Danube* and *Natalka-Poltavka*.
6. Alex J. Kay, "'The Purpose of the Russian Campaign Is the Decimation of the Slavic Population by Thirty Million': The Radicalization of German Food Policy in Early 1941," in *Nazi Policy on the Eastern Front, 1941: Total War, Genocide, and Radicalization*, ed. Alex J. Kay, Jeff Rutherford, and David Stahel (Rochester, NY, 2012), 101–29 (108).
7. Himmler's verbal orders were independently confirmed by the defendant Friedrich Jeckeln in the Riga Trial (1946) and by the witness Bach-Zelewski in the Nuremberg Trial (1946). See Christian Gerlach, *Kalkulierte Morde* (Hamburg, 1998), 52–53.
8. "Der Generalplan Ost," ed. Helmut Heiber, *Vierteljahrshefte für Zeitgeschichte*, 6/3 (July 1958), 281–325 (308, 312–18); Wolfgang Benz, "Der Generalplan Ost. Zur Germanisierungspolitik des NS-Regimes in den besetzten Ostgebieten, 1939–1945," in *Die Vertreibung der Deutschen in den besetzten Ostgebieten 1939–1945. Ursache, Ereignisse, Folgen*, ed. Wolfgang Benz (Frankfurt, 1985), 39–48.
9. See above, chapter 6.
10. On the Nazis' New Order policy, see Mark Mazower, *Hitler's Empire: Nazi Rule in Occupied Europe* (New York, 2008); Hein Klemann and Sergei Kudryashov, *Occupied Economies: An Economic History of Nazi-occupied Europe, 1939–1945* (London, 2013).
11. Kai Struve, *Deutsche Herrschaft, ukrainischer Nationalismus, antijüdische Gewalt* (Berlin, 2015), 222–24, 261, 524; Gregorz Rossoliński-Liebe, "The 'Ukrainian National Revolution' of 1941: Discourse and Practice of a Fascist Movement," *Kritika* 12/1 (Winter 2011): 83–114 (97–99).
12. Karel Berkhoff, *Harvest of Despair: Life and Death Ukraine, 1941–1944* (Cambridge, MA, 2004), 20–21.
13. NA IRI RAN, f. 2, razd. VI, op.6-35: Selivanov; 6-6-16: Lidiia Val'kova; 6-6-11: Anna Chernenko, all from Kharkov.
14. NA IRI RAN, f. 2, razd. VI, op.6-2A: Vladimir Gutsevich, Kharkov.
15. Nikolaev, diary (entries for August 28, September 18, October 22, and November 10, 1941), private archive of Timur Kurganov, Nikolaev's great-grandson, Kharkiv. While excerpts from Nikolaev's wartime diary have been published, the editors chose to use a version of the diary that Nikolaev heavily edited after Soviet forces liberated Kharkov: Lev Nikolaev, "Pod nemetskim sapogom (vypiski iz dnevnika: oktiabr' 1941 g.—avgust

1943 g.," *Coiuz Pisatelei* 12 (2010), https://magazines.gorky.media/sp/2010/12/pod-nemeczkim-sapogom.html. This chapter presents Nikolaev's diary in its original form.
16. Private archive of Timur Kurganov.
17. Nikolaev, diary (October 9 and 27, 1941; see also June 21, 1942).
18. Nikolaev, diary (October 21, 1941).
19. Nikolaev, diary (November 25, 1941). Nikolaev later crossed out these lines from his diary.
20. Nikolaev, diary (October 21, 1941).
21. Nikolaev, diary (October 24, 1941).
22. NA IRI RAN, f. 2, razd. VI, op. 6-13: Nina Pukalova; see also 6-6-58: Petr Ryiaka, both from Kharkov.
23. NA IRI RAN, f. 2, razd. VI, op. 6-22: Mariia Kulinich, Kharkov.
24. The siege of Leningrad, which cost up to a million lives, was the most striking example of this hunger policy. In Kharkov, the famine is believed to have taken well over the fourteen thousand lives counted by city authorities. Dieter Pohl, *Die Herrschaft der Wehrmacht. Deutsche Militärbesatzung und einheimische Bevolkerung in der Sowjetunion, 1941–1944* (München 2008, 192). The number would have been higher had the Germans not begun to recognize the utility of some Soviet laborers in early 1942. From the start, Germans expected their draconian policies to provoke hunger revolts. When revolts did not materialize this was interpreted as expression of Kharkov residents' "childlike trust," see Norbert Kunz, "Das Beispiel Charkow: Eine Stadtbevölkerung als Opfer der deutschen Hungerstrategie, 1941–42," in *Verbrechen der Wehrmacht: Bilanz einer Debatte*, ed. Christian Hartmann, Johannes Hürter, and Ulrike Jureit (Munich, 2005), 136–44 (140–41).
25. Nikolaev, diary (November 5, 1941).
26. Al'tman, *Kholokost na territorii SSSR*, 1,027–28; Andrej Angrick, *"Aktion 1005"—Spurenbeseitigung von NS-Massenverbrechen 1942–1945. Eine "geheime Reichssache" im Spannungsfeld von Kriegswende und Propaganda* (Göttingen, 2018), 57–60; see also NA IRI RAN, f. 2, razd. VI, op. 6-2a: Gutsevich; 6-6-6: Aleksandr Tereshchenko; 6-6-65: O. Gudimova, all from Kharkov; GARF, f. R-7021, op. 76, d. 974, l. 9 ob.
27. Nikolaev, diary (November 16, 1941).
28. The caption reads: "The bodies of six civilians hang from the balcony of a school on Sverdlov Street where they were executed by German troops of the 50th Army Corps. The signs around their necks read 'punishment for blowing up an explosives storehouse.'" Sverdlov Street was renamed Sumskaya Street under German occupation.
29. Nikolaev, diary (December 15, 1941).
30. Angrick, *Operation 1005*, 57–60; Al'tman, *Kholokost na territorii SSSR*, 1,028–29.
31. NA IRI RAN, f. 2, razd. VI, op. 6, d. 11: Chernenko.
32. Nikolaev, diary (December 13, 16, and 29, 1941, and January 1, 1942); for prices on Kharkov's markets, see Buchbender, *Das tönende Erz*, 265.
33. This did not apply to all professors. The Germans took great interest in the work of a group of nuclear physicists at the Ukrianian Institute of Physics and Technology (UFTI) and provided them with generous support, see NA IRI RAN, f. 2, razd. VI, op. 6, d. 39: Ivan Korolev; d. 56: Stanislav Trofal'chik, both Kharkov.
34. NA IRI RAN, f. 2, razd. VI, op. 6, d. 8: Ippolit Nagibin, Kharkov.
35. Nikolaev, diary (March 4, 1942).
36. *Znat' i pomnit'*, 258; Ulrich Herbert, *Hitler's Foreign Workers* (Cambridge, 1997), 125–26, 132, 170.
37. By Himmler's decree, the principal criteria for wearing the badge was whether a worker came from the "old Soviet Russian territories": "Decisive in the entire treatment of these workers is the fact that they have lived for decades under Bolshevik rule and have been systematically raised as enemies of National-Socialist Germany and European culture," https://www.bundesarchiv.de/zwangsarbeit/files/rd19-3_erl-osta-kennz-sw.pdf.

38. Only German farmers were allowed to hire Eastern workers on an individual basis, see Herbert, *Hitler's Foreign Workers*, 163–65, 179.
39. NA IRI RAN, f. 2, razd. VI, op. 15, d. 49: Nikolai Prilezhaev, Minsk; TsDAHOU, f. 166, op. 3, d. 246: Andrei Charugin, Stalino.
40. NA IRI RAN, f. 2, razd. VI, op. 6, d. 3: Mikhail Sakharov, Kharkov; TsDAHOU, f. 166, op. 3, d. 244: Vera Kal'nitskaia, Kiev.
41. Herbert, *Hitler's Foreign Workers*, 168–69.
42. TsDAHOU, f. 166, op. 3, d. 246: Tatiana Selinchuk, Chernigov region; Gosudarstvennyi arkhiv Respubliki Krym (GARK), f. 156, op. 1, d. 31: Khrisanf Lashkevich; NA IRI RAN, f. 2, razd. VI, op. 11, d. 9: Nikolai Driutskii, Zaporozhe region; *Znat' i pomnit'*, 259.
43. M. Polian, *Zhertvy dvukh diktatur. Zhizn', trud, unizheniia, smert' sovetskikh voenno-plennykh i ostarbaiterov na chuzhbine i na rodine*, 2nd rev. ed. (Moscow, 2002), 94.
44. TsDAHOU, f. 166, op. 3, d. 246: Selinchuk; see also d. 243: Florisa Galetskaia, Gor'kii; d. 258: Akulina Golovchenko, Kirovograd region; GARK, f. 156, op. 1, d. 38: Koval'chuk; *Znak ne sotretsia. Sud'by ostarbaiterov v pis'makh, vospominaniiakh i ustnykh rasskazakh* (Moscow, 2016).
45. TsDAHOU, f. 166, op. 3, d. 246: Selinchuk; 166-343: Galetskaia; 166-3-245: Palazhka Ponomarenko, Cherkassy; NA IRI RAN, f. 2, razd. VI, op. 22, d. 21: Zinaida Shidlovskaia, Mogilev; GARK, f. 156, op. 1, d. 38: Koval'chuk.
46. Herbert, *Hitler's Foreign Workers*, 195.
47. German food rations had been cut in April 1942. Adam Tooze, *The Wages of Destruction: The Making and Breaking of the Nazi Economy* (New York, 2006), 541.
48. Herbert, *Hitler's Foreign Workers*, 202.
49. TsDAHOU, f. 166, op. 3, d. 258: Golovchenko.
50. Eastern workers—men and women—had to work factory shifts of twelve, sometimes sixteen hours, while other foreign laborers worked eight (women) or twelve (men) hour shifts. German men, a Soviet laborer remarked, worked ten-to-twelve-hour shifts, and German women had workdays of five to eight hours (TsDAHOU, f. 166, op. 3, d. 243: Galetskaia).
51. Herbert, *Hitler's Foreign Workers*, 214.
52. Benedikt Erenz, "Mythos, Hitler, Spiel und Spass," *Die Zeit*, July 17, 1987, 2.
53. *Psikhologicheskaia voina na Donu. Mify fashistskoi propagandy. 1942–1943*, eds. S. I. and M. I. Filonenko (Voronezh, 2006), 150.
54. Babette Quinkert, *Propaganda und Terror in Weissrussland, 1941–1944* (Paderborn, 2009), 270; *Psikhologicheskaia voina na Donu*, 152–57.
55. Vasilii Baranov, diary (September 6, 1943), https://prozhito.org/person/619; see also NA IRI RAN, f. 2, razd. VI, op. 6, d. 3, Sakharov; Quinkert, *Propaganda und Terror*, 258n35. German authorities printed special postcards for use by "Eastern laborers," see: https://collections.arolsen-archives.org/en/archive/7-2-1-1_721100003 (e.g. DocID: 126735336).
56. Herbert, *Hitler's Foreign Workers*, 169–70. Misery of the Eastern workers traveled not only through their letters; it was also imprinted on the bodies of those whom potential German employers rejected as "unfit to work" and sent back to their places of origin. According to German sources, a total of one hundred thousand workers were put on such "return transports" over the course of 1942. The sight of these emaciated and sick returnees frightened local residents. Herbert, *Hitler's Foreign Workers*, 175; Quinkert, *Propaganda und Terror*, 271.
57. Herbert, *Hitler's Foreign Workers*, 170, 174.
58. Nikolaev, diary (July 12, 1942).
59. Nikolaev, diary (August 16, 1942).
60. Nikolaev, diary (August 13, 1942).
61. NA IRI RAN, f. 2, razd. VI, op. 6, d. 8, Nagin; see also Berkhoff, *Harvest of Despair*, 130. Back in October 1941, when Kharkov lost running water and electricity, Nikolaev expected the Germans to restore these services within days. It took a full year before the

city had running water again, but it remained without electrical power. Nikolaev, diary (October 17, 1942).

62. NA IRI RAN, f. 2, razd. VI, op. 12, d. 13, Charugin; d. 7, Nikolai Pisarenko (both Stalino).
63. NA IRI RAN, f. 2, razd. VI, op.12-36: Pavel Artiukh, Stalino. In the initial months of the occupation, the attitude of Ukrainian peasants toward the Germans was mostly favorable, see Berkhoff, *Harvest of Despair*, 115–17.
64. Kenneth Slepyan, *Stalin's Guerrillas: Soviet Partisans in World War II* (Lawrence, KS, 2006), 118; Berkhoff, *Harvest of Despair*, 224; NA IRI RAN, f. 2, razd. VI, op. 6, d. 6, Tereshchenko (Kharkov); Miner, *Stalin's Holy War*, 132 (citing a November 10, 1943, report on Kharkov).
65. Nikolaev, diary (October 17, 1942).
66. NA IRI RAN, f. 2, razd. VI, op. 12, d. 14, Vasilii P'iankov, Stalino.
67. NA IRI RAN, f. 2, razd. VI, op. 12, d. 15, Tamara Kirillova, Stalino. On German soldiers harrassing and raping Soviet women, see Regina Mühlhäuser, *Eroberungen. Sexuelle Gewalttaten und intime Beziehungen deutscher Soldaten in der Sowjetunion, 1941–1945* (Hamburg, 2010).
68. These grievances were collected and ranked by an official from the German Ministry for the Occupied Eastern Territories in September 1942, see Herbert, *Hitler's Foreign Workers*, 173–74.
69. "We were speechless, when we saw how much and how often the Germans would resort to beatings," said Nadezhda Konashko, a worker from Kiev. NA IRI RAN, f. 2, razd. VI, op. 10, d. 20.
70. TsDAHOU, f. 166, op. 3, d. 245: Piasetskaia. As the witness went on: "We saw and understood full well that as soon as they finished with the Jews, they'd begin to do the same with us as well." Her addition makes clear that the woman beaten by the German was Jewish.
71. NA IRI RAN, f. 2, razd. VI, op. 9, d. 8, Saik (Tarnopol).
72. NA IRI RAN, f. 2, razd. VI, op. 12, d. 13, Charugin; see also d. 5, Gladkoskok (both Stalino).
73. Berkhoff, *Harvest of Despair*, 132–33.
74. Nikolaev, diary (September 5, 1942).
75. A song made the rounds in Ukrainian villages in summer 1942: "The tsar in Russia abolished serfdom long ago / But here Hitler ordered slavery brought in," see Berkhoff, *Harvest of Despair*, 217.
76. NA IRI RAN, f. 2, razd. VI, op. 3, d. 1, Stepan Baranov (Tula).
77. NA IRI RAN, f. 2, razd. II, op. 4, d. 6, Mal'chevskii; d. 34: Pankratov.
78. NA IRI RAN, f. 2, razd. VI, op. 12, d. 11, Maria Gaivoronskaia (Stalino).
79. NA IRI RAN, f. 2, razd. VI, op. 12, d. 14, P'iankov (Stalino).
80. Nikolaev, diary (October 22, 1942; see also October 17, 1942).
81. *Sovetskaia propaganda v gody Velikoi Otechestvennoi voiny*, 328–30; see in addition 406–11, 416, 485–86.
82. Buchbender, *Das tönende Erz*, 270, cf. RW4/236, fol. 22, online at invenio.bundesarchiv.de.
83. Dallin, *German Rule in Russia* (1981 ed.), 152–54; Quinkert, *Propaganda und Terror*, 275.
84. The projection foresaw three hundred thousand soldiers from among Soviet POWs and two hundred civilians, Quinkert, *Propaganda und Terror*, 274–75. Even when promoting the recruitment of Russians, Wehrmacht officials continued to voice concerns about security. For example, auxiliaries, many of whom would be armed, were not to exceed 15 percent of any formation to which they were assigned. Polian, *Zhertvy dvukh diktatur*, 104.
85. Quinkert, *Propaganda und Terror*, 275, 295–96; Weissbecker, "Wenn hier Deutsche wohnten . . . ," 42–43.
86. Quinkert, *Propaganda und Terror*, 280–81.

87. Hitler, *Reden und Proklamationen*, 1,977.
88. Sven Steenberg, *Wlassow* (Cologne, 1968), 52, 73; Catherine Andreyev, *Vlasov and the Russian Liberation Movement*, 50, 55.
89. *The Secret Conferences of Dr. Goebbels: The Nazi Propaganda War, 1939–43*, 319–20 (January 5, 1943, conference).
90. Here and elsewhere, Germans used the designation "Russians" to refer to any ethnicity in Soviet territory as of October 1, 1939, aside from Distrikt Galicia and Bezirk Bialystok.
91. Berkhoff, *Harvest of Despair*, 138.
92. Dallin, *German Rule in Russia*, 148. Even after Rosenberg issued an official ban on corporal punishment throughout the occupied territories, this had little effect because Koch's subordinates knew Koch's real views. During office hours, they often kept a whip on the table. See Berkhoff, *Harvest of Despair*, 47.
93. Dallin, *German Rule in Russia*, 163. See also TsDAHOU, 166-3-245: Ponomarenko.
94. Der deutsche Soldat und seine politischen Aufgaben im Osten, Armeeoberkommando 4, Ic/A.B.O. Im Mai 1943: NA IRI RAN, f. 2, razd. VI, op. 8-44; For a similarly worded instruction, see *Znat' i pomnit'*, 64.
95. For instructions by other agencies using similar language, see Quinkert, *Propaganda und Terror*, 292.
96. Polian, *Zhertvy dvukh diktatur*, 193.
97. Sauckel noted that factory owners who on their own initiative increased food rations for their workers would no longer risk punishment. *Belorusskie ostarbaitery: ugon naseleniia Belarusi na prinuditel'nye raboty v Germaniiu, 1941–1944. Dokumenty i materialy v dvukh knigakh*, vol. 2 (Minsk, 1998), 140–45.
98. TsDAHOU, f. 166, op. 3, d. 244, Kal'nitskaia.
99. NA IRI RAN, f. 2, razd. VI, op. 11, d. 9, Driutskii (Melitopol'); see also op. 10, d. 6, Iurii Markovskii (Kiev).
100. TsDAHOU, f. 166, op. 3, d. 244, Kal'nitskaia.
101. TsDAHOU, f. 166, op. 3, d. 245, Ponomarenko. In Germany, Eastern workers were being incentivized. Those workers who met the labor norms were allowed to wear the "East" badges on their sleeve. All others had to continue wearing it on the breast; see Polian, *Zhertvy dvukh diktatur*, 94. Higher labor output also assured higher food rations, yet there was a sinister edge to this "performance-based nutrition": the added food given to the overachievers was deducted from the rations of those who did not meet the labor norms, see Tooze, *Wages of Destruction*, 530–31; Quinkert, *Propaganda und Terror*, 293.
102. Vasilii Maksimovich Baranov, at prozhito.org, https://www.prozhito.org/person/619; see also TsDAHOU, f. 166, op. 3, d. 244, Kal'nitskaia.
103. Stalin's appeal energized a movement that had started months earlier. Slepyan, *Stalin's Guerillas*, 16.
104. Quinkert, *Propaganda und Terror*, 271.
105. The commando was led by SS-1st Ltn. Oskar Dirlewanger, a former Freikorps activist who had fought Communists in Weimar Germany and joined the Nazi Party in 1923. After being freed from a two-year prison term for raping a fourteen-year-old girl, Dirlewanger sought rehabilitation by fighting in the Spanish Civil War, where he served in the Legion Condor. He was accepted into the SS in June 1940. See Hellmuth Auerbach, "Die Einheit Dirlewanger," *Vierteljahrshefte für Zeitgeschichte* 10, no. 3 (1962): 250–63 (251); and Knut Stang, "Dr. Oskar Dirlewanger—Protagonist der Terrorkriegsführung," in *Karrieren der Gewalt. Nationalsozialistische Täterbiographien*, 3rd ed. (Darmstadt, 2013), 66–75.
106. Longerich, *Himmler*, 625–28; Gerlach, *Kalkulierte Morde*, 922–23.
107. Gerlach, *Kalkulierte Morde*, 611; Ben Shepherd, *War in the Wild East: The German Army and Soviet Partisans* (Cambridge, MA, 2004), 121.

108. Alex J. Kay, *Empire of Destruction: A History of Nazi Mass Killing* (New Haven, 2021), 177–80.
109. *Hitlers Weisungen für die Kriegführung 1939–1945. Dokumente des Oberkommandos der Wehrmacht*, ed. Walther Hubatsch (Frankfurt, 1962), 201–9 (208; emphasis in the original).
110. Shepherd, *War in the Wild East*, 127.
111. Longerich, *Himmler*, 629; Herbert, *Hitler's Foreign Workers*, 231–36.
112. D. A. Zhukov and I. I. Kovtun, *Okhotniki za partizanami. Brigada Dirlevangera* (Moscow, 2013), 217–19.
113. Gerlach, *Kalkulierte Morde*, 949–50; Auerbach, "Die Einheit Dirlewanger," 250–63 (261); Polian, *Zhertvy dvukh diktatur*, 188–91.
114. *Sozhzhennye derevni Belorussii, 1941–1944. Dokumenty i materialy* (Moscow, 2017), 168–69. See also Gerlach, *Kalkulierte Morde*, 902. The agronomist was based in Vileika County Commissariat and was responsible for Cottbus within his county. In toto, Operation Cottbus brought in 6,346 heads of livestock.
115. Nuremberg Document NO-3028, *Trials of War Criminals before the Nuernberg* [*sic*] *Military Tribunals*, Case 11, "The Ministries Case" (Washington, 1952), Green Series, vol. XIII, 519.
116. Gerlach, *Kalkulierte Morde*, 950.
117. Gerlach, *Kalkulierte Morde*, n413.
118. Gerlach, *Kalkulierte Morde*, 951; *Belorusskie ostarbaitery*, 143.
119. Longerich, *Himmler*, 659.
120. Nuremberg Document NO-007, *Trial of the Major War Criminals before the International Military Tribunal* (Nuremberg, 1949), Blue Series, vol. XXXVIII, 210.
121. Jeff Rutherford, "The German 7th Infantry Division and Retreat from the Rzhev Salient, February-March 1943," in *Armies in Retreat: Chaos, Cohesion, and Consequences*, ed. Timothy G. Heck et al. (Fort Leavenworth, KS, 2023), 195–216 (207–8); Armin Nolzen, "'Verbrannte Erde,'" in *Besatzung. Funktion und Gestalt militärischer Fremdherrschaft von der Antike bis zum 20. Jahrhundert*, ed. Günter Kronenbitter et al. (Paderborn, 2006), 161–75; Christian Stein, "Kontrollverlust und unumkehrbare Tatsachen. Die deutschen Rückzüge an der Ostfront des Zweiten Weltkriegs," *Militärgeschichtliche Zeitschrift* 81 (2022): 91–115.
122. Polian, *Zhertvy dvukh diktatur*, 206n60. Seven hundred thousand Soviet forced laborers were brought to Germany between November 1942 and December 1943, see Herbert, *Hitler's Foreign Workers*, 279.
123. Herbert, *Hitler's Foreign Workers*, 296; Rolf-Dieter Müller, *The Unknown Eastern Front: The Wehrmacht and Hitler's Foreign Soldiers* (London, 2012), 155–254.
124. David Motadel, "The Global Authoritarian Moment and the Revolt Against Empire," *American Historical Review* 124, no. 3 (2019): 843–77.
125. Steenberg, *Wlassow*, 115–17.
126. Aleksandrov, *Mify o generale Vlasove*, 147; *Lagebesprechungen im Führerhauptquartier*, ed. Helmut Heiber (Stuttgart, 1963), 109.
127. Steenberg, *Wlassow*, 108.
128. D. Zhukov and I. Kovtun, *Russkie esesovtsy* (Moscow, 2010), 184–86, 208–10; Steenberg, *Wlassow*, 119–20; M. I. Semiriaga, *Kollaboratsionizm. Priroda, tipologiia i proiavleniia v gody Vtoroi mirovoi voiny* (Moscow, 2000), 474. For a partisan leaflet addressing Russian collaborators to defect to the Soviet side, see *Sovetskaia propaganda v gody Velikoi Otechestvennoi voiny*, 485–86.
129. "Das ist der Unterschied," *Das Schwarze Korps*, October 28, 1942.
130. "Speech of the Reichsfuehrer-SS Heinrich Himmler at Kharkow [*sic*] April 1943," in *Nazi Conspiracy and Aggression*, vol. 4 (Washington, DC, 1946), 572–78. Himmler's figure of 200 million was vastly overstated. It roughly corresponded to the total number of the Soviet population in early 1941 (198,712,700 people) and did not take into account either the 65 million Soviet citizens who fell into German hands after the start of

Barbarossa, or the enormous bloodletting of Soviet people between June 1941 and October 1943. See *Tsentral'noe statisticheskoe upravlenie Gosplana SSSR. Chislennost' naseleniia SSSR na 1/I—1941 goda*, at https://web.archive.org/web/20210502183748/http://istmat.info/files/uploads/50979/rgae_4372.41.189_l.19-20.pdf.

131. Nuremberg Document PS-1919, partial English translation in *Nazi Conspiracy and Aggression*, vol. 4, 558–72. Complete German transcript: "Rede des Reichsführers SS bei derSS-GruppenführertagunginPosenam4.Oktober1943," https://www.1000dokumente.de/pdf/dok_0008_pos_de.pdf.

Chapter 8: Liberation

1. For the text of the communiqué, see https://history.state.gov/historicaldocuments/frus1941-43/d452. "Unconditional surrender," the two Western leaders detailed in an earlier press statement, "means not the destruction of the German populace, nor of the Japanese populace, but does mean the destruction of a philosophy in Germany and Japan which is based on the conquest of other peoples." Undated Draft Statement to the Press (January 20–22, 1943), "Foreign Relations of the United States, The Conferences at Washington, 1941–1942, and Casablanca, 1943," U.S. Department of State, Office of the Historian, https://history.state.gov/historicaldocuments/frus1941-43/d448.
2. Warren Kimball discounts the significance of Stalingrad for the Casablanca meeting, noting that neither Churchill nor Roosevelt at the time had a full grasp of the Soviet victory at Stalingrad, and that even Stalin himself could not divine that the Red Army would wrest the strategic initiative from the Germans in the course of 1943. As he makes this point, Kimball overlooks the multiple references the Casablanca communiqués made to the Soviet war effort. Warren F. Kimball, *The Juggler: Franklin Roosevelt as Wartime Statesman* (Princeton, 1991), 70–71.
3. "Beispiellos harte Kämpfe im Raum von Stalingrad," *Völkischer Beobachter* (Vienna edition), January 23, 1943, 1–2, citing the Wehrmacht communiqué. Emphasis in the original communiqué. See also "Stalingrad—bisher schwerste Kämpfe der Ostfront," *Volks-Zeitung* (Vienna), January 23, 1943, 1. English translation at https://research.calvin.edu/german-propaganda-archive/stalingrad1.htm.
4. *Meldungen aus dem Reich. Die geheimen Lageberichte des Sicherheitsdienstes der SS, 1938–1945*, vol. 12, ed. Heinz Boberach (Herrsching, 1984), 4,716.
5. Marianne Sperl, *Tagebücher* 1939–1943. Walter-Kempowski-Archiv, Akademie der Künste (Berlin), BIO 2278 (January 22, 1943). For letters expressing similar fears, see Wolfram Wette, "Das Rußlandbild in der NS-Propaganda. Ein Problemaufriß," in Hans-Erich Volkmann, *Das Russlandbild im Dritten Reich* (Köln, 1984), 55–78 (76–78).
6. Domarus, *Hitler, Reden und Proklamationen*, 1,981.
7. "Letzter Widerstand im GPU.-Gebäude," *Völkischer Beobachter* (Vienna ed.), February 1, 1943, 1.
8. *Jochen Hellbeck, Stalingrad: The City That Defeated the Third Reich* (New York, 2015), 224, 226–61.
9. *Hitler, Reden und Proklamationen, 1932–1945*, ed. Max Domarus, 1,983n88.
10. Henry Picker, *Hitlers Tischgespräche im Führerhauptquartier, 1941–42* (Bonn, 1951), 124–26.
11. Orlando Figes, *A People's Tragedy: The Russian Revolution, 1891–1924* (London, 1996), 646; Hans-Ulrich Wehler, *Entsorgung der deutschen Vergangenheit? Ein polemischer Essay zum "Historikerstreit"* (Munich, 1988), 147–54.
12. Ju. Tsaruski (Jürgen Zarusky), "Porazhenie nemtsev v Stalingrade: reaktsiia nemetskogo obshchestva i natsistskogo gosudarstva," *Rossiia XXI* 2 (2013): 118–27 (125).
13. *Meldungen aus dem Reich*, 4,848 (report dated February 25, 1943).
14. In contrast, the German police surveillance among non-Soviet foreign laborers was spotty at best. Herbert, *Hitler's Foreign Workers* (Cambridge, 1997), 347–48.
15. Herbert, *Hitler's Foreign Workers*, 315. Prejudice among Western European forced laborers against Soviet fellow inmates was widespread. "To make matters worse, many

Soviet prisoners faced blanket hostility by prisoners from other countries, who denounced them as loafers, thieves, and murderers." Nikolaus Wachsmann, *KL: A History of the Nazi Concentration Camps* (New York, 2015), 507.

16. Tsaruski (Zarusky), "Porazhenie nemtsev v Stalingrade," 125.
17. *Meldungen aus dem Reich*, 4,850.
18. *Oldenburg im Zweiten Weltkrieg. Das Kriegstagebuch des Mittelschullehrers Rudolf Tjaden* (Oldenburg, 2010), 144 (February 23, 1943).
19. Herbert, *Hitler's Foreign Workers*, 345–46.
20. E. A. Brodskij, *Die Lebenden kämpfen. Die illegale Organisation Brüderliche Zusammenarbeit der Kriegsgefangenen (BSW)* (Berlin, 1968), 95. The flyer was dated April 18, 1943. Laura Eckl, "Der Widerstand sowjetischer Kriegsgefangener und Zwangsarbeiter*innen 1942–1943. Die Entwicklung der antifaschistischen Widerstandsorganisation 'Brüderliche Zusammenarbeit der Kriegsgefangenen' (BSW) innerhalb nationalsozialistischer Strukturen im Großraum München" (master's thesis, Free University of Berlin, 2019); Christian Streit, *Keine Kameraden. Die Wehrmacht und die sowjetischen Kriegsgefangenen*, 1941–1945, new ed. (Bonn, 1991), 259–60. Lieutenant Colonel Efim Brodskii was the first scholar to document the activities of the BSV. A historian by training, Brodskii discovered Gestapo files about Soviet-led resistance movements while working as a propaganda officer in Soviet-occupied Germany. The tortuous publication history of Brodskii's research is described in Seth Bernstein, *Return to the Motherland: Displaced Soviets in World War II and the Cold War* (Ithaca, NY, 2023), 169–72.
21. *Serdtse ty nashel maguchei strany* // You found a mighty country's heart
    Tebe vechno my budem verny. // We'll be faithful to you forever,
    Ataku liubogo vraga otrazim. // We'll repel any enemy's attack.
    Liubov'iu svoeiu ty nas odaril. // You made us a present with your love.
    Izvergov ty nenadivish i b'esh' // You hate and beat the monsters
    Nam zhe ty vechnoe schast'e // You give us eternal happiness.
22. As he corresponded with Galetskaia, Zheleznov appealed to her as a member of the intelligentsia to politically enlighten other "Eastern workers," for the most part uneducated peasant youth. Her task was to make them embrace the mission of "liberating the Russian and Ukrainian peoples from their enslavement." TsDAHOU, f. 166, op. 3, d. 243, interview with Florissa Galetskaia, December 12, 1945. Zheleznov was the nom de guerre for Nikolai Nikolaevich Shevchenko, a history teacher from Chernigov who would join the staff of Chernigov's Historical Museum after the war and in that capacity build an archive about Soviet anti-fascist resistance inside Germany (see NA IRI RAN, f. 2, razd. VI, op. 22, d. 28, containing Shevchevnko's correspondence with Isaak Mints and other members of the Commission on the History of the Great Patriotic War, 1949). Seth Bernstein treats Shevchenko's and Galetskaia's accounts of their resistance activities at arm's length, believing that they largely served the goal of securing their author's postwar repatriation into the Soviet Union. Bernstein goes so far as to write that Shevchenko's resistance claims were invented. He also believes that the Nazis greatly exaggerated the size and threat of Soviet underground organizations (Bernstein, *Return to the Motherland*, 73–79, 172–82). Both these suppositions are belied by the consistency of the Soviet and the German documentary record. For the latter, see Efim Brodskii, "Iz arkhivov Miunkhenskogo Gestapo," *Novyi Mir*, no. 6 (1964): 258–76.
23. *Die Tagebücher von Joseph Goebbels*, II/7, 514 (March 9, 1943).
24. *Die Tagebücher von Joseph Goebbels*, II/7, 514–15.
25. Dr. Joseph Goebbels, "Nun, Volk, steh auf, und Sturm brich los!, Rede im Berliner Sportpalast 18. Februar 1943," at http://ia802607.us.archive.org/4/items/WolltIhrDenTotalenKrieg/GoebbelsJoseph-Rede-WolltIhrDenTotalenKrieg194315S.pdf.
26. Goebbels, "Nun, Volk, steh auf, und Sturm brich los!," Goebbels's appeal carried beyond the walls of Berlin's Sports Palace; relatives of soldiers who had gone missing in Stalingrad circulated chain letters to families of other "Stalingraders" demanding that Ger-

many take revenge on the "6–7 million Jews in our hands" should Moscow's "Jewish rulers harm our captured soldiers," Frank Biess, *Homecomings: Returning POWs and the Legacies of Defeat in Postwar Germany* (Princeton, 2006), 32.

27. The picture of this soldier was also used in the SS-sponsored picture book, *The Subhuman* (*Der Untermensch*, 1942), to highlight the contrast between upright and healthy Aryans and demonic-looking "Jewish-Bolshevik" types. See also Mareike Otters, "Fotografien sowjetischer Kriegsgefangener aus dem Konzentrationslager Sachsenhausen. Eine Untersuchung antisowjetischer, Propagandabilder,'" in *Besatzung, Vernichtung, Zwangsarbeit* (Berlin, 2017), 105–36.
28. Himmler issued his order on July 19, 1942. According to German data, 2,284,000 Jews lived in the General Government in hundreds of ghettos dispersed all over the country. Yitzhak Arad, *Belzec, Sobibor, Treblinka: The Operation Reinhard Death Camps* (Bloomington, IN, 1987), 44–47. More than eight hundred thousand victims were murderd in Treblinka. Only after operations in Treblinka wound down during 1943 did Auschwitz become the main killing ground of Jews. Wachsmann, *KL*, 307.
29. Arad, *Belzec, Sobibor, Treblinka*, 81; Vasily Grossman, "The Hell of Treblinka," in Vasily Grossman, *The Road: Short Fiction and Articles* (London, 2011).
30. Arad, *Belzec, Sobibor, Treblinka*, 165n67. There is no official record of the visit, see *Die Organisation des Terrors. Der Dienstkalender Heinrich Himmlers 1943–1945*, ed. Matthias Uhl et al. (Munich, 2020).
31. Angrick, "*Aktion 1005*," vol. 1, 346, 375.
32. Arad, *Belzec, Sobibor, Treblinka*, 167, 173; Grossman, "The Hell of Treblinka"; Angrick, "*Aktion 1005*," vol. 1, 247.
33. Ilya Ehrenburg and Vassily Grossman, *The Complete Black Book of Russian Jewry* (New Brunswick, NJ, 2002), xxi.
34. The Jewish fighting organization (ZOB) cited as its precursor a Communist "Antifascist Bloc" that had been founded in the ghetto in early 1942 and called on ghetto residents of fighting age to join partisan formations in the forest, as was practiced in the Minsk ghetto. German arrests terminated the Antifascist Bloc before it could take meaningful action. While the organization did not survive, its operational design and activist ethos lived on in the ZOB. Havi Dreifuss, "The Leadership of the Jewish Combat Organization during the Warsaw Ghetto Uprising: A Reassessment," *Holocaust and Genocide Studies* 31 (2017): 24–60 (25–26).
35. Marek Edelman, *The Ghetto Fights: Warsaw 1943–1945* [1946] (London, 1990), 71–72.
36. A facsimile of the report (minus its appendix) is available at https://catalog.archives.gov/id/6003996. The report mentioned seventeen Axis soldiers and policemen killed, in addition to ninety-three wounded, all of them listed individually, with rank, occupation, and date of birth (2–6).
37. A facsimile of the report, which is located in the National Archives and Records Administration (NARA), can be found at https://catalog.archives.gov/id/596657.
38. Ibid., 11 (18 in the PDF of the facsimile). The report refers to Treblinka II as "T. II."
39. It was "high time" to confront the "steadily growing terrorism" by "removing as fast as possible" all remaining Jews from the General Government, Goebbels dictated to his diary on April 25, fully aware that "removing" spelled "killing." Goebbels, *Tagebücher*, II/8, 163 (April 25, 1943); *Dieter Pohl, Nationalsozialistische Judenverfolgung in Ostgalizien, 1941–1944: Organisation und Durchführung eines staatlichen Massenverbrechens* (Munich, 1996), 256.
40. These cumulative raids killed an estimated 80,000 Jews. Pohl, *Nationalsozialistische Judenverfolgung in Ostgalizien*, 263. In late June, Higher SS and Police Leader Fritz Katzmann produced a leather-clad report that resembled Stroop's earlier report and echoed its flush of victory. "Galicia is free of Jews!" Katzmann proclaimed. Claudia Koonz, "On Reading a Document: SS-Man Katzmann's 'Solution of the Jewish Question in the District of Galicia,'" Raul Hilberg Lecture, University of Vermont, November 2, 2005, at https://web.archive.org/web/20150205021305/http://www.uvm.edu

/~uvmchs/documents/KoonzHilbergLecture002.pdf; Pohl, *Nationalsozialistische Judenverfolgung in Ostgalizien*, 262. On the bunkers, see Katzmann's Report, reprinted in *Trial of the Major War Criminals before the International Military Tribunal* ("Blue Series"), vol. 38, 391; Peter Longerich, *Heinrich Himmler* (Oxford, 2012), 664–65.

41. This was the number given in an official German report published in September 1943, *Amtliches Material zum Massenmord von Katyn* (Berlin, 1943). According to internal Soviet reports, 4,421 officers were executed at Katyn. *Katyn: A Crime Without Punishment*, ed. Anna M. Cienciala, Natalia S. Lebedeva, Wojciech Materski (New Haven, 2007) 1, 240–41, 332.
42. John Fox, "Der Fall Katyn und die Propaganda des NS-Regimes," *Vierteljahrshefte für Zeitgeschichte* 30, no. 3 (1982): 462–99 (463); *Amtliches Material zum Massenmord von Katyn*.
43. Claudia Weber, *Krieg der Täter: Die Massenerschießungen von Katyn* (Hamburg, 2015), 175–78.
44. Weber, *Krieg der Täter*, 179; *Soviet Government Statements on Nazi Atrocities*, ed. Viacheslav M. Molotov (London and New York, 1946), 127–28.
45. *Die Tagebücher des Joseph Goebbels*, II/8, 126 (April 18, 1943); Fox, "Der Fall Katyn," 465.
46. Fox, "Der Fall Katyn," 464; Weber, *Krieg der Täter*, 104.
47. Herf, *The Jewish Enemy*, 201, 207.
48. *Die Tagebücher des Joseph Goebbels*, II/7, 382, 418 (February 22 and 26, 1943); II/8, 104 (April 14, 1943).
49. Sensing the propagandist exploitation of their travel to Katyn, several of the European pathologists refused to give interviews to German press after their return to Berlin as they feared to appear like Nazi stooges. Fox, "Der Fall Katyn," 487.
50. Berkhoff, "Total Annihilation of the Jewish Population," 89.
51. *Amtliches Material zum Massenmord von Winniza* (Berlin, 1944). As in Katyn, locals had informed the Germans about these mass graves as early as in 1941.
52. *Amtliches Material zum Massenmord von Winniza*, 103–8. In the town of Ovruch and elsewhere in Ukraine, German authorities allowed local activists to erect monuments to local victims of Communist repression in the 1930s. By October 1943, substantial funds were also raised for a monument in Vinnitsa, but it was not built. Serhii Stelnykovych et al., "Nazi Occupation and the Dismantling of Communist Monuments in Ukraine during World War II," *Intermarum* 8 (2020): 76–88 (83–84).
53. *Nove Ukrains'ke slovo*, July 31, 1943, quoted in Weiner, *Making Sense of War*, 267–68. As with Katyn before, the Soviet information bureau shot back, asserting that the Germans were responsible for the murder of the people exhumed in Vinnitsa. Sovinformbiuro sarcastically invited the Germans to continue their work and "uncover" the enormous number of Soviet victims of fascist terror who had been executed in Kiev's Babi Yar ravine. "Ocherednaia provokatsiia fashistskikh liudoedov," *Krasnaia Zvezda*, August 12, 1943, 1.
54. Pavel Lomakin and Grigorii Loiko (Kharkov); Ivan Romanchenko (Lvov), NA IRI RAN, f. 2, razd. VI, op. 6, dd. 42 and 45; TsDAHOU, f. 166, op. 3, d. 246.
55. Oleksandr Maevs'kyi, "Vydobrazhennia vynnits'koi tragedyi v dzerkaly natsysts'koi propagandy," *Ukrains' kyi Istorychnyi Zhurnal* 19 (2017), illustration no. 15.
56. Tarik Cyril Amar, *The Paradox of Ukrainian Lviv: A Borderland City Between Stalinists, Nazis, and Nationalists* (Ithaca, NY, 2015), 138. See also TsDAHOU, f. 166, op. 2, d. 214, Vasilii Vavrik (Lvov).
57. TsDAHOU, f. 166, op. 3, d. 246, Ivan Romanchenko (Lvov); d. 245, Mariia Piasetskaia (Lvov).
58. Illustration 65, https://collections.ushmm.org/search/catalog/irn543893. The poster was also produced with "Vinnitsa" in the Russian spelling.
59. Amir Weiner, "The Making of a Dominant Myth: The Second World War and the Construction of Political Identities Within the Soviet Polity," *Russian Review* 55/4 (October 1996): 638–60 (656).

60. NA IRI RAN, f. 2, razd. VI, op. 14, d. 4.
61. Claudia Weber, "'Stalin's Trap': The Katyń Forest Massacre between Propaganda and Taboo," in *Theatres of Violence: Massacre, Mass Killing and Atrocity Throughout History*, ed. Philip Dwyer and Lyndall Ryan (New York, 2012), 170–85 (174); *Katyn. Mart 1940 g.—sentiabr' 2000 g." Rasstrel. Sudby zhivykh. Ekho Katyni. Dokumenty*, ed. Natalia S. Lebedeva (Moscow, 2001), 423–25; Janina Struk, *Photographing the Holocaust: Interpretations of the Evidence* (London, 2004), 48.
62. On the building of the legal front against Nazism, see chap. 9. Goebbels saw in the American and British refusal to embrace the truth about Stalin's crimes added confirmation of a global Jewish conspiracy against Germany (Herf, *The Jewish Enemy*, 203, 240).
63. This visit and operation is extensively covered in Angrick, *"Aktion 1005,"* vol. 1, 346–99.
64. NA IRI RAN, f. 2, razd. VI, op. 10, d. 27, Vladislav Kuklia; d. 24, Nikolai Panasik (both Kiev); Karel C. Berkhoff, "Babi Yar," Online Encyclopedia of Mass Violence, https://pure.knaw.nl/ws/files/1653911/Berkhoff-2015-BabiYar-OnlineEncyMasViolence.pdf.
65. NA IRI RAN, f. 2, razd. VI, op. 10, d. 1; Ainsztein, *Jewish Resistance*, 690–91.
66. Angrick, *"Aktion 1005,"* vol. 1, 190–91, 373. ("*Hier liegen meine 30,000 Juden.*")
67. Angrick, *"Aktion 1005,"* vol. 1, 373–78.
68. Angrick, *"Aktion 1005,"* vol. 1, 373–78.
69. Angrick, *"Aktion 1005,"* vol. 1, 354.
70. NA IRI RAN, f. 2, razd. VI, op. 10, d. 24, Nikolai Panasik.
71. Angrick, *"Aktion 1005,"* vol. 1, 391; Ainsztein, *Jewish Resistance*, 690–96 (provides a different escape date).
72. *Petr Andreevich Zaionchkovskii. Sbornik statei i vospominanii k stoletiiu istorika*, ed. L. G. Zakharova et al. (Moscow, 2008), 146. Zaionchkovsky would after the war become a preeminent historian of Late Imperial Russia.
73. I. Erenburg, "Delo sovesti," *Pravda*, October 29, 1943.
74. I. Erenburg, "2 sentiabria 1943 g.," in idem, *Voina. 1941–1945*, ed. B. Ia. Frezinskii, (Moscow, 2004), 462–66; I. Erenburg, "Delo sovesti."
75. Ilya Ehrenburg, "Something I Can Never Forget," *New York Times Magazine*, December 26, 1943, 22.
76. I. Erenburg, "Izgnanie vraga," *Krasnaia Zvezda*, September 9, 1943.
77. Ehrenburg provided Hauster's military postal code: 11 981. This code belonged to a convoy within Infantry Regiment 172 (75. Inf. Div.) that retreated across north-central Ukraine from Romny to Priluki and Kiev. Norbert Kannapin, *Die deutsche Feldpostübersicht 1939–1945*, Bd. 1: Nrn. 00001-20308 (Osnabrück, 1980), 241.
78. I. Erenburg, "Delo sovesti"; Ehrenburg, "Something I Can Never Forget." Ehrenburg's archive includes a photograph that he took of dead cows in the liberated Soviet territories. See *Ilja Ehrenburg und die Deutschen*, ed. Peter Jahn (Berlin, 1997), 72.
79. Joshua Rubenstein, *Tangled Loyalties: The Life and Times of Ilya Ehrenburg* (London, 1996), 195; Berkhoff, "Total Annihilation," 69.
80. The piece appeared in the November 4, 1943, issue of *Einikait*, the newspaper of the Jewish Anti-Fascist Committee. It was subsequently republished as "Nemetskie fashisty ne dolzhny zhit," in *Birobidzhanskaia zvezda* (November 26, 1943), a Russian-language paper for Soviet Jews in the autonomous republic of Birobidzhan. Vassily Grossman's famous essay, "Ukraine Without Jews," did not appear in *Einikait* until November 25, 1943, with a second installment following on December 2, 1943. Grossman's observations may have been partly prescribed by Ehrenburg's. The Jewish Anti-Fascist Committee is discussed in chapter 10.
81. Martin J. Blackwell, *Kyiv as Regime City: The Return of Soviet Power after Nazi Occupation* (Rochester, NY, 2016), 19; NA IRI RAN, f. 2, razd. VI, op. 10, d. 17, Nina Riabchenko; d. 20, Nadezhda Konashko (both Kiev).
82. NA IRI RAN, f. 2, raz. 6, op. 10, d. 17, Riabchenko; d. 31, Natalya Gubar'kova (Kiev).

83. NA IRI RAN, f. 2, razd. 6, op. 10, d. 15a and 15b: Solomon Pekker; d. 15v: Ol'ga Mukhortova-Pekker (both Kiev).
84. NA IRI RAN, f. 2, razd. VI, op. 12, d. 2a, Fedor Starovoitov (Stalino); op. 6, d. 44, Aleksei Simonov (Kharkov); Artem Latyshev, "Almost Soviet: Integration of the Liberated Territories of the USSR, 1942–1944," *Jahrbücher für Geschichte Osteuropas* 3, no. 4 (2020): 378–402 (381–84); Serhy Yekelchyk, *Stalin's Citizens: Everyday Politics in the Wake of Total War* (Oxford, 2014), 74–75; Blackwell, *Kyiv as Regime City*, 140; Livshin, *Sovetskaia propaganda v gody Velikoi Otechestvennoi voiny*, 676–81, 694–97.
85. Yekelchyk, *Stalin's Citizens*, 70.
86. NA IRI RAN, f. 2, razd. VI, op. 11, d. 2, Vassili Filippovskii (Melitopol'). Filippovskii's initial wariness wore off when he saw people arrive with red flags and portraits of Stalin that they had stashed away when the Germans arrived in 1941.
87. This liberation script had roots in the early Soviet revolutionary tradition. Consider the Reds' recapture of the city of Ufa from the Whites in June 1919, as narrated by former Red Army commissar Dmitry Furmanov. Within hours after the storming of the city, "a huge quantity of leaflets was distributed among the population, explaining the situation. Wall newspapers covered the walls of the houses, and from the morning of the next day on, the divisional newspaper was regularly issued every morning. Improvised meetings were held in all corners of the town." Dmitrii Furmanov, *Sobranie sochinenii*, vol. 1 (Moscow, 1961), 277. In the civil war, and then again during the Second World War, Soviet leaders banked on the personally and collectively empowering effects of their ideology of political liberation, which they held up against the "reactionary" ideology of their foes. "They conduct unceasing agitation," a White officer said, grudgingly acknowledging the success with which the Red Army's political workers campaigned among their recruits; "[They take] advantage of every available opportunity and [exploit] even the most trivial fact to highlight the benefits that the Bolshevik regime has brought to their lives." Mark Von Hagen, *Soldiers in the Proletarian Dictatorship: The Red Army and the Soviet Socialist State, 1917–1930* (Ithaca, NY, 1990), 98, 113.
88. N. S. Atarov, "Panshin voinu ob"iasniaet," in idem, *Voennaia publitsistika i frontovye ocherki* (Moscow, 1966), 438–50 (445–46); Alexander Werth, *Russia at War, 1941–1945* (New York, 2017), 608–10.
89. Paula Chan, "Seeing Like the Stalinist State: The First Wave of War Crimes Investigations in Krasnodar, Stavropol, and Orel," unpubl. ms., 18–19, 37; Nathalie Moine, "La commission d'enquête soviétique sur les crimes de guerre nazis: entre reconquête du territoire, écriture du récit de la guerre et usages justiciers," *Le Mouvement social*, no. 222 (2008): 81–109 (89). The spontaneous, ground-level creation of these documents was also their weakness: only few of them identified exact enemy units that had perpetrated a given crime or came with sufficiently precise dates to qualify as legal documents.
90. The survivor, Vladimir Davydov, didn't come alone. Together with several other former inmates, he delivered to the NKVD three Ukrainian guards who had tormented the prisoners in the Syrets camp. "Zapyska kolyshnikh uviaznenykh Syrets'koho kontstaboru D. Budnyka, V. Davydova, Z. Trubakova, I. Dolinera, V. Kukli," May 20, 1945, in *Derzhavnyi arkhiv Kyivs'koi oblasti*, f. P-4, op. 2, spr. 85, ark. 176–82, http://www.kby.kiev.ua/book1/documents/doc85.html; see also *Babi Yar. Chelovek. Vlast'*, 140.
91. Blackwell, *Kyiv as Regime City*, 131–32; "Zapyska kolyshnikh uviaznenykh Syrets'koho kontstaboru."
92. Aleksandr Zviagintsev, *Rudenko* (Moscow, 2008), 57. Born in 1907, Roman Rudenko had served as procurator of the Donetsk (renamed Stalino in 1938) region between 1937 and 1940. In that function he took a lead part in extrajudicial sentencings and executions of several thousand presumed "counterrevolutionary elements," most of them Soviet citizens of German, Polish, Latvian, or Finnish nationality. Rudenko personally attended many of the shootings. See "Troika v biografii," *Kommersant*, February 1, 2020, https://www.kommersant.ru/doc/4241117.

93. Steiuk's interrogation protocols, https://victims.rusarchives.ru/protokol-doprosa-svidetelya-yaa-steyuka-o-prestupleniyakh-nemecko-fashistskikh-zakhvatchikov-v; https://victims.rusarchives.ru/protokol-doprosa-svidetelya-steyuka-o-prestupleniyakh-nemecko-fashistskikh-zakhvatchikov. Ilya Ehrenburg and Vasily Grossman, *The Complete Black Book of Russian Jewry* (New Brunswick and London, 2002), 11–12.
94. Gvardii Maior I. Stadiuk, "Ubiitsy zametaiut sledy. Babii Iar otkryl strashnuiu tainu," *Muzhestvo* (271), November 18, 1943, 1. See also https://www.berkovich-zametki.com/2013/Zametki/Nomer1112/Gluhovsky1.php.
95. Gennadii Glukhovskii, "Zhizn' Iakova Shteina," *Evreiskii obozrevatel'* 10, no. 250 (October 2013), https://jew-observer.com/puti-i-sudby/zhizn-yakoba-shtejna-2/.
96. NA IRI RAN, f. 2, razd. VI, op. 10, d. 24. Andrej Angrick laments the fact that the Soviet state did not protect its crown witnesses against Nazism and moreover insinuates that the fourteen survivors were drafted into the Red Army against their will. Four of them would die in battle. Angrick, *"Aktion 1005,"* vol. 1, 203, 398.
97. Ainsztein, *Jewish Resistance*, 767–69. Not every survivor who wanted to fight was allowed into the Red Army. Newly recruited soldiers from the formerly occupied regions first underwent a screening process to test their political reliability. Artem Latyshev, "Almost Soviet: Integration of the Liberated Territories of the USSR, 1942–1944," *Jahrbücher für Geschichte Osteuropas* 3, no. 4 (2020): 387.
98. Brandon Schechter was the first scholar to size up the emotional charge and reach of these vengeance meetings. Brandon M. Schechter, *The Stuff of Soldiers: A History of the Red Army in World War II Through Objects* (Ithaca, NY, 2019), 113–14.; S. S. Koz'min, *O liubvi i voine. Vospominaniia* (Ekaterinburg, 2018): 31–32.
99. "Sestry zhdut," *Muzhestvo* (271), November 18, 1943, 1.
100. Schechter, *The Stuff of Soldiers*, 112–15.
101. Ehrenburg and Grossman, *The Complete Black Book*, 185.
102. Arkadi Zeltser and Erina Megowan, "Differing Views Among Red Army Personnel About the Nazi Mass Murder of Jews," *Kritika: Explorations in Russian and Eurasian History* 15, no. 3 (2014): 563–90 (587).
103. *Sovetskie evrei pishut Il'e Erenburgu*, 132 (letter dated March 25, 1944); see also Ehrenburg and Grossman, *The Complete Black Book*, 185–88.
104. Schechter, *The Stuff of Soldiers* 114; see also Manfred Zeidler, *Kriegsende im Osten*. Die Rote Armee und die Besetzung Deutschlands östlich von Oder und Neiße 1944/45 (Munich, 1996), 131.
105. "Miting v osvobozhdennom Kieve," *Muzhestvo*, December 8, 1943, 1. Soon Oleksandr Dovzhenko's documentary film about Ukrainian wartime suffering and liberation came into Soviet cinemas, though not under Dovzhenko's proposed title, *Ukraine in Flames*. The words invited suspicion of nationalist agitation. Ukrainian intellectuals like Dovzhenko actively promoted the theme of Soviet Ukraine's liberation as a way of articulating their national feelings, and in Moscow-controlled narratives of the war, Ukraine rose to second place, following Russia, in the Soviet hierarchy of nations (Weiner, *Making Sense of War*, 336). But Moscow censors clamped down on any appearance of a Ukrainian nationalism that either vied for equality with the Russian big-brother nation or was regarded as asserting itself independently of the Soviet Union. See Yekelchyk, *Stalin's Empire of Memory*, 38–40. Ukrainian officials themselves were highly aware of the need to articulate their national faith in fundamentally different terms than their nationalist competitors who had been collaborating with Nazi Germany.
106. This episodic acknowledgment, and simultaneous withholding on conceptual grounds, of Jewish suffering may help explain why the Jewish theme alternatively appeared and disappeared in the Soviet wartime press. In toto, Mordechai Altschuler shows robust coverage of Jewish themes in the Soviet wartime press and posits a break merely for the postwar years. Mordechai Altshuler, "The Holocaust in the Soviet Mass Media during the War and in the First Postwar Years Re-examined," *Vad Yashem Studies* 39, no. 2 (October 2010): 121–68.

107. Lev Bezymenskii, "Informatsiia po-sovetski," *Znamia* 1998, no. 5, 192–93. Even though the report nominally dealt with German atrocities in Kiev, its opening sections made clear that the subject was suffering Ukraine: *Soviet Government Statements on Nazi Atrocities*, 136–40.
108. For the case of Soviet Estonia, see Paula Chan, "Red Stars and Yellow Stars: The Soviet Investigation of Klooga Concentration Camp," *Holocaust and Genocide Studies* 33, no. 2 (2019), 197–224.
109. "O zlodeianiiakh nemtsev na territorii L'vovskoi oblasti," *Krasnaia zvezda*, December 23, 1944.
110. A White Book on Katyn, filled with photos, forensic findings, and testimonies, appeared in Berlin in September 1943: *Amtliches Material zum Massenmord von Katyn. Im Auftrag des Auswärtigen Amtes aufgrund urkundlichen Beweismaterials zusammengestellt* (Berlin, 1943).
111. *Katyn'. Mart 1940 g.—sentiabr' 2000 g.*, 429–30.
112. *Katyn'. Mart 1940 g.—sentiabr' 2000 g.*, 430–31. Some scholars have treated Burdenko's rendition of his discovery with considerable suspicion: M. Iu. Sorokina, "Operatsiia 'Umelye ruki', ili chto uvidel Akademik Burdenko v Orle?," in *In memorium: Sbornik pamiati Vladimira Alloia*, ed. T. B. Pritykina and O. A. Korostelev (St. Petersburg, 2005), 361–89. The American journalist Edmund Stevens was one of several foreign observers who were invited to the Katyn forest to observe the forensic work of Burdenko's commission. Even in his 1946 memoirs Stevens did not doubt that the Germans had murdered the Polish officers. Edmund Stevens, *Russia Is No Riddle* (New York, 1946), 167–71.
113. "Military Rites Held at Reburial of Poles," *New York Times*, February 1, 1944, 3. After the retaking of Vinnitsa by Soviet troops in March 1944, the crosses that had been put up to commemorate the victims of Soviet terror were replaced by a pillar inscribed: "Here victims of fascism lie buried." Irina Paperno, "Exhuming the Bodies of Soviet Terror," *Representations* 75, no. 1 (2001): 89–118 (103).
114. *Pravda*, January 26,1944, 2–4; English translation: *Soviet Government Statements on Nazi Atrocities*, 107-36; *Katyn'. Mart 1940 g.—sentiabr' 2000 g.*, 433–37.
115. In conversations with other commission members, Burdenko voiced astonishment at how carelessly the Germans must have performed their forensic work to overlook easily obtainable evidence that disproved their own claims. See *Katyn'. Mart 1940 g.—sentiabr' 2000 g.*, 434.
116. Prior to Burdenko's discovery, Sovinformbiuro had made the same observation vis-à-vis the exhumed victims in Vinnitsa, remarking on the German trademark style of killing people with shots in the nape of their necks. "*Ocherednaia provokatsiia fashistskikh liudoedov.*"
117. *Meldungen aus dem Reich*, October 7, 1943; Herbert, *Hitler's Foreign Workers*, 472n169.
118. Herbert, *Hitler's Foreign Workers*, 345.
119. Eckl, "Der Widerstand sowjetischer Kriegsgefangener und Zwangsarbeiter*innen 1942–1943"; Herbert, *Hitler's Foreign Workers*, 355–56.
120. TsDAHOU, f. 166, op. 3, d. 243.
121. Two hundred survived until the end of the war. Arad, *Belzec, Sobibor, Treblinka*, 337; Selma Leydesdorff, *Sasha Pechersky: Holocaust Hero, Sobibor Resistance Leader, and Hostage of History* (New York, 2017).
122. NA IRI RAN, f. 2, razd. VI, op. 8, d. 9. Barutchev was interviewed in Moscow on December 25, 1944. See also Arad, *Belzec, Sobibor, Treblinka*, 368.
123. Herf, *The Jewish Enemy*, 232; Arad, *Belzec, Sobibor, Treblinka*, 372–73.
124. Daniel Blatman, *The Death Marches: The Final Phase of Nazi Genocide* (Cambridge, MA, 2011), 58.
125. Details from Konstantin Simonov's essay, discussed below.
126. K. Simonov, "Lager' unichtozheniia," *Krasnaia Zvezda*, August 10–12, 1944.

127. David Shneer, "Is Seeing Believing? Photographs, Eyewitness Testimony, and Evidence of the Holocaust," *East European Jewish Affairs* 45, no. 1 (2015): 65–78 (70–72).
128. Simonov's article covered the November 3, 1943, massacre in Majdanek in detail. His account was likely provided by the Armenian doctor Barutchev, who mentioned to Mints's team of historians that he had been interviewed by the writer in the liberated camp. See NA IRI RAN, f. 2, razd. VI, op. 8, d. 9, Barutchev.
129. Berkhoff, "Total Annihilation of the Jewish Population," 92; Shneer, "Is Seeing Believing?," 77n23. Simonov's complete account was published in English as *In One Newspaper: A Chronicle of Unforgettable Years*, ed. Ilya Ehrenburg and Konstantin Simonov (New York, 1985), 405–30.
130. *Tsena kadra. Sovetskaia frontovaia kinokhronika, 1941–1945 gg.* (Moscow, 2010), 846–47.
131. *Tsena kadra. Sovetskaia frontovaia kinokhronika*, 846–47; "Lublin Extermination Camp Called 'Worst Yet' by Writer," *Daily Worker*, August 14, 1944, 8. See also Natascha Drubek-Meyer, *Filme über Vernichtung und Befreiung. Die Rhetorik der Filmdokumente aus Majdanek, 1944–1945* (Wiesbaden, 2020); Victor Barbat, "Un opérateur en guerre: le parcours de Roman Karmen, 1941–1945," in *Par le fil de l'image. Cinéma, guerre, politique*, ed. Sylvie Lindeperg (Paris, 2018), 109–26. According to Barbat, Karmen enjoyed a degree of artistic freedom that was unusual for a filmmaker of the Stalin period.
132. Anita Kondoyanidi, "The Liberating Experience: War Correspondents, Red Army Soldiers, and the Nazi Extermination Camps," *Russian Review* 69 (2010): 449–52. The response that the Soviet discoveries met in various parts of the world was ambivalent, however. When the British Moscow correspondent Alexander Werth sent the BBC a detailed report on the discovery of the Majdanek camp in August 1944, his editors in London turned it down, thinking it was a Soviet propaganda stunt. It was not, Werth remarks in his memoirs, until the "discovery in the West of Buchenwald, Dachau and Belsen that Western media became convinced that Majdanek and Auschwitz were also genuine." Alexander Werth, *Russia at War, 1941–1945* (New York, 1964), 890.
133. The soldier apologized to Ehrenburg for writing in Yiddish, explaining that his mastery of Russian was poor. *Sovetskie evrei pishut Il'e Erenburgu*, 169–70.
134. On the different estimates given about the prisoners killed at Treblinka, see Angrick, "*Aktion 1005*," vol. 1, 244.
135. Grossman, "The Hell of Treblinka," in Vasily Grossman, *The Road*, ed. and trans. Robert Chandler (New York, 2010).
136. V. S. Grossman, "Treblinskii ad," 127.
137. Grossman, "The Hell of Treblinka."
138. This was the case in Kharkov's Drobitsky Yar. Angrick, "*Aktion 1005*," vol. 1, 359–60.

Chapter 9: "Here She Is, Accursed Germany!"

1. Tar inscription on a half-destroyed house along the Berlin highway, 1945. Oleg Budnitskii, "The Intelligentsia Meets the Enemy: Educated Soviet Officers in Defeated Germany, 1945," *Kritika. Explorations in Russian and Eurasian History* 10/3 (2009), 629–82 (630).
2. "Prikaz Verkhovnogo Glavnokomanduiushchego 1 maia 1944 goda," *Pravda*, May 1, 1944, 1.
3. Elke Scherstjanoi, *Rotarmisten schreiben aus Deutschland. Briefe von der Front (1945) und historische Analysen* (Munich, 2004), 46.
4. *The Kremlin Letters: Stalin's Wartime Correspondence with Churchill and Roosevelt*, ed. David Reynolds and Vladimir Pechatnov (New Haven, 2018), 263–64, 267–70.
5. Peter Caddick-Adams, *Sand and Steel: A New History of D-Day* (New York, 2019).
6. "Tov. Stalin o vtorzhenii soiuznykh voisk v Severnuiu Frantsiiu," *Krasnaia zvezda*, June 14, 1944, 1; Reynolds and Pechatnov, *The Kremlin Letters*, 281–82.
7. Il'ia Erenburg, "Nachalos'!," *Krasnaia zvezda*, June 8, 1944.

8. Declaration of the Three Powers, December 1, 1943, https://avalon.law.yale.edu/wwii/tehran.asp.
9. John Erickson, *The Road to Berlin* (London, 1983), 214–27.
10. *Die Tagebücher von Joseph Goebbels*, part 2, vol. 1, 400 (November 30, 1941).
11. Volkogonov, *Triumf i tragediia*, vol. 2, 363–64; *Velikaia Otechestvennaia voina, 1941–1945: Kn. 3: Osvobozhdenie*, ed. V. A. Zolotarev (Moscow, 1998), 457.
12. "Svidetel' veka—17 iiulia 1944 g," https://vk.com/video-173751070456239069. Photographs and map of the itinerary at https://rg.ru/201 9/07/17/rodina-marsh-pobezhdennyh-glazami-arhivistov-istorikov-i-pisatelej.html.
13. The march through Kiev comprised thirty-seven thousand prisoners, compared to the fifty-seven thousand who had marched through Moscow. Clearly, the Ukrainian officials in charge were at pains not to tip the scale of Soviet imperial power. "'Eti liudi imeiut zdorovyi vid.' O konvoirovanii nemetskikh voennoplennykh cherez gor. Kiev," *Rodina*, no. 4 (2005), 70–73.
14. "'Eti liudi imeiut zdorovyi vid'"; V. A. Panteleev and K. S. Polbitsova, "Operatsiia 'Bol'shoi val's'. Iz istorii konvoirovaniia v SSSR," *Penitentsiarnoe pravo. Iuridicheskoe pravo i pravoprimenitel'naia praktika*, 16, no. 2 (2018), 122–26. A secret police report took note of an apple that was thrown out of a window of 34 Horowitz Street while the prisoners passed underneath. NKVD operatives established that the apple had been thrown by a woman named Andriantseva. The report specified that her husband had been arrested as an "enemy of the people" and that she had lived in Kiev during the Nazi occupation. On another incident, where tobacco and bread were given to the prisoners (10 Horowitz Street), the report noted that the case was being investigated. Serhy Yekelchyk, "The Civic Duty to Hate," in *Stalin's Citizens: Everyday Politics in the Wake of Total War* (New York, 2014), 543–44.
15. Gerd Ueberschär, Die sowjetischen Prozesse gegen deutsche Kriegsgefangene 1943–1952," in *Der Nationalsozialismus vor Gericht. Die alliierten Prozesse gegen Kriegsverbrecher und Soldaten, 1943–1952*, ed. Gerd Ueberschär (Frankfurt/Main, 2000), 240–61 (248–49).
16. "Prokliatie i smert' gitlerovskim palacham! Ubiistvo Zoi Kos'modem'ianskoi," *Pravda*, October 24, 1943, 3.
17. Lidov, "Piat' nemetskikh fotografii," *Pravda*, October 24, 1943, 3; see also: "Nemetsko-fashistskoe zver'e," *Krasnaia Zvezda*, September 8, 1943, 1, 3.
18. Moine, "La commission d'enquete," 83–84.
19. Paula Chan, "Seeing Like the Stalinist State: The First Wave of War Crimes Investigations in Krasnodar, Stavropol, and Orel," unpubl. ms., 37.
20. *SSSR i Niurnbergskii protsess. Neizvestnye i maloizvestnye stranitsy istorii*, ed. N.S. Lebedeva (Moscow, 2012), 12. This commission had been created by the Western Allies; the USSR did not join as Soviet leaders felt outnumbered by Britain and its dominions India, Australia, Canada, each being given a separate seat and vote. The Western powers rejected Stalin's demand that the six Soviet Union republics that had suffered under Nazi occupation be counted separately.
21. The proposal was made during the German offensive at Stalingrad and motivated in part by Soviet fear that Great Britain might pact with Germany and build up an anti-Bolshevik axis. Lebedeva, ed., *SSSR i niurnbergskii protsess*, 7–9.
22. Lebedeva, ed., *SSSR i niurnbergskii protsess*, 8–11.
23. Alexander V. Prusin, "'Fascist Criminals to the Gallows!': The Holocaust and Soviet War Crimes Trials, December 1945–February 1946," *Holocaust and Genocide Studies* 17, no. 1 (2003): 1–30 (5).
24. "October 1943. Statement on Atrocities," The Avalon Project, n.d., https://avalon.law.yale.edu/wwii/moscow.asp.
25. The Kharkov tribunal was the first wartime trial with German soldiers and policemen standing in the dock. The earlier Krasnodar trial in July 1943 mainly targeted Soviet citizens who were accused of collaborating with the Nazis. Several Germans,

including Richard Ruoff, Commander of the 17th Army, and Kurt Christmann, head of Einsatzkommando 10a, were tried in absentia. Greg Dawson, *Judgment Before Nuremberg: The Holocaust in the Ukraine and the First Nazi War Crimes Trial* (New York, 2012).

26. Edmund Stevens, *Russia Is No Riddle* (New York, 1946), 111. Moreover, watching the Nazi defendants, Stevens came to reassess his earlier skepticism about the Moscow Show Trials. "Weren't the charges in all of the cases real?" he wrote. And hadn't subsequent events "proved that the charges and admissions at the Treason Trials, fantastic as they may have seemed at the time, were not fiction?" Ibid, 114–16.
27. *Sudebnyi protsess o zverstvakh nemetsko-fashistskikh zakhvatchikov na territorii gor. Khar'kova i Khar'kovskoi oblasti v period ikh vremennoi okkupatsii* (Moscow, 1943).
28. *Sudebnyi protsess o zverstvakh*, 50. No van outfitted with the deadly gas pipes was ever seized by any of the Allied powers. The vans were easy to change back into standard models with virtually no signs of their previous function. Jerzy Halbersztadt, "Gas Vans," http://www.deathcamps.org/gaschambers/gaschambersvans.html.
29. *Sudebnyi protsess o zverstvakh*, 25, 33–35, 87. The Russian defendant, Mikhail Bulanov, accepted full responsibility for the charges brought against him. Ibid., 89–90.
30. Wording of April 19, 1943, https://victims.rusarchives.ru/ukaz-prezidiuma-verkhovnogo-soveta-sssr-no-39-o-merakh-nakazaniya-dlya-nemecko-fashistskikh-zlodeev.
31. Bazyler, *Forgotten Trials of the Holocaust*, 34; for the August 7, 1941, hangings in Zhytomyr, see above, chapter 3.
32. "I. Erenburg glazami D. Zaslavskogo," *Lekhaim*, July 2006 (December 19, 1943).
33. "I. Erenburg glazami D. Zaslavskogo," *Lekhaim*, July 2006 (December 10, 1943).
34. I. Erenburg, "Ubei!," *Krasnaia zvezda*, July 24, 1942. One line from this article is often cited: "If you haven't killed at least one German in the course of the day, your day's worthless." What gets lost in these citations is Ehrenburg's broader argument about Soviet morality versus German fascist inhumanity, which runs through this and many other of his wartime writings.
35. Il'ia Erenburg, "Opravdanie nenavisti," *Pravda*, May 26, 1942.
36. Il'ia Erenburg, "Spravedlivost.' Svideteli," *Krasnaia zvezda*, December 19, 1943.
37. Il'ia Erenburg, "Shagi Nemezidy," *Krasnaia zvezda*, November 7, 1943; idem, "Spravedlivost.' Svideteli." Edmund Stevens reached a strikingly similar conclusion, maybe because he spent much time together with Ehrenburg on the train back from Kharkov to Moscow. As Stevens wrote in his dispatch from Moscow, the Kharkov Trial had put on brutal display the total lack of any "moral repentance or shame" on the part of the German defendants. "Perhaps this destruction of individual conscience and individual moral responsibility among his followers is Hitler's greatest crime of all." Edmund Stevens, "Kharkov Rebuilds on Ruin Left by Nazis," *Christian Science Monitor*, December 24, 1943, 1, 6 (6). For Stevens's fascinating description of Ehrenburg, see: Stevens, *Russia Is No Riddle*, 130–42.
38. Il'ia Erenburg, "Vse," *Krasnaia zvezda*, January 26, 1944.
39. Joshua Rubenstein and Vladimir Naumov, *Stalin's Secret Pogrom: The Postwar Inquisition of the Jewish Anti-Fascist Committee* (New Haven, 2001), 17–18.
40. Il'ia Erenburg, "Oni k nam prishli—oni ot nas ne uidut," *Na razgrom vraga*, February 6, 1944.
41. Erenburg, *Voina*, 783.
42. J. V. Stalin, "Order of the Day, No. 55," February 23, 1942, https://www.marxists.org/reference/archive/stalin/works/1942/02/23.htm. Morré, *Hinter den Kulissen des Nationalkomitees*, 31.
43. *Flugblätter aus der UdSSR, Nationalkomitee freies Deutschland, 1943–1945: Bibliographie, Katalog*, ed. Klaus Kirchner (Erlangen, 1996), 456.
44. "Obrashchenie obshchestvennykh i politicheskikh deiatelei Germanii k germanskomu narodu," *Krasnaia zvezda*, January 30, 1942, 2.
45. Lew Hohmann, *Friedrich Wolf. Bilder einer deutschen Biographie* (Berlin, 1988), 243.

46. Morré, *Hinter den Kulissen des Nationalkomitees*, 31–33; *Flugblätter aus der UdSSR, Nationalkomitee freies Deutschland, 1943–1945*, 458.
47. Morré, *Hinter den Kulissen des Nationalkomitees*, 43–46.
48. Gerd R. Ueberschär, "Das NKFD und der BDO im Kampf gegen Hitler, 1943–1945," in *Das Nationalkomitee "Freies Deutschland" und der Bund Deutscher Offiziere*, ed. Gerd R. Ueberschär (Frankfurt 1995), 31–51.
49. "Manifest des NKFD an die Wehrmacht und an das deutsche Volk," https://berlin.museum-digital.de/singleimage?imagenr=67350&noiiif=1.
50. Jochen Hellbeck, "Breakthrough at Stalingrad: The Repressed Soviet Origins of a Bestselling West German War Tale," *Contemporary European History* 22, no. 1 (2013): 1–32.
51. *Die Front war überall. Erlebnisse und Berichte vom Kampf des Nationalkomitees "Freies Deutschland"* (Berlin, 1978), 170–74. Kügelgen's article appeared in *Freies Deutschland* on November 15, 1943.
52. *Die Front war überall*, 170–74.
53. Hohmann, *Friedrich Wolf*, 255; Leutnant Heinrich Graf von Einsiedel, "Zurück in die menschliche Gemeinschaft," *Freies Deutschland*, November 7, 1943.
54. Jennifer Taylor, "Propaganda as an Art Form? Some Reflections on Friedrich Wolf's Work in the Soviet Union in 1942," *German Life and Letters* 38 (January 1985): 138–54 (139).
55. Hohmann, *Friedrich Wolf*, 243, 255.
56. *Flugblätter aus der UdSSR, Nationalkomitee freies Deutschland, 1943–1945*, xxxvi; Hohmann, *Friedrich Wolf*, 251.
57. Erickson, *The Road to Berlin*, 178–79.
58. *Das Nationalkomitee "Freies Deutschland" und der Bund Deutscher Offiziere*, ed. Gerd R. Ueberschär (Frankfurt, 1995), 288–89.
59. *Das Nationalkomitee "Freies Deutschland,"* 235–36.
60. *Flugblätter aus der UdSSR, Nationalkomitee freies Deutschland, 1943–1945*, 458; *Das Nationalkomitee "Freies Deutschland,"* 31–51.
61. Leonid Reschin, *Feldmarschall im Kreuzverhör. Friedrich Paulus in sowjetischer Gefangenschaft, 1943–1953* (Zweibrücken, 2002), 113–15.
62. Reschin, *Feldmarschall im Kreuzverhör*, 118–20.
63. Reschin, *Feldmarschall im Kreuzverhör*, 119.
64. *Das Nationalkomitee "Freies Deutschland,"* 39–42.
65. Karl-Heinz Frieser et al., *Die Ostfront, 1943–44: Der Krieg im Osten und an den Nebenfronten. Das Deutsche Reich und der Zweite Weltkrieg, Bd. 7* (Munich, 2007), 612.
66. I. Ehrenburg, "Velikii den'," *Krasnaia zvezda*, October 24, 1944. Ehrenburg had formulated this reminder many times, including in "Nakanune," *Krasnaia zvezda*, August 7, 1944; and "Otvet ledi Gibb," *Krasnaia zvezda*, October 15, 1944.
67. Zeidler, *Kriegsende im Osten*, 126; Il'ia Erenburg, "Gore im!," *Krasnaia zvezda*, August 19, 1944.
68. As soldiers crossed into Germany, they walked past signs that marked Germany as the "Fascist Lair" and reminded soldiers that the "hour of revenge" had struck! "Jetzt wird Selbstbeherrschung verlangt," *Der Spiegel*, May 11, 1975.
69. The words were from Ehrenburg's widely published January 1944 article, discussed above. Iurii Rubtsov, *Shtrafniki ne krichali: "Za Stalina!"* (Moscow, 2012), 246.
70. Manfred Zeidler, "Die Rote Armee auf deutschem Boden," in *Der Zusammenbruch des Deutschen Reiches 1945: Die militärische Niederwerfung der Wehrmacht*, ed. Rolf-Dieter Müller (Stuttgart, 2008) 713–14.
71. See Vojin Majstorović, "The Red Army in Yugoslavia, 1944–1945," *Slavic Review* 75, no. 2 (2016): 396–421.
72. Some researchers project 1.1 million rape cases for the East German provinces. See Barbara Johr, "Die Ereignisse in Zahlen," in *Befreier und Befreite. Krieg, Vergewaltigung, Kinder*, ed. Helke Sander and Barbara Johr (Frankfurt, 2005), 46–73 (58, 61). Recent research has identified heightened incidences of sexual violence among forcibly recruited units of soldiers lacking prior cohesion. Sexual violence is seen as creating

among the soldier body bonds of loyalty amid an environment of fear and mistrust. See Miranda Alison, "Wartime Sexual Violence: Women's Human Rights and Questions of Masculinity," *Review of International Studies* 33, no. 1 (January 2007): 77; Regina Mühlhäuser, "Between 'Racial Awareness' and Fantasies of Potency: Nazi Sexual Politics in the Occupied Territories of the Soviet Union, 1942–1945," in *Brutality and Desire: War and Sexuality in Europe's Twentieth Century*, ed. Dagmar Herzog (Basingstoke, 2009), 201. While this interpretation is helpful in explaining how and why sexual violence in the Red Army formed from the ground up and often took place in plain view, according to its logic the Red Army, sorely fractured by war's end and lacking primary group cohesion in all units, would have committed massive acts of sexual assault in any theater of the war. This was not the case. Outsize acts of sexual violence took place only in Germany, closely followed by Hungary. Unforgiving hatred toward the "fascist" enemy drove this violence. For an excellent discussion of Soviet troop violence in multiple contexts, see Mark Edele, "Soviet Liberations and Occupations, 1939–1949," in R. Bosworth and J. Maiolo, ed. *The Cambridge History of the Second World War* (2015): 487–508 (489–94). See also Norman M. Naimark, *The Russians in Germany: A History of the Soviet Zone of Occupation, 1945–1949* (Cambridge, MA, 1995), 107–10; Majstorović, "The Red Army in Yugoslavia"; Andrea Petö, "Women as Victims and Perpetrators in World War II: The Case of Hungary," in *Women and Men at War: A Gender Perspective on World War II and Its Aftermath in Central and Eastern Europe*, ed. Maren Röger (Osnabrück, 2012), 81–96.

73. This was the soldier's last letter; he would die during the storming of Königsberg. Scherstjanoi, *Rotarmisten schreiben aus Deutschland*, 39–40; see also Budnitskii, "The Intelligentsia Meets the Enemy," 632–47.
74. Zeidler, "Die Rote Armee auf deutschem Boden," 708. As he sought to gauge the mood of Red Army soldiers, Zeidler heavily cited from a collection of Soviet letters that were captured and analyzed by Wehrmacht military intelligence. He does not reflect on how the views of the German investigators may have guided their selection of these letters. Zeidler, "Die Rote Armee auf deutschem Boden," 706–9.
75. [Iurii Uspenskii,] "Die Tagebuchaufzeichnungen eines russischen Artillerieoffiziers in Deutschland im Frühjahr 1945," ed. Peter Gosztony, *Wehrwissenschaftliche Rundschau: Zeitschrift für die europäische Sicherheit*, 9 (September 1969), 512–24 (514, January 12, 1945).
76. [Uspenskii,] "Die Tagebuchaufzeichnungen," 517, 519 (January 24 and 26, 1945).
77. Zeidler, "Die Rote Armee auf deutschem Boden," 717–20; Schechter, The Stuff of Soldiers, 174.
78. [Iurii Uspenskii,] "Die Tagebuchaufzeichnungen," 519–20 (January 27, 1945).
79. Budnitskii, "The Intelligentsia Meets the Enemy," 639; see also Scherstjanoi, *Rotarmisten schreiben aus Deutschland*, 29, 46, 52, 65, 68, and many more pages.
80. N. N. Inozemtsev, *Frontovoi dnevnik. Vtoroe izdanie* (Nauka, 2005) 209. The quoted passage contains several unintelligible words likely describing Soviet acts of violence against German civilians. Inozemtsev probably struck them out when he reread his diary after the war.
81. Inozemtsev, *Frontovoi dnevnik*, 210.
82. E. S. Seniavskaia, "*Osvoboditel'naia missiia Krasnoi Armii v Evrope v 1944–1945 gg. v kontekste istoricheskoi pamiati. Novye arkhivnye dokumenty i ikh interpretatsiia,*" *Metamorfozy istorii* 13 (2019), 206–37.
83. Elena S. Senjavskaja, "*Deutschland und die Deutschen in den Augen sowjetischer Soldaten und Offiziere des Großen Vaterländischen Krieges,*" in Scherstjanoi, *Rotarmisten schreiben aus Deutschland*, 247–66 (258–59).
84. German military intelligence archive, FHO, at https://commons.wikimedia.org/wiki/File:SovietOrder1945-00.png.
85. "Nashe mshchenie," *Krasnaia zvezda*, February 9, 1945.
86. Lev Kopelev, *Khranit' vechno* (Ann Arbor, MI, 1975), 128.

87. Scherstjanoi, *Rotarmisten schreiben aus Deutschland*, 59–60.
88. Gennadij Bordjugow, "Wehrmacht und Rote Armee—Verbrechen gegen die Zivilbevölkerung," in *Verführung der Gewalt. Russen und Deutsche im Ersten und Zweiten Weltkrieg*, ed. Karl Eimermacher et al. (Munich, 2005), 1213–60 (1257); Nicole Eaton, *German Blood, Slavic Soil: How Nazi Königsberg Became Soviet Kaliningrad* (Ithaca, NY, 2023), 144, 150.
89. E. Zhirova, "Chast' naseleniia konchaet zhizn' samoubiistvom". Doneseniia stalinskikh spetssluzhb," *Vlast'* 6 (2000): 45–47 (Emma Korn).
90. Bordiugov, "Wehrmacht und Rote Armee," 1230; Scherstjanoi, *Rotarmisten schreiben aus Deutschland*, 123–25.
91. Scherstjanoi, *Rotarmisten schreiben aus Deutschland*, 31.
92. Scherstjanoi, *Rotarmisten schreiben aus Deutschland*, 39–40, 60, 181; Zeidler, "Die Rote Armee auf deutschem Boden," 710, Schechter, *The Stuff of Soldiers*, 224–39.
93. Scherstjanoi, *Rotarmisten schreiben aus Deutschland*, 81–82. Zeidler, who consistently emphasizes the brutality of Red Army soldiers, quotes from the woman's letter at length but leaves out the demeaning "pig" reference at the end. Zeidler, "Die Rote Armee auf deutschem Boden," 711.
94. For insightful explorations of the cultural gradient structuring relations between German women and Red Army men, see Atina Grossmann, *Jews, Germans, and Allies: Close Encounters in Occupied Germany* (Princeton, 2007), 92; see also Naimark, *The Russians in Germany*, 69–76, 78, 114.
95. *Krasnaia zvezda*, February 22, 23, and 25, 1945.
96. I. Erenburg, V. Germanii, *Krasnaia zvezda*, February 22, 1945; see also Il'ia Erenburg, "Sozrela i nastupaet," *Krasnaia zvezda*, March 11, 1945.
97. The major was likely Iakov Zakharovich Rozenfel'd (1922–1988); see jewmil.com (Internet-proekt po uvekovechivaniiu pamiati voinov—evreev), https://www.jewmil.com/biografii/rozenfeld-yakov-zakharovich.
98. Leonid Reshin, "Tovarishch Erenburg uproshchaet." Podlinnaia istoriia znamenitel'noi stat'i "Pravdy," *Novoe vremia* 8 (1994): 50–51.
99. Reshin, "Tovarishch Erenburg uproshchaet"; Berkhoff, *Motherland in Danger*, 193.
100. Domarus, ed., *Hitler, Reden und Proklamationen*, 2000.
101. Domarus, ed., Hitler, *Reden und Proklamationen*, 2083–84.
102. *Die Deutsche Wochenschau* 727, August 10, 1944.
103. *Der Nationalsozialismus. Dokumente 1933–1945*, ed. Walther Hofer (Frankfurt, 2nd ed., 1957), 252–53.
104. Waldemar Besson, "Zur Geschichte des nationalsozialistischen Führungsoffiziers," *Vierteljahrshefte für Zeitgeschichte* 9 , no. 1 (1961): 76–116 (105).
105. Stargardt, *The German War*, 454.
106. Bernhard Fisch, "Nemmersdorf 1944. Ein bisher unbekanntes zeitnahes Zeugnis," *Zeitschrift für Ostmitteleuropa-Forschung* 56, no. 1 (2007); 105–14 (109–10).
107. "Der Blutterror der Sowjets," *Völkischer Beobachter* (Vienna ed.), October 31, 1944, 1; Eaton, *German Blood, Slavic Soil*, 107–9; Bernhard Fisch, *Nemmersdorf, Oktober 1944. Was in Ostpreußen tatsächlich geschah* (Berlin, 1997), 173. Unlike Katyn in 1943 and Lvov in 1941, Nemmersdorf was too close to the front lines to serve as a physical exhibition site; no German soldier-tourists came to visit. The Nazi exhibit design remained entirely virtual.
108. Upon learning about the concocted flyer, Ehrenburg responded in his trademark style, by firing off a sarcastically worded column. Il'ia Erenburg, "Belokuraia ved'ma," *Krasnaia zvezda*, November 25, 1944.
109. Ehrenburg had gained notoriety in the Nazi press more than a year earlier, on the heels of the Sixth Army's rout at Stalingrad. At that fateful moment, multiple German papers recalled his 1923 novel *Trust D.E.* ("D.E." standing for "Destruction of Europe"), the novel in which Ehrenburg depicted the ravaging of Europe at the hands of American bankers and Europe's corrupt old elites. The Nazi press recast Ehrenburg's satire as an

expression of his personal desire. JEWISH FANTASIES OF HATRED. EUROPE TO BECOME A DESERT, *Völkischer Beobachter* headlined its front page. "Only a Jew is able to harbor such absolute hatred against Europe's culture," the paper declared. "Ehrenburgs Wunschtraum," *Oberdonau-Zeitung*, February 24, 1943, 2; "Jüdischer Haß in Wunschträumen. Europa soll zu einer Wüste werden," *Völkischer Beobachter* (Wien), April 13, 1943, 1. For a discussion of *Trust D.E.*, see above, chapter 2.

110. "Tagesbefehl des Führers an die deutsche Wehrmacht," *Völkischer Beobachter*, January 2, 1945, 1. During the final year of the war, German military intelligence translated several of Ehrenburg's essays from *Red Star* and reported them up the chain of command. National Archives and Records Administration (NARA), T78/483.
111. Zeidler, "Die Rote Armee auf deutschem Boden," 724–25.
112. Joseph Goebbels, "Wir lassen nicht von unserem Anspruch auf Leben und Freiheit," *Völkischer Beobachter* (Vienna Edition), March 1, 1945. English translation at https://research.calvin.edu/german-propaganda-archive/goeb89.htm.
113. Michael Geyer, "Endkampf 1918 and 1945: German Nationalism, Annihilation and Self-Destruction," in *No Man's Land of Violence: Extreme Wars in the 20th Century*, ed. Alf Lüdtke and Bernd Weisbrod (Göttingen, 2006), 57.
114. Rüdiger Overmans, *Deutsche militärische Verluste im Zweiten Weltkrieg* (Munich, 1999), 238–43, 265–79.
115. Christian Goeschel, *Suicide in Nazi Germany* (New York, 2009), 161.
116. Goeschel, *Suicide in Nazi Germany*, 156–64. Another suicide wave followed the Red Army's arrival.
117. Bordjugow, "Wehrmacht und Rote Armee," 1228, 1252; Eva Hahn and Hans Henning Hahn, *Die Vertreibung im deutschen Erinnern: Legenden, Mythos, Geschichte* (Paderborn, 2010), 263, 280; Bastiaan Willems, *Violence in Defeat: The Wehrmacht on German Soil, 1944–1945* (Cambridge, 2021), 202.
118. Ingolf Spickschen, "Flucht aus Ostpreussen," in *Alltag in Trümmern. Zeitzeugen berichten über das Kriegsende 1945*, ed. Stephan Hebel (Berlin, 2005), 172–73.
119. *The Expulsion of the German Population from the Territories East of the Oder-Neisse Line*, ed. Theodor Schieder (Bonn, 1956), 141–42.
120. Daniel Blatman, *The Death Marches: The Final Phase of Nazi Genocide* (Cambridge, MA, 2011), 168.
121. NARB, f. 750-P, op. 1, d. 119, Budaeva; NA IRI RAN, f. 2, razd. VI, op. 8, d. 18, Ust'ianova.
122. NA IRI RAN, f. 2, razd. VI, op. 8, d. 15, Govorushko; Simone Erpel, *Zwischen Vernichtung und Befreiung: Das Frauen-Konzentrationslager Ravensbrück in der letzen Kriegsphase* (Berlin, 2005).
123. Saul K. Padover, *Experiment in Germany: The Story of an American Intelligence Officer* (New York, 1946), 110–12, 115–18.
124. Stargardt, *The German War*, 513.
125. Herbert, *Hitler's Foreign Workers*, 319–20, 359; Irina Kalimova, " 'Ia ne smeiu govorit . . .' Vospominaniia moego deda A. A. Kalimova o fashistskom plene (1941– 1945)," in *Tsena pobedy. Rossiiskie shkol'niki o voine* (Moscow, 2005),359; Stargardt, *The German War*, 514.
126. Herbert, *Hitler's Foreign Workers*, 360–62.
127. *Hans Maršálek, Die Geschichte des Konzentrationslagers Mauthausen. Dokumentation* (Vienna, 4th ed., 2006), 346–47; David Wingeate Pike, *Spaniards in the Holocaust: Mauthausen, the Horror on the Danube* (London, 2000), 167–72, 398.
128. Blatman, *The Death Marches*, 100–2, 404–5.
129. Stargardt, *The German War*, 517.
130. Herbert, *Hitler's Foreign Workers*, 375–6. Kammler committed suicide by taking cyanide on May 9, 1945.
131. Ronald Matthews, "Sabotage in Town of Sullen Eyes," *The Daily Herald* (London), April 7, 1945, 4. This report predated reporting about the first Nazi camp in Germany to be

liberated by the Western allies—the forced labor camp Ohrdruf, which was freed on April 4 and first made the news on April 11, 1945.

132. "Muenster Prelate Assails 'Russians", *New York Times*, April 7, 1945, 4; see also "Germany: Chaos—and Comforts," *Time*, April 16, 1945, http://content.time.com/time/subscriber/article/0,33009,775573-2,00.html. On April 13, 1945, von Galen formally complained to American military authorities about liberated Red Army soldiers raping German women and pillaging German and Allied property. *Bischof Clemens August Graf von Galen—Akten, Briefe und Predigten, 1933–1946,* ed. Peter Löffler (Paderborn, 2nd. Ed., 1996), 1104.
133. Kalimova, "'Ia ne smeiu govorit, . . .," 361. For Kalimov's earlier fate, see chapter 5. On vigilante justice among liberated prisoners, see Seth Bernstein, *Return to the Motherland: Displaced Soviets in World War II and the Cold War* (Ithaca, NY, 2023), 90.
134. Title of a *New York Times* editorial, May 4, 1945, 18.
135. Evan Mawdsley, *The Second World War,* 400–1.
136. David M. Glantz and Jonathan M. House, *When Titans Clashed: How the Red Army Stopped Hitler* (Lawrence, KS, 1995), 256.
137. Il'ia Erenburg, "Razviazka", *Pravda*, April 4, 1945.
138. Il'ia Erenburg, "Pered finalom," *Krasnaia zvezda*, April 7, 1945.
139. Il'ia Erenburg, "Khvatit!", *Pravda*, April 9, 1945.
140. The massacre was carried out by soldiers of Waffen-SS division "Das Reich," an elite unit of political soldiers which had recently been transferred from the Eastern Front. See Sarah Farmer, *Martyred Village: Commemorating the 1944 Massacre at Oradour-sur-Glane* (Berkeley, 1999), 47–48.
141. Soviet authorities counted 628 Belarusian villages in which the Germans attempted to annihilate all residents, killing a total of 83,000 people. As part of their anti-partisan operations, German forces carried out massacres in more than 4,500 other Belarusian villages. Kay, *Empire of Destruction*, 173.
142. Belzec was on Polish soil, but almost half of the more than 500,000 Jews who were killed there hailed from the Lvov region that the Soviet Union had annexed in 1939.
143. "Sabotage in Town of Sullen Eyes," *Daily Herald*, April 7, 1945.
144. I was unable to locate this *Daily Telegraph* article.
145. Ilya Ehrenburg, "Khvatit!," *Pravda*, April 7, 1945.
146. Jonathan Walker, *Churchill's Third World War: British Plans to Attack the Soviet Empire 1945* (Stroud, 2017).
147. These numbers depart from those provided by David Glantz and Jonathan House, see note 136 in this chapter.
148. *The Kremlin Letters: Stalin's Wartime Correspondence with Churchill and Roosevelt*, ed. David Reynolds and Vladimir Pechatnov (New Haven, 2018), 579 (Stalin to Roosevelt, April 7, 1945).
149. Reynolds and Pechatnov, eds., *The Kremlin Letters*, 582–83.
150. G. Aleksandrov, "Tovarishch Erenburg uproshchaet," *Pravda*, April 14, 1945.
151. Scherstjanoi, *Rotarmisten schreiben aus Deutschland*, 145.
152. Domarus, ed., *Hitler, Reden und Proklamationen*, 2223–224.
153. Diaries of Aleksandr Reziapkin, April 21, 1945, and Nikolai Bunda, April 21, 1945, prozhito.org.
154. E. Gekhman, "Po Berlinu—ogon'!," *Krasnaia zvezda*, April 24, 1945.
155. Diary of Vladimir Stezhenskii, April 24, 1945, https://www.prozhito.org.
156. Ernst Volland, *Das Banner des Sieges* (Berlin, 2008); Jeremy Hicks, *Victory Banner over the Reichstag: Film, Document and Ritual in Russia's Contested Memory of World War II* (Pittsburgh, 2020).
157. "Prikaz Verkhovnogo Glavnokomanduiushchego No. 20," *Krasnaia zvezda*, May 1, 1945, 1.
158. The official number of 8.7 million military deaths cited by the Russian Ministry of Defence, in line with G. F. Krivosheev's research, is widely considered as an under-

count. G. F. Krivosheev, *Soviet Casualties and Combat Losses in the Twentieth Century* (Barnsley, 1997), 157. See S. N. Mikhalev, *Liudskie poteri v Velikoi Otechestvennoi voine 1941–1945 gg. Statisticheskoe issledovanie,* 2nd ed. (Krasnoiarsk, 2000), 26–28; Viktor Zemskov, "O masshtabakh liudskikh poter' SSSR v Velikoi Otechestvennoi Voine," *Voenno-istoricheskii arkhiv* 9 (2012): 59–71.

159. Diary of Vladimir Stezhenskii, May 2, 1945, https://www.prozhito.org.
160. Hitler, *Politisches Testament*, in NS Archiv, https://www.ns-archiv.de/personen/hitler/testament/politisches-testament.php.
161. Transcript of speech, recorded in DRA, https://web.archive.org/web/20141020150011/http://www.dra.de/online/hinweisdienste/wort/2005/dezember24.html.
162. Klaus-Dietmar Henke, *Die amerikanische Besetzung Deutschlands* (Munich, 1996), 675–79, 686.
163. Henke, *Die amerikanische Besetzung Deutschlands*, 684.
164. Michael Jones, *After Hitler: The Last Days of the Second World War in Europe* (New York, 2015), 259.
165. Leonid Poritskii, "Akt o voennoi kapituliatsii Germanii," *Zerkalo nedeli* 17, no. 392 (2002): 11–17, https://web.archive.org/web/20090209003740/http://www.zn.ua/3000/3150/34695/; "Surrender of Germany (1945)," National Archives, https://www.archives.gov/milestone-documents/surrender-of-germany#transcript.
166. *Germany surrenders, 1945* (Washington, DC, 1989); Poritskii, "Akt o voennoi kapituliatsii Germanii."
167. Volker Ullrich, *Eight Days in May: How Germany's War Ended* (London, 2021), 235–36.
168. Blatman, *The Death Marches*, passim.
169. NARB, f. 750-P, op. 1, d. 119, Budaeva.
170. Ustianova was interviewed in the German town of Neubrandenburg in June 1945. NA IRI RAN, f. 2, razd. VI, op. 8, d. 18.
171. NA IRI RAN, f. 2, razd. VI, op. 8, d. 12, Trush; d. 15, Govorushko. Hundreds of thousands of Jews across Europe, from Transnstria and Hungary to Austria and Germany, owed their survival to the advancing Red Army. Vojin Majstorovic, "Red Army Troops Encounter the Holocaust: Transnistria, Moldavia, Romania, Bulgaria, Yugoslavia, Hungary, and Austria, 1944–1945," *Holocaust and Genocide Studies* 32, no. 2 (Fall 2018): 249–71.
172. Internal Soviet reports dated late April 1045 noted a "strong decline" in the indiscriminate raping and killing of German civilians compared to the earlier East Prussian campaign. Bordjugow, "Wehrmacht und Rote Armee," 1257.
173. Diary of Vladimir Stezhenskii, May 2, 1945, https://www.prozhito.org; see also Scherstjanoi, *Rotarmisten schreiben aus Deutschland*, 160.
174. Vasily Grossman, A *Writer at War: A Soviet Journalist with the Red Army, 1941–1945*, ed. Antony Beevor (New York, 2007), 326–27, 340.
175. Bavarian parish records serve as a source basis in Miriam Gebhardt, *Crimes Unspoken: The Rape of German Women at the End of the Second World War* (Malden, 2017). Johannes Kuber has explored priest reports from the archdiocese of Freiburg: Johannes Kuber, "'Frivolous Broads' and the 'Black Menace': The Catholic Clergy's Perception of Victims and Perpetrators of Sexual Violence in Occupied Germany, 1945," in *War and Sexual Violence: New Perspectives in a New Era*, ed. Sarah K. Danielsson (Paderborn, 2019), 183–208.
176. Gebhardt, *Crimes Unspoken*, 81–85.
177. *Das Ende des Zweiten Weltkriegs im Erzbistum München und Freising*, ed. Peter Pfister (Regensburg, 2005), 835.
178. Hitler on November 12, 1944, in Domarus, ed., *Hitler, Reden und Proklamationen*, vol. 1 (Würtzburg, 1962), 2164.
179. Il'ia Erenburg, "Pobeda cheloveka," *Izvestiia*, May 16, 1945.
180. "Befehl des Chefs der Besatzung der Stadt Berlin," facsimile at https://asset.museum-digital.org/berlin/images/34/71177-100580/100580/100580-71177.jpg.

181. Gerhard Keiderling, *"Gruppe Ulbricht" in Berlin April bis Juni 1945. Von den Vorbereitungen im Sommer 1944 bis zur Wiedergründung der KPD im Juni 1945* (Berlin, 1993), 260; Naimark, *The Russians in Germany*, 41–42.
182. "O chudovishchnykh prestupleniiakh germanskogo pravitel'stva v Osventsime," *Pravda*, May 7, 1945; "Osventsim: Ubiitsy detei," *Pravda*, May 8, 1945, https://0gnev.livejournal.com/1709637.html. *Pravda*'s first lengthy report on the Auschwitz camp, based on the escapee reports, dated back to October 1944: "Lager smerti v Osventsime," *Pravda*, October 27, 1944. The liberation of the camp on January 27, 1945, was immediately followed by Boris Polevoi's emotional feature: "Kombinat smerti v Osventsime," *Pravda*, February 2, 1945.
183. "Ungeheure Verbrechen der Nazis im Todeslager Auschwitz," *Tägliche Rundschau*, May 17, 1945, 2–3.
184. Diary of Anne-Marie Durand-Wever (May 18, 1945), cited in Grossmann, *Jews, Germans, and Allies*, 15.
185. "Germany: Chaos—and Comforts," *Time*, April 16, 1945.
186. Ronald Matthews, "Sabotage in Town of Sullen Eyes," *Daily Herald* (London), April 7, 1945, 4. This lack of remorse on the part of the Germans was noted by many returning or visiting German émigrés, including Friedrich Wolf and Hannah Arendt. Friedrich Wolf had high hopes for a reformed Germany when he returned from Moscow to Berlin shortly after war's end. His play, *Doctor Mamlock*, had its German premiere at the Hebbel Theatre in Berlin's American sector in 1946. Yet Wolf felt that most of his countrymen were unreceptive to change. The Germans, he wrote in 1947, were a "screwed-up, self-righteous, unteachable people." See Manfred Karge and Hermann Wündrich, *Erstürmt die Höhen der Kultur! Umkämpftes Theater in der DDR* (Mainz, 2020), 40; Hannah Arendt, *Besuch in Deutschland* (Berlin, 1993).
187. The Soviet officials duly recorded the questions: Scherstjanoi, *Rotarmisten schreiben aus Deutschland*, 121.
188. Frank Biess, *German Angst: Fear and Democracy in the Federal Republic of Germany* (Oxford, 2020), 31–32.
189. *The Jews in the Secret Nazi Reports on Popular Opinion*, ed. Otto Dov Kulka and Eberhard Jäckel (New Haven, 2010), 655.
190. *The Jews in the Secret Nazi Reports on Popular Opinion*, 657.
191. Like Ehrenburg, historian Michael Geyer surmises that the Germans kept on fighting the Soviet enemy until the end on the strength of feelings of guilt for "unspoken [German] atrocities" in the East. Geyer, "Endkampf 1918 and 1945," 57. But the reason that these atrocities remained unspoken was that they did not register as crimes in the German mind. Nazi Germans were taught to imagine the Bolsheviks as subhuman aggressors, and Germans as their ultimate victims. This left no place to think of Soviet citizens as victims of German actions, which inherently counted as acts of self-defense.

Chapter 10: Erasure

1. R. L. Karmen, "Doklady o Niurnbergskom protsesse" (April 1, 1946), https://nurnberg.rusarchives.ru/documents/karmen-roman-lazarevich-doklady-o-nyurnbergskom-processe
2. *Trial of the Major War Criminals Before the International Military Tribunal. Nuremberg 14 November 1945–1 October 1946*, vol. 1 (Nuremberg, 1947), 153.
3. The four Allied judges discussed their sartorial preferences before the beginning of the trial. Soviet Judge Iona Nikitchenko dismissed as "medieval" the black gown on which the French judge insisted. The judges ended up agreeing that each side should wear what they considered appropriate. Ann Tusa and John Tusa, *The Nuremberg Trial* (New York, 2010), 138–41.
4. Genêt (Janet Flanner), "Letter from Nuremberg," *New Yorker,* March 30, 1946, 76–82 (77–78).

5. *Trial of the Major War Criminals Before the International Military Tribunal*, vol. 7, 151–53. The song quoted by Rudenko was entitled "The Rotten Bones Are Trembling" and composed by Hans Baumann in 1932. A recording from 1938 is available at https://archive.org/details/78_es-zittern-die-morschen-knochen_reichsmusikzug-des-reichs-arbeitsdienstes-hans-baum_gbia0376121a.
6. Rudenko's French colleague François de Menthon was the only other prosecutor to place central emphasis on race: a double effect of Republican identification with Enlightenment values and the French experience of Nazi occupation. While highlighting the Nazi murder of the Jewish people as a whole, de Menthon did not dwell on the fate of French Jews.
7. A fifth witness was the Czech physician Dr. František Bláha, who had been imprisoned in Dachau. Shortly before his interrogation in court, Blaha had submitted an affidavit in which he detailed the many medical experiments—virtually all of them deadly, he emphasized—that Nazi doctors in Dachau had performed on prisoners. In court, the U.S. prosecutor chose to read out the affidavit, rather than to interrogate Blaha, declaring that this approach would save the court a lot of time. *Trial of the Major War Criminals Before the International Military Tribunal. Nuremberg 14 November 1945–1 October 1946*, vol. 5, 167. The sixth witness was Austrian Erwin von Lahousen, an officer who had worked for the German military-intelligence service and participated in the resistance movement against Hitler. For a list of all witnesses to the International Military Tribunal, see *NMT. Die Nürnberger Militärtribunale zwischen Geschichte, Gerechtigkeit und Rechtschöpfung*, ed. Kim C. Priemel and Alexa Stiller (Hamburg, 2013), 813–25.
8. *Trial of the Major War Criminals Before the International Military Tribunal*, vol. 7, 227.
9. *Trial of the Major War Criminals Before the International Military Tribunal*, vol. 6, 295.
10. *Trial of the Major War Criminals Before the International Military Tribunal*, vol. 6, 295–96.
11. This collection remains the largest photographic record of an SS camp in operation. It is stored in the History Museum of Catalonia; portions of it are available online at https://www.mhcat.cat/enmhc/exhibitions/online_exhibitions/francesc_boix_from_the_concentration_camps_to_photojournalism/history_of_the_collection. Boix was a Communist loyal to Moscow, and his political views differed from those of other Spanish Republicans who were interned in Mauthausen, including another Spaniard who worked with him in the camp's photo lab. Using the memoirs of his detractors, David Pike sides with the Republican fighters who opposed Stalin and paints Boix in a very negative light. What gets lost in his account is the ability of Stalinist and their Trotskyist critics to engage in joint resistance against Nazism. David Pike, *Spaniards in the Holocaust: Mauthausen, the Horror on the Danube* (London, 2000), especially 128–32, 162–66.
12. *SSSR i Niurnbergskii protsess. Neizvestnye i maloizvestnye stranitsy istorii*, ed. N.S. Lebedeva (Moscow, 2012), 318–21; *Niurnbergskii protsess: uroki istorii. Materialy mezhdunarodnoi nauchnoi konferentsii. Moskva, 20-21 noiabria 2006 g.*, ed. N.S. Lebedeva et al. (Moscow, 2007), 160. The initial long list included six witnesses who were explicitly mentioned as Jews, including four Babi Yar witnesses. Of the ten survivors whom the Soviets brought to Nuremberg, nine spoke at the trial. The tenth was David (Dovid) Budnik, a survivor of the Babi Yar prison commando. Why he was not summoned into the courtroom is unclear. See Abraham Sutzkever, *From the Vilna Ghetto to Nuremberg: Memoir and Testimony*, ed. and trans. Justin D. Cammy (Montreal, 2021), 239, 246–47.
13. Sutzkever, *From the Vilna Ghetto to Nuremberg*, 283–84; Laura Jockusch, "Justice at Nuremberg? Jewish Responses to Nazi War-Crime Trials in Allied-Occupied Germany," *Jewish Social Studies: History, Culture, Society* 19, no. 1 (2012): 107–47 (120).
14. De Menthon indirectly referred to Vaillant-Couturier as he addressed the Nuremberg court: "France . . . asks you, above all in the name of the heroic martyrs of the

Résistance, who are among the greatest heroes of our national legend, that justice be done." *Trial of the Major War Criminals before the International Military Tribunal*, vol. 5, 367. Vaillant-Couturier represented the Communist Party in the Constituent Assembly and would be bestowed with the Legion of Honour upon returning from the Nuremberg tribunal.

15. Jockusch, "Justice at Nuremberg?," 122. After the trial, Jackson reiterated his distrust toward testimony offered by any aggrieved party with a "strong bias against the Hitler regime." Donald Bloxham, "Jewish Witnesses in War Crimes Trials of the Postwar Era," in *Holocaust Historiography in Context: Emergence, Challenges, Polemics and Achievements*, ed. David Bankier and Dan Michman (Jerusalem, 2008), 539–53 (541–42).
16. Drew Middleton, "Films Back Charge of German Crimes," *New York Times*, February 20, 1946. Göring reacted in his own way: When an erroneously inserted reel disrupted the presentation of the Soviet film, showing the liberated survivors of Auschwitz standing on their heads, Göring burst out laughing and looked around to see if others in the audience were laughing as well. Nobody was. A U.S. psychologist who was charged with studying the German defendants established the documentation's shattering effect on most of the Nazis standing trial. Only Göring kept denouncing the film as a forgery, maintaining that the Soviets were blaming their own atrocities on the German side. By contrast, Göring found the U.S. documentary believable. G. M. Gilbert, *Nuremberg Diary* (New York, 1947), 46–50, 152–53.
17. I thank Anna Nath for coining the term "witness justice." See also Jeremy Hicks, *First Films of the Holocaust: Soviet Cinema and the Genocide of the Jews, 1938–1946* (Pittsburgh, 2012), 191, 205. The French and Soviet display of witness justice challenges Annette Wieviorka's influential thesis that the Nuremberg trial marked the triumph of the written over the oral and that the "era of the witness" came to the study of the Holocaust only with a significant delay. Annette Wieviorka, *The Era of the Witness* (Ithaca, NY, 2006).
18. "The Sinews of Peace ('Iron Curtain Speech')," March 5, 1946, International Churchill Society, https://winstonchurchill.org/resources/speeches/1946-1963-elder-statesman/the-sinews-of-peace/.
19. "Interv'iu tov. Stalina s kor. 'Pravdy' otnositel'no rechi g. Cherchillia," *Pravda*, March 14, 1946, 1.
20. D. Zaslavskii, "Lobyzanie Gebbel'sa", *Pravda*, August 1, 1946, 4; Joseph Goebbels, "Das Jahr 2000," *Das Reich*, February 23, 1945, 1–2.
21. Francine Hirsch, *Soviet Judgment at Nuremberg: A New History of the International Military Tribunal after World War II* (Oxford, 2020), 245.
22. Raymond Daniell, "Göring Defends Nazi Suppression from Witness Stand in Nuremberg," *New York Times*, March 14, 1946, 1, 7.
23. Hirsch, *Soviet Judgment at Nuremberg*, 264–65.
24. This was established during the testimony of Friedrich Paulus, the star witness for the Soviet side. Prior to commanding the German Sixth Army, Paulus had presided over the planning of Operation Barbarossa. In his court testimony, Paulus made clear that detailed plans for the attack on the Soviet Union dated back to at least summer 1940. Göring was heard shouting to his lawyer while the General Field Marshal made his deposition: "Ask that dirty pig if he knows he's a traitor! Ask him if he has taken out Russian citizenship papers!" Gilbert, *Nuremberg Diary*, 139.
25. Hirsch, *Soviet Judgment at Nuremberg*, 322, 343.
26. Hirsch, *Soviet Judgment at Nuremberg*, 326–34.
27. Hirsch, *Soviet Judgment at Nuremberg*, 334. *The New York Times* reported on each side's witness testimony in a way that made either party appear credible.
28. Irina, Schulmeister-André, *Internationale Strafgerichtsbarkeit unter sowjetischem Einfluss. Der Beitrag der UdSSR zum Nürnberger Hauptkriegsverbrecherprozess* (Berlin, 2016), 511–17.

29. Schulmeister-André, *Internationale Strafgerichtsbarkeit unter sowjetischem Einfluss*, 525.
30. Bosley Crowther, "Goering with Swagger Lacking, in 'Nuremberg Trials,' at Stanley," *New York Times*, May 26, 1947, 24; J. P., "The Nuernberg Trials-Stanley," *New York Herald Tribune*, May 26, 1947, 16.
31. Levering, *American Opinion and the Russian Alliance*, 194–99.
32. Les K. Adler and Thomas G. Paterson, "Red Fascism: The Merger of Nazi Germany and Soviet Russia in the American Image of Totalitarianism, 1930s–1950s," *American Historical Review* 75, no. 4 (1970): 1046–64 (1053).
33. Ralph Levering, *The Cold War: A Post-Cold War History* (Malden, MA, 2016), 33–34.
34. David S. Foglesong, "Roots of 'Liberation': American Images of the Future of Russia in the Early Cold War, 1948–1953," *International History Review* 21, no. 1 (1999): 57–79; Kevin Gotham, "A Study in American Agitation: J. Edgar Hoover's Symbolic Construction of the Communist Menace," *Mid-American Review of Sociology* 16, no. 2 (1992): 57–70.
35. Hicks, *First Films of the Holocaust*, 216–17. Both the American and the Soviet atrocity films shown at Nuremberg would be used by Israeli prosecutors in the Eichmann trial. Lawrence Douglas, *The Memory of Judgment: Making Law and History in the Trials of the Holocaust* (New Haven, 2001), 99.
36. Daniel J. Leab, *I Was a Communist for the F.B.I.: The Unhappy Life and Times of Matt Cvetic* (University Park, PA, 2000).
37. Joshua Rubenstein, *Tangled Loyalties: The Life and Times of Ilya Ehrenburg* (London, 1996), 231–40.
38. Ilya Ehrenburg, "Visiting Russian Sums Up His Trip," *New York Times*, June 26, 1946, 10.
39. Joshua Rubenstein, "Ilya Ehrenburg—Between East and West," *Journal of Cold War Studies* 4, no. 1 (Winter 2002): 44–65 (49).
40. Rubenstein, "Ilya Ehrenburg—Between East and West," 44–65 (49).
41. Rubenstein, *Tangled Loyalties*, 265.
42. Rubenstein, "Ilya Ehrenburg Between East and West," 53–54; Il'ia Erenburg, "Nasha kliatva," *Pravda*, October 2, 1949, 2. Ehrenburg's depiction of U.S. media in the throes of anti-Soviet hysteria was not off the mark. A case in point is *Collier's* magazine's preview of a nuclear war fought by the United Nations under American leadership against the Soviet Union. In the course of this "holy war," which the magazine detailed over 132 pages in its special 1951 issue, U.S. forces would detonate thousands of atomic bombs over Soviet cities and in the end occupy a decimated Russia. Bernd Greiner, "Antikommunismus, Angst und Kalter Krieg. Eine erneute Annäherung," in *"Geistige Gefahr" und "Immunisierung der Gesellschaft." Antikommunismus und politische Kultur in der frühen Bundesrepublik*, ed. Stefan Creuzberger and Dierk Hoffmann (Munich, 2014), 29–42 (37–39).
43. Timothy Johnston, "Peace or Pacifism? The Soviet 'Struggle for Peace in All the World,' 1948–54," *Slavonic and East European Review* 86, no. 2 (2008): 259–82 (271, 277–78).
44. Alexander V. Prusin, "'Fascist Criminals to the Gallows!': The Holocaust and Soviet War Crimes Trials, December 1945–February 1946," *Holocaust and Genocide Studies* 17, no. 1 (2003), 7; *Niurnbergskii protsess: uroki istorii*, 159.
45. B.N. Kovalev, "Velikolukskii protsess 1946 goda v osveshchenii sovetskoi pressy," *Uchenye zapiski Novgorodskogo gosudarstvennogo universiteta* 13, no. 1 (2018): 1–4.
46. "Minsk, Kishinev, Sevastopol' . . . Khronika 20 otkrytykh sudebnykh protsessov v SSSR nad voennymi prestupnikami i ikh posobnikami," at https://rg.ru/2021/01/18/hronika-20-otkrytyh-sudebnyh-processov-v-sssr-nad-voennymi-prestupnikami-i-ih-posobnikami.html; see also Manfred Messerschmidt, "Der Minsker Prozeß 1946. Gedanken zu einem sowjetischen Kriegsverbrechertribunal," in *Vernichtungskrieg. Verbrechen der Wehrmacht, 1941–1944*, ed. Hannes Heer and Klaus Naumann (Hamburg, 1995), 551–68.
47. Prusin, "'Fascist Criminals to the Gallows!'"

48. "Iz protokola doprosa na Kievskom protsesse v kachestve svidetelia spassheisia ot rasstrelov D. Pronichevoi," in *Babii Iar: Chelovek, vlast', istoriia. Kniga 1: Istoricheskaia topografiia. Khronologiia sobytii*, ed. Tat'iana Evstaf 'eva and Vitalii Nakhmanovich (Kyiv, 2004), 277–80; Karel Berkhoff, "Dina Pronicheva's Story of Surviving the Babi Yar Massacre: German, Jewish, Soviet, Russian, and Ukrainian Records," in *The Shoah in Ukraine: History, Testimony, Memorialization*, ed. Ray Brandon and Wendy Lower (Bloomington, IN, 2008), 291–317.
49. Peter Novick, *The Holocaust in American Life* (New York, 1999); Wieviorka, *The Era of the Witness.*
50. "Babii Iar. Kontekst. R13/ Dina Pronicheva," https://www.youtube.com/watch?v=XjwdMi5n_EQ; Ilia Levitas, *Pravedniki Bab'ego Iara* (Kyiv, 2001).
51. Shimon Redlich, *War, Holocaust and Stalinism* (New York, 1995), 177–83. Kiev was a predominantly Russian-speaking city at the time of Ehrenburg's birth.
52. *Gosudarstvennyi antisemitizm v SSSR. Ot nachala do kul'minatsii, 1938–1953*, ed. G. V. Kostyrchenko (Moscow, 2005), 40–44.
53. *The Black Book: The Nazi Crime Against the Jewish People* (New York, 1946); Albert Einstein, "Unpublished Preface to a Blackbook," in Einstein, *Out of My Later Years* (New York, 1950), 258–59.
54. Among the executed was Dovid Hofstheyn. Just before his arrest in September 1948, Hofshteyn had called on Golda Meir, Israel's minister plenipotentiary to the Soviet Union, to revive Hebrew in the USSR. See Dovid Hofshteyn, in *The Yivo Encyclopedia of Jews in Eastern Europe*, https://yivoencyclopedia.org/article.aspx/Hofshteyn_Dovid.
55. Rubenstein, *Tangled Loyalties*, 272–76.
56. For an exploration of the compound Jewish-Soviet identity, see Yarden Avital, "The Jewish Anti-Fascist Committee between Universal Being and Particular Suffering" (PhD diss., Rutgers University, 2022).
57. Richard Sheldon, "The Transformations of Babi Yar," in *Soviet Society and Culture: Essays in Honor of Vera S. Dunham*, ed. Terry L. Thompson et al. (Boulder, 1988), 124–61.
58. Yevgeni Yevtushenko, "Babi Yar," translated by Benjamin Okopnik, https://remember.org/witness/babiyar. Yevtushenko's poem was likely inspired by an earlier poem on the Babi Yar massacre, penned by Ehrenburg. Ehrenburg first published his untitled poem in *Novyi mir* in 1944, without referencing the Kiev ravine by its name. For the poem's republication in 1959, Ehrenburg added a title: "Babi Yar." Maxim D. Shrayer, "Jewish-Russian Poets Bearing Witness to the Shoah, 1941–1946," *Studies in Slavic Languages and Literatures* (2010): 59–119 (74–75).
59. Sheldon, "The Transformations of Babi Yar," 141–42.
60. Sheldon, "The Transformations of Babi Yar," 146; see also Joan Peterson, "Iterations of Babi Yar," *Journal of Ecumenical Studies* 46, no. 4 (2011): 585–98.
61. "Mass Shootings at Babyn Yar (Babi Yar)," at https://encyclopedia.ushmm.org/content/en/article/kiev-and-babi-yar.
62. Lisa Kirschenbaum, *The Legacy of the Siege of Leningrad, 1941–1995: Myth, Memories, and Monuments* (Cambridge, 2006); Mischa Gabowitsch, "Victory Day Before the Cult," in *The Memory of the Second World War in Soviet and Post-Soviet Russia*, ed. David L. Hoffmann (London and New York, 2021): 64–85. As Arkadi Zeltser has recently shown, memorials to the murdered Soviet Jews did go up in numerous Soviet towns and villages, particularly in Ukraine, in the years and decades after the war. These included many monuments that referenced Jewish suffering by name. Their decidedly local character saved many of these Jewish initiatives from pushback by Soviet officials. Arkadi Zeltser, *Unwelcome Memory: Holocaust Monuments in the Soviet Union* (Jerusalem, 2018).
63. The standing of ethnic Russians in official Soviet storytelling of the Great Patriotic War changed markedly over time. Russian leadership in the forging of the Soviet family of nations was a strong theme in the late 1930s and the early phase of the war, before ceding to the myth of a "Soviet nation" forged in the fight against tribal fascism. The idea of ethnic Russian leadership resurged for a brief time after the end of the war, only to be

discredited in subsequent decades. Until the end of the Soviet era, the official war cult invoked pan-Soviet internationalism as its guiding idea. Jonathan Brunstedt, *The Soviet Myth of World War II: Patriotic Memory and the Russian Question in the USSR* (Cambridge, 2021). See also David Brandenberger, *National Bolshevism: Stalinist Mass Culture and the Formation of Modern Russian National Identity, 1931–1956* (Cambridge, MA, 2002).

64. Anthony Austin, "U.S. Unit, at Babi Yar, Stunned by Soviet Silence on Jews," *New York Times*, August 4, 1979, 2.
65. Weiner, *Making Sense of War*; idem, "The Making of a Dominant Myth: The Second World War and the Construction of Political Identities within the Soviet Polity," *Russian Review* 55, no. 4 (October 1996): 638–60.
66. About five hundred thousand Soviet citizens, predominantly from the borderlands that the Soviet Union had annexed in 1939 and 1940, opted not to return to the USSR. Nick Baron, "Remaking Soviet Society: The Filtration of Returnees from Nazi Germany, 1944–49," in *Warlands: Population Resettlement and State Reconstruction in the Soviet-East European Borderlands, 1945–50*, ed. Peter Gatrell and Nick Baron (London, 2009), 89–116 (96); Bernstein, *Return to the Motherland.*
67. I. V. Govorov, "Fil'tratsiia sovetskikh repatriantov v 40-e gg. XX vv.: Tseli, metody i itogi," *Cahiers du Monde russe* 49, no. 2/3 (2008): 363–82 (377–78).
68. Baron, "Remaking Soviet Society," 105. Govorov, using figures from the Leningrad region, provides higher numbers: Govorov, "Fil'tratsiia sovetskikh repatriantov v 40-e gg," 380.
69. Baron, "Remaking Soviet Society," 106.
70. Immediately following his liberation, Mints inventoried the archive of the anti-fascist committee, listing detailed information about individual prisoners in Fallingbostel, including those who had served the Germans. With help from the British, he loaded the material on trucks and drove it to the Soviet zone. NA IRI RAN, f. 2, razd. VI, op. 22, d. 2.
71. "Mints Maks Grigor'evich," https://www.sakharov-center.ru/asfcd/auth/?t=book&num=2066.
72. Artem Latyshev, "Almost Soviet," *Jahrbücher für Geschichte Osteuropas* 68, no. 3/(2020): 378–402 (385–88).
73. Irina Kalimova, "'Ia ne smeiu govorit . . .' Vospominaniia moego deda A. A. Kalimova o fashistskom plene (1941–1945)," in *Tsena pobedy. Rossiiskie shkol'niki o voine* (Moscow, 2005), 362–63.
74. Kalimova, " 'Ia ne smeiu govorit . . .," 363.
75. Weiner, "The Making of a Dominant Myth," 659.
76. Gabowitsch, "Victory Day Before the Cult," 74–77.
77. "*Interv'iu tov. Stalina s kor. 'Pravdy.'*" The Red Army's exact losses in the war against the Axis powers were being kept secret at the time: In June 1945, the Red Army's General Staff worked out a detailed statistic: 6.3 million killed personnel, more than 3 million captured and missing soldiers, and 14 million injured. S. N. Mikhalev, *Liudskie poteri v Velikoi Otechestvennoi voine 1941–1945 gg. Statisticheskoe issledovanie*, 2nd ed. (Krasnoiarsk, 2000), 13.
78. *Istoriia Velikoi Otechestvennoi voiny, T. 6* (Moscow, 1965), 30.
79. Soviet courts tried an estimated seventy-two thousand Nazi Germans during and after the war, compared to five thousand cases against Nazis brought forth by the Western Allies. Andreas Hilger, "'Die Gerechtigkeit nehme ihren Lauf.' Die Bestrafung deutscher Kriegs- und Gewaltverbrecher in der Sowjetunion und der SBZ/DDR," in *Transnationale Vergangenheitspolitik. Der Umgang mit deutschen Kriegsverbrechern in Europa nach dem Zweiten Weltkrieg*, ed. Norbert Frei (Göttingen, 2006), 180–246 (191–94).
80. Hilger, "'Die Gerechtigkeit nehme ihren Lauf,'" 225–26, 240–43.
81. Gerhard Wettig, "Die Entlassung der Kriegsgefangenen aus der Sowjetunion 1955—Folge der Verhandlungen mit Adenauer? Untersuchung auf der Basis neuer

Archivdokumente," *Historisch-politische Mitteilungen* 14, no. 1 (2007): 341–52; Robert Moeller, *War Stories: The Search for a Usable Past in the Federal Republic of Germany* (Berkeley, 2001), 105–22. The decision to free the last German prisoners predated Adenauer's visit to Moscow. Khrushchev made it in support of Soviet security interests in Europe. Beate Ihme-Tuchel, "Die Entlassung der deutschen Kriegsgefangenen im Herbst 1955 im Spiegel der Diskussion zwischen SED und KPdSU," *Militärgeschichtliche Mitteilungen* 53 (1994): 449–65 (453).

82. Alexander V. Prusin, "The 'Second Wave' of Soviet Justice: The 1960s War Crimes Trials," in *Rethinking Holocaust Justice: Essays Across Disciplines*, ed. Norman Goda (New York, 2017), 129–57.
83. Vanessa Voisin, "The 1963 Krasnodar Trial: Extraordinary Media Coverage for an Ordinary Soviet Trial of Second World War Perpetrators," *Cahiers du Monde russe* 61, no. 3 (2020): 383–428 (403–4).
84. Voisin, "The 1963 Krasnodar Trial," 410. Rudenko's career encapsulates the gradual legal turn of the Soviet judicial apparatus after the Second World War, a function in part of its exposure to Nazism. Six months after he had been appointed Procurator General of the Soviet Union, and nine months after Stalin's death, Rudenko asked Khrushchev to critically investigate the legal basis of Stalin-era sentencings and executions. This plea paved the way for Khrushchev's Destalinization policy. See "Troika v biografii," *Kommersant*, February 1, 2020, https://www.kommersant.ru/doc/4241117. On the legal turn in Soviet postwar jurisprudence, see Katrin Boeckh, *Stalinismus in der Ukraine. Die Rekonstruktion des sowjetischen Systems nach dem Zweiten Weltkrieg* (Wiesbaden, 2007), 291–327, 541–42; Mark Edele, "The Soviet Culture of Victory," *Journal of Contemporary History* 54, no. 4 (October 2019): 780–98 (788–89).
85. In 1961, The State Criminal Police Office (*Landeskriminalamt*) of Baden-Württemberg opened a lawsuit against the surviving former head and another former member of GFP 626. See Stegerer, *Die Geheime Feldpolizei im Dritten Reich*, 331–33.
86. Jasmin Söhner, "After Nuremberg: The Appearance of Soviet Victims of Nazi Atrocities as Witnesses in Postwar Trials in West Germany, 1964–1969," *Jahrbücher für Geschichte Osteuropas* 68, no. 3–4 (2020): 432–54. Soviet witnesses regularly appeared in East German courts.
87. Söhner conjectures that victims' reluctance to travel to West Germany was merely an official excuse by Soviet authorities who did not want the witnesses to leave the Soviet Union. Söhner, "After Nuremberg," 437, 448.
88. Berkhoff, "Dina Pronicheva's Story of Surviving Babi Yar," 300.
89. Söhner, "After Nuremberg," 449.
90. Söhner, "After Nuremberg," 448–49.
91. Ingo Müller, Die Verfolgung der Nazi-Verbrechen in Ost und West, in Gedenkstätten Forum, https://www.gedenkstaettenforum.de/aktuelles/publikationen-rezensionen/details/die-verfolgung-der-nazi-verbrechen-in-ost-und-west.
92. Cooperation started slowly, peaking between 1968 and 1973. Most of the approximately 280 Soviet citizens who were interrogated in the presence of West German prosecutors and judges within the framework of a legal assistance procedure gave their testimony in the Soviet Union. In contrast, Soviet citizens regularly testified in East German courts. Söhner, "After Nuremberg," 433.
93. Eveline Passet, "Im Zerrspiegel der Geschichte: Deutsche Bilder von Ilja Ehrenburg," *Osteuropa* 57, no. 12 (December 2007): 17–48 (19–26).
94. Frank Biess, *Homecomings: Returning POWs and the Legacies of Defeat in Postwar Germany* (Princeton, 2006), 154–67.
95. *Documents on the Expulsion of the Germans from Eastern-Central Europe* (4 vols.), ed. Theodor Schieder (Bonn, 1953–1960); Moeller, *War Stories*, 64–66.
96. Christina Morina, *Legacies of Stalingrad: Remembering the Eastern Front in Germany Since 1945* (Cambridge, 2011), 90–91. Original transcripts of Adenauer's declarations in Moscow, https://www.konrad-adenauer.de/seite/dokumente-zur-moskaureise/.

97. K. Taradankin, "Pravda ob Oberlendere," *Izvestiia*, April 6, 1960, 4; Tuviah Friedman, "*Der Nazi-Minister Theo Oberländer begann als erster mit den Massen-Erschießungen der Juden in Lemberg, Anfang Juli 1941*," Institute of Documentation in Israel for the Investigation of Nazi War Crimes (Haifa, 2004). Oberländer himself claimed to have fallen victim to a plot by Eastern European secret services. Philipp-Christian Wachs's examination of the documents largely sides with Oberländer's defense. Philipp-Christian Wachs, *Der Fall Oberländer (1905–1998). Ein Lehrstück deutscher Geschichte* (Frankfurt, 2000).
98. Weiner, *Making Sense of War*, 176–78; Alexander Statiev, *The Soviet Counterinsurgency in the Western Borderlands* (Cambridge, 2010).
99. Amir Weiner, "The Empires Pay a Visit: Gulag Returnees, East European Rebellions, and Soviet Frontier Politics," *Journal of Modern History* 78 (June 2006): 333–76 (368–70).
100. Paula Chan, "Documents Accuse: The Post-Soviet Memory Politics of Genocide," *Journal of Illiberalism Studies* 1, no. 2 (2021): 39–57 (41, 43, 47).
101. Jenelle Davis, "Marking Memory: Ambiguity and Amnesia in the Monument to Soviet Tank Crews in Prague," *Public Art Dialogue* 6, no. 1 (2016): 35–57.
102. Lars Peder Haga, "Coming to Terms with Europe," in *Socialist Internationalism in the Cold War: Exploring the Second World*, ed. Patryk Babiracki and Austin Jersild (New York, 2016), 19–48.
103. James Mark, "Antifascism, the 1956 Revolution and the Politics of Communist Autobiographies in Hungary 1944–2000," *Europe-Asia Studies* 58, no. 8 (2006): 1209–40. Official campaigns against the Hungarian "fascists" enjoyed robust support in Soviet society; see Weiner, "The Empires Pay a Visit," 352.
104. Masha Hamilton, "Soviets Admit Pact with Nazis to Gain Baltics, *Los Angeles Times*, August 19, 1989, https://www.latimes.com/archives/la-xpm-1989-08-19-mn-496-story.html.
105. Davis, "Marking Memory."
106. The Bronze Soldier monument in Tallinn replaced a preceding wooden memorial that had been blown up by two young Estonian resistance fighters to avenge the prior Soviet destruction of memorials to the Estonian War of Independence. The youths were sent to the Gulag. Martin Ehala, "The Bronze Soldier: Identity Threat and Maintenance in Estonia," *Journal of Baltic Studies* 40, no. 1 (2009): 139–58. Outside the Soviet Union, anti-fascism retained social legitimacy in countries or areas that were not occupied by Soviet forces. Yugoslavia is a case in point.
107. Svetlana Alexievich, *The Unwomanly Face of War* (New York, 2017); see also Daniel Bush, "'No Other Proof': Svetlana Aleksievich in the Tradition of Soviet War Writing," *Canadian Slavonic Papers* 59, no. 3–4 (2017), 214–33.
108. Gorbachev rounded up the exact number provided by the commission—26.6 million dead. On the work of the commission, see *Vserossiiskaia Kniga Pamiati. 1941–1945: Obzornyi tom* (Moscow, 1995), 395–96; *Naselenie SSSR. 1922–1959* (Moscow, 1993); V. N. Zemskov, "O masshtabakh liudskikh poter' SSSR v Velikoi Otechestvennoi Voine (v poiskakh istiny)," *Voenno-istoricheskii arkhiv* 9 (2012): 59–71.
109. "Upheaval in the East; Soviets Admit Blame in Massacre of Polish Officers in World War II," *The New York Times*, April 13, 1990, 1.
110. M. S. Gorbachev, "Uroki voiny i pobedy," *Izvestiia*, May 9, 1990: 1–2.
111. *Chernaia kniga* (Kiev: MIP "Oberig", 1991).
112. James E. Young, "America's Holocaust: Memory and the Politics of Identity," in *The Americanization of the Holocaust*, ed. Hilene Flanzbaum (Baltimore, 1999), 68–82 (73).
113. Museum Press Kit, U.S. Holocaust Memorial Museum, https://www.ushmm.org/information/press/press-kits/united-states-holocaust-memorial-museum-press-kit/.
114. "Final Solution—1940 to 1945," https://www.ushmm.org/information/exhibitions/museum-exhibitions/permanent/final-solution-1940-to-194.5.
115. Young, "America's Holocaust," 79.
116. For visitors' responses, see A. Stone, "In the Museum, Silent Disbelief," *USA Today*, April 27, 1993; photograph of shoes at USHHM, https://m.facebook.com/holocaustmuseum/photos/a.423860602676/10157693716637677/?type=3&p=90.

117. See page 5 of the USHMM's Museum Guide, https://www.ushmm.org/m/pdfs/Visitor_Guide_General_Museum_brochure_42412.pdf.
118. In recent years, the museum has expanded the section dedicated to the liberation of the camps by installing three monitors that continuously show Soviet, British, and American film footage of camps liberated by the Red Army (Majdanek and Auschwitz), British forces (Bergen-Belsen), and the U.S. Army (Dachau, Ohrdruf, Buchenwald). An accompanying text points out that the liberations were not the actual goal, but a by-product of the goal of defeating Germany and its allies. This comment was possibly added to explain why the Soviets were the first Allied power to liberate the death camps. The claim is debatable; recall Stalin's message of May 1, 1944, in which he called on the soldiers of the Red Army to liberate their "brothers and sisters" who had fallen under the "yoke of the German oppressors."
119. "What Other Groups Did the Nazis Target and Why?," https://encyclopedia.ushmm.org/content/en/article/mosaic-of-victims-an-overview#what-other-groups-did-the-nazis-target-and-why-1.
120. These nine biographies include six of Jews who hailed from Poland and the Baltic republics and became Soviet citizens only after their countries were annexed by the Soviet Union in 1939 and 1940. The three others were from core areas of the Soviet Union. They included two Jews who served in the Red Army and died in German captivity (Iosif Kirzhner and Isaac Sandler), and a Russian girl (Alexandra Schicharva) who was deported to Germany as an "Eastern worker" and survived the war. See https://encyclopedia.ushmm.org/landing/en/id-cards.
121. "What Conditions, Ideologies, and Ideas Made the Holocaust Possible?," Holocaust Encyclopedia, at https://encyclopedia.ushmm.org/content/en/question/what-conditions-and-ideas-made-the-holocaust-possible.
122. "Remarks of President William J. Clinton at the Dedication Ceremonies for the United States Holocaust Memorial Museum," April 22, 1993, https://www.ushmm.org/information/about-the-museum/mission-and-history/clinton.
123. I. Erenburg, "Opravdanie nenavisti," *Pravda*, May 26, 1942.
124. See the May 1945 poll that was undertaken by the French agency IFOP, https://www.herodote.net/Textes/ifop-victoire-1945.pdf; see also *Tsena kadra*, 1018–32.
125. For a sympathetic account, see Timothy Snyder, *Bloodlands: Europe Between Hitler and Stalin* (New York, 2010).
126. Rod Nordland, "Where the Genocide Museum Is (Mostly) Mum on the Fate of Jews," *New York Times*, March 30, 2018.
127. Stefan Troebst, "23 August: The Genesis of a Euro-Atlantic Day of Remembrance," *Remembrance and Solidarity. Studies in 20th Century European History 1* (2012): 15–53, https://enrs.eu/article/23-august-the-genesis-of-a-euroatlantic-day-of-remembrance.
128. Katrin Hammerstein and Birgit Hofmann, 'Europäische "Interventionen": Resolutionen und Initiativen zum Umgang mit diktatorischer Vergangenheit', in *Aufarbeitung der Diktatur—Diktat der Aufarbeitung? Normierungsprozesse beim Umgang mit diktatorischer Vergangenheit*, ed. Katrin Hammerstein et al. (Göttingen, 2009), 189–203 (196).
129. See OSCEPA, *Declaration of the OSCE Parliamentary Assembly and Resolutions Adopted at the Eighteenth Annual Session* (Copenhagen, 2009), https://www.oscepa.org/en/documents/all-documents/annual-sessions/2009-vilnius/declaration-6/261-2009-vilnius-declaration-eng/file (Articles, 10, 11); "Resolution on Stalin Riles Russia," BBC News, http://news.bbc.co.uk/2/hi/europe/8133749.stm. In September 2008, the European Parliament had proclaimed August 23 a Europe-wide Day of Remembrance for the Victims of All Totalitarian and Authoritarian Regimes, https://www.europarl.europa.eu/doceo/document/TA-6-2008-0439_EN.html.
130. "MOTION FOR A RESOLUTION on the 80th anniversary of the start of the Second World War and the importance of European remembrance for the future of Europe," European Parliament, https://www.europarl.europa.eu/doceo/document/B-9-2019-0098_EN.html.

131. Sergey Radchenko, "Vladimir Putin Wants to Rewrite the History of World War II," *Foreign Policy*, January 21, 2020, https://foreignpolicy.com/2020/01/21/vladimir-putin-wants-to-rewrite-the-history-of-world-war-ii/.
132. "At Katyn Memorial, Putin Calls for Poland, Russia to 'Move Toward Each Other,'" RFE/RL, April 7, 2010, at https://www.rferl.org/a/Putin_Speaks_At_Joint_Commemoration_Of_SovietEra_Massacre/2005357.html.
133. "Istoricheskaia neprikosnovennost," https://www.kasparov.ru/material.php?id=4A38F4044148E.
134. Interview with Elina Chuianova, https://beta.baltija.eu/news/print/4264. The Presidential Commission was folded again in 2012.
135. Formerly, the military parade on May 9 took place every five years, commemorating the big anniversaries. Olga Malinova, "Political Uses of the Great Patriotic War in Post-Soviet Russia from Yeltsin to Putin," in *War and Memory in Russia, Ukraine and Belarus*, ed. Julie Fedor et al. (London, 2017), 43–70 (53).
136. Andrii Nekoliak and Elizaveta Klochkova, "Weaponizing Russia's Memory Law: On Russia's Mnemonic Dissidents," *VerfBlog*, July 11, 2023, https://verfassungsblog.de/weaponizing-russias-memory-law/.
137. Shaun Walker, "Replica Reichstag Stormed at Russian 'Military Disneyland,'" *The Guardian*, April 24, 2017, https://www.theguardian.com/world/2017/apr/24/russians-storm-replica-reichstag-military-disneyland-patriot-park.
138. Jochen Hellbeck, "Das zerklüftete Gedenken," *Frankfurter Allgemeine Zeitung*, May 5, 2015. Ukraine left the CIS in 2018.
139. Jochen Hellbeck, Tetiana Pastushenko, and Dmytro Tytarenko, "'Wir werden siegen, wie schon vor 70 Jahren unsere Großväter gesiegt haben.' Weltkriegsgedenken in der Ukraine im Schatten des neuerlichen Kriegs," in *Kriegsgedenken als Event. Der 9. Mai 2015 im postsozialistischen Europa*, ed. Mischa Gabowitsch, Cordula Gdaniec, and Katja Makhotina (Paderborn, 2017), 41–66; Dmytro Tytarenko, "Der Feind ist wieder in unser Land einmarschiert [...]: Der Zweite Weltkrieg in der Geschichtspolitik auf dem Gebiet der Donecker Volksrepublik (2014–2016)," *Jahrbücher für Geschichte Osteuropas* 68, no. 3/4 (2020): 508–56.
140. Another law, passed at Poroshenko's behest and in effect to the present day, condemns "the Communist and Nazi totalitarian regimes in Ukraine and bans propaganda of their symbols." For the most part, however, the law focuses on the Soviet era. All that it has to say about Nazism is that its racial theories drove certain groups out of their professions. It makes no mention of the mass murder of Jews, let alone the participation of Ukrainians in these atrocities. The law glorifying the World War II–era Ukrainian insurgent army was drafted by the army's commander surviving son. Jochen Hellbeck, "Ukraine Makes Amnesia the Law of the Land," *New Republic*, May 21, 2015, https://newrepublic.com/article/121880/new-laws-ukraine-make-it-illegal-bring-its-ugly-past. Ukraine left the CIS in 2018.
141. Francine Hirsch, "Ukraine and Russia Are Both Looking to the Nuremberg Trials—But Finding Different Lessons in the History," *Time*, May 26, 2022, https://time.com/6181464/ukraine-war-crimes-nuremberg/.

Image Credits

Page 12: Courtesy of the author
Page 28: Russian State Library
Page 32: GL Archive / Alamy Stock Photo
Page 44: Süddeutsche Zeitung Photo / Alamy Stock Photo
Page 46: Sammlung Museum für Hamburgische Geschichte
Page 54: United States Holocaust Memorial Museum Collection, The Abraham and Ruth Goldfarb Family Acquisition Fund
Page 58: Bundesarchiv, Bild 183-R96360
Page 58: Bundesarchiv, Bild 102-02920A
Page 65: Stadtarchiv Göttingen; Photograph by A. Blankhorn
Page 68: © The Heartfield Community of Heirs / Artists Rights Society (ARS), New York, 2025
Page 81: Poster Collection, GE 391: Der Bolschewismus—Grosse antibolschewistische Schau in den Messehallen Stettin vom 25. bis 10 Okt. 1937, Hoover Institution Library & Archives.
Page 82: Shawshots / Alamy Stock Photo
Page 83: Deutsche Digitale Bibliothek
Page 87: Bundesarchiv, Plak 003-018-053 / Graphic artist: Christian Minzlaff
Page 105: NS-Dokumentationszentrum der Stadt Köln
Page 115: *Warum Krieg mit Stalin? Das Rotbuch der Anti-Komintern* (Berlin and Leipzig, 1941)
Page 118: Museum Berlin-Karlshorst
Page 130: Landesarchiv Speyer. Nachlass Walter Gottschalk, Photographer: Walter Gottschalk
Page 156: Süddeutsche Zeitung Photo / Alamy Stock Photo
Page 157: United States Holocaust Memorial Museum Collection
Page 166: National Archive, Prague
Page 172: © André Zucca / BHVP / Roger-Viollet
Page 175: Süddeutsche Zeitung Photo / Alamy Stock Photo
Page 182: Top, Süddeutsche Zeitung Photo / Alamy Stock Photo; bottom, RGAKFD
Page 186: Georg Schmidt, courtesy of Bundesarchiv, Bild 101I-010-0919-34
Page 187: Bundesarchiv, Bild 77-138-27A
Page 188: © Museum Berlin-Karlshorst / Photo by Albert Dieckmann
Page 202: Yad Vashem
Page 205: Arkhiv svidetelei Minskoi istoricheskoi masterskoi
Page 228: RGAKFD
Page 234: Copyright © Arkady Shaikhet Estate, Moscow; Courtesy of Nailya Aexander Gallery, New York

Page 240: Pictorial Press Ltd / Alamy Stock Photo
Page 247: Universal Images Group North America LLC / Alamy Stock Photo
Page 254: Central State Audiovisual and Electronic Archive
Page 260: United States Holocaust Memorial Museum, courtesy of David Mendels
Page 264: Top, © Bundesarchiv, Bild 183-R70660; bottom, Interview-Archiv "Zwangsarbeit 1939–1945"
Page 270: Timur Kurganov
Page 277: Bundesarchiv, Plak 003-040-051
Page 282: Bundesarchiv
Page 283: Bundesarchiv, Bild 121-1736
Page 287: Friedrich Zschäckel, courtesy of Bundesarchiv, Bild 101III-Zschaeckel-189-35
Page 298: Mjölnir [Hans Schweitzer], courtesy of Bundesarchiv, Plak 003-029-043
Page 305: United States Holocaust Memorial Museum Collection, gift of the Katz Family
Page 318: United States Holocaust Memorial Museum, courtesy of Belarusian State Archive of Documentary Film and Photography
Page 322: Bundesarchiv, BA58/213 Blatt 545
Page 332: Mikhail Trakhman, courtesy of TASS
Page 333: Yevgeni Umnov, courtesy of Natalia Feldman
Page 338: RGAKFD
Page 347: RGAKFD
Page 359: History and Art Collection / Alamy Stock Photo
Page 360: Christian Minzlaff, courtesy of Bundesarchiv, Plak 003-029-048
Page 375: Georgi Petrusov, courtesy of the Alex Lachmann Collection
Page 383: United States Holocaust Memorial Museum, courtesy of Robert Kempner
Page 387: United States Holocaust Memorial Museum, courtesy of National Archives and Records Administration, College Park
Page 388: Courtesy of Hadas Kalderon and the Sutzkever Estate
Page 417: United States Holocaust Memorial Museum

Index

Page numbers in *italics* refer to photo captions.

Abel, Theodore, 21–22, 24, 35, 48, 59–60
Adamovich, Ales, 414
Adenauer, Konrad, 408, 410–11
Africa, 103, 250, 292
Agitprop (Department of Agitation and Propaganda), 218, 234, 317
Aktion 1005, 306–7, 317–18, *318*
Aleichem, Sholem, 310
Aleksandrov, Georgy, 218, 234–35, 317, 370–71, 378
Alexievich, Svetlana, 414
Allenstein, 352
Almuzlino, Haim, 145
Altenkirchen, 295
Altona, 50
Angriff (*Attack*), 45, 65, 152, 161, *162*
Anti-Bolshevik League, 29
Anti-Comintern, 84, 87, *87*, 97, 161, 171, 175
anti-Semitism, 58, 189, 257, 410
  of Hitler, 2–3, 35–38, 221, 392, 399
  in Nazi Germany, 13, 16n, 23, 171
  in Poland, 110, 111
  in Soviet Union, 3, 27, 96, 111, 195, 220, 311–12, 401–3
Antonescu, Ion, 136–37, 141
Antonov, Alexei, 374
Anvaer, Sofiya, 179
Arco auf Valley, Anton Graf von, 33–34
Ardennes forest, 366
"Asiatic" people, 2, 10, 14, 16n, 20, 31, 32, 83, 114, 115, 118, 125, 135, 138, 139, 171, 184, 187, 220, 240, 276, 286–91, 356, 410, 419
Attack (*Angriff*), 45, 65, 152, 161, *162*
Auschwitz, 9, 13, 167, 169–71, 323, 346, 361–62, 379, 385, 389, 392, 394, 404, 409, 421
Austria, 29, 94, 95, 146

Babi Yar, xxiii, 389
  massacre at, 1, 135, 163, 219, 261, 306–7, 311, 313–14, 317, 326, 328, 333, 341, 343, 347, 368, 387, 398, 400, 409
  massacre memorial, 402–4
"Babi Yar" (Yevtushenko), 402–3
Bach, Johann Sebastian, 342
Bach-Zelewski, Erich von dem, 129, 131, 255, 281–83
Baden-Württemberg, 409
Bagerovo, 235
Balamut, Nikolai, 365
Balkans, 138
Balti, 125
Baltic states, 10, 30, 31, 37, 113, 128, 129, 132, 157, 187, 189, 193–94, 361, 366, 384, 398, 411, 421, 423
  independence of, 413, 415
  see also Estonia; Latvia; Lithuania
Bandera, Stepan, 424
Baranov, Vasily, 279–80
Baranovichi, 131
Barutchev, Suren, 179, 184, 322–23
Bastian, Claus, 55
Bavaria, 59
Bechtolsheim, Gustav von, 281
Beethoven, Ludwig van, 239, 342
Beimler, Hans, 55
Belaya Tserkov, 268–69

Belgium, 98, 103, 144–45, 149, 249, 255, 369, 396
Belgrade, 144–46, 348
Belorussia (Belarus), xxiii, 10, 20, 111, 129, 131, 177, 179, 189, 195, 197, 206, 207, 218–21, 254, 272, 274, 281, *282*, 285, 308, 310, 315, 317, 346–49, 367, 384, 398, 399, 405, 414, 420
  Operation Bagration in, 331, 345
Belorussian Pioneer, 202
Belzec, 368
Berdichev, 327
Beria, Lavrenti, 120
Berlin, 9, 10, 15–17, 42–44, 48, 54, 55, 58, 58, 60, 131, 150–51, 154, 156, 157, 158, 160, 176, 212, 297, 366, 374–75, 377, 378, 380, 390
  Battle of, 370–72, 376, 378, 412
  exhibitions in, 173, *174*, 175, *175*
  Goebbels's Sports Palace speech in, 297–99
  memorial park in, 412
  Olympics in, 88
  Soviet workers in, 266, 267, 269, 297
  Stalin and, 366, 369
Berzarin, Nikolai, 378–79
Bessarabia, 100, 125, 135–36, 157
Bialystok, 128–29, 132, 200
Bielefeld, 150
Birkenau, 13, 169, 170, 323, 416
Birobidzhan, 109, 221n
Black Book, The, 341, 400, 401, 415
Blobel, Paul, 134, 306–7, 317, 328
Bloch, Ernst, 94
Bogdanovka, 137
Böhme, Franz, 147–48
Boix, Francesc, 386–87
Bolshevism and Judeo-Bolshevism, 10, 19, 21–60, 67, 69–71, 73, 75–81, 95–97, 101, 102, 105–6, 111, 113, 114, 116, 126–35, 143, 145, 156–58, 255, 258, 261, 270, 276, 286–89, 298, 304, 356–60, 365, 390, 391, 411, 418, 419, 421, 425
  Axis coalition and, 87–88
  Bolshevik and *Bolshevist* terms, xxiii
  as catalyst for extermination of Jews, 13
  as driving force of war, 15–16
  European Jews and, 5, 143
  European survival and, 171–72
  in France, 147
  German effort to recruit Russians in fight against, 276–77, *277*
  German exhibitions on, 3, 81–84, *81*, *82*, *83*, 88, 102, 171–76, *172*, *174*, *175*, 302
  German labor recruitment drives and, 263, 267, *268*
  German publications on, 84–87, 114–15, *115*, 124
  German war against, turned into war against all Jews, 159
  Great Britain and, 88, 171
  Hitler and, 2–3, 24, 35, 37–39, 41, 52, 59, 61–63, 77–80, 82, 83, 102, 103, 123–24, 151, 153, 254, 276, 355, 365, 371, 373, 419
  intelligentsia and, 197
  Judeo-Bolshevism concept, 2–3, 5, 13, 24, 221
  Katyn massacre and, 301–4
  non-Jewish Soviet citizens and, 5, 178, 221
  Operation Barbarossa and, 4, 5, 13, 113–16, 118–35, 171
  reprisal killings and, 147–49, 154, 160, 163
  Russian auxiliary forces and, 276, 278
  Russian revolution, 25–26, 29, 39, 57, 76, 111, 158, 198–99, 202, 249, 250, 406
  and Soviet attitudes toward anti-Semitism, 27, 96, 195
  and Soviet leaders' depictions of Nazism, 220
  Soviet POWs and, 178–80, 185–89, 192, 193, 196–97
  women and, 185, 203
bone-grinding machine, 300, 317–18, *318*
book burnings, 65, *65*, 70, 102, 419
Braemer, Walter, 207
Braunschweig, 48–49
Bredel, Willi, 72
Bremen, 144, 366
Brest, 179, 193, 217
Brezhnev, Leonid, 407, 418
Britain, *see* Great Britain
Brown Book on the Reichstag Fire and Hitler Terror, The (Münzenberg et al.), 65–69, 93, 94
Bruskina, Maria, 200–203, *201*, *202*
Bryansk, 177, 279, 286, 316
BSV (*Bratskoe sotrudnichestvo voennoplennykh*; Fraternal Cooperation of Prisoners of War), 296, 321
Buchenwald, 56, 404
Budapest, 171

Budayeva, Elena, 375–76
Budyonnovka, 241
Büge, Emil, 165–66
Bukharin, Nikolai, 70–72, 94–95
Bukovina, 136
Bulanov, Mikhail, 337, *338*
Bulgaria, 98, 218
Bunin, Ivan, 25
Bunka, Jean, 194–95
Burckhardt, Carl J., 103
Burdenko, Fedor, 319–20, 324
Buryn, 308

Canaris, Wilhelm, 183
Carter, Jimmy, 404
Casablanca Conference, 292
Caucasus, 248, 249, 269
Central Asia, 285
Central Association of German Citizens of Jewish Faith, 35
Central Committee for the Liberation Struggle of the Enslaved Peoples in Fascist Germany, 297, 321
Césaire, Aimé, 396
Chamberlain, Neville, 97
Cheka, 37, 71, 131, 164, 194
Cherkasy, 344–45
Chernenko, Anna, 261
ChGK, 319–20, 328, 336, 379
Chiang Kai-shek, 92
China, 27, 31, 37, 58, 92, 115
Christian Science Monitor, 337
Churchill, Winston, 11, 26, 30, 153, 226, 245–47, 249–50, 366, 389, 390, 394
  at Casablanca Conference, 292
  Iron Curtain speech of, 389–91, 396
  Katyn massacre and, 306
  Stalin and, 249, 330, 390, 391, 407
Civil Rights Movement, 404
Clinton, Bill, 418
Cold War, 394, 396, 405, 419
Cologne, 152, 295
Columbia University, 21, 22
Come and See, 414
Comintern (Communist International), 26, 62, 64–66, 69, 74, 75, 78, 79, 88, 92, 94, 100, 127
  Anti-Comintern and, 84, 87, *87*, 97, 161, 171, 175
  Stalin's abolition of, 342–43
commissars, 112–19, *118*, 125, 136, 139–41, 143, 163, 165, 170, 178, 186, 192, 298, 304
Committee of State Defense, 215
Commonwealth of Independent States, 424
Communists, Communism, 5, 15, 74, 80, 96, 98, 100–102, 111, 144–46, 185, 219, 246, 277, 311, 350, 368–69, 379, 391
  Churchill and, 390
  in France, 146–47
  in Germany, 2, 15, 23, 24, 34, 35, 39–40, 42–48, 50, 53–54, 58–59, 58, 66, 73, 77, 101, 212, 342, 343
  Hitler and, 2, 4, 16n
  identity concealed by, 196, 197
  in Minsk, 196, 197, 199, 200, 203, 204, 206, 207, 209–10, 300
  mobilizing power of, 178–79
  in Niemöller quote, 11–12
  opponents of, as fascist, 412
  politsai and, 189
  reprisal killings of, 147–49
  Soviet, *see* Soviet Communism
  in Spain, 79, 82, 126, 185
  in Ukraine, 269, 305, 400
  U.S. fears of, 394–97
  World War II scholarship and, 13–14, 20
Compiègne, 149, 170
concentration camps, 2, 9, 13, 24, 55, 57, 66, 72, 96, 101, 137, 144, 146, 148, 154, 169–70, 288, 298–301, 321–23, 369, 375, 379, 382, 392
  Auschwitz, 9, 13, 167, 169–71, 323, 346, 261–62, 379, 385, 389, 392, 394, 404, 409, 421
  Birkenau, 13, 169, 170, 323, 416
  Buchenwald, 56, 404
  Compiègne, 149, 170
  crematoriums of, 165, 167, 323–24
  Dachau, 55, 57, 163, 404
  destruction of evidence at, 299–301, 317, 323, 324, 327–28
  gas chambers in, 167–68, 299, 323, 324, 417
  inmates moved west in advance of Red Army, 323–24, 361–62
  inspectors of, 163–64, 169
  Janowska, 317–18, *318*
  liberation of, 9, 346, 369, 384, 416–18, 421
  Majdanek, 9, 169, 184, 322–26, 350, 389, 417
  map of, xx–xxi

concentration camps (*cont.*)
Mauthausen, 166–67, 363, 386–87, *387*
in Minsk, 198, 199, 210, 219
nape-shot killing method in, 161–65, 176
Nuremberg tribunal and, 384–86, 391, 392
Oranienburg, 55–57, *56*, 163, 165
Poniatowa, 322, 323
prisoner-of-war, 162–71, *166*, 176, 178, 180–85, *182*, 187–91, *188*, 194, 196, 197, 286, 296–97, 321, 364, 365, 385
Ravensbrück, 362, 385
recording of deaths in, 307
Sachsenhausen, 57, 163–66, *166*, 168, 169, 176, 286, 298
Sobibor, 321–23
Sonnenburg, 389
Trawniki, 322, 323
Treblinka, 298–301, 321, 323, 327–28, 387, 392
uprisings in, 321–22
Counterattack, 65
Cracow, 105–6, 346
Crimea, 285
Croatia, 144
Czechoslovakia, 75, 97–98, 146, 218, 369, 412–13, 423

Dachau, 55, 57, 163, 404
Daily Mail, 49
Daily Telegraph, 368
Daladier, Eduard, 98
Darmstadt, 409
Davydov, Vladimir, 313, 317, 328
D-Day, 330–31, 419
Defeat of the German Troops near Moscow, The, 248
Defeat the Enemy!, 342
de Gaulle, Charles, 367
Democratic Party, 394
Denikin, Anton, 28–29
Denmark, 87, 98, 373
Depression, Great, 71
Dimitrov, Georgi, 66–69, 73, 75, 93, 94, 98, 372
Dirlewanger, Oskar, 281–83
Dobromil, 195
Donbas, 211–12, 270, 334, 424
Donetsk (Stalino), 270, 271, 273, 424
Dönitz, Karl, 373, 381, 384
Drancy, 146
Dresden, 280
Drexler, Anton, 36
Dr. Mamlock's Exit (Wolf), 73, 97
Drobitsky Yar, 260–61
Drozdy, 196–97
Druzhina Brigade, 286
Dubno, 129, 152
Du Bois, W. E. B., 396
Dulles, Allen, 394
Dunkirk, 103, 104
Durand-Wever, Anne-Marie, 379
Dvinsk, 190–91
Dwinger, Edwin Erich, 119–20

Eastern Europe, 389–91, 396, 408, 411–13, 420–22
Eastern Front, 3, 16, 373, 374
death toll in, 5, 330, 360, 407, 414, 418, 419
final fighting on, 366
as Great Patriotic War, 20, 214, 403–4, 413–14, 423
maps of, xi, xiii, xv, xvii, xix
turning tide in, 295, 327
Western scholarship on, 13–14, 20
see also Operation Barbarossa; *specific places*
East Prussia, *347*, 366, 370
Soviet offensive in, 345–52, 354–56, 361, 376
Eberhard, Kurt, 134
Ebert, Friedrich, 30, 55–56, *56*
Eden, Anthony, 247
Ehrenburg, Ilya, xxiii, 6–7, 70–72, 90, 94–96, 212, 213, 218–19, 221, 237–45, *240*, 249, 308–10, 326–28, 330, 347–48, 353–55, 366–71, 373, 377–78, 380, 399, 409, 419
Black Book and, 341, 400, 401, 415
death of, 415
The Extraordinary Adventures of Julio Jurenito, 71
on German denial of guilt, 353–54
Hitler and, 358
Jewish Anti-Fascist Committee and, 399–401
Jewish identity of, 399–401
memoirs of, 409–10
Nazi war crimes and, 339–42
New York Times pieces of, 251–52, 395
at Nuremberg tribunal, 387–89
on photographs of German violence, 237–38
Red Army and, 18, 255, 308, 315–16, 326, 341–42, 347, 354–55

on Soviet advance into Germany, 9, 10, 346–47
on Soviet treatment of Germans, 354
Stalin and, 74, 355, 358
Sutzkever and, 387–88
The Thaw, 401–2
Trust D.E., 71
United States and, 395–97
Wehrmacht flyer and, 358, 410
at writers conferences, 70, 92
Yevtushenko and, 403
Ehrenburg, Irina, 415
Ehrich, Lore, 361
Eichmann, Adolf, 146, 404
Eicke, Theodor, 163–66, 288–89
Einstein, Albert, 400, 401
Einsatzgruppen, 126–31, 134, 141–42, 384, 416
Einsatzkommandos, 398, 408
Eisenhower, Dwight, 366, 374
Eisenstein, Sergei, 101
Eisner, Kurt, 33–35
Engels, Friedrich, 70, 342
Enlightenment, 3, 20, 65, 419
Esterwegen, 56–57
Estonia, xxiii, 31, 100, 160, 181, 188, 190, 194, 365, 411–13, 415
European Parliament, 421, 422
European Union, 421, 422, 424
explosions, 1, 134, 136, 259
Extraordinary Adventures of Julio Jurenito, The (Ehrenburg), 71
Extraordinary State Commission for Establishing and Investigating Crimes Committed by the German Fascist Invaders (ChGK), 319–20, 328, 336, 379

factories, 17, 246–47, *247*, 262, 265, 269, 280
Fallingbostel, 406
fascism and anti-fascism, 6, 8, 39, 49, 62, 65, 69, 70, 73–75, 88–96, 98, 99, 101–2, 218, 222, 243, 296, 300, 311, 316–18, 339, 354, 372, 395, 405–15, 419, 424
National Committee for a Free Germany and, 343–45
racism in U.S. and, 395–96
"red fascism," 393
Soviet repatriation and, 405–6
FBI, 394–95
Feuchtwanger, Lion, 93–94
FHO (*Fremde Heere Ost*), 78
Filippovsky, Vassilii, 312–13
filtration camps, 405, 406
Finland, 100, 172
First Anti-Fascist Partisan Brigade, 286
Flanner, Janet, 382
Flossenbürg, 167
flu pandemic, 29
France, 6, 29, 30, 39, 65, 78, 79, 87, 98–100, 104, *105*, 144–45, 147, 149, 255, 257, 395, 396
Communist Party in, 146–47
Germany and, 103, 109–10, 172, 212, 246, 249, 367, 369
Nuremberg tribunal and, 381, 382, 385–88, 419
Revolution in, 3, 67
Russia invaded by, 214
Soviet Union and, 75
Franco, Francisco, 88–91, 98
Frank, Hans, 76, 108, 381
Franke, Lothar, 340
Fraternal Cooperation of Prisoners of War (*Bratskoe sotrudnichestvo voennoplennykh*; BSV), 296, 321
Freikorps, 31–34, 55, 113–15, 364
Fritsch, Werner Freiherr von, 77–78
Fritzsch, Karl, 167
Frunze Military Academy, 355

Galen, Clemens von, 125–26, 365, 368–69
Galetskaia, Florisa, 265, 296–97, 321
Galicia, 120, 121, 285, 301
Gamarnik, Jan, 91
gas chambers, 167–68, 299, 320, 323, 324, 417
mobile, 168, 209, 260, 266, 306, 337, 362
Gatchina, 340
Gaubschat, 266, 267
Gautherot, Henri, 146
Gelsenkirchen, 364
Geneva Convention, 183, 331
George VI, King, 249
German Soldiers See the Soviet Union, 124
German Workers' Party, 36
Germany, 6
economy of, 39, 47, 78
Nazi, *see* Nazi Germany
reclamation from Nazi ideology, 342–45
Revolution of 1918 in, 29–30
Weimar, 2, 33, 47, 54, 176
West, 17, 408–11
in World War I, 22, 29–30, 32–33, 35–36, 40, 41, 52, 61, 290, 297, 369
World War I reparation payments by, 35, 39

Gestapo, 1, 5, 95, 144, 169, 176, 204, 261, 282, 296, 308, 311, 313, 315, 321, 363, 391, 408, 420
Gide, André, 74, 92–93
Gil, Vladimir, 286
Glagolev, Vasily, 348
Glubokoe Monastery, 191
Glücks, Richard, 166, 169
Goebbels, Joseph, 19–20, 44–45, 65, 76, 82–84, 86, 95, 110, 119, 122, 124, 150–57, 159, 160, 171–73, 212, 218, 254, 313, 358–59, 372, 373, 378, 390
  Katyn massacre and, 302–4
  Molotov's note and, 222–23
  Russians and, 276–77
  Sports Palace speech of, 297–99
  Stalingrad and, 293–94
  suicide of, 373
  worker unrest and, 297
Goethe, Johan Wolfgang von, 67, 96, 102, 232, 239, 339, 342, 378
Gorbachev, Mikhail, 16–17, 414–15, 418
Göring, Carin, 46
Göring, Hermann, 46, 53, 54, 59, 68–69, 76–77, 183, 218, 254, 279, 283, 391
  Nuremberg tribunal and, 381, 384, 388
  partisans and, 281–82
  Stalingrad and, 293
Goslar, 77
GPU, 81, 113, 114, 122, 133, 152, 161, 164, 174, 260, 294, 302
Great Britain, 8, 26, 97–100
  Bolshevism and, 88, 171
  Germany and, 97–98, 104, 109–10, 213, 224, 290, 366
  India and, 253
  Jewish resettlement plans and, 109
  Nuremberg tribunal and, 381, 382, 384, 388, 391, 392
  Soviet Union and, 30, 63, 97, 245–51
  women encouraged to do war work in, 246–47, *247*
  U.S. aid to, 247
  in World War I, 29–30
  Yalta Conference and, 366
Great Depression, 71
Great Patriotic War, 20, 214, 403–4, 413–14, 423
  see also Eastern Front
Greece, 144
Greife, Hermann, 85–86
Grenzschutz Ost, 31
Grichanik, Mikhail, 199
Grossman, Vasily, 327, 328, 376–77, 401, 419
Gross-Rosen, 167
Gruppe Baum, 175–76
Gubarkova, Natalia, 311
Gumbinnen, 349
Gutterer, Leopold, 150–51
Gzhatsk, *188*

Hague Convention on Warfare, 222
Halifax, Edward Wood, Viscount, 97, 99
Halder, Franz, 113
Hamburg, 50, 152, 158, 362, 366
  Minsk and, 207–9
Hammerstein-Equord, Helga, 62, 66
Hammerstein-Equord, Konstantin, 61, 62, 102
Hammerstein-Equord, Marie-Therese, 62
Hartmann, Helmut, 119, 189
Harvest Festival operations, 282, 322–23
Hauster, Johann, 309
Heartfield, John, *68*, 69
Hegel, Georg Wilhelm Friedrich, 342
Heidelberg, 367
Heilmann, Ernst, 55–56, *56*
Heine, Heinrich, 239
Heinrici, Gotthard, 32–33
helots, 275
Henderson, Nevile, 79
Heydrich, Reinhard, 107–8, 126–28, 131, 132, 140, 145, 151–52, 154, 157, 159–61, 163, 164, 168, 169, 209, 384
Hilger, Gustav, 47
Himmler, Heinrich, 32, 55, 77, 107, 112, 128–29, 131, 132, 140, 154, 155, 158, 159, 169–70, 176, 207, 226, 254, 300, 306, 322, 384, 398
  and annihilation of Jews, 299, 300
  camp death list system of, 307
  dead zones and, 284–85
  and distinction between German and Soviet Jews, 158–59
  Gaubschat plant and, 266
  Generalplan Ost of, 255
  in Kharkov, 287–88
  labor recruitment and, 262
  partisans and, 280–83
  Posen speech of, 288–91
  Russia Center depopulation instructions of, 254–55
  speeches and orders to SS, 288–91, 299
  Treblinka visited by, 299, 327–28
Hindenburg, Paul von, 50, 52, 53

Hitler, Adolf, 22, 23, 34–44, *44*, 47–54, 57, 59, 60, 61–65, 74, 78, 90, 96, 119, 129, 135, 151, 169, 170, 173, 175, 189, 212, 218, 219, 221, 224, 239, 245, 252, 270, 276, 279, 286, 297, 327, 330, 344, 357, 369, 378, 382, 419, 323
annihilation of Jews prophesized by, 102–3, 133, 151, 159, 176
anti-Bolshevism of, 2–3, 24, 35, 37–39, 41, 52, 59, 61–63, 77–80, 82, 83, 102, 103, 123–24, 151, 153, 218, 219, 254, 276, 355, 365, 371, 373, 419
anti-Semitism of, 2–3, 35–38, 221, 392, 399
appeasement of, 97
appointed chancellor, 51–52, 61
art and, 83–84
assassination attempt against, 345
birthdays of, 176, 371
commissars and, 113–14
Communism and, 2, 4, 16n
coup attempted by, 39–40, 61
deportation of Jews authorized by, 152–54, 157
Dimitrov and, 69
Ehrenburg and, 358
euthanasia program of, 125–26, 365
generals addressed by, 61–62, 64, 94, 99, 102, 112
Germans' break with, 342–45, 354
Göring and, 46
Katyn massacre and, 302
Keitel and, 147
Leningrad and, 5, 153
Mein Kampf, 34–35, 38, 40–43, 63, 383
Minsk and, 210
Moscow and, 331
Mussolini and, 39
Olympic Games and, 88
Operation Barbarossa and, 2–5, 20, 112–14, 117, 122–24, 128, 136, 139–42, 153–54, 213, 227
partisan warfare and, 281
Paulus and, 294, 345
plans for conquered Soviet lands, 253–54
Poland and, 106, 108, 110, 112
rise to power, 6, 13, 52, 64
Rosenberg and, 37–38, 284
Soviet advance and, 355–56, 371
Spain and, 79
speeches of, 61–62, 64, 76, 79–80, 89, 94, 99, 102–3, 112–13, 127, 139–40, 176, 276
Stalin and, 6, 11, 14, 95, 153, 225, 246, 342, 371, 390
Stalingrad and, 293–94
Stalin's pact with, 2, 14, 100–103, 110, 114, 116, 119, 120, 136, 144, 181, 211, 212, 245, 391, 421
suicide of, 372–73
on visual propaganda, 43
Wolfschanze headquarters of, 153, 160
Zionism and, 155
Hitler Youth, 80, 356, 363
Hiwis (Russian auxiliaries), 275–76, 278, 286, 289
Hodgson, Vere, 246–48, 251
Hofshteyn, Dovid, 400
Holland, 98
Holocaust, 11, 14, 141, 404, 421, 425
denial of, 417
scholarship on, 14–15, 16n, 165
United States Holocaust Memorial Museum, 11–12, *12*, 415–18, *417*
Homburg, 365
Hoover, J. Edgar, 394
Höss, Rudolf, 167
Hoth, Hermann, 113
House Committee on Un-American Activities, 394
humanism, 7, 74, 102, 112, 219, 318, 351
Hungary, 34, 98, 171, 172, 412, 423

India, 253, 285
Inozemtsev, Nikolai, 351
Insterburg, 349
Institute for the Study of the Jewish Question, 84
internationalism, 41, 96, 102, 187, 191, 202, 206, 220–21, 402
international law, 112, 114, 183, 219, 222, 281, 384
Iron Curtain, 389–91, 396, 408
Israel, 401
Istra, *234*
Italy, 39, 88, 98, 251, 320, 369, 396
Sicily, 330
I Was a Communist for the FBI, 394–95
Izvestiya, 6, 62, 72, 90, 96, 212, 237

Jackson, Robert, 381–82, 388
Janowska, 317–18, *318*
Japan, 63, 64, 88, 92, 247
Pearl Harbor attacked by, 159, 227
Jeckeln, Friedrich, 134, 158, 162–63, 397–98
Jelgava, 185

Jewish Anti-Fascist Committee (JAC), 399–401
Jews
Bolshevism and, *see* Bolshevism and Judeo-Bolshevism
deportations of, 151–54, 157–58, 160, 170, 199, 207, 208
distinction between German and Soviet, 158–59
German, as enemies, 150–57
German remorse over treatment of, 380
global conspiracy belief about, 13, 126
Hitler's prophecy of annihilation of, 102–3, 133, 151, 159, 176
identifying armbands and stars for, 5, 27, 108, 117, 145, 146, 151–52, 154–56, *156*, *157*, 197, 198, 208, 361
in Niemöller quote, 11
Nuremberg tribunal and, 384, 388
as racial-political enemy, 5, 15–16
resettlement proposals for, 108–9
Soviet identity of, and Soviet accounts of war, 219–21, 317, 325, 399–401, 403–4
Western focus on suffering of, 404
Zionism and, 111, 155, 400, 401
see also anti-Semitism
see also commissars
Judgment of the Nations, 393
Jurisdiction Decree, 115–16

Kahn, Rudolf, 60
Kalimov, Aleksandr, 181, 190, 365, 406–7
Kamenev, Lev, 91, 93
Kammler, Hans, 363–64
Kapustiansky, Aleksandr, 228
Karmen, Roman, 227–28, 325–26, 381, 388, 393, 419
Kataev, Valentin, 237, 239
Katyn massacre, 110, 301–6, 318–20, 324, 357, 378, 391–92, 415, 422
Kaunas, 157, 158
Keitel, Wilhelm, 145, 147–49, 183, 226, 374–75, *375*, 381, 419
Kerch, 235, *236*, 368, 389
Kersten, Captain, 238, 239
Kharkov (Kharkiv), xxiii, 153, 162, 168, 186, 219, 256–62, 266, 269, 270, 285, 287–89, *287*, 304, 389
closure of academic and political institutions in, 261
food in, 258–59, 261, 262
Germans' looting in, 258
hangings in, 259
Himmler's visit to, 287–88
labor recruitment drives in, 262, 266–67
land mines in, 259
mass shootings in, 259–61
mortality rate in, 261
NKVD in, 257–58
POWs in, 273–74
Sumskaya Street, *260*
war crimes trial, 336–40, *338*, 397
Kharkov University, 287
Khrushchev, Nikita, 305, 313, 332, 333, 402–3, 408, 410
Kieper, Wolf, 130–31, 339
Kiev (Kyiv), xxiii, 130, 134–36, 141, 162, 198, 238, 253, 304, 306, 309, 311–13, 316, 329, 332–34, 341, 399, 400, 424
Babi Yar, *see* Babi Yar
explosions in, 1, 259
German occupation of, 1, 134, 153, 180, 198
German POWs in, 332–34
labor recruitment drives in, 262–63, 279
Soviet liberation of, 18, 308, 310–12, 317
war crimes trial in, 397, 398
Kiev Opera House, 253, *254*
Kindler, Helmut, 409–10
Kircher, Grete, 23
Kleist, Peter, 98–99
Klemperer, Eva, 155
Klemperer, Victor, 154–55
Klimov, Elem, 414
Klin, 247
Kluge, Günther von, 185
Koch, Erich, 254–55, 278, 346–47
Kogan, Moshe, 130–31, 339
Koltsov, Mikhail, 94
Komsomol, 111, 127, 202, 229, 231–32
Konev, Ivan, 371
Königsberg, 279, 346, 367
Korsun, 344–45
Kosmodemyanskaya, Liubov, 232, 233
Kosmodemyanskaya, Zoya ("Tanya"), 229–33, *230*, 334–36
Kovalchuk, Anastasia, 265
Kozelets, 309
KPD (Communist Party of Germany), 2, 15, 23, 24, 34, 35, 39–40, 42–48, 50, 53–54, 58–59, *58*, 66, 73, 77, 101, 212, 342, 343

Krasnodar, 320
Kristallnacht, 13, 40, 96, 97
Kube, Wilhelm, 207–10, 279, 284, 398
Küchler, Georg von, 113
Kügelgen, Bernd von, 343–44
Kun, Bela, 34
Kursk, 285
Kutuzov, Mikhail, 232
Kyiv, *see* Kiev

Lampe, Maurice, 386
Langheld, Wilhelm, 338, *338*
Latvia, xxiii, 28, 31–32, 100, 132, 185, 188, 190, 194, 411, 413, 415
League of Nations, 74, 75
Lemberg, *see* Lviv
Lend-Lease, 8, 245, 247
Lenin, Vladimir, 2, 25, 29, 43, 70, 76, 158, 173, 200
Leningrad, 5, 153–54, 162, 215, 224, 301, 347, 349
Leninism, 13, 244, 342, 343
Lenin Mausoleum, 225
Levina, Basya, 196
Levitan, Yuri, 213–14, 419
Ley, Robert, 79–80, 126
Liady, 315
Lidov, Pyotr, 229–32, 334–36
Liebknecht, Karl, 30, 33
Life, 171
Lippe-Detmold, 50–51
Lithuania, Lithuanians, xxiii, 28, 31–32, 63, 100, 132, 187, 188, 197–99, 349, 411, 413, 415, 416, 420–21
Lodz, 157, 158
Löhning, Günther, 90
Löhr, Alexander, 106
Lohse, Hinrich, 129–30, 209
London, 250
Lublin, 169, 184, 279, 323
Luce, Clare Boothe, 394
Luck, 129
Ludwigslust, 373
Luftwaffe, 78, 106
Luhansk, 424
Lutsk, 152
Luxembourg, 157
Luxemburg, Rosa, 33
Lvov (Lemberg, Lwów, Lviv), xxiii, 28, 104, 120–24, 127–29, 150, 152, 171, 193, 271, 304–5, 360
  Janowska concentration camp in, 317–18, *318*

Madagascar, 109
Magic Flute operation, 282
Maizles, Etta, 203–6
Majdanek, 9, 169, 184, 322–26, 350, 389, 417
malinas, 203–4
Maly Trostinets, 368
Mann, Heinrich, 65
Mann, Klaus, 74
Mannheim, 367
Marcuse, Ludwig, 74
Mariupol, 344
Marx, Karl, 43, 70, 76, 96, 342
Marxism, 3, 13, 15, 22–24, 33, 38, *44*, *46*, 67, 69, 70, 76, 105, 112, 161, 173, 244, 342, 343, 350
  as model for Nazism, 42–43, *42*
Mattner, Walter, 132–34, 143, 184–85, 226
Mauthausen, 166–67, 363, 386–87, *387*
Mayakovsky, Vladimir, 73, 232
Mayer, Arno, 16n
Mein Kampf (Hitler), 34–35, 38, 40–43, 63, 383
Melitopol, 278, 312
memorials and monuments, 407, 411–15
  Memorial to the Murdered Jews of Europe, 421
  United States Holocaust Memorial Museum, 11–12, *12*, 415–18, *417*
Mikhoels, Solomon, 221
Ministry of Information, 246, 249
Minsk, 157, 158, 165, 168, 173, 191, 195–210, 216, 279, 282, 284, 296, 321
  children in, 204–5
  Communists in, 196, 197, 199, 200, 203, 204, 206, 207, 209–10, 300
  concentration camp in, 198, 199, 210, 219
  Hamburg and, 207–9
  malinas in, 203–4
  mass killings in, 157–58, 199, 203–5, 208–10, 219
  November action in, 157–58, 198–99, 203, 204, 208
  underground in, 200–210
  war crimes trial in, 397, 398
Mints, Isaak Izrailevich, 18–19, 233, 244, 312
Mints, Maks, 177–78, 189, 191–93, 405–6
Mogilev, xxiii, 132, 134, 143, 184, 315
Molotov, Viacheslav, 96, 100, 213–15
  note on Soviet POWs, 222–23, 233, 248
Montgomery, Bernard L., 373

Moosburg, 377
moral compass, 225, 269–74, 339–40
Morning Post (London), 25
Moscow, 6, 18, 23, 69–70, 73, 74, 139, 153–54, 157, 159, 172, 215, 216, 221, 224, *234*, 247, 272, 276, 331, 349
  Battle of, 227–39, 248–49
  German POWs in, 331–32, *332*, *333*, 334, 378
Moscow City Council, 224–25
Moscow Conference, 336
Moscow Congress of Writers, 342
Moscow Museum, 424
Moscow Strikes Back, 248, 394
Mozhaisk, 229
Mukhortova-Pekker, Olga, 1, 311–12
Munich, 34–39, 55, 57, 97–98, 176, 296, *322*
Münster, 181
Münzenberg, Willi, 65, 69, 94
Museum of Occupation and Freedom Fights, 420–21
Mussolini, Benito, 39
My Political Awakening (Drexler), 36

nape-shot killing method, 161–65, 174, 176, 260, 302, 319, 320, 355, 378, 392
Napoleon I, 214, 330
Napoleonic Wars, 331
Narochnitskaya, Natalya, 423
National Committee for a Free Germany (NKFD), 343–45
Nazi armed forces
  Army Group Center, 129, 133, 284, 331, 374
  Nuremberg tribunal and, 382, 392
  prisoners of war from, 331–34, *332*, *333*, 336, 343–45, 378, 408, 410
  Secret Field Police, 337, 340, 356
  Volkssturm, 356, 363, 363
  see also Wehrmacht
Nazi Germany
  Allied bombing of, 290, 320, 362, 380
  Allied soldiers in, 362–69, 377–78
  in Axis coalition, 88
  Baltic states and, 413
  birthrate in, 254
  Britain and, 97–98, 104, 109–10, 213, 224, 290, 366
  demise of, 12, 20, 369, 375, 425
  Eastern workers in, 262–69, *264*, 271, 278–80, 282–84, 286, 320–21, 362–64, 368, 377, 391, 405
  Eastern workers' uprisings in, 295–97, 320–21, *322*
  economy of, 78
  euthanasia program of, 125–26, 365
  evidence of crimes destroyed by, 299–301, 306–8
  France and, 103, 109–10, 172, 212, 246, 249, 367, 369
  Gestapo of, 1, 5, 95, 144, 169, 176, 204, 261, 282, 296, 308, 311, 313, 315, 321, 363, 391, 408, 420
  living space for, 41, 62
  military buildup in, 74–75
  quality of life in, 353
  racial ideology of, 2, 3, 9, 33, 40, 76, 77, 84, 218, 219, 353, 382–84, 390, 392, 397
  refugees from, 360–61
  repatriation of Soviet citizens from, 405–6
  SA (storm troopers) of, 23, 38, 43, *44*, 45, 47–50, 53, 55, 58, *58*, 60, 68, 73, 96, 97, 362–63, 408
  Security Police (Sipo) of, 107, 109, 126, 127, 129, 145, 147–49, 158, 267, 283, *283*, 288, 398
  social hierarchy in, 219, 265
  Soviet Communism compared to, 421–23
  Soviet nationalization and universalization of victims of, 325, 399
  Soviet Union invaded by, *see* Operation Barbarossa
  SS of, *see* SS
  suicides in, 9, 352–53, 360
  surrender of, 292, 372–75, *375*
  swastika symbol of, 36, 45, 50, 63, 76–77
  U.S. and British journalists in, 364
  vagrants in, 362–63
  vigilantes in, 363
Nazi Germany–Soviet relations, 2, 3, 14, 63, 69, 211–13
  nonaggression pact, 2, 14, 100–103, 110, 114, 116, 119, 120, 136, 144, 181, 211, 212, 245, 391, 421
  war, *see* Eastern Front; Operation Barbarossa
Nazi Party, 17, 150, 159, 173, 342, 364
  autobiographical essays by members of, 21–24, 35, 59–60
  former Nazis, 408, 409, 411
  founding and rise of, 13, 21, 22, 24, 36, 40, 50, 53, 54, 70, 71, 102
  Marxism as model for, 42–43, *42*

in occupied territories, 255–56
rallies and marches of, 44–45, *44*, 47, 48, 75–76, 79–82, 89, 96, 102, 114, 297
Nazi propaganda, 21, 22, 31, *32*, 43–48, *46*, 50–52, *51*, 54, *54*, 78–87, *86*, 117, 122, 124, 125, *156*, 171–72, *187*, 195, 239, 240, 284, 304, 305, 312, 356, 358, 382
exhibitions, 3, 81–84, *81*, *82*, *83*, 88, 102, 171–76, *172*, *174*, *175*, 302
Katyn massacre and, 302, 303, 306
posters, 31, 43, 45–46, *46*, 50–51, 82, *82*, 83, *83*, 253, 262, *263*, 267, 298, *298*, 304, *305*, 359–60, *359*, *360*
and recruitment of Russians to fight Bolshevism, 276–77, *277*
Soviet fears of, 220
for work recruitment, 267, *268*
Nazi war crimes, 336, 408
Ehrenburg's views on, 339–42
execution for, 339
Jurisdiction Decree and, 115–16
Kharkov trial, 336–40, *338*
Moscow Declaration and, 336
Nuremberg International Military Tribunal on, 10–11, 381–89, *383*, 391–93, 397, 404, 419
Soviet trials of, 306, 313, 334–40, 397–99
UN War Crimes Commission, 336
West Germany and, 409, 410
Nebe, Arthur, 128–29
Nemmersdorf, 356–58
Netherlands, 103, 110, 144–45, 255, 373
Neubrandenburg, 376
Neukölln, 266
Neurath, Konstantin von, 61
New Yorker, 382
New York Herald Tribune, 393
New York Times, 10, 25, 49, 59, 80, 89, 97, 223, 248, 251–52, 389, 393, 395, 404
Nibelungen Verlag, 84–86, 114
Niemöller, Martin, 11–12
Nikitchenko, Iona, 392–93
Nikolaev, Lev, 257–62, 266–67, 269–70, *270*, 272–74
NKFD (National Committee for a Free Germany), 343–45
NKVD (Narodnyi komissariat vnutrennykh del), 86, 91, 94, 102, 120, 121, 128, 129, 134, 136, 171, 177, 211, 215, 231, 241, 257–58, 289, 313–14, 332–34, 352, 405, 420
Katyn massacre by, 110, 301–6, 318–20, 324, 357, 378, 391–92, 415, 422
Vinnitsa graves and, 304
Nolte, Ernst, 16
Normandy, 330–31, 395, 419
North Africa, 250, 292
Norway, 87, 138, 369
Novgorod, 309, 353
Nuremberg, 321, *322*
labor office in, 265, 296
rallies in, 47, 48, 75–76, 79–82, 89, 96, 114, 297
Nuremberg International Military Tribunal, 10–11, 381–89, *383*, 391–93, 397, 404, 419
Nuremberg Laws, 13, 76–77

Oder River, 366
Odessa, 136–37, 305
Ohlendorf, Otto, 384
Okun, Zinovy, 206
Oldenburg, 295
Olympics, 88
Operation Bagration, 331, 345
Operation Barbarossa (German invasion of Soviet Union), 3–7, 13, 15, 16n, 20, 104–6, 112–43, 144–46, 150, 151, 153–55, 159, 171, 177, 181, 194, 211–52, 254, 356, 380, 390, 393, 410, 419
Bolshevism and, 4, 5, 13, 113–16, 118–35, 171
dead zones in, 284–85, 328
destruction and looting in, 258, 282–85, 308, 309, 315, 328
German defeat in, 10, 251, 252, 346–71, 378, 379
Germans' contempt and violence toward Soviet civilians in, 271–72, 274, 280, 284
Germans' destruction of evidence of, 299–301, 306–8, 317
Germans' increased pace of killing in, 320
German soldiers' letters and diaries during, 237, 240–44, 309, 380, 409
Germans' targeting of civilians in, 193–99
Germany's planning of, 2, 77–78, 98–99, 213
hangings in, 230, *230*, 237, 259, 272, 313, 334–36
Hitler and, 2–5, 20, 112–14, 117, 122–24, 128, 136, 139–42, 153–54, 213, 227

Operation Barbarossa (German invasion of Soviet Union) (*cont.*)
Jewish identity and, and Soviet accounts of war, 219–21, 317, 325, 399–401, 403–4
life in occupied territories, 253–91
naming of, 112
Operation Bagration and, 331, 345
partisans and, 191, 209, 229–34, 280–86, *282*, *283*, 286, 290, 305, 313, 314, 331, 334–35, 409
recruitment of workers in, 262–69, *264*, 271, 278–80, 282–84, 286
Soviet advance and liberation of occupied areas, 285, 292–328, 329–31, 336
Soviet advance into Germany, 9, 329, 346–71
Soviet documentation of German violence in, 213, 216–24, 226–45, 306, 328
Soviet food production and, 254, 277–78
Soviet identity and, 274
Soviet Jewish identity and, 221, 403–4
Soviet oral history of, 18–19, 233, 312
Soviet public informed of, 213–14
Stalin and, 213–16, 219, 224–26
see also specific places
Operation Cottbus, 282–84
Oradour, 367
Oranienburg, 55–57, *56*, 163, 165
Organization for Security and Cooperation in Europe (OSCE), 421
orphanages, 204
Orsha, 179, 183
Ortenberg, David, 226, 228
Oryol, 319, 320
Ostland, 129–30
Ostrovskaia, Elena, 201
Oswiecim, 170

Pacific theater, 159, 227, 247, 248
Pale of Settlement, 141, 310
Palestine, 83, 344, 400, 401
Panasik, Nikolai, 314
Paniavin, Grigori, 190–91
Papen, Franz von, 50–52
Paris, 6, 73–75, 96, 109, 146, 147, 149, 171, 212
World's Fair in, 88–89
partisans, 191, 209, 229–34, 280–86, *282*, *283*, 286, 290, 305, 313, 314, 331, 334–35, 409
Paulus, Friedrich, 294–95, 345–46
Pavlichenko, Liudmila, 250
peace congresses, 396
Pearl Harbor, 159, 227
Pechersky, Alexander, 321
Pekker, Solomon, 18, 311–12
People's Commissariat for Defense, 217
Petrishchevo, 229–31
Petrograd, 30
Picasso, Pablo, 396
Pirna, 167
Pisactor, Erwin, 49
Pius XI, Pope, 59
Plague in Russia! (Rosenberg), 37
pogroms, 28–29, 128, 136, 195, 199, 203, 204, 209–10, 225
Pokrovsky, Yuri, 388–89
Poland, Polish, 10, 13, 14, 28, 29, 40, 63, 95–96, 98–100, 104–13, 116, 119, 129, 132, 138, 141, 146, 148, 149, 152, 193, 209, 213, 218, 323, 369, 370, 422, 423
anti-Semitism and, 110, 111
Himmler and, 255
Katyn massacre of soldiers, 110, 301–6, 318–20, 324, 357, 378, 391–92, 415, 422
Soviet liberation of, 325
workers, 266, 413
Polar Sea, 160, 161
Poleshchuk, Anna, *264*
Politburo, 75, 100, 319, 397, 407
politsai, 189
Poltava, 142, 168, 272, 308
Polytechnical Institute, 200
Ponary, 368
Poniatowa, 322, 323
Ponomarenko, Panteleimon, 219, 220
Popular Front, 75, 91, 93, 98
Poroshenko, Petro, 424
Portugal, 87, 172
Posen, 288–91
Prague, 58, 154, 157, 390, 411–13
Prague Spring, 412
Pravda, 75, 93, 94, 96, 214, 217, 220, 221, 226, 228–32, 237, 308, 310, 320, 334–35, *335*, 367, 370, 379, 390
Presidential Commission to Counter Attempts to Falsify History to the Detriment of Russia's Interests, 422–23
Pripyat Marshes, 131
prisoners of war
Geneva Convention and, 183, 331

German, 331–34, *332*, *333*, 336, 343–45, 378, 408, 410
Soviet, *see* Soviet POWs
Pronicheva, Dina, 398–99, 409
propaganda, 90
British, 246
Nazi, *see* Nazi propaganda
Protocols of the Elders of Zion, 27–28, 38, 41
Soviet, 27–28, *28*, 85–86, 212–13, 239, 240, 256, 310, 317, 393
Proskurov, 28, 180
Protocols of the Elders of Zion, 27–28, 38, 41
Pruslina, Khasya, 195–97, 203–5, *205*, 209–10
Prussia, 31, 50, 53, 68
East, *347*, 366, 370
East Prussian offensive, 345–52, 354–56, 361, 376
Przemysl, 108
Pskov, 275
Pushkin, Alexander, 378
Putin, Vladimir, 422–25

Radek, Karl, 62–63, 94
Radova, Emma, 203
Rasch, Otto, 134
Rastenburg, 354
Ravensbrück, 362, 385
Rawa-Ruska Stalag, 385–86
Red Army, 4, 6, 8–10, 16, 18, 19, 26, 30–31, 50, 72, 78, 82, 87, 91–92, 110, 113, 114, 117–19, 124, 129–41, *140*, 144, 172, 177, 181, 183, 196, 200, 209, 212–14, 216, 222–29, *228*, 233–35, 241, 244, 245, 247–49, 251, 252, 256, 273, 276, 287, 288, 329, 372–74, 380, 384, 393, 410, 414, 419, 420
advance and liberation of German-occupied areas, 285, 292–328, 329–31, 336
advance into Germany, 9, 329, 346–71
at Berlin, 370–72
burial sites of, 412
camps liberated by, 346, 417–18, 421
D-Day and, 330–31
Eastern European presence of, 389–91
in East Prussian offensive, 345–52, 354–56, 361, 376
Ehrenburg and, 18, 255, 308, 315–16, 326, 341–42, 347, 354–55
German looting and, 285
at Moscow, 18
9-Millimeter Cure and, 161–62, *162*
in Operation Bagration, 331, 345
prisoners from, *see* Soviet POWs
Reichstag and, 372, 423
reorganization of, 6
repatriation and, 405
at Stalingrad, 8, 18, 20, 248–52, 274–76, 286–87, 292–97, 299–301, 307, 321, 327–28, 342, 355
surrender as viewed in, 190
survey of soldiers in, 368
vengeance and, 8–9, 244, 314–16, 326–27, 339, 349–54, 378
violence, destruction, and sexual assaults by, 348–59, 377–78, 423
women in, 185–87, *186*, *187*
Red Megaphone collective, 43
Red Menace, The, 394
Red Star, 9, 217, 219, 226, 235–41, *238*, 243, 310, 324, 330, 346, 353–55
Reichenau, Walter von, 135, 220, 221, 226
Reichstag, 30, 48, 52, 372
elections in, 45–48, 50–52, 54, *54*, 58, *58*, 71
fire at, 53–54, *54*, 66–69, 73, 82, 372
Red Army's storming of, 372, 423
replica of, 423–24
Reims accord, 374
Reinecke, Hermann, 181, 183
reprisal killings, 147–49, 154, 160, 163
Republican Party, 394
Return from the USSR (Gide), 92–93
Retzlaff, Reinhard, *338*
Revolution Betrayed, The (Trotsky), 91
Rhine, 363, 366
Ribbentrop, Joachim von, 97, 100–101, 381, 391
Riefenstahl, Leni, 80, 88
Riga, 31, 142, 157, 158, 163, 184, 194, 384, 397–98
Ritz, Hans, 338, *338*
Rohatyn, 301
Rolland, Romain, 74
Romania, 87, 98, 135–37, 146, 172, 251, 305, 423
Röntgen, Wilhelm, 34
Roos, Anton, 104–6, *105*, 109, 122, 138, 142–43, 186, 226
Roos, Elisabeth, 104, 105, 122, 142, 186
Roos, Gustav, 138
Roosevelt, Franklin Delano, 176
at Casablanca Conference, 292
death of, 370
Katyn massacre and, 306
Stalin and, 369–70

Rosenberg, Alfred, 37–38, 76, 114, 284, 289
Roser, Paul, 385–86
Roslavl, 178, 178, 191
Rostov, 235, 241, 389
Rote Fahne, 47
Roth, Leo, 62, 94
Rovno, xxiii, 129, 131
Rozenfeld, Major, 354
RSHA (Reich Security Main Office), 146
Rudenko, Roman, 314, 381–84, *383*, 386, 408
Ruederer, Ludwig, 335–36
Ruhr, 363, 365
Rumbula, 163
Russia, 100, 317, 325, 399, 405, 413, 420, 424
  civil war in, 7, 25, 27, 34, 37, 47, 185, 390
  corporal punishment in, 272
  historical defeats of, 63–64
  Patriotic War of 1812 in, 214
  revolution in, 25–26, 29, 39, 57, 76, 111, 158, 198–99, 202, 249, 250, 406
  war against Ukraine, 424–25

SA (storm troopers; *Sturmabteilung*), 23, 38, 43, *44*, 45, 47–50, 53, 55, 58, *58*, 60, 68, 73, 96, 97, 362–63, 392, 408
Sachsenhausen, 57, 163–66, *166*, 168, 169, 176, 286, 298
Salaspils, 184
Saloniki, 144
Sambor, 195
Sunstein, Maks, 193
Sauckel, Fritz, 279, 283, 284, 381, 391
Sauerland Forest, 363
Scheer, Paul Albert, 398
Scheidemann, Philipp, 30
Schiller, Friedrich, 96, 102, 239, 342
Schleicher, Kurt, 51
Schmidt, Friedrich, 241–43, 409
Scholz, Hermann, 340
Schönherr, Hans, 23, 47–48
Schwabach, 321
SD (*Sicherheitsdienst*), 107–9, 126, 127, 134, 145, 150, 163, 207, 209, 286, 288, 293, 295, 380, 408
Security Police (Sipo), 107, 109, 126, 127, 129, 145, 147–49, 158, 267, 283, *283*, 288, 398
Seghers, Anna, 396
Selvinsky, Ilya, 235–37
Serbia, 144, 146–49, 168
Sevastopol, 19, 301
Seydlitz, Walther von, 345–46
Shawcross, Hartley, 382, 384
Shcherbatsevich, Olga, 200–201
Shcherbatsevich, Vladlen, 200, 201, *201*
Shelest, Petro, 407
Shevchenko, Nikolai, 321
Shirokaya camp (Minsk), 198, 199, 210, 219
Shumilov, Mikhail, 294
Shvernik, Nikolai, 319
Siberia, 64, 72, 80, 85, 160, 173, 194, 218, 227, 235, 255, 356, 371, 378
Sicily, 330
Signal, 171, 172
Silesia, 366, 370
Simonov, Konstantin, 324–26, 412
Sipo (Security Police), 107, 109, 126, 127, 129, 145, 147–49, 158, 267, 283, *283*, 288, 398
Slavs, 218, 219–21, 253, 254, 289
SMERSH, 334
Smolar, Hersh, 200, 203, 206
Smolensk, 110, *188*, 190, 215, 275, 288, 301, 302, 319, 320, 334
  Katyn, 110, 301–6, 318–20, 324, 357, 378, 391–92, 415, 422
  Soviet liberation of, 319
Sobibor, 321–23
Social Democratic Party of Germany (SPD), 24, 30, 31, 46–50, 53–57, 59, 66, 84, 101
socialism, 93, 94, 97, 111
Sonnenburg, 389
Sonnenstein, 167
Soviet armed forces, 214–16
  see also Red Army
Soviet Communism, 2–3, 12, 30, 111, 126, 127, 212, 274, 420
  criteria for Party admission, 244
  Komsomol, 111, 127, 202, 229, 231–32
  Nazism compared to, 421–23
Soviet–Nazi Germany relations, 2, 3, 14, 63, 69, 211–13
  nonaggression pact, 2, 14, 100–103, 110, 114, 116, 119, 120, 136, 144, 181, 211, 212, 245, 391, 421
  war, *see* Eastern Front; Operation Barbarossa
Soviet POWs, 5, 9, 10, 119–20, 125, 177–93, 206, 201, 224, 313, 369, 386, 411, 419
  in camps, 162–71, *166*, 176, 178, 180–85, *182*, 187–91, *188*, 194, 196, 197, 286, 296–97, 321, 364, 365, 385
  cannibalism among, 184, 191
  deaths of, 178, 184, 190–91, 222, 273, 275, 386

escapes of, 189–93, 222, 307–8, 363, 364, 368
ethnicities of, 187–89
food and water for, 181–85, *182*, 191, 196, 222, 273, 364
increase in violence toward, 363
Jewish or Bolshevik, 178–80, 185–89, 192, 193, 196–97
as laborers, 191
minefields and, 180, 222
Molotov's note on, 222–23, 233, 248
Nuremberg tribunal and, 385–87
photographs of, 387, *387*
policies on treatment of, 181, 183
in *politsai*, 189
public abuse of, 272–75, 333
repatriation of, 405, 406
segregation of, 187
and Soviet prosecution of Nazi war crimes, 336–38
SS and, 179–80, 184
treatment of, compared with Soviet treatment of German POWs, 333
Wehrmacht and, 181, 185, 188–89
women, 185–87, *186*, *187*
Soviet propaganda, 27–28, *28*, 85–86, 212–13, 239, 240, 256, 310, 317, 393
Soviet Union
anti-Semitism in, 3, 27, 96, 111, 195, 220, 311–12, 401–3
arrests and purges in, 7, 17, 91, 92, 94–95, 99, 274, 304
Baltic states annexed by, 413
Britain and, 30, 63, 97, 245–51
Cheka in, 37, 71, 131, 164, 194
China and, 92
Cold War and, 394, 396, 405, 419
collapse of, 17, 413
collectivization in, 7, 64, 85
corporal punishment in, 272
deportation of German Jews to, 108–9, 151–53
Eastern Europe and, 389–91, 408, 411–13
famine in, 7, 64, 85
food production in, 254, 277–78
France and, 75
Five-Year Plan in, 72, 78
German invasion of, *see* Operation Barbarossa
GPU in, 81, 113, 114, 122, 133, 152, 161, 164, 174, 260, 294, 302
Gulag in, 154, 160, 173, 394, 394
industrialization in, 17, 63, 64, 85, 215, 269
internationalism in, 96, 102, 187, 202, 206, 220–21, 402
Iron Curtain and, 389–91, 396, 408
Israel and, 401
Jewish identity in, 220–21, 317, 325, 399–401, 403–4
in League of Nations, 74
military preparedness in, 6, 64, 215
Nazism's victims universalized in, 325, 399
Nazi war crimes trials in, 306, 313, 334–40, 397–99
Nuremberg tribunal and, 381, 382, 384, 387–89, 391–93, 397, 419
NKVD of, *see* NKVD
Poland and, 110–11
Politburo of, 75, 100, 319, 397, 407
in postwar period, 405
repatriation of citizens to, 405–6
show trials in, 91, 93–95, 337, 411
Spain and, 79, 92
Thaw in, 401–2, 412
Ukrainian nationalists and, 411
U.S. aid to, 8, 245
war crimes of, 422
Western views of, 10–11, 13–14, 20, 245–46, 393–94
West Germany and, 408, 410–11
Yalta Conference and, 366, 371
Sovinformbiuro, 240, 246, 249
Spain, 79, 82, 88–91, 97, 98, 126, 172, 185, 386
SPD (Social Democratic Party of Germany), 24, 30, 31, 46–50, 53–57, 59, 66, 84, 101
Speer, Albert, 79, 89, 384
Spring Festival operation, 282
Sputnik agitatora, 211
SS (*Schutzstaffel*; *Sturmstaffel*), 4, 15, 17, 45, 55, 56, 77, 96, 97, 108, 109, 112, 113, 127–29, 131–35, 141, 145, 146, 148, 155, 157, 158, 160, 162–67, 169, 195, 254, 286–88, 322, 328, 344, 358, 363, 367, 375, 408
American soldiers and, 377
Babi Yar and, 306–7
bone-grinding machine of, 317–18
Division Leibstandarte, 297
Einsatzgruppen, 126–31, 134, 141–42, 384, 416
Einsatzkommandos, 398, 408
former members of, 409
Harvest Festival operation of, 322–23

SS (*Schutzstaffel*; *Sturmstaffel*) (*cont.*)
  Himmler's speeches and orders to, 288–91, 299
  Jewish ghettos raided by, 301
  at Majdanek, 324
  in Minsk, 198–99, 208–10
  Panzer Corps, 287
  partisans and, 280–82, *282*, *283*
  POWs and, 179–80, 184
  at Ravensbrück, 362
  Russia Center depopulation and, 254–55
  SD (intelligence service), 107–9, 126, 127, 134, 145, 150, 163, 207, 209, 286, 288, 293, 295, 380, 408
  Waffen-SS, 281–83, 285, 287, *287*, 288
  in Warsaw Ghetto, 300–301, 321
  war crimes trials and, 337, 338, 340, 383, 384, 386, 387, 397
Stadtler, Eduard, 29
Stahlecker, Franz Walter, 129–30
Stalin, Joseph, 7, 20, 63–64, 74, 75, 81, 85–88, 91, 92, 98–100, 120, *140*, 162, 212, 213, 216, 230, 231, 256, 262, 270, 304, 312, 318, 358, 370, 373, 374, 389, 414–15, 418, 421
  anti-Semitism condemned by, 96
  Berlin and, 366, 369, 371
  Casablanca Conference and, 292
  Churchill and, 249, 330, 390, 391, 407
  Comintern abolished by, 342–43
  death of, 401
  Dimitrov and, 69
  Eden and, 247
  Ehrenburg and, 74, 355, 358
  Eisenhower and, 374
  German military directive quoted by, 225, 226
  German POWs and, 331–33
  Germany's invasion and, 213–16, 219, 224–26
  Hitler and, 6, 11, 14, 95, 153, 225, 246, 342, 371, 390
  Hitler's pact with, 2, 14, 100–103, 110, 114, 116, 119, 120, 136, 144, 181, 211, 212, 245, 391, 421
  industrialization program of, 17, 63, 64, 85, 215, 269
  Jewish state and, 400
  Katyn massacre and, 306, 318, 319, 391–92, 422
  message to armed forces from, 329
  partisan warfare and, 280, 284
  Poland and, 110
  purges of, 6, 17, 91, 92, 94–95, 99, 274, 304
  Red Army violence and, 352
  Romania and, 135–36
  Roosevelt and, 369–70
  speeches of, 214–15, 224–26, 249–50
  at Teheran Conference, 331
  writers and, 70
Stalingrad, 153, 327, 348
  Battle of, 8, 18, 20, 248–52, 274–76, 286–87, 292–97, 299–301, 307, 321, 327–28, 342, 355, 395
Stalino (Donetsk), 270, 271, 273, 424
State Department, 396
Statue of Liberty, 252
Steiuk, Iakov, 314, *314*, 317, 328
Stevens, Edmund, 337
Stezhensky, Vladimir, 372, 376
Stowe, Harriet Beecher, 265
Stroop, Jürgen, 300–301
Strunnikov, Sergei, 229, 334
Stülpnagel, Otto von, 147, 149
Stürmer, 3, 81
Sudetenland, 97–98
suicides, 9, 352–53, 360
Susloparov, Ivan, 374
Sutzkever, Abraham, 387–88, *388*
Sviridovsky, Mikhail, 180
swastika, 36, 45, 50, 63, 76–77
Sweden, 367
Switzerland, 98
Syrets, 307
Syria, 285

Taganrog, 241, 288, 309
Tägliche Rundschau, 379
Tallinn, 181, 412
"Tanya" (Zoya Kosmodemyanskaya), 229–33, *230*, 334–36
Tarasov, Vasily, 223–24
Tarnopol (Ternopil), 104, 271
Tartu, 194
Tashkent, 220
TASS, 213, 235, *236*
Tatars, 285, 315
Taubert, Eberhard, 84–85
Tchaikovsky Museum, 247, 248
Teheran Conference, 331
Tess, Tatyana, 237, 239
Thaw, The (Ehrenburg), 401–2
Thirty Years' War, 284
Thule Society, 33, 34, 36, 37
Tikhonov, Ivan, 229
Times (London), 75, 392

Tippelskirch, Kurt von, 373
Tiraspol, 349
Tito, Josip Broz, 145–46
Tolstoi, Aleksei, 218
Tolstoy, Leo, 232, 248, 257
Topola, 148
Torgler, Ernst, 66, 67, 69
total war, 216, 356
Trawniki, 322, 323
Treaty of Brest-Litovsk, 29
Treblinka, 298–301, 321, 323, 327–28, 387, 392
Trier, 104
Triumph of the Will, 80
Trotsky, Leon, 26, 27, 91, 93, 94
Truman, Harry, 389, 394
Trusov, Kirill, 200, 201, *201*
Trust D.E. (Ehrenburg), 71
Tschammer und Osten, Eckart von, 196, 197
Tukhachevsky, Mikhail, 75, 91, 94, 95
Tula, 233, 272
Tusk, 422
Tyszelman, Samuel, 146

Ukraine, Ukrainians, xxiii, 10, 20, 28–30, 109–11, 120–22, 128–31, 133–35, 137, 142, 160, 186, 193, 195, 198, 207, 218, 221, 255, 256, 258, 270, 274, 278, 288, 306, 308, 310, 312–13, 315, 317, 334, 343, 348, 371, 384, 399, 405, 411, 424
  Communist Party of, 269, 305, 400
  dead zones and, 284, 285
  Donbas, 211–12, 270, 334, 424
  Kharkov, *see* Kharkov
  Kiev, *see* Kiev
  nationalism and, 411
  Soviet liberation of, 18, 308, 310–12, 316, 317, 325
  POWs, 187–89
  Russia's war with, 424–25
Uncle Tom's Cabin (Stowe), 265
Union of Soviet Writers, 69–70
United Nations, 374
  War Crimes Commission, 336
United States, 224, 249, 290, 320
  Bolshevism and, 26
  Civil Rights Movement in, 404
  forces in Germany, 10, 377–78, 362–67
  Germany's declaration of war against, 159
  Lend-Lease program of, 8, 245, 247
  Nuremberg tribunal and, 381–82, 384, 389
  racism in, 395–96
  in World War I, 29
  Yalta Conference and, 366
United States Holocaust Memorial Museum (USHMM), 11–12, *12*, 415–18, *417*
University of Munich, 34
Unwomanly Face of War, The (Alexievich), 414
Ural Mountains, 191, 224, 235, 254, 269, 276, 290, 353
Uspensky, Yuri, 349–51
Ustyanova, Yevdokiya, 376
Uzbekistan, 220

Vaillant-Couturier, Marie-Claude, 385, 388
Valkyrie plan, 321
Vallejo, César, 89–90
van der Lubbe, Marinus, 53, 66, 67, 69
Velikie Luki, 397
vengeance, 8–9, 244, 314–16, 326–27, 339, 349–54, 378, 381–82
Versailles Treaty, 35, 48, 63, 74, 76
Victory Day (May 9), 407, 42, 424
Vienna, 29, 154, 157, 173
Viljandi, 181
Vilna, 387, *388*
Vilnius, 249, 420
Vilnius Declaration, 421
Vinnitsa, 304, *305*, 357, 407
Vistula River, 346
Vitebsk, xxiii, 282
Vlasov, Andrei, 275–76, 286
Vogt, Paul, 340
Völkischer Beobachter, 36, 37, 45, 54, 76, 122, *123*, 152, 218–19, 302–3, *303*, 357
Volkssturm, 356, 363, 363
Volokolamsk, 228–29, *228*, 347
von der Goltz, Rüdiger, 31, 32
Voronezh, 320
Voroshilov, Kliment, 72
Vorwärts, 49

Wäckerle, Hilmar, 55
Waffen-SS, 281–83, 285, 287, *287*, 288
Wagner, Richard, 101
Wall Street crash of 1929, 47
Wall Street Journal, 246
Wannsee Conference, 13, 160, 161, 169
war crimes
  Nazi, *see* Nazi war crimes
  Soviet, 422
Warsaw, 106, 299, 321, 346, 389, 416
  SS in, 300–301

Warsaw Pact, 412
Warsaw Synagogue, 300
Warstein, 364, 365
Wehrmacht, 5, 80, 94, 103, 106, 108, 112, 117, 127, 128, 131, 134, 135, 137–39, 141, 146, 147, 149, 153, 173, 199, 209, 224, 227, 243, 275, 276, 278, 283, 287, 288, 305, 351, 378, 408
  captured soldiers from, 343–45, 408
  dead zones and, 285
  Ehrenburg and, 358, 410
  Katyn and, 301–2, 392
  Kharkov trial and, 337, 338
  Luftwaffe, 78, 106
  NKVD massacres and, 301–2, 304
  partisans and, 281, *283*
  refugees and, 361
  Russian auxiliaries to (*Hiwis*), 275–76, 278, 286, 289
  Soviet POWs and, 181, 185, 188–89
  at Stalingrad, 8, 18, 20, 248–52, 274–76, 286–87, 292–97, 299–301, 307, 321, 327–28, 342, 355
  surrender of, *375*
  Valkyrie plan of, 321
Wehrmacht, *170*
West Germany, 17, 408–11
Westminster College, 389–90
White Ruthenia, 208, 209, 279
Why Fight Stalin?, 114–15, *115*
Wielun, 106
Wiesel, Elie, 404
Wilhelm II, Kaiser, 30
Wittenberg, 265
Wolf, Friedrich, 72–73, 89, 97, 342, 343
Wolfschanze, 153, 160
women
  Bolshevism and, 185, 203
  in Britain, 246–47, *247*
  German soldiers' behavior and, 270–71
  in Red Army, 185–87, *186*, *187*
  in underground, 200–204, *201*, *202*
World Bolshevism, 78
World Congress of Intellectuals for Peace, 396
World War I, 2, 26, 46, 52, 70–71, 74, 78, 100, 140
  Germany in, 22, 29–30, 32–33, 35–36, 40, 41, 52, 61, 290, 297, 369
World War II, 8, 17, 64, 292, 404, 420
  Allied invasion in, 8, 250, 330–31, 395, 419
  beginning of, 106
  Casablanca Conference and, 292
  D-Day, 330–31, 419
  Germany's appeal to Allies in, 10
  Germany's defeat in, 12
  legacy of, 408
  Pacific theater of, 159, 227, 247, 248
  Western scholarship on, 13–14, 20
  see also Eastern Front
writers and publishing, 6, 69–75, 80, 84–87, *86*, 89–90, 92–93, 102, 172–73
  Soviet, and German invasion, 217–18, 239–45

Yalta Conference, 366, 371
Yanukovych, Viktor, 424
Yaroslavsky, Yemelyan, 214
Yeltsin, Boris, 423
Yevtushenko, Yevgeny, 402–3
Yugoslavia, 98, 145–46, 213, 255, 348, 369, 395

Zagreb, 144
Zaionchkovsky, Pyotr, 308
Zaitsev, Vasily, 244–45
Zakopane, 104
Zessner, Günther, 341
Zhdanov, Andrei, 70
Zheleznov, Comrade, 296–97
Zhitomir, 130–31, *130*
Zhukov, Georgy, 347–48, 371, 375
Ziereis, Franz, 166, 176, 363
Zinoviev, Grigory, 26, 91, 93
Zionism, 111, 155, 400, 401
Zucca, André, 172